A HISTORY

OF THE

SEPOY WAR IN INDIA

1857-1858.

W0033264

BY

JOHN WILLIAM KAYE, F. R. S.

IN THREE VOLUMES

VOL. III.

Published by

Gyan Publishing House
5, Ansari Road
Daryaganj, New Delhi-110002
Phone: 011-47034999, 9811692060
E-mail: books@gyanbooks.com

Distribution Network
gyanbooks.com
India, USA, Canada, UK, Australia, France

© **Publisher**

All rights reserved. No part of this work may be reproduced, stored, adapted, or transmitted in any form or by any means, electronic, mechanical, photocopying, micro-filming, recording or otherwise, or translated in any language, without the prior written permission of the copyright owner and the publisher.

ISBN: 978-81-212-8191-1 (Set)
978-81-212-8188-1 (PB)
First Published, 1876

2nd Impression 2023

Printed at: Gyan Press, Delhi.

The book is sold subject to the condition that it shall not, by way of trade or otherwise, be lent, resold, hired out, or otherwise circulated without the prior publisher's written consent.

A HISTORY OF THE SEPOY WAR IN INDIA, 1857-1858 (VOL. III.)
Author: JOHN WILLIAM KAYE

A HISTORY

OF

THE SEPOY WAR IN INDIA.

1857—1858.

A HISTORY

OF THE

SEPOY WAR IN INDIA.

1857—1858.

BY

JOHN WILLIAM KAYE, F.R.S.,

AUTHOR OF THE "HISTORY OF THE WAR IN AFGHANISTAN."

VOL. III.

LONDON:

W. H. ALLEN & CO., 13, WATERLOO PLACE.

Agents in India :

CALCUTTA : THACKER, SPINK, AND CO. BOMBAY : THACKER, VINING, AND CO.

1876.

PREFACE.

In the autumn of last year, I hoped and believed that this volume of the History of the Sepoy War would be laid before the public in the course of the following month of November. But it was otherwise ordained. I was compelled to lay aside the pen, when I thought myself most capable of using it; and not until the dawn of the next summer was I permitted, or, indeed, able, to resume my work, with a feeling that I was equal to the task. Some had exhorted me to finish it any-how; others, to get some one to help me. I could only answer that I would rather not finish it at all, if I could not put my best powers of workmanship into it; and, whatever the toil and travail might be, write every line myself. So I waited patiently for the hour and the hour came. My old love of historical research came back upon me, and with it my power of sustained work.

Let no man deceive himself as to the nature of that work. There is no such thing as the easy writing of History. If it be not Truth it is not

History; and Truth lies very far below the surface.
It is a long and laborious task to exhume it. Rapid
production is a proof of the total absence of conscientious investigation. For History is not the
growth of Inspiration, but of Evidence. It is scarcely
reasonable, therefore, to complain of delay, when
without delay, or in other words, protracted inquiry,
there can be no approximation to the Truth. I cannot, therefore, apologise for that to which these
volumes owe any little value that they may possess
in the eyes of the present or a future generation.

As I went further into the depths of this strange
story I found that the difficulties of narration, to
which I had referred in my second volume, had
greatly increased. Materials were superabundant.
I cannot sufficiently express my gratitude to friends
and strangers (strangers only in the flesh) who provided me so freely with memorials of one of the most
wonderful episodes in the history of the British
nation. But the very wealth of these materials increased my difficulties. It is comparatively easy to
describe a series of events. But I had not to do
with events rising out of, or following each other in
succession, but with a multitude of detached and
almost contemporaneous incidents, the only connecting link being the universal fact that the Black man
had risen against the White. As illustrative materials, some of them of the most interesting character, were showered upon me, it became increasingly
difficult to deal with such a mass of details, without
extending the dimensions of the work far beyond
the limits that would be acceptable to the Public. I
have endeavoured to give prominence to the most
significant and suggestive events. I cannot hope
that I have altogether succeeded; but I trust that I

have not wholly failed. Doubtless, many an exciting adventure which would have stirred the heart of the reader, and many an act of personal gallantry, which it would have been a delight to me to narrate, has found no record in these pages. Nothing but the stern laws of necessity have compelled these omissions. It will be said, perhaps, that greater compression in some parts might have afforded larger space for amplification in others. But compression, though doubtless a virtue, is, like some other virtues, not always very interesting; and every man must write his books in his own way. It might have been better for me if I had not undertaken this work ; but having undertaken it, I was bound to complete it, with all the power I had in me, at any cost of worldly fortune, or health, or even of life itself.

I have been told by one or two friends, to whom I have shown some passages of this volume, that they will "excite controversy and give pain." No one can be more unwilling than I am to cause unnecessary suffering. There is no greater literary crime than the infliction of pain, without thorough inquiry into the painful statements made and ample proof of their truth, except to stand by them after their falsehood has been made manifest. And, assuredly, it is pleasanter to praise than to blame. "But," I am told, "admitted that it is all true, it is injudicious to publish the truth, and there will be much controversy arising out of it." The Historian who shrinks from controversy has mistaken his vocation. I have told and I intend to tell the truth, so far as I can discern it, after laborious and conscientious inquiry, without any regard of persons. As I would speak of a stranger I would speak of a friend; and as I would speak of a friend, I would speak of a brother or of a son—of living and of dead alike. If a man is not prepared to do this, and to take the consequences, let him write novels and travels in the manner of Gulliver and leave History alone.

The present volume, like its predecessors, contains three books. The FIRST of these relates to affairs in Bengal and Behar, including some account of the excitement at Calcutta, of the rising in Shahabad, the mutiny at Dinapore, the defence and relief of Arrah—together with some notices of Lord Canning's defensive and suppressive measures and of the general policy observed by the Government in the earlier days of the rebellion. In the preparation of these chapters I have been much aided by the private correspondence of Lord Canning, by a mass of documents, printed and manuscript, lent to me by Mr. William Tayler, Commissioner of Patna, and by the simple, manly narratives of Sir Vincent Eyre. The SECOND (Book VIII.) contains a narrative of the several risings in the North-Western Provinces, the wide-spread subversion of British authority, the bearing of the principal Native Princes and Chiefs, and the defence of Agra up to the period of Mr. Colvin's death. My information with regard to these events is principally derived from Mr. E. A. Reade, Sir William Muir, who had charge of the Intelligence Department, Mr. Charles Raikes, Major Weller of the Engineers, and the Confidential Reports of the several civil and political officers whose narratives were called for by Government after the suppression of the insurrection. The THIRD part (Book IX.) is devoted, firstly, to affairs in Oude, the general state of the Provinces, the risings in the Districts, the siege and defence of Lucknow, the death of Sir Henry Law-

rence, and subsequent events up to the time of the
first relief of the Residency by Havelock and Outram ; and secondly, to the final and victorious siege,
assault, and capture of Delhi. These last chapters have
caused a greater expenditure of time, labour, and
thought, than any other part of the work. And I
cannot be too grateful to those who have enabled me,
in some measure, I hope, to overcome the difficulties
of the task. Among these, I may mention the late
Sir Archdale Wilson, the family of the late Colonel
Baird Smith, Sir Neville Chamberlain, Colonel
George Chesney, and Colonel Welby Greathed of
the Engineers, Sir Edward Greathed, so highly distinguished in subsequent operations against the insurgents in the North-West, Sir Charles Reid, who
held so long the Picket at Hindoo Rao's, and Sir
Henry Daly, then of the Guides. Among artillerymen, from whom I have derived the most important
assistance, are Sir James Brind, Sir Edwin Johnson,
General E. W. Scott, and my brother, Lieutenant-
General Edward Kaye. From such authorities as
these I must have evolved a large measure of truth,
amounting almost to perfect accuracy. But I wish
the reader to understand that I have not pretended
to write a MILITARY history of these or any other
operations—that my narrative was not intended to
bear "a stamp exclusive or professional," but to command the common interests and catholic sympathies
of all classes of readers. It is, therefore, necessarily
deficient in personal and statistical details, such as
may be gathered from old Army Lists or the official reports of the day. And I have purposely ab-
stained as much as possible from technical phrase-
ology, though having had the advantage of a military

education and having served my apprenticeship to
the profession, such language would have come
readily from my pen.

I had intended in this volume to have included
some account of the first relief of Lucknow : and, indeed, the narrative of Havelock's operations were
already in print; but not only did I find that the
fulfilment of this design would have swollen the
volume to an inconvenient bulk, but it appeared to
me on reconsideration that it would be more advantageous to the entire work to embrace in one conse-
cutive narrative the story of the campaign of Havelock and Outram and the final operations of Sir
Colin Campbell.   This will form a not unimportant
part of the next volume, which will contain also,
if I am suffered to complete it, some account of
Delhi within the walls, of the Trial of the King and
others implicated in the slaughter of our people, a
history of the Central-Indian Campaign under Sir
Hugh Rose, of later events in Agra and Rajpootana
—of the risings in Western India, of affairs in the
Deccan, and of the general pacification of the country ; concluding with a chapter on the Fall of the
East India Company, the proclamation of the Queen's
Government throughout the country, the remedial
policy of Lord Canning, and the manner in which
our promises and pledges, given in the day of danger,
have been, in the day of safety, fulfilled.

J. W. K.

Rose Hill, Forest Hill.

CONTENTS OF VOL. III.

CHAPTER III.

LUCKNOW IN JUNE AND JULY.

CHAPTER IV.

THE SIEGE OF DELHI.

CHAPTER V.

CAPTURE OF DELHI.

ERRATA.

[In First Edition of Vol. II.]

Page 79, *note*, for "Buktawuss Sing" read "Buktawur Khan."

Page 88, lines 4 and 5, for "officers of the Bengal Artillery" read "officers of the Ordnance Commissariat Department."

Page 169, line 10, for eight-pounders" read "nine-pounders."

Page 187, line 5 from bottom, for "having moved down from Bolundshuhur" read "having moved up from Bolundshuhur."

Page 266, line 13, for "Moole-gunj" read "Mootee-gunj."

Page 376, line 12, for "stimulate" read "simulate."

Page 395, line 5, for "Kooshen Gardens" read "Khoosroo Gardens."

Page 397, *note*, for "short" read "shot."

Page 426, line 3 from bottom, for "Punjabee troops" read "troops in the Punjab."

Page 447, 6 lines from the bottom, for "Inniskillen Dragoons" read "Twenty-seventh Foot (Inniskillens)."

Page 667, Appendix (quotation), line 10 from bottom, for "Accountant Commissioner" read "Assistant Commissioner."

HISTORY OF THE SEPOY WAR.

BOOK VII.—BENGAL, BEHAR, AND THE NORTH-WEST PROVINCES.

[June—July, 1857.]

ERRATUM.

Page 429, top line, for " Mr. Colverly Jackson," read
"Mr. Coverley Jackson."

THE BARRACKPORE REGIMENTS—THE GREAT CALCUTTA PANIC—ARREST OF THE KING OF OUDE—SIR PATRICK GRANT—FINANCIAL DIFFICULTIES OF THE CRISIS.

WHILST the incidents recorded in the preceding books were occurring—whilst Havelock and Neill were pushing on from the South to the relief of Cawnpore and Lucknow, and John Lawrence was pouring down from the North all his available military strength to the attack of Delhi—events were developing themselves, in many different parts of the country, which showed how wide-spread was the disaffection, and how momentous was the crisis, with which the head of the British Government was called upon to contend. To Lord Canning, who wisely continued to reside in the capital, the month of June was one of intense anxiety and vexation—anxiety

1857.
June.

The Governor General at Calcutta.

for the fate of his countrymen in the Upper Provinces, vexation engendered by the attitude assumed by some influential classes of the European community at Calcutta, who grievously misunderstood his character, and continually condemned his conduct.

The lull which immediately followed the outbreaks at Meerut and Delhi had now been rudely disturbed. Every post was freighted with tidings of some new manifestation of the all-prevailing excitement in the Native Army of Bengal, and made more clear to him the enormous difficulties which now threatened the security of the Empire. The North-Western Provinces were in a blaze. Not only was the whole Native Army falling away from him, but the fabric of civil government was in many places crumbling to pieces. Whether this disorganisation were the result merely of the ravages of the soldiery, and the love of rapine natural at all times to the predatory classes, or whether the discontents of our trained fighting men were shared by the peaceful communities, and the country was ripe for civil rebellion no less than for military revolt, was not at that time apparent. But it was certain that the first efforts of the Government must be directed to the suppression of the mutinous activities of the Sepoy Army. And to the accomplishment of this, Lord Canning, never disguising from himself or from others the magnitude of the danger to be grappled with, had put forth all his personal strength, and evoked all the resources of the State.

That on the first receipt of intelligence of the capture of Delhi by the insurgent army, the Governor-General addressed himself, with the utmost promptitude and vigour, to the work of collecting troops from all available sources, has been shown in the first volume of this History. The looked-for succours were of two kinds: those already on the Indian establishment, which could be easily gathered up and brought speedily to the scene of action by his own authoritative word; and those which lay at a distance under the control of other authorities, and for which he could do no more than ask. The first, it has been seen, soon began to pour in, and they were despatched to the Upper Provinces with all possible speed. That the Government were taken by surprise, that the available means of transport were inconsiderable, and that the Military Department at the Presidency was not strong during the first month of trouble, is not to be denied. But it is equally clear to me that Lord Canning neglected no means at his disposal to despatch European troops to the endangered provinces with all the speed which could be attained by the functionaries under him, who had never before been prepared for such an emergency, and were not likely now to be in an abnormal state of preparation. With what success these primal efforts were attended has been shown. Benares and Allahabad were saved by the succours sent upwards from Calcutta. But Cawnpore was lost; Lucknow was still in imminent danger; and the flames of rebellion were spreading all over North-Western India.

And there was a never-ceasing source of dire affliction to him in the thought that all he could do at such a time was but little and light, weighed against what needed to be done. "It is enough to break one's heart," he wrote in June, "to have to refuse the imploring prayers of the Europeans at out-stations for protection by English troops against the rising of the Sepoys in their neighbourhood, or against the savage marauders and mutineers who are afoot. But to scatter our small force over the country would be to throw away every chance of a speedy success."

Throughout the whole country, there was no place, the perilous environments of which had been regarded with profounder anxiety by Lord Canning, than the cantonment of Cawnpore. All his letters written in the month of June express the painful uneasiness with which he contemplated Wheeler's position, and the eagerness with which he sought to relieve him by succours both from below and from above. Benares and Allahabad being secured, he desired that all the reinforcements sent up from the southward should pass on to Cawnpore; and he wrote to Sir Henry Barnard, urging him to send down a regiment from the Delhi Field Force.* "Benares," he wrote in the middle of June, "has been made safe. So has Allahabad, I hope, but only just in time. Henceforward, the reinforcements will be pushed up still further—to Cawnpore; but the disorganised state of the country between Allahabad and Cawnpore may interpose delay; and both telegraph and dawk from any place north of Allahabad is now cut off from Calcutta. I cannot, therefore, speak so confidently of the time when help will reach Sir Hugh Wheeler. It may not be for four or five days, or even more.† This makes it all the more urgently necessary that you should push down an European force immediately. When it reaches the Cawnpore Division, it will, ac-

---

* It has been shown (vol. ii. p. 136) that he wrote at the same time to Mr. Colvin, desiring him to make every effort to despatch southwards all the troops that Barnard could spare.

† I have not the original of this letter before me; perhaps it does not exist. The passage is correctly transcribed from the copy, in the private secretary's handwriting, kept by Lord Canning. There is some reason, however, to suspect the word "days" is a clerical error for "weeks." If not, it is difficult to understand the context.

cording to the instructions which have been sent to you, pass under Sir Hugh Wheeler's command. And with him will rest the responsibility of relieving Lucknow and pacifying the country from Cawnpore downwards. It will be for you to judge what your own movements should be. All that I require is that an European force, as large an one as you can spare, shall be sent southwards with the least possible delay, and that it should not be detained an hour for the purpose of finishing off affairs at Delhi, after once the great blow has been struck." Whether this letter ever reached its destination is uncertain.* If it did, it must have been received with astonishment on the Delhi Ridge. And it was not merely in that direction that the expectations of the Governor-General were overleaping the stern realities of the position. The succours from Allahabad, by which first Cawnpore and then Lucknow were to be saved, were almost as remote contingencies as those summoned from the northward. This misconception resulted not from a want of sagacity, but from a want of information. The magnates of Calcutta were groping hopelessly in the dark. The difficulties of their position had been rendered still more difficult by the interruption of postal and telegraphic communication between Calcutta and many of the chief stations of Upper India. Nearly all the country above Allahabad was sealed to them. News from Agra, from Delhi, from the Punjab, came in by many devious channels after long intervals, and was often little to be relied on when it came. Again and again news came that Delhi had fallen. Not only in Calcutta, but in Allahabad,

---

* It was drafted on the 10th of June, but was not despatched till the 21st. Lord Canning retained it, after a duplicate had been made, until that day, probably in uncertainty as to whether the accounts which reached him of the fall of Delhi were true or false.

1857.
June.

Agra, Cawnpore, Lucknow, all our chief British posts, the cheering report came down only to disappoint and to mock our people; and in some places royal salutes were ostentatiously fired in honour of the auspicious event.

Lord Canning's correspondence.

In spite, however, of postal interruptions—often only delays—Lord Canning received many letters, at this time, from officers in responsible positions, who rightly took upon themselves, in total disregard of official proprieties, to write directly to the Governor-General; and from others, too, upon whom the crisis had conferred no such right, but who were eager to offer advice to the head of the Government. These letters were of very different kinds and characters. In many there was serviceable information of the best kind; in others, sound good sense, often too late to be of any service to the chief ruler, as it related to the causes of the revolt, not to its remedies. In some there was blatant folly. Military reformers and religious enthusiasts spoke out freely, and the Adjutant-General and Armageddon alternately figured in these volunteer despatches. Many, it may be supposed, counselled the most sanguinary retributory measures. All these letters Lord Canning attentively perused, and then handed them over to his Private Secretary, to be duly docketed and properly pigeon-holed. Often he answered them. When good service was done he was prompt to recognise it. Those who said that he was cold-hearted because he was cool and collected in danger, little knew the warmth which he threw into his more private correspondence. Sometimes this warmth took the shape of reprobation rather than of applause—reprobation of principles asserted, not approval of actions performed. But even in this repro-

bation there was generally some recognition of the
zeal and loyalty of the man, though the counsel
offered to him was of a kind altogether foreign to
his own sentiments and opinions. Thus to one correspondent, who recommended that measures of a most
vigorous (or otherwise sanguinary) character should
be taken for the purpose of overawing the Native
soldiery, he wrote: "You talk of the necessity of
striking terror into the Sepoys. You are entirely
and most dangerously wrong. The one difficulty,
which of all others it is the most difficult to meet, is
that the regiments which have not yet fallen away
are mad with fear—fear for their caste and religion,
fear of disgrace in the eyes of their comrades, fear
that the European troops are being collected to crush
and decimate them as well as their already guilty
comrades. Your bloody, off-hand measures are not
the cure for this sort of disease; and I warn you
against going beyond the authority which Government has already given to you, and even that authority must be handled discreetly. Don't mistake
violence for vigour." And these sentiments were
shared by the wisest and most heroic of Lord
Canning's Lieutenants. Sir Henry Lawrence, both
by word and deed, strove to allay the fears of the
timid, to encourage the loyalty of the wavering, and
in all to reward the good rather than to punish the
evil. Sir John Lawrence, in pure, intelligible vernacular, said that he believed it was "all funk" that
was driving the soldiery into armed opposition to the
Government, and that the greatest difficulty with
which he had to contend, was that our measures of
repression had a necessary tendency to prolong the
crisis by increasing the general alarm. And Sir
James Outram rebuked an officer who had recom-

mended sanguinary measures of retaliation, by saying that he had always observed that men the most blood-thirsty in council were the least gallant and courageous in action. There were, doubtless, times and seasons in the development of this revolt, when the cruelty of the hour was the prescience of enlarged humanity—when, to strike remorselessly at all, taken red-handed, in the first flush of rampant crime, would be merciful to the thousands and tens of thousands who were waiting for the encouragement of a successful beginning to fling themselves into the troubled waters of rebellion. But this dire and deplorable necessity differed greatly from the vindictive eagerness which longed to be let loose, not only upon proved murderers and mutineers, but upon whole races of men guilty of the unpardonable offence of going about with dark skins over their lithe bodies.

And already, indeed, Lord Canning was beginning to fear that this intense national hatred was bearing bitter and poisonous fruit. The tidings which he received directly or indirectly from Benares and Allahabad filled him with apprehensions, lest the wild justice of the hour, which was running riot in the Gangetic Provinces, should become a reproach and a misery for years. He feared that the great powers which had been given both to soldiers and to civilians were already being abused; and yet he felt that he could not arrest the hand of authority without paralysing the energies of the very men to whom he most trusted to crush the rebellion which was destroying the lives of our people and threatening our national supremacy. There had been no feeble humanitarianism—no sentimental irresolution —in Canning's measures. It has been seen that, on the 30th of May, an Act had been passed sweeping

away many of the old legal fences, and giving extraordinary powers to officers in the trial and execution
of offenders; and now, on the 6th of June, another
Act was passed extending these powers of life and
death.* That the Governor-General should have
watched the result of this exceptional legislation with
anxious forebodings is not strange. But that the
head of a Government, which had given what it
rightly described as " enormous powers" to individual Englishmen, for the suppression of mutiny
and rebellion by hanging the Natives of the country,
with scarcely the formality even of an impromptu
trial, should have been charged, as he was, with not
appreciating the gravity of the position, is, rationally
considered, one of the strangest facts in the whole
history of the war.

The strangest things, however, are not always un-
accountable. The self-esteem of the Calcutta citizens
had been wounded; and egotism often affectionately
adopts what reason contemptuously discards. Lord
Canning had not accepted the first offer of the European community of Calcutta to enrol themselves into
a Volunteer Corps for the protection of the City; and
it was thought or said, therefore, that he could not
see the dangers which beset our position. But even
this ground of reproach was now to be removed. In
the second week of June, the reconsideration of the
question, which had been decided adversely in the
preceding month, was urged upon Lord Canning by
the ablest of his counsellors. Very earnestly, and
with a great show of authority, Mr. Grant, on the
10th of June, pressed the Governor-General to recall
his refusal. His memory grasped the fact that, three
years before, the whole question of Volunteer Corps

* This is given in the Appendix.

1857.
June.
for the protection of the chief cities of India had
been discussed and minuted upon by Lord Dalhousie's
Government. That was the time of the Crimean War;
and the Governor-General saw but too plainly that
whenever English troops might be wanted for purposes
of European warfare, little thought would be given
to the requirements of the great Indian dependency.
It had, therefore, been held worthy of consideration
whether in all the large towns in which Europeans
and Eurasians congregated in sufficient numbers to
enrol themselves into Volunteer Corps of respectable
strength, the movement might not wisely be encouraged by the State. And the views of the Government of the day had been received with favour by
the East India Company. This weighty precedent
being now exhumed, the papers recording it were
put together and circulated after the wonted fashion,
and with the papers, which thus brought up the
Governor-General of yesterday to bear witness against
the Governor-General of to-day, Mr. Grant despatched
a note to Lord Canning, saying: "I entreat your
Lordship to read so many of the papers in this box as
I have put at the top of the bundle. It is not a
quarter of an hour's reading. You will see that the
general question of having a Volunteer Rifle Corps
here, when the Europeans come forward, has been
settled both by the recommendation of Lord Dalhousie's Government and the Court's decision thereon.
Now, not only have these inhabitants come forward,
but they are grumbling at their offer having been
virtually declined. Certainly an emergency has occurred infinitely greater than was contemplated at
the time by any member of Lord Dalhousie's Government."* And he added to this that it was highly

---

* In this letter Mr. Grant thus
describes the situation with all its
probabilities of danger. I do not think
the language exaggerated. "I think

probable that if a Volunteer Corps were not raised in such a crisis as was then before them, the Home Government, after what had passed a few years before, would ask the "reason why." Lord Canning was not a man to be moved by any apprehensions of this kind; but the persuasive utterances of his colleague induced him to reconsider the whole question, and to reverse his former judgment. Perhaps he was not sorry to prove to the Christian community of Calcutta that they had erred in believing that he had rejected their former offer with studied contempt. In the middle of June, as in the middle of May, it was still his impression that a body of amateur soldiers, with other interests and other responsibilities, would not materially augment the military strength at his disposal, or enable him to release a single company of Regulars from the immediate defence of the capital.*

it is one thing to show alarm gratuitously and another thing to make all secure against bad weather, when the glass falls below stormy. In reality, as well as in appearance, we are very weak here, where we ought to be—and if we can't be, should at least appear to be—as strong as possible. We have as enemies three Native Infantry regiments and a half, of which one and a half are the very worst type we know; one, two, three (for no one knows) thousand armed men at Garden Reach, or available there at a moment; some hundred armed men of the Scinde Ameers at Dum-Dum; half the Mahomedan population; and all the blackguards of all sorts of a town of six hundred thousand people. Against these we have one and a half weak regiments, most of whom dare not leave the Fort. There is no reason to expect real help in real danger from the Native Police. The insurrection is regularly spreading down to us. Is this an emergency or not? My conviction is that even a street row at the capital would give us an awful shake—not only in Bengal, but in Bombay and Madras —at this moment." — MS. Correspondence.

* "Another sedative to the fears of Calcutta has been the acceptance of the offer of Volunteers. They resented being made special constables, and objected to act with the Police. They have now been enrolled as Volunteer Guards. Arms have been given to them, and their present duty is to patrol at night. After a little training they will make a very useful patrol guard, when needed; but I was not long in finding out that any duty which should take them away from their homes for any length of time—such, for instance, as garrisoning the Fort in place of European troops—would be strongly objected to by three-fourths of them. The truth is, that Calcutta does not furnish men idle enough and independent enough to be able to give themselves to that duty continuously."—Lord Canning to Mr. Vernon Smith, June 19, 1857, MS. Correspondence.

1857.
June.

But he consented to the enrolment and the arming of the citizens, and he sent for Colonel Cavenagh, the Town-Major, and instructed him to make immediate arrangements for the organisation of the force, and to take the command of it himself.

And it is to the honour of the community that, notwithstanding what they considered to be a rebuff in the first instance, they again made offers of their services—not so numerously, not so enthusiastically, as in the month before, but still in sufficient force to constitute two serviceable bodies of Horse and Foot. Lawyers and merchants, covenanted and uncovenanted civilians, tradesmen and clerks of all kinds and degrees, turned out to drill in the worst seasons of the year, in scorching heat and in steamy damp; and we can take just account of what they did and suffered only by remembering the quiet, easy, monotonous lives from which many suddenly emerged into a forced and unnatural activity. One thing at least was certain—the enrolment of these volunteer bands had an assuring effect on the minds of the community at large. They seemed to start suddenly into life, as by a wave of the enchanter's wand. Cavenagh went about his work with promptitude and energy of the best kind, and although he was soon afterwards honourably relieved from the command, on account of the urgent pressure of other duties, it is hard to say how much the efficiency of the Volunteer Corps was due to his first efforts.

Restrictions on the Indian Press.

But that which of all causes of vexation vexed Lord Canning most in this month of June was the language of the Indian Press—the malignant outpourings of the Native and the unguarded utterances of the European journals. That, for some time past, the former had been overflowing with sedition was certain; but the latter had always been loyal, if not to the local governments, at least to the Crown and the Nation. The Native newspapers, printed in Persian or Nagari characters, or sometimes only lithographed as rude fly-sheets, were generally supposed by the European communities to be of small circulation and smaller influence. But with a partially educated and a generally poor people, the influence of a published journal is out of all proportion to the number of copies printed. Not only did every impression of a Native newspaper pass through a number of hands, but each one of the numerous recipients read it aloud, or recited its contents to a still larger audience. And as every reader and every hearer was, in an extreme degree, credulous and suspicious, every lie uttered and printed was believed as gospel, and other lies were encrusted upon it. There were, doubtless, some exceptions, especially in Bengal; but the majority of Native journals were either intentionally hostile and false to the British Government, or they scattered abroad, with reckless prodigality, lying rumours, which were perhaps more dangerous in their insidiousness than the utterances of open sedition. Though generally disregarded, as I have said, by Englishmen in India, these manifestations of an unquiet spirit in the depths of Native society had attracted, during a long series of years, the attention of some shrewd observers; and it was sometimes prophetically said that the fidelity of the Native Army could not long survive the establishment of a Free Press. And it is not improbable that not one of those shrewd observers, from Sir Thomas Munro downwards, ever discovered half the mischief lurking beneath the ambiguously worded articles and enigmatical paragraphs of the Native journalists.[*]

The European journals, on the other hand, which were for the most part conducted by educated English gentlemen holding a good position in society, prided themselves on being intensely English. A large proportion of their readers, and a still larger proportion of the purchasers of these journals, were either "in the services," or members of the commercial communities of the large towns. That there was also a Native Public for these writings is true; but the English journalist and the Hindoo or Mahomedan reader were commonly brought together by the medium of translations in the Native papers. The classes, therefore, for which the English newspapers were edited were those most interested in the maintenance of good order and the supremacy of the British Government. But Anglo-Indian editors, whilst loyally fulfilling their duty to the Public and to the State, on the whole with praiseworthy conscientiousness, were not exempt from the besetting infirmity of their craft—an intense craving for news. The fault was not in the Journalist so much as in the Public. The journal that published a lying report one morning was held in greater esteem than the contemporary who contradicted it on the next. Anything was more acceptable than dulness; and to be cautious is always to be dull. And this not only with respect to facts, but also with respect to opinions. A critical conjuncture not only generates an extreme desire for news on the part of the public, but an ex-

---

[*] Sir Thomas Munro's famous minute has been often quoted, but this narrative would be incomplete without some more particular refer-ence to it. I have, therefore, given some remarkable passages in the Appendix.

cessive tendency towards strong writing on the part of the public instructor. The excited journalist naturally throws out at such times the angry sparks of his peculiar national tendencies with a freedom which, however gratifying to himself, cannot be otherwise than embarrassing to the State. His patriotism is not to be doubted. He is English to the backbone. He will fight and die for his country. He will do all things for it—but one. He will not be reticent when he ought to be; he will not forego the privilege of saying just what he likes.

But there are times and seasons when even the honourable impulses of loyal journalists may wisely be held in restraint, and assuredly such a time had arrived in the month of June, 1857. In the official language of the day, "The Bengal Native Army was in mutiny; the North-Western Provinces were for the moment lost; the King of Delhi and our treacherous Sepoys were proclaiming a new empire; small bodies of gallant Englishmen were holding out for Government in isolated stations against fearful odds; the revolt was still extending; and the hearts of all Englishmen in India were daily torn by accounts of the massacre of their brethren, and the massacre, and worse than massacre, of their women and children."* In a word, there was a great crisis, and European journalism did not sufficiently take account of it—did not sufficiently consider that, whatever in ordinary times might be the uses of plain-speaking, a little reticence at such a season as this might be advantageous to the general interests of the Public and not dishonourable to public writers themselves.

It may be said, that when everybody else is excited,

* The Government of India to the Court of Directors, July 4, 1857.

it is not to be expected that the journalist should be free from excitement—that if, in the midst of general tribulation and confusion, he maintains serenity of mind and moderation of speech, he is superior to the majority of his fellows. But it is not to be forgotten that he assumes a superiority —a superiority, on the strength of which he criticises and controverts the acts and opinions of the highest officers of the Government, even of the Government itself—and that he, above all others, therefore, is bound, as a self-appointed public teacher, to set an example to the community. The responsibility which he takes upon himself is great; and he must stand or fall as he proves himself worthy or unworthy to be invested with it. If an individual communicates important information to the enemy—if he spreads abroad false reports tending to endanger the interests of the State and to jeopardise the lives of his countrymen—if he inflames and alarms the minds of those whom his Government are striving to pacify and to reassure—every journal in the land forthwith denounces him as a pestilent spy, a dangerous agitator, and a public foe; and calls for condign punishment to be inflicted upon him. But the newspaper that does these things is not a single spy—a single agitator—a single foe; but a legion of spies, and agitators, and foes. Its emissaries spread themselves all over the country, and do their mischief in the most remote as in the nearest places. The treason is of the most dangerous kind, and none the less so because it is unintentional.

It seemed, therefore, to Lord Canning and his colleagues in the middle of the month of June, that the malignant hostility of the Native and the reckless unreserve of the European Press were evils which it was the duty of the State to arrest. When the Press was liberated, some twenty years before, it had been one of the most cogent arguments in favour of the liberation — one, indeed, which had disarmed the hostile and encouraged the wavering—that, in the event of a critical conjuncture of affairs calling for such a measure, the Government of the day might in the course of an hour reimpose such restraints as it might think fit upon the Press. That circumstances might arise to render the reimposition of such restraints a salutary measure, and that it would be not only justifiable, but commendable on the part of Government to exercise the power vested in it, was never questioned even by the most liberal contemporaries of Sir Charles Metcalfe. And those exceptional circumstances, calling for exceptional measures, were now present to the Governor-General and his counsellors.

The Legislative Council of Calcutta was then composed of the members of the Executive Government and others especially appointed thereto, including the Chief Justice and one of the Puisne Judges. The legislators who met the Governor-General on the 13th of June consisted of four covenanted civilians, one military officer, and three English lawyers. The English element, therefore, of which the Governor-General, who had been little more than a year in India, was a conspicuous part, was certainly not overborne by the "services." The Governor-General brought in the Bill and proposed its first reading, which was seconded by Mr. Dorin, as senior member of Council. Lord Canning made a brief and emphatic speech, taking the whole responsibility on himself; but Chief Justice Colvile frankly declared his willingness to share that responsibility with the head of the

1857.
June.

Executive Government. There was not a dissentient voice in Council. There was not, indeed, any reluctance or any reserve on the part of a single legislator in that assemblage. Even Sir Arthur Buller, a Liberal of Liberals, accorded his assent as freely as Mr. Dorin and Mr. Grant. And Mr. Peacock was equally convinced that the *salus populi— suprema lex* demanded the exercise of exceptional powers for the suppression of an exceptional evil. The Act was passed, placing for a year the whole Press of India under penal restraints. Thenceforth no printing-press, within that time, was to be kept without a license from Government—if so kept, in defiance of the law, it might be seized and confiscated; —and the Executive Government was vested with full power to suppress at will, by an announcement in the Government Gazette, any publication which might be considered injurious to the interests of the State.

June 13.

Ever since the days of John Milton, Englishmen, in all parts of the world, have had a just reverence for the privilege of "unlicensed printing." It is not surprising, therefore, that the law passed on the 13th of June—No. XV. of 1857—excited a howl of indignation at the time, and by later writers has been severely condemned. It was forthwith christened the Gagging Act, and loaded with every term of reproach. The prompt cries of the daily papers were followed by the more deliberate execrations of the weeklies. It is unnecessary to examine in detail what was written under the influence of intense excitement, and would hardly now be justified by the writers themselves. But there is one statement, repeated in calmer moments, that may be noticed here. It has been said that by passing this Act Lord

Canning insulted the whole European community at a time when it was his special duty to conciliate them. But it is stated by the assailants of the Governor-General that the Company's civilians prompted the measure; so they were not insulted. It has been seen that the most eminent lawyers in Calcutta voted unhesitatingly in favour of the Bill; and it is not to be believed that they would have deliberately sanctioned a measure regarded as an offence to the whole legal profession. The sentiments of the merchants and traders are not equally apparent in the retrospect. But as they had a greater interest in the preservation of order and the protection of property, and were more largely connected with the Native inhabitants than any other class of Europeans, it must not be hastily assumed that a measure intended to allay public excitement and to moderate antipathies of race, was an abomination to the commercial community.* Moreover, to have drawn a distinction in such a case between the European and the Native Press would have been an insult to the loyal Native

---

* A letter before me, written a week after the Act was passed (by a high civil officer, one not likely to deviate from the truth), says: "I don't know what you will think of the Press Act, but no one ought to object to it who has not given a week to the study of the Indian newspapers. Sir Henry Lawrence tells us that the English Press has done us more harm in the Native mind than the Native Press, and that no paper has done us more harm than the *Friend of India*, which preaches the duty of spoliation in so many words, and almost in terms recommends forcible conversion, or the next thing to it. . . The sensible part of the European public approve of the Act. The good Native Press openly approves of it." The remarks of Sir Henry Lawrence, as contained in a letter to Lord Canning, were these: "Whatever may be the danger from the Native Press, I look on it that the papers published in our language are much the most dangerous. Disaffected Native editors need only translate as they do, with or without notes, or words of admiration or exclamations, editorials from the *Friend of India* (on the duty of annexing every Native State, on the imbecility, if not wickedness, of allowing a single Jagheer, and of preaching the Gospel, even by commanding officers), to raise alarm and hatred in the minds of all religionists, and all connected with Native principalities or Jagheers. And among the above will be found a large majority of the dangerous classes."

inhabitants who were supporting the Government in all parts of India. I think that the highest praise that can be bestowed on Lord Canning is that he never lost sight of the fact that he was Governor-General of India —that India was a great country, inhabited by vast millions of people, of different races and different religions, and that although it was his duty to maintain by all just means the Empire which he had been commissioned to govern, it did not become him to keep prominently before the Natives of the country the fact that they were a conquered people—a subject race—bound by other laws and amenable to other conditions than those recognised by their white-faced conquerors.

But no man knew better than Lord Canning that distinctions, which he was himself disinclined to draw, would be drawn by others both in India and in England; and he wrote to the President of the Board of Control, saying: "Another step taken last week, and which will provoke angry comment at home, is the check put temporarily upon the Press. The papers which go to you show the grounds on which this has been done. As regards the Native Press, I shall be surprised if even in England there are two opinions as to the propriety of the measure. The mischief which such writings as these which I send to you do amongst the ignorant and childish, but excitable Sepoys, and the fanatical Mahomedans of every class, will be easily understood, especially when it is known that they are eagerly sought and listened to by the Native soldiers. I consider that this evil is one which cannot, in the present state of India, be allowed to continue without positive guiltiness on the part of the Government. Therefore, I have not hesitated to take the power of arresting it by the only means which will be summary and efficacious. As to the English Press, it has no claim to exemption. If it were read only by English readers, something might be urged in its defence. Such an article as appeared in the *Friend of India* four weeks ago, pointing out our temporary weakness and the opportunity which it affords to our enemies, might then be harmless enough. But the articles of the English newspapers are translated into the Native languages and read by all. Again, as regards the announcement of facts, where a very little trouble of inquiry would avoid error, this morning (June 19) the *Hurkaru* states that European troops have been sent to Berhampore to arrest the Nawab of Moorshedabad, who, with his principal officers, has been discovered, through papers which the Government have seized, to be deeply implicated in the rebellion. This is wantonly false. The Nawab has hitherto been perfectly faithful, but how long he may remain so, if this paragraph meets his eye, is very doubtful. Of its effect upon the bigoted Mahomedan population of Moorshedabad there can be no doubt. They are ripe for revolt, and have already tampered with the Sepoys at Berhampore, and unless the means which have been taken to prevent any copy of the newspaper reaching Moorshedabad shall be successful, the risk of a rising against the Europeans will be most imminent; for the post will arrive there two days before the troops, who have been sent for no other purpose than to protect the station."*

* The displeasure of the Government was naturally very much increased by the recollection of the fact that the Calcutta journalist was freely supplied with information from Government House, in the shape both of actual news and the verifica-tion or correction of current rumours. "He has," wrote Lord Canning, "all information of interest supplied to him daily by the Government, and all his questions receive immediate answers; and yet he puts in a paragraph for which there is not a shadow of

1857.
June.

Perhaps now that Time has allayed the popular excitement and moderated the rash judgments of men, the sober conclusions of most people resemble these. I am aware that they are mere commonplaces; but they are the commonplaces of common sense. That it is the duty of a Government, in the general interests of the community, at periods of great popular excitement, to obtain the sanction of the Legislature for the exercise of exceptional powers, has never been questioned. The Liberty of the Subject and the Liberty of the Press are blessings to which every Englishman holds fast as to an inalienable birthright. But there are times and seasons when the most constitutional of Governments impose restrictions on the former, by suspending the Habeas Corpus Act, and do so without reproach when the public safety seems to demand a temporary suspension of the ordinary laws of the land. It is necessary to the justification of such a measure only that the crisis should be one of extreme urgency, and that the violence of persons should be sufficient to demand such violent interference with their liberties. And the same with respect to liberty of speech. Now the urgency of the crisis in this case was unquestioned and unquestionable. The only consideration was, whether the unrestrained utterances of the Anglo-Indian Press had been such as to increase, or to threaten to increase, the danger which menaced the State and the lives of the Christian community? Lord Canning thought that they were. All the members of his Council thought that they were. The most eminent lawyers in Calcutta thought that

foundation, and has not the sense to see that he is perilling the lives of a whole community of unprotected Europeans. Such editors in such times as these, and in this country, need to be controlled, whether they be European or Native."

they were. The Governors of the other Presidencies
thought that they were. Not because the attitude
of the Press was hostile to the Government, for, indeed, the general tendency of the most influential
portion of it was to support the British authorities—
but because — notwithstanding the loyalty, which
had never been suspected, which, indeed, was English
to a fault—it had manifested signs of a dangerous
want of caution, both in the dissemination of facts
and the utterance of opinions tending to expose
the weakness of the British Empire, to inflame the
passions of the people of India, and to excite alarm
among her Princes and Chiefs."

But it has been said that, although the circumstances were such as to justify the Government of the
day in placing restrictions upon the liberty of the
Press, as upon the liberty of the Subject, the same
results might have been attained in a less offensive
manner. In other words, a censorship might have
been established. But a censorship is, at all times,
an inconvenient and embarrassing affair, and, in
times of great popular excitement, the difficulty is
increased almost to the point of impossibility. For it
is in such times that a Government has most need of
the services of every one of its best officers; and it is
only to one of its best officers that the work of a
censorship can be safely intrusted. To take away any
such officer from his normal duties to watch the im-
prudences of the Press, would have resembled the
great evil which all men were bewailing at the time
—the necessity of employing European regiments
in keeping watch over suspected Sepoy battalions.
" Better disarm them at once !" was the cry. But
Lord Canning had another and still more incisive
reason for rejecting the alternative of the censorship.

If he had an officer whom he could spare for this difficult and delicate duty, he had not one to whom, he thought, he could safely intrust the performance of it. " I should have had to do it myself," he said afterwards to a gentleman who discussed the question with him ; and this may be considered conclusive.

But it is not to be doubted that this and other measures, however little understood, increased Lord Canning's unpopularity with some classes of the European community. To say that he was indifferent to it would not be true. No man can be altogether indifferent to the opinions of his countrymen. But he bore up bravely against it. It is more than probable that a certain feeling of contempt, which he could not suppress, contributed to the strength of his endurance. Perhaps, he had formed too low an estimate of the courage and constancy of the men by whom he was surrounded, and that he was too prone to draw general conclusions unfavourable to his countrymen from a few isolated facts. This was, doubtless, in some degree at least, to be attributed to the peculiarities of his position. For the head of the Government often lacks information of what is passing beyond the walls of Government House, and knows little or nothing of the tone and temper of general society. Those who sought his presence—I do not speak of the official functionaries, who had daily access to him—commonly came, with much excitement of manner, to tell alarmist stories, which he did not believe, or to suggest defensive measures, which he could not approve; whilst of the calm, quiet courage of those who stood aloof he probably heard nothing. Even those who liked him least and reviled him most never asserted that he showed the slightest symptom of fear ; and it must be admitted by the warmest of his admirers that he was not tolerant of those who did. It has been said, too, that his high personal courage, in which there was nothing boastful, sometimes led him into errors, which, though the errors of a noble nature, one may see reason to regret. This may not be wholly untrue. But the greater part of the charges brought against him— charges, which after ample circulation on the spot were sent home to friends in England, and by them published in the London newspapers, were based upon allegations absolutely, and in some instances ridiculously, false. Even Lady Canning, who was as little afraid as her lord, but who was full, to over-flowing, of sympathy and compassion towards her distressed countrymen and countrywomen, did not escape the mendacious censoriousness of Calcutta. It was said of her that she had spoken of the "poor, dear Sepoys;" and, though no such words had ever passed her lips, the rumour ran from house to house and found its way to England, and the unpopularity which had gathered so thickly around Lord Canning began also to encompass his wife. And lies grew apace—how, no man knew; for every one believed, who uttered them.

In the first week of June, and in the earlier part of the second, there appears to have been some sub-sidence of the excitement, the manifestations of which, in the latter part of the preceding month, had aroused such bitter feelings of indignation in the breast of Lord Canning; but ere the second week had expired, there was a renewal of the alarm, in a more exag-gerated form, and for a little while a great fear of the armed Sepoys took absolute possession of large num-

1857.
June.

bers of Christian people. There had always been a loud cry for the disarming of the Native regiments in Bengal, to the extreme limits of that province up to the great military station of Dinapore, hard by the city of Patna, not seldom in a state of Mahomedan fermentation. Of this I shall speak presently; but first must be recorded the events which occurred at the Head-Quarters of the Presidency Division of the Army.

The Barrack-pore regiments.

Whilst the first reinforcements of European troops were pouring into the great Presidency town, at Barrackpore the Sepoys seemed to be recovering from the epidemic which had recently assailed them. On the 25th of May, the Seventieth Regiment of Native Infantry had made offer of their services to march against the rebels at Delhi. Struck by this evidence of loyalty, and eager by all means to encourage it, for he believed that many might yet be reclaimed by generous proofs of confidence on the part of Government, Lord Canning, without loss of time, had driven to Barrackpore, where the regiment was drawn up to receive him, and in a brief, stirring address thanked them for their offer, and said that they should march up the country. The example of the Seventieth was soon followed by the Forty-third, who requested also that their regiment "might be allowed to proceed against the mutinous regiments at Delhi." And in the first week of June all the corps at Barrackpore besought the Government to supply them with the new Enfield rifle. Outwardly it was wise to accept this movement as another proof that the Sepoys had cast out their old suspicions, and were prepared faithfully to serve the Government, whose salt they had so long eaten. But to comply with the request, if compliance were possible, might have been to strengthen the hands of our enemies by placing in them a new and formidable weapon, which ere long might be turned against us. Whether such were the hidden purpose of the request, or whether the regiments who, from the first, had been swayed backwards and forwards by varying gusts of confidence and fear, of loyalty and infidelity, were at that time sincere in their protestations, can never be satisfactorily determined.* There was, fortunately, no need that Government should unravel this knotty question. The difficulty was cut through at once by the opportune fact that there was no supply of Enfield rifles in store that could be served out to the three regiments.

And before another week had spent itself, the whole complexion of things was changed. Instead of thinking of marching the regiments to Delhi with Enfield rifles in their hands, the authorities were now busy with the thought of dispossessing them even of the old clumsy instrument known among British soldiers as " Brown Bess." On the night of Saturday, the 13th of June, an express arrived at Government House from General Hearsey, stating that the Sepoys at Barrackpore had conspired to rise in the course of the night, and that he had sent for the Seventy-eighth Highlanders, who were then at Chinsurah, to disarm the suspected regiments, if the measure were approved by Government. The sanction to the disarming was reluctantly given. General Hearsey had " shown such firmness and nerve before," that Lord

* The words of the Native officer of the Seventieth are worth quoting. " We have thought over the subject, and as we are now going up country, we beg that the new rifles, about which so much has been said in the army and all over the country, may be served out to us. By using them in its service, we hope to prove beyond a doubt our fidelity to Government ; and we will explain to all we meet that there is nothing objectionable in them, otherwise why should we have taken them ? Are we not as careful of our caste and religion as any of them ?"

1857.
June.

June 14.
The regi-
ments dis-
armed.

Canning "could not resist the appeal." He was never satisfied that the measure was necessary. But he issued instructions with all promptitude, and that night one European regiment was marching up from Calcutta, and another was coming down from Chinsurah, to enforce the disarming.*

The night passed quietly in the Lines, though anxiously in the English bungalows; and, perhaps, not without some efforts on the part of the worst-disposed of the Sepoys to excite their comrades to an immediate outbreak, this quietude was maintained. About five o'clock on the morning of the 14th the Highlanders marched into Barrackpore. Misled by a guide, they had gone out of their way; and when they made their appearance at Head-Quarters, weary and footsore, and in many instances only half dressed and accoutred—according to contemporary chroniclers, some without shoes and stockings, and some in their sleeping drawers—the time had passed for immediate action. The day was spent quietly, as the night had been, and when towards evening the Native regiments were suddenly warned for parade, and marched to the parade-ground, they found themselves face to face with a line of guns, and with a body of Europeans on each of their flanks. Then General Hearsey addressed them, tenderly and kindly, in his wonted

* A week afterwards he wrote to Mr. Vernon Smith, saying: "I am not now satisfied that there was any sufficient ground for a general disarming; and, although all Calcutta is delighted at it, I look forward with some apprehension to the effect which the measure will have at the several stations in Lower Bengal. I have always foreseen this danger in disarming at the Presidency. I shall rejoice if my fears prove groundless —but already several desertions have taken place since the disarming, and some of the men are making their way to Barrackpore with the news. The Forty-third, the best behaved regiment in Bengal, against which there has never been a breath of reproach, is completely panic-stricken, and the men are deserting one day and coming back the next, not knowing what to do with themselves, but confident that some further disgrace or injury is intended to them."— *MS. Correspondence.*

manner, and told them that it was the order of Go-
vernment that they should lay down their arms, lest
they should be incited by ill-disposed persons to acts
of mutiny and rebellion. They obeyed, promptly
and patiently, with the air of men who had been
wrongfully treated rather than baffled in an iniquitous
design. They were fearful and sorrowful, and many
of their English officers were well-nigh heart-broken
by what they considered the unjust punishment and
humiliation of their men. Some asked that the
Sepoys' arms might be restored, whilst the Sepoys
themselves, believing that they would be massacred
by the Europeans, deserted in large numbers, glad to
escape even with their lives.

The Sepoy guards in Calcutta, at Fort William,
and in the suburbs of the great city, were furnished
from the regiments at Barrackpore. If the main
bodies of the several battalions at the Head-Quarters
of the Division were to be disarmed, it could not be
otherwise than necessary to subject to similar treatment the offshoots on scattered duty elsewhere.
Whilst, therefore, the disarming parade was being
held at Barrackpore, the detachments at the Presidency were disarmed. It was effected without resistance. The work was easily done ; and in the same
quiet orderly manner the Sepoy guards at Dum-Dum
were deprived of their arms by a party of the Fifty-
third sent up for the purpose.

Meanwhile, on that 14th of June, there was   "Panic Sun-
great excitement in Calcutta. It was reported   day."
that the Sepoys at Barrackpore had risen in the
night; and soon the rumour ran that they were in
full march upon Calcutta. Then also went abroad
the story, and ready credence grasped it, that the
Oude people at Garden-Reach were to rise at the

same time, and to join in the threatened massacre of
the Christian people. So the hearts of many failed
them through fear, and some, terror-stricken and bewildered, left their homes, seeking refuge wheresoever
safety could be found. From an early hour in the
morning a great shudder ran through the capital,
and soon the confused activity of panic flight was
apparent. The streets, in some parts of the city,
were alive with vehicles. Conspicuous among them
were those great long boxes on wheels, known as
"palanquin carriages." Within might be seen the
scared faces of Eurasians and Portuguese, men,
women, and children; and without, piled up on the
roofs, great bundles of bedding and wearing apparel,
snatched up and thrown together in the agonised
hurry of departure. Rare among these were carriages of a better class, in which the pale cheeks of
the inmates told their pure European descent. Along
the Mall on the water-side, or across the broad plain
between the City and the Fort, the great stream
is said to have poured itself. The places of refuge
which offered the best security were the Fort and
the River. Behind the ramparts of the one, or in the
vessels moored on the other, a safe asylum might be
found. So these fugitives are described as rushing
to the gates of the Fort, or disgorging themselves at
the different ghauts, calling excitedly for rowing-
boats to carry them to the side of ship or steamer.
There was a prevailing feeling that the enemy were
on their track, and that swift destruction would overtake them if they did not find shelter within the
earthworks of Fort William or the wooden walls of
the shipping on the Hooghly.* Hard work had

* An informant, resident in Cal-   flight as "what might have been seen
cutta at the time, who describes the   if a modern Herculaneum had been

Colonel Cavenagh to dispose of all these refugees— harder still to persuade them that all the wild stories with which they were full to bursting were nothing more than the figments of an excited imagination. But he contrived to dismiss them at last, and sent them back to their homes.*

It is recorded, too, by contemporary chroniclers and correspondents, how, in the securer parts of the city, other Christian people were garrisoning their houses and giving ingress to friends, who, living in remoter places, or in residences less capable of defence, sought shelter from the coming danger—how doors

1857.
June 14.

evacuated in broad daylight on the approach of a visible eruption from a neighbouring volcano," says: "The whole line of the ghauts was crowded with fugitives, and those who could find no shelter in the ships took refuge within the Fort, of which the squares, the corridors, all the available space everywhere, indeed, were thronged by many, who passed the night in their carriages."—*MS. Memorandum.* [As some guarded statements in my second volume have been contradicted on the authority of Dr. Mouat, it is right that I should state that the writer of the above is Dr. Mouat himself.]

* Very contradictory accounts of the rush to the Fort having reached me, I think it right to record the evidence of the highest official authority on this point. Colonel Cavenagh, early on the morning of the 14th, had ridden to Government House to receive instructions from the Governor-General: "On my return home," he has recorded in his journal, "I found my house besieged by all sorts of people wishing to obtain shelter in the Fort, and all full of rumours of the worst description from Dum-Dum and Barrackpore. I endeavoured to reassure them to the best of my power; but

I am sure that many left under the impression that I was misleading them. However, in time I pacified them and sent them away." This was written at the time. Subsequently, in reply to my inquiries for fuller information, Colonel Cavenagh wrote: "I took my ride in the evening to visit the different guards, and satisfy myself that my orders had been duly executed. I noticed that there were, comparatively speaking, few carriages on the Course, but did not observe any unusual number of vehicles in the Fort. Being Sunday, there may have been a few drawn up on the roads leading to the church, but none on the parade-grounds, for I am certain I should at once have ordered them off. In the forenoon, two ladies, perfect strangers to me, had asked for shelter. I told them that they were welcome to the use of my drawing-room, but that I thought they had better return home, upon which they departed. I believe that some of the officers in the garrison gave accommodation to friends, and I heard of one lady and gentleman coming during the night to the officer commanding the Main Guard, with whom, if I remember rightly, they were connected."

1857.
June 14.

and windows were fast closed; rifles and revolvers were loaded, and how some took down their hog-spears and placed them ready for the expected assault.* From the less fashionable outskirts, as Entally and the Circular Road, occupied mainly by the great world of clerkdom—the so-called "crannies," official and commercial, of Calcutta—the exodus is described as universal. The thoroughfares were as those of a city which had been smitten with a pestilence. Save by a few sturdy pensioners, who were to be seen unconcernedly smoking their pipes, the houses in that neighbourhood were wholly deserted. Many had been left with doors and windows open, at the mercy of any lawless citizens who might chance to covet their neighbours' goods.† A few active plunderers might have gathered a rich booty. But it seems as though even crime itself were bewildered and incapable on that Sunday afternoon; for not a house was entered for an unlawful purpose; not an outrage was committed in the streets.

There were others, who bore themselves bravely before their fellows, and, confident themselves, inspired confidence by their calm and resolute bearing. The ministrations of the Church were not neglected, and the pews were not empty, though many believed that our Christian temples would be the first points

* It has been stated (Red Pamphlet) that among the most panic-stricken were men highest in authority. "Those highest in office were the first to give the alarm. There were secretaries to Government running over to members of Council, loading their pistols, barricading the doors, sleeping on sofas; members of Council abandoning their houses with their families, and taking refuge on board ship; crowds of lesser celebrities, impelled by these examples, having hastily collected their valuables, were rushing to the Fort, only too happy to be allowed to sleep under the Fort guns." Compare note, p. 34.

† One informant (Dr. Mouat), who drove that evening through Entally, the Circular Road, &c. &c., tells me that "the very dogs and cats seemed to have vanished from the earth." He had never witnessed "a scene of such utter and absolute abandonment."

of attack for the furious raging of the heathen or the
wild fanaticism of the followers of the Prophet.* It
was on a Sunday that the great storm had first
burst upon us ; it was on a Sunday, three weeks
afterwards, that, as many believed, a far more desolating storm was to have swept over the country ;
and now again it was on a Sunday that, in the
excited imaginations of our people, their chief city
was to be given up to the cruel vengeance of barbarous
enemies. But these barbarous enemies were as much
scared as our Christian people. A great panic was
upon them. They were expecting that the European
soldiers who had recently arrived from beyond the
seas would be let loose upon the unarmed populace.
And many shut themselves up in their houses, bolted
and barred their doors and windows, and looked forth
furtively with frightened faces when they heard the
sounds of horses' hoofs or wheeled carriages in the
streets. But nothing came of these wild alarms.
The day, the evening, the night passed, and there
was no shedding of blood, no disturbance of the peace.
Never since Fear first entered the world had there
been a more groundless and unreasonable panic. No
demonstration was made by the Sepoys of the Presidency Division, and if any mischief had been designed by the Oude colony at Garden Reach, it
never developed into action. The promptitude of
Government strangled it in the womb.

It will be seen that, of the phenomena of this
"Panic Sunday," I have written more doubtfully,

1857.
June 14.

* Dr. Duff says, that "Almost all the ministers in Calcutta had expos-tulatory letters sent them, dissuad-ing them from preaching in the fore-noon, and protesting against their attempting to do so in the evening. And though, to their credit, no one, as far as I have heard, yielded to the pressure, the churches in the fore-noon were half empty, and in the evening nearly empty altogether."

after a lapse of years, than others whose knowledge of facts both time and place must have favoured. Contemporary chroniclers and correspondents who were in Calcutta, or the vicinity, on that 14th of June, have written, in graphic language, of the flight to the Fort and the Fleet; and others have narrated to me verbally some of the incidents of the great Christian exodus. But, on the other hand, men of high character and position have denied, with equal strength of assertion, the accuracy of these records and reminiscences of a reign of terror. After most diligent inquiry, I have come to the conclusion that the truth is to be found mid-way between the two extremes. That men of high official rank, whose first duty it was to set an example of confidence and constancy to the community, stained their manhood and disgraced their office by betraying the cowardice in their hearts, I have discovered no satisfactory evidence to convince an impartial historical inquirer.* But that there was no panic—no flight—no confusion; that there was little to distinguish the 14th of June from any other day; that the ordinary goings-on of social life moved in the accustomed groove; and that the outward signs of a great bewilderment were discernible only by the eye of imagination—are assertions equally remote from the truth. The excitement of the times drove men, otherwise honest and truthful, into excessive generalisation, and the shortcomings of a few were described as the failure of a whole community. On the other hand, after a

---

* It is to be borne in mind that even in ascertained cases of high functionaries having left their houses in the suburbs to dwell nearer the centre of business, the ostensible reason of the change was the inconvenience, at a time of frequent official references, of residing at so great a distance from Government House; and it would be uncharitable not to accept the ostensible reason as the real one.

lapse of years, there is a natural tendency to ignore
what cannot be spoken of with pleasure or with
pride, and broad denials take the place of broad
assertions, equally to the obscuration of the truth.*

1857.
June 14.

For some weeks the rumour had been gaining
ground that the King of Oude, or more properly the
people about him, had been tampering with the
Native soldiery, and instigating them to rebellion.
It was currently believed that the exiles of Garden
Reach were, in fact, the prime movers of the insurrection which was bearing such bitter fruits. It was so
inevitable that such reports should be in circulation,
and so probable that the truth, in such a case, should
be greatly exaggerated, at a time when everything
was magnified or distorted, that Lord Canning was
slow to credit all the stories which reached him,
sometimes from notorious alarmists. But as the
month of June advanced, it became more and more
apparent that the reports, which came to his ears,
were not wholly without the foundation of fact.† It

June 15.
Arrest of the
King of
Oude.

---

* It is a significant fact that, four days afterwards, the following graphic account was published as part of an editorial article (*Friend of India*, June 18, 1857), and I do not observe that it was contradicted: "Whilst the work of disarming was going on at Barrackpore, precisely the same process was being carried through at Calcutta, where it was rumoured that murder and mutiny were triumphant at the former place, and that a strong force of rebels was marching down upon the city from Delhi. The infection of terror raged through all classes. Chowringhee and Garden Reach were abandoned for the Fort and the vessels in the river. The shipping was crowded with visitors, and in houses which were selected as being least likely to be attacked, hundreds of people gladly huddled together, to share the peculiar comforts which the presence of crowds imparts on such occasions. The hotels were fortified; bands of sailors marched through the thoroughfares happy in the expectation of possible fighting and the certainty of grog. Every group of Natives was scanned with suspicion. . . . . Many years must elapse before the night of the 14th of June, 1857, will be forgotten in Calcutta."

† One incident in particular created a great sensation, in high places, at the time. A man had been caught tampering with a Sepoy

1857.
June 15.

was certain that people living within the great circle of the new Oude home on the banks of the Hooghly had endeavoured to corrupt the Sepoys in the Fort — and especially the sentries posted at its gates. Colonel Cavenagh, the Town-Major, had received repeated warnings from Mahomedan friends that mischief was brewing, that Mussulman Sepoys were frequently visiting the King's people at Garden Reach, and that some influential visitors from Oude, including the great Talookhdar, Maun Singh, had visited Calcutta, and held conferences with the King or his Minister.* Of his obese Majesty himself, it was generally said that he had not energy sufficient to take active part even in intrigue. But in his own indolent way, beguiled by large promises of restoration to his lost kingdom, he suffered the work to be done for him ; and it went forward—with what de-

in the Fort, had been tried by court-martial, and had been sentenced to death. The trial took place on the 14th of June; and the man was to have been hanged on the following morning. But in the course of the night he managed to effect his escape.—*See Note in the Appendix.*

* The fact of this visit to the King of Oude, and of the subsequent correspondence with Maun Singh, was asserted very unreservedly by a Native informant of Colonel Cavenagh, Town-Major of Fort William. See following extracts from that officer's journal : "*May* 21. My old friend Amir Ali called. He stated positively that the King of Oude had carried on a correspondence with Rajah Maun Singh, who had addressed him in the first instance, calling for his sanction to a rising in his favour, and on this being refused on the plea of the King's relations being in our hands, was reminded by the Rajah of the fact of Akhbar Khan having secured the release of

his father, Dost Mahomed, upon which a firman was prepared and despatched to Oude, authorising the movement proposed, provided he, the King, was not in any way compromised, and promising to remit three years' revenue to any one who should join his cause." . . . "*May* 27. Amir Ali called. He states that the letter from Rajah Maun Singh was despatched, though not by public dawk, to the address of Zemindar Mullyan Singh, and that the correspondence was carried on by cipher" (certain Persian letters being substituted for others of the same alphabet). "He asserts that Rajah Maun Singh has certainly reached Calcutta and been closeted with the King." Lord Canning did not then credit the story, and it was afterwards made clear that the Rajah was not in Calcutta at the end of May, being then under surveillance at Fyzabad. It is believed that he visited Calcutta earlier in the year. See *post*—Chapters on Oude.

vices we may never know, but certainly with such
activity as would have rendered it wrong in Government any longer to neglect it. So the resolution
was taken. The King of Oude, his chief minister
(Ali Nuckee Khan), and one or two others of the
principal people about him, were suddenly to be
made prisoners on the morning of the 15th of June,
and to be conveyed in custody to Fort William.

The performance of this duty was intrusted to
Mr. George Edmonstone. Bearing a name of high
repute in Indian history, he had well maintained
his hereditary title to distinction. The energy and
ability which had placed his father in the very foremost rank of a past generation of Indian statesmen,
and which, indeed, in a great measure had made the
reputation of the greatest of India's Governor-Generals, had descended to him unimpaired; and
there was not one of all Lord Canning's immediate
advisers whose counsel might be more safely trusted.
Holding the office—the most honoured of all under
the Governor-General in Council—of Political or
Foreign Secretary, it devolved upon him to transact
ministerially all the business of the Native States
and Native Princes of India—chiefly by correspondence; but, in some instances, as in this, by more
personal action. The mission on which he was now
sent was a delicate and a painful one. Firm, but
yet courteous in his bearing, he acquitted himself
with excellent address, and did the work intrusted
to him with all fidelity to the Government, and with
as little offence as possible to the exiled monarch
whom he was sent to arrest.

Accompanied by some officers of Lord Canning's
staff, and escorted by a considerable body of European troops, with a supplementary force of police,

Mr. Edmondstone.

The colony at
Garden
Reach.

1857.
June 15.
Edmonstone arrived under the outer walls of the King's residence in the first dim light of the dawn. Having surrounded the premises, so as to render escape impossible, he entered the compound with a detachment of the Fifty-third under Colonel Powell. A strange sight greeted him there. In the garden-grounds of Wajid Ali's new home a great village, or a small town, had arisen. The area was thickly covered with Native houses—a great confused mass of thatched buildings, huddling one upon another, without a symptom of arrangement or design. This rendered the advance and the disposition of the troops difficult; but there was small need for military coercion of any kind. There was not a sign of resistance, not even of preparation. The strong hand of the British had descended suddenly and unexpectedly on the new Oude colony, and the most active members of that great Mussulman community were rousing themselves in the early morning to respond to nothing more formidable than the Azan, or Mahomedan call to prayer. The troops had been warned not to use their arms unless there were signs of armed resistance. One man only was put under fixed bayonets and gently coerced to show the way to the residence of the chief minister; for the seizure of Ali Nuckee Khan was the first step to be taken. After some delay the Nawab came forth, and was at once arrested, with two other principal members of the suite—Ahsun Hoossein Khan and his son. These last, together with Tikaet Rao, the Dewan of the Chief Begum, were sent under a guard on board the *Semiramis*, which had been steaming down the river to Garden Reach whilst the troops had been marching along the road.

Arrest of the King.

It was now Edmonstone's duty to obtain ingress

to the King's apartments. This was a work of some difficulty and delicacy, and only to be accomplished after further delays. For there was a general reluctance to convey the unwelcome message to his Majesty's ears; and Wajid Ali had to bathe and to attire himself before he could receive the English gentlemen. But the regal ablutions and the toilet having been duly performed, Edmonstone and his companions were admitted to the presence of the King. Seated on a couch, and surrounded by members of his suite, he welcomed the Government Secretary with a sickly smile, shook him by the hand, and courteously received the other English officers. When they were all seated, Edmonstone spoke. He said that intelligence had reached the Governor-General, which had satisfied his Lordship that emissaries using his Majesty's name had spread themselves in all directions over the British dominions, and had instigated many of the Native soldiers of the Army to swerve from their allegiance. " It is the wish of the Governor-General, therefore," he added, " that your Majesty should accompany me on my return to Calcutta."

Roused by this address into something at least resembling energy of manner and emphasis of speech, the King replied that he had not been guilty of the offence imputed to him, and that if he had done anything to tamper with the loyalty of the troops, he would be deserving of any punishment which the British Government might be pleased to inflict upon him. Edmonstone answered that he had no authority to discuss the question, and requested his Majesty to prepare for departure. A number of his courtiers clamoured for permission to accompany him. Liberal compliance was accorded to them; and ere long the unwieldy, tottering exile was leaning on the arm of

1857.
June 15.

the British Secretary, who escorted him to the outer door, where the Governor-General's carriage was waiting to receive them.

On their way to the Fort the firmness of the King broke down. He seemed suddenly to awaken to the misery and humiliation of his position. Bursting into tears, he spoke of the dignity of his ancestors, his own heavy fall and wretched condition as an exile and a suspect, and asked whether, if he had ever intended to array himself against the British Government, he would not have done so when he had twenty lakhs of men at his back. "But ask General Outram," he added, "if I did not quietly submit to his authority, and deliver up my kingdom into his hands." He then subsided into silence, almost into insensibility; but presently he burst again into tears, protested his innocence, and pointing to an amulet, on which some passages of the Koran were inscribed, and which hung from his neck, he said, "When I read in the *Hurkaru* newspaper that I was accused of tampering with the troops, I swore upon this that I would keep clear of all such machinations." To this Edmonstone could only reply that justice would be done, and every consideration shown to his Majesty, by the Government which he represented. The rest of the journey was accomplished in silence, and about eight o'clock the King of Oude was placed, with becoming courtesy and respect, in the hands of Colonel Cavenagh, the Town-Major, who was prepared to receive him.

Thus, on the morning of June 15th, Wajid Ali, Ali Nuckee Khan, and three other members of the King's suite, were conveyed, state prisoners, to Fort William. There quarters were provided for them in the building known as the Government House—an edifice appropriated to many uses, but seldom or never to the one for which it was originally designed. Although on a limited scale, the accommodation was not ill-suited to the purpose to which it was now to be put; for there was at least one large state apartment, with several smaller ones opening into it, and there was a dignity in the name which may have rubbed off some of the degradation of the captivity. It was the best place that could be found as the temporary home of his Majesty of Oude and the wily ministers who directed his political movements. But little or nothing was brought to light to implicate the King in the alleged conspiracies against the British Government. If there were damnatory evidence in letters or documents at Garden Reach, it was not discovered. The premises could not be searched without violating the sanctity of the female apartments; and this an English officer, save in extremest cases, is ever bound to respect.*

The disarming of the Sepoys and the captivity of

* This measure calls for neither justification nor explanation; but I may as well place upon record Lord Canning's brief statement of his reasons, as contained in a letter to the Indian Minister at home : "The King of Oude and four of his suite have been placed in Fort William. The immediate grounds of this will be found in the deposition of a Sepoy, who was twice tampered with by a Mahomedan, who described himself as coming from the King's people, and although no complicity in the act has been fixed upon the King or his chief courtiers, I deem it necessary for the safety of the State that it should for the present be put out of the power of any one to seduce the State's soldiers by speaking in the name of the King of Oude, and that his name should not be made a rallying-point for disaffected soldiers. I think this the more necessary, because I know that offers of enlistment were made a few weeks ago by a person in the King's service to another supposed to be seeking employment. Of the four who are in the Fort, Ali Nuckee Khan is the King's minister ; Hoossein Khan is a notorious intriguer of the Court, of the worst repute from the time of Colonel Sleeman. Hassan Khan is his son ; Tikaet Rao is a Hindoo, a Dewan or steward in the Queen's service. His character makes him an object of suspicion."—Lord Canning to Mr. Vernon Smith, June 19, 1857.—MS. Records.

1857.
June.

the King of Oude restored for a time tranquillity to Calcutta. To this result the activity of the Volunteer Guards greatly contributed. Any doubts which might at first have been entertained respecting the practical efficiency of these citizen-battalions, were soon removed by the zeal which they continuously manifested. It was not permitted to them, as to Havelock's volunteers, of whom I have already spoken, or Henry Lawrence's, of whom I shall speak presently, to flash their sabres in the faces of an overwhelming enemy; but night after night, amidst all the inclemencies of the rainy season, they were found at their posts, ready for any service which they might be called upon to perform. Some hundreds of Infantry were thus enrolled under Major Davies, with a proportionate number of Cavalry under Captain Turnbull, whilst Captain Dickens of the Artillery organised the Ordnance branch of the brigade. Major Strachey of the Engineers had succeeded Colonel Cavenagh in command of the entire force. And all did their work so well that it was not long before Lord Canning took occasion publicly to express his appreciation of their "zealous and excellent services."*

---

* See reply to Address of Calcutta inhabitants, petitioning for martial law throughout the Bengal Provinces. At a later period Lord Canning wrote with reference to the Volunteers: "It has received every encouragement from the Governor-General, from the day of its formation, and has done useful service in patrolling the town and giving confidence. It is not to be denied that the mutinies, which then declared themselves, have grown into a more formidable revolt than was anticipated; but at the time . . . whilst every preparation was made to meet the growth of the danger, whatever dimensions it might assume, the Governor-General felt it to be urgently necessary to check panic in places where no real danger existed, especially in Calcutta, where it could not fail to be mischievous, both politically and commercially. There is not a doubt that the exaggerated fears, which a great part of the Calcutta population have exhibited on at least three occasions during the progress of the mutinies, have led the Natives to doubt our self-reliance and our strength, whilst nothing of safety has been gained to ourselves thereby."

The centenary of Plassey came and went. In
Calcutta, as in other parts of the country, apprehensions had been entertained that on that day there
would be a formidable rising ; and when it arrived
there was something more than the wonted vigilance
and preparation. But the most memorable incident
connected with that 23rd of June, was the publication, two days afterwards, in the Serampore journal,
of an article in celebration of that important anni-
versary—an article in which Mahomedan Princes
were reviled as "cruel, sensual, intolerant, unfit to
rule"—and Mahrattas and Sikhs were triumphed
over with equal insolence of self-laudation—an article
closing with the words, "the first centenary of
Plassey was ushered in by the revolt of the Native
Army ; the second may be celebrated in Bengal by
a respected Government and a Christian population."
There was not much in the words. Such words had
been often published before and smiled at complacently by the Government of the day. But there
was much in the time of publication. The article
was peculiarly calculated, in such a conjuncture, to
irritate the minds of the people, for it might bear a
meaning which perhaps the writer never intended to
assign to it. Straightway, therefore, the Government
"warned" the publisher of the *Friend of India.* This
brought forth a rejoinder, headed "The First Warning," still less discreet than its predecessor. And the
ablest journal in Bengal, which had always been
regarded as a model of respectability and discretion,
would have been suppressed, if some friends of the
absent proprietors had not come forward to protect
their interests, and guaranteed that the "officiating"
editor should no longer have it in his power to

1857.
June.

Military precautions.

sacrifice their property by his want of temper and want of tact.*

Meanwhile, every exertion was being made to expedite the movements and to secure the efficiency of the reinforcements despatched, or about to be despatched, to the North. The arrival of Sir Patrick Grant had infused new vigour into the military department of Government, and had afforded to the Governor-General himself most appreciable assistance and support.† The troops from the Coast and from the Persian Gulf had been despatched to the Upper Provinces before the end of the third week of June;‡ and now Lord Canning looked eagerly for the coming of the regiments which he had urged Lord Elgin and General Ashburnham to divert from the China Expedition. It was necessary to prepare for the arrival of these by providing all the necessary appliances of equipment and carriage; so orders were sent to

---

* I do not purpose to dwell any further upon the practical results of the passing of this law, which were, indeed, so slight, that it has been said of the Act that it was a "dead letter." It is right, however, thus to state, with respect to the *Friend of India*, which has always borne a high reputation, by no means confined to the place of its nativity, that the proprietors of the paper and the responsible editor were, at the time, absent from India, and that the literary management was then in the hands of a public writer of more ability than discretion, who has placed on record, in a permanent form, his impressions of the great events which were passing around him. ("Mead's Sepoy Revolt," published by Mr. Murray in 1857.) I have a conviction amounting to certainty, that if either of the absentees, to whom I have referred, had been in India in May and June,

1857, no such articles as those which brought temporary discredit on the *Friend of India* would ever have been written.

† Sir Patrick Grant arrived at Calcutta on the 17th of June.— Vol. ii. p. 281.

‡ "The European troops are being pushed up as quickly as possible. The whole of the Madras Fusiliers must now be at Allahabad, and the Eighty-fourth have passed beyond Benares, as also a portion of the Sixty-fourth. The last of the Seventy-eighth Highlanders leave by bullock-train to-morrow, the 20th, when the wing of the Thirty-seventh will be despatched. One European battery left by steam this morning, and another is preparing to follow. The detachment of the Royal Artillery will also be sent up by bullock-train." —*Memorandum of General Birch, June* 19.—The wing of the Thirty-seventh had come from Ceylon.

Madras to despatch immediately to Calcutta a large
proportion of the clothing and camp-equipage that
had been collected there, whilst the Bombay Government were called upon to procure from Bushire and
other places " as large a supply of horses as possible
for Cavalry and Artillery purposes." Efforts at the
same time were made to communicate to Agra the
instructions of Government that no exertion should
be spared in the North-Western Provinces to collect
carriage for the upward march of the troops. The
miserable want of conveyance for the sick and
wounded, which had so palpably presented itself to
General Neill at Allahabad,* was being supplied as
rapidly as possible by the artificers of Calcutta. If
there had before been any short-comings, omissions,
or delays, nothing now was neglected that could give
completeness to the military organisation by which
the succours received from beyond the seas were to
be turned to the best account. Nothing escaped the
practised eye of Sir Patrick Grant. His training had
been of the right kind to qualify him for the apt performance of the work in hand. His coming, therefore, supplied what was most wanted to give strength
to the administration, which had before been essentially wanting in military efficiency. Perhaps, if the
General had been moved only by his own natural
impulses, he would have proceeded at once to the
seat of war to take an active part in the great
struggle. But his better judgment taught him that
in no place could he, at that time, be so serviceable to
the State as at the seat of Government; and in this
opinion Lord Canning and all the members of his
Council concurred.† To the Governor-General it

* Vol. ii. p. 273.
† " I am of opinion that as soon as

the course of events shall tend to
allay the general disquiet, and to

1857.
June.

Succours
from Eng-
land.

appeared that his new colleague possessed most of the essential qualifications to be looked for in a man, to whom the chief command of the Indian Army, with the great after-work of reconstruction, might now be safely intrusted ; and he wrote letters to the Home Government urging the permanent confirmation of the provisional appointment. He was afraid of the coming of a stiff-necked Horse Guards General ; and dwelt emphatically on the importance, in such a juncture, of that knowledge and experience which can be acquired only by long years of residence in India and familiarity with its camps and cantonments.

From the first, Lord Canning, though hoping to gather up troops enough from our outlying colonies, or from the great highway of the ocean, to break the neck of the first revolt, felt that there would be much after-work to be done, which would demand the aid of large reinforcements from England. On the 19th of May, he had written to the President of the India Board, saying : " From England what I ask is, that you should immediately send out the regiments which are due to the full complement of Queen's corps in India without making us wait for the issue of events in China; and that you will give support to the demand for three new European regiments to be added to the Company's Army in place of the six which have now erased themselves from the Army List. You will see that there will be no additional

show to what points our force should be mainly directed, with the view of crushing the heart of the rebellion, it will be proper that his Excellency should consider anew the question of his movements. His Excellency's experience and high authority will then, in all probability, be most use-fully employed in the disturbed districts or their neighbourhood. For the present there will be the greatest advantage in his Excellency remaining at the seat of Government."— *Minute of Lord Canning, June 22,* 1857.

cost. I beg that you will grant me both these re-
quests." But ere the first week of June was at an
end, these moderate views had expanded under the
expanded significance of the revolt. The magnitude
of the work to be accomplished was now shown to be
far greater than it had appeared some two or three
weeks before. " Be the issue what it may," wrote
Lord Canning to Mr. Vernon Smith on the 5th of
June, " whether with the speedy fall of Delhi the
rebellion at once collapses, or whether before this
happens ravages extend and the Europeans are driven
from the Central Provinces, and those parts hence to
be recovered, I reckon that we shall require an additional force of twelve regiments of Infantry and one
regiment of Dragoons. We must not conceal from
ourselves that our Government must henceforth rest
much more openly than heretofore upon military
strength. There must be no arsenal, or strong places,
such as Allahabad and Delhi; no fanatical stronghold, such as Benares; no large tract of rich, defence-
less country, such as Lower Bengal, without a European regiment. No brigade of Native troops should
be without one. A strong force, not less than eight
regiments, should be always near the capital, ready
to be directed to any point in the Bay of Bengal.
Second and third-class arsenals and depôts must have
a defence of Europeans. Europeans must be seen in
Central India and Nagpore. We must for a time,
and no short time, make our European strength
visible and sensible to all India. Our power and
name have had a rude shock, and nothing must be
spared to make them firm again. Until this has been
done, no confidence, political, social, or commercial,
will be re-established. I have no hope that it can be
done by anything short of ten regiments to be added

1857.
June.

permanently, and at first I should greatly desire to have twelve." But, although he saw clearly the necessity, and thus urgently impressed upon the Home Government the duty, of immediately strengthening the European Force in India, he was careful not to make, under the influence of this pressure, such demands upon the military resources of Great Britain as might result in the infliction of a permanent burden upon India such as it would be difficult to bear up against on the restoration of peace. He saw clearly in the distance an immense strain upon the finances of the Indian Empire, and he was anxious not to increase it by any unnecessary military expenditure.*

Economical measures.

It was not, indeed, only the great trouble of the present that oppressed him. He was even then compelled, amidst all the distractions of the hour, to look the future of the Empire in the face. The mutiny—the rebellion—whatsoever it should prove to be, might be trodden down; but still it would leave behind it a great incubus of disorder and disaster, rendering the work of settled government difficult, for years to come. There was necessarily an enormous additional expenditure of money at a time when, in many parts of the country, the sources of revenue were being dried up by the fire of revolt; and how to meet all these extraordinary charges was a question of no very easy solution. The only certainty was, that it had become an absolute necessity to provide for the exigencies of the moment at any sacrifice of future efficiency and prosperity. There are seasons

---

* "I am very anxious," he wrote to Mr. Vernon Smith, "that we should not, under the present pressure, great as it is, rush into any superfluous expenditure for purposes of safety. The material progress of the country has at the best been pushed back many years, and every lakh unnecessarily spent upon military establishments will retard its advance." — *MS. Correspondence of Lord Canning, July* 3, 1857.

when nations, like individuals, must live from hand to mouth; when the struggle is for bare existence, and all principles of sound financial economy must yield to the exigencies of the crisis. It is a sore trial to a statesman to be compelled to cast away the means of large prospective gain in the pursuit of some necessary scheme of present retrenchment. And thus now was Lord Canning tried. He had to get money as he could; he had to save it as he could. To get it was not easy. That such a crisis as this must have greatly shaken the credit of the British Government was inevitable. The wonder is that it was so little shaken. "It is astonishing," wrote Lord Canning to Mr. Vernon Smith on the 3rd of July, "how little Government securities have suffered during the convulsion. Four-per-cent. paper at the beginning of June was at fourteen to fourteen and a half discount—an ordinary rate. About the 12th of June it reached its lowest depreciation—twenty to twenty-one discount. Since that it has been pretty steadily rising, and has got back to fifteen to fifteen and a half per cent. This does not look very bad." A five-per-cent. loan was then open. At this time the Governor-General reported that it had "stopped, or all but stopped, at close upon two millions sterling." It was obvious, therefore, that to meet the enormous military expenditure some extraordinary means must be resorted to, to raise the necessary finances. Whether to raise the money in India or in England was then the question. After much discussion, Lord Canning's Government determined that the wisest course would be to open a six-per-cent. loan in India, but to obtain the promise of the Court of Directors that they would be "prepared to help if need be, in order that it may be known here that we are not altogether at the mercy of the holders of money in this country." "I apprehend," added the Governor-General in his private letter to the President of the Board of Control, "that in order to be ready to help the Government in India, the East India Company must have recourse to Parliament for permission to borrow. At least I know not how any considerable sum can be forthcoming from the Court by any other means. Whether these means shall be had recourse to, you at home will decide. My belief is that we in India shall still be able to raise what we want (I put it at three crores) by offering six per cent.; but I am sure that the chances of being able to do so will be greatly increased if we have an assurance that in case of failure help will come from home."* Meanwhile, there was a pressing necessity to reduce the expenditure of the Government by every possible means, at any sacrifice of future advantages to the State.

So an order went forth for the immediate suspension of all the great reproductive public works, which

* What was actually done in Calcutta may be gathered from the following statement, which forms part of the comments of Lord Canning on the petition for his recall: "When the notifications of the 20th and 27th July were issued, the position of affairs was altogether changed. The mutiny had spread, the money market was daily becoming tighter, a falling off in the revenue had become certain, and on its thus being unquestionable that more favourable terms than five per cent. would be necessary to secure subscriptions to a loan, the arrangement for taking four, four and a half, and three and a half paper in part subscription to the five-per-cent. loan was resolved on, in preference to opening a six-per-cent. loan, chiefly out of consideration to the then holders of Government securities. That the credit of the Government was destroyed is proved not to be the case by the fact that cash subscriptions have been received since the 21st July to the amount of 97,81,390 rs., while the transfers have amounted to 96,09,710 rs., and this notwithstanding that the subscriptions in Calcutta have been greatly curtailed by the Bank of Bengal having, for a considerable period, refused any accommodation in the way of fresh loans. 'At the present date (9th November) the loan has reached three millions sterling."—It need not be added that loans were afterwards raised in London, on the security of the revenues of India.

would have added so much to the wealth of the 1857. Empire. How it pained him to do this may be July. gathered from his correspondence. Respecting what he had done, he wrote on the 3rd of July to the President of the India Board: "The stoppage of public works is made as absolute as possible. No new works of public improvement to be entered upon; many already in full swing to be abandoned, and nothing but the real necessities of the military and civil establishments to be provided for, and repairs. The Staff, too, will be reduced. This sounds prudent and economical. It is neither one nor the other. It is wasteful to the last degree—wasteful of money already expended—wasteful of much labour of organisation and discipline, and much dearly-bought experience; and, besides, disheartening to the invaluable Staff of officers who have been trained to the works, and humbling to the Government. But there is no choice for the present, at all events."

And still, as these cares pressed heavily upon him, Personal there were trouble and vexation at his own door. vexations. For the Christian communities of the capital continued to clamour for much that his deliberate judgment told him it would be unwise and unjust to concede. As weeks passed, and every week brought a fresh catalogue of crimes committed against our Christian people by Natives of the country, Mahomedans and Hindoos—and not all, not nearly all by men who had once worn the uniform of the British Government — as many, many households in the capital were mourning the miserable deaths of their nearest and dearest—nay, as fugitives came in from the Upper Country with dreadful stories to relate, and the horrors which they truthfully recited were magnified in repetition, till there was not a con-

1857.
July.

ceivable outrage which men or fiends could commit not laid to the charge of the black races—it was not strange that both fear and hatred should have grown stronger among our white people, and that there should have been a cry, ever increasing in strength, both for protection and for retribution.   To have yielded to the cry would, at that time, have won the hearts of the Christian communities of Calcutta. But he could not sacrifice his sense of duty to any yearning after popularity ; and though the imploring cries of his countrymen from all parts pained him deeply, and he grieved for the tribulation of the great English capital, he could not bring himself to concede all that they asked.   So as week followed week, the Governor-General grew more and more distasteful to the European communities of Calcutta, until there began to be much eager talk about a Petition to the Home Government for his recall.

Instructions to the Executive.

He bore up bravely against it, never for a moment thinking of yielding to the clamour.   Indeed, the louder it grew, the more convinced he was that it was his duty, in all ways and by all means, to resist it.   For every day it became more and more sadly apparent, that in all parts of the country the resentments of the Englishman had been roused to such a pitch, that he was ready on every possible opportunity and occasion to take the law into his own hands, and to execute upon the Native races the wild justice of revenge.   There was nothing in this to astonish Lord Canning, and he could not severely condemn it.   But he knew only too painfully, to what, if not arrested, this must tend ; and he bethought himself and invited the counsel of others as to the best means of arming the Executive with full power promptly to punish the guilty with-

out placing in their hands authority to smite un-
sparingly at every Sepoy who might cross their path,
and all suspected of abetting him. So, at the end
of July a resolution of Government was passed, em-
bodying instructions to officers in Bengal and the
North-Western Provinces to draw lines of discrimination between, firstly, Sepoys of regiments which
had not mutinied, not being found with arms in
their possession; secondly, Sepoys, unarmed, being
mutineers or deserters from regiments guilty of
simple rebellion, but not charged with the murder of
their officers or any other sanguinary crime; and
thirdly, mutineers or deserters, found to belong to
regiments guilty of the murder of their officers or
other Europeans, or of having " committed any other
sanguinary outrage." In the two former cases the
prisoners were to be sent for trial by the military
authorities; in the last they were to be tried by the
civil power, and the sentence passed upon them to
be carried out forthwith—with this reservation, however, that execution should be stayed, pending a
reference to the Government, if the accused should
furnish evidence of his not having been present with
his regiment at the time of the commission of the
crime, or that, if present, he had endeavoured to
prevent it. It had become all the more imperative
on Government to enforce the observation of these
distinctions, since it had become known that in some
instances Sepoys on leave from their regiments (it
was the furlough season of the year) had been seized
and executed when passing to and from their respective homes.

Having recorded these instructions with respect to
military prisoners of all classes, the Government
proceeded to define, but in less precise language, the

course to be pursued by the civil authorities "in
regard to acts of rebellion committed by persons not
mutineers." "It is unquestionably necessary," said
the Resolution, "in the first attempt to restore order
in a district in which the civil authority has been
entirely overthrown, to administer the law with such
promptitude and severity as will strike terror into
the minds of the evil-disposed among the people, and
will induce them, by the fear of death, to abstain
from plunder, to restore stolen property, and to
return to peaceful occupations. But this object once
in a great degree attained, the punishment of crimes
should be regulated with discrimination. The continued administration of the law in its utmost
severity, after the requisite impression has been made
on the rebellious and disorderly, and after order has
been partially restored, would have the effect of
exasperating the people, and would probably induce
them to band together in large numbers for the protection of their lives and with a view to retaliation—
a result much to be deprecated. It would greatly
add to the difficulties of settling the country hereafter, if a spirit of animosity against their rulers
were engendered in the minds of the people, and if
their feelings were embittered by the remembrance
of needless bloodshed." The district officers were in
this spirit exhorted, "without condoning any heinous
offences," to encourage all persons to return to their
usual occupations, and to "postpone as far as possible
all inquiry into political offences until such time as
the Government are in a position to deal with them
in strength after thorough investigation." The wholesale burning of villages was especially deprecated, as
tending morally to the general exasperation of the
people, and practically to the prevention of their resumption of the cultivation of their fields—"a point,"

it was added, "at this season of vital importance, inasmuch as if the lands remain much longer unsown, distress and even famine may be added to the other difficulties with which the Government will have to contend."

These instructions, the extreme moderation and plain practical good sense of which cannot at this distance of time be questioned, were not proclaimed or published, as was afterwards stated, but were sent, in the shape of confidential circulars, to the officers whom they concerned. A copy of them, however, was printed in a Calcutta paper. And the more violent section of the European inhabitants of the capital were roused to a high pitch of indignation by what they afterwards denounced as "indiscriminate forgiveness," though the avowed object and practical effect of the measure was to enforce a wholesome discrimination in the punishment of accused or suspected persons. "Lenity," it was added, "towards any portion of the conspirators is misplaced, impolitic, and iniquitous, and is calculated to excite contempt and invite attack on every side, by showing to the world the Government of India so powerless to punish mutiny, or so indifferent to the sufferings which have been endured by the victims of the rebellion, that it allows the blood of English and Christian subjects of Her Majesty to flow in torrents, and their wives, sisters, and daughters to be outraged and dishonoured without adequate retribution." It was forgotten that this adequate retribution, if it had been commendable and desirable, would, at the time when these orders were issued, have been impossible, from sheer lack of strength to execute it, and that the attempt would only have rendered greater the disproportion between the evil to be suppressed and the means of suppress-

1857.
July.

ing it. In fact, the retribution party were clamouring for that which would have aggravated their dangers and increased their fears, and that the policy which they advocated would, in its adoption, have been as fatal to the interests as damnatory to the character of the nation.

The sale of arms.

Another source of discontent was this: a new element of danger was supposed to have been discovered in the fact that there had been a large importation of arms into Calcutta, and that the Natives of the capital and of the surrounding districts were purchasing them freely from shopkeepers not disinclined to make money by the crisis. In truth, the Natives of the country were more alarmed than the Christian inhabitants; and when they saw our people arming themselves everywhere, and knew that we were disarming their military compatriots, they began to suspect that we should, at no distant period, use our rifles and revolvers for other than defensive pur-

July 20.

poses. On the 20th of July, the subject was brought to the notice of Government by the Town-Major. About the same time, the Commandant of the Calcutta Militia, Major Herbert, sent in reports to the effect that an English firm had imported a large quantity of arms, which had been sold to a Native dealer, and that they were being freely bought in the bazaars. On the 22nd, the Grand Jury, in the Supreme Court of Calcutta, made a presentment recommending that all the Native population of the capital should be forthwith disarmed, and that the sale of arms and ammunition should be legally forbidden. And on the following day, a number of the Christian inhabitants appealed to the Government to disarm all the Natives in the place. To this reply was given, two days afterwards, that it was not in-

1857.
July.

tended to disarm any class of the residents of Calcutta or the neighbourhood—that sufficient precautions had been taken for the safety of the city; and that a General Arms Bill was under consideration.*

This was not considered a satisfactory reply; but the sincerity with which it was given was beyond all question. For Lord Canning had up to this time refused to disarm his own body-guard—a body of picked Native soldiers, well armed and well mounted. He never went abroad without some of these troopers in attendance upon him. He was earnestly exhorted to disarm them; but he was reluctant, at this time, to consent to such a measure. Some said that it was "fool-hardy;" others argued that it was another proof that he did not understand the gravity of the position. But none could dispute that it testified his assured conviction that the general disarming of the people was uncalled for, and proved that he was not one to exhort others to manifestations of confidence of which he did not himself set a conspicuous example.

But in this disregard of his own personal safety Lord Canning may have erred. The persistent manner in which he long refused to change the Sepoy guard at Government House for one composed of European soldiers, is said, however commendable it might have been in a lesser man, to have been an indiscretion in the Governor-General. It was, doubtless, a noble example that he set. If he had dismissed his Sepoy guards at the commencement of our troubles, the news would have run, like an alarm-note, through all classes of the community, and there would have been a diminution of that confidence which it was so im-

Confidential Memorandum by Lord Canning—unpublished.

1857.
July.

portant to maintain in every quarter where Christian people were assembled. So, although oftentimes urged not to trust himself any longer to the dangerous guardianship of men whose comrades had stained their hands with the blood of their officers, he continued to confide in them, and could not be induced to order Europeans to be posted at his doors. Secretaries and members of Council deplored this; but they could not bend him to their will. At last,

Mr. Halliday.

Mr. Halliday, Lieutenant-Governor of Bengal, who had come down to the Presidency from Darjeeling, so wrought upon the Governor-General by telling him that his duty to his country demanded that he should take every precaution to protect a life, which at such a time was of incalculable value, that he began reluctantly to yield, and to bethink himself of consenting to the change which had been so often vainly pressed upon him.

It was no easy task that Halliday had set himself, and it was not easily accomplished. Time did something to mitigate the difficulty, for the general disaffection of the Bengal Army was every week becoming more apparent. But the personal influence of the Lieutenant-Governor did more. Lord Canning said of him afterwards, that for many months he had been the "right hand of the Government." A man of commanding stature and altogether of a goodly presence, he looked like one born to command. He had all his life been a steady, robust workman, and he had brought to his work no small amount of natural ability and administrative sagacity of the most serviceable kind. His lot had been cast in the hitherto tranquil regions of Bengal. No opportunity of proving his powers in action had been afforded to him; but his sufficiency in council had won the confidence of successive Governments, and in all that related to the Lower Provinces there was no man whose experiences were of greater value. To Lord Canning, who, wisely or unwisely, had been chary of his confidences to those immediately about him, the arrival of Mr. Halliday had been extremely welcome, and from that time there was no member of the Government whom he so frequently consulted or whose opinions he so much respected. But still only by repeatedly urging upon the Governor-General that his life belonged to his country, and that he had no right to expose it to any unnecessary risks, could his Lieutenant induce him to allow the order to be issued for European guards to be posted at Government House. It was not, indeed, until the month of August had expired that the European Guard marched into the compound of Government House, under the immediate orders of the Lieutenant-Governor.*

In the mean while events were developing themselves in the country below Benares, which seemed in some measure to confirm the apprehensions of the European community at Calcutta, and which doubtless rendered the Governor-General's outward calmness of demeanour, which they so grievously misinterpreted, more offensive and irritating to them than before. It seemed as though the toils were closing around them—that Bengal itself would soon be in a blaze, and murder and pillage rampant in the capital—whilst the head of the Government was complacently closing his eyes to the surrounding danger. But no one saw it more clearly than Lord Canning. Writing at the beginning of August to the Indian

1857.
July.

* This was either on the 31st of August or the 1st of September.

Minister at home, he said : " For the moment everything must give way to the necessity of arresting rebellion or general disorder below Benares.   If this is
not done our slender remains of revenue will be in
jeopardy, and every isolated regiment throughout
these provinces will mutiny ; for it is impossible to
reach them with any European force strong enough
to disarm them, without their having full warning of
what is coming upon them."   The events to which
reference is here made must now be fully narrated.

CHAPTER II.

THE BENGAL PROVINCES — CHARACTER OF THE POPULATION — THE CRY
FOR DISARMING — STATE OF THE DINAPORE REGIMENTS — CONDITION
OF THE PATNA DIVISION — ARREST OF WAHABEES — GENERAL LLOYD'S
HALF-MEASURE — MUTINY AT DINAPORE — DUNBAR'S EXPEDITION — THE
DISASTROUS RETREAT — GALLANT EXPLOITS.

THE India Bill of 1853 had placed the provinces
of Bengal, Behar, and Orissa under a Lieutenant-
Governor. They extended from the borders of the
Madras Presidency on the south to the limits of
the Nepaul country on the north. Of all our acquisi-
tions in Upper India, they had been the longest
under our rule ; and the people had become, therefore, most habituated to our systems. A peaceful,
pliant, plastic people, the genuine Bengalees were
easily intimidated, easily subjected, easily moulded.
They were, indeed, what the moist, relaxing climate
had made them, a feeble, languid race of men. They
did not recruit our armies ; but they were adepts in
trade. They could not fire a musket or handle a
sabre ; but they were the most litigious people in all
the world. Whilst they schemed and trafficked with
immense success, they did not hesitate to acknowledge, with self-condemning frankness, that, in the
active business of fighting, they were cowards. They
had, however, a passive kind of courage of their

1857.
The Bengal
Provinces.

own. They had great powers of endurance. They could lie down to be crushed to death under the wheels of Juggernauth, or they could swing from a high pole with iron hooks in their backs. In the aggressive business of insurrection, such a people could be no proficients. Their idea of a popular revolt was a great assemblage of people, sitting on their haunches, hungry and silent, and defying the Government by sheer force of utter inaction and inexhaustible patience.

Such was the general character of the population. But there are no places in which there are not exceptional elements of violence—it may be of an indigenous, it may be of a foreign character. In Bengal were large numbers of immigrants from all parts of the East—some settled and some transitory. The Bazaars of Calcutta were swarming with them—with men of all races, from the flat-faced, close-shaven Chinaman to the aquiline, bearded Afghan. The predatory classes were not absent from Bengal. Budducks and Kechucks, and other professional robbers, plied their trade with audacious success. The Police was about the worst in the world—part and parcel often of the predatory organisation—and certain, in the event of an insurrection, to side with the insurgents as the more profitable course. Notwithstanding, therefore, the non-military character of the rural population, there was some reason to regard with dismay the rising of the Native troops in the Lower Provinces, where no European battalions were posted; whilst higher up in 'the circle of the Lieutenant-Governorship were people of different instincts and habits from those of the populations of Bengal and Orissa.

Here, indeed, were some sources of reasonable in-

quietude. To one of the chief of these the moneyed
interests of Calcutta looked with intelligible anxiety.
If the rich indigo districts of Behar were overrun
by a mutinous soldiery, aided by the Budmashes
of the country, what would become of all the money
advanced upon the growing crops? This was a substantial ground of alarm to many of the merchants
and agents of the capital, but the ruin which would
have followed such incursions of rebels into the
indigo districts would not have been confined to
them. It would have been wide-spread and most
disastrous. Now, the apprehension of disturbances
in Behar was by no means the growth of the creative
powers of an excited imagination. The Lieutenant-
Governor had represented in June that there was
danger to be apprehended from the return of mutinous Sepoys to their homes in Behar—for, although
few Native soldiers were ever drawn from Lower
Bengal, further up in Behar were races of a more
warlike character—immigrants partly from higher
latitudes. Then there was the great city of Patna,
which had for long years been a not unreasonable
source of suspicion and mistrust to the ruling authorities. Mahomedanism was strong and rampant at
Patna; and it was the most active kind of Mahomedanism, for there we saw the followers of the Prophet
in the rejuvenescence of Wahabeeism. Then there
were three Sepoy regiments at Dinapore, and, although they were watched by Her Majesty's Tenth
Foot, it was still probable that they might suddenly
break into mutiny and escape, as others had escaped
before them. The result of this might have been
mischievous in the extreme. Already were there
great alarm and excitement. Strange rumours agitated the people. Mr. Tayler, the Commissioner of

Patna, had written to Mr. Secretary Beadon, saying: "The whole English community at Tirhoot have demanded protection, as they believe that the people will rise and the Nujeebs mutiny. All Buxar and Shahabad fled like sheep and flocked into Dinapore. . . . . Richardson, of Chuprah, writes that the whole country opposite his cutcherry on the Ghazepore Doab, and the people of all the districts to the west of Chuprah, are in open revolt." In this excited condition of the people, it was argued, if the Sepoys at Dinapore should rise and sweep down upon Patna, carrying off the treasure, looting the rich opium-godowns, and thence spreading desolation through the homes of the indigo farmers of Tirhoot, the contagion might spread lower and lower, Moorshed-abad might rise, in spite of the steadfast loyalty of the Nawab Nazim, and the insurgents gathering strength as they went, might pour themselves down upon the capital. Why, then, not prevent a calamity of so probable a kind by disarming the Dinapore regiments? It was a feat of no difficult accomplishment. The Tenth Foot, aided by some of the reinforcements passing up the river, which might have been detained a little while for this special service, could have easily overawed the Sepoy battalions, and deprived them of all means of offence. But the Governor-General believed that there was still greater danger in disarming, and so the Sepoys were left with arms in their hands; and a regiment of Europeans, when every English soldier was worth his weight in gold, was kept at Dinapore to watch them. And there were many in Bengal, who, admiring and upholding the Governor-General, and condemning the popular clamour which had been raised against him as intemperate and imbecile,

thought that he had erred in refusing, for so long a
time, to disarm the regiments at Dinapore.

It is right, however, that the arguments with
which the Governor-General sustained his declared
reluctance to disarm the Dinapore Brigade should be
recorded. If the question before him had related
only to the measures best calculated for the protection of the indigo districts of Behar, the disarming
of the regiments (its successful accomplishment assumed) might have been the stroke best tending
towards the deliverance of those whose lives and
properties there were in danger. But Lord Canning
had not merely to consider what was locally or in-
dividually best, but what was generally most condu-
cive to the interests of those under his charge. And
he could not but perceive that, however safe it might
be to disarm Native regiments in the neighbourhood
of European troops, the result might be dangerous
in the extreme to our people in other parts of the
country, where Sepoys abounded and not a detachment of Europeans was to be seen. He was looking anxiously for the arrival of fresh reinforcements,
when the game would be more in his own hands;
but in the then destitute state of the Lower Provinces, it seemed to him and to the members of his
Council to be sounder policy to temporise. It could
not be wise, he thought, to precipitate a crisis, which
he had not the power successfully to confront. All
parts of Lower Bengal were dotted over with Sepoy
detachments, waiting eagerly for news, perhaps for
instructions, from Head-Quarters, and ready to break
out into rebellion at an hour's notice. And it had
been industriously circulated among them that disarming was only another name for destruction, and
that when they had given up their muskets, they

1857.
June.

The Dinapore
regiments.

would either be shot down or sent as prisoners beyond the seas.

The intelligence, which Lord Canning had received from the General Officer commanding the Dinapore Division, tended to confirm him in the impression that an outbreak at that station was not to be expected. On the 2nd of June, General Lloyd had written to the Governor-General, saying : "Although no one can now feel full confidence in the loyalty of the Native troops generally, yet I believe that the regiments here will remain quiet, unless some great temptation or excitement should assail them, in which case I fear that they could not be relied upon."* A few days afterwards it seemed that the hour of temptation had come; for news had arrived from Benares of the disarming of the regiments there, and what had followed, and all the exertions of the Dinapore officers were needed to allay the alarm, which is so often the precursor of revolt. This passed; but ere many days had lapsed, General Lloyd, in reply to a suggestion from Government, wrote to Lord Canning that the opium-godown at Patna was in a good state of defence, and that he did not believe that there was any danger of an attack upon it, as no treasure was kept there. But, he added, "the temptation to an outbreak consists in the presence in the Collector's cutcherry at Patna of

* Writing at the end of May, the commandant of one of the regiments—an excellent Sepoy officer—said : "I am very happy to inform you that the three Native regiments here display the best temper, and all duties are being regularly carried on—parades, drills, and target practice every morning. Not a murmur is heard about cartridges. All commanding officers and others are doing their best to keep matters right, and the real state of the case fully explained to the officers and men ; and they are warned that the wild stories and lies purposely spread about by emissaries are only to alarm and disturb them. They have been told that if they can seize and give up any of these emissaries, they will be promoted and rewarded with a money present."

some twenty lakhs of rupees—money brought in
from Chuprah, and expected to arrive from Arrah,
under the escort of Captain Rattray's men, to-morrow
morning.* The Treasury is under the charge of the
Nujeebs, and a guard of Sikhs goes for its protection
during the night. The money is to be sent to Calcutta by the first downward steamer. . . . I believe
the worst feeling towards us prevails in Patna and
in Behar generally—particularly among the Mahomedan population and the sect of Wahabees. As
yet it is confined to words only; but a very little
more excitement would cause it to show itself in
deeds." The temptation, however, here anticipated
had been resisted, and the Native regiments, all
through the remaining weeks of June and the earlier
part of the month of July, had gone about their
accustomed duties without any outward manifestations of disloyalty. And General Lloyd had continued to report that he believed they would remain
true to their salt, unless some fresh temptation should
arise to elicit the momentary madness that had driven
so many others to perdition.

It was not to be doubted, however, that, as time
went on, there was, apart from these apprehensions of
the sudden falling of a spark upon the combustible
elements of Sepoy discontent, a not unreasonable
cause of anxiety in the chronic state of fear into
which the Native regiments had subsided, owing to
reports industriously circulated among them that
the river steamers passing upwards were crowded
with large numbers of European troops, who would
bring upon them swift destruction under cover of

* Rattray, with his Sikhs, reached   will be made of their excellent ser-
Patna in the early morning of the   vices.
8th of June. Subsequent mention

F 2

the darkness of the night. In vain their officers tried to reassure them. The panic grew. As had happened, and was yet to happen in other places, the strong instinct of self-preservation moved them to concert measures for their liberation from the toils which it was believed were closing around them. To allay these fears, orders were issued that each regiment should furnish a picket, to be posted at night in its Lines, ostensibly for the purpose of refusing ingress to mutineers or deserters from other regiments, and to seditious and intriguing persons of all kinds who might seek to corrupt them. This wise precaution was not without good results. It seemed for awhile to pacify the men. If it did not altogether restore confidence to them, it kept them quiet for awhile. And it was the desire of the General commanding to keep the Native regiments together at a time when the Government were straining every effort to send upwards, along the Grand Trunk Road, small detachments of Europeans in wheeled carriages; for an outbreak of the Native troops at Dinapore might have closed the road and delayed the advance of our reinforcements in the hour of our greatest need.

Excitement in the Patna Division.
Meanwhile, irrespectively of all military disloyalty, there was increasing excitement in Behar. It has been shown in an earlier chapter that, some years before the general outbreak of mutiny in the ranks of the Bengal Army, there had been dangerous plots developed, if not originated, in Patna for the corruption of our Sepoy regiments, as the first step towards the subversion of British power in the East.* In no place were large and influential classes of the Native com-

* Vol. i., p. 304—309.

munity better prepared for a rising of the soldiery; and nowhere, when the crisis came, was there more of the excitement of ill-disguised sympathy. As a link between them there were the Police—the Nujeebs —a hybrid race, but a power in the State. The fusion of the three, whichsoever might be the prime mover of sedition, was dangerous in the extreme; and it was certain that an inert policy would not be a successful one. So already the civil authorities were striking heavy blows at incipient rebellion, and endeavouring to overawe the suspected classes by repressive measures, which engendered as much hatred as fear.

The chief civil officer of the division was Mr. William Tayler, of whom mention has already been made. A man of varied accomplishments and of an independent tone of thought and speech, he had studied the Native character, as only it can be rightly studied, with large-hearted toleration and catholicity of sentiment. Fully alive to the melancholy fact of the great gulf between the two races,* he had often dwelt, in his public correspondence, on the evils attending the self-imposed isolation of his countrymen, and the want of sympathy, and therefore the want of knowledge, in all that related to the feelings of the people, of a large majority of official and non-official

1857.
June.

William Tayler.

---

* Nothing can be better than the following, which I extracted some years ago from one of Mr. Tayler's official papers: "Separated as we necessarily are from the millions around us, by our habits and ideas, we are still further, and without the same necessity, isolated from their hearts by the utter absence of all individual feeling or sympathy. The great mass see or hear of functionary after functionary coming and going, and holding the destinies of the people in the hollow of their hands, but they seldom, perhaps never, know what it is to feel that the minds of their rulers have ever been directed to understand or sympathise with the great heart that is beating around them. The result is an utter absence of those ties between the governors and the governed, that unbought loyalty which is the strength of kings, and which, with all his faults, the Native of India is well capable of feeling."

Englishmen in India. Nearly two years before the outbreak of the mutiny, he had reported to Government that, "owing to sundry causes, the minds of the people in these districts are at present in a very restless and disaffected state, and they have generally conceived the idea that there is an intention on the part of Government to commence and carry through a systematic interference with their religion, their caste, and their social customs." Utterances of this kind are never very palatable to Government; and Mr. Tayler was regarded in high places, if not actually as an alarmist, as a man who suffered his imagination to run away with him; and although it is impossible to govern well and wisely without it, nothing is more detestable to Government than imagination. So it happened that Mr. Tayler had fallen into disrepute with some above him, and had excited the resentments of some below him. He was a man of strong convictions, not chary of speech; and there was small chance at any time of a division under his charge subsiding into the drowsy, somnolent state which gives so little official trouble, and is therefore so greatly approved.

There was, a short time before the outburst of the revolt, one especial matter which had been a source of much conflict, and had resulted in the determination of the Lieutenant-Governor of Bengal to remove Mr. Tayler from the Patna Commissionership. It was a question of the establishment of an Industrial Institution, to be supported by the landholders of the several districts; and Mr. Halliday was of opinion that undue influence had been used to obtain the adhesion of the Zemindars to a scheme which they did not really approve. Into the merits of this question I do not purpose to enter. Mr. Tayler manfully declared

that it appeared to him, after the storm of trouble 1857.
had burst, to be so paltry a matter that it should be June.
dismissed from the consideration of the local officers.
But it is necessary to the right understanding of
what follows that the general position of affairs, as
thus described, should be known to the reader. It
was an unfortunate circumstance that the Commissioner's authority should have been weakened by the
notoriety of the displeasure of his Government. There
were undoubtedly two parties in Patna; and a house
divided against itself is always infirm. When hostile
multitudes are swarming around us, nothing but the
united action of such handfuls of Englishmen as we
can muster to oppose them, can ever work out perfect
deliverance.

The chief out-stations of the Patna Division were Alarm in the
at Chuprah, Arrah, Mozufferpore, Gya, and Mote- districts.
haree.* There resided the usual staff of administrators—judges, collectors, magistrates, and opium-agents
—and under their charge were the gaols, and treasuries, and godowns, the repletion of which bespoke
the activity wherewith they pursued their callings.
The guardianship of these was intrusted to the Police.
It would have been in favour of our people that no
detachments of Sepoys were posted at these stations,
if the Nujeebs had been trustworthy; but it was
generally felt that their fidelity would not survive
an outbreak of the soldiery, and they might, any
day, following the suit of their military brethren,
release the prisoners in the gaols, carry off the coin
in the treasuries, and murder every Christian in the
district. When, therefore, news came that Delhi

* The districts were Sarun, Shah- were at Patna, which gave its name
abad, Tirhoot, Behar, and Chum- also to a district.
parum. The civil head-quarters

was in the hands of the insurgents, and no news came, after waiting awhile for it, that the English had recovered the city and crushed the short-lived power of the Mogul, there was considerable uneasiness in the minds of all the English inhabitants of Behar. At first, there was the comforting reflection to sustain them, that the Native gentry were on their side—that the influential Zemindars and others would place all their resources at the disposal of our people. This belief, however, soon passed away. It is curious to mark in the private or demi-official correspondence of the day, how, as time went on, the confidence entertained by our civil officers in the loyalty of the local gentry gradually waned and at last disappeared. The month of May had not come to a close before stories began to reach the Commissioner from different out-stations, showing how great was the mistrust that was beginning to overshadow the minds of our public functionaries. Just ten days after the outbreak at Meerut, one wrote to Mr. Tayler, saying: "A Bazaar report was abroad that the Persian Army was close to Lahore, and hourly expected, and that all was up with the British in India. This is enough to alarm the loyal, as well as to encourage the disaffected. There is another story that I heard privately, and some weight may be attached to it, namely, that Maun Singh, the outlaw of Oude, is in Nepaul, and has been down on our frontier making observations and arrangements; that he excited the sympathy of many in our provinces, and that our great Rajahs in those parts are not to be depended upon for a moment; that they encourage revolt, though not, perhaps, ready to join in it, unless an invading army should come. . . . . I know the Hutwah man has a *mooktear* at Lucknow, For what possible object? . . . . You may depend upon it that the cartridge question is all fudge. Some deeper scheme than that has been laid." Early in June, one of our magistrates wrote from Gya to the Secretary to the Bengal Government, saying: " I have reason to believe that the Mahomedans throughout this province are greatly disaffected; they are anxiously looking out for news from the North-West, exaggerating matters, and publishing *pro bono publico* all they hear. In Gya this feeling has shown itself to a great extent." And again, some days later: "My last mentioned state of feeling up to 11th. From that time the people have become much more disaffected. Reports were duly received that Budmashes and numbers of the Mahomedan population, in parties, were strolling about, poisoning the minds of their neighbours with wild stories of our reign having come to its conclusion, the massacre of the Europeans in the North-West, &c.; and in many other ways was the animus but too apparent, and excitement was thus shown to be at its highest pitch, bordering upon an outbreak. . . . . It is reported from several places in my jurisdiction that men are wandering about in the guise of Fakeers and tampering with the villagers." And on the same day, the chief civil officer of Chuprah wrote to the Commissioner: "There is no concealing the present condition of the Chuprah people, and it requires but the tidings of a disturbance at Dinapore to make the Mussulmans, aided by the Nujeebs, rise."*

* Another letter, written from Chuprah (May 25th), said : "I have, these last two days, been visited by numbers of the Natives, and I have been explaining the whole matter to them—impressing upon the wealthy men that the first thing the Sepoys did in Delhi was to loot every wealthy man. I also informed them that the regiments which were on their way to China would now probably pay Calcutta a visit, and that in a few days there would be a European force there sufficient to conquer the

1857.
June.
Alarm at
Patna.

June 7.

At the chief station of Patna there was the greatest alarm of all. It was not unreasonably anticipated that if the Dinapore regiments should revolt, they would pour themselves upon Patna with a great destruction of property and of life. At the end of the first week of June the chronic alarm of the Europeans culminated in an acute paroxysm of panic. A report had arrived from Dinapore that the Sepoys were expected to mutiny in the course of the night, Then our people asked what was to be done? Mr. Tayler, to whom all resorted for guidance in this emergency, counselled concentration in his own house. And in a little while the spacious residence of the Commissioner and his family was gorged to repletion.* The moon rose that night on a scene of strange bewilderment and confusion. Outside the house, a large body of Nujeebs, in their dark-green dresses, were drawn up under their English chief;† and a guard, from Holmes's Irregulars, warlike and picturesque, was mounted at the chief entrance.‡

whole of India over again." . . . . "There are some disaffected people at work, and I only wish that I could get hold of them. I have my eye upon one or two; but they seem to be raking up all the old causes of complaint. Twice to-day I have been asked why the Government wish to cut off the prisoners' hair and beards, and though I explained to them that the Mussulman's beard was only to be clipped, and that four fingers' breadth was to be left, they were not satisfied, and said, 'One day it will be four, the next two fingers, and then it will be cut off altogether.'"

* "My wife and myself were in a curricle when we received the news; we drove off at once to the houses of the nearest residents and informed them quietly of the plan decided

upon, begging them to come over without delay, bag and baggage, to the rendezvous; messengers were at the same time despatched to warn the more distant residents. In less than an hour almost every man, woman, and child (excepting some few who lived close to the opium-godown and found refuge there) were hurrying helter-skelter to our house, followed by a heavy phalanx of beds, clothes, pillows, mattresses, and other domestic impedimenta."
—*Tayler's Patna Crisis.*

† Major Nation — whence they came, in the language of the province, to be called the National Guard.

‡ The head-quarters of Holmes's regiment was at Segowlie. An account of this corps will be found in subsequent pages of the narrative.

Inside, our people, men, women, and children, were huddling together, some confident and some scared. The usual strong contrasts that a season of danger commonly evokes were strikingly developed by the crisis. Some looked to the locks of their guns or felt the edges of their swords; some resigned themselves tranquilly to their fate. Some groaned in spirit; some laughed regardless of their doom. And whilst some elders were examining the ladders which led to the roof of the house, and preparing themselves for a sudden ascent, young men and maidens, in the Commissioner's garden, could not resist a little moonlit flirtation, although it might be their last.*

But there was no need of the ladders—no use for the guns. As the night advanced, the danger seemed to thicken. Letters from Dinapore had been received by the Nujeebs, saying that the Sepoy regiments were all of one mind, that they were coming down upon Patna, and that if the Police battalions would join them, success would be assured. With the exception of a few troopers from Segowlie, the Nujeebs were the sole protection of our people. The gloom, therefore, grew darker and denser. But never were the scriptural words, " Heaviness may endure for a night, but joy cometh in the morning," more signally verified than in this Patna crisis. There was hourly expectation of the arrival of Captain Rattray's well-known and much-trusted regiment of Sikh Irregulars. The Commissioner had already sent urgent missives to Rattray to hasten his advance, and on that very

* "On the garden side, our daughters, with some other girls and the juveniles among the gentlemen, in spite of the hubbub and ignorant of the real danger, were enjoying the open walks and moonlit grass of the garden, and somewhat scandalised the more nervous portion of the assemblage by their laughter and merriment. My wife was, as is her wont, engaged in ministering to the comfort of all who had taken shelter in the house."
—*Tayler's Patna Crisis.*

1857.
June.

afternoon he had despatched fresh messengers, in the light-wheeled carriages of the country, to urge and to assist the rapid progress of the regiment. And when about the hour of dawn, Rattray himself, with his picturesque accoutrements, his high jack-boots, and his long sword, clanked into the Commissioner's house, and announced that his men were behind him, there was a general feeling of deliverance. But in fact there was no danger from which the European community of Patna were to be delivered. The Dinapore regiments did not rise; and next morning the strange assembly of people that had been gathered together in the Commissioner's house returned, safe and hopeful, to their several homes.

Repressive
measures.

There was not a man in the country more disposed towards strenuous action than Mr. William Tayler. The instructions which he issued to his subordinates all through the months of June and July were of the most encouraging and assuring kind. He exhorted all men to put on a bold front, to maintain their posts, and to crush all incipient sedition with the strong arm of authority. It was in these words that he wrote to the chief civil officer of Tirhoot, and all his directions to others were in the same strain: "I don't think that you are in danger. The Sepoys, if they rose, would not go so far out of their way. Your own Budmashes, therefore, are all you have to fear. If you look sharp and raise your extra Police—keep your Sowars in hand—stir up your Darogah—tell that little Rajah to send you men in different parts to help you—keep a look-out at the ghauts, and at the same time quietly arrange for a place of rendezvous in case of real danger, where you may meet, all will go right. . . . . Make everybody show a good face—be plucky, and snub any fellows who are impudent. If any people talk sedition, threaten them with a rope, and keep a look-out on the Nujeebs. Try and form without any fuss a body of volunteers, mounted gentlemen, so that in case of any extremity they might all meet and pitch into any blackguards. If anything really bad were to happen, the branch volunteers should come into Patna and join the main body, and we would keep the province till assistance should come. These are only probabilities, so don't tell people they are anticipated. The word for Tirhoot just now is 'All serene.' "* And it was, doubtless, the true policy to betray no fear, but to be thoroughly awake to and prepared for all possibilities of surrounding danger.

I say it reluctantly—but I fear that it is to be said most truthfully—that all the Englishmen in the Patna Division were not of the same high courage as Mr. William Tayler himself. There had been sudden alarms and flights from some out-stations, and bewildered rushings into Dinapore. "Such a cowardly panic-struck set as have rushed in here yesterday and to-day I never saw," wrote General Lloyd to the Commissioner on the 9th of June. And the Commissioner himself had been compelled to rebuke some, who had shown too great an alacrity to leave their posts without sufficient reason for running away. But it must in all fairness be conceded, that there were some exceptional grounds of apprehension on the part of the European residents in Behar. Already, in general terms, has mention been made of these. The sources of danger were of two kinds— external and internal—military and civil. Not only

* M.S. Records.

was it clear that into the Patna Division would pour all the Sepoy deserters and refugees from the Lower Provinces, but that large numbers of the influential local gentry were disaffected to the core, and were watching the movements of the soldiery with grateful anticipations of a time of trouble to the English. The fact that Sepoys of nine different regiments were known to have fought against us in Shahabad, afterwards afforded substantial proof of the former. The plots which were actually discovered, and the treasonable correspondence which was intercepted at the time, left no doubt of the latter ; and if any had remained, subsequent revelations would have thoroughly dispersed it. Apart from the indigenous sedition— the sedition of "fanaticism" as it has been called (for a sincere belief in other creeds than our own is always fanaticism in the Christian vocabulary)— there were foreign influences at work to stimulate the Mussulman inhabitants of Patna and the neighbourhood to rise, whenever a fitting opportunity should present itself, against the British Government. Foremost among these were the sinister influences that issued from Lucknow. The annexation of that country had sent to Patna a small Oude colony with all kinds of embittered resentments against the British Government, and there was an active correspondence continually going on between the Mahomedans of the two great cities ; whilst in the districts intrigue was incessantly at work to weaken, and eventually to overthrow, the hateful power of the Feringhees.

Arrest of
Waris Ali.
One incident deserves special narration. About the end of the third week of June, intelligence reached the authorities of Tirhoot that one of their Jemadars of Police, Waris Ali by name, said to have been of the blood-royal of Delhi, was in trea-

sonable correspondence with some disaffected Mahomedans of Patna. The Magistrate, seeing at once
the necessity of immediately arresting this man, who
was at a police-station in the interior of the district,
asked Mr. William Robertson, a young civilian of
two or three years' standing, if he would undertake the work. Robertson, a fine, high-spirited
youth, who seems at all times to have been cheery
and confident, and ripe for action, accepted the offered
duty with alacrity; and it was agreed that four
Englishmen of the district should be selected to share
the dangers and the honours of the enterprise. The
gentlemen finally selected were Messrs. Urquhart,
Baldwin, Holloway, and Pratt, indigo-planters of the
neighbourhood, "all of them," as Mr. Robertson
wrote, "steady, cool chaps, and yet fighting men."
All arrangements made, this little party of five, well-
mounted and well-armed, rode for Mr. Baldwin's
factory, some three miles from the police-station,
where they dined and matured their plans; and
before daybreak started, in high spirits, for the
Jemadar's quarters. Coming suddenly upon him,
they found Waris Ali in the act of writing a treasonable letter to one Ali Kureem, a Mahomedan of
wealth and influence, notoriously disaffected, who
was then living upon the road between Patna and
Gya. The culprit was seized with all his correspondence. He had evidently girded up his loins for immediate flight; and if William Robertson had swooped
down upon him an hour later, the prey would have
been lost. His horse—a remarkably fine one—stood
saddled in the stable, with holsters at the pommel.
Carts, already laden for a journey, with the draught
cattle beside them, were standing in front of the
house. Every article of furniture, down to the cook-

ing pots and pans, were heaped up ready for departure. There was no doubt of the man's guilt. Taken *flagrante delicto*, he resigned himself to his fate. He was carried a prisoner to the station, and soon afterwards he was hanged. It is said that at the foot of the gallows he cried aloud, "If there is any friend of the King of Delhi here, let him come and help me."

Flight of Ali Kureem. The correspondence found in the house of Waris Ali clearly implicated Ali Kureem. It was sent to the Commissioner, who determined to apprehend this man. A party of Sikhs, with ten mounted troopers, under Captain Rattray, and accompanied by Mr. John M. Lowis, the Magistrate, were despatched to his house; but either warned of the movements of the English, or scared by the capture of his friend, Ali Kureem had placed himself on the back of an elephant and taken flight. What now was to be done? The answer was obvious. The troopers, with one of the English officers at their head, might have gone in pursuit and captured him. But in an evil hour, Mr. Lowis suffered himself to be persuaded by his Nazir, of whose treachery there was afterwards little doubt, not to take the horsemen with him. So he started in a wheeled carriage ill-suited to rapid travelling, and when Ali Kureem caught sight of his pursuers he astutely forsook the open road and struck across the fields, where the elephant made good progress but the ecka could not follow. On this, Lowis, still eager in the chase, left the carriage and followed on foot. But everything was against him. The sympathies of the people were clearly on the side of the fugitive.* They rendered the English officer no assistance; but

* Mr. Tayler ("The Patna Crisis") says: "The villages not only gave him no assistance, but actually removed a tattoo (pony) that he had secured."

on the other hand actively impeded the pursuit. So 1857. next day he returned, "wearied and disheartened," June. leaving his Native assistant to follow up the chase. But the heart of the Nazir was with the enemies of the Nazarene, and the fugitive escaped. A reward of five thousand rupees was afterwards offered for Ali Kureem's head.

Meanwhile a crisis was approaching in the city of Patna itself. Profoundly mistrustful of the popula- tion of that great city, especially of its Wahabee inhabitants, some of whom were men of wealth and influence, Commissioner Tayler had from the first endeavoured to overawe the disaffected by vigorous measures, only to be justified by the extremity of the danger to be combated. The practice which he pur- sued was described in the rough vernacular of the day, as "hanging right and left." There was some exaggeration in this; but the policy was, doubtless, one of intimidation, and the process of intimida- tion necessarily involved a somewhat slender regard for proofs. Of calm judicial investigation there could be none at such a time. To strike promptly was to strike successfully; and to be suspected was often to be condemned. Arrest followed arrest. A great panic arose among the Mahomedans of Patna. No one knew whose turn would come next, or what form the offensive movements of English authority would take. The Commissioner was equally cou- rageous and adroit. Though he fought openly and struck boldly, he did not despise the aid of stra- tagem. One story, of the arrest of some of the principal Wahabee suspects, is worthy of narration.

There were three Moulavees in the city, believed to exercise, by means of their reputed saintliness, great influence over many of the townspeople. They

Excitement in the city.

Arrest of the Moulavees.

were described by Mr. Tayler as "little, shrivelled, skin-dried men, of contemptible appearance and plain manners," but with "a large body of followers, who would sacrifice everything at their beck." There was reason to believe that these men were busily intriguing against us. So Tayler determined to arrest them. "I felt sure," he wrote afterwards, "that with their necks at my disposal, and their persons under the drawn sabres of the Sikhs, not one genuine Wahabee in the district dare stir a finger." It was obviously, however, a thing to be done as quietly as possible. A violent seizure of these holy men in the heart of the city might have precipitated an outbreak, which would have had inconvenient results. So the Commissioner bethought himself of a device whereby this danger might be avoided. He sent a Circular to all the most respectable Natives of the city inviting them to visit him on the following day, "for consultation on the state of affairs." At the appointed time they assembled in considerable numbers, and the three Moulavees were among them. When they were seated around Mr. Tayler's long dining-table, the Commissioner with his Civil Staff entered the room. With them also entered Major Nation, Chief of the Police, Captain Rattray, of the Sikh Regiment, and Soubahdar Hedayat Ali, of the same corps. The long swords of the two last in their steel scabbards clanked ominously on the floor, as they took their seats near the little Moulavees. The performance then commenced. There was some talk about the troubled times and the measures to be most expediently adopted for the safety and welfare of all classes of the community. When sufficient time had been given to the decencies of the sham, the Native gentlemen were formally dismissed; but, as the party

was breaking up, the Moulavees were requested to
remain, as the Commissioner had a few private words
to say to them.

So the little shrivelled men, who had been sitting
very uncomfortably during the conference, with their
legs tucked up on Tayler Sahib's chairs, and who
had clearly foreseen what was coming, resigned themselves to their fate. The Commissioner told them
that he considered it his duty, in the interests of the
public safety, to keep them under arrest until the
coming of more quiet times. No resistance was attempted or thought of for a moment. There was
not even a word of complaint. With the quiet
dignity habitual to them, they courteously addressed the British Commissioner, saying, " Great
is your Excellency's kindness—great your wisdom.
What you order is best for your slaves. So shall
our enemies be unable to bring false charges against
us !" To this the Commissioner responded with
equal courtesy. Then, " smiles and salutations"
having been exchanged, the wretched men, bearing
up bravely under their lot, were escorted to their
palanquins, and under a guard of Sikhs conveyed to
the Circuit-house, not without some apprehension of
being hanged.

"To this day," wrote Mr. Tayler, a year afterwards, " I look at the detention of these men as one
of the most successful strokes of policy which I was
able to carry into execution." But it can hardly
escape the consideration of any candid mind that
what is thus regarded as a successful stroke of policy,
when executed by Englishmen against Mahomedans,
would, if Englishmen had been the victims of it,
have been described by another name. To invite
men to a friendly conference, and when actually the

guests of a British officer, to seize their persons, is not only very like treachery, but is treachery itself. If these little shrivelled men had resisted, they would, perhaps, have been cut down; and if they had been, a Mahomedan historian would, doubtless, have described the successful policy of Commissioner Tayler in language similar to that in which I described the treacherous assassination of Sir William Macnaghten by Sirdar Mahomed Akbar Khan. The exigencies of a great crisis justify exceptional acts in the interests of the national safety; but I do not know any excuses that may be pleaded or arguments that may be advanced by a British officer in such a case, that might not, and doubtless have been pleaded and advanced, by Native chiefs in like circumstances, and freely echoed by the popular voice.

But, whatsoever other successes this stroke of policy may have wrought, the tranquilisation of Patna was not one of them. Following closely upon the arrest of the Moulavees, an attempt was made to disarm the city of Patna. Like all attempts of the same kind, it was only partially successful. There was a limited surrender of offensive weapons; but many more were concealed. And the fanatical hatred of the Mahomedan population seems to have been increased by these acts. On the evening of the 3rd of July they rose. A large body of Mahomedans, bearing aloft the green flag, and summoning others to join them by the beating of drums, marched through the streets of the city and attacked the house of a Roman Catholic priest. The Sikhs were at once ordered out, and an express was sent to Dinapore for European troops. Meanwhile, Dr. Lyall, with praiseworthy but incautious zeal, had mounted his horse and ridden down to the scene of

tumult, thinking by his influence to pacify the crowd.
He had scarcely appeared on the scene when he was
shot dead. But when Rattray with his men came
down upon them, the victory of the mob was at an
end. Hating with a bitter hatred these Mahomedans, they struck out with hearty goodwill. The
rioters were soon dispersed, and quietude was restored
to the city.

A number of the most notorious malcontents were
arrested in the course of the next few days. Among
these was one Peer Ali—a Mahomedan bookseller,
whose professional acquaintance with the amenities
of literature may have sharpened his intellect, though
it had by no means mollified his manners. He was
brave and unscrupulous, and he hated the English.
He had been a long time plotting against us, now in
communication with Delhi, now with Lucknow—
mainly, indeed, with the latter city, of which he was
a Native. When his house was searched much
treasonable correspondence was found in it. One
document said : " The state of affairs at Patna is as
follows. Some respectable persons of the city are in
prison, and the subjects are all weary and disgusted
with the tyranny and oppression exercised by Government, whom they all curse. May God hear the
prayers of the oppressed very soon !" It was generally said that this man had shot down Dr. Lyall
with his own hand. He was tried and sentenced to
death. Brought before the Commissioner and other
English gentlemen, " heavily fettered, his soiled garments stained deeply with blood from a wound in
his side," he was asked whether he had any information to give that might induce the Government to
spare his life. With dignified composure, such as
our own people did not always maintain under excit-

ing circumstances, he confronted his questioners, and replied : "There are some cases in which it is good to save life—others in which it is better to lose it." He denounced the oppression of the English, especially of the Commissioner, and added, " You may hang me, or such as me, every day, but thousands will rise in my place, and your object will never be gained." After some further conversation, throughout which, except when he spoke of his children, he betrayed no emotion, Peer Ali was taken out to execution. He salaamed respectfully to the Commissioner, and went forth " unmoved and unconcerned." He was hanged. His house was razed to the ground, and his property was confiscated.

Arrest of
Lootf Ali
Khan.

But Peer Ali was not a rich man. And Commissioner Tayler was thoroughly convinced by " the fact that men had been kept for months on pay regularly distributed, under a conditional compact to come forward when called for," that "some wealthy party was at the bottom of the intrigues, that were shown to have been carried on for months." He had no difficulty in naming the man. There was one Lootf Ali Khan, a wealthy banker, against whom there was a strong suspicion by no means confined to the Commissioner. One of the men arrested and executed for the outrage which had resulted in the death of Dr. Lyall, was this man's Jemadar. He was known to have harboured a Sepoy of the Thirty-seventh Regiment that had revolted at Benares ; and he was suspected of being in communication with Sepoy regiments, and to have supplied, for rebellious purposes, the money distributed by Peer Ali and others. When the Magistrate went to the banker's residence in the city, accom-

July 5.

panied by a guard of Sikhs under an English officer,   1857.
to arrest him, Lootf Ali came forth, and being in-   July.
formed that he was to accompany the Magistrate to
the Commissioner's house, blandly assented, and at
once ordered his carriage to be brought round. After
the manner of his tribe, the coachman was absent
when he was called for; so Lootf Ali, having requested
the English gentlemen to take their seats in the carriage, mounted the box and drove his captors to
Mr. Tayler's door—a manner of arrest, perhaps, un-
precedented in the annals of police.* The banker
was formally tried by Mr. Farquharson, the Judge;
but the evidence adduced was insufficient to convict
him, and in due course he was released.† If the
majority of English residents were not surprised,
they were exasperated and alarmed by the acquittal.‡

* As this statement has been questioned, upon high authority, I give the following confirmatory passage from Mr. Lowis's official report: "One of the chief events to be noted is the capture of Syud Lootf Ali Khan, a wealthy banker, whom I, at the request of the Commissioner, Mr. W. Tayler, arrested on the night of the 5th instant. I was accompanied by Lieutenant Campbell with a guard of Sikhs, who surrounded the house, but the precaution was needless, as there was no show of resistance or attempt at escape. He at once came out to meet me, and when informed that he had been summoned by the Commissioner, ordered his carriage, and, as the coachman was not forthcoming, got himself on the box, and drove us to Mr. Tayler's house."

† The Sepoy whom he had harboured was hanged—as well as (as stated in the text) Lootf Ali's servant, who was known to have taken an active part in the murder of Dr. Lyall.

‡ One letter before me, after stating what had been proved against Lootf Ali, says: "We" (the residents at Patna) "knew all this, which was afterwards proved upon his trial, and doubted not of his fate; but to our astonishment and mortification and disgrace, he was acquitted and borne away from court in triumph by his supporters. This was sufficiently alarming, one would suppose, to the supporters of order; but this was not the climax. A few days after his release, the man who, with hardly one exception, the Europeans of Patna and Dinapore considered a rebel of the blackest dye, was received with all the honours due to a highly faithful and meritorious subject by his late acquitting judge, in his then merely temporary position of Acting Commissioner. Could any act of a single man have alienated me from the allegiance due to our Government, this would have done it. I would rather we had been all driven from house and home by an open rebellion in Patna than that this moral victory should have been yielded."—MS. Correspondence.

Stories were freely circulated to the effect that the great wealth of Lootf Ali had carried him triumphantly through the ordeal. It was said that large sums of money had been remitted to Calcutta for the purpose of working out his deliverance. That deliverance, when it came, was quite an ovation. The pæans of party were resonant from Calcutta to Dinapore. The great Mahomedan capitalist, who, a little time before, had been suspected of holding large numbers of armed men in his pay to exterminate the Nazarene, was now welcomed and consoled as a martyr to the prejudice of an individual. Received with favour by some of the Government officers, and invited to their houses—an act of toleration only too rare in official circles—he could afford to laugh at the malice of his enemies, and so he expanded into greater exuberance than before. As to the guilt or innocence of the man, it still remains a subject of controversy; but it is right that history should give him the benefit of the popular doubt, and, still more, the benefit of the judicial acquittal. It is to be remembered that in those days, not only in the Patna Division, but throughout the whole country, a strong anti-Mahomedan feeling pervaded the minds of the English communities; and that many fell under suspicion of complicity in treasonable designs upon evidence far more slender than that on which the Patna banker was arrested. If we cannot blame Judge Farquharson for acquitting him, it is equally certain that we must not condemn Commissioner Tayler for committing him.

After the anti-Mahomedan demonstrations above recorded, there was, as the month of July wore to a close, a season of comparative quietude at Patna; and outwardly the Sepoy regiments at Dinapore maintained the order and discipline habitual to them in the most tranquil times. But ever was flowing on an undercurrent of disaffection and intrigue in the towns and through the districts; and, as weeks passed, and still no tidings came of the recovery of Delhi—but instead of this intelligence so cagerly looked for and confidently expected by the English, fresh stories of defeat and disaster fatal to the British rule came huddling on each other—when it was known that Cawnpore had fallen, with a great massacre of Christian people, that Lucknow, the only spot in Oude still held by us, was beleaguered, that Agra was in peril, and nearly all parts of the North-Western Provinces in a great blaze of rebellion— when all these things were known, and many wild exaggerations were associated with these truthful reports in the mouths of the inhabitants of Behar, it became more and more apparent that the thoughts of the Native gentry were turning, with vague expectancy, to a coming time, when they would recover their ancient dignities and privileges; whilst men of less note were summing up the offences committed by the English against Mahomedans and Hindoos, and prophesying the approach of a day of retribution.

In this excited state of the public mind, when all were watching with eager interest the movements of the soldiery at the Dinapore Head-Quarters, and still they gave no sign of open mutiny, the long-anticipated crisis was evolved in a most unexpected manner. The cry for the disarming of the Dinapore regiments had been resisted; but it had not been stilled. An advantageous opportunity for the successful accomplishment of this design was presented in the middle of July by the arrival at Calcutta of the Fifth Fusiliers, which was to be sent up at once to recruit General

1857.
July.

Mutiny of the
Sepoy regi-
ments.

Havelock. The detention of this regiment would have been a great evil. But the Calcutta Government, urged onwards by the importunities of the commercial communities, consented to allow its stoppage for a little space at Dinapore, just, in the language of the day, "to polish off the Sepoys," in conjunction with its brethren of the Tenth, and then to pass on to its destination. So, on the 15th of July, Sir Patrick Grant wrote confidentially to General Lloyd, saying: "The first detachment of Her Majesty's Fifth Fusiliers left Chinsurah this morning on flats towed by steamers in progress towards Benares, and the remaining portions of the regiment will follow by the same means of transit to-morrow and Friday. If, when the regiment reaches Dinapore, you see reason to distrust the Native troops, and you entertain an opinion that it is desirable to disarm them, you are at liberty to disembark the Fifth Fusiliers to assist you in this object; but it is imperatively necessary that the detention of the regiment should be limited to the shortest possible period. If you decide on disarming, it should extend to all three regiments, and it should be carefully explained that it is merely a measure of precaution to save the well-disposed from being led to commit themselves by the evil machinations of designing scoundrels, some few of whom are always to be found in even the best regiment. If resistance to authority is exhibited, the most prompt and decided measures for its instant suppression should be adopted." Although these instructions were very clear, they left, to a certain extent, the responsibility in the hands of General Lloyd; and General Lloyd was one of those who shrunk from responsibility. And for some days after the receipt of this letter he was minded to do nothing.

But on the 24th of July, in an evil hour, General Lloyd, feebly halting between two opinions, bethought himself of a compromise.   Still reluctant to disarm the regiments, yet unwilling to turn a deaf ear to the increasing implorations and remonstrances of the Europeans of Bengal, now at last, after long delay, supported by Government, he fell back upon the fatal folly of a half-measure.   There was nothing to command success, in those days, that had not inscribed upon it the great watchword of "Thorough." But General Lloyd did not see clearly that to give to his men all his confidence or none—to do the thing all in all or not at all—was the only way to success. He shrunk from the decided act of taking away from his men their muskets and their pouches.   But he thought that he might render their possession harmless by depriving the regiments of percussion-caps. So taking advantage of the arrival of two companies of the Thirty-seventh Foot on the 24th of July, he ordered a parade of the Europeans for the following morning, and directed arrangements to be made for carting away all the caps in the magazines. *

At the appointed time the parade was held.   The European troops and the Artillery were drawn up in the great barrack-square; and two bullock carts were

1857.
July.

July 25.

---

* These companies had come round from Ceylon to Calcutta. Lord Canning had written urgently to Sir Henry Ward (sending his letter by Major Bazeley on a special steamer) to despatch the whole of the Thirty-seventh; but both the Governor and the Commander-in-Chief of the colony had demurred to the proposal thus to strip the island of all European defence. "I entirely agreed," wrote Sir Henry Ward, " with Major-General Lockyer's view that nothing would justify us in parting with the whole of the Thirty-seventh Regiment, and in thus placing the colony at the mercy of a regiment of Malays and Sepoys, who may, I think, be relied upon as against the Natives, if kept in check by a proper admixture of the European element, but who may also, though all now appears to be gained, be brought under those mysterious influences which have worked so fatally upon the Bengal Army."— *MS. Correspondence.*

sent to the magazines to bring the percussion-caps to the English quarters. Between the magazines and the square were the Sepoy Lines—so the laden carts, which told the story of the present disgrace, and, perhaps, the coming destruction of the Native regiments, had to pass beneath their eyes. As they crossed the Lines, there was a great commotion among the Sepoys of the Seventh and Eighth Regiments; but the Fortieth appears to have been quiescent on the side of mutiny, if not active on that of "order and discipline."* The Seventh, who were being paraded for guard at the time, were the most tumultuous. They are said to have cried out for the murder of the Sahibs and the rescue of the ammunition. But their officers went among them and pacified them; and the danger for the moment was tided over.† The two cart-loads of percussion-caps were stored away under charge of the Europeans. The officers went home to their breakfasts, and the General issued some supplementary orders to his Staff, of such small importance he thought, as not to require that he should see them executed himself.

---

* General Lloyd says: "The Fortieth Native Infantry made a decided demonstration towards the cause of order and discipline, being ready to oppose any attempt to rescue the caps." Colonel Cumberlege, who commanded the Fortieth, says: "About six A.M. on the 25th of July, 1857, the Fortieth Regiment had just been dismissed from parade, when a cart containing percussion-caps for the three regiments, taken from the magazines, passed along the road in front of our parade-ground; an angry buzz of voices had arisen amongst the men in the lines on our right, and some of the men of the Seventh Regiment Native Infantry were rushing in a disturbed and excited manner, and some tried to make across the corner of our parade to intercept the carts. In this they were most decidedly opposed and turned back by the men of our grenadiers and right wing— our men meanwhile keeping perfectly quiet and orderly."—*Parliamentary Papers*.

† In the official statement of Brevet-Colonel Templer (*Parliamentary Papers*) there is no mention of these threats. The colonel says, "The Seventh Regiment under my command, for the first time showed a mutinous spirit to exist in some of the men on the morning of the 25th of July, 1857, by the regimental guards (at guard-mounting) dispersing, instead of obeying the orders of the officer of the day to wheel into column."

The supplementary orders related to the percussion-caps which were already in the possession of the Sepoys—those which had been served out to them for immediate use, together with the corresponding rounds of ball-cartridge. Had there been no signs of disaffection in the early morning, these few caps might have been left with the men, and fired away, in course of ordinary duty, without exciting suspicion; but the bearing of the Sepoys rendered it expedient that prompter action should be taken. So a parade was ordered at noon, at which it was to be explained by the Native officers to their several companies that the measure then ordered was "merely one of precaution to save the well-disposed from being led away to commit themselves by the evil machinations of designing scoundrels"*—and then the caps were to be collected. It was easier, however, to empty out the magazines than to take this little residue out of the clutches of an excited soldiery.

A little after the hour of noon the regimental parades were held. The soothing explanations were given. But when the time came for them to surrender their caps, the Seventh and Eighth Regiments broke out into open mutiny. Rushing towards the bells-of-arms they seized their muskets and fired at all the Europeans they could see. They took their regimental colours and their regimental treasure, and prepared themselves for flight. The Fortieth, however, hesitated. There was still some sense of duty left in them. The Native officers and non-commissioned officers, and some of the Sepoys, formed and marched into the square with their colours and treasure, intending to defend them; and it is possible that the whole regiment might have stood fast; but in a critical moment of doubt and perplexity

* Regimental Orders of the Seventh Native Infantry, July 25, 1857.

some Europeans of the Tenth fired upon them from the roof of the Hospital, and panic completed what disaffection had only half done. So the three regiments went off together *en masse*—taking their arms and accoutrements, but not their uniforms, with them. And the Commander of the English forces put himself on board a steam-boat in the river.

How it happened that, at such a time, the General could have abandoned his proper post it is not easy to explain. He was old and infirm. He was grievously afflicted with the gout. He could not walk. He could not ride. But he could sit upon the deck of a steamer, and there dimly survey the operations on the shore. Perhaps the feeling of thorough helplessness reconciled him to a desertion which could not be regarded as otherwise than discreditable. Had he confessed his physical inability to cope with the crisis, and made over the command to the officer next in seniority, there would have been a far better result. But the crisis had arrived at Dinapore; and there was no responsible officer on the spot to confront it.*

---

* It is right that General Lloyd's own words should be quoted. The following is from a letter written to his brother and published in a London newspaper: "I had no horse in cantonments. My stable was two miles distant, and being unable at the time to walk far or much, I thought I should be most useful on board the steamer with guns and riflemen, in which I proceeded along the rear of the Native lines—the river being only two hundred yards, or thereabouts, distant from the right of the advancing column of guns and Europeans, and expecting to get some shots at the Sepoys on shore or escaping by the river. Considering that I had fully previously given instructions for the attack and pursuit of the Sepoys by the guns and Her Majesty's Tenth, under their respective commanding officers, I left it to them to follow up the mutineers by land." The letter from which this passage is quoted will be found complete in the Appendix. There is no incident detailed in this volume regarding which I have had more travail in elucidating the truth than this story of the Dinapore mutiny. I had been led to believe by previous published statements that General Lloyd went on board the steamer *before* the regiments had mutinied. His own statement, however, distinctly refutes this—whether to his advantage or not I leave the reader to determine. I confess that his apology appears to me to be altogether unsatisfactory.

It had been supposed that in any emergency of this kind the European force at Dinapore would have been more than strong enough to turn a mutiny of the Native regiments into something like a massacre of insurgents. There was the Tenth Foot, less two companies; and there was a battery of Foot Artillery, but wanting some of its guns and gunners, which had been sent to Benares; and there were two companies of the Thirty-seventh Foot. The assembly was sounded in the barrack-square, and the English Infantry and Artillery were mustered under their commandants, Fenwick and Huyshe. But the Sepoys' power of flight was greater than our soldiers' power of pursuit. The state of the country was in favour of the Natives. The parade-grounds were mostly under water, and the country beyond was a great swamp. The Sepoys in their scanty undress, literally with their "loins girt about for flight," traversed easily the familiar morasses. But our Infantry floundered in them, and our Artillery stuck fast. Both fired when it was too late at "impossible distances,"* and the Sepoys made good their escape almost to a man. Full notice had been given to them, and they had wisely spent the morning in making their preparations for a triumphant exodus, whilst the Europeans made only a feeble effort at pursuit; and as they could not overtake the fugitives, set fire to their huts and halted for further orders. The General was missing. No one liked to take the responsibility upon himself; no one, perhaps, knew what was to be done. The emergency that had now come upon our people had been anticipated for months, and yet when it came no one seems to have had any conception of the way in which it was to be met.

1857.
July 25.
Flight of the Sepoys.

* These are General Lloyd's words.

1857.
July 25. It was not so with the Sepoys. Some few made the mistake of taking to the Ganges, where their boats were fired into and run down by the steamer, and some of their inmates shot or drowned. But the majority hastened to the river Soane, which skirts the south-east boundary of the district of Shahabad, dividing it, for some fifteen miles, from the Patna district, and emptying itself into the Ganges about ten miles south of Dinapore. It was the object of the mutineers to enter this district of Shahabad, from which it is said that the Dinapore regiments had been largely recruited.* On the banks of the river, they had it all to themselves. It was not without some trepidation that they looked at the waters swollen by a month's rain, and thought that it would go hard with them if the English should arouse themselves into aught approaching the activity of pursuit. But any apprehensions which they may have entertained were shown to be groundless. There was not a white man on their track. Everything, indeed, was in their favour. They had friends before them; and no enemies behind. All that they wanted was a little time; and the complacency of the military authorities at Dinapore afforded them even more than they required. So they crossed the river with as much ease and comfort as they could desire, some in boats and some by the public ferry; and then they set their faces towards Arrah, the official capital of Shahabad.

* Mr. Trevelyan, in his graphic account of the defence of Arrah, relates that "the men were all drawn from the notoriously turbulent district of Shahabad, of which Arrah is the official capital, and were united by the bond of an undefined allegiance to Kower Singh, who was recognised as chieftain by the Rajpoots or soldier-caste of that region." This, perhaps, may be a little too broadly stated; but it is not to be doubted that a large number of Rajpoot Sepoys were drawn from Shahabad. If the Dinapore regiments contained an exceptional number of these recruits, it was a grievous mistake to post them at Dinapore at all—still more grievous not to watch them more closely.

There was nothing there to oppose the insurgent
Sepoys but the pluck of a few English civilians—
public functionaries, indigo-planters, and railway engineers, and a handful of Sikh mercenaries, who
might or might not be faithful to their employers.
On the side of the Sepoys there was a friendly
country, auxiliaries from other mutinous regiments
flocking to meet them, and, more than all, that
which had so often been wanting to give due effect
to the efforts of the mutineers—a leader ready to
place himself at their head. He was an old man.
The burden of some fourscore years was upon him;
but he had retained some remnant of the energy of
his younger days. His name was Kower Singh. He
was of Rajpoot stock; and he was, or he had
once been, the owner of great estates. It was said
that the revenue systems of the English, the tendencies of which were so much towards the Dead
Level, had greatly impoverished him; but, if it were
so, his influence in the district had survived his
wealth, and he was still a power in Shahabad. The
story ran that he had been for weeks past maturing
his plans to cast in his lot with the rebellious Sepoys
—that he had intrigued largely with the mutinous
regiments of the Lower Provinces—and that he had
even been in communication with the Nana Sahib.
It is not easy to ascertain the exact amount of truth
in these contemporary stories. The popular voice of
the English at the time proclaimed him a miscreant.
The usual strong colours, with which we are wont
to daub our enemies, especially when they are successful, were freely used in our portraiture of this
man. But there was afterwards, as often happens in
such cases, a reaction of sentiment; and he grew
into a veteran warrior; a hero and a deliverer;

rising from a sick-bed, forgetful of his infirmities, regardless of the approaches of death; eager to redress the wrongs of his countrymen and to smite the persecutors of his race; arming himself for the strife and going forth to the battle.

But the truth lay midway between these two extremes; and the story of Kower Singh must be told in less ambitious language. A little while before the Dinapore revolt, the old Baboo had been held in high esteem for his loyalty by the Patna Commissioner. On the 14th of June, Mr. Tayler had written to Government, saying: "Many people have sent me letters, imputing disloyalty and disaffection to several Zemindars, especially Baboo Kower Singh. My personal friendship for him, and the attachment he has always shown me, enable me confidently to contradict the report." Again on July 8th: "Baboo Kower Singh would, I am sure, do anything he could; but he has now no means. He has written to me several times to express his loyalty and sympathy." It was, perhaps, true that he had no means for good; but he had immense means for evil, for the hearts of the people were against us. But his position was a critical one. The good opinion of Kower Singh entertained by the Commissioner was shared by the Magistrate 'of Shahabad, who wrote to the Government of Bengal, saying: "With regard to the Baboo, there have been, ever since the commencement of the present disturbances, reports, some of them tending to implicate him seriously. . . . I have no reason to believe them. The Commissioner has the highest opinion of his loyalty, and I see no reason to doubt it." But there were officers in other districts who knew, and who did not hesitate to report that there were many influential Zemindars watching the movements of Kower Singh, and prepared to follow his example. He was a man in such times to be narrowly watched; and so Commissioner Tayler wrote to him, inviting him to come into Patna (of course for the Baboo's own good), and sent an officer of the Commission to visit him and personally to observe the state of affairs. But the wily old Rajpoot, who knew that this was only a courteous mode of making him a prisoner, pleaded age and infirmity, and was not to be lured from his sheltered home in Jugdespore. He made, however, specious promises of attending to the Commissioner's wishes at some future period of restored health, knowing very well that something would happen in the interval to prevent their accomplishment. The old man was waiting and watching. He had "a case" of his own, about the issue of which he was anxious in the extreme; and it is possible that if this had gone well for him, he might not have desired to precipitate the convulsions which seemed to afford a shorter, if a more rugged way, out of the jungle of his difficulties. The embarrassed state of his affairs had, some time before, caused the intervention of Government. His estates were in liquidation, and it required the support of official authority to carry him successfully through the ordeal. At a critical moment, when Kower Singh was in doubt and perplexity as to the part he should play in the great historical drama which he saw clearly in the foreground of the future, an adverse decision was communicated to him. The support of Government was suddenly withdrawn. There was but one thing that could have kept the old Rajpoot free from the entanglements that surrounded him, and that one thing was such aid from Government as would have enabled him to end his days in quietude and peace, and to leave an honourable name behind him in the district. But instead of this, he was, like many others, driven to despair by that miserable want of imagination and lack of sympathy which characterised the action of our " Boards."* So as the saving hand of Government was not to be extended to him, he betook himself to the other way out of his difficulties; to the new and shorter road to the coveted release which lay through the troubles sweeping over the country.† There were many about him to counsel this course of action—many who, eager for rebellion themselves, turned for a leader to

* As some readers may wish to have a more specific account of this transaction, it may be briefly stated that Kower Singh had engaged to obtain an advance of money, to the extent of twenty lakhs of rupees, for the payment of his debts. There was to have been a gradual process of liquidation from the proceeds of his estates through the Collector of Shahabad. This loan had not been actually negotiated. But the capitalist had promised that the money was shortly forthcoming. There were some delays, as there commonly are when money is to be advanced—but in the meanwhile some smaller sums had been advanced by other parties, and some advantageous compromises had been arranged. Affairs were in this state when suddenly the Sudder Board of Revenue sent through the Patna Commissioner " a peremptory message to Kower Singh that unless he obtained the entire loan within a month (which was impossible) they would recommend the Government to withdraw all interference with his affairs and to abandon the management of his estates."

† This opinion was entertained by Mr. Wake, the local magistrate, who, writing to Government on the 19th of July, said : "He is nominally the owner of vast estates, whilst in reality he is a ruined man, and can hardly find money to pay the interest of his debts. As long, therefore, as law and order exist, his position cannot improve : take them away, and he well knows that he would become supreme in this district. I do not think he will ever openly oppose the Government as long as he thinks that Government will stand, but I do think that, should these districts be ever the scene of a serious outbreak, he may take it into his head that it is time to strike a blow for his own interests, and his feudal influence is such as to render him exceedingly dangerous in such an event. I am narrowly watching his conduct, and the Commissioner has sent for him to Patna to speak to him on the subject of the reports about him; he is said to be ill, and I dare say will object on that plea, but I have heard that he has stated that he will not go to Patna, and will resist if he is sent for. I hope soon to be able to speak with more certainty on the subject." The Bengal Government officially described him as "the ruined owner of vast estates, who would become supreme in the district on the occurrence of disorder, but who, so long as law and order prevailed, could barely find the means to pay the interest of his debts."

this venerable chief. So he consented to cast in
his lot with them ; and his name became great in
Shahabad. When the Dinapore regiments revolted,
the whole district rose, and the Jugdespore man fell
naturally into the place of leader of the insurgents.

Whilst, in those last days of July, the old Rajpoot chief was up and doing, the old English General
was thinking what was to be done. Under the
powerful influence of Kower Singh, the insurgents had
marched on Arrah, released all the prisoners in the
Gaol, plundered the Treasury, and but for the wisdom and bravery of the European inhabitants (of
which more will be said presently), would [have
butchered them all to a man. But Lloyd, though
not so far stricken in years, could only think and
think wrongly. It appears that his first idea was to
assume the defensive and to intrench himself at
Dinapore. He expected that the mutineers, having
possessed themselves of Arrah and slain all the white
men in the place, would return flushed with conquest, under the leadership of Kower Singh, and
attack the great military station. But Commissioner
Tayler, to whom the General referred the proposal,
protested against such an exhibition of weakness, and
urged the immediate despatch of a strong force into
the Shahabad district to crush the insurrection, and,
if not too late, to rescue our people.

This was on the 26th. All through the previous
day there had been great excitement at Patna. The
firing of the guns at Dinapore had been distinctly
heard. The English residents had chuckled over the
thought of the victory that our people were achieving, and had counted up the "butcher's bill." The

slaughter of the mutineers was variously estimated at from five hundred to eight hundred men. But as the hours passed away, and the sound of the guns passed away too, doubt and anxiety began to take the place of the first expectation of a great carnage. Then a rumour came that the mutineers were escaping, and that the English soldiery could not follow them through the swamps which stretched out before them. Before nightfall there was a gathering of all our people at the Commissioner's house ; and a little force was improvised, consisting of Sikhs and Nujeebs, and a few English gentlemen, which went out at night, in the hope of being able to cut off stragglers, and perhaps to intercept a diversion of the enemy towards Patna. But as the following day broke, news came which gave a new complexion to affairs. "Whilst it was yet scarcely daylight," wrote the Commissioner, "a note was brought to my bedside. By the imperfect light I could just distinguish the words, 'Major Holmes and his wife.' I felt at once what it was, and shall never forget the sensation of pain and horror with which I read the announcement of this gallant and chivalrous officer's murder. I immediately," added the writer," recalled our volunteer detachment." A new difficulty had come upon us from a most unexpected quarter.

Major Holmes and his regiment.

At Segowlie was a regiment of Irregular Horse (the Twelfth), commanded by Major James Holmes, an officer made of the right heroic stuff. A man of an ardent temperament, eager, impulsive, and bold as a lion, he shrunk from 'no responsibility, and was ready, in the hour of difficulty, to assume authority, which he did not rightfully possess, and to trust for future indemnity to the generosity of his masters. As soon as the first developments of insurrection rendered it certain that our positions in Behar would be threatened, he placed himself in direct communication with Lord Canning, and expressed his opinions with a freedom rarely seen in similar correspondence. Like Commissioner Tayler, he was all for prompt action and vigorous repression. "If every one," he wrote on the 25th of May to the Governor-General, "is true to himself and to the Government, and does his duty with smiling cheerfulness, all things will go well. I have endeavoured to impress this on the civilians of the district. I have also pointed out the necessity of their informing the wealthy Natives and Zemindars that the chief object of the turbulent Sepoys is plunder, and that it is their interest to seize any mutinous person and hand him over for punishment." "It is absolutely necessary," he added, "to strike terror by putting such 'persons to death by military law, and this power should, I think, be granted. If any person already discharged for mutiny from the Army should make such attempt, I would act on my responsibility."* What Lord Canning replied to this has been already shown.† But notwithstanding this plain expression of the opinions of the supreme authority, the fiery commander of Irregulars took upon himself the responsibility of placing the entire districts of Tirhoot, Chuprah, and Chunparum, as well as Azimgurh and Goruckpore, under martial law. "As a single clear head," he wrote on the 19th of June, "is better than a dozen in these times, and as military law is better than civil in a turbulent country, I have assumed absolute military control from Goruckpore to Patna, and have placed under absolute

---

* MS. Correspondence.   chapter, p. 7, was addressed to
† The letter quoted in the last   Major Holmes.

military rule all that country, including the districts of Sarun, Chunparum, and Tirhoot. The Governor-General having requested me to write to him direct, I do so daily, and have informed his lordship on this head." The Commissioner reported that Major Holmes had done this "with the knowledge and concurrence of the Governor-General." But this was a mistake—at least it was only half true. Major Holmes had written to the Governor-General, saying: "Hearing that some seditious letters and speeches have been coming into the district, I have thought it proper to order my patrolling parties to proclaim martial law over the districts of Goruckpore, Sehwan, Chunparum, and Tirhoot, and that I shall punish with instant death the following offences, namely:

" 1. Openly bearing arms against the State.

" 2. Seditious speaking, or exciting others to rebellion, or any expression of disaffection to the Government.

" 3. Concealing rebels, or even hearing others talk treason, and not immediately reporting to the nearest authorities.

" 4. Plundering—if caught *in flagrante delicto*.

"All this," he added, "may not be lawful; but I don't care for that. There are times when circumstances are above the law. I am determined to keep order in these districts, and I'll do it with a strong hand."* Nothing can be plainer than this—nothing more certain than that Holmes proclaimed martial law, with the subsequent knowledge of the Governor-General. But the Government promptly repudiated these unauthorised publications.†

* Major Holmes to Lord Canning, June 15, 1857.—*MS. Correspondence*. In a letter to Mr. Tayler, he wrote that it had been said that this hot-headed Major would not be content till he had strung up a high civilian.

† I cannot find the slightest trace in Lord Canning's correspondence of any sort of concurrence in

Major Holmes had full confidence in the fidelity of his men. He commanded a model regiment, supposed to be proof against all temptation. There was not a civil officer in the district who did not covet the protection of a few sabres from Holmes's Incorruptibles; and he freely scattered them about in little parties of fifty or thirty, never doubting that they were true to the core. "My parties now," he wrote to Lord Canning on the 14th of June, "patrol the whole country from Goruckpore and Azimgurh to Tirhoot, Chuprah, and Patna; and I believe that at the present not a word of sedition is spoken on the banks of the Ganges. I have proclaimed that I shall punish with instant death civilians as well as soldiers for one word of mutiny; and all know that I shall keep my word. In consequence all is quiet. Last night, at nine P.M., two unfortunate Sepoys of the Seventeenth,* mutineers, were sent into me from Sehwan. Within an hour I had hanged them both. I enclose copy of court-martial, that your lordship may understand how I act. It is vile, dirty, unsoldierly work; but at the present moment I should hang or shoot my own brother under similar circumstances. My party with the treasure have escaped with honour, for they retired by word of command from Captain Palliser, when overpowered by eight hundred Sepoys and gaol-birds, and three guns. They escorted the officers to Benares, and

Holmes's act; I presume, therefore, that he must have leaped hastily to the conclusion that silence gave consent. I believe that the Governor-General only wrote one letter to him—the one referred to above—in which he cautioned him against going beyond the authority already given to him. In that letter (May 30th) the Governor-General did not request Major Holmes to write to him directly. He merely in reply to that officer wrote, "I shall be glad to hear further from you, especially on matters within your own observation. I cannot undertake," he added, "to answer your letters, for I have no time for writing."—*MS. Correspondence.*

* This was the Azimgurh regiment. See *ante*, vol. ii. p. 213, *et seq.*

returned to their post at Goruckpore in good order."
And so letter after letter was written—now to the
Governor-General, now to the Commissioner, all in
the same confident strain—the fearless utterances of
a strong, bold man, who believed that all things
would yield to the force of his own resolute will.

But those were days when appearances were most
delusive, and the most reasonable hopes were often
doomed to bitter disappointment. One evening
Major Holmes was taking his accustomed drive, accompanied by his wife. The lady had once been
known as Dinah Sale, and afterwards as the wife of
Sturt the Engineer.* She had survived the horrors
of the retreat from Caubul, which had made her a
widow, and had become the wife of another brave
man, to confront greater dangers than those which
she had escaped. Neither thought so at that moment;
for they believed that, though all else might be false,
Holmes's troopers were as true as steel. But suddenly
the truth was revealed to them. A party of Sowars
rode up and fell upon them with their sabres. The
butchery was brief but effectual. I cannot give the
details of it. But a little time after the murder,
Mrs. Holmes's Native ayah (or tire-woman) went to
the spot where the crime had been committed and
saw the bodies of her master and mistress. The
corpses of both were headless. The troopers, in
whose devotion he had trusted to the last, had decapitated their late commander, and carried off his
head as a trophy and a witness to their comrades.
The lady's head lay still there; and the ayah bent
reverently over it, lifted the streaming hair, rich and

* Daughter of Sir Robert Sale— Sale, who gave us so vivid an ac-
distinguished in the Afghan and count of the former in her published
Sikh wars—and of the heroic Lady journal.

beautiful in its abundance, and cut it off, as a memorial to be cherished by those who had loved her.* Meanwhile, a party of troopers had completed the work thus begun by murdering the other Europeans at Segowlie. Dr. and Mrs. Garner were sitting in their bungalow, when the Sowars rushed in upon them and cut them down, with one of their two children.† The other, a little girl, escaped from the house, and was rescued by a Native functionary. The house was then fired, and the bodies of the doctor's family were burnt. Mr. Bennett, the Deputy-Postmaster, also fell a victim to the fury of the troopers. The great body of the regiment broke out into open mutiny of the worst kind; but some scattered branches stood fast, and a detachment of them did good service under Captain Johnson in the subsequent operations in Oude.

In the mean time, what had been done at Dinapore to compensate for the first great failure? The mutinous Sepoys had been suffered to escape towards the most dangerous district of the whole great province of Behar. At first it was thought that their flight to Shahabad might be arrested by the difficulty of crossing the Soane, as what were called " precautions" had been taken to have all the available boats removed to the other side of the river. But though this wise project had been conceived, the right man had not been found to accomplish it; and so the surging insurrection met with no check, and the flood poured on uninterruptedly. On the 26th, a feeble and unsuccessful effort was made to send a detachment of riflemen on board a steam-boat after the fugitives;

Proceedings at Dinapore.

---

* The bodies were afterwards carried into Matchuree by the police, as was also that of Mr. Bennett.

† Dr. Garner was, I believe, a relative of Major Holmes, whose name was James Garner Holmes.

but it came back, having accomplished nothing.* Another effort was then made with equal want of success. On the 27th, a steamer with a detachment of the Thirty-seventh was again despatched towards the Soane, with intention to land our men at a point some nine miles from Arrah, and "to bring away the civilians there besieged." This vessel did not return to Dinapore, but it stuck fast upon a sand-bank, not without suspicion of foul play on the part of a Native pilot. General Lloyd would then have recalled the detachment. But against this the Commissioner had protested, and had urged, on the other hand, the expediency of despatching another steamer with a strong reinforcement to pick up the stranded vessel, and then for the united force to march upon Arrah. Another steamer had come in, most opportunely, from Allahabad. It was full of passengers escaping to Calcutta. That this vessel should be turned, for present purposes, into a troop-ship, and that the Dinapore Protestant Church should be converted into a great caravanserai during the employment of the vessel on this special duty, was then determined by the military authorities, and arrangements were made to give effect to the design.

The departure of this third body of English troops was to have taken place at daybreak on the 29th;

---

* The following is taken from General Lloyd's letter to his brother, to which reference has already been made : "It is, perhaps, to be regretted that some (English troops) were not sent that night or next morning, but only a small party in comparison to the strength of the mutineers could have been detached —no guns could have gone, and as the mutineers avoided the road and kept to the fields, where they could scarcely have been followed by a small party of Europeans, they would probably not have been of much use. However, as the readiest means of following them to prevent them crossing the Soane, I next day (the 26th) sent off some riflemen in a steamer up that river, expecting that at this season there would have been sufficient water—but unfortunately the steamer could not get up high enough, and returned in the evening without having effected anything."

but when the men of the Tenth had been marched
down to the river-side, it was found that the steamer
was full of sleeping passengers, and the captain was
reluctant to disturb them.* Then it was discovered
that the steamer could not take so large a number of
men, as it was designed that she should also take in
tow the boat that was stranded with the detachment
of the Thirty-seventh.† So one-half of the men of
the Tenth were sent back to their barracks, and
Colonel Fenwick, who was to have commanded, made
over the charge to Captain Dunbar. A hundred and
fifty Europeans were thus embarked; and with them
went some seventy Sikhs under Lieutenant Ingleby
—a spirited young officer of one of the revolted regiments, who had volunteered for this service.

And there were other volunteers. On the 29th,
the Commissioner was at Dinapore supporting on

* Mr. Tayler's statement on this subject is too distinct and detailed not to be given in illustration of the narrative in the text: "Colonel Fenwick appealed to the General for authority to have the sleepers turned out, which was promptly given; the word was passed on to the non-com-missioned officers, and from them to some of the privates. In another minute, it was discovered that the steamer could not tow her own flat as well as that of the *Horungutta*, which it was arranged she was to take on, and consequently only half the force told off could go. Colonel Fenwick retired in disgust, and the command was delegated to Captain Dunbar. From that moment all was confusion. No progress was made, no one took upon himself to disturb the happy sleepers. As Civil Commissioner, I had no au-thority in matters purely military, but I could not quite refrain from interference. I saw the man, appa-rently a sergeant, to whom the order for turning out the passengers was given, but who, after Colonel Fen-wick's departure, had done nothing in the matter. I went up to him and suggested that if he would send three or four hard-hearted men to turn the passengers out, 'neck and crop,' if necessary, it would be a beneficial move, and they would never get off if he didn't; he had just said, 'All right, sir,' with much alacrity, and was telling off the men to set to work, when some-body called out to him, 'Hallo! you may knock off, you're not to go!' The man, a splendid specimen of a soldier, turned short off, mut-tering, and, with several others, went away in no good humour. *Several hours* elapsed before the final start was made, and the steamer did not get clear away till about half-past nine!"—*The Patna Crisis.*

† It should be explained to the English reader that what is com-monly described as a "steamer" consists of a flat, or large pinnace, with good accommodation, towed by a steam-vessel.

1857.
July 29.

the spot his protests in favour of a forward movement.* Mr. M'Donell, the Magistrate of Chuprah and Mr. Ross Mangles, Assistant to the Patna Commissioner, went with him. Both were eager to accompany any force that might be despatched to the relief of Arrah. For such men there was great attraction in the enterprise; firstly, for love of a

Mr. Wake.

friend, who was in peril there; secondly, out of that strong love of action and adventure, that irrepressible ardour of generous youth, which will not suffer it to be quiescent when danger is to be faced and work to be done. With the means already at the disposal of the military authorities, and fresh reinforcements continually coming up the river, what could be looked for but a successful—a glorious crusade? But these well-founded expectations were most delusive. Human calculations were as nothing in this emergency. The energy, the sagacity, the fertility of resource, which Englishmen were now displaying in many parts of the country, were wanting at Dinapore, as they had before been wanting at Meerut. Not only did misfortune track our steps, but grievous incapacity obstructed us at every stage. How it happened that Dunbar was selected for the command of such an expedition it is not easy to conjecture. General Lloyd did not hesitate to declare his opinion that the leader of this expedition was chosen by his commanding officer on account of his incompetency.† He had been a regimental pay-

---

* Mr. Tayler says that he went to Dinapore on the evening of the 29th, which must be a mistake, as he was obviously there on the morning of the 29th, when Dunbar's detachment embarked. The date should be the 28th.

† General Lloyd's letter will be found complete in the Appendix. I was guided to it, as to other very valuable references, by Mr. Montgomery Martin's work. It is observable, however, that that painstaking writer, by a clerical or typographical error, makes it appear that the General hinted that Colonel Fenwick was " *una*ware" of Dunbar's incompetence. The word is " aware."

master, and he had but scant knowledge of military 	1857.
operations in the field. But he took the work upon 	July 29.
him readily as a brave man, and went forth to his
doom.

About half-past nine, the vessel put off amidst Dunbar's ex-
cheers from the river-bank. "The gallant appearance pedition.
of the men," wrote one who watched their departure,
" the eager countenances of the officers, the anticipation of certain success in the enterprise, gave the expedition a character of bright and buoyant hopefulness."* But a terrible sentence was written down
against it. It appeared as though nothing prosperous
could ever come out of Dinapore. At every stage
there was mismanagement of the worst type. The
men embarked hungry; and hungry they were suffered to remain. There was abundance on board, but
neither food nor drink was served out to them; and
when some hours after noon, having picked up the
stranded vessel, and obtained the assistance of some
roomy country boats,† they disembarked at the nearest
point to Arrah, they went fasting and feeble on a
service which demanded all the spirit and strength
that could be imparted to them by generous internal
stimulants. They had a long march before them, and
nothing was to be obtained on the way.

It was about seven o'clock before the whole of the
troops were landed. The early moon was shining
brightly, and, aided by it, Dunbar made his military
dispositions, and, having secured a guide, marched on
with the Sikh detachment in front. At a distance of
two or three miles from their destination, they came

* Tayler's "Patna Crisis."
† Mr. Trevelyan says: "It was
the height of the rainy season,
and much of the country was under
water. Accordingly, on arriving
nearly opposite Arrah, the troops
left the steamer and embarked in
some large boats, in which they followed the course of a nullah, which
brought them some miles nearer
their point."

upon a bridge which seemed well suited for a halting-place. Here the leader of the expedition was recommended to serve out some rum and biscuits to the troops, and to bivouac for the night. But Dunbar determined to push on to Arrah. The moon was now waning, and, before midnight, darkness closed upon the advancing force. The Sikh skirmishers had been drawn in, and our people were moving forward, unsuspicious of the presence of an enemy, when, in the vicinity of a dense mango-grove, a tremendous fire was opened upon them. They were then marching on a raised causeway terribly exposed; whilst their assailants were concealed by their leafy shelter; so none knew how to return the fire. The white uniforms of the Europeans were seen through the darkness of the night, but the dusky Sepoys in undress, little short of nakedness, could not be discerned among the trees. It was plain now that our people had been drawn into an ambuscade. And it was a fatal one to our relieving force. Officers and men fell fast beneath the fire of the concealed enemy. One of the first to receive his death-wound was the commander of the expedition. If Dunbar had erred, he paid dearly for the error. He was never seen alive after this first discharge.

From the front of our column, from the right flank, from the left flank, came through the darkness, with fatal effect, the heavy shower of musket-balls. What the strength of the enemy was at that point it is hard to say.* But it was plain to our people that they were surrounded by a multitude of Sepoys,

---

* Some statements fix the number at two thousand—others at three thousand or even five thousand. It is obvious that if only the Dinapore regiments were there, the number could not much have exceeded the former amount. There were unquestionably, however, in Shahabad at this time many men from other revolted regiments, and many Sepoys on furlough.

and that their ranks were being rapidly thinned.
The sudden attack, followed by the fall of their
leader, had thrown them into confusion, and, straggling as they were, they could not return the enemy's
fire, in the darkness, without imminent risk of shooting down their own comrades. After a time, however, they rallied, and were got together by the
bugle-call in an enclosed field, at some little distance
from the grove, where they found shelter in a hollow,*
and there they might have lain in comparative safety
if our men could have been restrained from firing;
but the occasional crack of our rifles revealed our
position, and brought back bullets with destructive
interest.† Thus the night passed miserably with our
people, hungering for the dawn. But daylight
brought no relief to their sufferings—no confidence
to our afflicted people. There were those who counselled the prosecution of the march to Arrah; but a
retrograde movement was determined upon, in utter
despondency of heart.

A disastrous retreat was now to be commenced by
the survivors of this luckless expedition. Fatigued
and famished, and sore at heart, for the grievous
necessity of leaving the wounded behind them was
theirs, they set their faces again towards the river.
That morning's march will never be forgotten by the
few who live to think of it. As they went, it seemed
to them that the enemy were ubiquitous—that they
started up on every side; from copses and coverts of
all kinds, from walled enclosures and mud villages,
from hollows and ditches and the roofs of houses,

1857.
July.

The retreat.

* Mr. Trevelyan describes it as an empty tank, which is confirmed by Mr. M'Donell, in a narrative pub-lished in the *Times*.

† " Young Anderson, a very nice young fellow of the Twenty-second Native Infantry, a volunteer, was standing up behind the hedge; he was shot through the head, and jumped up like a buck—of course killed on the spot." — *M'Donell's Narrative*.

came with destructive activity the fire of the insurgents. Against it our people, if far less exhausted and dispirited, could have done little or nothing. For when they formed and fired, as they sometimes did, there was no enemy to be seen ; the aim of our people was directed only towards the puffs of smoke which indicated the position whence the fire had come, and every rebel volley was followed by a rapid retirement of the enemy. But these efforts soon ceased. Our retreat became a rout. Men thought of little but their own lives. All things were against them but one. As our men dropped by the wayside, the ammunition of their assailants was running short. This was a great deliverance. But for it, scarcely a man would have escaped.

July 30.   As it was, only a wretched remnant of the party that, flushed with the thought of victory, had left Dinapore on that July morning, returned to the nullah which they had crossed by the light of the rising moon. Happily the boats were still there, on the left bank, as we had left them. But the sight of them, presenting, as they seemed to do, the means of escape, extinguished the little discipline that was left in the retreating force. There was a scene of wild confusion—of crowding and huddling—at the ghaut, each man seeking his own safety, and, with a few bright exceptions, caring but little for his fellow-men. It was not strange, for the enemy were upon them— firing upon the fugitives from all sides, and striving hard to burn or to sink the boats. In this they were only too successful. Some of our people were shot ; some were burnt; some were drowned. The commands and entreaties of their officers were of no avail. Many threw away their arms and accoutrements—some stripped themselves to the skin, and flung themselves

into the water.   It is stated that the last man to leave
the shore was Lieutenant Ingelby, who had volunteered to lead the Sikhs to Arrah.   He stepped into a
burning boat, as it was putting off, and ere it was
half-way across the stream, the flames had so spread
that all on board were compelled to take to the water.
Ingelby was struck on the neck by a musket-ball and
went down ; but rising again to the surface, he threw
up his arms, cried aloud, " Good-bye, Grenadiers !"
and sunk—never to be seen alive again.

Those, who reached the opposite bank of the
nullah, were now safe.   The steamer and flat were
soon gained ; and back the diminished party went to
the cantonment of Dinapore.   Our people there had
looked anxiously for their coming—eager to welcome
the victors and to congratulate the rescued—never
doubting that there would be a great ovation; and
now as the vessel appeared in sight, the inmates of the
Barracks went out, men and women, to the river-side,
straining eyes and ears to catch a sight of the crowded
deck and the sound of triumphant exultation proclaiming the success of the expedition.   But not a shout was
heard as she steamed on ; and there was little sign
of life on board.   All indeed was ominously quiet.
People asked each other what it meant.   But when
the vessel came-to beside the Hospital, there was no
need for further questioning.   The silence was the
silence of disaster and death.   The whole sad story
was soon known; and then there was such a wail
from the women as those who heard it can never
cease to remember.   Some beat their breasts and
tore their hair in the wild excitement of their grief,
and called down the judgment of God on the
authors of this great calamity.   It is said that if
General Lloyd had appeared amongst them at that

I 2

moment, they would have torn him to pieces. Of the four hundred men who had gone out on the day before, full of health and hope, one-half had been left behind to gorge the vultures and the jackals, and of those who returned only about fifty were unwounded.*

Heroic
exploits.
But disastrous as was the retreat, it was not all disgraceful. There will always be acts of individual heroism when Englishmen go out to battle. It may be a soldier, or it may be a civilian, in whom the irrepressible warrior-instinct manifests itself in some act of conspicuous gallantry and devotion—but it is sure never to be wanting. In those days well-nigh every man was more or less a soldier; and there were few better soldiers than the members of the Bengal Civil Establishment. The traditions of the old Indian Service gave them a pride in their profession, and they held that nothing was incompatible with its duties that tended to maintain the honour and security of the Anglo-Indian Empire. Accustomed, in most instances, from boyhood upwards, to the use of fire-arms, with firm seats in the saddle, and often mighty hunters of the boar and the tiger, rejoicing in the perilous excitement of such sport, these men, especially in the earlier stages of their career, were well braced up for vigorous action, and had little to learn to fit them for the front of the battle. From the days when Charles Metcalfe headed the attack at Deeg, and Mountstuart Elphinstone rode side by side with the Wellington of the future at Assaye, the Indian Civil Service had been fertile in heroes. But never before the convulsions of 1857 had the martial energies of our civilians been so

---

* The official return says: 2 captains, 2 lieutenants, 3 ensigns, 3 sergeants, 10 corporals, 3 drummers, 112 privates killed; 1 lieutenant, 2 ensigns, 3 sergeants, 3 corporals, 2 drummers, and 49 privates wounded.

largely reduced; never had the pen so often been laid aside for the sword or the rifle. It has been already shown in these volumes how George Ricketts fought the Nabha guns on the bank of the Sutlej, how John Mackillop kept the well at Cawnpore, and how other soldierly deeds were done by men whose cutcherries were closed and whose judgment-seats were empty. And many more such stories will be told as the narrative proceeds. Two at least lighten up the record of the retreat from Arrah. They have been told before and better than I can tell them. But this History would be incomplete without the recital.

I have said that with Dunbar's relieving force went Mr. M'Donell and Mr. Ross Mangles, of the Civil Service. They did excellent service on the way. The local knowledge of the former enabled him to act as a guide, and the rifles of both were in constant requisition. In the first attack on our columns, Mangles had been stunned by a musket-ball, but he soon recovered himself, and was helping the surgeon who accompanied the force to bind up the wounds of his comrades, or carrying water to them in their agony. When morning dawned he shouldered his piece and stepped on with the rest towards the nullah, resolute to sell his life dearly. In the flower of his youth, a man of a fine presence, with a long stride and a firm hand on his two-barrel, our men looked to him, in the morning light, as to one who, though without official command, had natural right to be obeyed; and he did much good service as he went by his animating influence upon others and by his own personal prowess.* Though by reason of

* Mr. Trevelyan says that "he succeeded in keeping together a small knot of men, who supplied him with a succession of loaded muskets. As he was a noted shikaree, a dead hand at bear and antelope, the Sepoys thought proper to keep their distance."

his stature a conspicuous mark for the enemy, and "though dozens of poor fellows," as he wrote afterwards, "were knocked over close to him," by the blessing of God he escaped unharmed. He escaped to do a noble deed. A soldier of the Thirty-seventh, who had been struck down and was left helpless on the ground, where he would presently have been murdered by the Sepoys, implored the young civilian not to desert him. So amidst a destructive fire of musketry, Ross Mangles the Younger halted and knelt down, bound up the man's wounds, hoisted him on his back, and strode on with his burden. He had fasted for twenty-four hours; he had watched for forty-eight; but notwithstanding this want of food and rest, he declared afterwards that he had "never felt so strong in his life." And well was it that the invigorating sense of a great duty so sustained him. For the man whom he bore was as big as himself, and the enemy were close upon his track. Compelled, now and then, to lay his burden down, he stood over the wounded man, and if opportunity offered, turned the interval of rest to account by taking a shot at the insurgents. And the good God watched over this deed of mercy and love; for young Mangles carried the wounded soldier, over rough and swampy ground, for a space of six miles, till he reached the nullah; and then swimming out and holding up the helpless man in the water, he reached a boat, laid his charge safely in it, and soon had the delight of seeing him in good hands at the hospital of Dinapore, with leisure to thank God and his preserver for his almost miraculous deliverance.*

* The man's name was Richard Taylor. He was not dismissed from hospital till the 19th of November, and he was then invalided and sent to England. This story has a remarkable sequel. It was the first deed of the kind that eventually solved the question as to whether

119

Differing in kind, but not in degree, from this
heroic exploit, was another act of daring self-devotion
done by Mr. M'Donell, of the same service. It was
in no small measure owing to his representations and
to his offer to act as a guide to the relieving force,
for he knew the country well, that General Lloyd
consented to send the European detachment into
Shahabad. Always in the front, always in the thick
of the battle, he did excellent service, as I have
said before, on the march. Many a mutineer sunk
beneath the fire of his rifle. He was beside Dunbar
when he fell, and was sprinkled with the life-blood of
the luckless leader. Wounded himself, he still fought
on gallantly during the retreat, and reached the

1857.
July 30.

civilians could share with their military brethren the honour of the Victoria Cross. Those were days when, in the all-prevailing excitement, heroic acts were often overlooked at the time. And it was not until the lapse of more than a year that official notice was taken of this honourable incident; and then it was brought to the attention of Lord Canning by Sir James Outram. Both were men, who, courageous themselves, had a keen appreciation of courage in others, and never neglected an opportunity of recording their admiring approval. It was not before the summer of 1858 that Outram was made acquainted with the exploit above narrated. It had been his first thought to recommend young Mangles for the Victoria Cross. But meanwhile another gallant deed, done by an uncovenanted civilian in Oude (hereafter to be recorded), had been recommended for this reward, and the decision was that members of the military and naval services alone were entitled to this distinction. Believing this to be final, the Governor-General, on receipt of Outram's letter, wrote a letter to the Home Government,

forwarding it for their information, and emphatically indorsing its contents. The letter adds, " The modesty which has allowed the event to remain unknown to those in authority until after the lapse of a twelve-month it was brought to light by the journal of a surgeon recording the gratitude of the wounded soldier, is not the least remarkable feature in the story." Lord Canning wrote also to the younger Mangles saying, "It is a satisfaction to me to tell you with what pleasure I have done this ; but the pleasure would have been greater if (as ought to have been the case) my official letter could have been addressed to your father." Mr. Ross Mangles the Elder had vacated the Chair of the Court of Directors in April, 1858, and had been succeeded by Sir Frederick Currie. The whole question of the claim of civilians to the Victoria Cross was afterwards with reference to this and the Oude case (Mr. Kavanagh's) finally decided in favour of the claim of soldier-civilians—and I feel that there was not a soldier in the service who did not rejoice in the withdrawal of the invidious distinction.

nullah with a stiffened limb, but with no abatement of vigorous courage. There, having done his best to assist others more helpless than himself, he entered the last of the boats; and deliverance seemed to be at hand. But the insurgents had taken away the oars and had lashed the rudder, and though the breeze was favourable for the escape of our people, the current carried the boat back to the river-bank, and fast and furious came the shower of musket-balls from the pieces of the enemy. The boats were the large covered boats—the "floating haystacks"—of the country, which afforded excellent shelter to those who huddled together beneath the clumsy thatch. There were thirty-five European soldiers on board the boat; and M'Donell, seeing the difficulty and danger which the impossibility of steering the vessel brought upon them, called upon the men to cut the lashings of the rudder. But no man stirred. So M'Donell went out from the shelter, and climbing on to the roof of the boat, perched himself on the rudder and cut the lashings, amidst a very storm of bullets from the contiguous bank. It was truly a providential deliverance that he escaped instant death. Coolly and steadily he went about his perilous work, and though some balls passed through his hat, not one did him any harm. Thus the rudder was loosened, the boat answered to the helm, and by M'Donell's gallant act the crew were saved from certain destruction. The good deed was not forgotten. It afterwards earned for the noble-hearted civilian the crowning glory of the Victoria Cross.*

* The following is the official account of the exploit as given by Captain J. W. Medhurst, of the Sixtieth Rifles, previously of the Tenth Foot: "On the ill-fated expedition retiring from Arrah on the morning of the 30th July, 1857, and on arriving at the village and stream of Bherara, as is well known, the men, exhausted and dispirited, broke

1857.
July 30.

Nor was heroism of this best kind confined to our officers in high position, whose exploits are ever sure to find chroniclers, whilst the doings of humbler men are often obscured at the time, or afterwards forgotten. In the ranks of our luckless army, beaten as they were, driven back disastrously to their boats, by an enemy whom a little while before they had despised, were some stout-hearted English soldiers, who, in the midst of that confused flight for life, could think of the sufferings of their wounded comrades, and pause to aid them amidst the thickest fire of the enemy. Among the officers shot down during the retreat was Ensign Erskine, of the Tenth Foot, a good soldier, who had risen from the ranks. As he lay there in his helplessness, to be bayoneted or brained by the Sepoys, two men of the Tenth espied him and carried him off, thus encumbering themselves at the risk of their own lives. Erskine died, but one at least of these true noblemen survived to receive the honour for which some of the greatest

and made for the only six large country boats moored close to the right bank. After assisting some wounded men into the furthest boat, and being myself pulled in, I saw that Mr. M'Donell, who was one of our number, was exerting himself with a sergeant to move the boat into the stream. It being discovered that the boat was bound to the bank, one or two men jumped out and loosened the rope, and the boat moved. Assisted by the less exhausted of my party, I was keeping up a fire of Enfields on the enemy, whose musketry was very galling. Whilst so employed, I heard Mr. M'Donell call out for a knife to cut away some rope which bound the rudder to the right, causing the lumbering boat to veer round into the right shore again, and for a time causing it to stick fast. On looking round I saw him seated on the stern extremity of the boat in full view of the enemy, and quite exposed to their fire. He cut away the mentioned rope, and guiding the rudder himself, a fortunate breeze carried our boat across the stream, grounding at about ten yards from the left bank, whereby all those who were alive were enabled to jump out and reach the steamer in safety. The number of men thus saved was about thirty-five; and during the passage across three men were shot dead, one was mortally, and two or three slightly, wounded. I may safely assert that it was owing to Mr. M'Donell's presence of mind, and at his personal risk, that our boat got across on that day."

1857.
July 30.
captains of the age would have willingly surrendered their crosses and collars. For this and other subsequent acts of valour, Dennis Dempsey, of the Tenth Foot, was decorated with the Victoria Cross.*

One more episode of this Dinapore mutiny must be narrated. I wish that it were as honourable to the national character as those which have preceded it in the record. It happened that amidst the almost general defection of the Native troops at Dinapore, a few Sepoys of the Fortieth Regiment were found true to their colours. When their comrades had deserted they remained at their post—doubtless believing that their loyalty would be respected. But it appears that the fact of their fidelity—the truth that these few men had remained "faithful among the faithless"—sufficed not to countervail the other patent fact that these people had dark skins. So, when this little residue of loyal Sepoys, having been burnt out of their huts, were gathered together beneath a tent, or some other temporary shelter, it befel that under cover of the night a party of European soldiers rushed suddenly upon them with fixed bayonets and thrust out among them, striving to kill as many as they could. What the actual result was in killed and wounded it is not easy to ascertain. From authority which it would

* The following is the official record of the cumulative services which obtained for Dennis Dempsey the Victoria Cross: "Private Dennis Dempsey, Tenth Regiment: for having, at Lucknow, on the 14th of March, 1858, carried a powder-bag through a burning village with great coolness and gallantry, for the purpose of mining a passage in rear of the enemy's position. This he did exposed to a very heavy fire from the enemy behind loopholed walls, and to an almost still greater danger from the sparks which flew in every direction from the blazing houses. Also for having been the first man who entered the village of Jugdespore on the 12th of August, 1857, under a most galling fire. Private Dempsey was likewise one of those who helped to carry Ensign Erskine, of the Tenth Regiment, in the retreat from Arrah in July, 1857." The chronological arrangement of these incidents favours the supposition that, in the mind of the compiler, History should be read backwards.

be almost presumption to question, I learn that none were killed by the onslaught. Bayonet-wounds are seldom mortal. But this matters not. The intent to kill was palpable ; and it was a brutal and dastardly act. By reason of their own inactivity, or the ineptitude of their officers, these British soldiers, having suffered our enemies to escape, disgraced their uniform and stained their manhood by quietly bayoneting our sleeping friends, because they were of the same colour as the people who had baffled them.*

1857.
July 30.

* I have been informed, since the above passage was written, that the men of the Tenth were not moved to this act solely by their resentment at the thought that the mutineers had escaped. They had a personal wrong to revenge, for not long before some men of the regiment, having come upon a party of Sepoys sitting in consultation one night, under cover of the darkness, had been brutally assaulted by their Native comrades, and I believe that one of the Europeans was killed. This may not give a much fairer complexion to the story ; but it imparts a more intelligible meaning to the act.

CHAPTER III.

THE ENGLISH AT ARRAH—FORTIFICATION OF BOYLE'S HOUSE—APPEARANCE
OF THE MUTINEERS—PROSECUTION OF THE SIEGE—GALLANT DEFENCE BY
THE GARRISON — MAJOR VINCENT EYRE — IMPROVISATION OF A FIELD
FORCE—DEFEAT OF THE ENEMY—RELIEF OF ARRAH—FLIGHT OF KOWER
SINGH—DESTRUCTION OF JUGDESPORE.

1857.
July.
The English
at Arrah.

MEANWHILE the little party of English residents
at Arrah was holding out, against tremendous odds,
with a stern resolution worthy of Sparta in her
prime. Anything more hopeless, on the face of the
enterprise, than an attempt to defend a house or a
cluster of houses against some two thousand Sepoys
and a multitude of armed insurgents, perhaps four
times the number of the disciplined soldiery, could
not well be conceived. The almost absolute certainty
of destruction was such that a retreat under cover
of the night would not have been discreditable.
Reason suggested it. Nay, indeed, such was the
value of European life at that time, that what are
called the "claims of the public service" were all in
favour of what seemed to be the safer course. But
the European residents at Arrah had other thoughts
of their duty to the State. There were about a
dozen Englishmen, official and non-official, and three
or four other Christians of different races. Already
the women and children had been sent away to

places of comparative safety, and some few of the
male sex had departed in expectation of a coming
crisis in Shahabad. So what was left was of the
best stuff of muscular Christianity, and there was
nothing of a feebler kind to cling to its skirts and
encumber it. Still it was so very little in bulk, and
so weak in physical power of resistance, that self-preservation would have been impossible, but for a
happy circumstance which amplified and strengthened
the little garrison in the hour of its need. Commissioner Tayler had despatched to Arrah a party of
fifty Sikhs, of whose fidelity he had no doubt. At
such a time, indeed, the Grunth was the next best
thing to the Bible. There were fifty good fighting
men cherishing no sympathy with Poorbeahs of any
kind, and plenty of honest pluck under English
leaders to make a vigorous defence against any odds.
So it was resolved that there should be no flight, but
that the issue should depend upon the arbitrament
of hard fighting.

The centre of defence had been wisely chosen.
The works of the East Indian Railway were then in
course of construction, and at the head of the staff
so employed in the neighbourhood of Arrah was Mr.
Vicars Boyle, à gentleman who with the best knowledge of the civil engineer combined some acquaintance with military science, especially in the serviceable branch of fortification. The premises which
Boyle occupied contained two houses.* The smaller
one—a two-storied building with a flat roof—appeared to him to be best suited for purposes of de-

Fortification of Boyle's house.

---

* In the old days of English
hospitality in India it was a common
practice to erect within the " compound," or premises of the general
dwelling-house, a smaller supplementary building, to be used as a
guest-house. In this instance the
principal apartment had been used,
before Mr. Boyle's time, as a billiard-
room.

fence; and he had been for some time, in contemplation of the storm which had now burst, fortifying and provisioning this structure. If they could hold out for a few days—or it might be only a few hours—against a sudden incursion of mutinous Sepoys aided by the Budmashes of the place, all would be well; for who could doubt that relief would speedily arrive from Dinapore. So Boyle set to work and brought in stores of flour, grain, biscuits, beer, and other provender that would not spoil by keeping in that July weather—with water enough to supply seventy men for a fortnight. He got together, too, as much ammunition as he could find; and by building up the lower parts of the house, sufficient loopholes being left, and ranging sand-bags on the roof, he not only provided shelter for our people, but the means of operating freely against an enemy outside the walls of his little fortress. Nor was this all. Seeing that use might be made by the insurgents of the other and larger house in the compound, some fifty yards off, he had razed its front parapet, which would have afforded shelter to our assailants and aided their means of attack. When, therefore, news came that the Dinapore regiments had broken into rebellion and were streaming down upon Arrah, these wise precautions and preparations had determined the Government officers not to desert their post, but to hold out within the improvised fortifications so long as a pulse of life should beat in their bodies. So they gathered themselves together in the " chota ghur" in Mr. Boyle's compound, and braced themselves up to give a warm reception to the insurgents.

Commencement of the attack.
On the 27th of July, the bulk of the Dinapore mutineers, after doing, on the way, as much damage

as they could to all that belonged to the white men, poured into Arrah, and did according to the authorised Sepoy programme—they plundered the Treasury and released the prisoners in the Gaol. Having thus recruited themselves with the sinews of war and the rough material of murder, they made for Boyle's little fortress, the inmates of which seemed to them like so many rats in a cage. But marching up with a bold front, and maintaining a smart fire, as they advanced, they met with such a welcome from the British garrison as to check their confidence for a while, and make them think that it would suit them better to fight behind walls or trees. As the foremost men fell beneath the fire of our rifles or muskets from the loopholed walls or from the well-sheltered roof of the small house, the military order in which the insurgents had advanced was broken up, and they dissolved into scattered groups, looking lovingly towards the big house or the trees which studded the compound. And soon they had disposed themselves in this safer manner, eschewing the open, and taking up their head-quarters in or about Boyle's house. But it happened that the smaller house had a command of fire over the larger, and whenever one of the mutineers exposed himself for a moment, it was fortunate for him if a bullet, from behind the sandbags on the roof, did not put an end to his temerity.

It has been shown that there was not an English military officer in the garrison; but never was a most unequal defence more gallantly or more skilfully conducted. Herwald Wake, the Magistrate, took command of the Sikhs, and they had confidence in their leader, as he now had confidence in them. And yet their fidelity was sorely tried. Since the annexation of the Punjab to our British-Indian Empire, there had been a considerable enlistment of Sikhs into many of our Sepoy battalions, and in the Dinapore regiments were some who had cast in their lot with the Hindostanees. These men were now used as decoys. They called upon their comrades to join them; they offered large sums of money—readily payable from the spoil of the Treasury—to each Sikh soldier who would desert the English; but the answer returned went from the muzzles of our rifles and carbines, and was more eloquent than the best of words.

This hope having now departed from the besiegers, they bethought themselves of new devices. Our little fortress with its seventy fighting men might be treated like a wasp's nest: the garrison might be smoked into torpor and death. So under cover of the night our assailants brought together a large quantity of combustibles, such as straw, and fagots, and bamboos, and heaped them up under our walls. Next morning these inflammable materials were ignited, and on the burning pile were thrown all the chillies—the raw material of cayenne pepper—that could be culled from the gardens of Arrah, where they were growing abundantly in aid of the savoury dishes of both races. The pungency of the smoke so raised was distressing to the besieged, and in time they might have been suffocated by it; but, not for the first time in our national history, a providential wind arose and frustrated the knavish tricks of our opponents. The peppery smoke was swept away, before it had grievously affected our garrison; and the only tangible result of the attempt was that the remains of an adventurous insurgent, who had been active in the creation of the bonfire that was to have

smoked our garrison to death, were found charred
and calcined amidst its ashes. A bullet from our
little fortress had penetrated the pile and killed the
stoker in the midst of his work.

Another device was tried. It was not a dainty
one. The Sepoys may have heard of the use of
stink-pots. But it was not easy to make them; and
they thought that they could produce the same results in a simpler manner. The horses of Herwald
Wake and Vicars Boyle and others were at the
mercy of the enemy, if their masters were not; and
it occurred to the Sepoys that the English warriors
might be subdued by their own steeds. So they
shot the Arabs where they stood, hastily picketed,
and left their carcasses to rot under the walls of
our fortress.* It was calculated that the delicate
sensibilities of the Sahib-logue could not hold out
against the effluvium of the putrefying horseflesh,
supplemented by a few corpses of Sepoys, who might
more materially aid the siege in death than in life.
It was, indeed, a very heavy trial of their powers of
endurance. Unfortunately, those useful scavengers,
the vultures and the jackals, who would soon have
left only bleached skeletons, as studies of comparative anatomy for Dr. Hally, one of the garrison, were
scared away by the incessant firing from our rifles
and carbines and fowling-pieces, and compelled to
glut themselves on such carrion as they could find
at a distance. But again a favouring breeze sprung
up, and swept the foul stench away from the defenders. And they fought on none the worse for
any of these devices.

The next tactical experiment was this. The sturdy

* The horses were shot at the commencement of the siege, after our
first brush with the enemy.

veteran, Kower Singh, had dug up a couple of guns of small calibre. To what extent the soil of India was fertile with root-crops of this kind it is difficult to ascertain; but it is certain that, in many parts of the country, arms of various kinds were hidden underground, to be exhumed when occasion might require them. So the old Rajpoot brought these buried treasures to the surface. It was said afterwards, as a complaint against the Governor-General, who had been slow to pass the Act restricting the sale of arms, that these guns had been bought in Calcutta. The truth of the matter is as I have stated it. It is plain, indeed, that if, with malice prepense, there had been a purchase of guns at the great Presidency city, it would not have escaped the sagacity of Kower Singh that guns are not of much use without ammunition. But it happened at Arrah that the old Rajpoot having dug up the guns, was sorely perplexed by want of the means of loading them. Only a very few round shot could be found, and these were soon exhausted. But the Natives of India are an ingenious people. Having occupied Mr. Boyle's house, they were not slow in turning its contents to account. They had thrown up a battery in the compound, constructed out of the most substantial bits of furniture to be found in the sitting-rooms and bedrooms of the Engineer, and behind this they had sheltered themselves whilst working their guns. But the happiest thought of all was the discovery of implements of offensive warfare in these articles of domestic utility. Whatever metal could be found on Boyle's furniture was promptly converted into ammunition; and it was no small source of merriment to him to find that the enemy were firing into his fortress the castors of his wife's piano and his own easy-chair. But although the assailants did the best that they could with their guns—soon to be supplied with more suitable ammunition — and tried their effect from different points, including the roof of the big house, they could not bombard our people out of the fortress.

But there was an enemy more formidable than the Sepoy battalions—more formidable than Kower Singh and his followers. That enemy was Time. As days passed and still no relief came, it was impossible altogether to suppress the thought that the prospects of the besieged were gloomy. They fought on stoutly as before ; and they talked cheerfully to one another ; but as they saw both their water and their ammunition running short, and there were no tidings of the looked-for succours, even the bravest felt the gnawings of inward care. They had heard the firing on the night and morning of Dunbar's disaster, and had rightly divined that the first attempt at relief had failed. Speculation had been afterwards turned into certainty by the arrival of a wounded Sikh soldier, who had contrived to crawl to the walls of our fortress, and being received within them, told the sad story of the repulse of our relieving force. It seemed scarcely possible that they would be left to their fate ; but no one could say what greater exigencies elsewhere might prevent the timely assistance which alone could save them.* Aid might come— but too late. All they could look to with any certainty was their own audacious self-reliance—their magnificent fertility of resource. If ball-cartridges were scarce, could they not be manufactured? If water failed them, could they not sink a well? So

* It should be stated that the garrison had determined, in the event of succours not arriving before the exhaustion of their provisions, to make their way to some ford on the river Soane. But this a correspondent describes to me as "a forlorn chance."

K 2

some took to casting bullets, and some to boring the earth for water. And soon the eyes of the Sikhs were gladdened with the sight of the welcome supplies. If every bullet had its billet, there would have been cartridges enough of home manufacture to erase the Dinapore regiments altogether; and there was good water at a depth of eighteen feet from the surface, dug down from a chamber beneath the house, to last out any possible length of siege. The digging, too, had double uses. Earth was wanted almost as much as water, for our defences were growing weaker under the fire of the enemy, and the soil thus excavated was very serviceable for earthworks. But there was still another difficulty to be encountered. Boyle had provisioned the garrison with grain of all kinds. But Englishmen cannot work day and night, for any length of time, upon rice and chupatties. The want of the accustomed animal food soon began to be severely felt. But how were the needed supplies of butcher's meat to be provided? Some sheep were still browsing about in the compound, wondering why they did not get their wonted allowances of grain to fatten them. But it would have been certain death to our people to have gone out to capture the animals, except under cover of the night, when the enemy might not be on the alert. So a nocturnal sortie was determined upon in aid of our empty flesh-pots. The sally was as successful as could have been desired. Four sheep, not much the worse for recent limitation to pure pasturage, were brought in amidst great rejoicing. Contemporary history is silent as to the manner in which, in the absence of butcherly experiences, the live animals were converted into joints; but we may be sure that this difficulty was gallantly overcome like the rest, and that the roast mutton was none the worse for the absence of any professional dissection of the carcass.

But the most formidable peril of all that threatened the lives of the garrison was this. Having tried every other means of expelling the English and their allies from their little fortress, the enemy bethought themselves of mining operations. There were signs of this, too significant to be neglected. So again Boyle's engineering knowledge was brought vigorously into work to frustrate the designs of the assailants. If the enemy could mine, the besieged could countermine. Rapidly and successfully the work proceeded to its completion; and it was felt that the safety of the fortress was secured. It was subsequently proved that the suspected danger was not imaginary. The enemy's mine "had reached our foundations, and a canvas tube, filled with gunpowder, was lying handy to blow us up."[*]

And thus a week passed. The second Sunday came round. From their look-out places the defenders could see, on that morning, that there was unusual excitement among the people of Arrah. Something evidently had happened, or was going to happen, which might for good or for evil have an important influence on the fate of the garrison. There was unwonted commotion in the vicinity of the town, " whence crowds of people were hurrying with carts, elephants, camels, and horses, laden with plunder."[†] The fire of the enemy was not silent, but it had somewhat slackened, and but few of the besiegers were to be seen. Then as the day ad-

[*] Report of Mr. H. C. Wake. The writer, however, adds : "I do not think they would have succeeded, for their powder was bad, and another stroke of their pickaxe would have broken into our countermine."

[†] Account of the Siege of Arrah, written to illustrate Mr. Tayler's picture.

vanced, the ears of the garrison were strained to catch what seemed to be the sound of a distant cannonade, and they asked each other what was its meaning. It might be the sound of a coming deliverance, or it might be a portent of greater danger. They listened and listened; they watched and watched; and, as the day advanced, all outward interpretations seemed to be in favour of the besieged. It was plain that the enemy were drawing off—that they had other work in hand; that the guns which had been heard were the guns of a relieving force, and that the Sepoy regiments had gone out to meet it. Before the sun had set the siege was

at an end. Next morning they welcomed their deliverers.

How the deliverance came to pass must now be told. There was in the Company's Army an officer named Vincent Eyre. He was a Brevet-Major of Bengal Artillery in the prime of his life; but, though as a subaltern he had come out of the disastrous war in Afghanistan with a good reputation, both as a soldier and as a military historian, and had subsequently been selected to organise and to command the Artillery of the new Gwalior Contingent, the fortunes of the service had given him nothing better in 1857, on his return from a visit to England on sick furlough, than a company of European gunners with a horse field battery of six guns. With this he had been sent into the obscurity of British Burmah at the beginning of the year; but the convulsions in Upper India called him and his battery away from the outlying province, and he arrived off Calcutta in the midst of the great panic of the 14th of June, and at once took the measure of the crisis. It was plain that there was work for him to do, and he was eager to do it. Intelligence of fresh disasters, each more grievous than the last, was coming in every day. There was no military station at which Eyre, with his sixty European gunners and his Light Field Battery, would not have been a valuable accession to our strength; but it was hard, amidst so many imploring cries for help, to determine to which first to respond. On the 10th of July the battery was embarked on a river-flat, and was being tugged up the Ganges on its way to Allahabad.

1857.
July 10-25.

On the evening of the 25th of July the steamer was off Dinapore. That very evening had witnessed the mutiny and the flight of Lloyd's regiments. So Eyre landed at once, and offered his services to the General, who accepted the loan of three guns for the night. But next morning they were re-embarked, and the Artillery company went on its way up the river, with instructions, if occasion should require, to succour the station of Ghazepore. Between Dinapore and Ghazepore lies the town of Buxar, near which the Company had one of their breeding-studs for horses, with an extensive establishment, but neither any Sepoy regiments nor any European troops. There Eyre learnt that the Dinapore mutineers had crossed the Soane, and had marched upon Arrah, where the lives of all the European residents were in imminent danger. So he at once determined to rescue them. A company of Artillery alone could not accomplish this. He resolved, therefore, to steam on to Ghazepore, and to borrow or barter a handful of European Infantry. At the latter place was a Native Infantry regiment, watched by only a hundred men of the Seventy-eighth Highlanders. It was not strange

Eyre impro-
vises a field
force.

that there should be some reluctance to part from any of these; for Ghazepore was one of the places on the river that was most in danger. Although the bulk of the coin in the Treasury had been removed, there was great wealth of opium in the Company's godowns, and a great temptation, therefore, to a rising of the Sepoys. But a couple of well-manned guns, with an Artillery officer to command them, might be considered to contribute as much to the safety of the place as twenty-five foot soldiers. So a bargain was effected. Eyre landed his only subaltern, with two guns, and the right complement of gunners, and took on board with him his little party of Highlanders, ripe and ready for the work before them. He then turned back to Buxar, where he had left some high-spirited officers, as eager as himself to go to the relief of Arrah, who had promised to beat up for volunteers, and to do all that they could to help him. But the Captain of the steamer had his duty to perform as well as the Commander of the Artillery, and that duty was to go forward, not to go backward. There was a heavy penalty payable to Government for every day's delay, and his destination was Allahabad. Eyre, however, was not a man to shrink from responsibility of any kind, so he took upon himself to hold the Captain and his employers harmless; and on his arrival at Buxar, put the guarantee in official documentary shape. There, to his delight, he found that a detachment of Her Majesty's Fifth Fusiliers—a hundred and sixty strong—had arrived during his absence. They were under the command of Captain L'Estrange. To him Eyre at once made requisition; and again was met with the question of responsibility. There are many men more afraid of the Government which they serve than of the Enemy whom they are

1857.
July.

sent to encounter. Eyre was not one of them. He addressed, therefore, a public letter to Captain L'Estrange, ordering him to place the detachment of Fusiliers at his disposal, and to make ready for a march upon Arrah. This done, he had to provide draught cattle for his guns. He had necessarily left the horses of his battery at Burmah; and now he had to fall back upon the old rejected beasts of burden, and to take bullocks from the plough to flounder on with his field-pieces. His ammunition-boxes and his commissariat stores he placed on a number of country carts; and by the evening of the 30th of July he was fully equipped for the march.

The twenty-five Highlanders borrowed from Ghazepore having been ordered to return to that station, where they were much needed, Eyre's force consisted of a hundred and fifty men of the Fifth Fusiliers, fourteen mounted Volunteers, and thirty-four Artillerymen, with three guns—in all, two hundred fighting men, wanting two. Captain Hastings, whose acquaintance Eyre had made on his first visit to Buxar, and who had helped him to beat up for volunteers,* was appointed staff officer of the force. At five o'clock on the evening of the 30th of July, the little party set out in high spirits, never doubting the issue. Being one of those men who are by nature inclined "just to scorn the consequence and just to do the thing," Eyre reported to Divisional General Lloyd what he was going to do, and straightway proceeded to do it, leaving the sanction of higher authority to follow after him, or not to come at all, as the case might be.

---

* Eyre says in a family letter: "The Honourable Captain Hastings (as fine a fellow as ever breathed) entered enthusiastically into my plans, as likewise did Lieutenant Jackson in charge of the stud."

1857.
July—Aug.
The march to
Arrah.
After five or six weeks of heavy rain, the country between Buxar and Arrah was not likely to be very favourable to the passage of gun-carriages and heavy-laden carts. The bullocks, too, resented the new kind of work that had been imposed upon them, and were not easily persuaded, or stimulated practically, to recognise the necessity of prompt movement. Still Eyre contrived to make progress; and after a two days' march he came in front of the enemy. On the second day he had learnt the disaster that had over-taken Dunbar's relieving force. This had increased his eagerness to reach his destination and to release our beleaguered people. It was plain to him now that Providence had assigned this good work to him, and, despite the odds against him, he never doubted its successful accomplishment.

August 2.
In the early dawn of Sunday, the 2nd of August, he had just commenced his third morning's march, when the familiar notes of the "assembly," as sounded by our buglers in the Company's Canton-ments, came from a wood in his front; and soon his two hundred English fighting men were in the pre-sence of thousands of the enemy. It was plain that they were extending themselves on both sides, so as to outflank and to surround us. So Eyre drew up his force and offered them battle. There were three things now in our favour to counterbalance the im-mense disparity of numbers; we had Artillery, the enemy had none; our Infantry were armed with Enfield rifles, whilst the insurgents had only Brown Bess; and we had a Commander equally skilful and intrepid. The well-directed fire of the guns soon disconcerted the insurgents; and the skirmishers of the Fifth Fusiliers, pressing forward, sent such mes-sages of death to them, with unerring aim from long distances, that the Sepoys were not minded to ad-

vance. Profiting by this, Eyre concentrated his fire upon their centre, and on the grand old principle of *aut viam inveniam aut faciam,* cleared the way and marched through them with all his baggage. Having extricated himself from the wood, he pushed forward towards the village of Beebee-gunj, which lay on his road to Arrah. But there the enemy had destroyed the bridge, by which alone he could pass a deep stream, intersecting his route; so he was compelled to make a flank movement, which brought him clear of the nullah and on to the works of the unfinished railway on the direct line to Arrah. Meanwhile, the Sepoy regiments were marching down on the opposite side of the stream, eager to intercept his further advance, whilst Kower Singh, with a large body of armed retainers, was following his track. It was plain now that another battle, and a harder one than the first, was inevitable before the end of morning prayer in our churches.

The line of railway gained, Eyre drew up his force, and the fight speedily commenced. Awed by the foretaste they had had in the morning of our Enfield rifles and our field-guns, the enemy again sought shelter in a wood, from which they poured a galling fire on our people. Our want of numbers was now severely felt. There was a general want of fighting men to contend with the multitude of the enemy, and there was a special want, almost as great, which rendered the service of a single man, in that conjuncture, well-nigh as important as a company of fusiliers. Eyre had left his only Artillery subaltern at Ghazepore, and was compelled, therefore, himself to direct the fire of his guns when he would fain have been directing the general operations of his force. More than once the forward movements of the Infantry had left the guns without support; and the

1857.
August 2.

Sepoys, seeing their opportunity, had made a rush upon the battery, but had been driven back by showers of grape. Another charge made in greater force, and the guns might, perhaps, be lost to us. The Infantry were fighting stoutly and steadily, but they could not make an impression on those vastly superior numbers, aided by the advantage of their position. The staff officer, Hastings, indeed, had brought word that the Fusiliers were giving way. The moment was a critical one. Nothing now was so likely to save us as the arbitrament of the cold steel. So Eyre issued orders for a bayonet-charge. With the utmost alacrity, Hastings carried back the order to the Commander of the Infantry; but not immediately finding L'Estrange, who was in another part of the field, and seeing that there was no time to be lost, he " collected every available man," placed himself at their head, and issued the stirring order to charge. L'Estrange, meanwhile, had come up with another body of Fusiliers, and the whole, sending up as they went a right good English cheer, cleared the stream, which at this point had tapered down to the breadth of a few feet, and charged the surprised and panic-stricken multitude of Sepoys. It was nothing that they had our numbers twenty times told. They turned and fled in confusion before the British bayoneteers; whilst Eyre poured in his grape, round after round, upon the flying masses. The rout was complete. They never rallied. And the road to Arrah was left as clear as though there had been no mutiny at Dinapore—no revolt in Behar.*

---

* Among the foremost in the charge under L'Estrange was Arthur Scott, then a young Captain in the same regiment, who had recently been under hot fire in the capture of the Redan at Sebastopol. I am told that he said that this day's work was far the more trying of the two.

So they marched on along the line of the railway until, as the shades of evening were falling upon them, they came upon a rapid stream—another branch of the Beenas nullah—over which Eyre could not cross his guns. It was necessary, therefore, after some fashion or other, to improvise a bridge for the occasion. It was a fortunate circumstance that the railway works supplied abundance of bricks. To span the stream with a bridge of masonry in a single night was an effort beyond the reach of human power. But by casting large numbers of bricks into the nullah they so narrowed the extent of water to be passed, that by the help of the country carts, which they had brought with them, they formed a wooden bridge, across which the guns and the baggage were conveyed in safety; and on the morning of the 3rd of August they entered Arrah and marched upon Boyle's little house. The rapture of the moment, when Vincent Eyre learnt that he was in time to save the heroic garrison, must have been more than enough to compensate him for all the sufferings of his long captivity in Afghanistan. And it would be hard to say, when that little band of warriors, drawn from the two great services, met each other on that Monday morning, unshaven and unwashed, with the marks of battle on their faces, who were the prouder of the two—the Deliverers or the Delivered.

1857.
August 3.
Relief of
Arrah.

At Arrah, Eyre halted for a little space. He had need to recruit the strength of his weary force; and he had some accounts to settle with mutineers and rebels, otherwise than on the field of battle. A merciful, humane man, Vincent Eyre was not one to delight in "indiscriminate hangings;" but there were

Eyre's march
on Jugdes-,
pore.

stern duties to be executed within the pale of right-
eous retribution ; there were proved culprits to be
executed, and there were populations to be disarmed.
A week was spent in this work and in the better
equipment of his troops ; and then Eyre, reinforced
by two hundred men of the Tenth Foot from Dinapore, and a hundred of Rattray's Sikhs, prepared
himself again to take the field against the rebels of
Behar. With him went Herwald Wake, at the head
of the fifty Sikhs who had formed the bulk of the
old Arrah garrison ;* whilst others of the European
defenders enrolled themselves as troopers in Jackson's Volunteer Horse.

Kower Singh had taken up his position in the
neighbourhood of Jugdespore, where he owned an
ancestral castle or mansion, of large dimensions and
considerable strength. Within its walls he had stored
up vast quantities of grain, the collection of which
had grievously afflicted the people, and he had brought
together munitions of war on a scale sufficient to
enable him to stand a protracted siege. It might well
have been asked, "Who would have thought that
the old man had so much blood in him?" He had
obviously made great preparations for a campaign ;
and there had flocked to his standard not only the
Sepoys of the revolted regiments, but men who were
on furlough from other corps, and even the old pensioners, who were living on the bounty of the Company, in Behar. It was shown by the accoutrements
found upon the field that men of no less than nine
regiments had fought against Eyre at Beebee-gunj.
And this was the feeble, sick old man, who when

---

* There was glorious compensa-
tion in this, for Wake, before the
siege, had distrusted the Sikhs, and
begged that none might be sent to
Arrah.

William Tayler had invited him to Patna, could not stir from his couch. This was the friendly " Baboo" whose fidelity, in the fulness of our national self-complacency, had not been questioned or suspected, and who might have arrayed himself on our side if he had been better treated.

On the afternoon of the 11th of August, Eyre's force commenced its march to Jugdespore. On the following morning they found themselves before a "formidable jungle," covering the approaches to the town. The enemy were drawn up near the village of Dulloor—the Sepoy battalions being on the right and Kower Singh's Irregular levies on the left, but so sheltered by broken ground and dense jungle as to be scarcely discernible by our people as they advanced. But the fire of our skirmishers presently revealing their position, a shower of grape was poured in upon them from our nine-pounders; and then the enemy, after some temporary confusion, began to shift their line to the right. On this the men of the Tenth Foot, maddened by recollections of the past, became almost ungovernable in their eagerness to fling themselves on the insurgents. It would not have been wise to restrain such impetuosity, so the word was given to charge; and on they went, headed by Captain Patterson, with a ringing cheer, hoping that the enemy would stand the shock of the attack. But when our people, showing such a front as to portend that, notwithstanding the fewness of our numbers, there could be nothing but death and destruction in the impact, were within some sixty yards of the enemy, the Sepoys turned and fled, some seeking safety in the jungle, some the shelter of the walls of Dulloor. And thither the Tenth pushed on and pursued them.

Meanwhile, Kower Singh's levies had been closing in upon the right flank of Eyre's force, and L'Estrange's Infantry, with Wake's Sikhs and the Volunteers, were gallantly holding them in check. Happily, the howitzer had been left with this part of the British column, and, directed by Staff-Sergeant Melville, it opened upon the rebels with destructive effect. The result was that ere the fighting had lasted more than an hour, both the Sepoys and the Irregulars were in full retreat upon Jugdespore, pursued by Patterson and L'Estrange. Two of the enemy's guns fell into our hands during the pursuit; and an hour after noon, the British force had entered the stronghold of Kower Singh. The town was almost deserted, and of the rebel Rajah himself no tidings could be learnt. But on the following day it was known that Kower Singh had deserted his stronghold, just before Eyre's arrival under its walls, and had sought refuge in the jungle. There, at a distance of some seven miles from Jugdespore, he had an umbrageous retreat, to which, it was reported, he had betaken himself; so L'Estrange was sent to beat up his quarters. But whilst the old Rajpoot knew every path and winding of the jungle, and could rapidly make his way through it, the English officer, having no such knowledge, was comparatively slow of movement; and ere he reached the place of refuge, Kower Singh had fled onwards to Sasseram, with the remnant of the Fortieth Regiment. So L'Estrange destroyed the evacuated asylum, and marched back to Jugdespore.

Destruction
of Jugdes-
pore.
Having found good quarters for his force in the commodious residence of Kower Singh, Eyre halted them there for a little while, determined to leave no shelter for the enemy after his departure from

it. He undermined all the chief buildings, and whilst the work was going on, he distributed among the villagers the large supplies of grain that had been stored up in the Rajah's mansion,* and destroyed all the munitions of war that he could not take away with him. On the 15th of August everything was ready for the explosion. About mid-day the force marched out of the Jugdespore quarters, and soon afterwards the mines were sprung. All the principal buildings within Kower Singh's premises were soon heaps of blackened ruins; and a Hindoo temple, on the Rajah's estate, shared the fate of the other edifices.

The destruction of the temple excited some adverse comment. Major Eyre was censured for this act of severity by the Commander-in-Chief of the Army.† But it is probable that the case was not understood at Head-Quarters. The temple which Eyre destroyed was not an ancient fane, held in veneration for ages by the people of the surrounding country. It was little more than what we are wont to describe as a "hobby" or "folly"—an edifice recently built, at considerable cost, by Kower Singh himself. It was, indeed, a sort of private chapel, or pantheon, by the

* In Major Eyre's statement, as taken down by Mr. Gubbins at Lucknow, it appears that "Kower Singh had collected within his walls *stores of grain sufficient to have subsisted* 20,000 *men for six months.*" I thought that there must be some exaggeration in this. But Sir Vincent Eyre has assured me that this was the calculation made at the time by the Commissariat officers and civil officials: "Supposing each man to consume one pound of rice per diem, the total supply for six months for 20,000 men would be 45,000 maunds. The surrounding villagers complained

that Kower Singh had seized all their stores of grain to hoard up at Jugdespore, and the quantity found seemed to justify their complaint."

† No such censure was ever transmitted to Major Eyre by his superiors; but Sir Colin Campbell, while expressing his satisfaction to the Governor-General at Major Eyre's military proceedings, hesitated to extend his praise to so unusual an act as the destruction of a temple. Lord Canning, with a fuller knowledge of the circumstances, approved of it.

erection of which—at least as Eyre believed—the old Rajpoot sought to glorify himself rather than the deities which he had idolised there. The distinction thus drawn must not be denied its just weight. It is one thing to destroy an ancient religious edifice, in which generations after generations have worshipped, and another to demolish a modern fane, reared, in ostentation, by a living individual. Kower Singh was, doubtless, grievously pained and shocked by the demolition of his cherished temple; but the feelings of the peaceful inhabitants of the country were not outraged by it, as they would have been by the destruction of a popular shrine.*

The destruction of Kower Singh's stronghold was in effect the termination of Eyre's short and brilliant campaign. He marched on the 16th in pursuit of the enemy towards Sasseram; but he received on the way instructions to return to Arrah—his force being required for other and more urgent service. But already in that fortnight he had done such work as fairly to secure for him a place among the foremost soldiers of the war. He had rescued from certain destruction our beleaguered people. He had broken, at least for a time, the neck of the rebellion in Behar. He had dispersed the Sepoy mutineers, and shown, brilliantly and unmistakably, that there was still a robust vitality in the British Army, and that the sun of the Company's "*ikhbal*" had not set for ever in disaster and disgrace. He had restored

---

* Since the words in the text were written I have chanced upon the following passage in a private letter from Sir Vincent Eyre to Mr. Tayler: "It was curious to see how the Hindoos in my camp seemed rather to delight than otherwise in the sacrilege of its destruction. I suppose the fact is that they care as a rule only for public fanes such as Juggernauth, and are indifferent as to the fate of private ones, built like this one for self-glorification. I regarded the act at the time as necessary to injure Kower Singh's prestige, and I think it had that effect."

tranquillity and confidence to the British residents in
districts where before there had been excitement and
alarm. And over and above these local influences,
there was the great fact that these successes opened
out our communications, by road and river, with the
capital, which otherwise would have been disastrously
closed. These were the results palpable at the moment of victory. It was left for time to develop the
full benefits of Eyre's noble exploits. What those
who followed him in the track of victory owed to his
audacity will appear as the narrative proceeds.*

1857.
August.

---

* I must acknowledge my obligations, at the close of this chapter, to
an excellent article on Sir Vincent
Eyre's operations, in the *Calcutta
Review*, vol. xliv., which has, since
these pages were printed, been acknowledged by Colonel Malleson,
and republished in his " Recreations
of an Indian Official." I am also
indebted to a narrative written by
Mr. Martin Gubbins, from Eyre's
dictation, and published at the end
of the history of the "Mutinies in
Oudh." Sir Vincent Eyre's private
and public correspondence have
enabled me to verify these printed
statements.

CHAPTER IV.

MR. TAYLER'S WITHDRAWAL ORDER—STATE OF AFFAIRS AT GYA—RETREAT
TO PATNA—RETURN OF MR. MONEY—THE MARCH TO CALCUTTA—GO-
VERNMENT CENSURE OF MR. TAYLER—THE QUESTION DISCUSSED—
ARRIVAL OF SIR JAMES OUTRAM—APPOINTMENTS OF MR. GRANT AND
MR. SAMUELLS.

1857.
July.
Mr. Tayler's
withdrawal
order.

THERE is no part of this vast comprehensive history, in which the lights and shadows do not alternate. Whilst all men were rejoicing in this assertion of British pluck, a cloud came over the prevailing joy; for tidings ran through the country that elsewhere there had been a great collapse. To the astonishment of most men, it became known that William Tayler, the Patna Commissioner, on learning that Dunbar's expedition had failed, had issued an order instructing the few remaining civil officers at the out-stations to withdraw their establishments to Patna. To do this, it was said, was to abandon much Government property, to leave the gaols at the mercy of the populace, to sacrifice the good name of the British Government, and to give an impetus to rebellion in Behar, that it might take long months to suppress. That Commissioner Tayler, who had in the months of June and July restrained the fugitive propensities of men under his control, should have

commanded a precipitate flight to the Civil Head-   1857.
Quarters, was something strange and incredible; but   July.
it was a fact. Mr. Tayler believed that there was no
hope for Arrah, and that as the fall of this important
station would be the forerunner of other similar
disasters, there was nothing left for him but to save
the lives of the Christian people in the districts. So
he resolved to direct the chief officers at Mozufferpore and Gya to withdraw their establishments to
Patna, where the Chuprah officers, having abandoned
the station on learning that Holmes's regiment had
mutinied at Segowlie, had already sought safety. In
this resolution, he recorded a Minute, stating fully
his reasons for the step; and then he sent a copy of
it to the Bengal Government, with a brief recital, in
the form of an official letter, of the motives which July 31.
had actuated him.*

When this order reached Mozufferpore, the head- Mozufferpore.
quarters of the Tirhoot district, there had already
been some discussion as to the expediency of withdrawal, and some difference of opinion had prevailed
among the chief civil officers respecting it. Mr.
Forbes, the Judge, had written to Mr. Tayler on the
29th, declaring that the station was in extreme danger, and that unless some better protection could be
afforded to them, the officials, "with due regard to

* The following is the text of have been in for some days; they
Mr. Tayler's letter: "Separated as made an attempt to return to Doori-
Englishmen are, and scattered in gunge yesterday, but returned when
small numbers over several districts, they heard of the defeat of our force.
with no sufficient protection what- I trust the Government will approve
ever, we can now expect nothing of the measures taken; whatever be
but murder and disaster. Concen- the temporary confusion caused by
tration for a time, therefore, appears this measure, the object appears to
an imperative necessity, and is the me to justify it. I have hitherto
only means of recovering our posi- endeavoured to encourage all public
tion. I have therefore authorised officers to stand fast, but I now con-
all the officials of the districts to sider that their so doing only income in to Patna. Those of Chuprah creases the danger to all."

their own safety," could "not reasonably be expected to wait before quitting the station;" but Mr. Lautour, the Magistrate, had "attempted to persuade the residents to remain" at their post. The non-official residents of Tirhoot had, on the same 29th of July, written to General Lloyd, saying, that "owing to what had recently taken place at Dinapore and Segowlic, the district was in the greatest danger"— that, on the outbreak of any active disturbance, the "whole district would rise," and imploring the General to send a few European soldiers for their protection, or at least a sufficient number to escort their families into Dinapore. In this state of almost general alarm, the orders of the Commissioner were received and acted upon without hesitation. But, in this instance, the anticipated results were not realised. The people did not rise. The Treasury was not plundered; the inmates of the Gaol were not released; the houses of the Europeans were not burnt. Perfect quietude, however, did not prevail. There was a detachment of Holmes's Irregulars at Mozufferpore, and when the European gentlemen departed, they broke out into open mutiny. If the Nujeebs had then joined them, the station would have been sacrificed and the district would have been overrun by Budmashes. But the Nujeebs stood up staunchly against the Irregulars, and defended the public buildings; so the troopers, being repulsed in their attempts upon the Government property, consoled themselves with the plunder of some private houses, and made off in search of further mischief. When, soon afterwards, Mr. Lautour returned to Mozufferpore, he found that his own residence had been despoiled, but that the station was quiet, and the people ready to welcome the re-establishment of Government authority, if it

could be said ever to have been effaced. So the
episode of Mozufferpore took but a minor place in
history ; not so the story of Gya.

The city of Gya, the chief civil station of the Behar
district, lay at a distance of fifty-five miles from
Patna, and two hundred and sixty-five miles from
Calcutta. It was a place of considerable antiquity,
instinct with historical associations, and a favoured
home of Brahminical superstitions.* In the month of
July, 1857, the two chief British officers stationed
there were Mr. Trotter, the Judge, and Mr. Alonzo
Money, the Magistrate of Behar. There had, ever
since the commencement of the convulsions in Upper
India, been indications in the district of an unquiet
spirit, pervading more or less all classes of the community, and strongest perhaps among the Hindoo
Zemindars. In the city itself the Brahmins had been
busy, industriously disseminating the fiction, so rife
in all parts of the country, of the mixture of the bones
or blood of swine and oxen with the *atta*, or flour, in
the bazaars. It seemed to be one of their principal
objects to corrupt the Sikh soldiery who were posted
there, and to win them over to the rebel cause by
these infamous fabrications. When it was found that
this was of no avail, they ostracised the Sikhs, de-

---

* Mr. Edward Thornton, to whose
"Gazetteer of India" every writer
on Indian subjects is much indebted,
says that "the town consists of two
parts, one the residence of the priests
and the population connected with
them ; the other, the quarters of the
great bulk of the population. This
last was much enlarged by Law, and
thence denominated Sahib-gunj." In
a note Mr. Thornton says : "Law
commanded the French force in this
part of India from 1757 to 1761."
But I suspect that the Sahib thus
commemorated was Mr. Thomas Law
—a genuine Englishman—who presided for many years over the Company's establishments at Gya, in the
latter part of the last century. He
has been described (perhaps in imitation of the famous description of
Boyle) as "the Father of the Permanent Settlement and the brother
of Lord Ellenborough." He was
uncle of the second Lord Ellenborough, formerly Governor-General
of India, who died in December,
1871.

claring them to be Christians, and refusing to smoke from the same hookah with them. It became necessary to suppress these machinations with a strong hand; so a carpenter, against whom there was proof of having attempted to corrupt two Sikh soldiers, was

hanged in the most public manner before all the troops and the police in the place. And the example had a salutary effect in the city.*

But still the Gya Magistrate felt that he was surrounded by enemies only waiting the signal to rise. Writing on the 24th of July, he said: "There are rumours of hostile preparations on the part of Kower Singh in Arrah. Though he belongs not to my district, I have taken steps to ascertain the truth. A rise on his part would be felt here. A messenger from him three days ago went to the Deo Rajah in this district, and came on to Moodenarain Singh. For myself, I believe that half the people in the district would rise against us, were they not afraid. I hear constantly of ryots being instructed by their Zemindars to hold themselves in readiness." And in another letter he said: "If Kower Singh goes, half Behar would follow." Strange rumours were afloat of hostile movements on the part of other great landholders. Moodenarain Singh was reported to have exhumed numbers of buried guns, to have enlisted and armed a large body of retainers, and to have put his castle in a state of defence; and it was added that the Rajah of Benares had been in communication with the great Zemindar. There was nothing improbable in this; but when it was stated that this was a hostile conspiracy against the British Raj, there was a violent

---

* "The punishment," wrote Mr. Money, "appeared to have a great effect. One or two executions, I believe, strike terror and do good. But I hope not to have many. I am confident that the daily repetition of such scenes (where the people are against us) hardens and aggravates."

presumption not justified by ascertained facts. The Rajah of Benares had not swerved from his allegiance to the British Government, and it may be fairly conjectured that any movement upon his part was against the insurgents.*

When news reached Mr. Money that the Dinapore regiments had revolted, he bethought himself of active measures of defence. "The mutiny at Dinapore," he wrote to the Bengal Government, "has thrown Gya into a ferment. There is nothing, however, to be apprehended from the townspeople. They are surrounded by a new and strong police, and have a wholesome dread of the forty-five English and one hundred Sikhs. The present causes of apprehension are two: the inroad of any large number of Dinapore mutineers, or the approach of the Monghyr and Deoghur Fifth Irregulars, who are sure to rise, I imagine. . . . If the mutineers, or any portion of them, come this way, they will either remain in the district and be joined by disaffected Zemindars, or they will make for Gya. There are plenty of Zemindars who would join them if they once got the upper hand; but there are none, I think, who will hazard life and property before that. The following is our plan of operations: any body of the mutineers under three hundred or three hundred and fifty, are to be met about two miles from the town; forty-five English, one hundred Sikhs, and forty Nujeebs, besides four or five residents, will oppose them. I shall put the Nujeebs between the Sikhs and the English, so they

1857.
July.

July 28.

* See *ante*, vol. ii. page 231; and the Memorandum by Mr. E. A. Reade in Appendix to same volume. The information respecting Moodenarain Singh and his guns was communicated to Mr. Tayler, who wrote to Money on the subject. Money was eager to go out against the Zemindar and beat up his quarters, but he admitted that the facts did not justify the inference of treason, and the issue proved that he was correct.

must be staunch or be cut to pieces. The mutineers would be dejected and tired after a long march,
and I have no doubt of giving them a good thrash-
ing. If they come in large numbers, I shall place
the treasure in a pucka house, which is being provisioned, and we will defend it with the same
numbers as above." The man who wrote this must
have had the right stuff in him; he was sure not to
be wanting when the hour of danger should come.

Affairs were in this state when, news of Dunbar's
disaster having reached Patna, Mr. Tayler issued the
orders of which I have above spoken. How those
orders were received at Gya cannot be better told
than in the words of the Magistrate himself. "On
the 31st of July," wrote Mr. Alonzo Money, not long
afterwards, "I was sitting in my room, talking to the
Soubahdar of the Nujeebs, when a letter marked
'urgent' and 'express' was put into my hands. I
opened it. It was from the Commissioner. It contained an electric telegraph message from the Government and an order for me. The message spoke of
the defeat of Dunbar's party at Arrah, and continued: 'Everything must now be sacrificed to holding the country and the occupation of a central position.' The order decided me and the other civil
authorities to come with all our force to Patna,
making our arrangements as promptly and quickly as
possible. It contained an injunction to remove the
treasure, if doing so endangered not personal safety.
'What does the Commissioner Sahib say?' asked the
Soubahdar. I made some excuse, and after a minute
or two sent him off. I then despatched a circular
round the station, and within an hour every one was
present. It was agreed that we should start at five
that evening. . . . . At six we started." They went,

leaving everything behind them—seven or eight lakhs of rupees in the Treasury, and a gaol gorged with criminals. They went, leaving the station and all that it contained under charge of the Darogah and the Soubahdar of the Nujeebs, and set their faces towards Patna, in obedience to the orders they had received. But the orders were that they should not abandon the treasure unless their lives were endangered by the attempt to remove it, and there were those at Gya who thought that they might have safely remained to complete their measures for the safe custody of the coin.

But they had not ridden more than two or three miles, when Alonzo Money fell into conversation with a gentleman of the Uncovenanted Service, named Hollings. He was an officer attached to the Opium Agency, and he had no duty demanding his return to Gya. But he felt acutely the degradation of this sudden abandonment of the station. Mr. Money was moved by kindred feelings. So these two brave men determined to return to Gya and see what could be done to save the property of the Government, and to lessen the discredit of this precipitate retreat. Whilst, therefore, the rest went on to Patna, Money and Hollings went back to the station which they had so lately quitted. They found things nearly as they had left them. The treasure remained intact; the Gaol held fast its prisoners. Up to this time the Nujeebs had faithfully fulfilled their trust.* The

* On the 1st of August Mr. Money wrote to the Government of Bengal: "The abandonment of the Government property and almost certain giving up of the district and town to anarchy and plunder was repugnant to me. I felt that I could personally be of very little use at Dinapore. At Gya I might preserve order. Mr. Hollings was also anxious to return. We rode back together, having gone about three miles from the town. All was quiet. We went first to the Gaol; and I called out the Nujeebs and addressed them. They all professed loyalty. We then

return of the Magistrate seemed to give confidence to
the people. Many of the most respectable inhabitants
waited on Mr. Money, and welcomed him back with
expressions of joy. But when, as a measure of precaution not unwise in itself, he burnt the Government
stamped paper, the first feelings of confidence subsided, and presently the Nujeebs rose against us.

It was now plain that the position of these gallant
Englishmen was one of no common difficulty and
danger. Not only was there, so far as their information then extended, a prospect of being visited by the
Dinapore mutineers and the insurgent rabble under
Kower Singh, but they were threatened more im-
minently by an incursion of mutineers from Hazara-
baugh, where the Native troops had revolted. The
first step, therefore, to be taken was to recall the detachment of Her Majesty's Sixty-fourth, which had
left Gya just before the European exodus; and, this
done, the treasure was to be secured. Every effort
was made to collect carriage for the transport of the
coin; and on the 4th of August the convoy was ready
to depart. But in what direction was it to proceed?
The order (it has been shown) which Money had
received, was that he should convey the treasure
to Patna, if it could be done without endangering
European life. And this was the course which, in the
first instance, he had resolved to pursue. But when
false rumours came from Dinapore that a body of
mutineers was marching upon Gya, and that martial
law had been proclaimed in all the Behar districts,
there seemed to be little hope of so small a party,
heavily encumbered, reaching Patna in safety.* It

rode to the Treasury, and there
again I addressed the Nujeebs. We
had been absent three hours from
the town (for the stoppages had

been numerous), and I was glad to
find all quiet."

* " The next day (August 3rd)
brought a letter to Captain Thomp-

was determined, therefore, at a council of civil and military officers that the better course would be to take the Grand Trunk Road to Calcutta—a far longer but a safer journey. So the treasure-party moved out from Gya, under command of Captain Thompson, and Money prepared to join them. He was rescuing a few of his household gods from the certain wreck which would follow his departure, when a noise of shouting and yelling was heard, which needed not the explanation of a servant who presently ran in to announce that the Gaol was broken into and the prisoners loose. It was added that already they were streaming down upon the Magistrate's house. No time was then to be lost. His horse stood ready saddled in the stable. Nothing could be saved but life. So Money mounted, and rode with all speed to join the convoy.*

That night our little party was attacked by a mixed crowd of gaol-birds and gaolers. The escaped prisoners and the Nujeebs, who should have forbidden

1857.
August 4

son, written by an officer at Dinapore of his own corps. It contained these words in pencil : ' For God's sake look out. The Eighth Native Infantry mutineers have marched upon Gya, they say, with one gun.' The news of martial law proclaimed in all the Behar districts reached us the same morning. I called another council, and told Captain Thompson he was now the principal authority in the district. I gave him my opinion that, encumbered with treasure, we were too weak to run the risk of meeting so large a body of mutineers, and recommended falling back on the Grand Trunk Road. All coincided in the view of the case."—*Mr. Alonzo Money to Secretary to Bengal Government.*

 * " I had been busy all day (August 4th) with the carriage of the troops, the loading of the treasure, &c., and having seen the convoy started safe out of Gya, I returned to my own house to save a few things of value. I was shutting down a small portmanteau, when I heard shouts and yells, and a servant ran in saying the Gaol was loose and the prisoners near. I had just time to get to the stable and mount my horse, which fortunately was saddled. A minute's delay would have prevented my escape. I got away, but with the loss of everything. I have not even a change of clothes. However, I have, I trust, saved the Government property. If I succeed in conveying it safely to Calcutta, I shall feel quite satisfied."—*Alonzo Money to Secretary to Bengal Government.*

their escape, had made the expected combination ; and now, with the Government arms in their hands, they came down to seize the treasure. It was not to be expected that such a temptation would be resisted. So, although it was a night-attack, it was not a surprise. Thompson's men were ready for them, and they gave the would-be plunderers such a reception that they were soon in a state of hopeless panic, some of them shot down, and the rest glad to carry their lives back with them to Gya. Of course it was an easy victory over such a rabble. From that time Money, with the treasure he had saved, escorted by the detachment of the Sixty-fourth, went on his way, uninterrupted and unmolested ; and in the middle of August he rode into Calcutta, and delivered over to Government the large amount of treasure which he had rescued from the clutches of the insurgents. And among the exploits of the War, scored down to the credit of the Bengal Civil Service, there are few which at the time excited more enthusiasm than this. The Governor-General and his colleagues commended the conduct of Alonzo Money, and sent him back to Gya with enlarged responsibilities and increased emoluments. Mr. Hollings also had substantial reasons for being convinced that his conduct was approved by the higher authorities. To Money Lord Canning wrote on the 5th of August : "I should reproach myself if I lost a day in expressing to you, not my approval only, but my admiration of the manly and wise course which you chose for yourself. Happen what may at Gya, 'you have done your duty nobly in the face of heavy discouragement, guided by sound sense and a stout heart, and without a superstitious fear of responsibility. You and Mr. Hollings have acted in a manner to secure to

you both the respect of all who know the circum- 1857.
stances in which you were placed." This was written August.
before it was known that Money had made good his
march to Calcutta and saved the treasure. The com-
mendation was afterwards repeated, and the Governor-General, announcing to him his promotion, wrote:
" I am heartily glad that there is an opportunity of
enabling you to carry with you an unmistakable
mark of the approval and confidence of the Government."*

But whilst Authority was thus extolling and Mr. Tayler's
rewarding Alonzo Money's exploit, a great storm dismissal.
of official disapprobation was overtaking Commissioner Tayler. The Government of Bengal, with a
little more haste, perhaps, than was decorous in such
a case, pronounced the conduct of the Commissioner
to have been disgraceful, and forthwith dismissed
him ignominiously from his post. "It appears
from a letter just received from Mr. Tayler," wrote
Lieutenant-Governor Halliday, on the 5th of August,
" that whilst apparently under the influence of a
panic, he has ordered the officials at all the stations
in his division to abandon their posts and to fall back
on Dinapore. Had it not been for the spirited and
judicious conduct of Mr. A. Money, the Collector and
Magistrate of Behar, who, in spite of his orders, and
with only Mr. Hollings to bear him company, determined on remaining at Gya even after all the other
residents and troops had left the place, this act of
Mr. Tayler's would have entailed at that station
alone the certain loss of eight lakhs of rupees in the
Treasury, besides other public and private property,
the release of many hundreds of determined convicts
from the Gaol, and the risk of the whole town and

* MS. Correspondence.

district being thrown into anarchy and confusion. What has happened elsewhere is unknown; but there is the strongest probability everywhere of disaster arising from this unhappy measure. Under these circumstances, I have determined at once to remove Mr. Tayler from his appointment of Commissioner of Patna."* It is patent on the surface of this paragraph, that when the Lieutenant-Governor dismissed Mr. Tayler, he was imperfectly acquainted with the facts of the case. But the historical inaccuracies which it contains were caught up in London; and an eminent public writer,† whose name carried, and rightly carried with it, immense weight in all discussions relating to India, indorsed these errors, and they were disseminated by the leading journal of Europe. Mr. William Tayler was a man pugnacious to the backbone; one who never could be brought to understand the great truth contained in the aphorism that " speech is silver; silence is gold;" and such a flood of controversy arose, as would have sufficed to drown not only the patience, but the reason, of any man not endowed with large powers of endurance, who might be condemned to breast it. No incident of the Sepoy War has elicited such an ocean of words. The great Whig Chancellor who wrote that India is a country in which " eloquence evaporates in scores of paragraphs," might have added " and energy also." Mr. Tayler's mode of battle was to fight upon his stumps and to slay the slain; so the storm of controversy, which his removal from Patna excited, has scarcely been stilled

up to the present time; and the usual effect has been produced by the conflict. There is still an anta-

* Parliamentary Papers.
† Sir Charles Trevelyan—" Letters of Indophilus," originally published in the *Times* newspaper.

gonism of opinion. And it is probable that if Mr.   1857.
Tayler had written less, he would have been more   August.
appreciated and more applauded.

On the whole, it appears to me, on mature consideration, that the orders issued by Mr. Tayler were
not of such a character as to merit the condemnation
which Government passed upon them. It is not to
be questioned that up to the time of the mutiny of
the Dinapore regiments, the whole bearing of the
Patna Commissioner was manly to a point of manliness not often excelled in those troubled times. He
had exhorted all his countrymen to cling steadfastly
to their posts. He had rebuked those who had betrayed their fears by deserting their stations. His
measures had been bold; his conduct had been courageous; his policy had been severely repressive. If
he had erred, assuredly his errors had not leaned to
the side of weakness. He was one of the last men
in the service to strike his colours, save under the
compulsion of a great necessity. But when the
Dinapore regiments broke into rebellion—when the
European troops, on whom he had relied, proved
themselves to be incapable of repressing mutiny on
the spot, or overtaking it with swift retribution—
when it was known that thousands of insurgent
Sepoys were overrunning the country, and that the
country, in the language of the day, was "up"—that
some of the chief members of the territorial aristocracy had risen against the domination of the English, and that the predatory classes, including swarms
of released convicts from the gaols, were waging
deadly war against property and life—when he saw
that all these things were against us, and there
seemed to be no hope left that the scattered handfuls
of Englishmen at the out-stations could escape utter

destruction, he deemed it his duty to revoke the orders which he had issued in more auspicious times, and to call into Patna such of our English establishments as had not already been swept away by the rebellion or escaped without official recall. In doing this he generously took upon himself the responsibility of withdrawal, and absolved all the officers under him from any blame which might descend upon them for deserting their stations without the sanction of superior authority. It was not doubted that if there had been any reasonable ground of hope that these little assemblies of Englishmen could hold their own, that they could save their lives and the property of Government by defending their posts, it would have been better that the effort should be made. But their destruction would have been a greater calamity to the State than their surrender. It was impossible to overvalue the worth of European life at that time, and the deaths of so many Englishmen would have been a greater triumph and a greater encouragement to the enemy than their flight. It was the hour of our greatest darkness and our sorest need. We know now how Wake and Boyle and Colvin and their comrades in the "little house" held the enemy in check, and how Vincent Eyre taught both the Sepoy mutineers and the Shahabad insurgents that there was still terrible vitality in our English troops. Of this William Tayler knew nothing. But he had palpably before him the fact of Dunbar's disaster, and he believed that nothing could save the little garrison at Arrah. The probabilities at the time were that the Dinapore regiments, with Kower Singh and his followers, having done their work in that direction, would move, flushed with conquest and gorged with plunder, upon Gya and other stations, carrying destruction with them wheresoever they might go. What the Commissioner then did was what had been done and what was being done by other authorities, civil and military, in other parts of the country; it was held to be sound policy to draw in our scattered outposts to some central point of safety where the enemy might be defied. In this I can perceive no appearance of panic. If Tayler had not acted thus, and evil had befallen the Christian people under his charge, he would have been condemned with a far severer condemnation for so fatal an omission.

But events so greatly in favour of the nation were all against the Patna Commissioner. Eyre's triumph was Tayler's disgrace. The apprehensions of the latter were not realised. So it would have been better, in the issue, if the withdrawal order had been held in abeyance. Still if the order were an error—the error of one not 'a prophet—I can hardly think that in itself it merited the official punishment which it brought down upon the Commissioner—a punishment which involved the total non-recognition by the Crown of all the previous services which he had conferred on the country in the earlier stages of the rebellion in Behar. But the Bengal Government was not at that time in a temper to overlook any failure on the part of Mr. William Tayler. He had given dire offence to his superiors by his "highhanded" mode of conducting the duties of his office. Not only was it his wont to do his work in his own way without consulting any one—to do it first and to write to Government afterwards; but sometimes, in the hurry and crush of overwhelming business, he did it without reporting it at all; and this irritated superior authority. The same thing was being done

M 2

on a larger scale elsewhere; but Patna was comparatively near to Calcutta, and Calcutta had not yet released itself from the coils of the Red Tape. Those were days when men — the best of our men—the men, indeed, who saved the country, thought more of doing than of writing. But Bureaucracy was still fain to assert that there could be no duty on the part of a public functionary more urgent than that of reporting his proceedings to Government. It is not too much to say that if this duty had been generally recognised we should have lost India. But, although at such a time great toleration should have been shown towards the errors of men called upon to act promptly, in sudden emergencies, with imperfect information before them, Mr. Tayler's conduct was stigmatised by his Government, and he was summarily removed from his office. All appeals against this decision were fruitless. The Governor-General, the Court of Directors, the Crown Government, all recorded adverse decisions; and Mr. Tayler withdrew from the service of the State. But I cannot, after full consideration of all the circumstances of the case, resist the conviction that if there was not, in this instance, a miscarriage of justice, there was a lack of that generous disposition to overlook occasional errors of judgment committed by men who had done good service in critical conjunctures, which is a distinguishing characteristic of Indian Government. Happily such instances as these are few—if, indeed, there be any other of a like, character; or there might be a fear that, warned by the fate of William Tayler, if a great storm should again overtake us, the masters of our vessels might be found sitting quietly in their cabins, with their pens in their hands, minuting and recording, asking leave to save the ship after the most approved fashion, and trying to still the troubled waters with the oil of official correspondence.

But the story of Mr. Tayler's disgrace would be incomplete, if one special reason alleged for his condemnation were not noticed and examined. It was said at the time that the Wahabee conspiracies of which he spoke were phantoms of his imagination. Time sets all things right—whether by illustrating truth or by unmasking imposture. The Commissioner of Patna was said to have ill-treated innocent Wahabee gentlemen. It is hard for a man who has been stripped of fame and fortune to wait patiently, during long years, for his vindication. Mr. Tayler did not wait patiently; but he waited long, and the vindication came. It was patent in rebellions and wars; in secret plots and open assassinations. It was pronounced by high courts and solemn tribunals. It was proved that there was a network of Wahabee conspiracy all over the land, and that " the centre of this truly bitter and formidable conspiracy was Patna."*

This ought to have been no unknown history in Calcutta, at the time of the events of which I have written; for in the Government archives were two minutes of that great minute-writer Lord Dalhousie, in which his sagacity was shown by exposing the

---

* Sir Herbert Edwardes to Mr. Tayler. " The Bengal Government," wrote this most able of public officers, and most upright of judges, " was determined not to believe in the Wahabee conspiracy, and punished you for your vigour. Time has done you justice, shown that you were right, and hanged or transported the enemies whom you suspected and disarmed." It may be observed here that Mr. Otto Trevelyan, in his admirable historical chapter " Cawnpore," sneers at that " favourite bugbear of the Calcutta alarmists," " the city of Patna," and says that after Mr. Tayler's removal " Patna was as quiet as Madras." Later experiences of life have doubtless satisfied this brilliant young writer that the places in which conspiracies are quietly hatched are not those which see their violent developments.

1857—1865. dangerous character of the Wahabee combinations even then existing. But the new doctrine of 1857 was, that the Wahabees were the least dangerous communities in the country—and at Patna especially to be encouraged. But not long afterwards it was apparent to the whole of India that the Patna Propagandists were fomenting frontier wars; that they were sending forth missionaries to preach destruction to the infidel; and that they had in the city a cunningly contrived asylum, in the penetralia of which were secret chambers and passages alike for concealment and escape.* It would be foreign to the purpose and design of this history to narrate the incidents of the frontier wars provoked by rebel colonies deriving their strength from the great forcing-house of Patna. It is enough to state that a

The Um-
ballah trials.
famous trial was held at Umballah in 1864, and another at Patna in 1865. The first was presided over by Sir Herbert Edwardes, before whom eleven prisoners were brought charged with "attempting to wage war and abetting the waging of war against the Queen." Five of these prisoners were residents of Patna. The arch-offender was one Yahiya Ali, "high priest of Patna." Sir Herbert Edwardes said of him: "It is proved against the prisoner that he has been the mainspring of the great treason which this trial has laid bare. He has been the religious preacher, spreading from his mosque at Patna, under

* See Mr. William Hunter's most interesting volume on the "Indian Mussulmans:" "They (the Wahabees) converted the Patna Propaganda into a caravanserai for rebels and traitors. They surrounded it with a labyrinth of walls and outhouses, with one enclosure leading into another by side-doors and little secret courts in out-of-the-way corners. The early caliphs had threatened to resist the magistrate's warrant by force of arms, but their successors found a less dangerous defence in a network of passages, chambers, and outlets. When the Government at length took proceedings against this nest of conspirators, it found it necessary to procure a plan of the buildings, just as if it were dealing with a fortified town."

the most solemn sanctity, the hateful principles of the Crescentade. He has enlisted subordinate agents to collect money and preach the Moslem Jehad. He has deluded hundreds and thousands of his country-men into treason and rebellion. He has plunged the Government of British India, by his intrigues, into a frontier war, which has cost hundreds of lives. He is a highly-educated man, who can plead no excuse of ignorance. What he has done, he has done with forethought, resolution, and the bitterest treason." This man was sentenced to death, with two others. But the Judicial Commissioner, Mr. A. Roberts, a man of rare attainments, whose early death was greatly deplored, observed, when reviewing the pro-ceedings, "The particular treason of which these pri-soners have been convicted is no new thing, but has been going on uninterruptedly for the last forty years, although the Government has had full cogni-sance of its existence. Ever since Syed Ahmed ap-peared on the Peshawur border in 1823-24, and pro-claimed a religious war primarily against the Sikhs, but also in fact against the British Government, whose allegiance he threw off, a continuous stream of men and money, supplied by an extensive and well-organised system, having its centre at Patna, has been flowing up from Bengal and Hindostan to the fanatic colony across the border.* Influential

* Mr. Hunter gives, as an eye-witness, the following graphic ac-count of a Wahabee missionary—which I am doubly willing to quote, because a very experienced and well-informed reviewer laughed at the generic description given, in a former volume, of the grey-bearded emis-sary and his pony : "Generally speaking the Wahabee missionary has little to fear from the magis-trates of the districts through which he passes; and, indeed, his fa-vourite preaching-ground is the open space thronged with suitors outside the magistrate's court. The first preacher whose acquaintance I made was encamped in the avenue of the Commissioner's Circuit House. It was only an old man talking to a group of Mussulmans under a pepal-tree. Close by an undersized reddish

members of the family to which the prisoners Yahiya
Ali and Abdool Ruhmeen belong, have from time to
time, up to the year 1862, gone forth from Patna,
and passing through the British provinces, have
almost openly joined the hostile band. Those who
have remained behind have been active, as Yahiya
Ali is proved to have been, in furnishing their
brethren with men and money." He, therefore,
recommended the commutation of the punishment to
transportation for life, and confiscation of property.

But the work of retribution was not then complete. There was yet another arch-conspirator to be
brought to the judgment-seat. This was the Moulavee
Ahmed-oollah, of Patna—brother of the above-mentioned Yahiya Ali. He was one of the three Wahabee
Moulavees whom Commissioner Tayler had arrested in
his dining-room in June, 1857—and was their spokesman on that occasion.* After Tayler's degradation,
Moulavee Ahmed-oollah was fondled by the Government officials of Bengal. He might have been seen
shaking hands at Belvedere with the Lieutenant-
Governor, in the presence of the Viceroy. It was
said that the inoffensive Wahabee gentlemen, whom
Tayler had arrested, were mere " book-men ;"† and
for awhile they laughed among themselves at the
pleasant credulity of the English. But when Captain
Parsons, in 1864, swept up a number of these Wahabee martyrs, and carried them off to Umballah to

pony with a large head fixed on a
lanky neck, was trying to switch off
the flies from a saddle-gall by means
of a very ragged tail. . . . . The
old man had a fresh complexion and
a long white beard."

* *Ante*, page 83. I wish the
reader who refers to this passage
to bear in mind, that I objected
therein only to the manner of arresting the Moulavees,

† There could not have been, for
exculpatory uses, a more unfortunate designation than that of
" book-men," for the most desperate of the Patna rebels, Peer Ali,
was a bookseller (*ante*, page 85),
and one of the chief agents of the
Patna conspiracy of 1845, as described in my first volume, was
a " wandering bookseller."—See
book ii. chapter iv.

be tried for their lives, on charges of high treason, the position of Ahmed-oollah—the official pluralist, high in honour, drawing the money of the State—did not seem to be quite so secure.* It was doubtful whether the good fortune, which had compassed him for so many years and enabled him to laugh at his enemies, would much longer sustain him in prosperity. Parsons came down to Patna, and for two months was helping the Magistrate, Ravenshaw, to hunt out evidence against the harmless "book-man." Nothing could be clearer or more convincing than the fact that he had aided and abetted the making of war against Her Majesty the Queen. He was tried at Patna, before Mr. Ainslie, the Sessions Judge, and convicted mainly upon the evidence of one of his fellow-conspirators, who had been tried and sentenced at Umballah. The Sessions Judge awarded the punishment of death; but the High Court commuted it to transportation for life and confiscation of property. So the honoured guest and favoured friend of the Patna Commissioner and the Lieutenant-Governor of Bengal was sent to the Andamans, where he had the satisfaction of seeing the Viceroy of India assassinated by a brother-convict.

1857.

---

* "He was appointed member of a committee under Act XX. of 1856, on the 15th of October, 1862, and again under Government Orders No. 2577, of 21st September, 1860, he was appointed Deputy Collector and Income Tax Assessor on a salary of two hundred and fifty rupees per month. He had also been appointed a member of the Patna Committee of Public Instruction, so that he was in office during the greater part of the time this treason was being carried on, and the business of the Committee on Treason at Sadikpore was carried on simultaneously with his employment as Deputy Collector."—*Report of Mr. G. F. Cockburn, Commissioner of Patna.* In the same report the Commissioner writes with respect to the arrest of the Moulavees by Mr. Tayler, that "his information appears to have been correct, though the propriety of the arrests was called in question at the time." "Subsequent to the mutinies," it is added, "these Patna Moulavees redoubled their exertions, and brought about the frontier war in the latter end of 1863."—*Published Correspondence.*

It has been shown that the events recorded in the preceding chapters made a strong impression on Lord Canning's mind, and that for awhile even the recovery of Delhi seemed to be of less importance to the State than the restoration of tranquillity to Behar. It was becoming clearer and clearer to him every day, that there was something more to be grappled with than a mutiny of the Bengal Sepoys, and that it would demand all the best energies of England's foremost soldiers and statesmen to prevent the flames from spreading in every direction, or rather—for it was hard to say where the conflagration raged not—to tread them out in one place whilst they were gathering strength in another. The crowning difficulty was this, that the very measures which seemed to be best calculated to overawe and to suppress had in them an inevitable tendency to increase the evil, by arousing the fears and suspicions both of the soldiery and of the people, and it was patent that among all the sources of rebellion not one was more cogent than terror. "The mismanage-

ment of the disarming at Dinapore," wrote Lord Canning to Mr. Vernon Smith, "is the greatest evil that has befallen us since Delhi was seized. The consequences of it will be that revenue will be more than ever crippled, and that the means of strengthening Havelock's force, Allahabad and Cawnpore, must be directed to pacifying Behar and Bengal. I told you some time ago of the difficulty and risk which would at any time attend the disarming of the Native regiments scattered singly or in detachments through Bengal, at stations far removed from, and, in some cases, inaccessible to European troops. This risk is unfortunately increased by the misconduct of General Lloyd at Dinapore. To some of the stations it is physically impossible to send aid. At others, it is a question whether the approach of Europeans will not precipitate the outbreak of the Native troops, and lead to the calamity which it is desired to avert.* Each case has to be judged by itself, and the decision to be taken upon each, together with the general question of weakening the main column of European troops, in order to meet such cases, are subjects of painful anxiety, which will now increase daily."

In the circle of the Bengal Lieutenant-Governorship, other troubles than those in Behar, of which I have written, disturbed the mind of the Governor-General. Some distressing episodes of accomplished facts were, from time to time, reported to him; and there were some peculiar sources of anxiety in the Eastern Bengal districts which kept his mind continually on the rack. I cannot write of all these; but one or two suggestive episodes may be narrated in this place. At Rohnee, in Deoghur, was posted the Fifth Irregular Cavalry. Major Macdonald was commandant. Sir Norman Leslie was Adjutant of the regiment. These officers were sitting one evening, with the Regimental Assistant-Surgeon Grant, in Macdonald's compound, drinking their tea and talking in all the tranquillity of perfect confidence, when three Sowars, in undress, with swords in their hands, rushed suddenly into the enclosure by the rear of the house and fell upon them with deadly ferocity. One struck at Macdonald's head and scalped him; Grant was severely wounded; and Leslie, who was sitting in an easy-chair, was cut down—or as the Commandant afterwards reported, "literally cut to ribbons." He lived for half an hour, and then

1857.

Rohnee.

June 12.

* A very similar opinion was expressed by Sir John Lawrence.

1857.

"quietly died." The murderers were detected by the help of some faithful men of the regiment; were tried by a drum-head court-martial; and executed with the utmost promptitude. But Macdonald, who had at first been most reluctant to believe that the assassins were men of his own regiment, still reported that the bulk of the corps were staunch in their fidelity, and would stand by him to the last.*

There was nothing more observable at this time than the fact that, while the British Government were utterly unable to despatch European troops to the outlying stations, the Native regiments posted in those stations were in a fever of alarm, under the belief that the white troops were coming down to disarm or disband—perhaps to fall upon them and massacre them. Propagated by designing persons with fitting circumstantial embellishments, these stories wrought upon the minds of the Sepoys, and made them consider and consult whether it would not be better for their own safety to rise at once before the threatened invasion could come upon them. From Cuttack came announcements that the Mussulmans

Cuttack.

* The cool, almost humorous manner in which Macdonald narrated this tragic incident, so far as regarded himself, is worthy of notice. "I am as fairly and neatly scalped as any Red Indian could do it. Grant got a brace of ugly cuts, but Leslie was literally cut to ribbons; he lived half an hour, poor fellow, and quietly died. We were sitting in front of my house, as usual, at eight P.M., taking our tea, when three men rushed quietly upon us, and dealt us each a crack. I was scalped, Grant cut on the elbow, Leslie, sitting in his easy-chair, appeared to fall at the first blow. I got three cracks in succession on the head, before I knew I was attacked. I then seized my chair by the arms, and defended myself successfully from two of them on me at once; I guarded and struck the best I could, and at last Grant and self drove the cowards off the field. God only knows who they were, and where they came from, but they were practised swordsmen. Leslie was buried with military honours; and had the burial service read over him at Deoghur, in Ronald's garden." In another letter he writes: "When you see my poor old head you will wonder I could hold it up at all. I have preserved my scalp in spirits of wine—such a jolly specimen!"

were tampering in this manner with the Native 1857.
soldiery. That station being on the extreme southern
limits of the Bengal Presidency, was guarded by
Madras troops; and the lie was insidiously framed
so as to meet the peculiar circumstances of the coast
army. They were told that the European troops
were coming to disarm them, and then to march
them off to a distance of many hundred miles. Now
the Madras soldier, as already explained, carries his
family with him;* so this was a most alarming
rumour. But the thought of the family, if a source
of alarm to the soldier, was a source of safety to the
State. The Madrassees would not listen to the voice.
of the charmer, whose wisdom overleapt itself. Some
of them answered that they were "bound by both
hands; in one they had their wives, in the other
their children."† Those wives and children were
hostages for their fidelity. If the families of the
Bengal Sepoys had followed them in camp and cantonment, they would not have gone into revolt.

But the place of all others, in which the isolation Julpigooree.
of a body of English officers with a Native regiment, May—Aug.
far from any possibility of European support, caused
most serious apprehensions to the Government, was
Julpigooree, which lies at a short distance from the
borders of Bhootan. There Colonel George Moyle
Sherer commanded the Seventy-third Regiment. It
was a piece of rare good fortune that such a man .
should have been at the head of the corps. He
understood the Sepoys well, and he had the decision

---

* Vol. i., p. 291. "The family
of the Madras soldier followed his
regiment, whilst the belongings of
his Bengal comrade remained in
their native village. The removal
of the family from one station to
another was a sore trouble and a

heavy expense to the Madras Sepoy,
and whatever increased the distance
to be traversed was, therefore, a
grievance to him."

† Letter from Captain W. D.
Short, Madras Engineers, in published papers.

of character and the conciliatory manners which at once invite respect and confidence. From the first he determined that he would trust his men, and that he would let them know that he trusted them. He felt that vague alarms and groundless suspicions, rather than any discontent or any hatred of the English, were hurrying the Sepoys into rebellion; and that all depended, under Providence, on the belief of his men in the good intentions of the British Government and its officers. For all sorts of rumours were flying about to the effect that European troops were coming in vast numbers to disarm and destroy them. Disarming had come into fashion, not without good reason, and, every time the post was delivered, Sherer expected to receive orders to apply the universal prophylactic to the case of his own men.* But so resolute was he not to betray the least want of confidence, that when the postal wallet was one day being unpacked in his presence, seeing that there was a despatch to his address from Division Head-Quarters, he turned to his second-in-command, and said: "If this, as I suspect, is an order to disarm our men, nothing will induce me to do it; I would rather lose my commission." From this decisive settlement of the grave question some about him dissented, and he was urged by his brother officers to obtain possession of the muskets, to place them on board boats, which would be got ready for them on the Teesta, and to send them off to a place of safety.

As the month of June advanced, sinister rumours of disaffection increased in significance; and it was

---

* Two troops of Irregular Cavalry, believed to be staunch, were at Julpigooree. Sherer said that they were sharpening their swords, and eager to be led against the Infantry. Two companies of the Seventy-third, who mutinied, were at Dacca.

known that there were emissaries in the Lines from
Meerut and Lucknow—one in the well-known guise
of a wandering fakeer—who were endeavouring to
corrupt the men. But there were no alarming symptoms until the 25th, when these disturbing reports
took shape and consistency in the statements of the
men of two companies of the Twenty-third, who had
arrived from Dacca, and who spoke, as from their
own knowledge, of the dangers to come. It was
affirmed that two hundred European soldiers were
marching from Calcutta to disarm them. There was
then great excitement in the Lines. The men were
swearing that they would not surrender their arms,
and some were meditating an immediate rising. It
seemed, indeed, that the time had come when Julpigooree, like other British stations, would be running with Christian blood.

When tidings of this excitement were brought to
Sherer on the following day, he at once ordered a
parade, sent for his horse and galloped to the Lines.
He heard as he approached them that murmur of
many voices which bespeaks the general excitement,
and he knew that the regiment was in the first throes
of a great convulsion. Everything then depended
upon the answer given to the question, "Are the
men to parade with their arms?" "Yes," replied
the Colonel, "by all means—with their arms, loaded
as they are." Every man had ten rounds of ammunition in his pouch, and one ready for mischief then in
his musket. The parade was formed ; and there was
not a word spoken or a movement made inconsistent
with the strictest discipline. Confidence, in this
instance, was triumphant.

But, although the crisis of the hour was past,

and there was less reason to apprehend a general
rising of the Sepoys at Julpigooree, the danger was
not surmounted. There were, from time to time,
signs of individual discontent, and even dribblings of
open mutiny. Suspicion, though temporarily allayed,
was easily re-awakened. Signs and symptoms were
eagerly watched, and commonly misunderstood.
When Sherer sent a number of elephants to Darjeeling to bring down the office-establishment of
the Lieutenant-Governor, with bag and baggage, to
the plains, a rumour ran through the Lines that the
carriage had been sent to convey European troops to
Julpigooree to overawe the Sepoys and disarm them;
and again there was fear of a sudden outbreak. By
blended kindness and vigour, by rewarding some and
punishing others, Sherer still kept the rebellion of
the regiment in check. But there were traitors in
the heart of it; and he had to grapple with a succession of plots for the murder of the English officers. '
The fidelity of some of the Native officers brought
these conspiracies to light, and acting on each occasion with the utmost promptitude and decision, he
struck terror into the hearts of the disaffected, whilst
he encouraged the more loyal of his followers by
regimental promotions and pecuniary rewards. Some
men were brought, without warning, to court-
martial, sentenced to imprisonment and dismissal,
and sent in irons to Calcutta. Others, who were
known to carry loaded pistols, waiting their opportunity, were attacked in their huts. One man was
shot through the head. Another, who in abject fear
had malingered in hospital and attempted to starve
himself, took to the river and was drowned. And so
month followed month, with occasional alarms, but
the regiment remained true to the leader whom they

loved; and Sherer lived to receive the honours, somewhat overdue, which he had fairly earned by the masterly manner in which, under the most trying circumstances, he had kept his regiment faithful to their colours.*

Other troubles had Lord Canning to contend with, at his own doors—new vexations arising from the discontents of the English in Calcutta. It has been said that a General Arms Bill was under considera-tion. It was thought better that some restrictions should be imposed upon the free possession of offensive weapons. Mr. Barnes Peacock, the Law Member of Council, had sketched out a draft Act, which he enclosed in a letter to Lord Canning. It was brought forward, after some delay, which seemed to bespeak reluctance in the Legislative Council, by Mr. Dorin, and was generally called Mr. Dorin's Act.† But, instead of affording any contentment to the European inhabitants of Calcutta, it filled them with intense disgust. It had the same fatal blot, in their eyes, as the detestable "Gagging Act." It affected all races alike. The Englishman and the Bengalee, if not in the exceptional clauses of the Bill, were alike to provide themselves with licenses for the carrying of arms. It was considered by the Govern-ment that, as the Native communities contained large numbers of men of all ranks, who had declared their fidelity to the British Government, and whose sub-stantial interests were so much mixed up with our own as to render it almost a certainty that their pro-

* If it had not been for the in-stitution of the Star of India, Sherer would have gone unrewarded to his grave. It was ruled that as his services were not services against an enemy in the field, he could not receive the honour of the Bath. He did not destroy his regiment, he only preserved it.

† Finally sanctioned Sept. 11.

1857. testations were genuine, it would be an injustice and
an insult to our Native fellow-subjects to draw the
line that was desired by our own countrymen. Lord
Canning, as I have said before, conceived that, as
Governor-General of India, he was the protector alike
of the black and the white races, and that it was neither just nor politic to impose restrictions only on the
latter, at a time when there was nothing to show that
the non-military communities of Bengal were not as
true to the Government as the Christian populations.
And there is nothing plainer than the fact that
to have disarmed the Native population, at a time
when Government were serving out arms gratuitously
to Europeans, would have created a panic of that dangerous kind which is so often the precursor of revolt.
But this reasoning was by no means convincing to
the European inhabitants of Calcutta. So, whilst
Lord Canning was laying up for himself such a store
of national honour as has seldom been amassed by
any statesman in any period of the world, his name
in the mouths of many was always coupled with a
term of reproach.

Demand for
proclamation
of Martial
Law.
 And there was soon another cause of offence.
The Christian communities, in the fulness of their
mistrust, were anxious that the whole of the Bengal
Provinces should be proclaimed under Martial Law.
This Lord Canning firmly resisted. Hints and suggestions were thrown away upon him. So a public
memorial was addressed to the Governor-General in
Council by two hundred and fifty-three of the inhabitants of Calcutta and the suburbs, setting forth
that, having viewed with deep sorrow and alarm the
calamities which had overtaken British India in its
Bengal Presidency, "they had the painful conviction
forced upon their minds that the disturbances might

soon extend in all their horrors over the yet quiet
portions of Bengal, even to Calcutta itself." They
declared that they had no confidence in the Native
Police, either of the Mofussil or of Calcutta, on the
contrary, total distrust of them, as men who would
co-operate with the insurgents ; and that as the great
Mussulman Festival of the Mohurrum was approaching, the danger had become imminent. The peti-
tioners, therefore, earnestly prayed that his Lordship
in Council would be pleased to ordain that Martial
Law be at once proclaimed throughout the Bengal
Presidency. To this, on the 21st of August, the
Governor-General made reply, through Mr. Secretary
Beadon, that he had given the most careful consideration to the petition, but that he was "unable
to come to the conclusion that the circumstances of
Lower Bengal, and especially of Calcutta, were such
as to require the proclamation of Martial Law, or
that such a measure would in any way be expedient
or useful." It was pointed out that large and exceptional powers to deal with heinous offences had
already been conceded by the extension of the Acts
of May and June to the whole of the Lower Provinces, and by the issue of Commissions in such district for the purpose—that it was wholly impossible
that European military troops could take the place
of Native Police in the Mofussil, their number being
quite inadequate for the purpose, and the interests of
the Empire demanding that reinforcements should be
otherwise employed. "In Calcutta," it was added,
"there are troops enough for the protection of the
city and its suburbs against any disturbance. There
are also the Volunteer Guards, whose zealous and excellent services the Governor-General in Council is
glad to have an opportunity of recognising. And

1857.   there is a numerous and trained Police, a considerable number of whom are Europeans, and all
under European direction and control, who, whatever
may be the impression entertained of their fidelity
and efficiency, have hitherto discharged their duties
in a satisfactory manner. The retention in Calcutta
of a European Military Force sufficient to take a
share in the duties of the Police is impossible, if it
were desirable." In fact, it was altogether a wild
project to think of proclaiming Martial Law over a
vast tract of country, where there were no European
regiments to enforce it. Nothing can be clearer than
this. But still the Europeans of Bengal resented the
refusal, and Lord Canning became more and more
unpopular every day.

False reports.   Meanwhile he was tantalised by reports of the fall
of Delhi, which poured in upon him from time to
time, even as early as the month of June. At first,
he was disposed to afford some credence to them,
and sent home the glad tidings without expressing
his doubts of the authenticity of the story. "The
latest news from Delhi," he wrote to the President
of the Indian Board on the 4th of July, "is that the
town was in our hands on the 14th (of June); that
there had been great slaughter of the rebels; and
that those who remained of them had retreated into
the Palace, or Fort. This is by telegraph through
Central India."* At that time there seemed—and
not only in Calcutta—to be no reason why such
news should not be true. And it might have been
true, for on that 14th of June an assault upon the
city was to have been delivered. But the movement

---

* Colonel Durand sent the mes-   by whom it was forwarded from
sage from Indore, through Major   Benares.
Erskine, who sent it to Mr. Tucker,

was arrested by an accident. How the story which 1857.
anticipated the fact by exactly a quarter of a year
first obtained currency it is not easy to discover, but
it was believed at the same time in Oude in the
Punjab, and in other places, and was the first of a
numerous family of false reports of the same kind.*
And whilst sometimes he was tantalised by tidings Want of information.
of events that never happened, communicated to him
perhaps without due discretion by over-zealous functionaries, he was also disturbed by the feeling that
what had happened was not always reported to him
with the promptitude which he had a right to expect.
Whether from accident, or from remissness, he was,
for the space of nearly a month, without any communication from the Lieutenant-Governor of the
North-Western Provinces; and as many private
letters had come in from Agra, Lord Canning was
stung by what he conceived to be Mr. Colvin's
neglect.† The truth appears to be that the Lieutenant-Governor was deterred from writing by the consideration of the extreme uncertainty of his letters
ever reaching Calcutta, and that although he and
others might not be greatly concerned about private
communications falling into strange and perhaps
hostile hands, he thought it expedient not to incur
the risk of correspondence of a more important character between two of the highest State functionaries
being intercepted by the enemy on its way.

* At Allahabad a royal salute was
fired on the 26th of June, for the
fall of Delhi.

† Lord Canning to Mr. Vernon
Smith. MS. Correspondence, July 4,
1857. On looking over the letters
received from Mr. Colvin by Lord
Canning, I find an entire blank between the 1st and 21st of June, and
as the communication of the latter
date begins with the words, "The
dawks are so completely closed, that
we can only try our chance of a letter
reaching you by the circuitous course
of the western coast, through Jyepore," I think it very probable that
no letters were sent in the interval
to the Governor-General,

1857.
Arrival of
succours.

But ever was there to be seen, breaking through these great clouds of gloom, some gleams of consolation and encouragement. As time went on the hopes of the Governor-General rose. For he saw at no remote distance the incoming of the ships which were to bring the desired reinforcements, by which he knew that he could tread down mutiny and rebellion in our provinces, so long as the Native States of India should continue true to their allegiance. The great deliverance to which he looked so eagerly was close at hand. From the first day of the outbreak the cry had been, "Send us more English troops;" and now from all quarters were coming the welcome responses, for there was not an Englishman in authority who was not willing to strip his own colony or dependency to succour the great Eastern Empire that was so fearfully endangered. " I cannot express to you," wrote Sir Henry Ward from Ceylon, " the pain with which I have received your despatches by Major Bazeley. The need must, indeed, have been great that made you write so urgently, and I should take shame to myself, as an Englishman, if I were to allow any consideration of responsibility to stand in the way of an immediate compliance with your request to the utmost extent of my power." He had but one regiment—the Thirty-seventh—some eight hundred strong. Of these he despatched to Calcutta four hundred and fifty, with fifty artillerymen from Trincomalee, and a large complement of officers.

Lord Elgin
and the
China force.

But the most saving help of all that was to come to him was that which he expected to receive from the diversion of the troops, which were on their way to China. It has been shown how earnestly he wrote, on the first outbreak of the rebellion, to Lord Elgin and General Ashburnham, and how manfully he took upon himself the whole responsibility of the 1857. diversion.* It does not seem that Lord Elgin, in the first instance, took in the full dimensions of the danger which threatened our Indian Empire. He received the Governor-General's letters at Singapore on the 3rd of June; and on the following day† he replied: " I greatly regret that we can do so little for you— but we are doing our best. It is not quite impossible that troubles in India may re-act upon China and add to our difficulties in that quarter. I hope, therefore, that it will not be necessary to remove any troops from Hong-Kong. Indeed, the European force there is so small that it could not, I apprehend, be reduced without positive danger. . . . . I shall await your next letters with the greatest anxiety. Meanwhile, I can only express my earnest hope that you may get well out of your difficulties." This was a hurried private letter. In his subsequent official letter Lord Elgin says, that having since seen a letter from Lord Canning to the Governor of the Straits Settlements, " in which you (the Governor-General) suggest that it might perhaps be expedient that means should be taken to arrest the troop-ships for China in their passage through the Straits of Sunda," he had put himself in communication with the senior naval officer on the station, in order that, with his assistance, he might effect that object. "Such," he added, " are the measures which we have adopted for the moment, subject, of course, to modification in the event of my receiving from your Lordship intelligence to the effect that the pressing necessity for reinforcements in India, which existed when your

---

* *Ante*, vol. i. pp. 605—606.
† Probably this should be "on the same day." The original letter, however, is dated June 4. Another (official) communication, also dated June 4, says: "I wrote a hurried line to your lordship yesterday."

1857.

Lordship's despatch under acknowledgment was written, had passed away." The regiments which he considered available for the assistance of Bengal were the Fifth from the Mauritius and the Ninetieth from England. Mr. Blundell, the Governor of the Straits Settlements, took resolutely in hand the work of arresting the troop-ships. He chartered a private steamer to proceed at once to Batavia, with a despatch to the Governor-General of Netherlandish India, requesting him to send on board the transport the orders of Lord Elgin and General Ashburnham to stop them on their way through the Straits. The General set his face towards China on that day. The Envoy remained at Singapore, awaiting the arrival of the *Shannon.*

Captain Peel and the *Shannon.*

That vessel was commanded by Captain William Peel—a son of the great Minister, whose career had been cut short by one of those lamentable accidents which at a later period deprived Protestant England of one of the best of her religious teachers. The *Shannon* was "a magnificent ship-of-war carrying sixty sixty-eight-pounders." She was described by her commander as "the fastest sailer he had ever been on board of, and with the best set of officers."* At break of day on the 11th she reached Singapore. On the 24th, having embarked Lord Elgin, she sailed for Hong-Kong, at which place she arrived on the 3rd of July. On the 14th, Elgin received further letters from the Governor-General—not with better, but with worse news of the situation of affairs. It was plain that nothing could be done at that time in China to exact reparation from the Court of Pekin,†

---

* Lord Elgin's Journal.

† Lord Elgin's motives are so clearly stated in his "Letters and Journals," published by Mr. Wal-

rond, that I need only refer the reader to pp. 194 *et seq.* of that interesting work.

as the French troops had not arrived. So Lord
Elgin determined to start for Calcutta in the *Shannon*,
and to take council with Lord Canning, who had
promised him a most hearty welcome. On board the
Shannon went also three hundred marines, who had
lately arrived on board the *Sanspareil*.

But the *Shannon*, though a fast sailer, was still but
a sailing ship, and Lord Elgin regretted that he was
not on board a steamer. He reached the Indian
capital on the 8th of August. Lord Canning was
rejoiced to welcome his old schoolfellow and brother-
collegian. The community of Calcutta equally rejoiced in his appearance. The Governor-General was
then in the lowest depths of his unpopularity, and it
was insanely thought that Elgin might keep Canning
"straight." But Elgin saw at once that his friend
needed no help from him. "There was hardly a
countenance in Calcutta," he afterwards said, "save
that of the Governor-General, Lord Canning, which
was not blanched with fear." He had not much
speech of the ruler. "Canning is very amiable,"
wrote Lord Elgin in his journal, "but I do not see
much of him. He is at work from five or six in the
morning to dinner-time. No human being can, in a
climate like this, work so constantly without impair-
ing the energy both of mind and body, after a time.
. . . . Neither he nor Lady Canning are so much
oppressed by the difficulties in which they find themselves as might have been expected."

But there was an arrival more important than
that of the Chinese Commissioner—the vessels which
accompanied him to the Hooghly—the *Shannon*
commanded by William Peel, and the *Pearl* commanded by Captain Sotheby. They were the backbone of the great Naval Brigade, than which there was

1857.   none that held higher place among the succours sent to Calcutta at this time. The idea of this important auxiliary force seems to have emanated from General Ashburnham.* But it was readily adopted by Lord Canning and Sir Patrick Grant, and consented to by Lord Elgin, who wrote to the Governor-General on the 10th of August,† saying, " I have further to state that having learnt from your Lordship and Lieutenant-General Sir Patrick Grant that a body of seamen and marines, though roughly trained as artillerymen, conveying guns of heavy calibre, and commanded by an officer of energy and experience, may render important service at this conjuncture, on the line of communication between Calcutta and Delhi, and possibly at Delhi itself, I am prepared to place Her Majesty's ships *Shannon* and *Pearl*, with their respective crews, at your Lordship's disposal, on the condition that a suitable steamer be provided for the conveyance of myself and suite to China, and for my use there, until I can obtain the requisite accommodation in one of Her Majesty's ships of war." And thus the Naval Brigade, of which much mention will be made hereafter, was formed. And the heart of Lord Canning rejoiced.

* " I hope I have been to some extent instrumental in getting up a demonstration, which I trust will be of service. My great wish was to see a Naval Brigade sent you, which might keep open the river communication with Allahabad, manning and arming some of the river steamers. My plan has as yet been very incompletely followed out; but with Captain Peel once with you, I shall be surprised and disappointed if he does not afford greater assistance than now contemplated. We are both impressed with one idea, and both desire nothing better than to serve you and the imperial interests at stake." —*General A. to Lord C., July* 16, 1857, *MS.* It is worthy of record that in this letter General Ashburnham writes : " Let me also venture to remind you of the dangerous vicinity of Patna, with a large and highly disaffected population."

† The original letter is dated "Calcutta, July 10, 1857," which is obviously a clerical error. I have before observed that errors of this kind are numerous in the correspondence on which this history is based. Sometimes they are very bewildering.

Another source of comfort was this. As the Go- 1857.
vernment needed more troops, so also they needed
skilled generals to command them. And news had
come that one of the best of India's soldiers was close
at hand. Early in the month of June, Sir James
Outram, having brought to a successful termination
the war in the Persian territory, had received intelligence of the rising of the Bengal regiments. He was
then making arrangements for the re-embarkation of
his troops, and his own return to the political post
which he held as Governor-General's agent in Rajpootana. The stirring news gave a new complexion to his
thoughts. He felt that some more active work would
be required from him, than that which was likely to
arise out of the post to which he stood appointed in
the official list; and again his energies were revived
by the thought of the coming conflict. But there
was, at the same time, much to depress him. "More
shocked than surprised,"* as he wrote, by these evil
tidings, and seeing clearly the magnitude of the
danger, he was torn alike by public and by private
anxieties. His wife and son were at Aligurh, in the
midst of the disturbed districts, and he wrote that
he was "tortured by fears" for their safety. His
eagerness to return to India, and to be on the scene
of action, was intense. So, having as his first care
taken steps to communicate the news to England,
through Constantinople, by the electric wire, he
made all haste to Bombay, telegraphed thence to the
Governor-General for orders, but having received no
answer up to the 9th of July,† he embarked on

* The letter is quoted at p. 242, Canning, Sir James Outram says:
'vol. ii.
† In an autograph memorandum "After my departure from Bombay,
before me, written at the back of a the Governor-General telegraphed
draft letter of that date to Lord to Lord Elphinstone on the 15th of
June (July) to send me in command

board a steamer bound for Galle, and thence steamed up the bay to Calcutta.

On the first day of August Outram arrived at the capital. To the community at large, as to Lord Canning, his appearance was most welcome. It seemed to solve one pressing difficulty arising out of the great failure at Dinapore. "There is no need," wrote the Governor-General to the Chairman of the Court of Directors, "of his services in Rajpootanu, and I proposed to him to take the command of the two military divisions of Dinapore and Cawnpore, his first duty being to restore order in Bengal and Behar, for which purpose every European soldier not absolutely necessary for the peace of Calcutta and Barrackpore, would be at his disposal. He undertook the charge eagerly, and left Calcutta on his passage up the river on the 6th. For the moment everything must give way to the necessity of arresting rebellion or general disorder below Benares." And again in another letter: "Outram's arrival was a godsend. There was not a man to whom I could, with any approach to confidence, intrust the command in Bengal and the Central Provinces. Colonel Napier,* lately returned from England, would have been the officer whom I should have selected had Outram not been here, and none more able in his vocation. But he is an engineer, and the work would have been new to him."

From Calcutta Outram wrote to Lord Elphinstone at Bombay, saying: "It will take me a fortnight, they say, to steam up to Dinapore, where I have only a bullock battery. Another (Captain Eyre's) is

---

of the troops in Central India, but subsequently again telegraphed to send me to Calcutta."

* Afterwards Lord Napier of Magdala and Commander-in-Chief of the Indian Army.

somewhere between that place and Benares. I take   1857.
up a mountain train with me, but no artillerymen
are to be had, and I must extemporise a crew for the
guns as best I can from among the sailors and
soldiers. You will allow my prospects are not very
brilliant, but I will do my best to uphold my honour
as a Bombay officer, and to prove myself worthy of
the confidence you have always placed in me." In
the same letter Outram says: " Lord Canning is
bearing up wonderfully under all his anxieties. Sir
Patrick Grant is most ably supporting him, and is
an excellent fellow.* The Council, too, appear to be
cordially aiding, Low especially, who is in better
health than when he left England to return here,
and he stays till March, to my great delight. Even
had his seat in Council been vacant, I should have
deemed it my duty to tender my services where they
are about to be employed, for action not counsel is
now required."†

On the afternoon of that 6th of August, when Sir
James Outram embarked on the river steamer for
Dinapore, two officers of high repute in the Bengal
Civil Service embarked with him. One was Mr.
Samuells, who had been appointed to succeed Mr. The new
Tayler as Commissioner of Patna. He was a man Patna Com-
held in great esteem by the Government and by his missioner.
brethren in the service, as a prudent, sagacious officer,
with a judicial cast of mind, one never likely to
commit himself by any indiscretions of undue energy,
or to compromise the high reputation of his profession by any defects of personal character. He was

---

* A week after Outram left Calcutta, Sir Colin Campbell arrived
and took the chief command of the
army. But the deeds of this true
soldier belong to another volume.

† Outram had been nominated
to succeed Low in the Supreme
Council; and, being eager for action,
he was sorely afraid of a call to the
Board.

not a brilliant man, but it is the nature of brilliancy to contract stains, and Mr. Samuells' good name had not a stain upon it. In a word, he was a safe man, which Mr. Tayler was not; and for purposes of counteraction no better selection could have been made. To assist the new Commissioner in the labours which lay before him, a Mahomedan gentleman of good repute, named Ahman Ali, was appointed as Assistant-Commissioner. It was presumed that the object of this appointment was to signify to the world that Mr. Tayler, in distrusting the Mahomedan population of Patna, had committed a grave error. If it were so, it was a much graver error. But in itself there was nothing that ought to have elicited the yellings and howlings which it drew forth from the European community of Calcutta. No appointment more unpopular among the Europeans of the Presidency was ever made. They were greatly embittered, at that time, against the Native races, and most of all against the Mahomedans, whom they believed to be the prime movers of the insurrection; and they looked upon the elevation of a follower of the Prophet as a declaration of sympathy with the rebel cause. The interpretation was strained and preposterous in the extreme, but there were those who pronounced the head of the Government to be the greatest rebel in the land.

Appointment of Mr. Grant to the Central Provinces. The other fellow-traveller of Sir James Outram was Mr. John Peter Grant, a member of Lord Canning's Council. It has been said that his great abilities had not up to this time been much tested in situations of exceptional responsibility, demanding from him strenuous action in strange circumstances.[*]

---

[*] *Ante*, vol. i. page 389.

But although his antecedents, and to some extent, indeed, his habits, seemed to fit him rather for the performance of sedentary duties as secretary or councillor, there was a fund of latent energy in him, and he was eager for more active employment than could be found for him in Calcutta. When, therefore, the state of affairs in the Central and Upper Provinces was seen to be such as to require closer supervision and more vigorous control than could be exercised, in such a conjuncture, by the existing local authorities, and Lord Canning determined to despatch a trusted officer of high rank, with a special commission to the disturbed districts beyond the limits of the Lieutenant-Governorship of Bengal, he found Mr. Grant quite prepared to undertake the work at any sacrifice to self, and to proceed at once to the scene of action.*   "The condition of the country," wrote the Governor-General to the President of the Board of Control, "about Allahabad and Benares, where we are recovering our own, but where every man is acting after his own fashion, and under no single authority nearer than Calcutta, has made it necessary to put some one in the temporary position of Lieutenant-Governor, all communication between Agra and those districts being indefinitely cut off. There is no man in whose capacity for the task of re-establishing order I have so much confidence as Mr. Grant, and certainly none who will act more in harmony with the military authorities. The punishing, the pardoning, the escheating of lands and the re-appointment of them, need to be superintended by one head, and there is no time to be lost in appointing one. I have, therefore, sent Mr. Grant there in

* I believe that I am not wrong in saying that Mr. Grant himself suggested the appointment.

1857.   the character of Lieutenant-Governor of the Central Provinces. He will exercise precisely the powers which Mr. Colvin would exercise if the latter were not shut up in Agra, without means of communicating with those parts of his Government, and this will continue until Mr. Colvin is set free. Every exertion must now be made to set cultivation going on each acre of ground that we recover. If this be not done, we shall have famine and pestilence upon us in addition to our other calamities; and the chance of doing it depends upon a prudent, temperate, and, where possible, indulgent treatment of the Natives, both proprietors and cultivators. They must be encouraged and won back to their fields without delay, and our local officers, even the best of them, are too much irritated and excited with what has been passing before their eyes to do this as it ought to be done."

It is time now that I should speak of the events referred to in this letter, which had "shut up Mr. Colvin in Agra," paralysed the authority of the Lieutenant-Governor of the North-West Provinces, and rendered it necessary that another high officer should be sent to those districts, below the seat of Government, over which he had ceased to have any but nominal control.

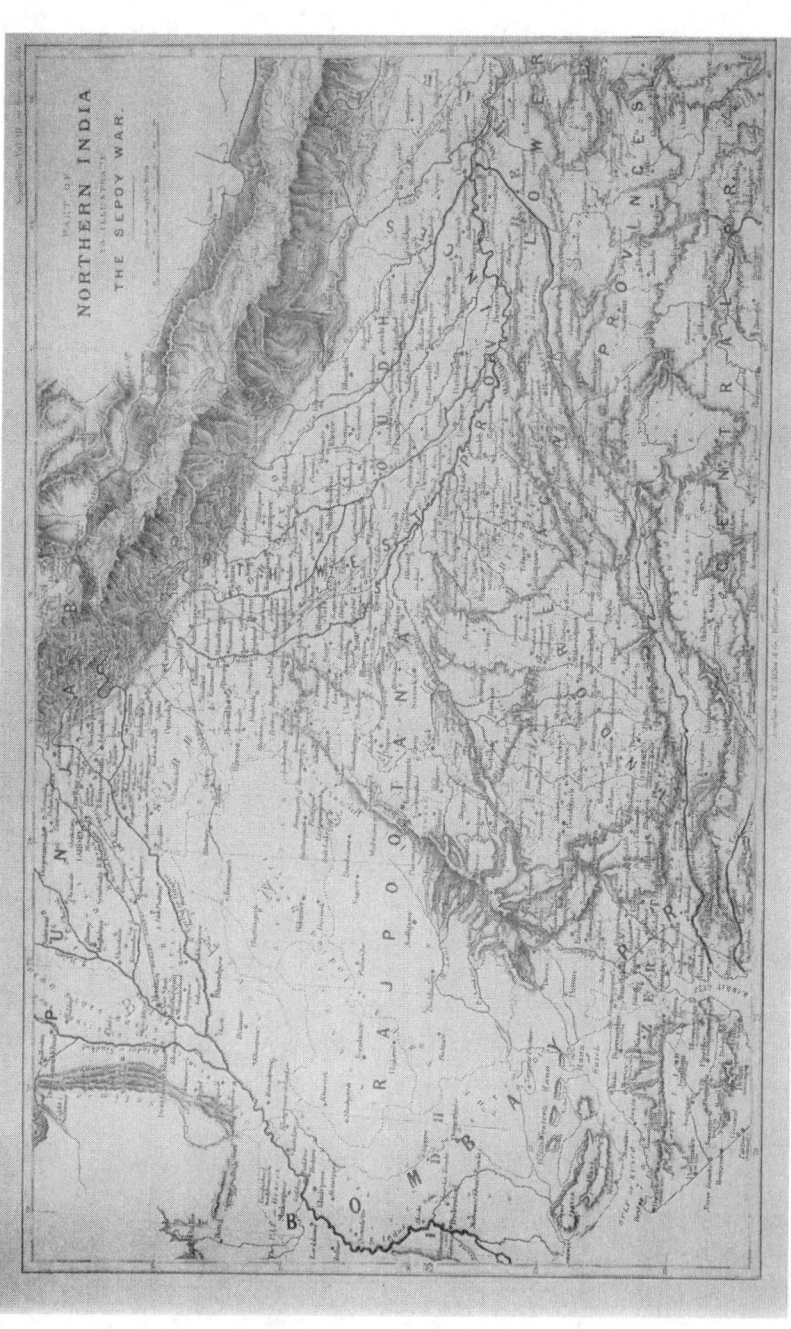

PART OF

NORTHERN INDIA

ILLUSTRATING

THE SEPOY WAR.

BOOK VIII.—MUTINY AND REBELLION IN THE
NORTH-WEST PROVINCES.

[MAY—SEPTEMBER, 1857.]

CHAPTER I.

THE NORTH-WESTERN PROVINCES — MR. COLVIN — CONDITION OF AFFAIRS
AT AGRA—COUNCILS AND CONFLICTS—MUTINIES AT ALIGURH—ETAWAH
AND MYNPOOREE—ALARM OF THE CHRISTIAN COMMUNITY AT AGRA—
MEASURES OF DEFENCE — MR. COLVIN'S PROCLAMATION — OPINIONS OF
LORD CANNING—DISARMING OF NATIVE REGIMENTS.

THE "North-Western Provinces of India," as then
administratively defined,* extended over an area of
more than a hundred and twenty-five thousand miles,
comprising the most important and the most interesting part of Hindostan. Stretching along the great
valley of the Upper Ganges, they reached from the
Kurumnassa on the South-East to the Sub-Hima-
layahs and the borders of the Punjab in the North-
West, and embraced nearly all the great historical
cities of Northern India. In the time of the Moguls
this country had afforded sites for their palaces and
encampments for their armies. And, in later days,
it had witnessed the triumphs of our military strength
and the successes of our political diplomacy. How

1857.
May.
The Govern-
ment of the
North-
Western
Provinces.

* Major Chesney, in his admirable
work on "Indian Polity," very truly
says, with reference to the official
designation of "North-Western Provinces," "As a geographical expression the appellation 'North-West'
is at the present day perfectly inac-
curate."

first one district and then another had passed by
conquest, or by cession, under British rule need not
here be narrated. Notwithstanding these diversities
of times and circumstances, there was a certain unity
and compactness about the whole. The people were,
for the most part, composed of the same races, having
the same cast of countenance, speaking the same
language, and conforming to the same usages. If the
population of any part of India Proper could rightly
be called a warlike population, the designation might
fairly be attached to the inhabitants of these provinces.* They were a handsome, athletic, robust
community of men, with finer qualities than those of
the timid and astute Bengalees ; and they freely supplied our army with fighting men. In no part of the
country was there so close an alliance between the
military and the agricultural classes ; and nowhere,
therefore, was a great movement among the former
more likely to evoke the sympathies of the latter and
to swell into a popular revolt. And in no part of India
was the population so dense. Official statistics show
that upwards of thirty-three millions of men, women,
and children were congregated in the towns and
villages.†

The general administration of these great provinces
was confided to a Lieutenant-Governor. He was
not, like the Governor-General or the Governors of
Madras and Bombay, assisted by a Council; nor had
he a separate army under his control. The troops
located in the North-Western Provinces were components of what had been once correctly designated the
Bengal Army, but which by the extension of our
Empire had been made wholly to outgrow the term.

* It will be understood that I say
India Proper, because the Punjab is
not properly a part of India.

† Of these, in round numbers,
twenty-eight millions were Hindoos
and five millions Mahomedans.

All the most important Divisions of the Army were
included in this tract of country, until the Punjab
became our border province, and the defence of the
frontier against foreign invasion by land became
the duty of the regiments that garrisoned it. Still,
however, the great Meerut, Cawnpore, and Saugor
Divisions were within the circuit of the North-
Western Provinces. The Meerut Division of the
Army included the great district from which it took
its name, and the important territories of Delhi,
Rohilkund, and Agra. The Cawnpore Division comprised the Allahabad and Benares districts and the
new province of Oude; and in the Saugor Division
were Jubbulpoor and Jhansi. The Civil Divisions
were more numerous. The administration was entrusted primarily to a number of English Commissioners, members of the privileged Civil Service,
under whom were Judges and Magistrates and Collectors of Revenue of the same class. The principal
Commissionerships were those of Delhi, Meerut, Rohilkund, Agra, Allahabad, Benares, Jubbulpoor, and
Jhansi. The Head-Quarters of the Civil Government
were at Agra.

The Lieutenant-Governorship of the North-Western Mr. Colvin
Provinces was then held by Mr. John Colvin. He
stood high in public estimation as one of the ablest
civilians in the country. He had been brought into
public notice as the Private Secretary of Lord Auck-
land, over whom he was supposed to exert an influence far greater than has since been exercised by any
officer in the same subordinate position. The disastrous results of the war in Afghanistan, of which he had
been supposed to be, if not one of the prime movers,
one of the most earnest supporters, had for a time
overclouded his reputation. He was held to be, though

a clever, a rather unsound and erratic statesman, and he had been sent to outlying protectorates, such as the Tenasserim Provinces, or to far-off frontier residencies like Nepaul, where no especial opportunities of distinguishing himself had been afforded to him. It was not until 1853 that his great administrative capacity was fairly recognised by his appointment to the Agra Government in succession to Mr. Thomason. Then he fully justified the opinion which had been formed of his capacity as an administrator, by the conscientious assiduity with which he superintended the internal affairs of the great provinces which had been committed to his care, and the success which had attended his efforts. Like others of his class, he had profound faith in the security of our Empire, and believed in the popularity of our rule. Perhaps, the recollection of the great historical episode of Caubul had rendered him especially unwilling to interfere in political affairs, and therefore, when news came to him that the Delhi Family were intriguing with Persia, he pigeon-holed the report, and was satisfied that it was all nonsense.* He did not see that the effete Mogul could possibly do us any harm, or that the people could have the least concern about the old dotard's doings. And when suddenly, on a quiet May day, tidings came to Agra to the effect that the Native troops at Meerut had broken into rebellion, he does not seem to have thought of the great political danger of the proximity of the mutineers to Delhi. But when those tidings were supplemented by further news to the effect that Behaudur Shah had been proclaimed Emperor of Hindostan, it was seen at once that the safety of the Empire was imperilled—that a crisis in our fortunes

* See *ante*, vol. ii. p. 38.

had arrived, the like of which had not been seen for
a hundred years. Sensible, however, as he was of the magnitude of the danger, he met its first approaches with a calm confidence, not unworthy of the man whose chief lieutenant he was; he looked forth, from the great centre of Agra where the storm found him, over the vast tract of country under his immediate care, and he comprehended, with a steady far-seeing eye, the peculiar perils and necessities of each of the great cities on the banks of the river, and of the outlying stations more remote from its banks. He saw that some of our populous towns, as Benares and Allahabad, were almost wholly barren of European troops, and that other important stations, where the central Civil authority of vast districts was established, the English Government and the English people might be swept away in an hour by the Sepoys, who had been charged with their protection. What the dangers were, and what the efforts made to counteract them, in the two great cities above-named, has already been told. But it was not only to the country below Agra, but all around and above the seat of Government, that Colvin turned his thoughts with apprehensions, every day growing into certainties, of fresh disasters—of mutinies merging into rebellions, of British Administration effaced or paralysed, and society everywhere convulsed.

Meanwhile, at Agra itself, as the month of May
advanced, there was great excitement, but no demonstration of active rebellion. This important city in the days of the old Mogul Emperors had been second in grandeur only to Delhi. The sinuous waters of the Jumna flowed beneath the great city, the fortress, and that wonder and delight of the East, the beau-

1857.
May.

tiful Taj-Mehal. The quarters of our English people lay more inland, extending in something like a semicircle, following the curve of the river, behind the City and the Fort. On the side of the Taj were the British Cantonments, including the barracks of the Europeans, the lines of the Sepoys, the bungalows of the officers, and the Protestant Church. Beyond the city was the civil station, with the Government House, the Government offices, the great Gaol, the College, the Roman Catholic Cathedral and Convent, and the residences of the chief civilians—the whole included within a circuit of some six miles, the Government offices being at one extreme end and the Sepoys' huts at the other. Between the Fort and the City was the bridge across the Jumna, leading to the great roads to Cawnpore and Aligurh.

The military force at Agra.

The military force then posted in the Cantonments of Agra consisted of a mixed body of Europeans and Natives. In the barracks were the Third Regiment of Company's Européan Infantry, commanded by Colonel Riddell, and near them were the European Artillery—a horse field battery under Captain D'Oyley. The Sepoy regiments were the Fortyfourth and the Sixty-seventh. The whole were commanded by Brigadier Polwhele.

First tidings of disaster.

Intelligence of the great events at Meerut and Delhi reached Agra on the 12th and 13th of May.* On the former day some precautionary measures had been taken. A company of Europeans had been ordered into the Fort,† and Englishmen had begun to look at

* The official report of Mr. Phillipps, magistrate of Agra, says, "On the 14th the news of the massacre at Delhi reached Agra." Mr. Raikes, who quotes from a journal kept at the time, says the 13th. Mr. Reade also gives the 13th as the date. I am inclined, therefore, to accept the latter statement.

† So Mr. Phillipps's official report. Mr. Reade says two companies, and adds, that the merit of the movement is due to Brigadier Polwhele. Mr. Harvey's report says "one com-

their revolvers. If any alarm arose, it was not
that there was a doubt of the power to suppress
at once all mutiny in the Agra Lines, for an English regiment and a company of English Artillery
could have readily disposed of two Sepoy corps. The
danger which threatened them was not danger from
this source. It was of a twofold character—danger
from the great city, the people of which might have
risen against us—danger from the outlying districts,
in which Sepoy regiments or detachments were posted,
without any European troops to hold them in check.
It was possible that these might stream down upon
Agra — possible, even, that the great rebel force
gathered at Delhi might march down to attack the
English capital in the North-West.

There were many stout hearts and clear heads in
Agra, and Colvin did well in turning them to the best
account. Among the leading civilians then at the
Head-Quarters of the North-Western Government were
Mr. E. A. Reade, Mr. George Harvey, then Commissioner of the Agra Division, Mr. H. B. Harington,* Mr.
(the Honourable) R. Drummond, Mr. William Muir,
Mr. Charles Raikes, and Mr. Cudbert Thornhill.
Never, perhaps, was the Bengal Civil Service, great
as it is in history, represented, on one spot, by seven
men of greater energy and intelligence. These men,
with the higher military authorities—as Brigadier
Polwhele, Colonel Fraser, Chief Engineer, and others
—were summoned to Government House to attend a

margin notes: 1857. May. — Precautionary measures. — May 14.

---

pany." I have since ascertained
from Colonel Riddell that only the
light company was sent, commanded
by Captain Patten.

* Mr. Harington had been appointed a member of the Legislative
Council of India, and was preparing
for his departure from Agra when

intelligence of the outbreak was received. He might easily have proceeded to Calcutta, and thus placed
himself and his family in a state of
comparative safety; but he cast in
his lot with his old comrades, and
remained at Agra till the danger
was over.

Council of War. Mr. Colvin stated that it was his intention, in the face of such great and pressing difficulty, to bring all the Christian families into the Fort, from which the Native regiments were to be entirely removed. The order, indeed, had actually gone forth. But against this measure Mr. Drummond, Mr. Harington, and others vehemently protested, and the order was recalled. It was then resolved that a general parade should be summoned for the following morning, and that the Lieutenant-Governor should address the troops. At the same time, it was determined that a body of European and Eurasian Militia should be raised; and that the minds of the community should be reassured by a system of patrolling which would enable even the most timid to sleep quietly in their beds.

The meeting then broke up. It had not been a decorous one. Men who had been summoned to the Council expressed their opinions with much warmth; and others, who had not been summoned, came unbidden with notes of alarm or warning; whilst letters from outsiders came pouring in, further to embarrass and perplex the Lieutenant-Governor. One who was present writes that Mr. Colvin handed him one of these missives with a smile. "It was from an able public officer, who had great opportunities of knowing what was going on in the city, and contained a solemn warning to His Honour to beware of the knife of the assassin. One officer rushed in to suggest that we should all retire to the Fort, another to ask what was to be done at the Gaol, a third to speak about provisions, a fourth about the Sepoy regiments in cantonments. Every man was anxious to do his best, but to do it in his own way."* It cannot be

* Charles Raikes.

truthfully denied that, even in the midst of the courage and confidence which were generally displayed, there was some trepidation. All men have not the same temperament, and among the large number of Christians at Agra there were some who were not able steadfastly to confront the perils of the situation.

To Mr. Colvin, the multitude of counsellors that assailed him on all sides must have been most distracting and perplexing. He was not merely a Civilian; he was a Civilian of Civilians. He stood by his order; for he had faith in it. And he had reason to have especial faith in the members of that order who surrounded him. But there were men of other experiences, whose counsel he neglected; and it was said that even among his own brethren of the Civil Service, he did not always choose his counsellors wisely. In Mr. Drummond, the Magistrate, he had a colleague able, active, and energetic; and he reposed unstinted confidence in him.* It was Drummond's belief, at the commencement of our troubles, that they would soon subside—that the disaffection was superficial and partial—and that the soundest policy was that which indicated the greatest confidence in the loyalty of the people. It has been said that this in a great measure may have been the growth of his antecedents; for he had served for many years in the Pillibhiet district, where the Mussulman population was abnormally abundant, and he had mixed largely with Mahomedans of the better class—the most thorough gentlemen on the face of the earth—who had made so favourable an impres-

* Writing to Lord Canning on the 29th of May, Mr. Colvin said: "With the invaluable aid of Mr. R. Drummond, the Magistrate here (whose energy, influence, and spirit are beyond all praise), I have been able to maintain order as yet in all the Agra district."—*MS. Correspondence.*

sion upon him, that he was slow to credit the stories of their perversion. When, therefore, unfavourable reports were brought to him—when first one story and then another of treasonable conspiracies in the city reached him—when it was said that even his own Native officials were hatching sedition against the State—he turned a deaf ear to these warnings, and could not be induced either to act or to inquire. It may be assumed that some of these stories were the effusions of an excited imagination; but the general tendency of Mr. Drummond's policy, and therefore of Mr. Colvin's, was to ignore the surrounding danger, and to avert all possible hostility, by appearing to be unconscious of it.

The Engineers at Agra.
There were protests raised against this policy of over-confidence, especially by the Engineer officers at Agra. Of all classes of public functionaries, perhaps, our Engineer officers in India were those whose lives had best fitted them to take an impartial and comprehensive view of the nature of the crisis that threatened the State, and of the best means of combating it. They were the flower, intellectually, of our military service—the *emeriti* of that now-effaced college at Addiscombe, which sent forth so many great men to fight our battles, and to direct our councils. Their duties lay midway between those of the soldier and of the civilian; and they were commonly free from those professional prejudices and jealousies which often raised conflicts of opinion and of action between the two branches of the public service. They had in many, if not in most instances, served in widely different parts of the country, and they had enjoyed peculiar opportunities, when employed in the districts, of ascertaining the feelings of the people. And when it is considered that with

this general knowledge were combined their own special scientific qualifications—their knowledge of the theory and often of the practice of modern warfare, and, most of all, of defensive operations—few will hesitate to admit that the crisis at Agra demanded that the advice offered by the Engineer officers should be received by the Lieutenant-Governor with the utmost deference and respect.

It was not so. And yet the Engineer officers at Agra were men of no common merit. The Chief Engineer was Colonel Hugh Fraser—a soldier of high professional attainments, greatly esteemed in his corps; a vigorous, cool-headed man, prompt in action and fertile in expedients. Many anecdotes, illustrative of his courage and energy, were current in the country.* If he lacked anything, it was power of expression to enforce his views in the most effective manner. But what he wanted was largely possessed by Major Weller, his comrade and friend, who ever went hand-in-hand with him, knowing his worth, and feeling that the day would come when it would be fully recognised. There were others of the same distinguished regiment, including Colonel Glasford, who at an early period was appointed Commandant of the Fort, and Captain Norman Macleod, Military

---

* I cannot abstain from giving the following, in the words of one who knew him well: "Many years before 1857—I think in 1836 or 1837—he was driving along the parade at Cawnpore, when he saw a crowd assembled. Always inquiring, and being very short-sighted, he asked his syce what was the matter. The syce said that there was a row, and Fraser got out of his buggy and walked to the spot. A Sepoy of the Seventh Native Infantry had shot a Havildar, and, having reloaded his musket, was standing at bay threatening to shoot any one who attempted to seize him. Fraser at once pushed through the crowd, and afterwards told me, 'Hang it, ——, what could I do but to collar him?' The man was, of course, tried and hanged; and I think it probable that no one less generally liked could have seized him with impunity." Another characteristic anecdote will be found in a subsequent chapter relating to events at Lucknow.

Secretary to the Lieutenant-Governor, whose gallantry had been approved before the gates of Ghuznee at the commencement of the great Afghan campaign.

When Colonel Fraser first learnt that the troops
at Meerut had broken into rebellion, he wrote a
Minute, or a series of "notes," setting forth the
course which, as he conceived, ought to be adopted.
The essence of the policy which he advocated was
contained in the first sentence : " If the news from
Meerut is bad, or none arrives from that place by
ten A.M., distrust everybody, and recognise the
emergency." Mr. Colvin afterwards said that he
" recognised the emergency" from the beginning;
but he assuredly did not support the policy of mis-
trusting every one. If Mr. Drummond's notion at
this time was not that it would be wise to trust
every one, it was assuredly his belief that we should
appear to trust every one. But the Engineers thought
differently. They recommended that all the treasure
should be conveyed to the Fort, and that all the
women and children should be ordered to take up
their residence within its walls—that the Lieutenant-
Governor with his Staff and all important records
should also be moved into the Fort—that one half of
our Artillery should be garrisoned there, and that "all
writers, pensioners, and Eurasians" should be armed
and sent thither with " magazine establishment complete." Other detailed suggestions were put forth,
and among them one to the effect that the Ninth
Native Regiment at Aligurh, believed to be faithful,
should be brought down to Agra, and should furnish
guards over the Treasury.* It was recommended

* The words are, "March the Aligurh down to the Treasury, put
Ninth Regiment Native Infantry at all women and children there, or in

also that General Wheeler, as one of the best Sepoy officers in India, should be summoned to Agra; and that the Cawnpore Brigade, under Brigadier Jack, should be ordered to Aligurh, there to be joined by any troops obtainable from Gwalior, and then to be marched upon Meerut. Viewed by the light of after events, these two last suggestions were of doubtful wisdom; but they were written when nothing more was known than that the Meerut regiments had revolted. Of the recommendations with respect to the internal defence of Agra, I cannot think otherwise than that they were wisely conceived, and that it would have been well if they had been adopted. Had all valuable property, public and private, been removed into the Fort, together with the public records, much would have been saved, the loss of which has since been bitterly deplored alike by individuals and by the State. But it was thought that such precautions would have betrayed a want of confidence, and so the advice of the Engineers was rejected.*

On the morning of the 15th, the troops were brigaded in cantonments. The Lieutenant-Governor and all the principal civil officers were present. Mr. Colvin,

1857.
May.

The Lieutenant-Governor's address to the troops, May 15.

nearest adjoining buildings, and let the commanding officer and civil authorities do their best—the civil authorities arranging for Sowar patrols in every direction." This does not seem to be quite consistent with the idea of "distrusting everybody."

* The following is from Mr. (afterwards Sir George) Harvey's official report: "It was unfortunate that occasion was not taken for inviting all residents to send in their valuables for safe custody. It was wholly a mistake to suppose that the Native mind would have imbibed impressions of alarm from such course. It would have been explained by the known occurrences at Meerut and Delhi, the certainty that we should have to wait for European reinforcements, and 'forewarned is forearmed.' Few bulky articles would have been sent in, and the terrible and irreparable destruction of private valuables, libraries, &c., to say nothing of important public records, would not have occurred. Mr. Drummond, a very able, energetic, and intelligent officer, opposed himself strongly to this scheme."

standing up in his carriage, first addressed the European regiment on parade. He told the men not to distrust their Native brothers-in-arms, but significantly
added that they had murdered a clergyman's daughter
at Delhi. The Europeans clutched the butts of their
muskets with a firmer grasp, and there was not,
perhaps, a man in the ranks who would not fain have
loaded at that moment and fired his piece into the
thick of the Native battalions. Then Colvin addressed
the Sepoys in Hindostanee, telling them that he had
full trust in their loyalty, but that if any man wished
to leave his colours, or had any complaint to make,
it was the desire of the Government that he should
come forward. Then the Sepoys set up a shout, or a
yell, but no man came to the front. It has been said
that they "looked with a devilish scowl" at our
people, and it is probable that even then there was
rebellion in their hearts. They were merely biding
their time—waiting their opportunity—seeing what
their brethren would do.

Having done what he thought best, in that first
week, to provide for the safety of his capital, Colvin
bethought himself of what might best be done for
the great country under his charge, or, in other
words, for the Empire. He had never taken a
desponding view of the situation. He knew that if
Delhi were not speedily recovered, the structure of
British rule would be shaken to its very foundation;
but he did not think that the mutineers even behind
the walls of the great city could make an effectual
stand against the troops that would be sent down
to expel them; and he wrote to General Anson, as
Lord Canning and Sir John Lawrence had written,
to urge him to lose no time in moving upon and
attacking Delhi. Meanwhile, efforts might be made

at Agra, to show that the British Government were not stunned or paralysed. If the enemy came down upon them, they would march out to give battle to the rebel force. And, in any case, something might be done to re-open the roads between Agra and Delhi, to give assurance to the neighbouring districts, and to ascertain the actual state of things in the country above. To accomplish these objects, Mr. George Harvey, the Commissioner, was selected by the Lieutenant-Governor. He readily accepted the office, and prepared himself at once to set out on his hazardous mission.* He started on the 20th of May, accompanied by some officers of the Customs departments and some employés of the East India Railway, and on the following morning was at Muttra, where he found a body of Bhurtpore troops.

It was of immense importance in such a conjuncture to secure the support, or, indeed, even the semblance of the support, of the Princes and Chiefs of India, who, at no great distance from Agra, were maintaining their Native Courts, and holding in their pay Native Armies. Although we had taken upon ourselves the entire defence of India, protecting the Native States against Foreign enemies, and not suffering them to make war among themselves, we

margin note: 1857. May.

margin note: Support of the Native Chiefs.

---

* " Mr. Colvin intimated to me a wish that, escorted by two hundred of the Gwalior Contingent and two guns daily expected, I should proceed towards Delhi by the right bank of the river, viâ Muttra. It was, he said, very desirable that the Governments of the North-Western Provinces should give some sign of life in this emergency; that the communications between Delhi and, through it, of Meerut should be re-opened; and that the actual truth of rumours causing dangerous excitement should be ascertained—whilst it was of essential importance that the movements and wishes of His Excellency the Commander-in-Chief should be known to Government. I was, on arrival, to take charge of the Delhi Agency, and to remain permanently in the appointment should I desire it."—*Official Report.* The Gwalior troops, however, were required for other service.

1857.
May.

had permitted these Princes and Chiefs to entertain
considerable bodies of troops, partly to give dignity
to their rule and partly to support the Civil administration of their respective territories. These had
not the high organisation and matured discipline of
our own troops; but though, as seen by the outward
eye, they lacked much of the military steadfastness
and regularity to which we are accustomed, they had
some good fighting qualities, and in partisan warfare
were by no means to be despised. And, besides
these purely Native troops, drilled and equipped
after the Eastern fashion, there were in some states
bodies of troops, known as Contingents, officered by
English officers and disciplined after the English
fashion. In the service of the Maharajah Scindiah
was a strong force of this description, with its head-
quarters at Gwalior — a force, the components of
which differed little from those of our own regiments. Of this Contingent I shall presently speak
more in detail. In the little state of Kotah, there
was also a Contingent, on a much smaller scale; and
at Bhurtpore, which lay nearer to Agra than either
of those places, there was a Native force in the pay
of the Rajah, composed principally of hardy Jháts.
The contiguity of these several military powers
might be a source of strength or a source of weakness to us at Agra.* In Colvin's eyes it was the
former. At that time the movement against the
British authority appeared to be mainly a Mussulman movement. At all events, at the great centre
of Delhi, it had taken the shape of a Mahomedan
revolution, culminating in the restoration of the

* It will be understood that I am   whose movements especially affected
speaking here only of those states   our position at Agra.

Mogul Empire. It was not likely that the Hindoo
States would sympathise with this movement. "Scindiah and Bhurtpore," wrote the Lieutenant-Governor
on the 15th of May, " will be heartily with us against
the new dynasty of the House of Timour." Both
Princes responded readily to the call, and, for good
or for evil, sent in their military aid. On the 15th
Captain Nixon, with a detachment of Bhurtpore
troops, occupied Muttra; and on the 16th some
details of Cavalry and Artillery from the Gwalior
Contingent made their appearance at Agra. Scindiah
afterwards manifested his loyalty and good feeling
by placing his body-guard at the disposal of the
Lieutenant-Governor. It was true that any or all
of these might follow, or even lead the way, along the
rough road of rebellion ; but still the mere fact that
their masters had sent them to aid us, and had thus
openly arrayed themselves on our side, could not
be otherwise than productive of a good moral effect.
There was nothing plainer to Colvin than that, if the
Princes and Chiefs of India were then to rise against
the British, no earthly power could save us from
destruction. It was sound policy to trust them—to
assume that the interests of the Mahratta, Jhát, and
Rajpoot powers were, in that crisis, identical with
our own. It flattered their pride to confide in them
as faithful allies and to seek their assistance in the
hour of our need. The presence of their troops at
Agra might be a source to us of immediate weakness
rather than of strength, by increasing the numerical
preponderance of the Native soldiery; but still, at
such a time, there would be gain to our cause
throughout the country in this exhibition of the
security of our Native alliances; and Colvin was not

thinking so much of the safety of the city in which he
lived, as of the general welfare of the great provinces
committed to his care.

An interval
of calm.
May 15—21.

Days passed, and there were still no overt signs of
mutiny. Things went on outwardly much as they
had been wont to do before the sound of that ominous
word had been heard. The formal routine of public
business was not suspended or broken through. The
Judge took his seat on the bench, and the Revenue
Officer went to his work after the wonted fashion.*
The Government and the Missionary schools were
attended as numerously as in the most tranquil times.
Not a pupil absented himself from his class, not a
lesson was foregone or neglected. And though the
elder and more thoughtful civil officers went about
their work with heavy hearts, thinking of friends and
relatives at a distance exposed to the fury of the
enemy, the younger military officers took their accustomed rides, played at billiards, swam in the river,
and were apparently as joyous and unconcerned by
day, and slept as soundly by night in the Sepoys'
lines, as though they were not, in all human probability, destined to be the first victims to the savage
hatred of the soldiery whom they commanded.† But
although the technical business of administration went
on with outward regularity, precautionary measures
were taken by the authorities to give confidence to
the weak and the wavering, and to prepare against
any sudden attack. Among these was the formation
of a Volunteer Cavalry Corps, for service beyond the
limits of cantonments—a corps that afterwards did
right good service—and the organisation of patrolling

---

* Mr. Raikes says with emphatic
force, " We had to grant injunctions
which nobody attended to, and to
pass decrees which no one could
execute."
    † Raikes.

bands for the immediate defence of Agra, intended to
assure the minds of the people if loyal, or to overawe
them if they brooded on mischief. It may be said
that every Englishman in the place joined one or
other of these forces, whilst many Christians of the
mixed blood enlisted cheerfully in them. Those who
had no ties of wife and children were glad to mount
their horses and to scour the surrounding country.
Those whose families were in Agra naturally preferred
service as town-patrols.

Affairs were in this state when, on the 21st of
May, tidings were brought to Agra that the Native
troops at Aligurh,* fifty miles distant, on the
other side of the river, had broken into rebellion.
The story, as subsequently developed, was this:—
Only a small Sepoy force was located at Aligurh.
A few companies, with the head-quarters, of the
Ninth Sepoy Regiment, under Major Percy Eld,
composed the garrison. On the 12th of May, news
of the Meerut mutiny reached the station. But the
troops did not seem to waver. A week passed away,
and the only symptom of disquietude was " the
burning of an empty bungalow." But that ever was
a sign of coming trouble. Reports of a most alarming and irritating character were in circulation—
some wholly false, and some having foundation of
fact with a vast superstructure of error. Among the
latter there was an exaggerated story of the unfortunate affair of the Sappers and Miners at Meerut.†
It was generally said, and currently believed, that
the English at that station had been altogether the

* The city is known as Coel, the   † *Ante*, vol. ii. p. 178.
fort as Aligurh.

aggressors, and that European troops were coming down to destroy the Sepoys at Aligurh.

It was plain, indeed, that, although all was quiet in city and cantonment, it needed but a spark to excite a general conflagration. Before the third week of May was spent, everything was ripe for an outbreak. It was a mere matter of accident what might be the immediate cause to precipitate it. One pitfall was escaped. A party of the Ninth had been sent out, under Captain D. M. Stewart, to suppress some alleged disturbances in the district; and with it had gone young Francis Outram, of the Civil Service, with a little party of Sowars, whom he had contrived to pick up at Aligurh. They found the stories of disorder greatly exaggerated—perhaps they were intentional exaggerations for the purpose of diverting our minds from what was passing in the city—and after a day or two they marched back to the station. As they passed through the butchers' quarter of the city, there was much excitement among the people, which communicated itself to the Sepoys, and there was that kind of noise to be heard in the ranks which indicates a suppressed consultation. The detachment, however, marched on, and nothing happened. It was known afterwards that the townspeople had endeavoured to persuade the Sepoys to murder their officers and fly, as the Europeans from Meerut had come in during their absence and massacred their comrades in Cantonments. And they would have fired at once into the backs of their officers, if a drummer of the mixed race had not told them that in a few minutes the Treasury would be in sight, and it would be seen whether the guard was in its accustomed place. So the detachment marched on, and it was presently apparent that everything was in the condition in which it had been left.

But, although this immediate danger was tided over, it can scarcely be said that the escape delayed the inevitable crisis. Whilst Stewart's detachment had been absent from the station, a new danger had arisen—not in the Sepoys' lines, not in the butchers' quarters, but in the rural districts. In a neigbouring village was a Brahmin of some influence, who had a relative in the Gaol-guard, and who was not unwilling to do service as an ambassador of evil between the villagers and the Sepoys. It was known that there were some seven lakhs of rupees in the Collector's treasury. If the Sepoys would rise, the villagers would come down and share in the plunder. It was proposed that at a given time a crowd of people, simulating a noisy marriage procession, should enter the city, that they should fraternise with the Sepoys, massacre the Europeans, and seize all the property of individuals and of the State.

The Brahmin began his work, and made proposals to two Sepoys, who told the story to their commanding officer. Major Eld ordered them to seize the rebel. They obeyed his orders, and the man was tried by a Native court-martial and sentenced to death. As the sun was setting on that day, the Brahmin was hanged, in the presence of the troops. Up to that time there was everything to encourage the belief that the Sepoys were true to their salt. But scarcely had swift punishment overtaken the high-caste offender, when the smouldering mutiny in the breasts of the Sepoys of the Ninth broke into a flame. A Brahmin Sepoy stepped from the ranks and cried aloud to his comrades, "Behold a martyr to our faith!" It was like the springing of a mine. The

explosion took place at once.   All discipline, all
fidelity, all loyalty were blown into the air.   Only a
tender compassion for the officers, who had ever
treated them justly and kindly, remained.   There
was a scene of terrible confusion, such as had been
seen before, and was destined often to be seen again.
The Sepoys spared the lives of their English commanders; but all were then compelled to escape; all
who in any capacity represented the Government or
the community of the Christian stranger.   Military
officers, Civil officers, and independent Europeans or
Eurasians, were driven to fly for their lives.

In the little party of Europeans thus expelled from
their homes was one, of whom every Englishman
must have thought tenderly and affectionately, when
he heard that Aligurh was in danger.   This was
Lady Outram, the wife of the great soldier, who had
just brought the war with Persia to a close, and to
whose return all men were looking, in this emergency, as to a very present help in trouble.   She was
making her preparations to spend the hot weather at
Nynee-Taal.   During the absence of her son with
Captain Stewart's detachment, Lady Outram had
been residing at the house of Mr. Dumergue, the
Judge, whose wife and daughter were the only other
English gentlewomen at the station.   But, on the
day of the outbreak, she had returned to her son's
bungalow, in another part of the cantonment, and
was superintending the arrangements for her departure, when the regiment broke into rebellion.
Frank Outram was, at that critical moment, in the
compound of the Magistrate's house, conversing, in
absolute peace of mind, with the officers of a detachment of Cavalry from Scindiah's Contingent, which
had come in from Gwalior, when some officers of the

1857.
May.

Ninth rushed in, crying out that the regiment had
"gone." Outram's pony stood saddled close at hand ;
so he mounted at once and rode for his bungalow,
where he found, with joyful surprise, that his mother
was safe, and in happy ignorance of the danger that
surrounded her.

Lady Outram was at that time, dressed for the
evening drive, awaiting the Judge's carriage, which
was to call for her. It then seemed that nothing
could save her but instant flight. So she mounted
the pony behind her son, and they made for the civil
lines. The journey was not a long — but it was
a dangerous one. They were soon compelled to take
to their feet, for the animal they rode resented its
double burden and was loth to proceed.* Their road
lay through the cantonments, where they saw the
Sepoys moving excitedly from place to place, with
their arms in their hands, all eager for the plunder of
the Christian bungalows. But no man pointed a
musket at them. So they passed on, unmolested, to
the civil lines, and soon found themselves amidst a
little assembly of their countrymen debating what
was to be done.

There was nothing to be done—but to seek safety
in flight. The Gwalior Cavalry had outwardly
remained true, but they were insufficient for the
recovery of our position, even if their fidelity could
have been relied upon. The only question then
was, whether our people should escape to Agra or
to Meerut. About this, there was either difference
of opinion or misunderstanding as to the decision
arrived at, for some went in one direction, some in

---

* Exaggerated stories of Lady
Outram's escape were at one time current. It was said that she escaped,
barefooted in her night-dress. She wore the ordinary light costume of
the hot weather, with thin shoes, of
which the rough road soon dispossessed her.

another. Lady Outram had a seat in the Judge's carriage, which took the direction of Agra; whilst Frank Outram and others, headed by Mr. Watson, the Magistrate, all well mounted, took to the Meerut road—a party of Gwalior Cavalry accompanying them. The former party reached Agra in safety. The latter encountered some adventures, and did right good service, to be narrated in a subsequent chapter of this narrative.

The English being thus driven from Aligurh, the mutineers and rebels proceeded to plunder the Treasury and other Government offices, and then to ignite the buildings. The seven lakhs of rupees in the Treasury were shared between the Sepoys and the Rabble. The former, carrying their coin with them, set their faces towards Delhi. The latter remained in possession of the place. The prisoners in the Gaol were set free, and every man helped himself to what he could get. Public and private property fell to the strongest and most active plunderers. The houses of the Europeans were gutted, and everything belonging to them either carried off or destroyed. For a time every trace of English authority was utterly gone from Aligurh. When some time afterwards it was partially re-established, it was seen how great the devastation had been. Of the first return to Aligurh, one present wrote: "A wonderful appearance it presented. The bungalows, gaol, &c., had all been burned and looted. The accumulation of laden bullock-trains and other carts, detained from further progress after the 12th, shared the same fate, and the miscellaneous character of the loot may be imagined. On our approach, the Natives had hastened to clear away all vestiges of booty out of their premises, in fear of search; and the roads for miles round, the jungles, and the wells, were covered and choked by the most extraordinary chaos of articles conceivable, from cases of champagne down to consignments of Holloway's pills (of which there seemed to be a carriage load or two)—from splendid kincaubs down to our old garments, plate, furniture, boxes, supplies of eatables—everything except hard cash."*

1857.
May.

Meanwhile, at Etawah, which lies on the road to Meerut, at a distance of seventy-three miles from Agra, the civil officers were watching, with a wise vigilance, the progress of events. A company of the Ninth Sepoys from Aligurh was posted there, but in the earlier part of the month there was no reason to doubt the fidelity of the men. The people of the district were prosperous and contented. Never, indeed, had there been more hopeful and encouraging signs of present tranquillity and future progress.† The Magistrate and Collector was Mr. Allan Hume—a son of the great English reformer—who had inherited the high public spirit and the resolute courage of his father. When news of the mutiny of the troops at

Etawah.
May, 1857.

* MS. Memorandum. Mr. Bramly's report states that "in this work (of plunder) Regsaal Khan, Khansaman (purveyor) of the Dawk Bungalow (traveller's halting-place), and Meer Khan, mail-coachman, distinguished themselves." It is not improbable that both had tasted the insolence of European travellers.

† "The fatal month of May opened in hopefulness and peace. Never, apparently, had the prospects of the district been so cheering. Crime was and had been for the previous two years steadily decreasing; the Revenue flowed in without a recourse to a single coercive pro-

cess; public libraries and numerous schools gave rich promise of future progress; new lines of communication were being rapidly opened out; the railroad was fast ripening; the great canal, with its daily multiplying branches, steadily diffusing fertility over an ever-widening area; and all classes of the community, though of course not without their minor grievances, on the whole were singularly happy and contented. Suddenly the mutiny burst upon us, effacing apparently in a day the labour of years."— *Report of Mr. Hume.*

Meerut and Delhi arrived from Agra, a day or two after the outburst, Mr. Hume's first thought was that he might arrest some of the mutineers either on their way to their homes or dispersing themselves over the country to corrupt other Sepoy regiments. Patrolling parties were, therefore, sent out to watch the roads, and on the night of the 16th of May a party, seven in number, of the Third Cavalry was arrested. Being well armed with swords and pistols, when taken to the Quarter-Guard and confronted with our soldiery, they made a vigorous resistance, shot Lieutenant Crawford, who commanded, in the shoulder, and would have murdered Lieutenant Allan, but that the assailant was killed by the Kotwal and a Sepoy of the Ninth. The guard was then ordered to turn out, and the mutineers were overpowered. Two were shot dead, two were cut down, and two escaped, one of whom was afterwards captured by the Police. And this was the first retributive blow that fell upon the mutineers of the Third Cavalry. They were all Mahomedans (Pathans) of Futtehpore.

A few days afterwards, another party of fugitives from the Third Cavalry made its appearance in Juswuntnugger, about ten miles from the chief station of Etawah, armed with sabres, pistols, and with a few carbines among them. They had come down in a capacious cart, which was stopped by the patrol upon the road. On being called upon to give up their arms, they first of all made a show of submission, and then shot down their captors. Having done this, they made their way to a Hindoo temple, at the end of a walled grove, and prepared to defend themselves.

When tidings of this movement reached Mr. Hume, he ordered his buggy to be got ready, armed himself as best he could, and, accompanied by Mr. Daniell,

started for Juswuntnuggur. It was then nine o'clock
in the morning; there was a fierce sun, a hot wind
like the blast of a furnace; and neither had broken
his fast. A brisk drive of an hour and a quarter
brought them before the asylum of the Meerut
troopers. It was a strong position in itself, and
admirably suited to purposes of defence. Everything
was in favour of the mutineers; they had shelter for
themselves, a command of observation and a command of fire in all directions; and whichsoever way
the intrepid Englishmen turned to reconnoitre the
position of the enemy, the Sepoys fired at them from
their cover with pistols or carbines. Moreover, the
townspeople were on the side of the mutineers. Hume
had invested the place with some troopers of the
Irregular Cavalry and some of his own Police; but
they could or would not keep the people from opening communication with the troopers in the temple,
and so the defenders were supplied with food and
ammunition. There was no hope, therefore, of
starving them into surrender, or rendering them
powerless by exhaustion of powder and shot. To
carry the place by assault seemed an almost hopeless
endeavour. For although there was a large body of
armed Police, none would go within reach of the carbines of the troopers. They were content to show
their zeal by firing from a distance in the air. Reinforcements had been sent from Etawah, but the
detachment of Sepoys despatched to their relief purposely missed their way. So the day wore on in its
fiery strength, and Hume and Daniell were without
support. The excitement among the townspeople—
for the most part a low class of Mahomedans—was
increasing. In a little while a rescue might be
attempted, and the retreat of the Englishmen might

be cut off. So they determined, as the sun was nearing the horizon, to make an effort to carry the place by themselves. Only one man followed them to the door by which an entrance was to be attempted. He paid for his fidelity with his life. Daniell was shot through the face, and fell senseless, amidst a yell of exultation from the townspeople, who were eagerly watching the affray from the side of a neighbouring hill. Then Hume, having vainly endeavoured to rally some of his followers, went to the assistance of his friend, and through the pressing crowd and the uproar of the streets led him safely to the spot where their carriage was posted. That night, in the midst of a violent storm, the mutineers escaped; but the double-barrels of Hume and Daniell had done some execution, for difficult as it had been to reach them, one of their party had been killed and another dangerously wounded.*

This was one of the first of those heroic deeds of which I have before spoken†—great deeds of heroism by which the civil servants of the Company—men not trained to arms or wearing any insignia of the military profession—bore noble witness to the courage and constancy of the national character. This English Magistrate and his Assistant, in the face of an insur-

---

* The following is Mr. Hume's very modest account of the affair: "Early in the morning of the 19th of May a number of the Third Cavalry were stopped at Juswunt-Nugger, about ten miles from the Sudder Station. On an attempt being made to disarm them, they shot one and wounded three more of the Police, and then took up a position in a neighbouring temple, small, but of great strength. Mr. Daniell and myself proceeded to the spot, and did our best to carry the place, but could obtain no support, owing to the extreme danger attending storming. At last, after a final attempt to force it by ourselves, in which Mr. Daniell was shot through the face, and the only man who accompanied us killed, I thought it advisable (especially as the whole body of the townspeople, mustering some two thousand low-caste Mussulmans, were becoming actively hostile, and the Police proportionately timorous) to return to Etawah."

† Ante, chapter ii., p. 116.

gent population, went out, resolute to bring to justice or to avenge themselves on the spot upon men who a few days before had foully murdered our people under the eyes of a brigade of Europeans; and with only a single follower they had laid gallant siege to a strongly defended place of refuge, and then had quietly walked back through the crowd with the confidence of strength and the assumption of victory. Habituated to rule and accustomed to do much great work single-handed, our large-hearted civilians, with any fearful odds against them, still regarded themselves as masters of the situation, and, with their double-barrelled guns or revolvers, made light of their lack of followers, and seldom shrunk from facing, unsupported, a multitude of enemies. It will become a familiar record, as this History advances; and yet so great is the number of these heroic deeds, that, under pressure of historical necessity, some acts of distinguished gallantry may meet with less than their merited applause.

On the following day, the head-quarters of the Ninth Regiment at Aligurh broke into rebellion; and when news of this disaster reached the Government officers, they saw at once that it was their first duty to keep the knowledge of the event from reaching the detachment at Etawah. Accordingly, Mr. Hume took counsel with the senior officer of the company of the Ninth, and it was determined that the detachment should be removed to an isolated position, where they were less likely to hear of the defection of their comrades. It was impossible to keep them long in ignorance of this event; but Hume had written for reinforcements, and it was of primal consequence to gain time. Accordingly, it was resolved that the Sepoys should be marched to

Burpoorah, a police station on the road to Gwalior. They marched out with apparent cheerfulness, but they had not proceeded more than two miles, when the greater number of them threw off the mask, broke into mutiny, and returned to Etawah. A few Native soldiers remained staunch, and, with their officers, the ladies, and the children, marched on to Burpoorah. The mutineers, meanwhile, re-entered Etawah, and, aided by the surrounding rabble, plundered the Treasury, broke open the gaols, released the prisoners, burnt all the public offices and the officers' houses (Mr. Hume's excepted), and for three or four days anarchy in its worst forms was triumphant; every trace of the British Government had disappeared. Happily, Hume's forethought had greatly diminished the evil—for on the first rumour of rebellion he had secured all the most important Government records by bricking them up secretly in a house in the city, and had sent one-half of the treasure to safe custody at Agra.

On the night of the 24th, our little party at Burpoorah were succoured by the arrival of Major Hennessy with the Grenadier Regiment of the Gwalior Contingent; and as day broke, on the following morning, the whole marched into Etawah and reoccupied the place. A miserable spectacle then presented itself to the eyes of our people. Riot and rapine had held high carnival during our absence, and the predatory classes, of whose inactivity the English Magistrate, a short time before, had great reason to be proud, were now suddenly warmed into new life and vigour. Not only the released convicts of the gaols, but others, who, under the strong arm of authority, had been driven to seek more lawful occupations, had returned to their old courses. Nor were

the criminal classes the only persons who were disposed to take advantage of the temporary obscuration of British authority. Those who had suffered
by the action of our Civil Courts were also beginning
to rouse themselves to reverse the decisions of men,
who, it seemed, could no longer enforce them ; and
in one village, the old Zemindars, who had ousted the
proprietor recognised by the British Government,
made manful resistance, and were put to the sword.*
For a while British authority, as represented by
Allan Hume, was again on the ascendant. But it
was hard to say how long the Gwalior Grenadiers
would continue faithful to the Raj of the Feringhees.
We were only maintained in our supremacy by the
mercenaries of a Native Prince.

At Mynpooree was another body of the Ninth Mynpooree.
Sepoys. The head-quarters of the regiment having
mutinied, it was not to be expected that the detachment would remain true to its colours. On the
evening of the 22nd of May, intelligence of the
rising at Aligurh was received, with exaggerated
accounts of the murder of the European officers;
and at once arrangements were made to convey the
Christian families to Agra.† At the same time it
was agreed between the civil and military officers

---

* See Mr. Hume's official report : "One village fort at Sumpther, where the old Zemindars, who had ousted the proprietor, pertinaciously refused to surrender, though offered pardon, and fired on our emissaries of peace, was carried by storm, burnt, and the garrison put to the sword." This is recorded as a solitary instance; but it is to be remembered that British authority had then been only three days in abeyance.

† Mr. Power, in his report o May 25, says : "Fourteen females, consisting of ladies, sergeants' and writers' wives, with their children (an unlimited number), left the station under the charge of Mr. S. W. Power, the Assistant-Magistrate, who accompanied them a stage towards Agra, which they reached safely in 'shegrams' (native carriages)."

that the question of the fidelity of the Sepoys should be at once put to the test by the issue of an order for their immediate march to Bhowgaon.*

The officers of the Ninth with the detachment at Mynpooree were Lieutenant Crawford and Lieutenant De Kantzow. The civil officers were Mr. Arthur Cocks, Commissioner; Mr. Power, Magistrate; his brother, Assistant-Magistrate; and Dr. Watson, Civil Surgeon. The Rev. Mr. Kellner, a missionary, was also at the station. In the early morning of the 23rd, whilst the civilians, with the exception of the younger Power, who was escorting the women and children on their way to Agra, were gathered together discussing the position, the military officers were endeavouring to induce their men to march to Bhowgaon. But they were not to be commanded or persuaded. It was plain that the experiment had failed. The Sepoys were breaking into revolt and threatening the lives of their officers. Upon this Crawford galloped back to the Magistrate's house, told him that the Sepoys were in open mutiny, that he believed that De Kantzow had been killed, and that it was his intention to ride into Agra. What now was to be done? Arthur Cocks, a brave and resolute man, saw that he could do nothing in the immediate crisis, and as Crawford gave it as his opinion that, in a military sense, there was nothing for them but retirement on Agra, and the Sepoys were shouting defiance and firing their muskets to threaten and intimidate the English, he declared that no one was bound to remain at Mynpooree ; and presently, accompanied by Mr.

---

* Mr. Cocks, in his official report, says, that the news came on the 19th. This is obviously an error, as the troops at Aligurh did not mutiny before the evening of the 20th.

Kellner, he set out, in a buggy, for the Jumna, with the intention of returning with reinforcements. But Power, the Magistrate, declared that he had determined to remain at his post; and the younger Power, having returned to the station, cast in his lot with his brother. Dr. Watson determined also to remain at Mynpooree.*

During this time nothing had been heard of De Kantzow. What was he doing? He was stemming single-handed the tide of mutiny. And it was mutiny of the most delirious kind. The Sepoys returned to the station dragging the Lieutenant with them. As they went, they fired into all the houses of Europeans that they passed. They broke open the Magazine—took possession of all the ammunition, amounting to some three hundred rounds a man—and then, proud of their wealth, proceeded to fire wildly in every direction. It was a mercy and a miracle that De Kantzow was not shot dead. Often was the piece of a Sepoy pointed at him, to be struck down or dashed aside by the hand of one of his comrades. The Sepoys had, according to their wont, made for the Treasury, where they were met by the Civil-guard, who would have fired upon the Sepoys had not De Kantzow wisely restrained them. There was then a scene of wild confusion. The Gaol-guards, few in number and badly armed, did all that they could to

1857. May.

* "The Sepoys were now approaching the station and firing off their muskets, and shouting like madmen. Mr. Power seemed to hesitate what he would do. I considered it no time for hesitation. I fairly told him I did not consider any one bound to remain; soon after which I ordered my buggy, and, with the Rev. Mr. Kellner, drove leisurely away, having told the people about that I hoped to return in a day or two with a force."—Report of Mr. Cocks, November 16, 1858. "Mr. Cocks and the Rev. Mr. Kellner immediately decided on leaving, and the former tried to induce me to leave also; as I informed him that I did not desire to leave my post, he honoured me by terming my conduct 'romantic,' and immediately departed in company with the Rev. Mr. Kellner."—Report of Mr. Power, May 25, 1857.

resist the Sepoys ; but against such a multitude their
defence, though faithful, was feeble. It is said to
have been "a fearful scene."* But in the midst of
this mighty peril, De Kantzow stood, firm and undaunted, imploring the soldiers to consider the
wickedness and folly of their course, and showing to
the wonder and the admiration of the surging multitude of Sepoys that a single English officer defied
them—that they might kill, but that they could not
conquer him. And so for three hours the young
English soldier breasted alone this great flood of
furious mutiny, and overawed his enemies by the
consummate gallantry of his bearing.†

When Mr. Power, the Magistrate, heard that De
Kantzow was thus perilously situated, he was eager
to join him with all the guards he could muster; but
he was dissuaded from this both by the Lieutenant
himself, who, in the midst of his own tribulation,
contrived to send a note to his friend, and by an
influential Native gentleman, the Rao Bhowanee
Singh (a relative of the Rajah of Mynpooree), who
had come in to our assistance with a small body of
horse and foot. This man, as brave as he was faithful, went unattended to the spot where De Kantzow
stood at bay, and used every art of remonstrance and
persuasion to pacify and subdue the mutineers. And
after awhile he succeeded. "He drew off and accompanied the rebels to the lines"—and the brave
English subaltern was saved, with the treasure which

* Mr. Power's Official Report,
May 25, 1857.
† The official account written by
Mr. Power says : " Left by his
superior officer, unaided by the presence of any European, jostled with
cruel and insulting violence, buffeted
by the hands of men who had received innumerable kindnesses from
him, and who had obeyed him a few
hours before with crawling servility,
Lieutenant De Kantzow stood for
three dreary hours against the rebels,
at the imminent peril of his life."

he had so nobly protected. Rife as is this narrative with records of great deeds done by the younger officers of the Company's Services, there is nothing more illustrative than this story of the grand self-reliance and self-devotion so often manifested in the conduct of untried men, when danger suddenly came upon them and girt them round as with rings of fire. Bravery such as this was sure to win the heart of Lord Canning, and to elicit from him prompt words of admiration. So, when he received Power's report he wrote at once to the noble-hearted young subaltern, saying, " I have read it with an admiration and respect which I cannot adequately describe. Young in years, and at the outset of your career, you have given to your brother-soldiers a noble example of courage, patience, good judgment, and temper, from which many might profit. I beg you to believe that it will never be forgotten by me."*

When news of these events reached Agra, there was great consternation among our people. Numbers of the Christian inhabitants rushed wildly to such houses and buildings as seemed most capable of defence. A brave-hearted Englishman then wrote to his brother, saying : " The panic here exceeds anything I have ever witnessed. Women, children, carts, gharries, buggies flying from all parts into the Fort, with loads of furniture, beds, bedding, baskets of fowls, &c. &c. The Europeans have all escaped from Aligurh. Lady Outram came in here, partly on horseback, partly on foot. . . . . One or two civilians here have behaved most shamefully. One of them

* Lord Canning to Lieutenant De Kantzow, June 7, 1857. MS. Records.

1857.
May.

went into his office, pale as his own liver, and told all the crannies to save their lives as they best could."*

Measures of
defence.

It was now obviously necessary to look the situation very gravely in the face. The Fort had been secured by the detachment of a body of Europeans to garrison it, and arrangements were being made to provision it for six months. There was not much apprehension of danger from the unaided efforts of the citizens; but the Native regiments were of very doubtful loyalty, and if they, or an incursion of the predatory classes in the neighbourhood, should release the prisoners in the gaols, there might be a popular rising. The European quarters, owing to their straggling nature and the wide space which they covered, at a distance from the European barracks, were not easily to be protected. In the Schools, the Convent, and the houses of the married civilians, were large assemblages of women and children. It was expedient, therefore, to organise some system of external defence, and Mr. Reade was called upon by the Lieutenant-Governor to do it. The task could not have been intrusted to better hands. He had,

* It does not appear that this account is at all overstated. Mr. Charles Raikes, in his published volume, gives the following graphic sketch of the general alarm. The picture of the calm steadfastness of the missionaries is very striking: "Every Englishman was handling his sword or revolver—the road covered with carriages, people hastening right and left to the rendezvous at Candaharee Bagh. The city folks running as for their lives, and screaming that the mutineers from Aligurh were crossing the bridge. The Budmashes twisting their moustaches, and putting on their worst looks. Outside the college all alarm, hurry, and confusion. Within calmly sat the good Missionary, hundreds of young Natives at his feet, hanging on the lips which taught them the simple lessons of the Bible. And so it was throughout the revolt. Native functionaries, highly salaried, largely trusted, deserted and joined our enemies, but the students at the Government, and still more the Missionary, Schools, kept steadily to their classes, and when others doubted or fled, they trusted implicitly to their teachers, and openly espoused the Christian cause."

at an earlier period, been of opinion that it would be
expedient to intrench the station; but this view had
not been supported, and he had abandoned it. He,
therefore, projected a system of rendezvous in case of
alarm, of defence-posts, and advance-pickets; so that
if danger threatened, early announcement of the
coming enemy might be received, and every non-
combatant might seek an asylum in one of the
appointed places of refuge. The principal public
buildings, as the Government House, the Post-office,
the Agra Bank, the Customs' House, the Medical
College, the Convent, and the Candaharee Baugh,*
with some of the private houses of civilians, were
fixed upon as places of resort, and arrangements were
made for their protection, extending from the Taj on
one side to the Cutcherry on the other. Defence-
posts, ten in number, so as to form a cordon around
the places of rendezvous, were to be manned in sufficient strength; and beyond these again another line
of defences, describing a larger semicircle, consisting
of fifteen outposts, five of which were to be of horsemen, to bring in promptly the first news of approaching danger, was to be established. But it was easier
for the Lieutenant-Governor to invite an officer, in
whose wisdom he had confidence, to organise a plan
of defence, and easier for that officer to perform the
important duty intrusted to him, than to induce
others to conform to the plan. Ever in such cases is
there disunion. Opposition to any scheme is to be
expected, unless it comes with all the force of an
imperial edict from the highest authority, and there
is something that must, not something that may, be
done. So it happened that Reade's plan of defence,

---

* This was a large brick-built
house, belonging to the Rajah of
Bhurtpore, and then occupied by
Mr. Morgan, of the Civil Service.

1857.
May.

which, read at this distance of time, seems at least to have upon it the stamp of the broad arrow of common sense, was by the multitude of councillors only partially accepted at the time,* and events were taking shape which soon rendered it an anachronism.

Meanwhile, Mr. Drummond, the Magistrate, was doing all that could be done to convert the City Police into a strong defensive force of Horse and Foot. Muskets and side-arms were served out from the Arsenal, and ammunition was freely supplied to them. But it was hard to say whether they were to be trusted, or, if true at the moment, how long they would remain staunch to their employers. Already they had begun "to scowl upon the Christians."†

Mr. Colvin's Proclamation.

Affairs were in this state, when the Lieutenant-Governor, tormented by doubts, seeing clearly what had already been done, and divining what would ere long be done, by mere force of example, in that great flock of Sepoys, whose nature it ever was to follow each other like sheep, bethought himself of doing something authoritatively to restore the fast-waning confidence of the soldiery by a public appeal to them. One of the ablest and most experienced officers of the

Colin Troup.

Sepoy Army had written to him, saying: "Having served, as I trust, faithfully a most liberal Government for upwards of six-and-thirty years, during which long period I have been associated with the Native soldier in every position in which he can be placed (some of them of very great difficulty), I am sanguine enough to believe that I have a correct and extended knowledge of all his habits, customs, and

---

* Mr. Reade himself states that, "It was partially adopted by the Magistrate and other residents—its effectiveness, however, being impaired by want of unity of purpose, by the wilfulness of some, who devised defensive measures of their own, and the neglect and carelessness of others."

† Raikes.

wishes, and, therefore, hesitate not, under the present trying events, to give it as my unqualified opinion, that in all that is said or done to the Native soldier during the present state of excitement no allusion should be made to the retribution or punishment awaiting those who have disgraced the name of soldiers; and I feel certain, if such can be done with propriety, that a proclamation from you to the effect that the past has been forgiven, and that the moment things are more settled those who have proved true to their Government shall not be forgotten, and that a commission of experienced European and Native officers will be formed to inquire into all their wants, and have everything so arranged as to put it out of the power of evil-disposed men to interfere with their rights and privileges for the future, would at this moment do more good than ten thousand European soldiers. For I have satisfied myself beyond all doubt that fear is the principal cause of all that is going on at present among the men of the Native Army." And he added: "Unless this comes direct from yourself or the Government (for the word of any intermediate authority would be of no avail), it will be of little use." The sentiments thus expressed by Colin Troup appear to have made a deep impression upon Colvin's mind. A strong conviction took possession of him that the old soldier was right; that the Native troops had been drawn into mutiny more by their fears than by their resentments, and that it was sound policy, in such a conjuncture, to endeavour by every possible means to reassure the minds of the Sepoys, who were huddling one after another, in panic-stricken confusion, like a flock of sheep, to destruction. And in this I must ever think that he was right. But the question was not whether the thing

1857.
May.

should be done, but how and by whom it should be done. To have reassured the minds of the Sepoys who had not yet broken into rebellion, and to have promised condonation of the offences of those regiments who had only mutinied—who had offended as soldiers, but had not stained their hands with blood —might in that conjuncture have been a wise measure. But it was absolutely necessary that in such a proclamation care should be taken most explicitly and emphatically to shut out from all participation in the promised amnesty every soldier of a regiment which had outraged its officers. And the proclamation should unquestionably have proceeded, not from the subordinate, but from the Supreme Government. But Colvin, though in communication with Calcutta by telegraph, took upon himself, without consulting the officers surrounding him,* to issue a manifesto in the following words, bearing date the 25th of May:

May 25.

" PROCLAMATION.

"Soldiers engaged in the late disturbances, who are desirous of going to their own homes, and who give up their arms at the nearest Government civil or military post, and retire quietly, shall be permitted to do so unmolested.

---

* Mr. Reade says: "Here I must briefly notice the proclamations issued by the Lieutenant-Governor. The first of these is dated May 15, and the original draft was sent to me, Mr. Harington, and others, before publication. It had our hearty concurrence, both for the tone it assumed and the line of policy it indicated. The subsequent proclamation of the 25th of May was framed and issued, so far as I have been able to ascertain, without reference to any one here at Agra. I see it stated in a republication from the Blue-book that it was sent everywhere as being thought by all here likely to have the best effect on the public mind; but this is altogether erroneous. It certainly took most persons at Agra by surprise, not from the objections made by the Supreme Government, which nobody knew of, but generally from its singular contrast with the proclamation issued only a few days before." Mr. Colvin, however, emphatically declared that the proclamation had been "universally approved" in Agra.

"Many faithful soldiers have been driven into resistance to Government only because they were in the
ranks and could not escape from them, and because
they really thought their feelings of religion and
honour injured by the measures of Government.
This feeling was wholly a mistake, but it acted on
men's minds. A proclamation of the Governor-
General now issued is perfectly explicit, and will
remove all doubts on these points. Every evil-
minded instigator in the disturbance, and those guilty
of heinous crimes against private persons, shall be
punished. All those who appear in arms against the
Government after this notification is known shall be
treated as open enemies."

These proceedings deeply pained Lord Canning.
Only on the 24th he had written to Mr. Colvin in
that warm language of gratitude and encouragement
which came spontaneously from his generous heart:
" I have never yet sufficiently expressed to you my
admiration of your cool courage and excellent judgment during all that has been passing. They have, I
know for certain, inspired confidence in those around
you, and I feel that it would be difficult to appreciate
at its true value the service which you have rendered.
To myself the satisfaction and comfort of feeling that
your charge is in such hands, is incalculable." And
now, three or four days afterwards, he was compelled
to repudiate, as chief ruler of the country, the most
important of the acts of his once-trusted Lieutenant.
Writing privately to Mr. Colvin on the 28th, he said :
" I never did an act that gave me more distress than
that of superseding the proclamation of the 25th. I
would have escaped, if I had thought escape possible,
and would have made any sacrifice to support the

one which had come from you. But I am strongly of opinion that it would not have been safe to leave that proclamation unaltered. The terms of the first paragraph opened escape to every man, and I cannot see that the door was closed to the most heinous offenders by the third paragraph. The soldiers who murdered their officers are not mentioned or indicated. There is no term which includes them among the most guilty. With that proclamation in their hands, every man of the Twentieth and Thirty-eighth Regiments might, so far as we know, have presented himself to you or to the Commander-in-Chief and have claimed liberty to go home. I use no exaggeration when I say that had any of these men availed themselves of it, the Government could never have held up its head again. I can guess, and, indeed, fully understand the difficulties which beset you, and which you have met so calmly, wisely, and with such dignity, but I do not gather that they are such as to compel us yet to offer free pardon to the murderers of our officers. Certainly nothing which you have sent me sets affairs in that light." "Do not suppose," he added, " that, sitting here in Calcutta, I wish to carry things with a high hand, without regarding the embarrassments and unavoidable weaknesses of those who are in the thick of the difficulties. I have no such desire. Menaces are unworthy of a strong and just Government, and dangerous to a weak one. I would use none. The proclamation now sent has less even of menace than your own. It gives even more distinctly a free and unconditional pardon to one section of the mutineers, and marks a difference between regiments, which strictly accords with justice and our duty towards our officers, whilst it may be expected to sow disunion at Delhi."

The proclamation which Lord Canning sent forth to supersede that which had been issued by Mr. Colvin, ran in the following words:

" Every soldier of a regiment which, although it has deserted its post, has not committed outrages, will receive a free pardon and permission to proceed to his home, if he immediately delivers up his arms to the civil or military authority, and if no heinous crime is shown to have been perpetrated by himself personally. This offer of free and unconditional pardon cannot be extended to those regiments which have killed or wounded their officers or other persons, or which have been concerned in the commission of cruel outrages. The men of such regiments must submit themselves unconditionally to the authority and justice of the Government of India. Any proclamations offering pardon to soldiers engaged in the late disturbances, which may have been issued by local authorities previously to the promulgation of the present proclamation, will thereupon cease to have effect. But all persons who may have availed themselves of the offer made in such proclamations shall enjoy the benefit thereof."

The Lieutenant-Governor was slow to acknowledge, and, therefore, it may be assumed that he was slow to see—for he was not one to simulate a belief that was not in him—that there was any material difference between the two manifestoes. And, perhaps, as Mr. Colvin intended his own proclamation to be understood, the difference was but slight. Verbally, however, the distinction was great and striking; and practically the embarrassments resulting from a strict interpretation of the Agra manifesto might have been immense. What Colvin had done, unintentionally, it would seem, was to exempt from punishment all but.

individual Sepoys known to have been "guilty of heinous crimes against private persons;" whereas the proclamation substituted by the Calcutta Government barred whole regiments, any members of which had been guilty of the murder of their officers or others. As it would have been difficult, if not impossible, save in rare instances, to prove blood-guiltiness against individual soldiers, the most probable result of the amnesty issued by the Lieutenant-Governor would have been the escape of numbers of actual murderers, and of many more, guilty in the second degree, as aiders and abettors. Nothing, moreover, could have been more infelicitous than the expression "private persons," for in no sense, with reference to the Sepoys, could their officers be so described. This, however, Lord Canning declared to be but a small part of the offence. "It is not," he wrote, "only a question as to the meaning of the term 'private persons' either in English or in Oordoo. Whatever may be argued on that point (and I confess that I do not like sailing very near the wind in interpretations upon which the lives of men and the honour of the Government depend), the apparent meaning and the real working of the proclamation will be the same. The vice of it, as I have already said by telegraph, does not consist in the words 'private persons' alone.* The whole burden of proof against each man is thrown entirely and at once upon the authority to whom he presents himself. To put a plain case. If twenty men of the

* Mr. Colvin stated afterwards that as rendered in the Native languages, the words literally represented "subjects of Government." Now, as understood in India at that time, "private persons" and "subjects of Government" were different classes of individuals. Mr. Colvin said that his intention was to discriminate between offences against the *State* and offences against persons— but surely offences against the servants of Government were offences against the Government.

Thirty-eighth Regiment leave Delhi and deliver up their arms to the nearest Magistrate, who knows nothing of them but that they belonged to that corps, can their unmolested liberty be refused to them? Assuredly not, unless the promise given in the proclamation is broken."

To such strictures by Lord Canning and others, Mr. Colvin, some weeks afterwards, replied in a letter to his brother: "The proclamation was universally approved here, though much that I have done since has been the cause of much difference of opinion. We here understood the vast extent of the danger that was opening on us, and the sincere and thorough delusion that the mass of the Sepoys were in, about the intentions of Government. Regiments were beginning to give way all round. To prevent the fatal mischief spreading, it seemed the wisest thing that could be done to mark that we desired to be just, and to offer the means of retreat to those not already desperately committed, and who had been betrayed into the rebel ranks by the insane apprehensions about religion, or by the inability of getting away from them. That those who had taken a leading or a deliberately malignant part in the revolt would ever seek to take advantage of the notification, we knew to be quite out of the question. The chance that seemed open (through the proclamation) of escape to such persons was what called forth the heavy censure at many distant points. But we who were nearer the scene, and knew the real spirit of the revolt, could not entertain such a supposition. The attempt to separate the comparatively innocent—to appeal through them to the feelings of the regiments yet in obedience—seemed in my deliberate opinion, and still seems, the right and useful thing to do at that time."*

Upon few events of those troubled times was so much useless controversy expended. For, notwithstanding all this logomachy, the proclamation was a very harmless proclamation. Nothing in effect came from it—except that the adverse criticisms passed upon it in Government House and in other places, high and low, had a wearing and depressing effect upon the Lieutenant-Governor's mind. In such times and in such circumstances, a man even with robust health and a strong nervous system on his side requires some external encouragement to sustain and to keep him up to the athletic standard which is necessary to the right discharge of great responsibilities. But Colvin's health was failing; his nerves were shaken. Whilst day after day, from beyond Agra, fresh tidings of disaffection and disaster came in to increase his perplexities and to aggravate his distresses, the difficulties which presented themselves to him at home, because more immediate and omnipresent, were still more vexatious and annoying. The differences of opinion, which arose among the many able and energetic officers who surrounded him, were continually distracting his mind and ministering to his irresolution. What he suffered no man can tell; but those about him saw more clearly every day that he was growing weaker both in body and in mind. It was plain that the burden upon him was greater than he could bear. He was a brave and honourable Englishman; but his lines had been cast in pleasant places. He had been sage in counsel; but he was not accustomed to face the responsibilities of prompt and strenuous action, and now he began slowly to

* MS. Correspondence.

succumb to the incessant pressure upon his brain; and those who watched him did not think that he would long survive to direct or to control them.

1857.
May.

Three weeks had now nearly passed away since the conflagration had commenced in the Upper Provinces of India; but although there had been many alarming rumours, there had been no reality of danger at Agra. The Native regiments had performed their accustomed duties, in obedience to their officers, who for the most part clung to the belief that their men would not turn against them.* And the principal civilians, whose counsels up to this time prevailed, were still preaching the expediency of maintaining an outward show of confidence, though in truth the faith itself, if ever honestly cherished, was rapidly passing away, and the Lieutenant-Governor was beginning to doubt whether he had not been ill-advised from the first.

May 30.
Mutiny at
Muttra.

But before the month of May had closed in upon us, a crisis had arrived in the affairs of Agra. There was a company of one of the Agra regiments (the Forty-fourth) at Muttra, a civil station some thirty-five miles distant; and it had been arranged

---

* It is probable that this belief was more strongly impressed on the minds of the elder than of the younger officers. When Sir Henry Durand was at Agra, on his way to Indore, at the end of March, he wrote to Lord Canning, saying : " Brigadier Polwhele spoke with dissatisfaction of the opinions and conversation of some of the younger officers, ascribing to unwise assertions on their parts the idea, more or less generally entertained, that the Sepoy corps sympathised with the Nineteenth Native Infantry, and he with a good deal of earnestness denied that the Sepoys here had given the slightest grounds for such a suspicion. There may of course be a lack both of experience and wisdom among young officers, but they are freer in their expression of opinion and the men less on their guard before them. Aged officers like Polwhele are slow to perceive and unwilling to admit anything not flattering to their own influence and authority."—*MS. Correspondence.*

that another company of the same regiment, and
one also of the Sixty-seventh, should be sent thither,
partly to relieve the old detachment, and partly to
bring away the bulk of the treasure. This amounted
to upwards of six lakhs of rupees. It ought to have
been, and it might easily have been, brought away
before. Mr. Colvin had been eagerly besought by
the Engineer officers to remove the treasure both
from Aligurh and Muttra; but these would have
been marks of no-confidence, which it was the policy
of the Government to disavow. There had been considerable excitement at Muttra. News had come
that the Delhi mutineers and others were marching
on Agra, and would pass through the Muttra station
on their way. The European women and children
had, therefore, been sent to the former place. In
the middle of the month the arrival of the Bhurtpore force, under Captain Nixon, though it alarmed
the Sepoys, did something to restore the general confidence.* It was believed that the Foreign Contingent was to be trusted; but it was merely a question, to be determined by some accident, as to which
should be the first to rise. The event proved that in
the race of rebellion they were destined to achieve
something like a dead heat. When, on the 30th of

* The following is from a letter
written by Captain Nixon (Muttra,
May 17): "On marching in, we
drove very thoughtlessly up to the
Treasury-guard, and, on arriving
near, the Sepoys turned out in a
dreadful fright. The fact is they
thought that they were going to be
attacked, as I had of course an
immense *sowarree* following me. I
was put in a very ticklish position,
and had to send back my *sowarree*,
as I saw the Sepoys commencing to
load. However, they immediately
stopped all hostile demonstrations
on my turning the *sowarree* back, and
we went and reassured them and
made them 'present arms.' The fact
is that my people had evidently been
threatening them, and they thought
that their time had come. I am
glad, for one or two reasons, that
this has happened—firstly, because
it is now quite clear to me that our
Sepoys and the troops of the Native
States will never coalesce, and secondly, because they are now frightened by an enemy from another
quarter." All this, as will presently
be seen, was an entire mistake.

May, the two companies marched in from Agra, there was a sufficient body of Sepoys at the place to seize the treasure without much fear of successful resist- ance. The moment was opportune; so as soon as the treasure was placed on the carriages, which were to convey it to Agra, the Sepoys broke into open rebellion. Lieutenant Boulton, who was superin- tending, with others, the transfer of the coin, was shot dead; Lieutenant Gibbon was wounded; and some of the civil officers narrowly escaped the fire of the insurgents. The Sepoys now had the rupee-bags securely in hand, and with them they started off for Delhi.

There was, however, some hope that those plans might be frustrated. At that time the Bhurtpore troops were at Hodul. Mr. Harvey, the Commissioner, was with them. In the early morning of the 31st of May, the Commissioner was apprised, by an incursion of fugitives from Muttra, that the troops had risen and were on their way to Delhi. His first thought was to intercept the progress of the insurgents. A plan of defence was, therefore, agreed upon between the civil and the military officers. The Bhurtpore guns were to be placed in position across the road, by which the mutineers were expected to advance. But all hope of a successful resistance was soon gone. Many of the artillerymen were Poorbeahs, deserters or discharged Sepoys from our own Infantry ranks; and their commanders told our officers that the men were not to be trusted. The Bhurtpore camp, indeed, was declared to be no place of safety for Europeans; and our people were, therefore, exhorted to depart. But they were slow to take this advice. For some hours they exerted themselves most strenuously to induce the regiments to do their duty. They offered

1857.
May 31.

liberal rewards on the part of the British Government. They reminded the troops that they would bring disgrace on their own Raj, if they forsook, in the hour of need, the allies whom they had been sent to succour. But no arguments, or persuasions, or promises could avail. The only result of these efforts was, that the Bhurtpore artillerymen pointed some of their guns threateningly at the group of Englishmen. There was now nothing more to be done but either to seek some safer place or to remain in the Bhurtpore camp to be murdered. So the party of Englishmen—some thirty in number—mounted their horses and rode off, carrying nothing with them but the arms in their hands and the clothes on their backs. Scarcely had they started, when the Bhurtpore troops broke into the wonted orgies of rebellion. The tents of the English gentlemen were almost instantly in a blaze. A few bungalows, which had been occupied by Customs' officials in our pay, were fired, one after another; and such property as our people had left behind them was plundered by our allies. And thus was the first rude shock given to our faith in the allied troops of the Native States—thus was all hope of the Agra Commissioner effecting the march to Delhi cut off from him for a time. Harvey's first thought was to endeavour to form a junction with the Sirmoor battalion, which was then moving upon Delhi. This, however, was not accomplished; and he eventually found himself in Rajpootana, where, in co-operation with the political officers in those states, he rendered excellent service to his Government.

Disarming of the Native regiments.

It was to be expected that news of these events would produce great excitement in Agra. The companies which had mutinied belonged to the Agra

regiments. There was little doubt that the main
bodies would follow the lead of these pioneers into
the jungle of rebellion. It was necessary, therefore, to act—and at once. The evil tidings had
been brought by a camel-express, and communicated
about midnight to Mr. Drummond. The Lieutenant-
Governor was at that time sleeping in the Magistrate's house. So Drummond roused him, and insisted that it was necessary to disarm the Sepoy
regiments on the coming morning at break of day.
If Colvin demurred for a little space, his reluctance
was soon overcome by the earnestness of the Magistrate. The order went forth; and at dawn on that
Sunday, the 31st of May, the Third Europeans were
brought down to the parade-ground, and Captain
D'Oyley's battery was drawn up ready for action.
When, therefore, the Sepoy regiments found themselves in dangerous proximity to the British Infantry
and the guns, they knew that certain destruction
was before them if they ventured to resist. The old
Brigadier, seated on his white charger, addressed a
few words to the Sepoys and gave the word of command. "Silent and sullen" the Sepoys obeyed the
order to "pile arms;" and they were marched back
to their Lines. Some applied for leave and went
to their homes. Others started off without leave for
Delhi. But any present danger to be apprehended
from them was gone; and, practically, two more
regiments were effaced from the Bengal Army List.

CHAPTER II.

STATE OF THE DISTRICTS — THE MEERUT AND ROHILKUND DIVISIONS — AFFAIRS AT MOZUFFERNUGGUR AND SAHARUNPORE—THE TWENTY-NINTH AT MORADABAD—MR. CRACROFT WILSON—MUTINY OF THE BAREILLY BRIGADE—KHAN BEHAUDUR KHAN—SHAHJEHANPORE AND BUDAON.

1857.
May—June. So the month of June dawned upon the Lieutenant-Governor and his colleagues, with at least one source of apprehension less. "The greatest good," wrote Mr. Colvin to Lord Canning, on the 1st of June, "has been done by the disarming of the two Native regiments here. Most of the men will slink away, chiefly from fear of what we may do to them, and we are well rid of them." In other parts of the country, this "slinking away" of disarmed Sepoys was called desertion, and men were hanged for the offence.* And wisely, too— for disarmed men, in such a state of things as then confronted us, soon became full-armed men. They had never to go far to re-equip themselves for the battle. And, therefore, a danger removed from Agra, or any central point, was only a danger sent to reappear on some other spot, and perhaps with redoubled cogency for evil. It was commonly said that Sepoys who had mutinied or deserted "went off to Delhi." But many halted by the way, scattering themselves over the

* *Ante,* vol. ii. page 482.

districts, some going straight to their Native villages with such share of the wages of rebellion as they might have succeeded in appropriating to themselves, and spreading abroad everywhere exaggerated stories of the evil intentions of the English, or of the speedy downfall of the British Empire.

Indeed, nothing was more certain at this time than that, whatever might be the improvement in the position of Agra itself, the North-Western Provinces were every day sinking into the profoundest depths of disorder. Before the end of May, Mr. Colvin had written to the Governor-General, saying : " The country is in utter disorder; but bold men, holding together, should still make their way through. The real reason, I regret to say, why messages do not get delivered is, that the belief in the permanence of our power has been very deeply shaken, and that men think that there is a better chance for them to take to open plundering than to engage in special risks for our service. . . . . The country north of Meerut (part at least of the Mozuffernuggur district) is at the mercy of the most daring and criminal. There are many good men, whose feelings are with us, but the vicious, the disappointed, and the desperate, are the most bold in all such convulsions of order, and on the whole there is (its police force being dispersed) no support to the Government. . . . . Aligurh and Etah, the two most important districts of the centre Upper Doab, are in a blaze of riot and ravage. . . . . It is melancholy to contemplate the fearful calamities which, at but a short thirty or forty miles from me, are causing the misery of our poor subjects, for whom we have thought and toiled with so many anxious cares. . . . . Such is the state of things in extremely opulent districts, which but three months ago I prided myself on having done so much to improve." Some of the more distant manifestations spoken of in this letter I must now proceed to relate.

In the districts of the North-Western Provinces situated above Delhi, British authority was threatened with greater violence than below. But the danger was not always of the same type. What we have hitherto traced in the shape of overt acts against the Government of the English, have been mutinous risings of the Sepoy soldiery, which their non-military brethren more or less aided and abetted. Into whatsoever dimensions, social or political, the movement may have afterwards swollen, its first activities were purely military. At all our great civil stations were detachments of Native Infantry regiments posted there mainly to protect the Treasury and other property of the Government. The revenue was collected, for the most part, in the silver coinage of the country, and at the head-quarters of every collectorate were treasure-chests groaning with rupees. No one, before the coming of this month of May, ever doubted that, under the charge of a guard of Sepoys, all this wealth was as secure as it would have been in Lothbury. But now it was clear that our strength had become weakness—our security had been turned into danger. The guardians of our public property had become its despoilers; and at most stations were doubt and apprehension, and a general wish that the property of Government and the lives of its servants had been in charge of the Civil Police of the district. But in some of the districts in the Meerut and Bareilly Divisions there was less fear of the soldiery than of the populace. The first threatenings came from the disaffected communities, whilst still the Sepoys were outwardly staunch.

At Saharunpore and Mozuffernuggur, in the Meerut

Division, and at Moradabad and Budaon, in the con- 1857.
tiguous Bareilly Division, this was especially appa- May—June
rent. At Saharunpore was a detachment of the
Twenty-ninth Sepoy Regiment, its head-quarters
being at Moradabad. It was a regiment of good
repute, believed to be loyal, and for some time it
maintained its character. But the guards at Mozuf- Mozuffer-
fernuggur were drawn from the Twentieth that had nuggur.
mutinied at Meerut, and there was, seemingly, small
hope of the continuance of its loyalty. It was probable, indeed, that on the arrival of the news from
head-quarters, the detachment would break into
instant rebellion. For three days, however, the
Sepoys were quiet. But those three days were fatal
to our rule. Before the soldiery had struck a blow,
there were signs of insurrection in the town. The
English Magistrate had closed all the public offices,
and hid himself in the jungle.* The most exaggerated
reports of the total collapse of British rule began to
spread through the district. Then all the discontented, the disappointed, and the down-trodden began
to take heart. The houses of our public officers were
burnt or attacked by armed bands; and it was believed that " the impoverished Syud Zemindars instigated the villagers to commit these excesses."† The
example having thus been set by the non-military
classes, the Sepoys rose. On the afternoon of the
14th, when it was proposed to move the treasure to a
place of greater safety, the guard refused to allow its
removal, broke into the chest, and gorged themselves
with the plunder.‡ Taking with them as much as
they could carry—about one-third, perhaps, of the

---

* In the official report by Mr.
R. M. Edwards it is significantly
said : " Mr. Berford at once ordered
that all the public offices should be
closed on that day. They were never
again opened."

† Official report.
‡ There were eighty-five thousand
rupees in the Treasury, and there
were only thirty-five Sepoys on the
Treasury-guard.

whole—they marched off triumphantly towards Moradabad. The rest of the coin was plundered by the townspeople, the Magistrate's servants, and it was more than suspected by the Native functionaries of the British Government. "Nobody," says the official report, "raised a finger to prevent them; everybody seems to have been paralysed."

But there was something still more surprising than this. Overcome by unmanly fear for his personal safety, the Magistrate determined to strengthen his own body-guard by releasing the prisoners in the Gaol, and withdrawing the guards that were protecting it. This crowning instance of the paralysis of British authority gave the finishing stroke to all law and order in the district. Whilst the Magistrate was sheltering himself in a suburb of the city, with a guard of Sepoys around the house in which he lay, the Government offices and officers' bungalows were burnt, the public records were exultantly destroyed, the empty Gaol was pulled to pieces, and the doors, and shutters, and railings carried off as plunder by the villagers, and from one end to the other of the district the tidings ran that English rule was at an end, that the English were hiding themselves for fear of their lives, that a reign of anarchy had commenced, that every one might do as he liked, and take what he could get, that the race was to the swift and the battle to the strong, and that every man was his own judge and collector.

Saharunpore.   And thus the prevailing faith of Mozuffernuggur soon became the prevailing faith of Saharunpore. I am glad to change the scene, for in the latter district English manhood was not utterly at its last gasp. All men are not alike, and even on the fair countenance of our national manliness may sometimes be

seen ugly blotches and unseemly tumours. The 1857.
difficulties of Saharunpore were increased by the May—June.
failure of Mozuffernuggur. In the former district
there had been some bad symptoms from the commencement, and when it was known that English
authority was prostrate in the latter, the audacity of
the people increased.* The Magistrate, Mr. Spankie,
on first learning that the Meerut troops had risen,
summoned a Council, and it was considered whether
the English should abandon the station or hold on to
the last. There was energy enough in the little con-
clave to carry a vote in favour of the manlier course.
This done, all the ladies and children of the station
were sent under safe escort to Mussoorie, on the Hills.
There was no expectation that the district would
remain quiet. Its population was a dangerous population. Its "plundering tribes" were prominent in
its statistics, and a general feeling of the inability of
the English any longer to maintain order, stimulated
every man to take the law into his own hand. There
was a company of the Twenty-Ninth Sepoys in the
station, guarding the public property; but the fear
was not of the soldiery, but of the populace. Whilst
the soldiery were at least outwardly tranquil, among
the people were throes and spasms of feverish emotion.

* See statements of Mr. Dundas Robertson, Joint-Magistrate of Saha-runpore, in his work, entitled "Dis-trict Duties during the Revolt in the North-West Provinces of India" (1859), one of the best of many valuable books, illustrative of scat-tered passages of the rebellion. See also Mr. Spankie's official report: "During this period of uncertainty (May 13-14), whilst speaking to several would-be well-disposed Na-tives, who it was easy to observe visited me more with the view of extracting than of furnishing in- formation, I was much struck with their evident satisfaction in the generally unfavourable nature of the news, and with the promise of mis-fortune to the English." Again : "In the Mozuffernuggur district (May 18-20), some thirty miles dis-tant, British authority had almost ceased to exist, and was but feebly pulsating in the southern portion of our own, bordering on Mozuffer-nuggur. . . . The whole surround-ing country was in a state of the most complete anarchy."

1857.
May—June.

Mr. H. D.
Robertson.

Class rose against class; the strong against the weak; the debtor against the creditor; the beaten defendant against the successful plaintiff. The greatest joy of all was to reverse, by stretching forth a mailed hand, the decisions of the English Courts.

But underlying all this internecine strife there was a hatred, strong though subdued, of British rule. And a shrewd observer—a man equally sagacious and brave, who nobly upheld the British character in Saharunpore—had, before the close of the month, assured himself, by a full consideration of his experiences, that "the Zemindars were one with the lower orders—that rebellion, not plunder alone, actuated the mass of the population." It was as surprising as it was deplorable. "Troops might mutiny," said the Joint-Magistrate, "but I could hardly realise this rapid change amongst peaceful villagers."* The change was sadly apparent everywhere. In the city men were closing their shops and burying their valuables. There was an almost entire suspension of business, whilst on the public roads, which a little time before had been "crowded to excess" with travellers of both races and an extensive traffic, there was now something like a solitude, broken only by a few bands of armed men. There was no longer any security for life or property. The civil power was utterly prostrate. Yet, all this time, there was no danger from the Sepoys. "The Sepoy Treasury-guard continued true to their duty."

Indeed, when towards the end of the month it was proposed to go out and take the offensive, a strong party of Sepoys, accompanying the English gentlemen and the horsemen of the District Police, went out

---

* Robertson's "District Duties during the Revolt." "A few days preceding the 23rd of May, we ascertained that several of the larger villages had combined to attack us."

to coerce the rebel villages. The detachment of the 1857.
Twenty-ninth had, by this time, been strengthened May—June.
by Sepoy reinforcements from Umballah, both Horse
and Foot.* Whilst in some parts the authorities
were eager to rid themselves of the great danger of
the Sepoys, here they were regarded as elements of
safety, and our people sought their protection against
the enmity of the inhabitants of the towns and villages—and this at no great distance from Meerut and
Delhi, where military mutiny was rampant.

Meanwhile, in the Rohilkund Division were to Rohilkund.
be seen similar manifestations of contempt for and
defiance of British authority. It was soon apparent throughout the districts that there was an uneasy, restless feeling among the people, and that
the national heart was turned against the English.
There was, indeed, no part of the country under
charge of the Lieutenant-Governor from which accounts were looked for with greater anxiety than
from that important province. For there, the Mahomedan population was strong both in numbers and
in influence—especially in the great towns. A fine,
hardy, warlike race of men were the Pathan Rohillas,
and there were chiefs among them with unforgotten
hereditary claims and unextinguished hereditary rancours. It was well-nigh certain, therefore, that the bulk
of the Mahomedan population would cast in their lot
with the military rebels; that if the Rohillas did not,
as was probable, set the example of insurrection, they

* " I felt that I required help
from without, and I wrote to Mr.
Barnes, Commissioner of Umballah,
who did all he could ; and Mr. Plow-
den, Assistant-Commissioner of Umballah, then quartered at Jugadhree,
crossed the Jumna with a party of
the Fourth Light Cavalry, under
Captain Wyld, and a company of Infantry (Fifth Native), under Captain
Garsten. The appearance of the
troops was most opportune, and
confidence for a time restored."—
Mr. Spankie's Report.

would instigate the Sepoys to cast off their allegiance to the British Government, and strike for the restoration of the Mogul Empire.

Moradabad.   At Moradabad the main body of the Twenty-ninth* Sepoy Regiment was posted; and neither their own officers nor the chief civilians in the district showed any sign of want of confidence in them.   There was fortunately then at the station a high civil functionary of immense energy and courage, a man equal to any emergency and capable of any act of daring. Mr. Cracroft Wilson was Judge of Moradabad.   In that capacity he had no official control over executive details.   But he had large experience of that part of the country; he was highly respected by the Native inhabitants of all classes; and it was with no undue appreciation of his own influence and capacity for good that he applied to the Lieutenant-Governor to enlarge his powers.†   The application was promptly granted; and Wilson began his work with characteristic resolution and sagacity.   The Twenty-ninth was a regiment of good repute, and it was believed that by firm and judicious management it might be kept true to its allegiance.   When news of our disasters at Meerut came in, Wilson, with the consent of the military authorities, went into the Sepoy Lines and conversed freely with the Native officers and privates, telling them that their comrades had been misled by lying reports, and that to follow the noxious example of these misguided men would

* As another instance of the manner in which writers may be misled by following official documents, it may be stated that Mr. Dunlop, in his public reports, calls this regiment the Twenty-third.

† It should be observed that the Magistrate, Mr. C. B. Saunders, had been very recently appointed to Moradabad, and therefore was comparatively unacquainted with the district. He was an officer of the highest promise—since abundantly fulfilled by his attainment to some of the most important political offices under the Government of India.

be to bring ruin upon themselves. Again and again 1857.
he went among them with reassuring words. And it May—June.
seemed to him that the majority of the Sepoys were
by no means disposed to swerve from their allegiance,
although great efforts were being made by some disaffected Mahomedans in the town to induce them to
depart from it.* There was, however, a detachment
of a Native battery of Artillery, the gunners of which
showed from the first unmistakable signs of an inclination to revolt.

During the earlier weeks of May the men of the
Twenty-ninth continued to obey orders. There was
work for them to do, as disorder began to develop
itself in the district, in opening the roads which had
been closed by the Goojurs, and arresting any dangerous rebels whose designs had become apparent. And
for this work they seemed to exhibit no disinclination.
But a far greater trial awaited the Twenty-ninth.

* A Hindoo Government translator, who from his propensity to
quote Shakspeare may be assumed
to have been educated at one of our
Government colleges, has written an
amusing account of the Moradabad
insurrection, which contains the following passage : "An old pretender
was now seen going towards the
cantonments with a few Mussulman
followers to tamper with the Sepoys.
It was Newab Niamut-oollah Khan,
formerly in Government employ—
viz., Moonsiff of Nugeenah in the
time of Mr. Judge Okeden, and subsequently a political pensioner. The
hoary-headed traitor, emerging from
his house in Mohullah Newab-ponah,
began to assure the townsfolk that
he, being a descendant of a former
viceroy, would soon take possession
of Moradabad, and govern it in the
name of the King of Delhi with
justice and peace. In order to gain
over the mutinous Twenty-ninth
Native Infantry, he sent them a
large quantity of parched grain with
goor, to serve as breakfast for them.
He sent bread and other kinds of
food to the Mussulman Sepoys. The
Sepoys, after accepting his presents
and thanking him, ordered him to
leave the lines on pain of death.
The ungrateful beast, thus disappointed, returned to his house with
indignation and shame." The writer
adds, with a self-denying naïveté
significant of truth, "Although I
knew a great deal, but being an in-
significant official, whose task was
only to translate into English heavy
civil suits, was never asked on any
subject, nor in the presence of a
large number of cunning Mussulman
officers of great influence, I had the
pluck to reveal anything successfully. Thus the treason of Newab
Niamut-oollah Khan was suffered to
pass unnoticed and with impunity,
until he openly became a Ghazee,
and was shot at Delhi on the day of
assault."

The test was a hazardous one. The detachment of the Twentieth (the mutinous Meerut regiment) which had risen at Mozuffernuggur was coming down upon Moradabad. On the evening of the 18th, intelligence was received of their arrival at the Gangun Bridge. Upon this it was agreed that a party of Irregulars then starting on an expedition to clear the roads should be reinforced by a detachment of the Twenty-ninth. So Captain Faddy and Lieutenant Clifford, two excellent officers, got their men under arms, and accompanied by Mr. Wilson and other civilians, they started for the encampment of the mutineers. It was starlight when they reached their destination. What followed it is not easy accurately to describe. The Sowars, of whose fidelity there was little doubt, had been wisely placed in front, and the detachment of the Twenty-ninth in the rear. The former were spread out so as nearly to surround the mutineers of the Twentieth, who at that time were taking their rest. Their slumbers were soon broken; and they started up surprised and bewildered, and wondering what had come upon them. Then Cracroft Wilson saw that the time had come for the Twenty-ninth to act; so he called upon Captain Faddy to advance. Soon there was a scene of confusion, in the midst of which it was apparent that Faddy's Sepoys, if not against us, were not with us. Some eight or ten of the mutineers were seized, and one was shot dead by a Sowar. The men of the Twentieth were heavily laden with bags of rupees, of which our people made a capture. The fastening cords of one or two of these bags were loosed, and then there was a scramble for the rupees, which put an end to active operations against the insurgents. The prisoners and the coin were carried towards Meerut,

and the bulk of the detachment went back to Morad- 1857.
abad, bearing with them the body of the slain May—June.
mutineer.

On the following morning some of the mutineers
of the Twentieth, who had escaped from the onslaught
on the Gangun, believing that nothing but fraternity
would be found there, entered the Lines of Moradabad. But they had miscalculated the amount of
security to be found there. One was shot dead by a
Sikh Sepoy of the Twenty-ninth, and four were taken
alive.* By a fatal error, living and dead were sent
to the criminal Gaol.† If they had been placed under
a military guard, as was Wilson's desire, they might
have escaped, or they might have been released, but
they alone would have recovered their liberty. But
it happened that the man who had been killed was a
relative of one of the Sepoys of the Twenty-ninth,
who incited a number of his comrades to proceed
with him to the Gaol to rescue the military prisoners
and to carry off the body of the slain. Then the
Nujeebs of the Gaol-guard fraternised with them,
declaring that carriages had been prepared to convey
the prisoners to Meerut to be hanged. So the Gaol
was entered, the mutineers were released, and with
them went forth, cheering and shouting, all the
prisoners confined by order of our criminal courts,
to carry devastation with them.

When news of this event was brought to Wilson
by the European officers, he mounted his horse and
accompanied them towards the Gaol. The escaped
convicts were then streaming about in all directions,

* Baboo Gunesh Pershad says
they were taken "by the City Police."
  † The Native chronicler above-
quoted says, "By whom and under
whose permission Heaven only
knows!" Mr. Wilson says that
they were sent there by the Adjutant of the Twenty-ninth.

and it would have been madness to have gone un-supported among them. Remembering, then, that there was in the neighbourhood a party of the Cavalry of the Nawab of Rampore, he rode off towards them and claimed their assistance, but they met him only with insulting refusals. So he rode back to the Lines. Meanwhile, the Adjutant of the Twenty-ninth had mustered a number of well-affected Sepoys, and gone in pursuit of the fugitive prisoners. Learning this, Wilson endeavoured to raise another levy of the same kind, and with a little party of eight or ten Sepoys and a few Rampore Irregulars, he went forth to capture the gaol-birds. These joint efforts were most successful. "A hundred and fifty men were recaptured and lodged in gaol." Returning about an hour after mid-day to the town, he found there an ominous silence. The shops were closed; the streets were deserted. No food had been cooked that day in the Lines. It was evident that every one had been waiting and watching for what was to come next. Wilson looked the crisis in the face. His first effort was to endeavour to enlist some of the principal townspeople on the side of the British Government. But even those on whom he had most relied held back in the hour of his need. So he determined to address the soldiery in the Lines. The Sepoy is easily wrought upon by brave words, aided by a manly presence and a confident demeanour. The resolute courage which the Judge had evinced from the beginning, had made a great impression on the Native soldiery, and now once more it was to be tested. As he rode towards the Lines he passed in front of the Artillery. The Golundauze, whose treachery had been known from the first, laid their guns and lit their portfires. Wilson's clear blue eyes calmly confronted the murderous design. Without a sign of fear on his face, he rode towards the guns, not from them, and waved his hat as a challenge to the gunners. Abashed and overawed by the bearing of the intrepid Englishman they slunk back, and Wilson was saved. Then he went on, accompanied by some officers, to the Quarter-Guard, but not a man had turned out on parade. It seemed that they were held back by a vague suspicion of treachery; but what these few Europeans could have done against so many it is hard to say. Still it was wise to remove the groundless fear ; so ball-cartridges were served out to the men of the Twenty-ninth, and they were ordered to assemble with their arms. Thus reassured they were drawn up in a hollow square, and Wilson went into the midst of them and addressed them. He told them that they had committed a great crime in the morning, but that only a portion of the regiment had been implicated, and that it was not right that he and others who had grown grey in the service should be ruined by the excesses of a number of unruly boys ; but that if they would swear to behave loyally for the future, he would recommend the Governor-General to forgive them. The Native officers asked if he would swear on the Bible to fulfil what he promised. To this he readily consented; mutual oaths were taken, and confidence was restored for a time. The shops were opened. The streets were thronged. The English ladies, who in this critical conjuncture had been wisely concealed, came forth from their hiding-places. And every one felt as if a load had been taken from his mind.

Meanwhile there were great commotions in the district. Against the non-military insurgents the

Sepoys did their duty well. On the 20th, a party under Lieutenant Clifford, with a few horsemen, went out and captured eighty Goojurs; and on the following day, Cracroft Wilson, having learnt that a disaffected Moulavee had summoned from Rampore a large body of Mahomedans, who were to come down upon Moradabad, raising the green flag, and to plunder the town, went out with a company of the Twenty-ninth, commanded by Captain Faddy, taking some Sowars with him, and arrested their advance. Their leader was cut down,* and several others of their chief people were captured, whilst the rest sought safety in flight.

But another and a far more severe trial was now to be forced upon them. A few days afterwards, news came that the two companies of Sappers, who had been left at Roorkhee, had mutinied on learning how their comrades at Meerut had been treated. These two companies were now marching upon Moradabad. Nothing had made so deep an impression on the minds of the Sepoys in the North-West as the story of the destruction of the Sappers—the story as told, with many exaggerations, in the Lines and Bazaars. A belief was gaining ground that the English intended to deal with all the Native regiments after the same fashion; and the Twenty-ninth had been discussing the incident with no little excitement. It was impossible, therefore, to feel any confidence that

---

* Mr. Wilson, in his official report, thus relates this incident: "We crossed the river Ram-Gunja at the Bareilly Ghaut, and seeing a man dressed in green on foot, I advanced towards him. Whilst speaking to him I knocked up the pan of his blunderbuss. He put it down. I then laid hold of the muzzle and held it firmly, pointing upwards. The fellow then drew a pistol from his belt, when a Sepoy, by name Kalkae Singh, of the fifth company, who had followed me unperceived, knocked him down; and then the Darogah of the bridge of boats gave him two sword-cuts across the back of his neck."

they would now operate against their comrades. About noon the advancing body of Sappers was seen from the roof of the Court-House. Captain Whish immediately ordered out two hundred men and two nine-pounder guns, and the civilians, with Wilson at their head, got together all the horsemen they could muster and joined the force. They were soon in front of the advanced body of the mutineers. The Sowars went in among the insurgents, endeavouring to persuade them to lay down their arms. The guns were loaded with shrapnel, and the port-fires were lit. But the position of some of our own people (purposely, perhaps) delayed the order to fire; and, when after a time the obstacle was removed, the mutineers "flung down their carbines and ran into the arms of the men of the Twenty-ninth Regiment, which by this time had come to within two hundred yards of the scene from the southward." But what was to be done with the prisoners we had made? Past experience had made us but too well acquainted with the danger of taking them to Moradabad. So they were deprived of their arms and ammunition, their money, and nearly all their clothes, and thus stripped and beggared, were cast adrift upon the world. The majority of them fled to Bareilly.

After this there was an outward appearance of order and discipline in the Lines; but in the surrounding districts there was an almost general defiance of law, and the Sepoys found employment in repeated expeditions to suppress these local disturbances. The Goojurs, the Mehwattees, and others took advantage of the opportunity, and improved the occasion, to the terror of the more peaceful inhabitants, whilst many of the more wealthy inhabitants of the city, though outwardly professing their loyalty

1857.
May—June.

to Government, secretly intrigued with the Sepoys, and told them that the British Raj was for ever overthrown. So the men of the Twenty-ninth waited and watched, and asked each other, "What news from Bareilly?"

June 1.
News from
Bareilly.

The month of June dawned ominously upon the little body of brave-hearted Englishmen at Moradabad. Ever since the commencement of our troubles their thoughts had turned anxiously towards Bareilly —the head-quarters of the division—where was a large force of Native troops surrounded by a hostile population. Of these several conditions I shall speak presently, when I come to write of what happened there. Here it need only be said that upon the movements of the Bareilly Brigade depended the safety of Moradabad; and now, on the 1st of June, the first sign of danger in that direction was given by the interruption of postal communication, which, up to that time, had been unintermittent. On that Monday morning no letters came from Bareilly; and there were rumours, both in the Lines and in the public offices, that the brigade had risen. Two hours after midnight, Wilson was roused from his sleep by the arrival of a messenger from the Nawab of Rampore, informing him that there had been mutiny and massacre at Bareilly, and urging him at once to seek safety in flight. To this the English officer demurred, saying that honour forbade such a course. There was no more sleep for him that morning. He rose, and went to the Adjutant of the Twenty-ninth, and at dawn the chief European and Native officers were assembled. Then Wilson stated unreservedly the information he had received, and explained that the only honourable course left for them was "to hold the district until the Bareilly

Brigade came to a distance of twenty miles of them, and that then they should march to Meerut with colours flying, taking guns and treasure with them." To this the Native officers consented, well knowing that the project was one which would never go further than the language in which it was spoken. Our people went to the Lines accompanied by the Native officers, and Wilson's brave words were "met with derision." They believed that to lead them to Meerut would be to take them to their doom, and one man openly reviled Wilson for conceiving this murderous design. Wilson told the man that he lied, which was true, and that he knew it, which perhaps was not true; but all felt that now the game was up at Moradabad, and that there was nothing left for our Christian people but to gird up their loins for flight.

It was a sore trial, but what else could be done? The townspeople were arrayed against us as virulently as the soldiery, and some influential noblemen in the neighbourhood were endeavouring to foment rebellion, and eagerly watching the progress of events in the hope of profiting largely by our discomfiture. There were two Nawabs, said to be men of ruined fortune, men who had been crushed by the padded feet of the English despotism, who now appeared on the scene with rival claims, each hoping to obtain supremacy, on our expulsion, as Governor of Moradabad under the Emperor. Their influence over the townspeople was far greater than that which they exercised over the soldiery, for the Sepoys, thinking that they might lose a portion of the perquisites of rebellion, resented the interference of these pretenders. Still, there was the dispiriting fact that we had no friends on our side, and that it was vain for

1857.
June.
us to contend against such multiplied antagonism. One of the Nawabs, eager to make a short cut to the desired supremacy at Moradabad, recommended the immediate execution of Wilson Sahib as "a great deed, equal to the destruction of half the Europeans in the Presidency of Bengal."* It was plain that from either quarter death might come suddenly; so, as the destruction of the English would have been great gain to the enemy, they came to the resolution above recorded, and prepared promptly for retreat.

But what was to become of the treasure? Virtually it was already lost to us. To carry it off to Meerut was impossible with the resources at our command. The only question was whether it were better to abandon it altogether, to be scrambled for by the soldiery and the townspeople, or to make it over quietly to the former. After some consultation, it was determined that it would be better to remove it from the Treasury, and to place the money-bags in tumbrils, under the Treasury-guard (which was in effect to surrender it to the Sepoys), as such a course "would remove all temptation to the Budmashes of the city to come out and join in the disturbance." So Wilson went to the Treasury with Charles Saunders, the Collector and Magistrate, and after

* The story, as told by the Native writer quoted above, is too characteristic and too amusing not to be recorded here. "The first Thakoor further proposed that it was the wish of his master that Mr. Wilson should be killed, because by killing such a great man and cunning officer, who possessed magic in his words, they would achieve a great deed, equal to the destruction of half the number of Europeans in the Presidency of Bengal. Such was the dread entertained by that villain or our old Mr. Wilson. I could not check myself, so, calling myself a Brahmin, I addressed the artillery-men in their own language, which I can speak very fluently, and used all the artful arguments of a Brahmin, and cited several Sanskrit verses on the impropriety and unrighteousness of the proposal of Abbas Ali. I openly told the artillerymen that Abbas Ali was a mere mean pretender. The Thakoor, being a rustic clown, was quite bewildered, and the artillerymen seemed pleased with my arguments, founded on the doctrines of the *Shasturs*."

some difficulty in forcing the locks, for one of the
keys was missing,* they proceeded to empty out its
contents. Whilst Wilson was handing out the bags,
Saunders was secretly destroying the stamped paper.
It was a service of no little danger, for the Sepoys
were hungry and impatient, excited and malignant,
and the amount of coin in the Treasury was found
to be less than they had expected. In this moment
of disappointment and exasperation, they would have
blown the Treasurer from a gun and shot down the
English civilians. Captain Faddy saved the former,
and the intervention of some faithful Native officers
rescued Wilson and Saunders from death.† There
was now nothing left to them but to trust for safety
to the horses on which they rode. So they made
their way to the house in which they had resided
since the commencement of the disturbances, and
made their arrangements for a retreat to Meerut.
There were four civilians, including the Civil Surgeon, with their wives. An escort of Irregular Cavalry—mostly leave-men—was ready; and so they

* The second key is always kept
by the Native Treasurer, who, in
this case, not without reason, was
slow to appear on the scene.

† Mr. Wilson's striking account
of this incident should be given in
his own words : " When all the
treasure was placed on the tumbrils,
the Collector, myself, and the (Native) Treasurer, came out into the
eastern verandah, and then began
murmurs as to the amount of treasure. The artillerymen forcibly
carried off the Treasurer towards
the guns, and were in the act of tying
him to one of them, when Captain
Faddy, who is deservedly a favourite
with his men, rescued him. By this
time the Collector and myself had
mounted our horses, when four
young Sepoys of the Treasury-guard
levelled their muskets at us. At
this instant Bohwanee Singh, Soubahdar, and Baldeo Singh, pay-Ha-
vildar of the grenadier company,
stepped between the muskets and
our persons and the former raising
his hand said, in an authoritative
tone, ' What ! do you wish to see
the flesh rot from your bones ? Did
you not take a most solemn oath not
to hurt a hair of their heads, and are
you now firing at them ?' The
muskets were lowered, and the Collector and myself rode off." It
should be mentioned, with respect to
the rescue of the Treasurer, that Mr.
Saunders, in his report, says : " I
succeeded in rescuing him from the
awkward position in which he was
placed."

made good, without accident, their way to the great military station.*

It had been Mr. Wilson's intention that the officers of the regiment should accompany him to Meerut, and due notice was given to them, but they went off to Nynee-Tal. The distance was shorter, the road was less perilous, and the place itself was more attractive. Thither, therefore, with their wives and children, they bent their way. But the Government clerks were not equally alert nor equally wise. At Moradabad was the usual staff of subordinate officials. Men of this kind—many of them Eurasians—strike deeper root in the local soil than Englishmen, soldiers or civilians, who are subject to more frequent changes of residence. The covenanted servant in the Mofussil is a bird of passage, and always ready for flight. The uncovenanted servant is, more or less, a fixture. He has manifold encumbrances and associations which bind him to the spot. He has relatives and connexions, a little house property and other belongings—the savings of a life—which he is unwilling to abandon, and so he commonly clings to his home to the last. So it had been, and so it was to be in other places. And so it was at Moradabad. When the military officers and the covenanted civilians started for Nynee-Tal and Meerut, the uncovenanted officials thought of their Penates, and were unwilling to gird up their loins for flight. Perhaps they conceived that the fury of the enemy was less likely to descend upon them than upon Christian men of higher degree, or of purer European blood. But it would have been well for them if they had betaken themselves to flight. For some, after a feeble defence

---

* The escort consisted of a Jemadar's party of the Eighth Irregulars from Bareilly, some twenty leave-men, and a few Sowars attached to the Magistrate of Moradabad.

in the house of an invalid officer named Warwick,* were killed whilst attempting to escape ; and others, after outwardly apostatising to Mahomedanism, were carried off captives to Delhi, where some of them, at least, were killed (it is believed, by our own people), at the capture of that fortress.

Bareilly was the chief city of Rohilkund. It was the Head-Quarters of the Civil Establishment—the Head-Quarters of the Military Brigade. It was a busy, stirring place, with no absence of the hum of peaceful industry among the people, though the germs of popular commotion were ever alive within them. The traders were principally Hindoos ; the dangerous classes were mostly Mahomedans. The conditions of which I have spoken, in reference to the general state of the province of Rohilkund, were peculiarly observable at the capital. A formidable insurrection had occurred there in 1816, when Mahomedans from different parts of the district—mostly Pathan Rohillas—had arrayed themselves against us, and it had been no easy work to subdue them. "Taxes" were the cause of this popular rising; but there were no military discontents at that time, and the soldiery were with us. But now, forty years afterwards, the English dreaded that dangerous combination which left a handful of European officers at the mercy of thousands of the people. For no Euro-

---

* Lieutenant Warwick was the only white man in the party. He had married a Native Christian woman, whose influence prevailed to induce him to remain. Being of a very unwieldy figure, and unable to run, he was soon overtaken and cut down. His wife, seeing what had befallen, turned back, and asked the murderer to deal with her in the same manner, and "she instantly fell a corpse at his feet."—*Narrative of Mr. Cracroft Wilson.* ·

pean troops were stationed at Bareilly. The warnings of 1816 had been utterly disregarded.*

In the hot weather of 1857, the troops stationed at Bareilly consisted of the Eighteenth and Sixty-eighth Regiments of Native Infantry, the Eighth Regiment of Irregular Cavalry, and a Native battery of Artillery. Brigadier Sibbald commanded the brigade. But at the first outburst of the mutiny in Upper India he was absent on inspection duty at Almorah, and Colonel Colin Troup, who had served in Afghanistan, and had been one of the British captives there, was then in charge of the station. There was a large cluster of civilians. Mr. Robert Alexander was Commissioner of Bareilly. Mr. David Robertson and Mr. George Davy Raikes were the Judges. Mr. James Guthrie was the Magistrate. There were many others of less rank employed in the Government service; and a considerable number of European or Eurasian merchants and traders. Altogether there were nearly a hundred Christians, exclusive of women and children.

State of the troops in May.

When the news of the risings at Meerut and Delhi first arrived at Bareilly, the temper of the troops appeared to be encouraging. Especial confidence was reposed in the Irregular Cavalry, who were believed to be true as the steel of their own sabres—so true, indeed, that their Commandant had been empowered to increase their numerical strength—and yet they had been largely recruited from among the Pathans

---

* It is curious to read the following in Hamilton's Gazetteer: "After the insurrection of 1816, Government thought it advisable to erect a small regular citadel on the plain to the south of the town, for the eventual protection of the European inhabitants should any similar commotion again occur. It is of a quadrangular form, has a good ditch, and two bastions projecting from opposite angles, an arrangement which gives the whole rather an odd appearance; but it is quite of sufficient strength for the object contemplated."

of Rohilkund and Delhi. As time advanced, even the Poorbeah regiments, though their demeanour differed from what it had been, were conceived to be rather timorous than malignant—agitated by vague fears, resulting from evil reports of the impending vengeance of the English. If assuring promises could be made to them—if they could be induced to believe that all who had not yet committed themselves would meet, not with punishment, but with favour from Government, all might yet go well. And it was in this conviction that Colonel Troup, with the concurrence of Brigadier Sibbald, addressed to Mr. Colvin the letter quoted in the last chapter.*

Meanwhile, in the city and in the surrounding districts there was visible excitement. The great idea of the "something coming" permeated all strata of society. All kinds of rumours were flying about, disturbing and irritating the public mind, and rendering men ripe for rebellion. On the 20th the Commissioner wrote to the Lieutenant-Governor, saying : "Things here are as uncertain as ever. This statement, as far as the military are concerned, is made on the authority of Colonel Troup. The Brigadier has come in to-day; he is old and ill, and has not the character or intelligence of the Colonel. The city is quiet; but on the *qui vive* at every rumour. The Kotwal behaving excellently. In the Gaol yesterday, a Jemadar was murdered by one of the prisoners. The intelligence of this has caused much sensation throughout the town—some people considering it as the prelude to an outbreak. . . . This morning Native officers have told Colonel Troup that it is believed that the prisoners in this Gaol have been

* *Ante,* page 230.

1857.
May.

beaten and kept without food for five days, and they say that they must go in and see them. The tale is but a pretext—but of course we are in the power of the men, if in a body they go to the Gaol. I have made a proposal that I should address them, giving them my word and my personal security—*i.e.* my person at their mercy, if a single man of their comrades is now in the Gaol. There is no question but that we must refrain from imprisoning the mutineers."*

May 21.

On the following day a general parade was held, and Brigadier Sibbald harangued the troops. He spoke of the uneasy feeling that had recently pervaded all ranks of the Native Army—of the discontent too plainly manifested by their demeanour; but he added that he looked upon all this as the result of their erroneous apprehensions, and that if they would resume the cheerful performance of their duty, the past would be forgiven to them, and the good old relations of mutual confidence would be thoroughly restored. Commissioner Alexander afterwards addressed the Native officers in front of the troops. He told them that they had been led astray by a great delusion, that the intentions of Government towards them were what they had ever been, and he besought them to dismiss from their minds all feelings of distrust and alarm. After this the Brigadier reported

May 23.

to Government that the troops were in a more happy and cheerful state, and, in their own words, had "commenced a new life." He asked for a formal assurance from the Lieutenant-Governor that the promises made to the troops would be confirmed. And he added, "were the men under my command

---

* MS. Correspondence. The wisdom of this is sufficiently proved by what took place at Moradabad—as above recorded—and, indeed, by previous events at Meerut,

fully convinced that the past would be forgotten, I
feel convinced that their loyalty and good conduct
may be relied upon." The Lieutenant-Governor lost
no time in sending the required assurances. The
Brigadier was authorised to inform the troops that
"nothing that had happened since the commencement of the recent agitation had at all shaken the
solid confidence of the Lieutenant-Governor in their
fidelity and good conduct." This was written on the
30th of May. Before the letter could reach Bareilly
the whole of the Native troops there had revolted,
and there was not a living European in the place.

For some days after this general parade there was
quietude in the Lines. On the 29th, a crisis was
imminent. Some men of the two Infantry regiments,
whilst taking their morning bath in the river, had
been overheard conversing about the massacre of the
English, which they had sworn to perpetrate at mid-
day. So the Irregular Cavalry were got under arms.
The cheerfulness and alacrity with which they obeyed,
with a full knowledge of the occasion, seemed to indicate that they would be true to the death. The day
passed without a rising in the Lines; but it was not
an uneventful one. A swarm of mutineers from the
Forty-fifth at Ferozepore appeared at Bareilly, scattering about terrifying rumours. Their comrades,
already prepared to believe that the English were
about to destroy them, grasped with ready credulity
the story now told by the refugees, that there was a
large body of Europeans—Horse, Foot, and Artillery—collected in the neighbourhood to crush the
Native Brigade. After this there was the wildest
excitement in the Lines—the intensest anxiety in the
bungalows of the British. The thoughts of all our
people turned with painful doubt to the attitude of

1857.
May.

May 29.

1857.
May.

the Irregular Horse, from whom alone could come the means of deliverance. The hope once entertained of their active succour was now passing away ; but it was believed that they would remain neutral, let the Infantry do what they might. There were some, indeed, who still cherished the belief that the regiments would not rise. But it was well to be prepared for the worst. So it was agreed that on the first sound of mutiny or rebellion, the English should hasten to the Cavalry Lines and there concert measures for their safety. An influential Mahomedan gentleman, of whom more will be presently narrated, had told Commissioner Alexander that the Sepoys had determined to revolt, and that there was nothing left for him but to " look out for his life." And, indeed, there was nothing else.

May 31.
Revolt of
the troops.

But the 30th of May passed, as its predecessor had passed, without any active demonstrations. And even on the morning of the 31st—the morning of that Sunday, which, it was said, and by many believed, had been fixed upon as the day of simultaneous rising against the white men in all our garrisons and cantonments—some of our chief military officers could not bring themselves to think that their regiments would turn against them. At nine o'clock the delusion prevailed. At eleven there was a sound of firing from the Artillery Lines. It was a signal for general action. The game commenced in the usual way. Parties of Sepoys of the Sixty-eighth went out to fire at the English bungalows. Their first object was to ignite the thatch of our houses. In that dry season of the year the work of incendiarism was easy. Fire and smoke soon rose from the burning straw. A strong, hot wind added fury to the flames, and the work of destruction was accomplished. Then they

turned their thoughts towards the destruction of
human life; and wheresoever they could meet a
white man, they shot him down with a yell of
triumph. Brigadier Sibbald, on the first sound of
firing, had mounted his horse, and ridden for the
appointed place of rendezvous attended by two
mounted orderlies. A party of Sepoys met him, and
he rode on with a bullet in his body. He is said to
have sat his horse till he reached the Cavalry Lines,
and then to have fallen lifeless from the saddle.*

The chief command then passed, by virtue of
seniority, into the hands of Colonel Troup. An abler
and a braver officer there was not in the service; but
what could he do in such an emergency as this? He
had gone down on foot to the appointed place of
assemblage, which was near to his own house, and
there he found the Commissioner and several other
officers, civil and military, congregated beneath a
camel-shed. Up to this time it was known only that
the Sixty-eighth and the Artillery had revolted. The
Eighteenth seem to have hesitated all through the
morning; and the Cavalry were making a show of
loyalty. The Commandant and Adjutant of the
Eighteenth, with some other officers, had gone down
to the Lines, and found the men in their normal
state of hot weather inactivity—neither armed nor
accoutred; and though apparently in a state of excitement, by no means bent upon mischief. They
were perplexed and bewildered, and did not know
what to do. Whilst they professed loyalty to the
Government and fidelity to their officers, they were
slow in obeying orders to fall in—little better than

---

* Some accounts state that he
was shot by one of his own orderlies.
But it is said also that he was
"shot through the chest." If he
had been shot by one of his orderlies
the presumption is that he would
have been shot through the back.

" a rabble professing devotion and sorrow,"* but with their hearts in the rebel cause. Meanwhile, the Cavalry were being put to the test. The officers assembled in their Lines had determined to retreat to Nynee-Tal. At first it seemed that the troopers would accompany them. They were mounted and drawn up on parade, and Troup called upon them to follow him. They had scarcely moved off, when Mackenzie represented that his troopers were eager to have " a crack at the mutineers." Troup, though doubtful of the expediency of such an attempt, consented, and the word was given. But the trial was too much for them. There was a fine open space before them, and a charge of cavalry would have been irresistible. But when they fronted the Sixty-eighth they saw the green standard of Mahomedanism, and it was seen at once that the game was up with the English. Whether a sudden impulse seized the troopers, or whether the movement was a preconcerted one, may never be known; but the Eighth Regiment of Irregular Horse forsook their English leaders, and drew up beside the mutineers. A few only found faithful in this emergency prepared to accompany the English in their flight. They were principally Native officers. Their conduct was above all praise. For they left their families and property behind them to succour the English gentlemen.

This important combination having been formed, the insurgent force determined that there should be no defaulters in the great hour of their triumph; and so they turned their guns upon the Eighteenth, which up to this time had been kept together by their officers, threatening to blow them to pieces if they did not join the national standard. Already

* See Captain Gowan's Narrative.

ripe for rebellion and eager for a share of the spoil,
they fell in with the mutineers. The whole brigade
had now revolted. There was no hope any longer
for the officers whom they had deserted. So Major
Patterson, Captain Gowan, and others, who had remained at their posts to the last, and who, on the
first outbreak of the Eighteenth had been concealed
by the men of their regiment, escaped into the country to endure great privations, and, in some cases,
eventually to suffer death. It would have been well
for them if their corps had revolted in the first instance with the other regiments, for then they would
have escaped to Nynee-Tal. But it happened that
Major Pearson, with four other officers, were killed
by the villagers of Ram-Puttee, whilst Captain
Gowan and some others, after months of distressing
concealment, were rescued by the heroic exertions of
Mr. Cracroft Wilson, of Moradabad.

The fate of the civilians was of the same chequered
kind. Some were killed—some escaped. Mr. Alexander, the Commissioner, who had been driven to his
bed by a severe spasmodic affection, was with difficulty removed from his house in a buggy, but after
awhile the emergency of the occasion compelled him
to mount a horse, and he reached the Cavalry Lines
in safety, eventually to escape to Nynee-Tal. Mr.
Guthrie, the Collector and Magistrate, also escaped.
The Judges, Mr. D. Robertson and Mr. G. D. Raikes,
were both killed. The former, with Dr. Hay and
Mr. Orr, took refuge in the house of the Moonsiff,
who promised to protect them, but they were both
murdered; whilst the latter, accompanied by Dr.
Buck, Principal of the College, was, by previous
arrangement, sheltered in the house of one Aman Ali
Khan, a Mahomedan gentleman of Bareilly. They

1857.
May 31.

Murder of
civilians.

were tracked and put to death by the connivance of a nephew of their host.* The Joint-Magistrates, Mr. Parley and Mr. Currie, escaped. Equally fortunate was Mr. Poynder, the Chaplain. Altogether nine members of the higher class of civilians, with several of the subordinate establishments, were slain. Many merchants and traders, with their wives and children, were massacred at the same time. It need not be added that, attending these murders, was the usual amount of plunder and devastation. The Treasury was emptied; the houses of the Europeans were sacked and burnt; and the Gaol, after a gallant defence by the officer in charge, who paid the penalty of his devotion, as will presently be narrated, was emptied of its criminal inhabitants. In these orgies the people of Bareilly were in nowise behind the military mutineers. The greater number of murders were committed by the former. The dominion of the English was at an end.

There were rival claimants to the Viceroyalty of Rohilkund. Both were of the old stock of Rohilla-Pathans—descendants of those hardy semi-Afghan tribes, against whom Warren Hastings sent our trained soldiery at the infamous bidding of the Wuzeer of Oude. One of these pretenders was Khan Behaudur Khan; the other was named Mobarik Shah. The latter was a man of good family and local influence, and personally possessed of some energy of character. But the former, though older and weaker, had superior claims upon the suffrages of the people, for he was a descendant of that Hafiz Rehmut Khan, who had been the first Pathan ruler

---

* The story of the English Judges at Bareilly having been subjected to a formal trial and deliberately hanged before Khan Behaudur Khan, seems to be a pure fiction.

of Bareilly, and who had fallen in battle killed by a round shot from an English gun.* He had, therefore, all the strength of old historical traditions on his side. That most iniquitous passage of our Anglo-Indian history, to which I have above referred, had never been forgotten in Rohilkund. Generation after generation may pass away, but the memory of blood feuds of this kind is not obliterated by after-years of peace and friendship and honest dealing. So these men came to the front, hating the English, and all the Mahomedans of Bareilly were ready to become their followers. Mobarik Shah, when he heard the firing that indicated the revolt of the soldiery, started at once for the Kotwali to proclaim himself Viceroy; but Khan Behaudur Khan had anticipated him, and it was plain that the majority of people had accepted him as their chief. So Mobarik Shah, with outward observance of friendship, but with enmity in his heart, joined the party of his rival, who was formally proclaimed.

The first act of the new Mahomedan ruler was to doom to death all the Christian people who had not already perished. This cruel decree had already been so prodigally anticipated by the unauthorised barbarity of lesser men, that there were not many victims to be dragged forth from their hiding-places and to be ruthlessly massacred before the eyes of the old Viceroy. The first to be brought to the shambles

1857.
May 31.

Massacre of Christians.

---

* I have taken this from an official report before me, but if the following passage of Bishop Heber's Journal contain the historical truth, the Rohilla chief must have been killed either by grape-shot or musket-balls. "When his nobles, at the head of their respective clans, either treacherous or timid, gave way, he remained almost alone on a rising ground in the heat of the fire, conspicuous by his splendid dress and his beautiful horse, waving his hand and vainly endeavouring to bring his army back to another charge, till, seeing that all was lost, he waved his hand once more, gave a shout, and galloped on the English bayonets. He fell *shot through and through.*"

were the family of Mr. Aspinall, a merchant. His two children were murdered in the presence of their parents, who were then put to death. To give further effect to this ghastly spectacle, the naked corpses of Englishmen slain in the first outburst of rebellion, having been dragged through the town, were brought into the presence and cast at the foot of the viceregal standard. Next day, Mr. Hansborough, the Superintendent of the Gaol, who had manfully defended himself throughout the whole of Sunday, was captured, and brought before Khan Behaudur Khan. Overcome, but not overawed, the gallant Englishman defied the new ruler, telling him and his followers, in a loud voice, that they might kill him and others, but that they would never destroy the British Government. He was presently cut to pieces. Some others of less note shared the same fate; but the old Rohilla was sorely grieved that there were so few victims for his knife.

Thus the English were in our expressive Anglo-Indian jargon *saf-kar'd*, or cleaned away. After a day or two there was no trace of them or their authority left. So Khan Behaudur Khan began at once to set his house in order—to organise his new Government. He had already made proclamation of his assumption of authority. He had paraded the streets of Bareilly on an elephant, with a number of followers, with bands and banners and other properties and paraphernalia of mock-royalty. And now he began to address himself to the establishment of an administration. The various posts in 'the Soubah were distributed. Justice was administered, and revenue was collected in the name of the Emperor. It was sound policy to utilise as much as possible of the old agency, and as there were few of our Native officers

who were not willing to take the rupees of the
restored Mahomedan Government, it was expected
that business would go on very much in the old
groove. But in this he was disappointed. The turbulent spirit which had been raised did not readily
subside. Disorder and violence were rampant everywhere; men rose against each other as ruthlessly as
before they had risen against the white men, and
were quite as unscrupulous in robbery and murder.

The main source of trouble, at the outset, to Behaudur Khan was the presence of the Sepoy Brigade.
The Viceroy was afraid of the soldiery. They had
shown no disposition, at the beginning of the rebellion, to fraternise with his political party. Their continuance at Bareilly would have been a source of
danger to the new Government. The Native Brigadier
was named Bukht Khan—a name afterwards distinguished in the annals of the war—and he had been
disposed to favour the pretences of Mobarik Shah
rather than those of his more successful rival. The
defeated candidate, however, had not given up the
game. He might obtain from the Emperor that which
he could not secure for himself. So he again opened
communications with Brigadier-General Bukht Khan,
persuaded him to march the troops to Delhi, and
having made a show of accompanying them, sent a
memorial to the Emperor by the hands of his friend,
petitioning His Majesty to appoint him Viceroy of
Rohilkund; and then he returned to Bareilly.

Whilst these terrible scenes were being enacted at
Bareilly, on that Sunday morning, there was a tragedy
in some respects even more painful, though more
limited in extent, going on at Shahjehanpore, which

lies at a distance of some forty-seven miles from the chief station, and had once been but little behind it in importance. Here was posted the Twenty-eighth Sepoy Regiment, commanded by Captain James. Mr. Mordaunt Ricketts* was the Magistrate and Collector. Mr. Charles Jenkins was his Assistant. There was the usual staff of subordinate Government officials, and a few Europeans or Eurasians engaged in the pursuits of mercantile life. There was not, with the exception of the commissioned and non-commissioned officers of the Native regiment, a single English soldier in the place.

When intelligence of the events which had occurred at Meerut and at Delhi first reached Shahjehanpore, there were great excitement and commotion in the city. The English dreaded a rising of the towns-people, but looked with confidence towards the sol-diery. It was rumoured—and the Sepoys carried the story to their officers—that, at the time of the Eed Festival, the citizens purposed to rise and to sack the Treasury. So it was determined that the station-guards should be increased, and that the sentries should be doubled. But this, which was intended as a compliment, was regarded as a penalty. Instead of pleasing the Sepoys, by thus manifesting the confidence that was placed in them, it excited their indignation. Vague fears and suspicions had taken possession of their minds. Some associated these extra duties with the greased cartridges; some thought it was a pretext only for keeping them away from the " méla " or great fair, which was being held

* I may avail myself of the men-tion of Mr. Mordaunt Ricketts's name in this place, to call attention to a clerical error in a note at page 511 of my second volume—where Mr. George Henry Ricketts, De- puty-Commissioner of Loodhianah, is described as Mr. M. Ricketts. The passage is a literal quotation from the "Punjab Mutiny Report," where the error occurred.

in the neighbourhood. And, viewed in this light, it was an outrage on their feelings, for it indicated want of confidence in the Sepoys. On the following day the order for the extra-guards was cancelled; but, although the officers of the Twenty-eighth believed that the bulk of the regiment would remain faithful, the Sepoys, as the month wore on to its close, were waxing every day more rebellious in their hearts, and ever and anon muttering sedition not to be misunderstood.

It was only a question of time—and the time soon came. On Sunday, the 31st of May, the troops rose. Many of our people were in church, for it was the hour of morning service, when the revolt commenced. It was the old story over again with scarcely a variation. The bungalows of the English were plundered and burnt. The Treasury was sacked. The Gaol was opened. The prisoners were released. The townspeople made common cause with the mutineers; and the surrounding villagers broke out into rebellion. An English factory, where sugar was refined and rum distilled, was attacked and devastated by the villagers. And, ere night had closed in upon the scene, new Native rulers had been formally proclaimed, and the dominion of the white man was at an end.

The fate of the English residents at Shahjehanpore has now to be recorded. The murder of our people was not a conspicuous feature in the programme of the mutineers of the Twenty-eighth. If the compact had been to destroy the English, root and branch, on that Sunday morning whilst engaged in the offices of their religion, it was very imperfectly fulfilled. A party of mutineers made for the Christian church; but it was to be counted only by units. Armed with swords and clubs, they rushed in, yelling. Mordaunt Ricketts was slashed by a Sepoy, but he carried his wound to the outer vestry-door, there to be cut down and slain.* A clerk in the Magistrate's office, named Le Maistre, was killed in this first onslaught. No other member of the congregation stained with his blood the floor of the Christian temple. But the agony of the women was great. These six or seven assassins might be the precursors of hundreds of remorseless insurgents from the Lines and from the city, all thirsting for Christian blood. Was it better, then, to endeavour to escape from the church, or to close the doors and prevent further ingress of the assailants? The Chaplain endeavoured to escape; but he was wounded as he left the church, and was afterwards killed by some villagers, together with a clerk named Smith, at a little distance from Shahjehanpore. After this the doors of the church were closed, and the shuddering women were removed to the Tower, where they abided in safety for a time.

Meanwhile, in the Cantonment, the Sepoys were in a state of wild excitement. But, as often happened, there was division amongst them. Captain James was shot on parade whilst endeavouring to pacify his men. Dr. Bowling, who, returning from his morning visit to the hospital, had found the regiment in rebellion, placed his wife and child and an European female servant in his carriage, and mounting the box beside the coachman, had made for the church. As they went a party of Sepoys fired at them, and Bowling fell dead from the box. Another bullet wounded his wife; but she escaped to reach the

* According to one account, " Mr. Ricketts was pursued and murdered in his own verandah." Mr. Jenkins says: " I saw Mr. Ricketts's body about thirty-five yards from the church vestry-door."

church, where other fugitives were assembling; and their Native servants, true to their salt, were bringing guns and pistols to their masters. If, at this time, there had been united action among the Sepoys, not one of our people could have escaped. But it happened that a party, scarcely less than a hundred strong,* rallied round our officers, and thus the Christian fugitives were saved. With this safeguard, those within and those without the church gathered themselves together and took counsel as to the means of escape. Mr. Jenkins recommended that they should make for Pohwaine beyond the Oude border, where it was believed that the Rajah of that place would shelter them. As by this time several horses and a carriage or two were assembled in the church-compound, the flight was not difficult. So they went. But the Pohwaine man declared his inability to protect them, and they went on to Mohumdee, one of our outstations in Oude. What afterwards befell them may be narrated in another chapter of this history. The tragedy of Shahjehanpore had not yet been acted out.

1857.
May 31.

There was another civil station in Rohilkund— Budaon—some thirty miles from Bareilly. The Magistrate and Collector was Mr. William Edwards, who had been for some years attached to the Secretariat, and had been personally familiar with the stirring events of the Governments of Lord Ellenborough and Lord Hardinge. There were few abler and few better men in the service. He had sat at the feet of Thomas Campbell Robertson, and had learnt from him lessons, the wisdom of which was now too miserably apparent.

Budaon.

* I believe that these were principally Sikhs.

He saw all around him proofs of the errors that had been committed by the new school of civil administrators. The country about him was rising against the British Government, and he had none to help him in the hour of his need.* He stood quite alone. He had not an English friend or comrade near him. There was one great consolation, however, in the thought that, foreseeing the danger to come, he had sent his wife and child to the safety of Nynee-Tal, though he might never see them again.

On the 25th (it was the time of the Eed Festival) it was reported to the Magistrate that there was to be a Mahomedan rising in the town at an appointed hour. So he invited to his house the chief Mussulmans of the place, and there taking counsel with them on the public safety, detained them until the hour was passed. Many of them were fierce and insolent, and all excited. The meeting was a noisy and tumultuous one; but the people calmed down after a time, and the day passed over without an outbreak. There was but one European gentleman to confront all this Mahomedan fury—a single white-faced Christian, a prayerful, God-fearing man, esteemed to be rather a Christian of Christians, with Native converts clustering around him as he ministered to them in his own house. But he was known

---

* "To the large number of these sales" (sales of estates by decrees of our Civil Courts) "during the past twelve or fifteen years, and the operation of our revenue system, which has had the result of destroying the gentry of the country and breaking up of the village communities, I attribute solely the disorganisation of this and the neighbouring districts. . . . The ancient landed proprietary body of the Budaon district were still in existence, but in the position of tenants, not proprietors. None of the men who had succeeded them as landowners were possessed of sufficient influence or power to give me any aid in maintaining the public tranquillity. . . . On the other hand, those who really could control the vast masses of the rural population were interested in bringing about a state of disturbance and general anarchy."—*Edwards's Personal Narrative.*

also to be a just man, tolerant and compassionate; and he had lifted up his voice fearlessly against the wrongs which had been done by our own Government, and injured himself by his plain-speaking. It might have been a consideration of this fact that saved William Edwards in that hour of danger; or it might have been that some sentiments of chivalry restrained them when they thought of the utter helplessness of that single white man among so many; but that day and the next day passed, and still the solitary Englishman sat and prayed, knowing that he could do nothing unaided, and fearing that no succour would ever come to him from a distance. He had a guard of Sepoys, consisting of about a hundred men of the Sixty-eighth from Bareilly, and these he was beginning to mistrust, for they had cast a covetous eye on the Treasury; and he had little more confidence in the Nujeebs of the Police. He knew that at a signal from the Suddur station the anticipated revolt would at once commence.

But on the third day, as he sat at his lonely dinner, he saw an Englishman ride up towards his house, escorted by a dozen horsemen; and presently he discerned the familiar features of his cousin, Alfred Phillips, the Magistrate of Etah.* He was the bearer of evil tidings; but still it was a joyous meeting—to Edwards most joyous, after those long dreary days of complete isolation. Etah is in the Agra Division of the North-Western Provinces, nearly opposite to Budaon on the other side of the Ganges. The district had risen. In Mr. Colvin's expressive language, it was in "a blaze of riot and ravage,"† and now the

1857.
May.

May 27.

Etah.

---

* Mr. Phillips in his official report says that he did not reach Budaon till the 29th.   † *Ante*, p. 245. The "riot and ravage" were increasing every day.

Magistrate was on his way to Bareilly to ask for military aid. The cry was for more Sepoys to help them against popular insurrections. The little party of the Ninth Regiment, the head-quarters of which were in rebellion at Aligurh and Etawah, with detachments in the same state at Mynpooree, had quietly joined their comrades; and Phillips, thus deserted, with only a few Sowars at his back, had crossed the river in the hopeless errand of obtaining reinforcements from Rohilkund, and passing through a dangerous country, not without risk of his life, had thus joined his cousin at Budaon.* Edwards told him that there was small hope of assistance from Bareilly, as he had himself applied for it in vain. But when it was known to him that the " town and rich mart of Bhilsea" were threatened by the marauders, he made another appeal to the Commissioner, and wrung from him a promise of help. It gladdened the hearts of Edwards and Phillips to learn that a company of Sepoys from the Bareilly Brigade, under the command of an English officer, were coming into the disturbed districts to aid them in the restoration of order. Every day the anarchy was becoming more extensive and more intense ; and it was thought that

* Mr. Alfred Phillips distinguished himself greatly on this occasion. At Kasgunj, he encountered a large body of insurgents who had been plundering in the neighbourhood—some armed with muskets, some only with lattics, or long clubs. "The whole," Phillips reported, "could not be less than five hundred men." "As soon as they saw us," he adds, " there was some hesitation apparent; on which, calling upon the Sowars to follow, I and the Jemadar charged them. They fired some shots as we advanced, but broke before we reached them. And the whole body took to flight. We followed for some distance outside the town, and killed many, but the ground was difficult for following dispersed footmen, and we were too small a body to separate far. Indeed, with the exception of the Jemadar, and two other Sowars, the rest showed little inclination to go forward. On this occasion the Jemadar behaved with undoubted gallantry. I saw him kill two men." Phillips says nothing of his own exploits, but William Edwards states that his cousin killed "three men with his own hands."

the Sepoys would bring deliverance with them. But
the joy of the English officers was soon turned to
mourning. For just as it was supposed that the
wished-for succours were at hand, news came that
the Bareilly Brigade had revolted, that all the English
officers at that Suddur station were either killed or
in flight, that the prisoners in the great Gaol had
been released, and that the surrounding country was
in the wildest state of confusion.

    What now was to be done? The news arrived
early in the morning; so Edwards at once aroused
his cousin, who, anxious to return to his post before
the roads were closed, mounted his horse and galloped
towards the banks of the Ganges. Soon afterwards,
the Magistrate was joined by a few of his scattered
countrymen from the districts—two indigo-factors
and another—which greatly increased the difficulty of
his position. Edwards himself determined to remain
at his post so long as there was a hope of being useful
to his Government. But he called the others together, and after they had joined with him in prayer,
exhorted them to seek safety in flight. But they
thought that their safety would be best secured by
remaining with the Magistrate, and they were unwilling to depart. Up to this time the Sepoys had
not broken into revolt. The Treasury-guard at
Budaon consisted of a party of the Sixty-eighth Infantry—one of the regiments that had revolted—
under the command of a Native officer. When news
came that the troops at Head-Quarters had revolted,
the Soubahdar, with solemn oaths, assured Edwards
that the Sepoys at Budaon had had no communication with their comrades at Bareilly, and that they
were determined to defend the treasure against the
Budmashes of the city. But on that very evening

1857.
May.

June 1.

the Sepoys rose, and the usual work of plunder and devastation commenced. A party from Bareilly came to fraternise with the Budaon guard; and the released prisoners, some three hundred in number, came yelling around the Magistrate's house. There was nothing now left for him but instant flight. So he mounted his horse, which had been saddled since the morning, in anticipation of a crisis, and, accompanied by three other Englishmen, rode for his life. He had not gone far when a Mahomedan gentleman of position and influence in the neighbourhood met him, with a band of retainers, and persuaded him to turn back and take refuge in his house, which lay at a distance of some three miles from Budaon. Hoping that by these means he might conceal himself until the mutineers and gaol-birds had scattered themselves over the country, and then return to re-establish his authority, Edwards readily accepted the proposal. He passed, as he went, his own house, and found that already it was being plundered—the Chuprassies, who had recently served him, being active in the work.* Thus escorted, he passed on safely to Sheckoopoor, and spent part of the night in the Sheikh's house. But it was obvious that the sole chance of safety lay in his speedy departure, so he went on into the howling wilderness.

The only representative of authority having thus departed, there was the usual license—the usual crime. The Sepoys—the townspeople—the released convicts—the predatory classes from the neighbouring villages scrambled for the spoil of the British Government and its officers, and execrations bitter and deep went up at the thought of the abnormal

---

* "The first man I saw was one of my own orderlies, and who had been a favourite of mine, with my dress sword on him."

emptiness of the Treasury—for Edwards, seeing what was coming, had wisely refused to receive, for a time, the instalments of revenue due from the Zemindars. But these primal excesses at the central point of action were but a small part of the riotous disorder in which the month of May closed on Budaon. The whole district was in a state of the wildest anarchy and confusion. Men rose against each other—against the existing order of things— against the decrees of the British Government. All our administrative errors then stared us in the face.* Here, as elsewhere, in Rohilkund and in the greater part of the Meerut Division, every trace of British rule was effaced. The Sepoys went off to Delhi, and left the work of rebellion in the hands of the rural population.† The authority of Khan Behaudur Khan was proclaimed and acknowledged. District officers of different grades were appointed; the revenue was collected in the name of the rebel Government; and the whole province remained to be reconquered.

It was necessarily a work of no common difficulty

---

* "In Budaon the mass of the population rose in a body, and the entire district became a scene of anarchy and confusion. The ancient proprietary body took the opportunity of murdering or expelling the auction-purchasers, and resumed possession of their hereditary estates . . . The rural classes would never have joined the Sepoys, whom they hated, had not these causes of discontent already existed. They evinced no sympathy whatever about the cartridges, or flour said to be made of human bones, and could not then have been acted upon by any cry of their religion being in danger. It is questions involving their rights and interests in the soil and hereditary holdings, invariably termed by them as 'jan see azeez'— *dearer than life*—which excite them to a dangerous degree."—*Edwards's Personal Narrative.*

† "Disturbances broke out in every direction, and anarchy and misrule completely obtained the upper hand. The roads were no longer safe for travellers, and opportunity was taken by the bands of armed men, who scoured the country in all directions, not only to satiate their lust for plunder, but to settle old feuds by an appeal to arms, or more frequently by the committal of cruel murders."—*Mr. Carmichel's Official Report.*

1857.   for the new Government at such a time to reconcile
all conflicting interests—especially antagonisms of religion. The faith of the dominant party was the
faith of a minority. Even in Rohilkund the Mahomedans formed but a small part of the population.
The impartiality of the British in dealing with these
several races was unquestioned. If they accused us
of persecution, as they insanely did at that time, it
was persecution of a catholic kind. If the Hindoos
did not think that they had more to fear from the
bigotry of the Mahomedans than from the bigotry
of the Christians, it was sound policy on the part of
the new rulers to anticipate such a feeling. So
Behaudur Khan issued a proclamation calling upon
all, Hindoos and Mahomedans, to combine for the
extermination of the Christians, and assuring the
first that " if the Hindoos shall exert themselves in
the murder of these infidels and expel them from the
country, they shall be rewarded for their patriotism
by the extinction of the practice of the slaughter of
kine." But, in the true spirit of Mahomedanism,
these promises were accompanied by threats. " The
entire prohibition of this practice," it was added, " is
made conditional upon the complete extermination
of the infidels from India. If any Hindoo shall
shrink from joining in this cause, the evils of revival
of this practice shall recoil upon them; and if any
person shall be guilty of acting contrary to the requirements of this proclamation, he shall be impri-
soned for six months with a fine." ' The Hindoos of
Rohilkund were, for the most part, a quiet, inoffensive people, engaged in industrial work, artificers or
agriculturists, or traders of different degrees, little
accustomed to the use of arms, and by no means
addicted to fighting. But the Mahomedans of that

country, on the other hand, were fierce and unscrupulous, skilled in the use of offensive weapons, and
ever ready to use them ; so, notwithstanding their
numerical inferiority, they were dominant in Rohilkund and the adjacent country, and felt that they
could issue their mandates without much fear of
resistance.

Still Khan Behaudur Khan and his advisers trusted
more to their guile than to their strength. It occurred to them that the Christians might endeavour
to checkmate the Mahomedans, by making similar
promises to the Hindoos. So they thought it wise to
anticipate the movement. " Should the English,"
said another proclamation, " with a view to neutralise
our proposal and make a similar agreement, and
urge the Hindoos to rise against the Mussulmans, let
the wise Hindoos consider that if the English do so,
the Hindoos will be sadly deceived. The English
never keep their promises. They are deceitful im-
postors. The Natives of this country have always
been tools in the hands of these deceitful Englishmen. None of you should permit this opportunity
to slip. Let us take advantage of it." There is much
of this, doubtless, plagiarised from our English modes
of assertion. As it was the prevailing faith of Englishmen that the Natives of India were liars, we had
no reason to complain that this slander was retaliated
upon us. Moreover, we were always reminding the
bulk of the people of what they had suffered under
Mahomedan rule, and assuring them that their only
hopes of happiness and prosperity resided in the permanence of the British Government. It was natural, therefore, and excusable, that the Mahomedans
should have copied us also in this matter, and told
the Hindoos that their true interests lay in the ex-

termination of the English and the support of Mussulman rule. A Bill of Indictment was brought against us. It was declared that the English were the " destroyers of the creeds of other nations." Then the Hindoos were reminded that we had sanctioned the re-marriage of Hindoo widows*—that we had forcibly suspended the rites of Suttee—that we had pressed the Natives of India to embrace our religion by promises of advancement—and that we "had made it a standing rule, when a Rajah dies, without leaving any male issue by his married wife, to confiscate his territory and not to allow his adopted son to inherit it."† " Hence it is obvious that such laws of the English are intended to deprive the Native Rajahs of their territory and property. They have already seized the territory of Nagpore and Lucknow.. Their designs for destroying your religion, O Rajahs, is manifest.‡ . . . Be it known to all of you, that if these English are permitted to remain in India, they will butcher you all and put an end to your religion." And whilst everywhere were going forth these appeals to the religious feelings of the Hindoos, the Mahomedans were called upon, in most inciting language, in prose and in verse, to commence a Jehad, or religious war, against the Feringhees. On the faith of the Koran, all true believers were told that by fighting against the infidels, or paying money to enable others to fight, they would secure to themselves eternal beatitude. It was the old story so often told, with some variations to suit the purposes

---

* The words were, that we had " promulgated that a Hindoo widow must re-marry."—See vol. pp. 188—189.

† See *ante*, pp. 70, *et seq.*

‡ Here follows a charge against the English with respect to the introduction of the new messing system into the gaols, to which reference is made at pages 195—196 vol. i.

of the hour. I do not know that ever before the 1857. commercial element was introduced into a proclama- June—Aug. tion of Jehad with so much pungency as in one which was found in the "dufter" of Khan Behaudur Khan, and translated by Cracroft Wilson. "He," it was said, "who will willingly give a pice in this cause will get from God on the day of judgment seven hundred pice. And he who will spend a rupee in this cause, and will use his sword also against the infidels, will get from God seven thousand rupees." It may be presumed from this that the "sinews of war" were wanting—that the great difficulty before the new Government was a paucity of rupees. But it is doubtful whether this figurative appeal to the moneyed interest produced the desired effect, for the money came in but slowly to the public Treasury, and more forcible means were resorted to for the abstraction of the public coin than these promises of enormous usufruct on the day of judgment. Still the Native Government went on from day to day, from week to week, from month to month, after a rude fashion of its own ; and nothing more was heard of the English except that here and there some wretched fugitive was hiding himself disguised in Oriental costume, and indebted for his life to the exceptional kindness of some Native of the country.

Meanwhile, there was the prologue of a dreadful Furruckabad. tragedy in Furruckabad—a district in the Agra Division of the North-Western Provinces. It is bounded on the north by Shahjehanpore and Budaon, from which it is divided by the waters of the Ganges. But though geographically and administratively severed from Rohilkund, the social conditions of the districts were nearly the same. The Mahomedan influences were there especially strong ; and the Pathan element

U 2

1857.

was largely represented among these followers of the Prophet. In the early days of British rule in India, this tract of country had been infamous for its lawlessness—for the supremacy of a race of bandits, who thought robbery insipid if it were not flavoured by murder. All this was gradually effaced under the administration of the English ; but although the outward conditions were greatly changed, there was ever beneath the surface the old hatred of the white man —the old desire to extirpate him, root and branch, from the land. They had long been biding their time ; and now the time had come.* Before the end of May the whole district was in rebellion. The Native regiment, the Tenth, had not then mutinied. " I traversed a great portion of the district during the first week of June," writes a trustworthy informant to me, "and I saw villages on fire, and being plundered on all sides. At that time the Tenth Native Infantry had not revolted. The rebellion had existed for a full month before the corps mutinied."

March.
Inquietudes
and alarms.

There had been, indeed, from the early part of the year great excitement in the Furruckabad district. In no part of the country had those monstrous fables of bone-dust flour and polluted wells been circulated more freely or with greater success. And there was at least one story more—one of which I have no knowledge of having been current in any other

---

* Mr. (afterwards Sir G. F.) Harvey, in his official narrative of events in the Agra Division, one that shows, perhaps, more literary skill than any in the collection, observes : "The (so to speak) Nawabee character of Furruckabad, the vast number of dissolute, desperate, and distressed Mahomedans there ; men who had lineage to boast of and old traditions to excite them, who were too proud to labour and too poor not to be discontented ; the very indolence and depravity, in short, of a large number of the Bungush family, made me always from the first feel more apprehension for the safety of Futtehgurh (Furruckabad) than for that of any district in the division."

district—it was believed that the English Govern-	1857.
ment had issued rupees of leather silvered over to
represent the ordinary coinage of the country. Major
Weller, of the Engineers, of whose good services at
Agra mention has been made in a preceding chapter,
was at Futtehgurh in March. A Native banker
called upon him to inquire into the truth of the
several stories about the bone-dust and other vile
designs of the English to destroy the religion of the
people. The English officer explained to him the
absurdity of these rumours. But the man was not
convinced. " But you know," he said, " that Government are issuing leather rupees, and intend to
gather up all the silver of the country." Major
Weller laughed at this story. But the credulous
banker shook his head, and said that he had seen the
leather rupees, and had some in his possession.
" Bring them to me," said Weller, " as many as you
can, and I will give you fourteen annas for each of
them." The Native banker took his departure, but
never produced a leather rupee. It is difficult to
declare, though it may be easy to conjecture, the
origin of this story. It was not a weak invention of
the enemy; it was in truth a very crafty device,
well calculated to excite the moneyed interests by
fears of a depreciation of the currency, and to alarm
those who still held to the belief that there was
desecration in contact with leather. Nothing could
better illustrate the unreasonable alarm pervading
the district.

The English station of Futtehgurh lies at a dis- Futtehgurh.
tance of about six miles from the town of Furruckabad. There was a fort—or some works which were
dignified by the name of one—within which was the
Gun-carriage Manufactory which Major Robertson of

the Bengal Artillery then superintended. The Tenth Regiment of Native Infantry was commanded by Colonel George Acklom Smith—a soldier of good repute. The confidence which he felt in his men— a confidence that was shared by most of his officers— was strengthened by the belief that the regiment was generally regarded by the Native Army as a collection of outcasts, with whom their brethren had no sympathy; for they had gone to Burmah across the " black water." In times of violent excitement, however, such distinctions are disregarded; and it was soon apparent that the Tenth were in communication with mutineers from other regiments. Indeed, there were too many scourings of mutiny and rebellion from neighbouring stations to permit any thought of safety. All Oude had risen. Rohilkund was in the throes of a great rebellion. What hope was there for Furruckabad? Not to have taken some precautions would, at such a time, have been madness. So Colonel Smith sent numbers of the women and the children and the non-combatants in boats, to drop down the river, and to make their way to what was then thought a place of safety, the great Cantonment of Cawnpore. On the 3rd of June, under cover of the darkness, some twelve or thirteen boats, " of various sorts and sizes," carried off about a hundred of the residents of Furruckabad, men, women, and children —the majority of them being Christian people, unconnected with the public service.

Occupation
of the Fort.
Meanwhile the regiment remained in a state of sullen quiescence. But a day, an hour, might change the complexion of affairs. And Colonel Smith, therefore, determined, if mutiny should surround him, to shut himself up in the Fort, with his officers and the Christian people who had either remained at, or had

returned to, Futtehgurh. It was hard to say what
was the temper of the men of the Tenth. They had
behaved well on the occasion of a revolt in the Gaol,
and had fired upon the insurgent prisoners, but, on
the other hand, they had prevented the removal of
the treasure into the Fort. At the end of the second
week of June all confidence—all hope—was at an
end. The waves of rebellion were closing around
Futtehgurh, and it was impossible that the Tenth
should resist the power of the great flood. The
troops that had mutinied at Seetapore in the Khyrabad Division of Oude* were approaching, and, feasted
and flattered on the way by the rebel Zemindars,
were holding traitorous correspondence with the
Tenth. Colonel Smith then saw the necessity of
destroying the bridge of boats across the river ; and
his regiment, with that strange outward inconsistency which sometimes indicates infirmity of purpose,
sometimes conceals deep designs, applied themselves
manfully to the work of destruction. This done, a
party of Native officers told the Colonel that their
" time was up," and that he and all under him had
better retreat into the Fort. So he gathered up his
people and prepared to defend himself against the
multitudes that might rise against him. There was,
indeed, a gloomy prospect before them. The Fort
was in a most miserable condition for all purposes
of defence. There was a glut of gun-carriages and
models of all kinds of ordnance. But there was a
dearth both of serviceable guns and of ammunition.
It is stated that there were six guns on the ramparts
and an eighteen-inch howitzer ; but that only thirty

* These were the Forty-first and one Infantry. The narrative of
Native Infantry, with two regiments this outbreak will be found in a
of Oude Irregulars, one Cavalry, subsequent book of this History.

1857.   round shots could be mustered. Of small-arm ammunition there was a better supply; but many of the cartridges were blank. Provisions were with difficulty obtained; but after awhile a flock of forty or fifty sheep were driven within the walls by the help of a Sepoy of the Eleventh. There was a population of about a hundred and twenty Christian people in the garrison—one-fourth of whom were men capable of bearing arms. The rest were women and children. There was only one Artillery officer—Major Robertson, of the Gun-carriage Agency—in the Fort. But Colonel Tudor Tucker, of the Cavalry, who had learnt the gun-drill at Addiscombe, was improvised into an Artillery Commandant, and right well he did his work.

June 18.   Whilst Colonel Smith was gathering up his people
Proclamation and concerting measures for their defence, the Sepoys
of the Nawab. of the Tenth were openly declaring themselves. They tendered their allegiance to the Nawab of Furruckabad, who had cast in his lot against us, and formally placed him on the Musnud under a royal salute. They opened the Gaol, and they seized the treasure, which they had pretended to guard.* But when the new Native Government demanded it, they resolutely refused to surrender a rupee. They were determined not to mutiny for nothing. And when the Sepoys of the Forty-first from Seetapore asked for a share of it, they refused to divide the spoil. From that time there was sharp contention between the two regiments. The Tenth seem to have had more greed for money than for blood. But the Forty-first having tasted the delights of murder, were eager for the

---

* Among other loot that fell   of the Maharajah Duleep Singh,
into the hands of the despoilers   who had an establishment at Futteh-
were the jewels and other property   gurh. (See note in Appendix.)

destruction of the English in the Fort, and implored
the Nawab to order the Tenth to lead the attack on
their old officers. Disappointed in this and in their
design up the treasure, they set fire to all the houses
in the Cantonment, and preluded their attack on the
Fort by an internecine conflict, in which several
Sepoys on both sides were left dead upon the parade-
ground. The Forty-first, when urged to display their
own sincerity by leading the attack, said that the
omens were not then favourable, but that the 25th
would be a propitious day. So on that day action
commenced. The Sepoys had two post guns, with
which they had pledged themselves to protect the
treasure; and the Nawab, who had flung himself,
with the deadliest animosity, into the active work of
rebellion, spared no pains to supply the besiegers with
the munitions of war, and hounded them on to the
destruction of the white men. He had received
favours from the English Government. He had
been rescued from ruin by their kindly exertions.
But nothing could efface the traditions of a by-gone
supremacy. He had assumed an air of friendliness
and an appearance of placidity, when he well knew
that the storm was brewing. But now the expected
hour had come ; and he found himself master of a
country in which before he had only been a pensioner.*

With desperate odds against them, our little garri- Gallantry of
son displayed a sturdy gallantry that could not be the defence.
surpassed. Day and night they toiled, weary but
undaunted, in the batteries. It was no new thing

* His family were in receipt of
arge compensatory allowances from
the British Government. But his
predecessors and himself had been
ruinously extravagant, and the
British Government, by the careful
management of the property, had
saved the family from absolute
beggary.

for our people to be driven to use strange ammunition with their artillery. The implements of the Gun
Manufactory, as screws, hammers, bolts, and axles,
were sewn up in gunny-bags and made to do service
as grape-shot. But rude as were these implements
of warfare, they did good execution among the besiegers, and many fell beneath the fire of our English
rifles. Colonel Smith, a noted marksman, picked off
the enemy with an amount of skill that would have
done credit to the prizemen of Wimbledon. Tudor
Tucker was shot by a Sepoy as he was looking out
through an embrasure, or loophole, to see the effect
of the last discharge of his gun. The Chaplain, Mr.
Frederick Fisher, alternated the duties of a soldier
with those of a Christian minister. He preached on
the text, "What time I am afraid I will trust in
thee;" and then went out to face the enemy. His
wife and boy were with him. They were secure
in the residence attached to the Gun-carriage Agency,
and it is related that little Phil. Fisher and the other
children were playing and singing as joyously as if
nothing were going on out of the common course of
events. The women prayed almost unceasingly for
the brave men who were defending them. They bore
up bravely in their passiveness—all but one. This
was the widow of a sergeant, or conductor, attached
to the Clothing Agency, who was shot dead at his
post. She was not one to sit down and weep. She
went out to work. She took a rifle and posted herself in one of the bastions, whence she is said to have
shot down many of the mutineers.* It was a most

* This was the story told to Mr. William Edwards by a Native in- formant, who, however, added that the woman had been killed at her work. From the official accounts it would appear that Sergeant (Con- ductor) Ahern was killed in the Fort, but Mrs. Ahern is said to have been murdered at Cawnpore.

unequal conflict. The besiegers were not strong in artillery, and their light guns could not make practicable breaches in the walls of the Fort. They delivered some unsuccessful assaults, and were driven back with heavy loss. But the Sepoys had learnt, from our teaching, lessons of warfare not to be neglected ; so they betook themselves to mining operations. They did not fight unaided—for many of the chief Mahomedan people had joined them, and were animating and aiding the assailants. In one of the attacks the foremost man was a Pathan, named Mooltan Khan, who had assisted the escape of Mr. Edwards. The Chaplain, Fisher, shot him dead on the crest of the breach, and those who followed him fell back in dismay. But gallant as were those thirty defenders, the defence could not be protracted with any hope of success or safety to the garrison. Their ammunition had failed, and there was no prospect of the arrival of any succours, though Smith had written imploringly for them. His letters reached Agra.* As the Native regiments there had been disarmed, a detachment of Europeans might have been spared from the seat of Government. Major Weller, who knew the country well, offered to lead it. But the detachment was not sent.† So it was resolved that the besieged should drop down into the boats on the river, under cover of the night.

There were but three boats for the party of a hundred Christian people, and they drifted out forlornly into darkness and unto death. This was the second exodus from Futtehgurh. How it had fared with

Evacuation of the Fort.

---

* One of them is now before me, written in French — or in such French as an old Indian officer, after years of absence from Europe, can commonly command—in very small characters, and on such thin paper that it might have been conveyed in a quill.

† See Appendix for further information on this point.

the first was not known. But the one idea was to escape to Cawnpore, that cruel Cawnpore, which was to witness the massacre of so many of our Christian people. It was a necessity that there should be some delay in embarking so many women and children with such requisites and appurtenances as could be gathered together for the river voyage. So the shades of night had well-nigh glimmered into dawn before the boats were fairly afloat. The difficulties and dangers of the escape were thus greatly enhanced. Colonel Smith, Colonel Goldie, and Major Robertson commanded severally the three boats. But ere long the three were reduced to two. Colonel Goldie's boat ran upon a shoal, and the rudder was smashed. A vain attempt was made to repair it, the result of which was that the villagers of Soonderpoor came down upon our people in great numbers and fired upon them. The blood of the gallant Englishmen was stirred by this assault. Then a little band of five Christian officers* went out and charged a throng of three hundred Natives, and drove them back to their village with the loss of some of their leaders. But it was plain that they could not wait any longer to refit, so the occupants of Colonel Goldie's boat betook themselves to Colonel Smith, and they pursued their perilous journey down the river.

Pursuit of the enemy.

The pursuit now became more active. The Sepoys took possession of the ferry-boats to follow the fugitives, and a gun was sent down on the right bank of the river to bear upon our unhappy people. The villagers on both banks, especially the dwellers

* These were Captain Vibart (Second Cavalry), Major Munro, Lieutenants Eckford, Sweetenham, and Henderson of the Tenth. Some accounts say that the armed villagers were from four hundred to five hundred in number. They came from three villages.

in the Mahomedan villages, fell upon them with equal ferocity. There had been small chance of escape, from the first, but when Major Robertson's boat grounded on a sand-bank opposite to Singee-Rampore, all hope was abandoned by its inmates. The Sepoys were coming down upon them in their boats, and the banks of the river were lined with enemies. There was acted over again, on a smaller scale, the dreadful scene of the massacre at the Cawnpore Ghaut. Men, women, and children flung themselves into the river, some to be drowned, some to be shot, some to be cut down. Three only of the boat's crew escaped with life and liberty.* Out of the general horror it is difficult to extract the miserable truth of individual calamities. It would seem that the gallant Chaplain, Fisher, severely wounded, leapt into the river with his wife and child in his arms. They were both drowned ; but he himself escaped immediate death by hiding himself during the night, and then making his way at dawn to Colonel Smith's boat.† Mrs. Robertson, her child, and Miss Thompson, who accompanied her, also lost their lives at this

* Major Robertson, Mr. Jones, and Mr. Churcher, two badly wounded.

† "Fisher was wounded, a ball passing through his left thigh. The Sepoys then came alongside to board the boat. Major Robertson now urged the ladies and children to get into the water to save themselves. They did so. Jones was still in the boat with other gentlemen, using their muskets. He cannot say to a certainty whether the ladies were mostly shot in the water or were drowned ; but when he jumped into the water himself he saw Mrs. Fisher, at some distance, up to her waist in water. The current was strong, and it carried her off her legs several times. Fisher was supporting her, and he had their child in his arms. He (Jones) thinks, from the appearance of the child in his arms, that he (little Philip Fisher) was probably drowned, for this was the fate of many children in the confusion of getting out of the boat. . . . . About four o'clock on the morning of the 5th (Sunday), poor Fred. Fisher hailed the boat. He was alone. Directly he got on board he burst into tears, and said, ' My poor wife and child were both drowned in my arms !' Where he had been all night, or what he had been doing, Jones did not hear."—*Rev. Mr. Spry, Chaplain at Allahabad, to Archdeacon Pratt. MS. Correspondence.*

1857.
June.

Noble
conduct of
Churcher.

place. One of Colonel Goldie's daughters fell at the same time. Major Phillott of the Tenth, and other officers of the same regiment, were also lost here, with several people attached to the Gun-carriage and Clothing Agencies.* Some were taken prisoners, and blown from guns by the Nawab of Furruckabad. Major Robertson, though painfully wounded, escaped with his life, by the generous aid of Mr. David Churcher, an indigo-planter, who secured an oar, on which the two supported themselves in the river until midnight, when they went ashore, and lay hidden in the village of Kulhour, where some herdsmen sheltered them and fed them. Then was witnessed another of those acts of heroic self-devotion of which the annals of the Sepoy War afford so many touching examples. Churcher might have made his escape, but Robertson was in such dire agony both of body and of mind that he could not rouse himself to the activity of flight. So Churcher determined not to leave him. For more than two months he watched over the stricken artilleryman, until death mercifully came to the relief of the sufferer. Then Churcher buried his friend, raised a mound of earth over his remains to mark the spot, and betook himself to the jungle, where Providence mercifully protected him, and enabled him, after awhile, to escape to Cawnpore.

In the meanwhile Colonel Smith's boat—the last of the little fleet, with all the survivors of the Futtehgurh Fort, dropped down towards Cawnpore—the

---

* Among those who perished were Dr. and Mrs. Heathcote. Mrs. Heathcote was a niece of Mr. Fisher, and sister of the wife of Major Darcy Todd—daughters of Dr. Sandham, Surgeon of the Sixteenth Lancers, who had married a sister of Mr. F. Fisher and of Colonel Fisher, whose sad fate at Sooltanpore shall afterwards be described. These murdered officers were sons of the Rev. Henry Fisher, Senior Presidency Chaplain for a long series of years.

desired harbour of refuge. And here authentic history fades into dim conjecture. What befel them on the way is not known. But it is too sure that they all perished at the place in which they had thought to find safety and shelter. That they fell into the cruel hands of Doondoo Punt, Nana Sahib, and were butchered at Cawnpore, has been already narrated.* It is known also that those who had preceded them in the flotilla which left Futtehgurh on the 4th of June, had been sent to the shambles before them. In all, more than two hundred Christian people—men, women, and children—who were in or near Futtehgurh at the beginning of June, died miserably on the dreary river voyage or at the place of their destination, where they had hoped to escape the malice of their persecutors.†

The English in Furruckabad having thus been expelled and destroyed, and all trace of their autho-rity effaced, an attempt was made to systematise the restored Native Government. But the Nawab, Tuf-foozul Hoosein Khan, was not a chief of super-abundant energy and activity, and it is doubtful whether he much delighted in the greatness which had been thrust upon him. He was a man of quiet habits and *dilettante* tastes, fond of painting and illuminating, and like others, both in the East and the West, of the same artistic tendencies, somewhat addicted to epicurean practices. He liked dancing

The Nawab of Furruck-abad.

---

* *Ante,* vol. ii. page 353.
† Colonel Williams, in his admirable report of events at Cawnpore, which I have before quoted from, says that those who left Futtehgurh on the 4th of June are supposed to have perished at Cawnpore on the 12th of that month. He states that Colonel Smith's boat reached Bithoor on the 9th of July, that the occupants were seized there and sent into Cawnpore, that the gentlemen (three excepted, Colonels Goldie and Smith and Mr. Thornhill) were killed on the 10th or 11th, and the women and children massacred on the 15th of that month.

girls better than soldiers, and had more pleasure in
the society of parasites than of public functionaries.
He had a traditional ascendancy in the province, and
that was all. He was a weak rather than a bad
man, and there were many people about him whose
hatred of the English was far more intense than his
own. He sat on a throne, and orders were issued in
his name for the collection of the revenue, and for
the definition of the processes of civil and criminal
law. The regulations did not differ much from those
which had been ordained in the time of British rule,
but they were enforced with greater stringency. It
was not to be expected that, here or elsewhere, after
long years of depression, Native administrators should
suddenly arise with systems and organisations of their
own. In such an emergency they were fain to pick
up, from the leavings of their predecessors, such
crumbs as they could find. Our old Native officials
were, for the most part, not unwilling—if not rejoiced—to array themselves under the Native Governments. Not being able to see into men's hearts,
I cannot say whether in this there was any spirit of
nationality, or whether it was merely an instinct of
greed. If they did not obtain higher pay—and in
most instances they procured at least the promise of
it—they had greater opportunities of illicit gains.
Our military retainers were as children, and, like the
children of all nations, they were cruel. But our
civil functionaries had the astuteness of maturity
about them, and were cold and calculating in the
midst of the general excitement. It was a necessity
of their very existence that they should cast in their
lot with the dominant power. And perhaps they did
not much care whether the White man or the Black
man were triumphant, so long as they retained their

places and preserved their pay. Some, however, held back—doubtful as to the final issue of the struggle—far-seeing men, who could afford to wait. And in time they had their reward.*

1857.
May—Aug.

I shall not pause here to attempt a full and impartial inquiry into the inner history—the moral anatomy, I may say—of this great movement against the White Man. But something may be briefly said about the character of the events recorded in the chapter now brought to a close—a chapter, the materials of which have been derived from the official reports of our own civil officers. In many parts of the North-Western Provinces there had been violent rebellion without the aid or presence of Sepoys—where Sepoys were few or none—before they had risen, or after they had left the disturbed districts. And in some instances our Native soldiers had actively aided the authorities in putting down popular insurrections. The violence of the Sepoys was commonly of a superficial kind, and such seeds of rebellion as they sowed took no root in the soil. Having plundered the treasuries, perhaps killed their

Character of the outbreak.

* Mr. C. R. Lindsay, in his very able and exhaustive report, says: " The conduct of the officials serving the British Government at the time of the outbreak was not praiseworthy. Out of the six Tehseldars (chief revenue officers) three took service with the Nawab. Out of eleven head police officers six accepted situations under the new Government. Amongst the nine Peshkars (officers next in rank to the Tehseldars), five gave in their adherence to the Nawab. The Canoongoes were all, save one, employed. All the collecting Sowars, with the exception of one, went over to the Nawab *en masse*. Of the other officials, such as Record-keepers, Mohurrers, Nazirs, Burkendauzes, Chuprassies, &c., all, or nearly all, tendered their services to the Government of the time. The Sheristadars of the criminal and revenue departments, and the Nazir of the former, did not accept appointments. The latter official got rather severely handled by the rebels. He was fined and plundered of a portion of his property."

officers and other Christian people, and opened the gaols, they made for their homes or betook themselves to Delhi. It was not on account of the violence of the Sepoys that the Lieutenant-Governor described the provinces under his rule as in "a blaze of ravage and riot," or that the Governor-General wrote officially that they were "lost to us" for the time. Where were no sources of complaint against the British Government other than of a military character, no grievances, no apprehensions, no alarms, where none but our trained soldiers were smarting under injuries, real or supposed, these uprisings made comparatively a slight and transient impression upon the country in respect of its government and administration; and our authority was speedily reimposed. But there were fears and discontents with which greased cartridges had no connexion, and uprisings not incited by thoughts of the spoliation of the treasure-chests. The fears and discontents of powerful classes, who felt that they had been downtrodden by the English, that their old dynasties had been subverted, their old traditions ignored, their old systems violated, their old usages contemned, and that everywhere the reign of annexation and innovation had commenced, and was threatening to crush out the very hearts of the nations, struck deep root in the soil, and it was a work of time to eradicate the evil growth. And all this, too, in the model provinces, the administrative conduct of which had been vaunted as the greatest triumph of British rule in the East.

It belongs to a later stage of this History, when the events of the Sepoy War shall have been more fully narrated, to prosecute this important inquiry to its legitimate termination. What has been now written is a commentary only on the contents of the present chapter. The brave heart of Lieutenant-Governor Colvin would not have been torn, as it was, if he had thought that the convulsions in the North-Western Provinces were confined to our military Cantonments.

CHAPTER III.

ANXIETIES OF MR. COLVIN—THE NATIVE CHIEFS—SCINDIAH AND HIS
CONTINGENT—EVENTS AT GWALIOR—OUTBREAK OF THE CONTINGENT—
ESCAPE OF THE ENGLISH—THE NEEMUCH BRIGADE—HOLKAR AND
TROOPS—OUTBREAK AT INDORE—WITHDRAWAL OF THE RESIDENT—
KOTAH—RAJPOOTANA.

1857.
May—June.
COLVIN suffered cruelly, but he bore up bravely,
though the silent approaches of death already were
casting their dark shadows over him.   Much of which
I have written was either not known at all, or but
dimly perceived at the Head-Quarters of the Supreme
Government.   But every day brought in some disastrous tidings to the Lieutenant-Governor, whose in-
timate knowledge of all local circumstances painfully
disclosed to him the full significance of the distressing
stories that came huddling on each other.   Those
which I have recorded are but excerpts from the
grim catalogue of "ravage and riot" which so dis-
tracted and distressed him.   And he felt that, bad
as was what he saw before him in the Present, there
might be worse in the Future to assail him.

To the bearing of the Native chiefs in this conjuncture, and especially of the Maharajah Scindiah
of Gwalior, whose capital lay at a distance of only
sixty-five miles from Agra, Colvin had looked from
the commencement of the rebellion with extreme

anxiety, and notwithstanding the promising signs and symptoms above recorded,* he was still racked by most painful doubts, which soon became most distressing realities. That great Mahratta Prince had a Contingent force of more than eight thousand men, with twenty-six guns,† under English officers, and a purely Native force of ten thousand men. The Contingent was little more than a local branch of our own military establishment, and there was small chance of the Gwalior soldiery being proof against the general alarm which was pervading the Native Army in all parts of the country. It was very soon apparent that they were tainted. But an army rebelling against its master, and without an acknowledged head, is one thing ; an army led to the battle by its sovereign prince is another thing, and one far more perilous to encounter. Everywhere it was asked, nervously, " What will Scindiah do?" The opportunity that lay before him was a tempting one. He might shake himself loose from the thraldom of the dominant Englishman; he might increase his territory, and increase his army, and become a more powerful and independent ruler than his ancestors had been in the palmiest days of the Raj. Every Native Prince is surrounded, more or less, by a crew of parasites and intriguers, whose game it is to foster the growth of every kind of corruption, and to shut him out from the good influences brought to bear upon him by honest and enlightened advisers. There were those, doubtless, who, still smarting under the losses sustained by their defeat at Maharajpore and

1557.
May—June

---

* *Ante*, page 208.
† There were two regiments of Irregular Cavalry—1158 men of all ranks—seven regiments of Infantry, aggregating 6412, four field batteries (each comprising five nine- pounders and a twenty-four-pound howitzer), and a garrison battery with two eighteen-pounder iron guns attached for field service. Twenty- six guns in all, with 748 artillery- men. See Appendix.

Punniah, would fain have persuaded the young Maharajah to array himself on the side of the enemies of the English now that all things seemed to be in their favour. It was not to be expected that being a man and a Mahratta, he should not, when assailed by the fierce temptation, sometimes have wavered in his allegiance, and, for a little while, yielded inwardly to the allurements that beset him. Perhaps, indeed, there was not a Native chief in India who was not sometimes minded to wait and watch at the outset of the great convulsion. And there were some personal circumstances, peculiar to the Gwalior chief, which rendered it especially likely that he would cast in his lot against the usurping Englishman.

At this time Scindiah was in his twenty-third year. His passion for military display had grown with his growth, and strengthened with his strength. Had he lived half a century earlier, this ambition might have been pregnant with great events. He might have ripened into a leader of armies, and made for himself a place in the history of the world. But all independent action of this kind had been crushed out of the Native Princes of India by the universal domination of the British. By the introduction of what we called our subsidiary system, it had come to pass that there was but one military power, but one military nation left on the great Indian Peninsula. The English soldier put down all internal conflicts, and took upon himself the general defence of the country. Neither Mahrattas, nor Rajpoots, nor Pathans, nor any other race, Hindoo or Mahomedan, within certain limits, were allowed to fight among themselves. So a Native Prince, with strong military instincts, had nothing to do but to play at soldiering. Of the

young Maharajah Scindiah, it was officially reported
in 1856, that he "seemed to enjoy no occupation save
drilling, dressing, ordering, transforming, feasting,
playing with his troops, and the unwearied study of
books of evolutions ; and he grudged no expenditure
connected with this amusement."*

A man of this character, if he had fallen into bad
hands, might have been dangerous to himself and to
others. Fortunately, he fell into good hands—hands
that gently but firmly restrained the restlessness of
his nature. At the most critical period of his life he
had Dinkur Rao at his elbow. That great Native The Dewan
statesman, who has shared with Salar Jung, of Dinkur Rao.
Hyderabad, the glory of being the Abul-Fuzl of the
nineteenth century, and from whom the best of our
English administrators have learnt many lessons of
wisdom, exercised a benign influence, not only over
the government of the Gwalior territory, which he
reformed and consolidated, but over the personal
character of Scindiah himself. He could not do this
without exciting some jealousy in the mind of the
Maharajah, and raising hostile cabals among a less
worthy class of Durbar servants. But, encouraged
and sustained by the British Political Agent, he
triumphed over these difficulties. In Major Charters Charters
Macpherson, our Government had at the Court of Macpherson.
Gwalior a representative in every way qualified both
to conciliate and to restrain a man of Scindiah's temperament. A member of a family, distinguished in
many different departments of the public service, he
had gained for himself an enduring reputation by his
successful efforts to suppress the great abomination
of Meriah sacrifice in Southern India. He was one
of the good old school of soldier-statesmen, with large

* Report of Major Charters Macpherson, December 13, 1856.

human sympathies and broad catholic political views. Few men, whom I have known and conversed with, have had less of that national self-love, which so often over-rides truth and justice in our estimate of and our conduct towards others. Essentially tolerant and many-sided, he could see how much of the evil, which we are wont to condemn in the Native States of India, is the growth of circumstances which have been developed in our own forcing-house. He felt that the young Maharajah was at least as good as, perhaps better than, we had any right to expect him to be; but he exerted himself to make him still better. The relations between the British Officer and the Mahratta Prince were of the most friendly kind. The cordiality between them had been confirmed by their visit to Calcutta in March, 1857, the incidents of which made a strong impression on Scindiah's mind. He saw at our English capital much that was new to him—much that was suggestive and impressive. And he returned to Gwalior with not only an enlarged estimate of the magnificent resources of the British Government, but with a more assured belief than he had ever entertained before of their friendly feelings and just intentions towards him. That was a time of almost general alarm among the rulers of the Native States of India ; and Lord Canning saw clearly the necessity of allaying it. So the Maharajah carried back with him to Gwalior the remembrance of assuring words spoken to him by the Governor-General at Calcutta, and 'had no more fear for the perpetuation of his dynasty. If he did not regard with much complacency the domination of the English, he felt that it was inevitable, and he reconciled himself to it, more contentedly than he could have done, when the air was alive with rumours of the annexation of the Native States.

It has been seen that, on the first outbreak of revolt, Scindiah had manifested his loyalty by placing his troops at the disposal of the Lieutenant-Governor of Agra. Major Macpherson had always doubted from the first whether the Contingent, composed as it was of the same materials as our own Native Army, would ever act against our Sepoy mutineers; and he represented that in no manner could the Maharajah testify his own devotion to the British so well as by sending to Agra his own body-guard, consisting mainly of Mahratta horsemen " of his own kindred or caste."* To this Scindiah had cheerfully responded. He saw the departure of his favourite phalanx with pride, and rode out some way to their camp. The Contingent, the Maharajah mistrusted as much as Macpherson had done; and he warned the British Agent that they had ceased entirely to be servants of the Government. Their hearts were with the mutineers of the Bengal Army. They were holding nightly meetings — taking oaths upon the Ganges water—receiving emissaries from Calcutta and Delhi —both accepting and propagating monstrous stories of our efforts to destroy the religions of the country and inculcating upon Hindoos and Mahomedans alike the duty of hastening the downfall of the British Government in India. But still Brigadier Ramsay and his officers, like their comrades of the Regular Army, believed in the fidelity of their men. Vainly were the views of the Maharajah and the Political Agent represented to him; he said that they were tinged with Mahratta intrigue and were not to be trusted. Still Macpherson insisted upon the duty of taking some precaution to insure the safety of the

1857.
May—June.
Bearing of Scindiah.

Confidence of the Contingent officers.

---

* Major Macpherson says of these men, "that they had been Scindiah's companions by day and by night inseparable from his pleasures and State."

1857.
May—June.

women and children in the event of a sudden out-break; and to this end it was arranged that the Residency should be fixed upon as a place of refuge, that the Contingent-guard posted there should be withdrawn, and Durbar troops substituted for them. But when the Political Agent represented that it would be expedient for the wives and children of the Contingent officers quietly and gradually to take up their abode in the Residency, the Brigadier protested against the movement as one that would indicate want of confidence in the fidelity of the troops.

May 28.
The first
panic.

But on the next day there was a great panic in Cantonments; and the women and children were flying for their lives to the Residency. It was ex-pected that the troops would rise that night; but it was a false alarm. When tidings of this movement reached Scindiah, he rode down, with a strong escort, to the Residency, posted troops securely around it, and urged upon Macpherson the expe-diency of bringing all the women and the children to a spacious mansion, built in the English style, attached to the Palace, where they would be pro-tected by his own people. So on the next day they were removed as quietly as possible to the asylum provided for them by the Maharajah; and there they ought to have been suffered to remain. But the Sepoys of the Contingent protested that the removal of our women and children was an imputation on their honour, and they prevailed with their officers to recall their families to Cantonments.*

* Major Macpherson telegraphed to Mr. Colvin to send back Scindiah's body-guard as there was danger of a rising; but Brigadier Ramsay having read this telegram, wrote to the Lieutenant-Governor that all was quiet and confidence increasing, and that he "considered that Scindiah was endeavouring to increase his own services at the expense of the Contingent."

The grievous error that had been committed was soon palpable. No sooner had " confidence been restored" at Head-Quarters than all the Contingent troops posted at the out-stations broke into rebellion. The first two weeks .of June saw all the country occupied by the Contingent in a blaze of mutiny and rebellion. One regiment revolted at Neemuch on the 4th, with all the Company's troops. On the 7th, revolt was inaugurated at Jhansi with the most fiendish orgies that the imagination could devise. At Sepree and Jubbulpore, the troops were showing unmistakable signs of a speedy rising ; and from our own provinces everywhere came disastrous tidings of regiments in mutiny, of Christian people murdered or . flying for their lives, of law and authority prostrate, of districts overrun by unscrupulous marauders.

There was now an almost general impression at Gwalior that the power of the English in India was at its last gasp. Among the very few who did not share this belief were Scindiah and his Minister. The difficulties with which they were beset were of a most embarrassing kind, for there was a constant flood of Mahratta intrigue ever pouring itself upon the Maharajah, and endeavouring to sweep away the influence and ascendancy of the Dewan, who was heart and soul with the English party. His most cherished friends and companions were active upon the other side. They had suffered by our domination ; they were eager for the overthrow of Dinkur Rao ; and they hoped to persuade Scindiah that, as his power would be vastly aggrandised by the expulsion of the British, it was folly to abstain from casting in his lot with the victorious army. He listened, made plausible answers, and talked of waiting ; but he never swerved from his allegiance. Amidst all

1857.
June.

Temper of the troops.

these sinister influences he remained true to us; and for awhile the Durbar Army continued to be loyal to its master. But it was plain that the Contingent at Gwalior might at any moment cast off the trammels of mock loyalty and break out into the violence of uncontrolled rebellion.

The outbreak at Gwalior.
The day, indeed, was close at hand. On Sunday, so often a fatal day to the English—Sunday, the 14th of June—our Christian people attended divine service in the church and took the Sacrament of the Lord's Supper. There had been a funeral in the morning. A little son of Captain Murray had been laid in the grave, and many of the European residents of Gwalior had attended the burial. The Sepoys saw them go and depart, and were respectful—almost sympathising in their demeanour. The day passed, and all was outwardly quiet. But on the evening of that Sabbath the Contingent rose. The crisis was precipitated after the wonted fashion. There was a cry that the Europeans were upon them—a panic in the Lines and then a general revolt. The Artillerymen rushed to their guns; the Infantry seized their muskets. The sound of firing and the sight of flames, breaking the stillness and the darkness of the night, proclaimed that the orgies of rebellion had commenced. Shouting, yelling, bugling, the Sepoys of the Contingent, in the wildest confusion, under the influence of a great fear, feeling that the time had come, roused themselves to the work of mischief. Their officers, who, in accordance with the early habits of the East, had either retired to their beds or were preparing for rest, rose up, hastily clothed themselves, and hurried down to the Lines. Many then left their homes never to see them again. All hope of quieting the general excitement had passed away. There was a furious multi-

tude, eager to cast off the domination of the British —some thirsting for the blood of the white-faced Christians. So when our officers went amidst the mutineers, in the darkness and confusion of the night, they were shot down by the men of the Contingent. Every commanding officer then at Gwalior was killed. Hawkins and Stewart of the Artillery, Blake and Sheriff of the Infantry, fell beneath the fire of the insurgents. The truth was soon known to all; and men, women, and children rushed from their houses to find safety where they could, or to perish by the way. The Sepoys in their fury spared none. Hawkins had his sick wife with him, a baby of a few days old at her breast, and four other young children. Mrs. Stewart and her children were also under his care. The fire of the enemy struck down the artilleryman, and when Mrs. Stewart bent over him and took his hand, a volley of musketry killed them both. Three of the children were also murdered. Here, as in other places, the inconsistency of the Sepoy character was marvellously manifested. Captain Stewart himself was wounded in the first nocturnal onslaught. Two of the men of his battery nursed him tenderly through the night; but when he had good hope of deliverance in the morning, he was taken forth and deliberately shot to death. Major Blake, Commandant of the Second Infantry Regiment—an officer much beloved by his men—a man as good as he was brave, who never feared death except for the sake of those he might leave behind him—was shot through the chest as he sat on his charger before the main guard, at the commencement of the outbreak. The Sepoys of his own regiment expressed profound grief, declared that he had been killed by the men of the Fourth, and tried to prove their words by giving him

1857.
June 15.

decent burial. The Superintending Surgeon, Dr. Kirk, was traced to an out-house, in which he had endeavoured to conceal himself, and there killed in the presence of his wife. The Chaplain, Mr. Coopland, having taken refuge with his wife in Major Blake's house, was dragged away from the arms of the beseeching women, hunted through Cantonments amidst volleys of musketry, and finally overtaken and cut down. Altogether on that night were killed seven officers, six sergeants and pensioners, with three women and three children.

A like number of officers—"some under showers of bullets, but favoured by a moonless night"[*]—escaped. And several ladies and children escaped with them. The majority of these made their way either to the Residency or to Scindiah's Palace. It seemed that, after the first outburst, the Gwalior Sepoys did not lust after the blood of women and children, although their greed compelled them to despoil the ladies of their rings and bracelets, and other ornaments on their persons. A party of five officers' wives—all but one[†] of whom had been made widows by the tragedy of that Sunday night—escaped in the morning with their children closely packed in a small carriage, which conveyed them in safety to Scindiah's Palace. There sufficient carriage was provided for them, and they were sent on towards the Chumbul. In the Dholepore country they were most generously protected and succoured by the

[*] Major Macpherson's Report.

[†] The exception was that of Mrs. Campbell, whose husband, Captain Campbell, was at Agra at the time of the Gwalior outbreak. She was a lady of great personal attractions, and, as she went, she excited the admiration of all—Sepoys and villagers — who saw her; but she was treated with the utmost respect. She had disguised herself in Native costume; but the disguise was soon penetrated. It is related that some who looked upon her exclaimed, with that appreciation of the beauty of small feet that seems to be inherent in nearly all nations : "See how well her feet look in Indian slippers!"

Rajah of that state, who provided them with an 1857.
escort, and safely conveyed them to Agra, where they June.
arrived on the 19th of June, some of them in a very
pitiable plight.*

When the news of these terrible events reached
Scindiah in his Palace, he was in an agony of
shame and grief, and in dire perplexity as to what
was to follow. Macpherson, not without risk of his
life, had hastened to join the Maharajah. On his
way he was attacked by a party of Ghazees, who
would have fired into his carriage, but for the
assurance of a Mahratta officer that the British Agent
was then on his way to Scindiah's presence as a prisoner, by the express orders of the Chief. When he
reached the Palace he found the Maharajah and
Dinkur Rao together. Brigadier Ramsay and others,
who had escaped from Cantonments, had already
arrived at the Phool-bagh. What now was to be
done? Scindiah and his Minister confessed their
inability to protect our people. Assured of this, they
had already ordered carriages and palanquins for the
conveyance of the fugitives to the Chumbul, or across
it to Agra. A party of the body-guard had been
warned to accompany them. Macpherson offered to
remain alone with the Maharajah; but against this
Scindiah protested. It might have been a needless
sacrifice of a precious life. It would certainly have
been an embarrassment to the Durbar. But it was
important that the Chief and his Minister should
take counsel with the British Agent as to what was
to be done after his departure. The anxiety of

* MS. Memorandum by Colonel tended to as far as our means per-
Riddell, who adds: "Accommoda- mitted." The services of the Rajah
tion was immediately provided for of Dholepore have been acknow-
those who had no friends in the ledged by the grant of a knighthood
garrison in one of the European of the Star of India of the highest
barracks, and every comfort at- grade.

1857.
June.

Scindiah was extreme. To him the crisis was one of almost unexampled difficulty. It was certain that the Contingent had gone. It was doubtful whether the Durbar troops would remain faithful. It was feared that they would coalesce with the mutinous Contingent, and call upon Scindiah to place himself at their head, to march upon Agra, and to drive the English out of the great capital of the North-West. To obviate this difficulty, it was the desire of the Maharajah to feed the mutineers largely with treasure, and to permit them to depart to their homes. But Macpherson saw clearly the evil of such a course. He implored the Maharajah to keep his troops together at Gwalior, and consented on the part of his Government that service should be given to them, so long as they might remain in their Lines. Scindiah promised to do all that could be done to conform with this advice, and for a while the troops of both branches of the service, having expelled the English, were kept together at Gwalior.

But, although there was for the present little apprehension of an attack upon Agra from the Head-Quarters of the Gwalior Force, there was threatened danger from another quarter, which Colvin and his colleagues could not disregard. It was reported that the Neemuch Brigade, which, as before said, had revolted, was about to march down upon Agra. Neemuch was a British Cantonment on the borders of Scindiah's territory, to which it had formerly belonged. It was one of the pleasantest and healthiest places in that part of the country—a "favourite station," at which a large body of troops was constantly posted.* Being on the western boundary of

* Mr. Pritchard, in his very in- in Rajpootana," says: "It is a
teresting account of the "Mutinies very favourite garrison for troops,

the territory administered by the Lieutenant-Governor of the North-Western Provinces, the regiments
of the Bombay Army had shared with their comrades
of Bengal the duties of garrisoning the station. It
was an unlucky circumstance that early in the year
some Bombay Infantry corps had been relieved by
Bengal regiments. On the first outbreak of the
mutiny the force at Neemuch consisted of a troop of
Native Horse Artillery, the left wing of the First
Light Cavalry, the Seventy-second Regiment of
Native Infantry (all of the Bengal Army), and the
Seventh Regiment of the Gwalior Contingent. No
European troops were in Cantonments, nor any
within a distance at which they could be available in
an emergency. At Nusseerabad were stationed the
Fifteenth and Thirtieth Regiments of Bengal Native
Infantry and a Native Horse Field Battery. They
had been for some time hovering on the brink of
mutiny. But there was a regiment of Bombay
Cavalry—the First Lancers, which was believed to
be staunch. But when, on the afternoon of the
28th of May, the Bengal troops broke into open
mutiny, the half-heartedness of their Bombay comrades was apparent. Ordered to charge and retake
the guns, they dashed forward, but when within a
few yards of the battery, they turned threes about
and left their officers to be slaughtered. Two were
killed and two were wounded. The different systems
of the several armies under the Company, to which I
have more than once referred, was prominently dis-

having the reputation of being one
of the healthiest stations in the
Presidency. The Cantonment is
built on an elevated ridge surrounding north-west and south-east; in
length about two miles and a half.
The soil is well adapted for horti-
culture, and most of the bungalows
had gardens attached to them. A
kind of fort, or fortified square, had
been erected for the protection of
the European inhabitants or garrison, and was generally used, I
believe, as a magazine."

played.   The Bombay troopers had their families with them.   They were alarmed for the safety of their wives and children—for if they had used their sabres against the Bengal Sepoys, there might have been a massacre in the Bombay Lines.   This accounted for the traitorous inactivity of the Lancers. It was now all over with our unfortunate people. They had nothing left to them but flight—men, women, and children—to Beawur, some thirty miles distant on the road to Deesa — all their property was abandoned; and the Sepoys had their usual " tomasha"—burning and plundering all the public and private buildings, and then marching off for Delhi.

The Nusseerabad troops, having revolted, there was small probability that the Neemuch force, which had long been suspected, would remain true to their colours. On the 3rd of June they broke into open mutiny, and revelled in the wonted plunder and devastation, but they spared their European officers and their families.   The only victims to their fury were the wife and children of a Sergeant of Artillery murdered in their own house.   The insurgents then made a movement to march on Delhi, taking Agra by the way, intelligence of which caused great consternation. It was soon known by the garrison of that place that the Neemuch Brigade had determined to march down upon them, and that there was little or nothing to interrupt their progress.   The distance, however, to be traversed was considerable, and there was an element of consolation in this.   More than three hundred miles of country lay between the mutineers and the capital of the North-West. Weeks remained, therefore, to prepare for the reception of the insurgents.   Moreover, the well-known vacillating character of the Sepoys rendered it at least possible that they would abandon their design of marching on Agra and strike off at once to Delhi. The danger, though formidable, and one afterwards fearfully realised, was not one of urgent pressure; and in the meanwhile other difficulties might present themselves and other complications were to be considered. Next to the bearing of Scindiah in this emergency, the propinquity of whose dominions was an immediate menace, that of Holkar was to be regarded. It follows, therefore, in due course to speak of the conduct of that chief.

1857. June.

Indore, the capital of the territory over which the Maharajah Holkar had sway, lies to the westward of his dominions, at a distance of four hundred miles from Agra, and some thirty miles less from Bombay. It is the chief seat of the representative of the British Government in Central India. The Residency is there; and the Agent to the Governor-General makes it his home during the greater part of the year. Thirteen miles from the capital, within Holkar's country, is the British Cantonment of Mhow. There in the hot weather of 1857 were posted the Twenty-third Regiment of Native Infantry—and the right wing of the First Native Cavalry. These were our weaknesses. Our strength lay in a Horse Battery of European Artillery commanded by Captain Townsend Hungerford. The commandant of the station was Colonel Platt of the Twenty-third.

Indore.

The officiating agent at Indore was Colonel Henry Marion Durand. He had earned for himself a high reputation, nearly twenty years before, when he

Colonel H. M. Durand.

and Norman Macleod, two splendid young Engineer officers, blew open the gates of Ghuznee. Having returned to England, after the first Afghan campaign, he was, on the nomination of Lord Ellenborough to the Governor-Generalship of India, appointed his Private Secretary.* He went out with the new ruler in the *Cambrian*, and was at the great man's elbow until his recall.   He was known then to be a man brave in battle and he was thought to be wise in council. Responsible appointments in the Civil and Political branches of the service were successively bestowed upon him. In 1857, he was acting as Governor-General's Agent in Central India—one of the highest political offices under the Supreme Government. The substantive appointment was held by Sir Robert Hamilton, a Bengal civilian of high repute, whom ill-health had driven to England. The two men were extremely dissimilar. They had different characters and different opinions. Sir Robert Hamilton had much tenderness towards the downtrodden Native princes and chiefs of India. He made great allowances for the evil circumstances surrounding a chief, especially in his younger days ; and he conceived that it was his duty, as the representative of the British Government, no less than it was his inclination as a man, to be tolerant, and by toleration to encourage all that was good in a chief rather than to suppress the evil by harshness. But Durand was not tolerant. He was a high-minded, conscientious English gentleman ; but he looked at every-

---

* It appears from the recently published correspondence of Lord Ellenborough that Durand was first appointed A.D.C. to the Governor-General. As mentioned in vol. i., the Private Secretaryship was offered to Lord Canning, and declined. It would seem, from a reference in the Ellenborough Correspondence, that Lord Charles Wellesley also received an invitation. However, Durand eventually became Private Secretary.

thing through the pure crystal of Christianity; he wanted imagination; he could not Orientalise himself. Had his lines been cast in other places, he might have been a great soldier.* He was not a good political officer, because lacking sympathy, he could not make allowances, and expected a Mahratta chief to be as leal as a Percy or a Campbell. This caused him to leap hastily to conclusions—as will presently be shown.

At this time, Holkar was in his twenty-first year.† He was a quiet, well-educated, intelligent man, of no great energy of character, and by no means addicted to warlike pursuits. He had been very carefully trained under the guidance of Sir Robert Hamilton, who placed over the young Maharajah as his immediate preceptor, a clever, well-instructed Brahmin, named Omeid Singh, who had been confidentially employed by Sir George Clerk on the Punjab frontier, and who had afterwards been Government translator at Agra. He was conversant not only with the languages of India, the Mahratta included, but also with English, both as spoken and as written. Sir Robert Hamilton's system was that, which has since been pursued in another Native state, with good promise of the best results.‡ He associated with the young Prince some of the sons of the chief people of Indore—boys of about his own age, who became his class-fellows and friends. When first the Maha-

1857. June.

The Maharajah Holkar.

---

* He was, perhaps, with one exception, the best writer of Military History whom I ever knew. He had not the fire and enthusiasm of William Napier, but no one ever understood more fully or explained more clearly great military operations than Henry Durand.

† Mr. Edward Thornton, in his very valuable *Gazetteer*, says that Holkar attained his majority in 1852. This would have made the Maharajah twenty-three years of age at the time of the mutiny.

‡ In Mysore, where Colonel Malleson is admirably exercising his powers, as guardian of the future ruler of that fine country (1873).

rajah came under tuition he was "an intelligent, bright boy, with an easy, self-possessed manner," but his attainments went little beyond his capacity to trace a few Mahratta characters on sand, after the custom of village schools. But he was exceedingly ductile and eager to learn, and he made good progress with his studies. Ere long he came to read and to understand English, but he never could write it freely. Long after his nonage was at an end— indeed up to the time of Omeid Singh's death —his correspondence was conducted by his old preceptor. But no letter went forth in his name, the contents of which he did not thoroughly understand.

It might have been right or it might have been wrong—I think it was right—but Sir Robert Hamilton encouraged the young Maharajah, when he came of age, and the chief people around him, freely to deliver their sentiments on all subjects, even though they might not be, in every case, very flattering to the British Government. It was the habit, therefore, at the Indore Durbar, when Hamilton returned to England, not without some mental inquietude as to the results of his absence, to speak out freely—to ventilate grievances, and to expound the supposed means of remedying them. But Durand could not tolerate this. A man of an imperious temper, with a profound belief in the immense inferiority of the Asiatic races, he esteemed it to be the worst presumption in a Mahratta prince or noble, to openly express an opinion of his own in the presence of the representative of the British Government. And, for this, or for some other reason, which I cannot even conjecture, he seems never to have had any feeling of personal kindness towards the young

Maharajah. There was an antipathy which, perhaps, was reciprocated. But no member of the British agency, during the first two months of trouble, ever spoke of the disloyalty of Holkar. Doubtless, he was sorely troubled in his mind. He knew that at Gwalior the Contingent had revolted. He knew that the British troops at Nusseerabad and Neemuch had declared for mutiny, and, if not drawn away towards Delhi and Agra, might disorganise his whole country. He saw, on his right hand and on his left, most terrible proofs of a general rebellion against the domination of the English. The whole of the North-Western Provinces were slipping away from our grasp. At Delhi we were still besieged by an insolent enemy. At Indore, all except those of his old class-mates, who were still attached to his Government or his person, were openly boasting the downfall of the British Raj, or muttering schemes of hostility, whereby they might rise on the ruins of the British Empire. But Holkar himself, though still young in years, was old enough in wisdom to have full faith in the durability of our power. He knew what were the resources of the State—what the energy of the English character; and there was a strong conviction within him that we should eventually be triumphant. And although he did not love Durand, there were those of our nation whom he did love, and he would not willingly have blackened his face before them.

So little was Holkar dreaming of war, that his troops were scattered over his country, and everywhere miserably equipped. His arsenal and magazine were almost empty. Early in June the Durbar sought the assistance of the British Agent, who wrote to Lord Elphinstone on the 5th of June for military supplies: "If the arms can be spared," he said,

" even to half the amount named,* a thousand fusils, Holkar would be gratified, for his Infantry are badly equipped, and would be much the better for reliable arms. So badly off is this Durbar for warlike prepara- tions, that although they have some good six-pounders and nine-pounders, they have no ammunition; and I have taken upon myself to order that they receive forty rounds per gun for each battery, the ammuni- tion being drawn from the Mhow magazine." No thought had Durand, at that time, that the Indore Government could ever turn against him. He be- lieved Holkar to be true ; and he sought to strengthen his powers of defence against the enemies of the British Government.

Up to this time, Durand had received assuring accounts of the state of the brigades at Nusseerabad and Neemuch. But it was impossible not to recog- nise the magnitude of the crisis. " Sir Robert Ha- milton," he wrote to Lord Elphinstone, " escapes a critical period. Central India is as yet all quiet ; but men's minds are excited, and anxiously awaiting news from Delhi, which I had hoped to receive to-day. Neemuch and Nusseerabad are reported all quiet, but the officers are evidently anxious, and not very confident. A well-struck blow at Delhi will prove an invaluable sedative. The present is even a more serious crisis than that which your Lordship announced from the signal-post at Madras, when the *Cambrian* hove in sight. It was a serious welcome.†

* The request made by Holkar's Vakeel was for two thousand fusils, three hundred pairs of pistols, and four lakhs of gun-caps.

† The semaphore announced, " Bad news." The *Cambrian* sig- nalled, " What news ?" When it was answered, that our troops had been driven out of Afghanistan, Lord Ellenborough drew a long breath of relief, and said to Durand that he had expected something worse — a mutiny of the Native Army.

But Lord Canning's present difficulties and responsibilities are still graver than those which beset all in high authority at the time I had the honour of being presented to you. It is matter of congratulation for all watching the course of events, that one of your Lordship's experience in India is at the head of the Bombay Government, and you may command my services in this sphere of action in any way you may deem necessary to the public service."

But even whilst he was writing that all things were quiet at Nusseerabad and Neemuch, the troops there were in the throes of active rebellion. He then trembled for the safety of Mhow. "I wish," he wrote on the 13th of June, "that I could give you a satisfactory account of the state of the troops at Mhow. The Twenty-third Native Infantry is, I think, more disposed to remain quiet than the wing of the First Cavalry. The troopers of the latter are said to be taunting and urging the Infantry to rise. Both, however, are in fear of the European battery, and also of the troops and guns here. They are in fear, too, of the column from Bombay, which they suspect to have a punitive mission for themselves. The officers are endeavouring to assure them that they have nothing to dread, provided they remain orderly and quiet. If the Mhow troops rise, it will probably be as much owing to the apprehensions so insidiously spread amongst ·them, of stern measures being in store for suspected corps, as to anything else. We sadly want the capture of Delhi to act as a sedative on Chiefs and People, and the smouldering spirit of Revolt." And so it was from all parts of India, the same despairing cry—Let the English triumph at Delhi, and the head of the great giant

Revolt will be crushed under the heel of the English-man.

And so the month of June wore to a close. The Nusseerabad and Neemuch Brigades were going off to Delhi. But the troops at Mhow had not risen, and no suspicion of the fidelity of Holkar had been entertained. By Colonel Platt, who commanded the station, the confidence system had been consistently maintained; not without some protests from the Artillery-man Hungerford, who urged upon the commanding officer wise, but not obtrusive precautions. All, however, had gone well. But, with the month of June, the prevailing quietude expired. Suddenly, a little before noon on the 1st of July, Colonel Platt received a note from Durand at Indore, saying, " Send the European battery as sharp as you can. We are attacked by Holkar."

The history of this sudden rising at Indore will, perhaps, never be revealed in all its naked truth.* But we know at least this much: on the morning of the 1st of July, Durand was writing a telegram to Lord Elphinstone, when the sound of firing was heard.† It was a startling surprise to him, for the

---

* Colonel Durand was of opinion that the arrest of General Wood-burn's column, which had been ordered to march on Mhow, brought affairs to a crisis; and this is extremely probable. Note the following: "When Lord Elphinstone notified by telegram the countermand of the advance of Woodburn's column, and asked me the probable effect on my charge—*i.e.*, Central India—I replied at once that I could not answer one hour for Central India, when it became known that Wood-burn's column was not to advance to Mhow. Unfortunately the contents of the telegram were known in Indore as soon as it arrived, and, being immediately followed by bad news from Delhi, Holkar's troops and city rose, attacked the Residency, &c., &c."—*MS. Memorandum by Colonel Durand.*

† Mr. McMahon and Mr. Butler, and some of the East Indian writers and Telegraph people, were killed. The following account of the Indore mutiny and massacre is borrowed from the letter of an eye-witness, published in a contemporary journal: "The slaughter of the inhabitants of the British Civil Station of Indore by the mutinous troops of Holkar commenced at eight o'clock A.M. on

guns which were roaring out their menaces, were some guns of Holkar's Artillery, which had been brought down, at his own request, for the defence of the Residency and the treasure.   It was soon ascertained that they had opened fire upon the pickets of the Bhopal Cavalry, and on the tents of the Bhopal Infantry.   Colonel Travers, who commanded the Bhopal Contingent, was soon in the saddle; but with the exception of half a dozen troopers, nearly all Sikhs, his Cavalry would not follow him, when he rode forward to charge the guns.   It is a miracle that his life was spared.   His horse was shot; the slings of his sword-belt were cut through, but he escaped both the grape-shot and the sabres of his assailants.   The Infantry of the Bhopal Contingent were equally inactive.   They refused to fire on the enemy—that is, upon those who had fired upon them; but levelled their pieces at the European sergeants, and seemed to be eager for the blood of their officers.   Two guns of the Bhopal Contingent were loyally worked; but they made little impression

the 1st instant. Three guns and the troops sent down by the Rajah for the protection of the Residency were the first to turn against us in the most unexpected and unprovoked manner; nor was the work of murder and destruction stayed until about twenty of the Christian residents had been slaughtered, and the pillage of the Government treasury, as well as the demolition of *all* public and private buildings had been accomplished. The Post Office was one of the first buildings attacked, and the wife, daughter-in-law, and child of the Postmaster, Mr. Beauvais, were shot down in their carriage whilst attempting to escape, before the eyes of the unhappy gentleman and his son, who providentially escaped unhurt amidst volleys of musketry. The following are the names of all those who are known to have escaped in safety from Indore : Colonel and Mrs. Durand; Colonel Travers; Colonel Stockley; Captain Ludlow; Captain Cobbe and wife; Captain Magniac and wife; Captain Waterman; Mrs. Captain Robertson and two children; Dr. Thompson; Mrs. Dutton; Lieut. and Mrs. Shakespeare and child; Dr. and Mrs. Rice; Dr. and Mrs. Knapp; and Messrs. Crawley, Hammond, Galloway, O'Brien, and Collins, of the Electric Telegraph Department."

1857.
July 1.

on the mutineers; and everything seemed to be against us.*

Departure of the English from Indore.

So Durand determined to gather up his people, and to fly from Indore. "Finding," he wrote, "that the Cavalry, who were loyal, though disordered and out of control, would be off on their own score, I very unwillingly gave the order to retire; and, mounting the ladies on the gun waggons, we made an orderly retreat, bringing off every European they had not killed, during the first surprise, and covered our withdrawal with the Bheel corps and the Cavalry of the Bhopal Contingent. The ladies went off from the Residency under a fire of grape from Holkar's guns, followed by a few farewell round-shots—but no damage was done to any of the riders on the waggons, though some had the pleasure of seeing their property burning before they got clear of the Residency."† It was the saddest hour of that brave man's life. "First," he wrote, some time afterwards, " came the humiliation of being forced to withdraw before an enemy that I despised, and who, could I have got anything to fight, would have been easily beaten back. As it was, with only fourteen Golun-

---

* The conduct of our auxiliaries in this conjuncture may be narrated in Colonel Durand's words: "I never expected to witness such wretched treachery and cowardice as drove us from Indore. . . . The Bhopal and Mehidpore Contingent Infantry would not fire a shot, or obey an order, and threatened to shoot their European officers. The Bhopal Contingent Cavalry never recovered the surprise, were panic-stricken, and from the first quite beyond the control of their officers. As for the Bheels, as fast as I put them behind pillars, or bays of windows, under cover for defence of the Residency, the moment my back was turned, or that of their own European officer, they used to collect together in the centre rooms." . . . "We could have repulsed the attack on the 1st easily, if we had had anything that could fight. But the Bhopal Contingent and Mehidpore Contingent fraternised with Holkar's troops. The Sikh Horse would neither form nor fight, and the only thing they thought of was keeping out of fire and bolting. It was the most painfully disgusting affair I ever underwent."—MS. Correspondence.

† Colonel Durand to Lord Elphinstone—Sehore, July 4.—MS. Correspondence.

dauze who would stand by their guns, we not only held our own for about a couple of hours, but beat back their guns and gained temporary advantage." So that "we retired unmolested in the face of superior masses, whose appetite for blood had been whetted by the murder of unarmed men, women, and children. Of all the bitter, bitter days of my life, I thought this the worst, for I never had to retreat, still less to order a retreat myself, and though the game was up, and to have held on was to insure the slaughter of those I had no right to expose to such a fate without an adequate hope or object, still my pride as a soldier was wounded beyond all expression, and I would have been thankful had any one shot me."*

Meanwhile, in the British Cantonment of Mhow, the Native troops, whom Colonel Platt had so greatly trusted, were in the first throes of rebellion. Hungerford, in contemplation of the rising of the Native troops, had urged the Colonel in the month of June, to allow him to take his battery on to the open plain, where they could be immediately manned and prepared for action. This had been granted; but when he further proposed that an artillery gun should be placed at the Fort Gate, and that shelter should be found behind its walls for our women and children, the old confidence cry was repeated. Self-assured of the loyalty of the Sepoys, the Commandant had refused to sanction a measure which might seem to imply suspicion of the fidelity of his men. The guns were parked in front of the barracks, but nothing

* Colonel Durand to Lord Lovaine, September 29, 1857.—*MS. Correspondence.*

1857.
July 1.

more had been done for our safety, when Hungerford received orders on the 1st of July to march down on Indore, as Holkar's regiments were in rebellion. In a little while his guns were clattering down to the capital.* As no escort had been ordered, two men for each gun and waggon were armed with muskets and mounted on the limbers. But Hungerford had not proceeded more than half-way to Indore, when he met a trooper of the Bhopal Cavalry bringing a pencil-note from Colonel Travers, stating that Durand and other Europeans had evacuated the Residency, and were retreating upon Sehore. The trooper added that Durand had not gone to Mhow, because the Cantonment was in Holkar's dominions, and an attack on our Cantonments was meditated in the course of the night. So the battery was counter-marched, and returned to the Cantonment of Mhow.

Then Hungerford went straightway to the Commandant and met him on the road. Having communicated the strange news, which had reached him on the route to Indore, he besought Colonel Platt to allow him to take his battery into the Fort, as he could defend the place for any time until succours should arrive. But Platt could not be brought to listen to the proposal. Consent was emphatically refused. And so the day wore on; and Hungerford, in spite of frequent refusals, continued persistently to advocate this course. The day was one of doubt and fear. Even the Commandant, as the shades of evening fell upon Mhow, ·began to think that he might have been mistaken. He then gave a reluctant assent to the movement, which had been so often pressed upon him; and Hungerford took his battery into the Fort. At this time there were manifest

Mutiny at
Mhow.

* See Colonel Durand's statement, *post*, page 344.

signs of an approaching crisis. The mess-house of
the Twenty-third was on fire. Other buildings in
the Cantonments were blazing and breaking through
the darkness of the night. This was ever the old
signal for the commencement of action; and soon
the ominous sound of firing came from the direction
of the Lines. At nine Colonel Platt was writing to
Durand, " All right, both Cavalry and Infantry very
khoosh (happy) and willing." At ten o'clock they
were in the spasms of revolt. The delusion was
suddenly dispersed. Platt mounted his horse, rode
into the Fort, and ordered Hungerford to turn out
his guns. He then, accompanied by Adjutant Fagan,
rode for the Lines. At the Quarter-Guard he drew
rein, and began to address his men. His appeal was
cut short by a volley from the faithful Twenty-third;
and both the Colonel and the Adjutant fell from
their horses, riddled with balls. About the same time
Major Harris of the First Cavalry was fired upon by
a party of his troopers, deliberately told off for the
purpose. The first volley killed his horse. Regain-
ing his legs, he attempted to escape through the
darkness—but he was shot down, and then gashed to
death by the sabres of his own men. These were
the only murders of the night. Other officers had
marvellous escapes.

Meanwhile Hungerford had been getting his guns
ready for action. The process was slower than it
would have been, if men and horses had not been
wearied by the march and counter-march of the
morning. Still, there was but slight delay on the
part of Hungerford's gunners. The Artillery Captain
had always said that it would take but little time and
trouble for him to crush any insurrection of the
Native troops, that might confront him at Mhow;

and now he went forth, confident of the result. But the difficulty was to find the enemy. As he made for the Lines, half a mile distant from the Fort, he was fired upon through the darkness, but he could not perceive his assailants. The bungalows of the English officers were in a blaze; but the Lines were in total obscurity. He was perplexed, too, by seeing nothing of the Commandant, from whom he had expected to receive orders. He did, therefore, the best thing that could be done. He opened fire upon the Lines. The roar of the guns frightened the Sepoys, Cavalry and Infantry; and they streamed out on the road to Indore, where they fraternised with Holkar's mutinous regiments, clamoured for the blood of our Christian people, and gutted the British Treasury. "Next day their Lines (at Mhow) were found full of their clothes, cooking vessels, &c., and many muskets, coats, &c., were found scattered for a great distance all over the country."* They had fled from our guns in a state of panic and bewilderment. Grape and canister were not to their liking.

Hungerford was now master of the situation. He was the senior officer at Mhow, and right gladly he took the command. The first thing that he did, after burying the bodies of the murdered officers, was to proclaim Martial Law "throughout the station." His first impression was that Holkar might be leagued with the mutineers. Ominous reports reached him, which he did not, over hastily, accept; but for a little space they enfeebled his former strong faith in the Maharajah. So he 'wrote to Holkar saying, "I understand from many Natives that you have given food to the mutinous troops. I have heard also, but I do not know whether to believe,

* Captain Hungerford's Report to Government, July 17, 1873.

that you have lent them guns and offered them 1857.
Irregular Cavalry, as assistance. These reports are July.
very probably much exaggerated. I do not believe
them. You owe so much to the British, and can be
so utterly ruined by showing enmity towards them,
that I do not believe that you can be so blind to
your own interest as to afford aid and show friendship to the enemies of the British Government." To
this Holkar promptly replied: " The accounts,
which you seem to have received of my assistance to
the enemies of the British Government are, as you
suppose, not only exaggerated but entirely false. No
one regrets more than I do the heart-rending catastrophes, which befel at Indore and at Mhow. . . . .
I have not, even in a dream, ever deviated from
the path of friendship and allegiance to the British
Government. I know their sense of justice and
honour will make them pause before they suspect,
even for a moment, a friendly chief, who is so sensible
of the obligations that he owes to them, and is ready
to do anything for them. But there are catastrophes
in the world, which cannot be controlled, and the
one that has happened is one of them."* Having
written, or caused this to be written, Holkar sent two July 12.
confidential officers to Mhow to explain all the circumstances of the outbreak of the 1st of July; and
Hungerford was satisfied and assured.

But it was hard to say what might not happen. Conduct of
No tidings came from Durand. All recognised poli- Captain Hun-
tical authority had swept itself out of the Indore gerford.
territory. The brave Artilleryman, who had taken

---

* In this letter Holkar says "but to offer them my own person,
that the mutineers demanded the but I would not allow the poor Euro-
heads of a few Europeans, whom he peans to be touched before being
had concealed in the Palace. " I had killed myself."
no alternative," added the Maharajah,

the reins into his own hands, took upon himself the
diplomatic, as well as the military, control of affairs.
He garrisoned and victualled the Fort. He blew up
the magazines in the Lines. He planted guns in
the embrasures of the Fort. He prepared himself to
stand a month's siege. And he waited for orders—
but he waited in vain. No orders came. He wrote
to Durand at Sehore—but he received no answers to
his letters. So he established himself as representative of the Governor-General in Holkar's dominion,
and opened a correspondence with the nearest Government—that of Lord Elphinstone at Bombay. He
was one of those men, who, little thought of in quiet
times, when opportunities were wanting, rose with
the occasion and went boldly to the front. He did
what he had "no right to do," and he was afterwards
severely rebuked by Durand. But History, rising
above all official formalities, must pronounce, that
the men who did what they had "no right to do,"
were those who saved the British Government in
India.

But what was Holkar doing all this time? The
roar of the guns surprised him as much as it surprised Durand, and perhaps it bewildered him still
more. He could not understand what it portended.
He did not know what to do. He knew that some
of his guns had opened fire, but for what purpose, and
in what direction, was not clearly known to him. All
the inmates of the Palace were in the wildest state of
tumult and confusion. First one story, then another,
was brought to him. No one could give him any
clear insight into this most unexpected and most
mysterious ebullition. It might have been directed

against the English, or it might have been directed
against himself. That in the first hour of the outbreak, he was astounded and paralysed is certain. But
no one can have followed me so far in this history of
the Sepoy War without discerning the patent, the
obstreperous truth that English soldiers and statesmen of the highest rank, were sometimes bewildered
and paralysed when first the storm burst upon them.
If, in the sudden confusion, when there were runnings
to and fro at the Palace, and the reports of one man
set at naught the reports of another, Holkar thought
more of himself and the Raj than of Durand and
the British Agency;* he did only that which in like
circumstances, any Englishman would have done.
His first duty was to his Raj, which he believed to be
as much imperilled as the lives of the little cluster
of Englishmen at his Court. But before the Maharajah had time to recover himself from the first confusion and stupor of this sudden outbreak, Durand
had fled from Indore—no one seemed to know
whither.

Still Holkar did not despair; he knew that his
face was irretrievably blackened in the eyes of the
representative of the British Government at his
capital. For Durand could justify his own departure, only by proving the consummate treachery

1857.
July.

* Holkar's own words are, "The tumult and confusion which prevailed were such, and alarm and fear so great, that it was impossible to procure an account of what had actually happened. I was utterly ignorant of what had brought about the outbreak, never entertaining for a moment the most distant idea that any troops, which had been posted at the Residency for its protection, had themselves proved mutinous. The first moment that I received even some confused intelligence of what was going on I ordered my Sowarree and was on the point of proceeding to you at once, but at that moment I learnt that you had left the Residency. I never dreamed, could never have dreamed, for one instant that you could have imbibed the shadow of a suspicion against me, or that the attack could have been directed by my orders."

z 2

of Holkar. Less than two hours had intervened between the first outburst of the guns and the eva- cuation of the Residency. It must have been a crisis of extraordinary magnitude that compelled the precipitate retreat of so brave and so wise a man with the best blood of England in his veins. All this the Maharajah knew to be fatally against him; but he knew also, that whatsoever might have been done, or not done, during those two delirious hours, there was yet time for him to prove his loyalty to the British Government by casting in his lot with them. And he did it. In what manner will presently be told.

Scarcely had the representative of the British Government turned his back upon Indore, when Holkar, having recovered from the first surprise and confusion attending that most unexpected outburst, began by many outward acts, not to be misunder- stood or misinterpreted, to demonstrate his fidelity to the paramount power of India. A few Europeans were still left alive in Indore. The Maharajah con- cealed them in the Palace, and the insurgents sent to him demanding their heads and those also of some Durbar officers supposed to be friendly to the British. They called on Holkar to come forth and show himself, and he rode out amongst them. They clamoured loudly, but their demands were resolutely rejected. He offered them his own person—but he would not suffer an Englishman to be hurt. They called upon him to place himself at their head, and to lead them against the English. They reminded him of the martial character of his great ancestor, Jeswant Rao, and taunted him with cowardice; but even this did not move him to join the ranks of our enemies. He told the insurgents that it was no part of the traditions of his family that they should murder women and children. He stood out boldly against all the entreaties and all the threats of his own soldiery, and then rode back to the Palace.

Already had the Maharajah addressed letters, on the day of the outbreak, to Colonel Durand and to Lord Elphinstone, assuring them of his fidelity, and he urged the immediate advance of the Bombay troops, under General Woodburn, for the suppression of disorder, and the pacification of the country. He gathered up the remains of the English treasure, and sent it under safe escort to Hungerford at Mhow. He sent thither also his own money and jewels, and Government securities and other property, and he despatched his most confidential servants to Hungerford to assure the British officers that he was as true as steel. And of this, the stout-hearted Artilleryman, who had doubted at first, was now fully convinced.

With sore distress and dismay the Maharajah heard that Captain Hutchinson, who held the post of Bheel Agent, under the Indore Resident, had been taken prisoner, with his family, by the Amjheera Rajah, and was confined in his fort. Mrs. Hutchinson was a daughter of Sir Robert Hamilton, and it was in no strain of Oriental hyperbole that the Maharajah declared that he regarded her "as his sister, and the whole family as his relations," for he looked up to Hamilton with filial reverence and affection. So he determined to send out a detachment for their rescue. Amjheera was tributary to Scindiah and to Holkar, therefore, was as foreign country. So he sought instructions from Hungerford, who promptly took upon himself the political responsibility. But Hutchinson and his party were not in captivity.

They were at Bhopawur, with other Europeans connected with the Bheel Corps, at the time of the
Indore revolt, tidings of which reached them on the
2nd of July, with the addition that Holkar had
placed himself at the head of the insurgents. All
the smaller chiefs in the neighbourhood were ripe
for revolt, and this startling intelligence from Indore
made them eager for the affray. At first Hutchinson
thought that he could defend himself and his people
with the help of a party of loyal Bheels, but this
hope soon passed away from him, and he saw no
chance of safety but in flight. And even that was
doubtful and precarious. They went forth disguised
as a party of Parsee merchants, with their families,
on the way to Baroda, and made a perilous journey
to Jubooah, where they were hospitably entertained
by the young chief and his family, who were of good
old Rajpoot stock, and would never betray those who
had sought sanctuary with them. When this was
known, the detachment, which Holkar had sent out,
was recalled, and an escort sent forward to bring
our people to Indore. "I had such implicit faith in
Holkar's friendship," wrote Hutchinson, "that I did
not hesitate to place myself and family under the
protection of his troops, for the purpose of proceeding to Indore to assume charge of the Residency,
during the absence of Colonel Durand, and by my
presence and advice to assure and guide Holkar
through the crisis." Thus was Hungerford relieved
from the political responsibility, which he had undertaken with so much promptitude and acquitted
himself of with so much address.

Reviewing, after a lapse of years, without prejudice or affection, this question of the retreat from Indore, it appears to me that the grounds upon which the abandonment of the Residency is to be justified are these, as set forth by Durand's friends: "That Holkar's force, which had opened fire on the Residency and attacked our people, and which Holkar was either unable or unwilling to control, were numerous and well-equipped—that the Residency was a building not calculated for purposes of defence—that some of the Contingent troops would not act against the enemy, and that the remainder were too few to resist them—that, by withdrawing at once, and falling back upon such support as he could find elsewhere, he would maintain the independence of the authority which he represented, and would be able to make his influence better felt by the several chieftains under his agency, and even by Holkar himself." The force of these considerations may be readily admitted. But it is added—"that no succour could be obtained from Mhow, where mutiny was known to be imminent, and, in fact, took place on the same day; the mutinous troops marching to Indore and plundering the Government Treasury;" and that "had Colonel Durand decided to remain, he could not possibly have withstood the combined attack of Holkar's troops and the Mhow mutineers. It could only have been by Holkar's being able and willing to control his own troops, and to use them against the Mhow mutineers, that the Residency could have been held." It is evident, however, from what has been already related, that succours from Mhow of the most serviceable kind were available; for Hungerford's European battery was rattling towards Indore, when news met it that Colonel Durand and all his people had departed. Had it arrived whilst the Residency was still occupied, the rising at Indore would most probably have been suppressed, and there would have been no combination of Holkar's troops with the Mhow mutineers. The Sepoys at Mhow were encouraged to revolt by the knowledge that nothing had been done to put down the insurrection at Indore. The evacuation of the Residency naturally caused it to be believed that Holkar was on the side of the insurgents. To have held on for a few hours would have given time for the Maharajah to recover from his first bewilderment, and to declare himself on our side, and it would have brought Hungerford and his battery to Indore.

To this Colonel Durand's answer was—in a letter written to Mr. Talbot, Lord Canning's Private Secretary, on the 16th of August—" I see, by the *Friend of India* of the 30th of July, that that paper, taking up the tone of a letter written from Mhow, talks of my inopportune flight, and repeats the nonsense and mis-statements about Hungerford's proceedings when shut up with the writer of the letter—a Captain Trower, of the Twenty-third Native Infantry—in the Mhow Fort. I should wish the Governor-General to know that Hungerford's battery — though my note to Colonel Platt, despatched from Indore at a quarter to nine, reached Colonel Platt by a quarter to ten— was not ready to move until noon, by the statement of its own officers. It then advanced to Indore at a trot, and had gone to the half-way village of Rao, where obtaining information that we had left Indore, Hungerford returned at a gallop or canter the whole way, and dashed with his battery straight into the Fort at three P.M.—the moment he arrived. Had he continued his course to Indore at the rate he moved away from Mhow, it would have been four P.M. at least before he reached the Residency, for they did not canter out. I retired from the Residency, after a two hours' cannonade, about half past ten."* That is three-quarters of an hour after the call for the battery reached Mhow. Now the battery could not have been equipped, mounted, and brought down to Indore, at full gallop, in three-quarters of an hour. So it is clear that Colonel Durand did not await even the possibility of the arrival, under the most favourable circumstances, of Hungerford and his guns. Indeed, Captain Hungerford's statement is that at eleven A.M. Colonel Platt called on him with a letter from Colonel Durand, begging that the battery under his command might be sent to Indore instantly. "I marched," added Hungerford, "my battery at once on Indore."† So it appears that Hungerford did not get his orders till after Durand had quitted the capital.

It is to the honour of Lord Elphinstone, whose whole conduct, as Governor of Bombay, during this momentous period, was distinguished by as much energy as sagacity, that he supported Hungerford throughout all his irregularities. There is a natural disposition on the part of Governors, where there is an official conflict, to side with the higher authority. Durand, at this time, had a great reputation throughout India. Hungerford was an unknown man—merely a Captain of Artillery—who, in the ordinary routine of regimental duty, had been sent to command a battery at Mhow. But Elphinstone could not resist the conviction that Durand had hastily condemned Holkar, and by his flight from

---

* MS. Correspondence.
† Captain Hungerford to Ad-

jutant-General, Bombay, July 4, 1857.

Indore, had brought matters to this issue — that either the Maharajah was a traitor, or that the British Agent had fled, without good cause, from Indore. That the Governor of Bombay, with all the facts before him, came to the latter conclusion, is certain. At Calcutta, where only the main outline of events was known, the honoured Patriarch of the Political Service, then a member of the Supreme Government, wrote that if the story of the abandonment of Indore were true, Durand ought to be removed from political employment. This was merely a first impression. What I have written will show Durand's reasons for the movements—which Lord Elphinstone could not endorse. But admitting that the sudden retreat was justifiable—or even commendable—I can see nothing to justify the after-treatment of Holkar by the Acting-Resident at Indore. There can be no question that Holkar was sacrificed to the justification of Durand.

Durand and
Holkar.
It is certain that in the brief interval between the first thunder of the guns, and the flight from the Residency, there was no time to ascertain, and no attempts made to inquire into the position of affairs, and to investigate the cause of the unexpected explosion. Durand had been warned by Holkar that the Durbar could not rely on the fidelity of their troops. This was not a proof of treachery. But on the 4th of July he wrote to Lord Elphinstone, saying, "The storm burst upon us earlier than I suspected, and from a quarter where gratitude and every other consideration rendered it most improbable. . . . No surprise could have been more complete, as Holkar's guns were there to aid in the defence of the Residency and the Treasury. The Cavalry never recovered from the surprise caused by Holkar's treachery.

Scindiah and Holkar appear to be allies. Scindiah's treachery, if there was any, never was palpable— but Holkar's has been of the true Mahratta stamp." It was Durand's argument, persistently repeated, that a Native Prince is responsible for the conduct of his troops. Whether this opinion be sound or unsound, as applied to ordinary times and circumstances, Justice and Policy should have dictated, at such a period of our history, entire reticence on this question of responsibility. For the great military revolt of 1857 was conceived, born, and developed in our own provinces. Our own disciplined troops led the way to the terrible revolts which convulsed and agonised the country. In the Native States the contagion of rebellion was caught from the Company's Army. It is scarcely to be doubted that the Sepoys of our own regiments at Mhow contaminated Holkar's troops at Indore. But blinded by that intense national self-love, of which I have so often spoken, Durand, like many other good men, could not discern the fact, that the great burden of responsibility for all these troubles was upon our own shoulders. He saw through a glass darkly our own errors and short-comings, but those of the Native States, face to face, or through a magnifying glass of enormous power. He knew that by some negligence or mismanagement of our own, we had set our house on fire and allowed the flames to spread; but when the fire, which we ought to have extinguished, extended to our neighbours, he held them responsible for the conflagration.

With what tenacity he clung to this doctrine was exemplified by the manner in which, not long afterwards, he treated the petty state of Dhar, when its mercenary troops, in the first days of the minority of the young Rajah, went into rebellion. He recommended the sequestration or the annexation of that ancient principality on the ground of the responsibility of the Durbar. And this most unjust and impolitic sentence would have been executed, but for the interposition of the Court of Directors of the East India Company, who wrote to the Government of India, saying, " We cannot consistently punish this or any other weak state for its inability to control its troops, when it is patent to the whole world that the more powerful states of Gwalior and Indore, and even the British Government itself, were unable to control theirs."*

After long and most deliberate consideration of all the circumstances of Holkar's conduct in that first week of July, I cannot resist the conviction, that he was thoroughly true to the British Government. The charge against him is that within two hours from the time when he was first startled by the roar of the guns, he had not assured the British Agent that he was in nowise concerned in the hostile movement. Durand was new to his work. If he had any knowledge of the Mahratta character it was only a half-knowledge. He had an obscure notion that all Mahrattas were by nature treacherous. But he did not fathom their treachery. He did not seem to know that from the days of Sivajee down to the time of Doondoo Punt, Nana Sahib, a Mahratta has always been most dangerous when simulating friendship. If Holkar had

* I do not know why Mr. Dickenson should so frequently, notwithstanding numerous proofs to the contrary, have called the despatch, from which the above passage is quoted, " Lord Stanley's despatch." I do not question that Lord Stanley, always just and logical, entertained the opinions thus expressed—but the passage was written and sent to India before Lord Stanley was appointed Secretary of State. I ought to be accepted as an authority upon this point of History—as I drafted the despatch myself, for the Court of Directors.

premeditated the attack on the Residency, he would have had a messenger ready to be despatched to Durand to assure the representative of the British Government of his loyalty. That this was not done, within the two first hours of the all-prevailing confusion, seems to indicate that Holkar was as much surprised as Durand.   So strongly impressed was Lord Elphinstone with the conviction that the Maharajah was true to us, that he wrote to Lord Canning on the 13th of July, saying, " It seems clearly proved that Holkar was not implicated in the outbreak.   He was unable to control his own troops, who were probably set on by the Bengal Sepoys at Mhow, and who attacked and plundered the Residency.   Colonel Durand appears to be under the impression that Holkar had turned against us, and that he was attacked by his orders.   This, however, is certainly not the case.   On the same evening Holkar wrote to Colonel Durand and to me, protesting his innocence and entreating that the march of General Woodburn's force should be hastened as much as possible."*   And some days afterwards he wrote to Colonel Durand, saying, " I led to believe that you still entertain doubts of Holkar.   All that has happened during your absence from Indore tends to acquit him of having been a party to the attack on the Residency.   Indeed, if he had been ill-disposed towards us, the whole country would have risen.   All the smaller chiefs seem to take their cue from him ; and even to the borders of Gujerat, the effects of his conduct would have been apparent. . . . . . This comes to me from too many sources to admit of a doubt . . . . . Let me, therefore, beg you not

1857.
July.

July 23.
1857

* MS. Correspondence of Lord same strain to Vernon Smith on Elphinstone. He wrote also in the the 14th.

1857.
July.'

to harbour any prejudices against Holkar, to whom I cannot but think that we are very much indebted for the preservation of the peace in Malwa, and also in Gujerat."*

But the prejudice never was overcome in the high places of the Supreme Government. Years passed and he was still more or less a suspect. The Star of India was conferred on him; but that which is most coveted by all as the highest honour—a grant of territory—was withheld from him though granted to Scindiah. He seems never to have recovered from this slight. Meanwhile he saw Durand elevated to the highest offices under the State—Foreign Secretary to Government—Member of Council—Lieutenant-Governor of the Punjab. One of the ablest men and best public servants that India has ever seen, and held deservedly in the highest honour even by those who differed from him in opinion. But we have still to mourn the fact that when the crown of his ambition was gained, Sir Henry Marion Durand died disastrously, in the prime of his life and the fulness of his reputation.

Another pregnant source of anxiety to the Lieutenant-Governor was the condition of that vast tract of country inhabited by the Rajwarrah races, and ruled by a great cluster of Rajpoot chiefs—sympathising little with each other, and many of them living in continual strife with the chief people of the principality—the " Thakoors"—whom they were supposed to govern. There was small chance of these Rajpoot chieftains sympathising with a movement,

* MS. Correspondence of Lord Elphinstone.

which if not in its origin a Mahomedan movement, had culminated in the recognition of the King of Delhi as the sovereign ruler of India. They had, on the whole, been well treated by the British Government, and were grateful in their own way.* But in all parts of the country were turbulent elements of one kind or another, and inconsistencies and discordances were as nothing when there was a common belief to be encouraged—a common object to be gained. In Rajpootana, as elsewhere, there was a prevailing faith that it was the intention of the British Government to destroy the religion of the country ; and some openly talked of the restoration of the *Badshah.*† All this was mere ignorance, and nothing was ever likely to come of it. But there was real cause of alarm in the fact that the legions of the great Rajpoot chiefs were composed very much of the same materials as our own Sepoy regiments. They were commanded by officers of our own army—but that had already been shown to be no safeguard. The probability of their breaking into rebellion, when time and opportunity should serve, was too patent to be disregarded by the statesmen of Agra, and they watched the event with the deepest concern.

The Governor-General's Agent in Rajpootana was Colonel George Fitzpatrick Lawrence, brother of Sir Henry Lawrence, whom he had succeeded in that important charge. He had seen more hazardous service and taken part in more exciting adventures than any officer in the country. Hair-breadth es-

---

* A short time before the outbreak of the mutinies, a report was circulated and pub'ished in the Indian papers to the effect that the Rajpoot States were to be annexed. I believe it to have been a malicious, as it was a very mischievous lie. I obtained the permission of the Court of Directors to contradict it on authority.

† See Prichard's "Mutinies in Rajpootana," p. 182.

1857.
July.

capes from death and long captivities seemed to be his portion. But he bore himself gallantly with a stout heart, a strong frame, and a noble spirit in every way worthy of the name he bore. He was doing his duty well in Rajpootana, when news reached him, on the 19th of May, of the commencement of our troubles. He wrote at once to all the principal officers under his control, urging upon them precautionary measures to be promptly executed. He called for a light field-force from Deesa ; and he pressed the Governor of Bombay to send up to Agra, by way of Gujerat and Rajpootana, "all available European troops returning from Persia." But a stronger hand had already been laid upon those troops. They were needed for other more pressing service than the defence of the North-Western capital. Lawrence then issued a proclamation to all the chiefs of Rajpootana calling upon them " to preserve peace within their borders, to intercept rebel fugitives, and to collect their followers on the frontiers." " This," says Lawrence, " was promptly replied to, and in one instance (Jouhdpore) anticipated by the most friendly assurances and promises of aid."*

It is a striking instance of the fact commented upon in an earlier portion of this narrative—the fact that well-nigh every man in authority thought only of the safety of his own immediate charge and of what could be done to insure it, regardless of the interests of others, or of the general welfare of the State—that the Lieutenant-Governor, who had authority over the Governor-General's Agent in Rajpootana, called upon Lawrence early in June " to march with all the European troops, officers, and

* Report of Brigadier-General Lawrence, July 27, 1858.

treasure he could collect, upon Agra, for the defence of that place."* It is impossible to conceive a wilder project than this, or one which would have been more fatal to British interests, if forced into execution. Lawrence was startled by the demand. But he was never for a moment doubtful of the direction in which lay his duty to the State. He would not abandon his charge. Like his brothers, Henry and John, he did not shrink from taking any responsibility upon himself. He saw clearly what would ensue in Rajpootana, if the whole country were evacuated by the British officers, whose influence in such an emergency was all to which we could trust for keeping the chiefs true to their allegiance, and holding the contingents in check. Such a movement, he said, would entail upon us the loss of Ajmere, with its important arsenal and stores, and lead to a general rise in Rajpootana. Representations to this effect, the force of which it was impossible not to recognise, had the expected result. Colvin saw that he had been wrong, and he did not enforce his request. Indeed, he soon perceived that it was his duty to strengthen Lawrence's hands, so he gave him entire command of the troops by appointing him a Brigadier-General.

And under George Lawrence worked a noble staff of officers. There was Major William Eden, Political Agent at Jyepore, a man of commanding presence; active and energetic in troubled times—firm, prudent, and sagacious in hours of peace. It may truly be said of him that he was the very backbone of Lawrence's Staff. Then there was Captain Charles Showers, our agent at Oodeypore, a man in whom

* "Reminiscences of Forty-three Years in India," by Lieut.-General Sir George Lawrence, K.C.S.I., C.B.

some fine qualities were united, but who, lacking others essential to a political officer, marred what he might have made a brilliant career. He had high courage, unquestionable ability, and a rare gift of speech. But he wanted judgment and discretion—especially that kind of discretion which recognises subordination as the main principle of all service and never gives way to the practical egotism, which men of strong convictions are, in defiance of authority, so prone to indulge. Then there was Captain Monck-Mason, Political Agent at Joudhpore—a man shrewd and sagacious, of a firm, well-balanced mind, but not incapable of rising to any height of daring, if strenuous action should be demanded from him. These were our British representatives at the principal ancient courts of Rajpootana. Beneath them were a cluster of younger political officers—many of great promise, who did their duty well and bravely in the emergency that had then risen.

But the most distinguished officer, connected with Rajpootana, was Colonel Dixon, of the Bengal Artillery, who now lay dying at Beawur. He had reclaimed Mhairwarrah from the state of lawlessness and barbarism in which he had found it many years before. The Mhairs were then little better than savages; he had reformed and civilised them. By gentle, kindly measures—by advice and persuasion—by conferring benefits on the people, teaching them what were their true interests, and showing them the blessedness of peace, he had gradually weaned them from their savage habits and converted what had before been a great congeries of robber-clans into a prosperous, thriving community. It was with mingled astonishment and admiration that the Mhairs had witnessed the vast improvement of their country—

and, as years passed, they also continued to improve
and never again fell back into their evil ways. And
now this wise and good man, stricken in years, lay
sick unto death, with all this great turmoil about
him. But he felt in his inmost heart that his Mhairs
would be true to the Government which had so be-
friended them. A Mhairwarrah Battalion of trusty
fighting men had been formed long ago ; and of all
the troops in Rajpootana they were those on whom
we could most confidently rely. " Do you think,"
they answered, when an attempt was made to tamper
with them, " that we will war against the Government which raised us from the dust and made us
what we now are?" Dixon died ; and, amidst the
clang of arms, little notice was taken of the peaceful
end of a man of peace ; but he left behind him an
abiding monument of his good deeds, such as few
have ever reared in India. He did not live to see
the staunch loyalty with which the Mhairs followed
us everywhere to the battle—but he never doubted
it and he died content.

The great Meywar chief— the Maharana of Oodeypore—was the acknowledged head of the Rajpoot
Confederacy. The traditional veneration in which
he was held, caused the other chiefs, in this crisis,
to turn their thoughts towards Oodeypore, in expectancy of some sign or portent aiding them the
better to shape their own measures. It was not a
propitious circumstance that George Lawrence, who
had preceded Showers as Political Agent, had been
involved in a sharp conflict with the Meywar Durbar,
and had recommended military coercion, the deposition of the Maharana and the banishment of some
of the principal chiefs under him. The policy then
recommended might have been right or might have

2 A 2

been wrong. But, right or wrong, its tendency might have been to alienate the confidence, if not to excite the animosity of the Meywar Durbar in this conjuncture. So it happened, that either for this reason, or from a foregone conclusion, that no good thing could come out of Oodeypore, George Lawrence could not believe in the fidelity of the Maharana and the chiefs. But Showers, the Political Agent, though recognising the probabilities of an adverse tone and temper in the Durbar, in no way despaired of success. The Maharana consented to meet him on the margin of the beautiful lake, with its glittering summer palace of white marble, and crossed over to an appointed place in one of his covered gondolas. " The result of this interview," wrote Showers, " was the Maharana giving in his open and declared adhesion to the British cause, and practically proving it by placing the most trustworthy troops at my disposal to take the field, sending his highest chiefs present at the capital and Durbar-officers to accompany me, and calling by proclamation on the loyal chiefs and district officers to afford every aid in our operations."

Whilst still at Oodeypore, tidings came to Showers of the mutiny at Neemuch, and the flight of our people. Barnes of the Artillery and Rose of the Infantry rode into the Residency and reported that a party of more than forty fugitives, women and children included, were gathered together in a village about fifty miles distant. Showers at once made his arrangements to start that night, accompanied by Barnes, with a party of Meywar Horse, for the prompt delivery of the captives. He found them in the last state of destitution—stricken by want and disease—sharing their place of refuge with cattle. He then placed them under the charge of

the Rao of Bedla, whom the Maharana had sent
with Showers as the most trusted of His Highness's
chiefs, whilst he himself pushed on in pursuit of the
Neemuch mutineers. The fugitives were brought
safely to the capital by the chivalrous Rajpoot, and
were lodged in one of the beautiful island-palaces on
the lake.

No doubt seems to have been entertained about
the fidelity of Jyepore. Eden placed himself at once
in communication with the Durbar; and on the 17th
of May he wrote to Mr. Colvin saying, "The Maharajah is ready to aid us with the troops to the utmost
of his ability and means;" and again, "I feel assured
that the Maharajah and the Sirdars will do all in their
power to meet the wishes of our Government." At
once they placed at Eden's disposal a large body of
troops of all kinds, good and bad; the latter greatly
preponderating; but it was not easy to decide what
was to be done with them. At that moment, however, the moral effect of such a declaration in our
favour was, perhaps, of more importance to us than
the troops placed at our disposal. The Jyepore detachment under Eden were to protect the Agra frontiers, and he wrote to Colvin for orders; but it was
not easy to give any definite instructions, when the
agency to be employed was of so uncertain a character. It was eventually resolved that Eden with his
five thousand Jyepore troops should march towards
the Muttra and Goorgaon districts "to maintain order
and aid in the re-establishment of the Civil Government." But it was apparent that the force had
in it too large a number of Hindostanees to render
success probable, and it soon appeared that they had
been tampered with by a discarded minister of the
Maharajah. So Lawrence was obliged to admit that

the assigned " duties were not fully discharged," and Eden, whose personal bearing had been of the most heroic kind, was compelled, after rescuing some European fugitives, to return to Jyepore.

Meanwhile Monck-Mason was calling upon Joudhpore for assistance, and prompt compliance was returned to the requisition. There was no doubt of the fidelity of the Maharajah, but long-standing internal feuds had weakened the State, and there was small likelihood of united action. Some of the great Thakoors, not long before, had been in armed resistance to the Maharajah. He now placed at our disposal two thousand Horse and Foot and six guns, hoping almost against hope that they would be serviceable to us. " Thus in all June and within a fortnight of the receipt of intelligence of the attack," wrote George Lawrence, " were the troops of Bhurtpore, Jyepore, Joudhpore and Ulwar co-operating with us in the field."* All this looked well at the outset, and Colvin's anxieties were relieved for the present by the aspect of affairs; but he clearly discerned the fact that although the Rajpoot Princes had no complicity either in Mussulman or Mahratta intrigues, they gave their daughters in marriage to the House of Delhi, made obeisance to the Mogul and coined money in his name. What the result was will be told in a later chapter of this History.

* It will be seen that there is no mention of Oodeypore in this recital. Oodeypore was ignored and Showers was ignored. But both did right well at the outset. A previous suspicion in the one case and a subsequent sharp contention surely afforded no just ground for the display of antipathies in respect to what had nothing to do with either the one or the other.

CHAPTER IV.

AGRA IN JUNE AND JULY—FRESH ANXIETIES OF THE LIEUTENANT-GO-
VERNOR—THE STORY OF JHANSI—ADVANCE OF THE NEEMUCH BRIGADE
—ILLNESS OF MR. COLVIN—THE PROVISIONAL GOVERNMENT—MUTINY
OF THE KOTAH CONTINGENT—THE BATTLE BEFORE AGRA—RETREAT OF
THE BRITISH FORCE—DESTRUCTION OF CANTONMENTS—LIFE IN THE
FORT.

THE Agra regiments, having laid down their arms, departed peaceably, with money, lawfully their own, in their waistbands. Many are supposed to have gone straightway to their homes; others may have fallen in with their mutinous comrades, and, newly armed by them, gone forth to fight for the Padshah. Whatever may have been the manner in which they disposed of themselves, the Lieutenant-Governor had no more anxiety from that source. They were swept out of Agra and there was an end of them, for the present, as agents of mischief, and an end also of Colvin's anxieties with respect to threatenings of internal revolt.

But there were many external sources of inquietude. Of the existing Native States within Colvin's circle—of their rulers and their armies—I have already written. Elsewhere were remnants of Native States—prostrate, down-trodden, whose ashes were

1857.
June.

still smouldering, whose fires a rude touch might at any moment revive. It was too much our wont, in the flush of our strength, in the pride of our egotism, to think that what it had pleased us to extinguish could never burst into a blaze again. But this was only one of our natural delusions. If there be one thing which the Natives of India thoroughly understand, it is the art of waiting. In their hearts, if not on their haunches, they sit *dhurna.* So it was in a Native State, of which I have written—a State our rulers had crushed. And the patience was more malignant, because the remains of sovereignty were represented by a woman.

Jhansi had been formerly a Native State. Lord Dalhousie had annexed it. It was, perhaps, the worst of all his annexations.* It was now to bear its bitter fruit. A pension of five thousand rupees a month, or six thousand pounds a year, had been offered to the Ranee, the widow of the last ruler. She had at first declined, but afterwards accepted, it; and property belonging to her late husband of the value of a lakh of rupees had been placed at her disposal and accepted. But she was thoroughly dissatisfied with her lot. Continuing to brood over the injury and the disgrace of Annexation, she hated the English with the deadliest hatred. And soon she began to cherish new-born grievances. Foremost among these was the killing of cattle by the English—an abomination in the eyes of her late subjects. On this injury she memorialised the British Government. The people of Jhansi did the same; but the answer was a repulse. Again, the Government were guilty of the extraordinary meanness of calling upon her to pay the debts of her late husband.

* In 1854—*ante,* vol. i. page 89 *et seq.*

The Ranee protested against this wrong—and Sir Robert Hamilton urged on Mr. Colvin compliance with Her Highness's request. But the Lieutenant-Governor was inexorable; and part of her pension was resumed or suspended. The Ranee pleaded, very reasonably, that as the debts were not her debts, she was not answerable for their payment out of her personal allowance, and she threatened to write to Government requesting permission to reside at Benares. I do not know what would have been the final issue; but the whole treatment of the Ranee was so ungenerous, and being ungenerous was so unwise, that Colvin must have shuddered, when he thought of the evil fruit that it was developing.* So her resentments grew stronger and stronger. A woman of masculine energy and feminine vindictiveness, she eagerly awaited the rising of the storm, well assured that her time would come. In 1857, she was a well-favoured woman of twenty-nine or thirty years of age. She was endowed with a keen intelligence — strong-minded and quick-witted—quite capable of discussing her affairs with a Commissioner or Governor. If she had any evil dispositions, she knew when to restrain the exhibition of them, and she tried to set bounds on her temper when conversing with a British officer. Evil things were said of her; for it is a custom among us *odisse quem læseris*—to take a Native ruler's king-

---

* Scarcely less irritating as a thorn in the flesh was the following act of spoliation, the circumstances of which are thus recorded in Captain Pinkney's official narrative. "The temple of Luchmee, situated outside the walls to the east of Jhansee, had long been supported by the Native rulers of the country, and an ancestor of Gungahur Rao had made over the revenues of two villages for its support. When he died Captain Francis Gordon, Deputy Commissioner, recommended that this arrangement should continue, but it was ordered that the villages should be resumed. This was strongly objected to by the Ranee and the case again referred to Government, with the same result. But before the resumption order could be carried out the outbreak at Jhansee took place."

dom and then to revile the deposed ruler or his would-be successor. It was alleged that the Ranee was a mere child under the influence of others, and that she was much given to intemperance. That she was not a mere child was demonstrated by her conversation; and her intemperance seems to be a myth.

The troops posted at Jhansi consisted of a wing of the Twelfth Regiment of Native Infantry, the headquarters and right wing of the Fourteenth Irregular Cavalry, and a detachment of Golundauze. They were under the command of Captain Dunlop of the Twelfth. The Commissioner, who had held the appointment from the first day of Annexation, was Captain Alexander Skene. How it happened that the Political Officer did not perceive that there were few places in the country where it was necessary at such a time to be cautious and vigilant and mistrustful of every one, that place was Jhansi, it is impossible to conjecture. But it seems never to have been thought that there were any smouldering animosities in high places or in low places—never thought that there was any one within the boundaries of the Commissionership, which had so lately been a petty kingdom, whose interests or antipathies were to be gratified by the subversion of the British power.

Skene had no belief that it was the intention of the Sepoys at Jhansi to rise, or that they were likely to be wrought upon by external influences. On the 18th of May he wrote to Agra, saying: "I do not think that there is any cause for alarm about this neighbourhood. The troops here, I am glad to say, continue staunch and express most unbounded abhorrence of the atrocities committed at Meerut and Delhi. They are commanded by a man (Captain

Dunlop) of the right sort, who knows how to manage Sepoys; and I do not anticipate any disaffection among them. As for the small Rajahs and Chiefs, they saw enough of rebellion, fourteen years ago, to give them a salutary dread of it. Then the Oorcha and Chutterpore and Ajeegurh men are children; the Dubbah man is off to Bithoor in a moribund state; the Sumpther man is mad and a prisoner in his own fort; the Chirkaree man and the Punnah men are almost the only chiefs worth mentioning, and they have kept out of everything of the kind hitherto —so I trust we are all safe . . . I am going on the principle of showing perfect confidence—and I am quite sure I am right." On the 30th of May, he wrote again in the same hopeful strain : " All continues quiet here, and the troops staunch. But there is of course a great feeling of uneasiness among the moneyed men of the town, and the Thakoors, who have never been well affected towards any Government, are beginning, it is said, to talk of doing something. All will settle down here, I feel perfectly certain, on receipt of intelligence of success." And again upon the 3rd of June : " We are all safe here as yet. I heard on Monday night of an intended attack on Kunchra by the Puan Thakoors. At midnight I called upon Dunlop to send a party to protect the town, and at eight A.M. a party of Infantry and Cavalry started in high spirits. They reached Kunchra at seven in the evening, but the Thakoors had got wind of the move and did not make the intended chupao. But for the feeling that this mutiny is universal I should say the men here are perfectly staunch." " The Sixty-seventh are the sister corps of my regiment the Sixty-eighth, and I have been watching with intense interest their conduct. I see the Sixty-seventh still promise loyalty. I trust the Sixty-eighth will evince it." And so little was it dreamt that there could be any political danger, that the Ranee obtained permission to entertain a body of armed men, as she said, for her own protection. With the true Mahratta instinct, she pretended that she was in danger from the enemies of the English, and thus intimated that her interests and desires were identical with our own, whilst she was plotting our overthrow.

It is remarkable that although Skene, on the 3rd of June, had expressed his belief in the staunchness of the troops, the wonted unmistakable signs of a coming outbreak had already begun to display themselves. A day or two before, in broad daylight, two bungalows in the Cantonment had been burnt. This was the warning to be ready; and on the 5th "firing was heard." It came from the direction of the Star Fort, which held our magazine and treasure. A party of Sepoys had possession of it and would not surrender it. It was plain now that the mutiny had commenced. So all the non-combatant Europeans betook themselves, with their families and such property as they could carry-off, to the Town Fort, whilst the officers of the Native troops remained in the Cantonments. Dunlop and his brother-officers did their best to soothe and pacify the Sepoys and to instil confidence into their minds. Of course, there was the old story over again. The Sepoys were loyalty itself; a few deluded men might have broken the bonds of discipline by occupying the Star Fort, but the rest were true to their salt. A parade was ordered for the following morning. It was attended by the Native officers and men of all arms of the Jhansi force. The men were respectful in their demeanour. What this meant was soon apparent. It

was only intended to lull us into the sense of a false
security. On this morning Skene and Gordon left
the Fort to visit Dunlop in Cantonments. What the
object of the visit or what passed at the conference
can never be known. Skene returned at once to the
Fort; Gordon breakfasted in his own house and
wrote letters to some of the neighbouring chiefs, in-
voking their aid—letters to which no answer was
returned—and then betook himself to the supposed
safety of the Fort. Early in the afternoon, the Ranee,
and a crowd of people, among whom were her chief
adherents, with two banners borne aloft, went in
procession from the Town to the Cantonments; and
a Mahomedan named Ahsun-Ali called all true believers to prayers.* Then the troops rose at once;
and fired upon their officers. All were killed, except
Lieutenant Taylor, who, though severely wounded,
mounted a horse and rode for the Town Fort.† The
massacre of the Cantonment officers having thus been
effected, in a manner most gratifying to the mutineers, they released the prisoners from the Gaol,
burnt the cutcherry; and then mutineers and gaol-
birds, together with the Police and Custom-house
officials, streamed into the Town and invested the
Fort.

Our people were now most lamentably in the
power of the mutineers, the rebels, and the followers
of the Queen. They had triumphed over the White
Man, who now lay prostrate and writhing at their feet.
Another day or two and all would be over. Jhansi
would be purged of the presence of the usurpers.
So the time had come for the apportioning of the
spoils. To whom was Jhansi, recovered after three
years of annexation, to belong? On the night of the

1857.
June.

Seizure of the district.

* Captain Pinkney's Report. † Colonel Malleson.

6th a meeting was held between the chief officers of the mutineers and certain delegates from the Ranee to settle this momentous question of the future Government of the country. Then came the great standing difficulty, which was doomed, before and afterwards, to cast a great cloud over the trium· phant joy of the victors, and sometimes to turn conflicts of opinion into internecine strife. The delegates of the Ranee and of the mutineers, after long disputation, could not come to any terms. The mutineer party bethought themselves of a somewhat clever piece of diplomacy. At Oonao, a village distant about twelve miles from Jhansi, dwelt a kinsman of the late Rajah, who had been one of the claimants to the Guddee of Jhansi. His name was Sadasheo Rao. If in this crisis he could be induced to adhere to the side of the Sepoys and to set himself as a rival of the Ranee, they might make better terms for themselves. So they invited this man to Jhansi. Meanwhile a Proclamation went forth, declaring that "The People are God's; the country is the Padshah's; and the two Religions govern."

The 7th of June was a day of sore tribulation to the ill-fated garrison of the Town Fort. The clouds were thickening above them, and there was small chance of their escaping the full fury of the storm. Their only chance of escape lay in the good offices of the Ranee. The English were reduced to the humiliating necessity of imploring the help of the woman whom they had so grossly wronged. In the morning Captain Skene sent three uncovenanted servants connected with the Commission—Mr. Scott and the two Purcells—to the Ranee to solicit safe-conduct after the exodus of our people from the Fort. They were

seized on the way by some of the Ranee's troops and
carried to the Palace. The Ranee sent them to our
own revolted Sepoys, who deliberately murdered
them. Afterwards, another uncovenanted servant,
Mr. Andrews, principal Sudder Aumeen, was butchered at the Palace door by the Queen's own servants. Skene and Gordon wrote often to Her Highness on that day—but no trace of their correspondence remains. It was a last hope and it was a vain
one. Two hours after noon the insurgents recom-
menced their attack on the Fort and continued the
firing; but they did very little damage, hurting none
of our people; whilst some of the insurgents fell
under the fire from the Fort. On that night the
besiegers were strengthened by the accession of more
guns supplied to them by the Ranee; and on the
morning of the 8th, with these increased resources
now more hopeful of success, they continued their
attack on the Fort. They attempted an escalade, but
it failed. Too many good shots were in the garrison
to render it safe for the assailants to expose themselves.

Now came the last struggle for life—the day of
their death or the day of their deliverance. Vigorous
and more vigorous became the efforts of the enemy
to carry the place by assault; and soon after noon
they established themselves on the lower works of
the Fort. The crisis of our fate seemed to be approaching. There was treachery within the walls no
less than fury without. An attempt was made to
open a gate of the Fort so as to admit the ingress of
the besiegers. It was happily intercepted in time—
though only to defer the final catastrophe for a few
hours. The traitors were disposed of by Gordon
and Burgess, but not before they had given Powis.

his death-wound. Meanwhile the siege continued. With all the heroism of despair our people worked on nobly in the defence of the Fort—Skene and Gordon sending many a message of death to the assailants.* But after a while a sad calamity befel us. Captain Gordon was looking through a window over the Fort gate, when his familiar face was observed by one of the enemy's marksmen, who took aim and shot him dead. He is described as "a gallant gentleman and an excellent officer, the life and soul of the garrison." When this lamentable event occurred, a great cloud of despondency gathered over the besieged. Provisions and ammunition were becoming scarce—the enemy were swarming around them. So it was felt that the defence could not be sustained—that there was nothing left for our people but to surrender. So Captain Skene hung out a flag of truce, or otherwise intimated to the besiegers that the garrison would treat for terms.

The leaders of the mutineers and of other insurgents came to the gate, and hearing what Skene had to say, they made oath, with the most solemn and sacred adjurations, a native doctor named Saleh Mohamed being the spokesman, not to hurt a hair of the heads of the British garrison, if they would lay down their arms and surrender the Fort. The terms were accepted; and our hapless people prepared to depart. As soon as they crossed the threshold of the Fort gate the enemy fell upon our unarmed people, and binding their arms, made captives of them. There could be no resistance. They were helpless as sheep. Through the town passed the melancholy procession; when just beyond the city

---

* It has been stated that Mrs. Skene loaded for them, but I have nothing authentic in proof of this.

walls some Sowars came up and said it was the order
of the Ressaldar that the whole should be put to
death. They then filed down, captors and captives,
to a place near which was a cluster of trees. The
Gaol-Darogah, who had been in the confidence of the
Superintendent and was never suspected of treachery,
was at the head of the party. But, presently a halt
was ordered. The murderous work commenced.
The Darogah cut down his old master. Then a
general massacre ensued. The women and children were separated from the men; but they shared
the same sad fate. Not one of those who left the
Town-Fort—man, woman, or child—was spared.*
The great crime accomplished, the bodies of some
three score of our Christian people were left for three
days on the road to rot. Then the men were cast
into one gravel-pit, the women into another, and
lightly covered over. Long afterwards, when we
again triumphed at Jhansi, the burial service was
read over their remains by a Protestant minister,
Mr. Schwabe, and Mr. Strickland, the Roman Catholic priest, attached to Sir Hugh Rose's army.

Thus the curtain fell upon the dismal tragedy
which was the antetype of the massacre of Cawnpore. Whether the Ranee instigated this atrocity,
or to what extent she was implicated in it, can never
be clearly known. I have been informed, on good
authority, that none of the Ranee's servants were
present on the occasion of the massacre. It seems to
have been mainly the work of our own old followers.
The Irregular Cavalry issued the bloody mandate
and our Gaol-Darogah was foremost in the butchery.

---

* The number of Christian people
slain in this final massacre was between fifty and sixty. The rest were
killed in Cantonments or during the
siege. Captain Pinkney gives sixty-
seven as the total number. Major
Erskine, Commissioner of Jubbulpore, says seventy-six.

1857.
June.

Measures of
the Ranee.

So long as the English were cleaned out of Jhansi and the country was left clear for the prosecution of her political intrigues—and she was bent on cleaning them out—it mattered not to her by what means the object was attained. They were all gone now; and the time had come for the settlement of the great political question—" Who is to be the future ruler of Jhansi ?" The mutineers had invited Sadasheo Rao to the city and he had gone thither, well disposed to bid for the Guddee. But the Ranee knew that there was nothing they so much coveted as money; so she produced a large sum in coin and promised further donations to the mutineers, who were thus brought to adhere to her cause, and then the Proclamation went forth : "The people are God's; the country is the Padshah's ; and the Raj is Ranee Lutchmee Baee's."* This accomplished, she threw all her energy and activity into the work of firmly establishing the Raj. She raised fresh troops; she strengthened her fortified places; she established a mint ; and she sent delegates to Doondoo Punt, Nana Sahib, with whom she had previously been in communication. It is stated, and apparently on the most trustworthy authority, that, at the same time, she "endeavoured to keep terms with our Government, by writing to the Commissioner of Jubbulpore and to others, lamenting the massacre of our countrymen ; stating that she was in no way concerned in it; and declaring that she only held the Jhansi district till our Government could make arrangements to reoccupy it."† But I have searched Major Erskine's exhaustive Report, and in the four hundred and forty-four para-

---

* Professedly she was only Regent—her adopted son, then a boy of eight years of age, being nominally the possessor of the Guddee.

† Captain Pinkney.

graphs to which it extends I cannot find a word upon the subject.*

Meanwhile at Naogong, where wings or detach-ments of the same regiments as those posted at Jhansi —namely, the Head-Quarters of the Twelfth Native Infantry, a wing of the Fourteenth Irregular Horse, and some Golundauze guns—were stationed, under the command of Major Kirke, very contradictory manifestations were apparent in the Sepoy Lines. From the 23rd of May to the 1st of June, it seems that they were waiting and watching. The Irregulars were lounging about in a careless, insolent, half-defiant manner, plainly indicating their belief that the end was near; whilst the Infantry putting on an outer garment of loyalty, protested their allegiance, and gave practical proofs of it, by offering to march against the mutineers at Delhi. On the 5th of June, Major Kirke held a parade of all the troops in Can-tonments. He then addressed them, commended them highly for their loyalty, and told them that the troops were in partial mutiny at Jhansi. Then came a most extraordinary scene—a preposterous piece of acting. The Sepoys were quite jubilant in their devotion to the British Government. The Go-lundauze hugged their guns in a paroxysm of en-thusiasm. The Infantry rushed to their colours. The Cavalry, with their wonted demeanour of outward insouciance, merely said that they would be true to their salt.† The officers were "much gratified." They did not seem to see that the violence of these

1857.
June.

Naogong.

* It should be mentioned here that, finding his claims disallowed, Sadashco Rao collected some three thousand men, seized the Fort of Kurrara, and issued a proclamation saying, "Maharajah Sadashco Rao Narain has seated himself on the throne of Jhansi at Kurrara." It was a very uneasy and unstable seat, for the Ranee despatched a body of troops against him and he was fain to escape into Scindiah's territory.

† Captain Scot's Report.

spasms clearly denoted the acted lie.   For some days everything was quiet.   But on the 10th, the play having been played out, the reality commenced.   A tall Sikh, followed by two others, walked up to the ground, where the guard of the Twelfth was being relieved, and deliberately shot the Havildar-Major. They then attempted to seize the guns ; there was no genuine resistance ; the Native Sergeant was over-awed and his followers were recreant to the core. Then was heard the rattle of musketry from the Lines, telling the old story.   The Sepoys had risen against their British officers, against the British Government ; they were mutineers and rebels of the worst kind, working out their ends by means of the basest falsehood and imposture.

The flight.   What now was to be done by the handful of British officers thus shamefully deserted?   It was hoping against hope to think, for a moment, that any efforts of theirs—any appeals to the Past, any promises for the Future, would lure them back to their allegiance. Some Sepoys of the Twelfth came forward, protesting their fidelity, and mustered in the mess-house of their English officers, but they were not strong enough to turn the tide of affairs in our favour.   There was nothing for them, therefore, but to remain at their posts to be massacred, like their comrades at Jhansi, or to attempt to rescue themselves by flight.   They chose the latter course—and wisely ; but it was a disastrous and a disorderly retreat.   The eighty-seven faithful Sepoys accompanied their officers, and the clerks of the Civil Establishment—some burdened with families—were among the number of the fugitives.   Their first thought had been to make their way to Allahabad, but this, on account of the state of the country about Banda, had been abandoned,

and they next set their faces towards Kalinghur and
Mirzapore. The story of their flight has been told in graphic detail by survivors of the retreat. It was a fortnight of misery and horror. The adventures which befel the fugitives on their perilous way much resembled, in many features, those which were encountered by others in like manner driven from their homes. And the same diversities of temperament and character were apparent. Major Kirke soon lost what little power of brainwork he possessed at the first outbreak of the mutiny. It is recorded of him that he had been in feeble health before this event and that " now from want of tea, and beer and wine, he was quite gone"—he sometimes "spoke of a mango, or something to eat and drink as if it were his life"; and he sent back two officers to Naogong to carry off the mess-stores. Occasional strange hallucinations overtook him. The first place to which they made was Chutterpore—a small state governed, like Jhansi, by a widowed Ranee as Regent for her son. It had escaped the great planing-machine of Lord Dalhousie's annexations. The Ranee behaved mercifully and generously to our people; and they passed on with some needed succours. But as they moved forward, it was discovered that Kirke was missing. He fancied that the Sepoys were plotting to murder him and had made off, unattended, by night, to Logassee, where he was received by a friendly chief. At this place Captain Scot and Lieutenant Townsend found him, maundering about new dangers and insisting that the Logassee chief was bent upon his destruction.

Meanwhile the Sepoys had gone on without their officers, greatly distressed by what they supposed to be either their death or their desertion. But on the

16th Kirke made his appearance with the cart-load of beer, wine, and tea, which he had sent his officers back to Naogong to heap up for him, and to satisfy his cravings. They then pressed on to Chirkaree, another friendly Bundelkund state, the chief of which received the fugitives with hospitality, and supplied them with money. The gleam of sunshine was but brief. A powerful gang of Dakoits came down upon them, and under promise of safe conduct to Kalinghur, eased them of a great part of their treasure, and then forthwith began to acquit themselves of their part of the compact, by killing as many of our people as they could. When Kirke and his followers pushed on, without the robber-chief, who had promised to guide them, they were fired upon from behind the cover of a cluster of trees and some adjacent hills. The Sepoys in return fired anywhere. They lost heart, whilst the Dakoits rose in their audacity and fired faster and faster on our people. In this crisis, the Major had a lucid interval of manhood. He went among the Sepoys, and eagerly exhorted them to carry the pass before them. But it was of no use. The brigands were masters of the situation. Their matchlocks carried far and well. Lieutenant Townsend fell dead with a bullet in his body. There was a great panic. The miscellaneous European or Christian community sought safety as best they could in flight—some on horseback, and some on foot—for the Dakoits had seized all our wheeled carriages. It was then necessary that the party should fall back on Mahoba. But Kirke did not live to reach it. After the passing excitement of which I have spoken, a terrible reaction came upon him, and within a few miles from the place of refuge, he fell from his horse and died.

Then Captain Scot became chief of the fugitive 1857.
June.
band. He was younger, stronger, more active than
the Major, and less dependent on mess-stores. He
seems, under most trying circumstances, to have
worked with almost superhuman energy for the preservation of the people thus committed to his care. But
death was busy among them. The fierce rays of the
June sun smote them terribly. Some were killed or
driven to madness by its power. Some were overcome by extreme exhaustion and fell by the wayside.
Others sought shelter, sank into stupor, and were left
behind. The great difficulty was the burden of the
women. There was but one wife of a commissioned Mrs. Mawe.
officer among them, but many wives of sergeants and
writers with children in their train, whom it was very
difficult to succour on the march. There would be
something almost ludicrous in the narrative of their
adventures, if it were not for the beautiful chivalry
of Scot, who went to the rescue of fat barrack-women
with as much heroic self-devotion as if they had been
princesses in the bloom of their youth and beauty.
He had two horses, for he had secured Townsend's,
and how best to utilise them was the difficult problem
which he had now to solve. Never, perhaps, was
back of horse put to stranger uses before. The
strangeness culminated in the circumstance that with
a nursery of children on one of his horses he was
compelled to find room for a wretched woman with
but little life left in her—if any. The back of the
horse was her death-bed, and the body was left to the
vultures.* Nor was Scot alone in these manifesta-

* See the following passage of a private letter from Captain Scot: "My work that day was terrible. I had to try to lug along two fat old women, whilst I carried three chil- dren on my horse and tried to keep back the Sepoys who were with me. The senior Havildar got more and more savage and wanted me to leave the children and the women; but I

tions of the chivalry and self-devotion of the true Christian gentleman. Lieutenant Jackson took up behind him the wife of a Sergeant of the Public Works Department, who rode astride lashed to her preserver, throughout four long days of weariness and pain—on one day riding forty miles—until they reached Adjighur, their numbers sadly diminished by the agonies of that dreadful march.

Before this, the eighty-seven faithful Sepoys had, by agreement, parted from their officers. They had become dissatisfied and hopeless of making good their way to British territory. The people along the line of flight were manifestly hostile to us. It was plain that our officers were encumbered with women and children, and the Sepoys could not appreciate the unselfish chivalry of those who sacrificed themselves to the weaklings who so impeded their progress. They proposed, therefore—whether in good faith or in bad faith it is hard to say—that the Europeans still remaining alive should give up their arms to the Sepoys, who should report everywhere that the white men were prisoners, whom they were taking to Banda. Our officers consented. For a time it succeeded. On pain of the displeasure of the King of Delhi townsfolk and villagers were called upon to supply food and forage to the little camp, and the requisition was obeyed. But the ruse was soon discovered, or the Sepoys said it was; so this state of things was

would not, and thank God, they did not leave us. I came at last to Mr. Smalley sitting beside his wife. She seemed dead, but it was doubtful, so I took her up before me and gave one of the children to my writer, who had got hold of my horse. It was a most arduous task to keep the utterly inert body on the horse, as I placed her as women ride. But after a while she seemed dead. I held a consultation about it and we left the body. I was lame from an awful kick of a horse and had but a strip of cloth on one foot; but poor Smalley was worse, and he got on my horse and Mrs. Tierney behind, her two children got seats upon the horses—and thus I reached the main body."

but of brief duration. The whole country, it was urged, was against us, and it was better that they should separate. So Scot gave them certificates of loyalty and they made their way to Allahabad; whilst the wretched remnant of the Naogong fugitives struggled on to Adjighur, whence they were passed on to Nagode and were saved. Mrs. Mawe, whose husband had died on the march, wandered to Banda, where her little daughter was restored to her by Scot, whose noble exertions had saved the child.*

1857.
June.

The month of July dawned darkly and ominously on the defenders of Agra. It was now certain that the Neemuch mutineers, swollen by detachments from other rebel hosts, were rapidly approaching. Colvin, whose health, strong man as he was, had for some time been breaking down under the continued pressure of external anxieties and internal dissensions, and the distressing sleeplessness which they engendered, was now said to be dying. He had many enemies among those who should have been his friends—many opponents among those who should have been his supporters. Some of his own officers, openly or covertly, conducted themselves, in this crisis, in a manner as disgraceful to themselves as it was cruel to their chief. Some were insolent and minacious to his face. Some wrote letters which ought never to have been written. Whilst others, taking advantage of the post by Bombay, addressed

July.
Agra.

Howlings of
our people.

* But for the necessities of space, I should gladly have told this story in greater detail, for it is a touching illustration of English heroism of the purest kind. A graphic narrative of the flight was written by Captain Scot and published in the *Times* newspaper of September 11, 1857. Mrs. Mawe, also, recorded her adventures, and the record is said to have been sent to the Queen by Lady Canning.

the Governor-General, denouncing the conduct of his lieutenant in no measured language, declaring his incompetency, and beseeching Lord Canning to remove him. Impeachments before Parliament were talked of and forcible arrests—indeed, there were no invectives, no threats, to which his assailants did not resort. Lord Canning spoke of these as " screeches from Agra"—and at Delhi, where many letters were received from these complainants, it was said, "There are the Agra-Wallahs howling again!" The Agra Garrison say that howlings came to them, as frequently from Delhi.

At the end of June it was clear that the Neemuch mutineers were approaching, and that it was necessary at once to concert detailed measures for their reception. So, on the 30th, a Memorandum was drawn up by the Brigadier, in which he very clearly defined our position and the dangers which threatened us; adding : " It is as well to observe that merely beating the mutineers is *comparatively* no material object gained. From the character of the enemy it does not seem likely that these mutineers would venture upon an attack on us, unless aided by any forces in the present neighbourhood, or by some promise of local treachery here, or by some other aid expected from the westward. The rise of the Chumbul river seems the best security we have against any early hostile movement of the troops at Gwalior." On the following day a Resolution was passed by the Lieutenant-Governor containing explicit instructions as to the movements of all branches of the Agra force; but when the time came for action, circumstances had changed and the Resolution became a dead letter.

Colvin had borne all the assaults upon him with

the finest temper and the truest Christian patience. But the malice of his enemies, and the unkindness of his own people struck at the very sources of his life, and on the 3rd of July alarming symptoms of apoplexy presented themselves. He was then compelled to make over the Government, for twenty-four hours, to a Council composed of Mr. E. A. Reade, Brigadier Polwhele, and Captain Macleod, Colvin's military secretary. The Council of Administration assembled on the 4th in the Brigadier's house, where Colvin, attended by his medical adviser, was lying in an adjoining room. Later in the day he brightened up a little and approved generally of the instructions issued by Reade and his colleagues. They made the most of their time and opportunity. One most important point was gained. The first paragraph of the Proceedings of the Council records: " The information regarding the movements of the Neemuch mutineers received through the Police being ambiguous and contradictory, volunteers were called for from the officers, who reported from personal observation the arrival of their camp within a distance of fifteen miles from Agra. Brigadier Polwhele had decided in the event of their advancing nearer, to meet and attack them." This would have been a great point gained, if there had been any certainty of a man, so vacillating as Brigadier Polwhele, clinging to his first resolution. For, a few days before, the Lieutenant-Governor had placed the Brigadier in full possession of all the circumstances of our position, and warned him of the dangers to be encountered. He had told Polwhele to take counsel with his principal officers, receiving their opinions as " to how far it would be prudent to advance from the cantonment and proximity of the Fort to arrest the advance of the enemy; whether it would be advantageous to employ the Kotah Contingent then encamped on the left bank of the Jumna, opposite to Agra; and whether it would be advisable to employ a force under our staunch adherent, the Newab Syfoollah Khan, to co-operate with us."

So Polwhele had assembled his officers and consulted them. It was determined that it would not be a wise strategical measure to move out the force so far in advance, as to necessitate its encamping. It would be better to await their coming and then to march out from the barracks to give battle to the enemy.* It was resolved, also, that the Kotah Contingent should be removed within the cantonment, "to take part in the defence," and that the services of Syfoollah Khan should be accepted.†

Mutiny of the Kotah Contingent. These last questions soon solved themselves. As the Contingent were stationed near the Europeans, it would have been easy to disarm them. This was counselled but the counsel was rejected. Vacillation was all dominant at that time. The Brigadier doubted and hesitated, whilst those whom he should have crushed were girding up their loins and arming themselves for the battle. At last, on the 4th of July, when it was clearly seen that their proximity might be inconvenient, if not dangerous, orders were issued by the Council of Administration for their removal from Agra. It was suggested by Major

---

* "The entire want of Cavalry with the force here," wrote Mr. Colvin, "was a main motive to this resolution, which I myself thought the best that could be adopted, under all the circumstances of our position."

† The sequel may be given in a note: "Lieutenant Henderson, having brought Nuwab Syfoollah Khan, after midnight, to the railway house to report the desertion of the Bhurtpoor Horse, and the Nuwab having acknowledged that his matchlock infantry were unfit to fight against mutineer soldiers, he was ordered to quit Shagunge at once, and to return to Kerowlee without delay." —*Proceedings of Council of Administration.*

Macleod that a test should be applied to them : "that
their guns should remain with the reserve of Europeans left for the protection of Cantonments, while
their Infantry and Horse should accompany the force
on its march out to meet and attack the mutineers."
At first the men of the Contingent seemed to be
satisfied with the arrangement; but when orders
were given to them to move their camp to the rising
ground on the road leading to Futtehpore Sikri, they
broke into open mutiny, shot down their European
Sergeant-Major, fired at other British officers, and
went off to join the Neemuch mutineers, in fear and
trembling lest they should be overtaken and cut up.
Captain Prendergast, a dashing soldier always on the
alert, with a party of Volunteer Horse, got in among
them, cut down some of the mutineers and captured
their camels and ammunition.   On the same evening it was discovered that some of the components
of Syfoollah Khan's force were equally treacherous,
so all that could be done was to render them
harmless as enemies, as they could not be useful as
friends.

The revolt of the Kotah Contingent rendered it Removal of
necessary that the Lieutenant-Governor should be Colvin into
moved into the Fort.   There was danger of an attack the Fort.
on the Brigadier's house, and a party of volunteers
and others had drawn up in front of it for purposes
of defence.   The Brigadier then insisted upon the
removal of Colvin to safer quarters; and the Lieutenant-Governor somewhat reluctantly consented to
the change.   He was removed under an escort; but
when he learnt that the Kotah Contingent had been
dispersed, he desired to return to the Brigadier's
house that he might be nearer the scene of action.
Reade carried the request to the Brigadier, but the

old soldier was peremptory and declared that he would not receive him. On the following day Colvin had a relapse so serious as to cause his friends and the general community the greatest anxiety. But he resumed the despatch of business as soon as his medical adviser reluctantly consented to his returning to his work.

It was not then very clearly known at what point the enemy were assembled; but on the 4th of July, it was felt that they must be close upon us. So before sunrise on the 5th, the Engineers, Fraser and Weller, went to Brigadier Polwhele and besought him to go out to meet the advancing enemy. " Give the Europeans their breakfasts," said Fraser, " then march out to find the enemy." But the Brigadier turned a deaf ear to these entreaties. He refused to move out and said that he would hold Agra against all comers. The lives of his Europeans, he said, were very valuable, and he would not needlessly expose them. He was a brave man ; but he was obstinate and wanting in judgment, and he was prejudiced against the Engineers. So Fraser and Weller left the Brigadier's quarters—disappointed and crest-fallen—lamenting the failure of their endeavours, but still hoping that another hour might bring forth better results.

Brigadier Polwhele was not the only military officer of rank who had refused advice tendered to him, in the presence of his advisers, and afterwards acted upon it as an original conception. Tidings that the enemy were at Shahgunj were brought in by Ensign F. Oldfield* at seven o'clock ; but it was not till two hours later that the Brigadier had determined to move out the troops, and about an hour afterwards

* This promising young officer Campbell's first advance on Luck-
was afterwards killed on Sir Colin now.

they were assembled on parade.* When Fraser
heard of this he went to the Brigadier and offered
his services as second-in-command. As he was the
next senior officer in the station this request could not
be refused. Weller volunteered at the same time for
service and joined the Europeans, as a Volunteer,
on foot. But there was still much hesitation and
delay; and before the force was ready to move, it
was known, not only that the enemy were in sight,
but that they had occupied the very position which
we ought ourselves to have held.

The rebel force consisted of more than two thousand Composition
of the enemy.
men; and many of them were among the best Native
troops, whom our English officers had disciplined.
There was the fourth troop First Brigade of Horse Artillery, known as Murray Mackenzie's troop.† There
was the Seventy-second Regiment of Native Infantry,
with its rifle company, that had done good service at
Mooltan—part of the First Native Cavalry, with
four troops of the Mehidpore Horse—and the Seventh
Regiment of the Gwalior Contingent. And to these was
soon added another host, on which we had relied as

* "However, on some information, we did not know what, probably
acquired after Colonel Fraser's interview, the Brigadier afterwards decided on going out; for about 9 A.M.,
when busily engaged in the Fort, I
was surprised, on meeting Mr.
Thornhill, Secretary to Government,
to learn that the Brigadier was
going out to fight the Neemuch
mutineers. I said it was impossible,
as Colonel Fraser had before sunrise
failed to persuade him to this course;
but on being assured it was true, I
at once hurried off to Colonel Fraser,
and we went to the parade ground
and found the troops assembled.
This was between 10 and 11 A.M.,
and Colonel Fraser at once solicited
from the Brigadier the privilege of
being his second - in - command,
which—as he was the next senior
officer in the station—could not of
course be refused. I was unable to
ride, but I had taken a gun and ammunition, and was allowed by Colonel Riddell, Commanding Third
Europeans, to fall in as a volunteer
with his regiment."—*MS. Memorandum of Major Weller.*

† At the time of the revolt of the
troop, Major Mackenzie was at
Delhi. It has been erroneously
stated in some narratives, that this
troop had rendered itself famous in
history, as a component of the "Il-
lustrious Garrison" of Jellalabad.
That was a Light Field Battery
(No. 6) commanded by Captain Au-
gustus Abbott.

our allies. The Kotah Contingent, who had been at our mercy on the preceding day and had gone into revolt, now joined the ranks of the enemy.

The battle of Shahgunj.
The camp of the mutineers was at a distance of some two miles from our Cantonment, planted obliquely on a metalled road with a village of mud-huts for their centre. One half of their Artillery was posted on one flank—one half upon the other—sheltered by low trees and walls, and natural earthworks. The camp and Cavalry were in the rear, hidden from our sight as we advanced. It was nearly two o'clock when Polwhele led his troops to the attack. Forming line and placing one half-battery under Captain D'Oyly on the right, and the other under Lieutenant Pearson on the left, he moved along the sandy plain on the right of the road leading to the enemy's position. Our force consisted of eight hundred and sixteen men, all in fine spirits and eager for the affray. D'Oyly, an excellent officer, and of the highest courage, had unbounded confidence in his guns and his gunners. He believed that it would be small work to silence the enemy's Artillery, and this done, the defeat of the rebels would have been easy. His influence with the Brigadier was great, and it is believed that the plan of attack was in accordance with his suggestions. There was underlying it a wise resolve, not to expose the Europeans. Riddell's regiment was eager for the battle, but it had seen little service, and at a time when the loss of a single English soldier was a calamity, it was deemed expedient to take every precaution against the possible results of rashness and impetuosity. Yet the boldest movement is often the least hazardous. Had the force advanced straight along the metalled road, upon the village, or had it moved in two lines, upon

both flanks of the enemy, success would have been certain. But when the mutineers saw our advancing troops, they opened fire upon us, from their cover, and then Polwhele ordered the Infantry to lie down, whilst D'Oyly's guns answered the fire of the rebel artillery. But the enemy were too well posted for us to do them any grievous injury, and the delay enabled them to get our range. They had been firing over our heads ; and if we had at once advanced, before they had got their guns to the right elevation, we might have fallen upon them, with comparative immunity, and they could not have stood the rush of the Europeans. But instead of thus utilising all branches of the service, the Brigadier trusted to his guns and wasted his ammunition.

Nothing could have exceeded the gallantry with which D'Oyly and Pearson worked their ninepounders. But some miserable accidents and miscarriages rendered their good service of but slight avail. D'Oyly's horse was shot under him at an early period of the engagement. This was a small disaster ; for he could command on foot, but at a later hour, whilst the intrepid artilleryman was endeavouring to right a gun, one of the wheels of which was in difficulty, a grape-shot from one of the enemy's batteries wounded him dangerously on the side. He was placed upon a tumbril, from which he gave his orders, suffering bravely the severest pain, until exhausted nature could no longer sustain him. Then thinking that the hand of death was upon him, he gasped out " I am done for. Put a stone upon my grave and write that I died fighting my guns."*

margin note: 1857.
July 5.

margin note: Our disasters.

---

* It is doubtful whether this was said on the field of battle or afterwards in hospital. It was probably repeated.

He was carried from the battle-field, and after some hours of pain expired in the Fort. One of his subalterns, Lieutenant Lambe, was dangerously wounded by a grape-shot, which shattered his right thigh.* He lingered for some weeks before death terminated the intensity of his sufferings. Lieutenant Patteson, who commanded the left half-battery, exposed himself with equal audacity. One of his guns was dismantled, the limber was blown up, and the gun-carriage ignited; but he and his men, exposed to a heavy fire, and molested by rushes of Cavalry, went to work to remount it as coolly as if they had been on the parade-ground of Dum-Dum or Meerut on a practice-day. It seemed that this battery, heroically as it was worked, was doomed to disaster, for, before the accident above recorded, a round shot from one of the enemy's guns exploded an ammunition waggon and its limber, and deprived us of that which was the very life of our power of attack, a loss which soon rendered our guns only an encumbrance to us. The rapid firing, with but small effect, at the commencement of our operations, now told most lamentably against us; for before the fortune of the day had been decided, or indeed even before the decisive action had commenced, our guns ceased firing. It is said that they had taken out ninety rounds of ammunition for each gun, but by four o'clock in the afternoon there was scarcely a shot to be fired.

Not until D'Oyly had reported that his ammunition was expended, did Colonel Riddell receive orders to advance with his Europeans. Then " two small columns" were thrown forward. The right

---

* Lambe was with the left half-battery.

was commanded by Major G. P. Thomas* of the
Third Europeans, and the left by Colonel Fraser
of the Engineers, with whom went his friend and
comrade Weller, both " with their shirt - sleeves
tucked up." They entered the village with a good
English " Hurrah !" all the more eager for having
been so long held back. After an obstinate defence,
and not without heavy loss on our side, the village
was carried. Here Major Thomas, whose horse was
shot under him whilst gallantly leading his men,
received his death-wound. Fraser's column forcing
an entrance into the village, with its " narrow lanes
and strong mud huts," was grievously assailed by the
firing of the enemy from roofs and doorways. It
was truly a critical moment. Fraser was eager to
hold the village against all odds, but it was a desperate undertaking; so after taking counsel with
Weller, he resolved at least to make an attempt to
bring up some guns; Weller, who, although on
foot, seems to have acted as staff-officer to the
Brigade, and to have been ready for any kind of
service, believing that Pearson had still a few rounds
of ammunition left, went off to him, to see whether
he could bring up his half-battery and render any
service in this emergency. But the artilleryman
shook his head. So many men and so many horses
had been killed, and so much damage had been
done, that it was impossible to go to the aid of the
Infantry. It was a happy circumstance that, in
one important respect, the enemy were in like
straits with ourselves; for they also had a scarcity

1857.
July 5.

* Major Thomas had been formerly in the Sixty-fourth Native Infantry, in which he had distinguished
himself at the commencement of the
Second Afghan War. He was a man of consummate courage as a soldier,
and, beyond this, he was a man of
genius. He was an artist and a
poet. I have pleasant recollections
of days passed in his society.

2 c 2

of Artillery, and their guns had been limbered up for flight.*

If then we had not been so miserably weak in the mounted branch all might have 'gone well. But all the Cavalry we possessed were some sixty mounted militiamen. They were men of all kinds—"military officers, whose regiments had mutinied or had been disarmed, members of the Civil Service holding appointments, salaried clerks in the public offices, sectioners, men drafted from the European regiments, pensioners, Christian drummers, musicians, &c., from Native regiments, and individuals not before in the service of Government."† To this strange list we may add, "horse-riders of a wandering circus from France." They had been exercised only for a space of ten days; but weak as they were in numbers and in discipline they were strong in loyalty and in courage. With such mighty odds against them, they could not conquer, but they took a glorious part in the defeat. Seven of their little party fell mortally wounded—among them Monsieur Jourdan, the chief of the equestrian troupe, who said that he went out to fight *pour l'honneur d'alliance*—and proved his sincerity by his death.

The enemy's Cavalry, on the other hand, were strong in numbers—more than as ten to one. And if they had been well commanded they might have cut us up root and branch. Some dim design of planting themselves between our position and the Fort, so as to cut off our retreat, seems to have been entertained for a time; but it was departed from in

---

* It seems that they had more sense than we had, and did not fire it all away. This may be gathered from the fact that they fired upon us during our retreat; but it has been stated that the last ammunition used against us consisted of bags of pice.

† Memorandum by Mr. E. A. Reade.

favour of another project. It was at that critical
period when Weller was endeavouring to bring up
Patteson's guns, that large bodies of horse were seen
to stream out from behind the village, as if to
threaten our rear and to render our retirement on
Agra perilous, if not impossible. But afterwards
perceiving that our two half-batteries were separated
and but imperfectly protected, they determined to
make an effort to capture our guns. So they charged
down, in two bodies, each on one half-battery—some
hundreds strong. Then was it that our mounted
militiamen showed the stuff of which they were
made. With audacity almost sublime they galloped
forward to meet the dense hosts of the enemy, but
they were "terribly shattered" and could make no
impression on the hostile multitude. But a volley
from the British Infantry covering the guns, delivered at a distance of seventy yards from the advancing enemy, threw confusion into their ranks;
and they wheeled off to the right, making for the
village, where a second volley from the Europeans
checked all their forward designs. The few troopers
who, with exceptional gallantry, got in among our
guns, were easily disposed of by our men.

Meanwhile the conflict in the village had not Conflict in
abated. Our two detachments were separated, and the village.
at one time had lost sight of each other. Fraser's
column had captured and spiked one of the enemy's
guns, and the rest had gone to the rear, limbered up
for flight. But the Infantry were strong and bold
behind cover. The mud-wall of a tobacco-field gave
them great opportunities of carrying on that particular style of warfare in which they most rejoice and
are most successful. We were in every way out-
matched, and it was soon apparent that we could

1857.
July 5.

only destroy our Europeans, every man of whom was of inestimable value at such a time, by continuing the unequal contest. So the attacking columns were withdrawn to join the main body,* and preparations were made for an orderly retreat of the brigade.

The retreat.

In all the force that went out on this disastrous expedition, there was not a braver man than the old Brigadier. He was always to be seen, conspicuous on his white charger, sitting composedly within reach of the enemy's fire. It was a sore trial to him to be compelled to give the order to fall in. Then there was great tribulation about carriage. Neither Pearson's disabled piece, nor the gun which Fraser had spiked could be carried from the field. Two elephants had been sent from Agra, but they were required to carry off the wounded; and the dead were left where they fell.† But when the Brigade had formed, it moved forward so steadily that the enemy for a time believed that we were returning to our quarters to obtain more ammunition and to renew the conflict. Under this impression, not thinking that the battle had been won and lost, they persistently harassed our retreat. Their Artillery galloped ahead, and with their little remaining ammunition fired into us again and again, whilst their Cavalry also rode forward to within a mile of the Fort, firing upon us from behind walls and village-houses. Still our people marched on "steady and confident, many even cheerful,"‡ halting ever and anon to fire upon the rebel Cavalry. There was very little slaughter in our ranks, and,

---

* "We found great confusion there—men and officers drinking greedily from a filthy buffalo-pool, which nothing but dire thirst and exhaustion could have induced them to touch."—*MS. Memorandum by an Eye-Witness.*

† A party of volunteers went out next morning; buried the dead bodies, and recovered Pearson's gun. The enemy had carried off their own piece.

‡ MS. Memoranda.

throughout that four miles' march, the column was never really in danger.

But although it was an orderly retreat—it was truly a great and pitiable disaster and a dire disgrace. The want of Cavalry was a grievous misfortune. But how often has inferiority of numbers been atoned for by superiority of pluck. It was not this misfortune that destroyed us. We were destroyed by the errors that were committed. The reserve ammunition, though packed, was not sent with our force or after our force; and our Infantry were not brought into action, until our guns had become unserviceable. It was madness of the worst kind to reserve the action of our Infantry until our Artillery had ceased to have the means of supporting them. But even of this madness we must speak tenderly ; for D'Oyly paid for it with his life, and Polwhele by the loss of his professional character.

With amazement and alarm our people in the Fort had marked the progress of the action. At first they could but dimly conjecture the issue of events from the sounds which reached them from a distance. They heard the booming of the artillery and the crashes of the great explosions, which had so crippled our action; and when the guns ceased firing and an ominous stillness ensued, the pause excited both wonderment and alarm. But, after a while from the Flagstaff, our brigade might be seen retreating, and soon the terrible reality was announced by the appearance of our beaten force making madly towards the Fort—all in the agony of thirst, eager to reach the canteen. There was then a scene of terrible confusion, such as those who witnessed it pray to God that they may never live to see again. It was not strange that in such a crisis the hearts of our people failed them through fear. But there were some, principally Eurasians and Portuguese, whose surroundings and belongings were such as to render departure from their old homes difficult and distasteful to them. They said that they had faith in their friends in the city who would protect them, and so they refused to betake themselves to 'the shelter of the Fort. But they had miserably miscalculated their chances of safety. The enemy's troopers, who had been foremost in the pursuit, had hounded on all the rascality of Agra and the surrounding villages to slaughter and to ravage our Christian people. More than twenty of these helpless ones were killed either on that evening or on the following day, mostly in their own homes. All our houses, except those immediately contiguous to the Fort, were

Burning of Cantonments.
gutted and burnt; the greater part of our public records were destroyed; and by the lurid light of the fires they had ignited might have been seen these savages dancing with frantic delight around the wrecks and ruins they had created. It was a "grand but melancholy sight." The mighty fire disported itself over a space of some six miles, "from the Civil Lines on our extreme right to the Khelat-i-Ghilzee Lines on the left." Everything of a combustible character was in flames; and our people looked out on the illuminated skies with a sickening sense of the sacrifice of their cherished goods, which the great conflagration portrayed.

It was a night never to be forgotten. Memorable on many accounts, it was memorable for nothing more than for the deep devotion with which the gentlewomen of Agra ministered to the wants of our wounded and weary fighting men. Ghastly sights were before their eyes to make them shudder and other sights from which feminine delicacy shrinks. But these brave-hearted, humane women were sustained by a solemn sense of duty to their God, and a great love for their fellow-creatures. " I think I see them now," writes an eye-witness after naming some who might rank with the Florence Nightingales of the Crimean War, " with the skirts of their gowns stuffed through their petticoats, waiting on the weary combatants of the 5th of July, at a table their own hands had prepared, and in turn taking to my poor and almost mortally wounded comrade, Richard Oldfield, lying at one end of the dining-room, or, in an inner room, to the dying hero of that fight, D'Oyly, whose last words were ' Tell them I died fighting my guns.' Never, whilst life lasts, can I forget those exemplars of unabated cheerfulness, active kindness, and readiness for any emergency."*

* " Then came the rush of weary soldiers to the canteen, which was close to our room and in the same barrack. Bloody, thirsty, covered with dust and smoke, the soldiers clamoured for drink. Beer, tea, wine and water were hastily given to them by the ladies of our party. I could overhear their remarks. ' Ah, my chummie, 'my townie!' said one whose comrade had been left dead on the battle-field. ' Faith ! and the Major (Thomas) went at 'em grand,' said another. The long string of hospital litters passed through the Fort gates. The gallant D'Oyly was carried in to die. Young Williams was undergoing the amputation of a limb in the hospital. Richard Oldfield, Under-Secretary to Government, was brought faint and steeped in blood to his young wife. I had a small tent near the barracks ; in this two wounded officers were lodged. A line of fire in the cantonments showed the course of the retreating enemy. Barracks, private houses, and bazaars, all were in a blaze."—*Raikes*. A touching incident connected with the return of Richard Oldfield has been narrated to me by Mr. E. A. Réade. It cannot be told better than in his own language. " Almost the last man brought in wounded was a relative of mine—R. C. Oldfield, shot down at the same time (as Monsieur Jourdan). His brother, H. T. Oldfield, and Lieutenant Lambe, with the Agra Militia Reserve, of their own accord marched up to the aid of the retreating European Regiment, and formed up as their rear-guard. As they passed up, the wounded brother was carried by (and they were loving brothers). One look was given to the civilian brother, to all appearances dying, and the soldier brother resumed his place at the head of his detachment."—*MS. Memorandum*.

CHAPTER V.

LIFE IN THE AGRA FORT—BESTOWAL OF OUR PEOPLE—ADMIRABLE AR-
RANGEMENTS OF MR. READE AND THE ENGINEERS—THE GOOD WORK OF
OUR GENTLEWOMEN—FORAYS OF THE VOLUNTEER HORSE—ANXIETIES
FROM THE WESTWARD—DEATH OF MR. COLVIN.

July, 1857.   THERE was nothing now to be looked at but the
Population of fact that the English were shut up in the Fort of
the Fort.
Agra, defending themselves against an enemy which
they had no longer any power to attack. Gathered
together within the walls and intrenchments were a
mixed population amounting in all to nearly six
thousand—men, women, and children. Of these the
larger number were Europeans and Eurasians. In
the census taken on the 27th of July, nearly fifteen
hundred Hindoos and Mahomedans were included.
In the earlier part of the month, there had been a
smaller body of these suspects in the Fort; but as
time went on and inconveniences accumulated, our
own people began to doubt whether every man with
a dark face must necessarily be an enemy. It was
thought at one time that our Europeans might minister to their own wants, or that Native Christians
might be employed. But the irksomeness of the
one recourse, and the insufficiency of the others, were
soon dismally apparent, The theory of self-help is

magnificent, but it must severely try an exotic European shut up in a hot fortress in the month of July. The Native Christians who could take service were few, and they proved themselves to be wonderfully unserviceable. So, little by little, we opened our doors to professional Native servants of all classes— to men who could cook, or wait at table, or help us at our toilets, or pull our punkahs, or bring us water, or sweep out and purify our abodes. It was the lesser evil of the two. Thus the number of our "enemies" within the Fort continued gradually to increase until it had attained the height which I have above stated. The Native Christians amounted in all to eight hundred and fifty-eight; but only two hundred and sixty-seven of these were adult males. Of the Europeans and Eurasians nearly half of the number were in this category. There were six hundred and twenty adult females—with some fifteen hundred boys and girls.*

Such was the population of the Agra Fort at the end of the month of July. It must have been difficult to find any accommodation for so large a body of people. It must have been difficult to distribute and assign the quarters without giving offence. But, after a while, these difficulties were overcome, and people shook themselves down in their appointed places, sometimes with an audible growl.† They

* Mr. Raikes says that in this motley assemblage were "unwilling delegates from many parts of Europe and America. Nuns from the banks of the Garonne and the Loire, priests from Sicily and Rome, missionaries from Ohio and Basle, mixed with rope-dancers from Paris, and pedlars from America. Besides these we had Calcutta Baboos and Parsee merchants. Although all the Christians alike were driven by the mutinous legions into the Fort, the circumstances of the multitude were as various as their races."—*Notes on the Revolt in the North-West Provinces of India.*

† On such occasions, much that is good and much that is bad in the human character are frequently evoked. If there was much selfishness there was also some unselfish-

1857.
July.

were strange quarters indeed. Some of the best were within the Palace of the Emperor Akbar—improvised little hutches, in the great arcades or galleries, separated from each other by screens of the substantial mat-work of the country,* whilst the different cells and nooks in this stately building were utilised in the most successful manner. Other dwellings were found of less romantic, but probably of a more convenient kind, in the different public buildings provided for the establishments maintained in the Fort. In a tiled barrack, on an elevation known as " the Mound," Brigadier Polwhele, the Sudder Judges, and the Engineers Fraser and Weller, were lodged.

Efforts of the
Engineers.

Those stalwart Engineers, and the advice which they offered to the chief military authority, had been thorns in the flesh of the old soldier. But, after the great failure of the 5th of July, he could no longer spurn their counsels. He made Fraser Second-in-Command, and Weller Brigade-Major of Engineers. There was much work to be done in strengthening the defences of the fortress. And from morning to night for weeks these officers laboured to bring the works into such a state as to withstand any possible siege. Embrasures were opened out, guns were mounted on the ramparts, the ground immediately

ness of a high order. One instance may be cited. To Mr. Reade, as next in rank to the Lieutenant-Governor, excellent accommodation was assigned. But, as his family were in England, he refused to make himself comfortable at the expense of others. His quarters were allotted to some wounded officers; and he contented himself with a shake-down on the floor of the marble hall of the palace. An old piano-forte cover and a hassock constituted all his bedding.

* " In huts hastily prepared, amongst the gates and galleries or the old palace of the Emperors, a motley crowd assembled. Matted screens were set up among the marble corridors, which in Akbar's time were hung with the silks or Persia and the brocades of Benares." —*Raikes*.

around the Fort, which might have afforded shelter
to the enemy, was cleared. Ammunition was placed
ready for immediate use, and the different components of the garrison told-off and warned, so that
every man might be at his appointed post as soon as
an alarm should be given. But that which was the
greatest source of anxiety to the Engineers was the
defence of the powder-magazines. It was suspected,
and not without reasonable cause of alarm, that there
were enemies in the Fort—wandering Fakirs and
other birds of passage, who were prowling about
to watch our movements, to ascertain the position of
our magazines, and opportunity offering, to destroy
us by a great explosion. It was proved that people
had been tampering with our prepared ammunition.
Shot and shell were changed to guns of different
calibre, and shell-plugs were jammed home, so as to
render the ammunition unserviceable. In this emergency it was above all things necessary to secure our
magazines against any hostile devices. There were
six or seven of these magazines, of which one only
was kept open as an expense magazine. The others
were walled round; their roofs were protected by
thick coverings of earth, the European sentries over
them were doubled, and they were continually visited
by the officers, who were responsible for their safety—
and who swept away all suspicious Natives who were
seen in the neighbourhood of the magazines.

Indeed, from the time of our defeat on the 5th of
July, Fraser became in all but name the actual commandant of the fortress. There was no kind of duty
which he was not eager to perform. He always went
the round of the hospitals to visit and to cheer the
sick and the wounded. He had a blunt rough manner,
but it was pleasing to our soldiers, and they loved him

for his kindness as much as they admired him for his bravery. More than once was he greeted by a sick soldier with the words, "And sure, Colonel, will you soon be tucking up your sleeves again at them mutineers?" He would, on almost every evening, go to Reade and say to him, "Come let us take a turn of the hospitals," and the soldier and the civilian would go out together, distributing kind words and often creature-comforts to the poor fellows, who looked eagerly for these visits, and who sent blessings after them as they went.

Defence of the Fort.

I have said that among the defensive measures of Fraser and Weller was the clearing of some space before the Fort, not open to the fire of our guns. Some houses were to be demolished; but it was just, as there was no proof of the enmity of the owners, that they should be compensated for the loss of their property. But who was to go outside the Fort and treat with the possessors? Reade, ever ready for service, undertook the duty. Fraser and Weller thought that the service was a dangerous one, and besought him to take a guard for his protection. But the civilian had no fear. He said laughingly, but logically, "They, at all events, will not kill me until they have got their money!" But the anxieties of the Engineers did not abate. Fraser and Weller were very careful for their friend—very careful for one who, in all civil affairs, was the very life of the defence. So one day when Reade was discussing terms of adjustment with a number of vociferous claimants, whose nature it was all to speak at the same time, a dead silence fell suddenly upon them. Turning round upon his saddle Reade saw a detachment of Europeans closely behind him. The householders, not unreasonably, thought that the white troops were coming down to destroy them; Reade thought that they were passing on to recover some property or perform some other duty, in no way connected with himself. But they drew themselves up behind him, and then he learnt that Fraser had sent the guard down for his protection. There was necessarily an end of all business. It was not possible that these Native householders should transact it under the bayonets of the Europeans. So Reade saw that the only thing that he could do was to ride back to the Fort; and he went with the guard behind him. Speaking of it afterwards, he said, "I have no doubt that the Natives thought at the time that they had taken me into custody." 1857. July.

Ere long the Fort of Agra was in a state of thorough preparation equally for defence and attack. But even an impregnable fortress is of small use, if it be not well provisioned. Orders had been issued at the end of June for supplying the garrison—to the extent of three thousand Europeans and fifteen hundred Natives—for six months. The general superintendence of this most important business devolved on Reade—the executive details being carried on by Lieutenant Chalmers, the Commissariat Officer. There would have been much difficulty and perplexity in pursuing these operations to a successful issue, if it had not been for the assistance of the great Army contractor, the well-known Jootee-Persaud, whose powers of organisation and extensive machinery of collection were invaluable in such a conjuncture. No one, after what had happened some time before, could blame him for insisting on payment in advance. Supplies were brought in freely; more abundant indeed than, as afterwards appeared, were needed. For when our first fears and suspicions were cast Victualling of the garrison.

1857.
July.

aside, and we ceased to see a foeman in every Mahomedan or Hindoo, supplies of every kind came in
freely from the city. Between the walls of the Fort
and the outer intrenchments was a space, which,
when cleared, was extremely useful to us, as a sort
of repository for our carriages and other heavy goods
which had been recovered from the wreck of the
cantonments. On this space, little by little, a flourish-
ing Bazaar sprang up: and our people were enabled
to purchase almost everything that they might require to satisfy their daily wants.

The women
of Agra.

And as time passed, the women of Agra shone
forth in all the lustre of good deeds, quietly but
vigorously prosecuted. There was much work to be
done and they were right willing to do it. Dr. Farquhar represented to Mrs. Charles Raikes that there
would be need of the establishment of a Civil Hospital, as the Military Hospital would soon be over-
crowded, and he asked her to take the management
of it. She consented, and then began to beat up for
recruits. There was a little paper published in the
Fort, and in this she inserted an advertisement, begging that any women, who wished to take part in this
good work, would send in their names. Before evening, numbers of women of all ranks had eagerly
offered their help. It was necessary, however, that
this beautiful regiment of Dorcases should be well
organised and disciplined. So Mrs. Raikes appointed
a goodly staff of gentlewomen, who superintended
the work of the numerous East Indian females who
had no other occupation. Besides visiting the hospital and ministering to the wants of the patients,
their principal work was that of making up clothing, bedding, bandages, &c., for the sick. The materials were supplied, by the Financial Commissioner,
from the Government stores. It was of necessity

that large indents should be made upon Mr. Reade ; and he well knew the importance of complying with them. But the Calcutta Financiers took another view of the matter ; and ignored this item as a public charge, and pronounced it to be one of " personal responsibility."

There were others of our English gentlewomen who did their good work in different directions, giving confidence to the desponding by cheerful looks and cheerful words—visiting the sick, teaching the young, and performing other Christian offices. Ominous reports of coming dangers had been set about by men, who, brave as lions themselves, took gloomy views of the position and were not slow to express them. " The space before the house occupied by the Deputy-Commissary," writes one who saw everything that was passing, and who has a rare power of putting his reminiscences into expressive words, " was one of often resort. Here was Lady Outram discussing the thousand and one rumours of the Fort, always cheerful, lightly treating the adventures of a walk, barefooted for many miles, on escaping from Aligurh, given to chaff the Financial Commissioner with some nonsense about our ' chief politician'—' as unshaken as the wind though busy in raising it'—sometimes borne on her ' taun-jaun', her son, Frank Outram, walking beside her. It was a delight to the European soldiers, scattered about Armoury Square, to see her, with her serene face always ready with a kind smile and a kind word. . . . . In Palace Square was Mrs. (now Lady) Muir with her five children, cheery as a sunbeam, energetic in promoting the employment and welfare of the Native Christians, with her neighbour, Mrs. C. B. Thornhill, enlisting other ladies in good work, stirring up

1857.
July—Aug.

subscriptions for the wounded and destitute of the North-Western Provinces. She and those above-mentioned, leaders in the social scale, were leaders also in the multiplied tasks of urging the well-disposed to active usefulness, relieving the poor, providing guardianships for waifs and strays of humanity, visiting and supporting schools, soothing vain alarms, repressing the vindictive feeling against Natives of the country, promoting charity among all."

I am afraid that this feeling of charity was not universal throughout the Fort. The Roman Catholic community kept themselves scrupulously aloof from the rest of the garrison.* Extensive quarters had been assigned to them—for they had many nuns and school-girls, priests, and monks, with a bishop at their head. This high ecclesiastical functionary, who lived in another part of the Fort, is said to have given much trouble, as he seemed bent upon making political capital out of the situation. At last it was held to be inexpedient to recognise him any longer as our referee, so Father Lewis was appointed to take his place. It has been written of this community that "their inner life was a sealed book. Their outward demonstration was a long promenade of pale sad faces, headed by two monks, whose jolly visages afforded a curious contrast to the rest." And it is added, "I do not remember that any of the nuns served as sisters of charity in the Hospitals; at least I never saw any."*

But our good Protestant Englishwomen knew little and cared less about differences of creed. Unless some accidental circumstance revealed the fact of

* I do not wish to infer that there were no exceptions to this rule. I am informed that Mrs. Vansittart, a Roman Catholic lady, was active in her ministrations.
† MS. Memorandum.

the patient's faith, those who ministered to the wants of the sick or wounded in the Hospitals, had no inkling of the creed of the patient. One poor fellow, whom Mrs. Raikes and others visited in the Hospital, was much pleased with the kindness of his lady-visitors and received them with grateful respect. He was very thankful for any newspapers or light literature that might be offered to him, but he refused to accept any of our religious books and would not listen to the reading of the Bible. One day Mrs. Raikes found his cot empty and saw him kneeling by the bedside of a Roman Catholic comrade to whom a priest was administering extreme unction. This accounted at once for the man's reluctance to listen to the Bible or to read our Protestant books.*

1857.
July—Aug.

* Mr. Raikes states in his "Notes on the Revolt," that the ladies were divided into watches and attended day and night. "To avoid teasing the men by too much nursing, they were in a small separate room, and, *at stated periods*, went round to give tea, jelly, soda-water, coffee, soup, or to help in dressing the wounds of the patients. All was done under the orders of the medical officers." There was sometimes a ludicrous side to the pictures of pain and sorrow presented to the eyes of the volunteer nurses. One story I may insert here, for it is so eminently characteristic of the Englishman in India. The man of whom this is told was a common soldier; but I have witnessed similar ebullitions from our English officers—and seen the man beaten for the blunderings of his master. I give the anecdote in the writer's words. The story relates to the period after the battle of the 10th of October, the story of which is reserved for the next volume. "Amongst them was a fine young artilleryman whose leg had been badly crushed by a heavy gun-carriage. His sufferings were intense, and, poor fellow, his temper at first very irritable. Much as I pitied him I could not help feeling amused one day when I found him threatening a hospital coolie who was bringing a chillumchee (brass basin) filled with water. Poor young Cumming was shaking his fists and saying alternately 'Put it down,' and 'Lee-jao' (take it away). The wretched coolie, though anxious to obey, was sorely puzzled by these conflicting orders. First he put down the water, then he took it up. Cumming was furious, until I interposed and said that the coolie did not know what was wanted. 'Yes, he does, lady; he wants to tease me and does it on purpose. I want him to put down the water and *go*, but he won't!' Poor Cumming! what a change came over him at a later day. He was quite a boy, and often spoke of his poor mother. From a lion he became a lamb. His constant words were, 'Don't leave me, dear lady, but offer up a prayer for me!' At last he sank while joining with us in prayer. One of

2 D 2

There were few, if any, among the women of Agra, who did not gratefully acknowledge the kindly aid, in all matters, rendered to them by Mr. Reade, and especially in the management of the financial affairs of those who were absent from their husbands, or who had been widowed by the great convulsions. To men and women alike shut up in Agra, the cheerful, but systematic manner, in which the "Financial Commissioner," for so they styled him without official sanction, administered the exchequer in a small apartment known as "the hole in the wall," whence he issued his warrants, which were taken to the Treasury and changed into rupees for present use, or if required into bills to be remitted to a distance, must have been very welcome to all his fellow *détenus*. Thus, as there was very little want of necessaries in the Fort, there was little lack of the means of purchasing them. Some special creature-comforts, however, were scarce. It is related that "you could buy millinery or perfumery, but not cheese, beer, wine, or tobacco."* On the whole, the burden of outward suffering to be borne by our people in the Fort was not very heavy or distressing. There were inconveniencies to be encountered, and privations to be endured—especially in respect of household accommodation and the more refined domestic appliances. The greatest evils of all were the over-crowding; the want of privacy on the one hand, and the want of ventilation on the other—the efforts to secure the former being necessarily antagonistic to

us wrote to his mother at Windsor to tell her he died happily. Another poor fellow who was sinking said, 'Lady, pray read to me of Our Lord walking on the water.' The men of the Ninth Lancers were all so gentle, indeed I may say all so gentlemanlike, that it was a real pleasure to read to them and to nurse them in their sufferings." This also was after the battle of the 10th of October.

* Raikes.

the latter. It was a curious sort of "board-ship
life," board-ship life on a gigantic scale, "stuffy,
stewy, aud vermin-infested ;" with a few state rooms
for families, and little side-cabins or hutches for
bachelors, and some open places, as cuddies or poop
decks, for common resort. Most providentially it
happened that the season was an unusually healthy
one, and there was probably not more than the
average amount of ill-health to distress the occupants of the Fort. Men and women alike missed
their ordinary morning or evening rides and drives
and " ate the air" under unfavourable circumstances.
But the air on the ramparts was wonderfully pure,
for the Fort stood high, and the river flowed beneath
it, and there was a luxury of their own in the evening
promenades. But it must be acknowledged that
their employments and diversions were of a somewhat monotonous character. The Engineers had
more than enough to do, to keep them at work from
sunrise to sundown ; and some had business, or made
it, in drilling troops for militia or volunteer service,
whilst many were driven to the undignified occupation of "loafing." There was no lack of books; but
the unwritten contemporary histories were those
most discussed, and when the curse of *ennui* sate so
heavily upon them, it is not strange that the *gup*, or
gossip, market was plentifully supplied, and that sometimes vague, wild rumours passed from mouth to
mouth and were] embraced or discarded according
to the temper of the recipients. But the evening,
perhaps, was the pleasantest time, when men met
each other at one or other of the numerous messes
that had been established, and ate their homely, but
abundant fare, with good appetites and cheery
faces. One of the best, if not the best of all, was

that presided over by Machell, the Ordnance Commissariat Officer, who had special means of purvey-
ing the best of fare that the place could supply.

Meanwhile, there was little in the aspect of affairs
beyond Agra to lighten the burden of trouble that
oppressed the Lieutenant-Governor. July passed and
August passed; but there was no appearance of the
capture of Delhi. Colvin was in close correspondence with Hervey Greathed; but the Commissioner,
though of a cheerful nature, could send no tidings
to gladden Colvin's heart. Delhi still in the hands
of the insurgents and Lucknow unrelieved, there was
no prospect of any aid from without to set free the
Agra garrison. The fall of the great stronghold of
the Moguls might virtually change the condition of
affairs throughout the whole of the North-Western
Provinces. But, as time went on, Colvin could but
see that the state of the country was growing worse
and worse. The tidings which came in to him from
all parts were not of an assuring character. He had
wisely organised an Intelligence Department, of which
William Muir had the chief direction. It was highly
important at such a time that reliable information
should be obtained from the officers of Government
themselves in place of the gossip of the bazaars or the
confused statements of frightened messengers. And
no man could have done the work better than Muir.
The demi-official or private correspondence that came
in, from day to day, was full of the most instructive
and suggestive details. It was said that he was a
little over-chary in the dissemination of the intelligence he obtained. But this can scarcely be regarded
as a fault when we consider how likely it was, amid
such a population as that of the Agra Fort, a story
once floated would be exaggerated or distorted, and

might rather add to the anxieties than strengthen the confidence of our people. There was, in truth, little or nothing of an exhilarating character to be communicated; so, perhaps, silence, at such a time, was of better metal than speech.

It was plain, indeed, that the situation was growing more and more perilous. The temper of the soldiery was worse, and their confidence, under the influence of continued success and impunity was waxing stronger every day. In the British districts and in the petty Native States there was a general upheaving of turbulent disorders. It was the great carnival of the dispossessed. And the area of disaffection was spreading largely; not only in the country under Colvin's care, but in other countries beyond the border of the North-Western Provinces; and the political significance of the movement was becoming, every week, more apparent. It had been hoped and, indeed, commonly believed, that the Bombay Army was staunch to the core. It was the fashion to speak of the mutiny of the Bengal Army, engendered by the accident of the greased cartridges. But now, as August dawned upon us, ugly rumours came of an outbreak in the Kolapore country and the mutiny of the Twenty-seventh Regiment. There could be nothing more significant than this. The outbreak did not come out of greased cartridges, but out of the Sattarah Lapse. "In 1849," wrote Lord Dalhousie in his celebrated Farewell Minute, "the principality of Sattarah was included in the British dominions by Right of Lapse."* The Rajah of Sattarah, a descendant of Sivajee, was the acknowledged chief of the Mahrattas. None questioned his su-

---

* See vol. i. page 71.

1857.
July—Aug.

premacy. The "Right of Lapse" was not very patiently admitted by the family, who memorialised the East India Company and sent an agent to England to advocate the justice of their claims. It happened that at this time, Azimoollah Khan was advocating, in London, for like purposes, the claims of the Peishwah family, of whom Doondoo-Punt, Nana Sahib, was the chief. To what extent the Mahratta and the Mussulman, not succeeding at all with the Directors of the East India Company, who at that time were the servants not the masters of Lord Dalhousie, took counsel together can only be conjectured. Rungo-Bapojee returned to India, by the help of the East India Company, for he was hopelessly insolvent; and he was soon busily at work in the Southern Mahratta country. That he was in communication with Bithoor may be assumed without any violent straining of the imagination. But whatsover the previous intrigue, on the last day of July the Twenty-seventh Regiment of Sepoys broke into mutiny at Kolapore. After what had happened "on the Bengal side," it was not strange that when tidings of this event reached Bombay there was something like a panic among the Europeans. As in Calcutta, some weeks before, "The European community in Bengal had taken alarm and numbers conveyed their wives and children to the shipping in the harbour. The civilians furnished Volunteer Horse that patrolled the streets at night; meetings were held to discuss points of rendezvous and best modes of defence; every one burnished up his weapons and there was a general feeling of distrust not lessened by the fact that, through the exertions of Mr. Forgett, the excellent and energetic Superintendent of Police, some of the Sepoys in garrison were found to be untrustworthy."[*] As in Calcutta also, the coolest head and stea- 1857.
July—Aug. diest pulse in Bombay was that of the Governor, Lord Elphinstone. He bethought himself at once of the best measures to be adopted and of the best man to give them effect. The man was Colonel Le Grand Jacob, who had recently returned from the scene of the Persian war, in which he had held command under Sir James Outram. He had a large knowledge of the political affairs of Western India, and he was a soldier of high courage and activity. Lord Elphinstone sent for him and gave him the supreme direction of affairs in the disturbed country. And at the same time he despatched from Bombay, the greater part of the way by sea, a detachment of European Infantry and Artillery. How well Jacob proved that the Governor had placed his confidence in the right man, and how subsequent events in Western India revealed the dangers which were lurking there, will be shown in a later chapter of this narrative. In this place it is enough to say that these tidings of disaffection in the Bombay Army must have fallen heavily upon Colvin. There was at least a likelihood that it would spread, and this likelihood was to be provided against by the Government, whose first duty it was to protect its own people; so there was small chance of the Agra dependencies being relieved, from Bombay, however pressing the need might be. The fidelity of the Bombay Army was a fountain of hope to the Lieutenant-Governor of the North-Western Provinces, and now it was dried up at its source.

But some stirring spirits were in the Agra garrison Agra.

[*] "Western India before and during the Mutinies," by Sir G. Le Grand Jacob. I shall write more fully of these Western risings in my next volume. Meanwhile the reader will do well to consult Jacob's book.

who believed that they might do something to help themselves. It was plain that an error had been committed after the battle of Shahgunj in shutting up the Fort so closely as to engender the belief outside that we had no power of further action left in us. The danger anticipated was quite visionary. There was less vitality in the insurgent army than in our own. So far from meditating an attack on the Agra Fort they had been glad to make their way in the direction of Muttra with the utmost possible despatch. The burning and sacking of the cantonments had not been their work. But there were some of our own people, who thought that they could do no better service than by firing wildly down on no one in particular, and thus preventing our friends from obtaining ingress to the Fort and affording us the information we most needed. But now the truth of this had become apparent, and there was a very general desire to go out and do something. Foremost among these were the gentlemen of the Volunteer Horse, who having little or nothing to do in the Fort were eager for some work beyond it. New councils were now prevailing and resolute action was taking the place of the old vacillation and total want of self-reliance that at one time had brought us to feebleness. Brigadier Polwhele had been superseded, and Colonel Cotton had taken his place. There was no cold blood in his veins. He is said, indeed, to have been a somewhat fiery warrior and to have been called "Gun-Cotton" by his comrades. He was easily wrought upon to send out a force to Aligurh to reoccupy that place,* where a rebel Government had

---

* Mr. Paterson Saunders, of the Volunteer Horse, says that he persuaded Cotton to send out the Force, and, doubtless, he did. But Cotton had no power, except that which was delegated to him by the

been set up by one Ghousa Khan, who proclaimed 1857.
himself as Soubahdar of the King of Delhi. "The July—Aug.
object of this movement was to give protection to
the important town of Hatrass, which has hitherto
escaped being plundered, to establish authority in
this portion of the Aligurh district, to give confidence
to the local Talookhdars, whose possessions are in
the neigbourhood of Hatrass, and to frustrate the
attempts of certain rebels to usurp the authority of
the British Government in other parts of the Aligurh
district."*

Major Montgomery, Brigade-Major of Agra, than Action at Ali-
whom there was no better officer in the garrison, gurh.
was appointed to command the Force. On the 20th
of August he went out taking with him three
companies of Europeans, three guns, a body of
Volunteer Horse,† and some Ghat horsemen raised by
Thakoor Govind Singh. Arthur Cocks went with
them, armed with special powers as Commissioner.
They started at 4 P.M. on the 20th of October.
On the 24th they were in the neighbourhood of the
insurgents. The enemy were composed chiefly of the

Civil authorities. It is understood that Arthur Cocks, aided by Reade and others, induced Colvin to give his consent. Mr. Saunders' words are: "I persuaded him, Cotton, to send out a party to attack him, (Ghousa Khan), otherwise the Soubahdar would have been his most formidable enemy."

* Memorandum of Instructions by Mr. E. A. Reade. The Lieutenant-Governor was too feeble to draw them up himself. But he countersigned the document.

† The uninstructed reader must be cautioned not to confound the Agra Militia with the Volunteer Horse—I believe that some of both were present. Mr. Reade says: "The Militia is composed of military officers of regiments which have mutinied, or have been disarmed, of members of the Civil Service holding appointments, of salaried clerks in the public offices, of sectioners, of men drafted from the European regiment, of pensioners, of Christian drummers, musicians, &c., from Native regiments, and of individuals not heretofore in the service of Government. It is an additional complication that some of the Agra Volunteer Horse now serve in the Militia, and that some of the Militia have been drafted into the recently constituted Rifle Company."

men raised by Ghousa Khan; but with them were some troopers of the notorious Third Cavalry. They had taken up their position in a walled garden; and it was not easy at first to accurately discern their location. But Saunders, who had ridden round the enclosure, " potted at," as he wrote, " by the enemy lining two sides of the square," carried information to Montgomery, which enabled him to make his dispositions. This was one of those actions of which it is difficult to give a comprehensive account with certainty of accuracy; for every man was so busy with his own work that he knew little of what others were doing at any given moment. The battle raged furiously for some time. All arms of our force fought with distinguished gallantry, and the enemy grappled with them in all the wild energy of desperation. Conspicuous on the field for deeds of daring were the Volunteer Horse; and conspicuous among the horsemen were Saunders and Tandy. Tandy was a man of whom all men knew that he was ready to dash into any dangerous enterprise, and to sell his life, not for the sake of the Government, for which he had less than no love at all, but for the sake of his murdered countrymen and their wives and children. Saunders went into battle with kindred sentiments. When he died, it was said of him that few men had more of the noble chivalry of the old times.* He was a bold, frank man; not chary of speech, and not chary of self. Tandy fell fighting gloriously; Saunders narrowly escaped the bullets to which he unflinchingly exposed himself. Many other brave men did their work well on that day; none better than Captain Murray. Saunders having, as above stated, learnt the

---

* It should be mentioned that his calling was that of an indigo-planter.

vulnerable point of attack, led that officer to it,
and now came the crisis of the action. Murray
charged into the midst of Ghousa Khan's people,
and was soon engaged in a desperate hand to hand
encounter with one of his leading followers. The
Englishman slew his man; and the enemy soon lost
heart. So completely were they routed that the
enterprise was abandoned, and they made the best of
their way from Aligurh.

It too often happens that in narratives of this kind
the good deeds of the humbler heroes of the hour
find no record. One instance may be cited here.
The telegraph wires had been recovered by the activity of the boys of the Department, and a line had
been laid between Agra and Aligurh; it being of
high importance that all the movements of Montgomery's force should be known in the Fort. One of
these boys, named Tayler, sat in a palanquin carriage, close to the field of action, and coolly telegraphed back to Agra all the incidents of the battle
as they occurred. There was great rejoicing when it
was known that the enemy had fled; and it is to be
hoped that the youngster was rewarded.

All this time Colvin was gradually wearing away. Last illness of
After the defeat of our troops on the 5th of July, and Mr. Colvin.
our withdrawal into the Fort, he seems to have lost
heart and hope. This slow fading away was perceptible to the devoted friends by whom he was surrounded; but he was reluctant to admit that he was
breaking down. Perhaps he thought it was sound
policy not to confess any apprehensions of the inner
dangers that threatened the life of the Lieutenant-
Governor. He would not cease to work. No entreaties, no remonstrances could induce him to spare

himself. He had a noble staff of officers under him, who were fully to be trusted; but even in minute details he toiled on to the last. Day after day, from all parts of the provinces, came in reports from his officers—often despairing cries for help, written in French or in Greek characters, and with difficulty to be deciphered. He issued instructions on each. I have them before me, and there are not many not endorsed in his familiar handwriting. Even paltry executive details far beneath the dignity of so high an officer to be concerned with were supervised by the Lieutenant-Governor with a rigid conscientiousness as uncalled for and undesirable as it was praise-

worthy in intention. Writing of the month of July, one who served under him, said: "Even now, if I wanted a sword or a pistol from the Magazine, Mr. Colvin's counter-signature was necessary."

This burden of toil alone might not have destroyed him, but it was aggravated a hundredfold by the burden of anxiety that oppressed him. Perhaps of all men in high position during that troubled year, he was the most severely tried. He saw district after district, under his government, passing away from him. He saw hundreds and hundreds of his fellow Christians —men, women, and children—pitilessly massacred. But he could do little to save the country or to rescue our people. Nothing, however, pained him more than the unkindness of those who ought to have sympathised with and aided him. One, who knew better than all others what was on, wrote to me, saying: "He had the mortification to find himself generally unable to exact respect or to enforce obedience. He proposed measure after measure only in too many cases to be met by excuses, evasions, or flat refusals. He attended one or two funerals of

officers beyond the entrenchments, he visited the
hospitals, traversed the ramparts, and had a kind
word for all. But it was of no use, his reception
was cold and sullen, when it was not actually dis-
respectful. He had brutally savage letters in his
box." He was emphatically a strong man; but
now, in this great extremity, shut up in Agra, with
no hope of succour, no chance of deliverance, and
little support, he felt that he was helpless as an infant.
So as the months of July and August wore on, and
the clouds grew darker and denser, it became more
patent to those about him, and especially to the chief
medical officer, Dr. Farquhar, that he was rapidly
breaking down. Yet Colvin himself was slow to
acknowledge that he was sensible of any diminution
of mental or physical energy, except in regard of
some impairment of his old powers of fixing his mind
even on small details, which he said greatly distressed
him. As far back as the 2nd of July his medical
attendant had apprehended an attack of apoplexy,
but this had been warded off by judicious prophy-
lactics; and he urged "the necessity of Mr. Colvin's
enjoying for a time perfect rest of body and of mind.
I am, therefore, desirous that on the first opportunity
he should proceed down country, and thence to England, for the recovery of his health."

But all this was denied to him. Beyond a temporary removal from the Fort to the Cantonment, the
purer air of which did him some good, there was no
possibility of effecting the desired change, even if
Colvin had consented to forego his labours. He
knew well that he should never see the old country
again. In this knowledge he touchingly quoted to
his private secretary, Captain Prinsep, the well-known
line of the Æneid : " Nec patriam antiquam nunc est

spes ulla vidęndi." He was rapidly growing worse, and in the first week of September it was plain that his end was approaching. On the 8th there was a consultation of medical officers, and it was unanimously agreed that " the state of Mr. Colvin's health was such that his continuing to attend to business was dangerous to his life." It was too late. The day of rest was, indeed, approaching—but it was beyond the grave. He was quite prepared for the great change. Mr. French, the Chaplain, who ministered to him at the last, found that he was quite tranquil and assured. He said that he could appeal to all who had watched his career and known his public character—and especially during the last months of sore trial and tribulation—that " he had not shrunk from bearing the burden which God had called upon him to sustain;" that he had performed his duty to the utmost of his ability; and that he had striven " to have always a conscience void of offence towards God and Man." " But it was not," adds the reverend writer, " the consciousness of integrity and honesty of purpose which was the pillow that supported his dying head. . . . He felt in the solemnity of the hour in which he was called to prepare to meet his God, that it was the atonement and intercession of Christ that he found to be ' an anchor of the soul both sure and steadfast.' These words emphatically repeated were some of the last that escaped his lips." He died on the 9th of September, and History rejoices to accord him a place in the front rank of those who died for their country, during that tremendous epoch, more painfully and not less gloriously than those who died on the battle-field—a true Christian hero of whom the nation must ever be most proud.

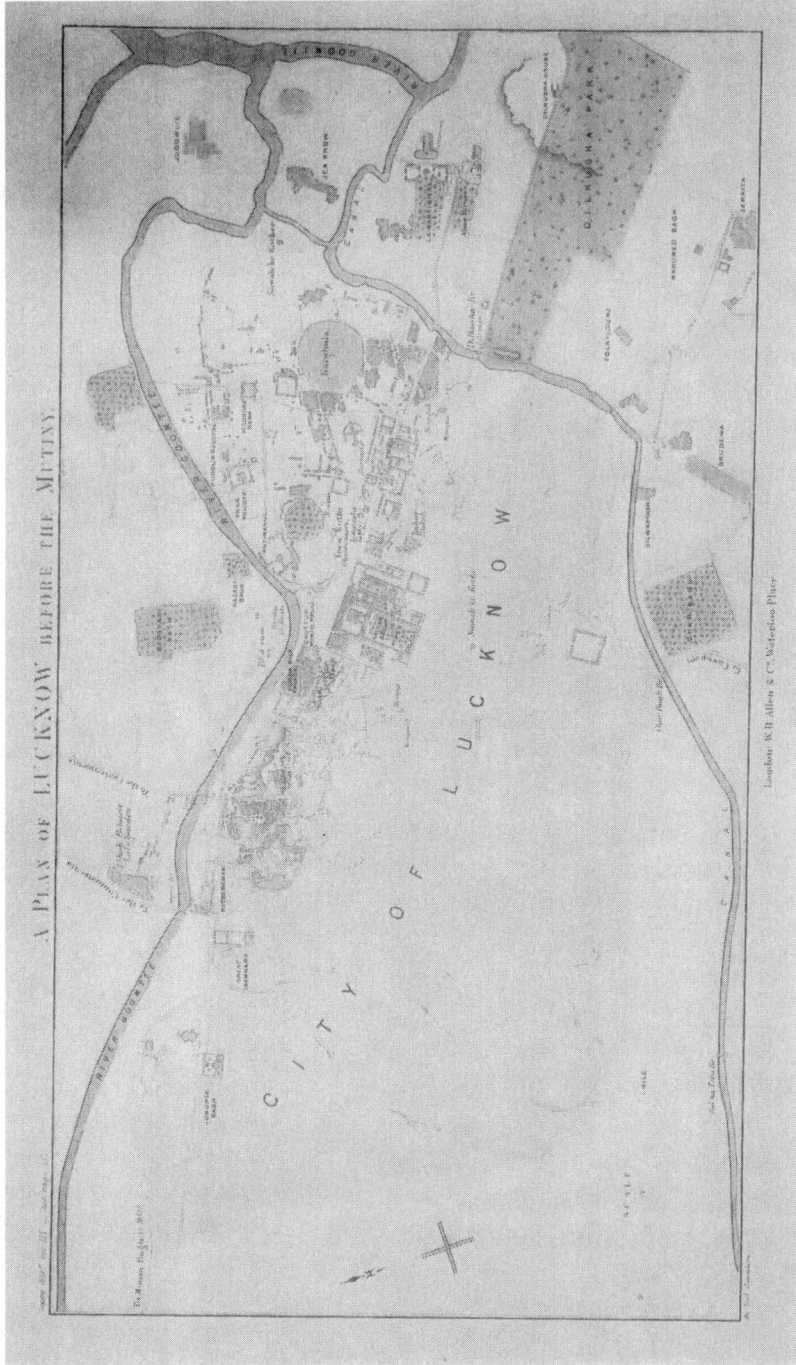

A PLAN OF LUCKNOW BEFORE THE MUTINY

London: W.H. Allen & Co, Waterloo Place

BOOK IX.—LUCKNOW AND DELHI.

[May—September, 1857.]

———◆———

CHAPTER I.

GENERAL STATE OF OUDE — CAUSES OF INQUIETUDE — RUIN OF THE IN-
FLUENTIAL CLASSES — THE NOBLES — THE GREAT LANDHOLDERS — THE
SOLDIERY — OVERTAXATION OF THE PEOPLE — LUCKNOW IN MAY —
THREATENINGS OF REVOLT — PRECAUTIONS OF SIR HENRY LAWRENCE —
DEFENSIVE MEASURES — PROGRESS OF MUTINY — THE OUTBREAK IN
CANTONMENTS.

FROM one end of India to the other, there was no
tract of country, the circumstances of which were
to be regarded with more reasonable anxiety and
alarm, than the great province of Oude. How, after
a long period of misgovernment by its Native rulers,
it had passed under the administration of the British,
and in what manner it had been governed during the
first year after its annexation, has been told in the
early part of this History. With the ordinary egotism of the English, blinded by our national self-
love, we had looked upon the seizure of Oude as a
grand deliverance of the people. It was boasted that
a line of Native tyrants had been cut off, and that
for their ceaseless cruelty and rapacity had been substituted the just and benevolent sway of the Christian
ruler. Law and order, it was said, were to prevail in
the place of anarchy and rapine. At the head of the
new administration were placed three "experienced

1856—57.

*General con-
dition of
Oude.*

1857.   civilians" from the North-Western Provinces, charged
with the duty of introducing into Oude the systems
which, in that part of the country, it was said, had
developed such encouraging results. It has been
already shown how these men frittered away their
energies in unseemly personal contentions with each
other, whilst much of the most important work of
Government was neglected, and dangers of all kinds
were suffered to gather unheeded around their doors.*
Either the sympathetic faculty was wholly absent from
their breasts, or they wilfully refused to see what
they knew to exist. Their theory was, that the great
masses of the people were with them, and that, therefore, the new Government was safe. There could not
have been a more fatal error. It is true that the
people might have eventually benefited by the new
rule. But in India the people have no potential
voice.† The *vox populi*, indeed, is little more than a
silence. What our statesmen, in such a case, should
have considered was, not the feeling engendered by
the revolution in the rural population, but the resentments which it was likely to arouse in the breasts of
the influential classes of the community. There was
a dynasty extinguished—a regal Court erased—a territorial aristocracy demolished—an army disbanded.
Out of any one of these might have come " votes for
troubles." Out of all combined it would have been
strange, indeed, if mighty mischief had not arisen to
disturb the " tranquillity" of which the English
boasted at the dawn of their dominion in Oude.

* It is pitiable to read the letters
addressed by the Chief Commissioner
to the Governor-General during the
first year of our occupation of Oude.
What a relief to turn from them to
those of Sir Henry Lawrence !

† It is to be remembered, however, that as the soldiery of the
Oude army and the retainers of the
great Talookhdars were drawn from
the rural population, even that class
suffered by the new rule.

The fortunes of Wajid Ali, the deposed King, have been traced in previous books of this History. To suppose that any individual sympathies, any tender regrets, any chivalrous feelings of personal devotion, followed the exiled monarch to the British-Indian capital, would be to take a romantic view of the position not probably justified by the fact. But whatsoever the weakness, the selfishness, the profligacy of the man may be, there is always a sort of reverential affection for the King, which neither political imbecility nor moral turpitude can destroy. Oude had seen a succession of Nawabs and Kings of the same family, differing little from each other in their love of self and their disregard of others. But these men, bad as they were, were Native rulers, Mahomedan Princes; and the country had become accustomed even to their abominations. Moreover, there was a large number of people who profited greatly by the extravagance and licentiousness of the Court of Lucknow. Money was freely spent—freely circulated—within the home circuit. It did not go out of the province—scarcely out of the capital. There were shoals of Court functionaries, of Court tradesmen, of titled pensioners, to whom the coffers of the King were accessible; and who were simply ruined when his Majesty was dethroned. The condition of some of these people was truly pitiable. Men and women of high birth, tenderly reared and luxuriously surrounded, were suddenly cast adrift on the world, without the means of subsistence. Some warded off starvation by selling their shawls and trinkets. Some are known to have gone forth into the streets to beg under cover of the darkness of the night.* The

* Mr. Gubbins, the Financial Commissioner, states this in his book with a candour and self-negation worthy of all praise: "But perhaps

2 E 2

1857.   usurpation of the English had sunk them into the
uttermost depths of humiliation; and there was no
one to listen to their despairing cries. Nothing was
further from the intention of Government than that
these privileged classes should suffer. But the fact
remains that they suffered miserably. Whilst the
Chief Commissioner and the Financial Commissioner
were indulging in contemptible conflicts of authority, the settlement of the Oude Pension List was in
abeyance; and nothing was done to provide the pensioners with *ad interim* allowances to keep them from
starving. It was, doubtless, a very difficult and com-
plicated business, and the complete disentanglement
of it must have been a work of time. The stipends
and pensions were of many kinds, drawn from many
sources; and in the first year of British administration, work was burdensome and distracting, and
much of it had to be learnt by our "experienced
civilians." Abler men were not to be found for the
performance of administrative duties in our settled
provinces; but in a country just rescued, as it was
phrased, from Native misrule, they were all astray in
the dark. Lacking sympathy with the nobility and
gentry of India, they seem to have looked upon the
question of the Oude Pension Lists as a problem to
be worked out on paper, not as an immediate matter
of food and clothing, dignity and modesty, indeed of

the class most entitled to sympathy
was the nobility itself, and the num-
berless relatives and friends who
hung upon it. The nobles had received large pensions from the Native
Government, the payment of which,
never regular, ceased with the introduction of our rule. Government
had made liberal provision for their
support; but before this could be
obtained, it was necessary to prepare
careful lists of the grantees, and to
investigate their claims. It must
be admitted that in effecting this
there was undue delay, and that for
want of common means of support
the gentry and nobility of the city
were brought to great straits and
suffering. We were informed that
families, which had never before been
outside the Zenana, used to go out
at night and beg their bread."

very life and death, to hundreds, whose misfortune it was to be off-shoots of an effete dynasty—perhaps minions of a corrupt Court—unable to dig and ashamed to beg, and therefore hopelessly stranded after the great wreck of the Native Government.* But Henry Lawrence, who carried with him to Oude the best of heads and the best of hearts, saw at once this terrible omission, and promptly proceeded to redress the wrong. Like many other good deeds done by good men, it was too late. The humiliation had been inflicted, the sufferings had been endured; and the bitter resentments which were festering in the breasts of these down-trodden nobles were not to be eradicated by this tardy instalment of justice.

And so naturally—reasonably, indeed—the people of the Court, of all kinds, came to hate us with a bitter hatred, and rejoiced when they heard that others had like reason with themselves to long for a day of retribution. They soon found that there were other influential classes who were exacerbated in an equal degree against the new dominion of the white men. Foremost among them were the great baronial The landed land-holders of the country, among whom the English aristocracy. Government had determined to let loose their settlement officers, with instructions to adhere closely to the practice observed in the provinces on the other side of the river. The principles of Bird and Thomason were to have pregnant expression. The Talookhdars were to be crushed down. The opportunity was

* I do not mean to attribute the immediate executive failure to the Financial Commissioner or his Superior. For the duty of supervising and administering the Pension Lists had been especially intrusted to Captain Fletcher Hayes, who had been appointed Political Assistant to the Chief Commissioner. He was a gallant soldier and an accomplished scholar, but he was dilatory and procrastinating, and he did not get on with his work. This is the official history of the case; but I do not see that it in any way exempts from blame the Chief Commissioner, whose duty it was to see that the work was done by his subordinate.

one most inviting to the disciples of the great levelling school; for, in truth, the Oude Talookhdars had a very evil reputation. Their faces had been blackened, past all hope of purification, by one who held the Thomasonian school in no sort of respect. Colonel Sleeman had printed, for official circulation, two volumes of a "Diary of a Tour in Oude," full of startling revelations of misrule, in which the territorial aristocracy of the country appeared as little better than bandits and outlaws. No one, indeed, had a good word to say for them; so they were sacrificed without remorse. In the new settlement that was made by the English officers they were treated as mere middle-men, and direct engagements were made with village proprietors who had before been content to occupy and to cultivate their lands under the old Talookhdars. Practically, the same results would have followed annexation, if these men had been better landlords and better subjects. But their evil reputation in our eyes, the fame of which had preceded our advent, gave zest to the employment, and barred the sufferers from sympathy. We had not sufficient toleration to discern the essential truth, that great as were the faults, perhaps the crimes of these men, they were the growth of a vicious system, of cankering circumstances, and that it needed only, as was afterwards shown, a better political atmosphere to develop the higher qualities which were latent within them.

But it was not simply through the circumstance of these "estates overthrown" that the germs of future danger lay embedded beneath the ruins of the territorial aristocracy. These great Talookhdars had large bodies of retainers; fighting men armed in a rude sort of way, who had been employed to defy the Government on the one side, and to coerce the cultivators on the other. They had mud forts, with dense jungly enclosures; and mounted guns, which might not have satisfied the critical perceptions of the skilled artillerymen of Dum-Dum and Meerut, but which could do some mischief when occasion required. On the assumption of the Government by the English, these forts were dismantled; these jungly barriers were cleared away; these baronial levies were disarmed and disbanded. Thus was the resentment of the Talookhdars further aroused, and the dangerous classes swollen by the addition of thousands of ruined retainers. The disarming of a country is something that looks well on paper. But in practice it is commonly a delusion. As long as Mother Earth is at hand to receive the iron, back again into her bosom, guns and swords will be buried and give no sign of their existence. It was the theory, too, that these fighting men would, at a moment's notice, return to the plough, and become peaceful tillers of the soil. A few of them, perhaps, did; but the majority were left without employment, chafing under the injury that had been done to them, and sullenly waiting the time to strike.

No one regarded this as any source of peril to the State; nor, indeed, was it supposed that there was any lurking danger anywhere at the bottom of the great revolution that we had accomplished. But there were other classes than the pensioned nobility and great landed gentry—the feudal Barons of Oude—whom the new supremacy grievously affected. There had been a large Native Army in the service of the King, which had necessarily been disbanded. The soldiery were drawn from the same classes as had recruited our own Army. But as

1857.

The soldiery.

1857.   soldiers they differed, in all essential conditions, from
their brethren in the Company's service. The relations between them and the Government were of the
most dissolute kind. Master and servant were equally
bad.   Where is irregularity of payment, there is
irregularity of discipline. Under the rule of Wajid
Ali, they were a sort of licensed banditti. Sixty
thousands of these men had to be disposed of when
the British Army was marched into Oude. Some of
these—about a quarter of the whole—were taken
into the service of the new Government. The rest
were cast adrift upon the province with small pensions or gratuities. Sullen, but not despairing, they
went off to their native villages, and talked to their
brothers and their sons about what was to be lost
and what was to be gained by the usurpation of the
English. It was natural to them that they should
wait and see. Even those who had been dismissed
with gratuities had money to spend for the present.
And to all had been paid the arrears due by the
Oude Government. So there was no need to stir at
once. This temporary quiescence was mistaken for
permanent content. But when Sir Henry Lawrence
was established in the Lucknow Residency, he saw
at once that there was danger to be looked for, not
only from the disbanded soldiery, but from those
who had been taken into the service of the British—
especially from the regiments that had been re-enlisted
en masse. "Our Punjab Irregulars," he wrote to
Lord Canning in April, " were mostly either men
who had fought under me, or Edwardes, or my
brother George, or were new levies recruited from
the villages. Here the Irregulars are bodies of men
who last year served the King, and who have been
taken in masses on their old foundations as regiments

with all their old associations. . . . It is quite a mistake to suppose that these regiments like our service better than the King's. The small extra pay (eight annas*) does not cover the extra bother—the pipeclay, and discipline, and duty. Besides, the officers and men have lost consideration and opportunites of plunder."†

But the innovations of the English, which thus struck at the very vitals of all the most influential classes in Oude, did not leave untouched the larger masses of the people. From among the causes of seditions set down in the great Baconian analysis, which stands as the motto or text of this work, "Taxes" are not omitted. The enthusiasm of our civil administrators was commonly directed towards the balance sheet. They had learnt, under Lord Dalhousie, that, on the annexation of a new province, it was expected that those, to whose its administration was intrusted, should demonstrate, by figured statements, that it would "pay." Perhaps the old " mercantile bottom " of the East India Company was, in some measure, answerable for this. I do not underrate the importance of the consideration thus suggested. But the mistake always lay in the attempt made to bring out results by a forcing process of unwholesome rapidity. Officers trained in the essential business of " settlement operations " had learnt that their efficiency as public servants was estimated in accordance with the success attending their efforts to screw up the revenue of their several districts to the highest possible pitch of productiveness. As long as the money was got, there was very little thought of the effect that might be produced on the minds of

1857.

New taxes.

---

* A shilling a month. Canning, April 18, 1857.—*MS. Cor-*
† Sir Henry Lawrence to Lord *respondence.*

the people by the manner of getting it. The black-and-white of demonstrable figures was greater in their minds than the animosities and resentments of an over-taxed people. So when Jackson and Gubbins went to Oude, they thought that they would gain great credit by making fine figured statements of forthcoming revenue from every possible source. The smoking of opium, or the enjoyment of the narcotic in some form or other, was almost as great a necessity to the people of Lucknow as to the people of Canton. So a heavy tax was laid upon opium. It created intense dissatisfaction. Opium-smoking, or opium-eating, or opium-drinking, is not, to any great extent, a prevailing taste of the English people; so it would have been a miracle if an English administrator, from the Regulation Provinces, had for the nonce put himself into the skin of a citizen of Lucknow, and, taking mentally a loan of his stomach, ascertained by sympathy what would be the effect of raising the price of the acquired necessity to what might be, and was in the case of many, a prohibition price.* Nor was the tax on opium the only financial experiment that pressed heavily on the people, especially of the large towns. The prices of other necessaries were raised, if not by direct imposts, by contract systems, which had equally injurious effects. And whilst our new revenue laws were thus disquieting the people, our new judicial regulations, with their increased formalities, and delays, and expenses, were causing scarcely less uneasiness and scarcely less popular dislike of the new Government,

* Mr. Rees (" Siege of Lucknow") says that " many who could not obtain it at the increased rates actually cut their throats in desperation." I do not vouch for the literal accuracy of this statement. But it is easy to understand the miserable depression of an enervated Asiatic deprived of his accustomed drug.

which was subverting everything with an unsparing 1857.
hand, and boasting of its beneficent improvements.

No man of healthy intellect can express a doubt Old and new
that the system of government which the English systems.
introduced into Oude was far superior to that which
was superseded by it. Order and security are, doubtless, great blessings. But time alone can teach people
unaccustomed to such enjoyments thoroughly to appreciate them. Like the beasts of the forest, or the
birds of the air, men are slow to conform themselves
to the tame domestic conditions. Food may be precarious—life itself may depend upon the will of some
stronger animal ; but the security, which brings restraints with it, is not appreciable at the outset. We
are too prone to bury this fact beneath a heap of
platitudes about Humanity and Civilisation, and to
complain of the ingratitude of those who do not rush
eagerly to embrace our proffered benefits. It is from
the intensity of our national ignorance that this great
moral cataract proceeds, blinding our eyes to the
truth, and causing us to stumble disastrously along
the great road of " improvement," which seems to us
to be so smooth and open, but which in reality is
everywhere beset with impediments and obstructions.
We are in too great a hurry to do good after our own
fashion. And so we introduce sudden changes, which
the people rarely understand, and often resent, until
resentment grows into resistance. It is commonly
beneath the dignity of our administrators to feel
their way to reformation. It is as though a general
were to endeavour to force his way into the unknown
country of an enemy, without an intelligence department and without pioneers. And so it was with our
civilians in Oude. They were not answerable for the
system. That originated in Calcutta. It was the

1857.

executive work of Mr. George Edmonstone. It bore the impress of the strong brain of Lord Dalhousie. The initial instructions to the Chief Commissioner, dated February 4, 1856, were distinguished by intellectual ability of a high order. They were clear, decided, exhaustive. But lacking the great essential of sympathy, they were utterly unsuited to the purpose. Nobody concerned in drafting the new code seems ever to have thought of the feelings of those whom our system would injuriously affect. There was an utter want of that dramatic perception which enables great statesmen, as it enables great writers, to see into the hearts of men and to know the effects of circumstances upon them. But even with this code before him, a Chief Commissioner of a different stamp—a man such as Outram or Lawrence—with less knowledge of Regulations and more knowledge of Men, might have gradually accommodated the scheme to the changing habits of the people. But these over-zealous civilians, instead of waiting, plunged at once into a great sea of "reformation," and raised a storm which could be subdued only by an overwhelming army.

Lucknow in April and May.

But to Sir Henry Lawrence all these things were clear ; and he never ceased to see in them the materials of which revolutions are made. He had always been a great master of the art of "letting people down easily ;" and his large sympathies had brought upon him the one great trouble of his life. He saw now with painful distinctness the grievous mistakes which had been committed by our Civilian Government during the first year of British administration ; and he deplored, as Lord Canning must then have deplored, the accident which had sent him to Rajpootana, whilst to Mr. Colverly Jackson was intrusted the work of introducing the new system into Oude. In April he had written to the Governor-General, saying : " This city (Lucknow) is said to contain six or seven hundred thousand souls, and does certainly contain many thousands (twenty thousand, I was told yesterday) of disbanded soldiers, and of hungry, nay, starving dependents of the late Government. There *must* be intrigue and disaffection in such a mass. . . . This very morning a clod was thrown at Mr. Ommaney, and another struck Major Anderson whilst in a buggy with myself. . . . The improvements in the city have gone on very fast—too fast and too roughly. Much discontent has been caused by demolitions of buildings, &c., and still more by threats of further similar measures. Also regarding the seizure of religious and other edifices, and plots of ground as Government property. I have visited many of these places and pacified parties, and prohibited any seizures or demolitions without competent authority. The revenue measures, though not as sweeping as represented by the writer, whose letter your Lordship sent me by Colonel Edwardes, have been unsatisfactory. Reductions have been made to the amount of fifteen, twenty, thirty, and even thirty-five per cent., showing how heavy was last year's assessment. The Talookhdars have also, I fear, been hardly dealt with. At least, in the Fyzabad Division they have lost half their villages—some have lost all." Well might he have exclaimed, "All these things are against me !" He derived no comfort from the thought that more than a year had passed without any great demonstration of discontent. For, as he wrote in the letter above quoted, "it is not the

1857.
April—May.

State of the
soldiery.

fashion for Natives to act energetically, or to commit themselves in a hurry." No people in the world know better how to *wait*.

"As long as we can perfectly trust our own people, there will be little danger from any others." This was the one drop of consolation that remained, and it was now fast being dried up. The tranquillity of Oude had been so settled a fact in the minds of our English statesmen, that well-nigh all the European troops had been removed from the province, and such hostilities as might arise from the numerous causes above recited were held in check by Native regiments, Regular and Irregular, at the capital and at the out-stations. At Lucknow there was one weak white regiment—the Thirty-second, under Colonel John Inglis. But such, in the face of so many and great dangers, was the confidence reposed in the general contentment of all classes of the people, that, with the exception of a weak company at Lucknow, there was no European Artillery from one end of Oude to the other. Often had Sir Henry Lawrence, publicly and privately, dwelt, with all the earnestness of his nature, upon the danger of thus falling asleep in the lap of a false security.* And now, as the month of May came in, he saw terribly before him the fulfilment of the old predictions which had been scoffed at by many and unheeded by all. Already has been shown, in an earlier part of this History, what were the first manifestations of an

---

* See the warnings quoted at page 453, vol. i. The Civilian Chief Commissioner was of opinion that no white troops were required in Oude. A wing of a European regiment was stationed at Cawnpore as a support to the Thirty-second at Lucknow. In the early part of 1857 the military authorities wished to remove this wing, and Mr. Jackson was consulted as to the safety of the measure. His answer was that they might take the wing and also the regiment at Lucknow, as he could hold the province with the Irregulars and the Police.

unquiet spirit in the Lines of Lucknow. Regulars and Irregulars were obviously on the brink of mutiny. Still he did not despair of the Sepoys. He felt that there were some soft spots in them which he would try to reach. If it were right and wise to punish those who had done evil, it was no less right and wise to reward those who had done well. There had been some conspicuous instances of loyalty and devotion to the British Government. Some good might come from a public recognition of these good services, and from an appeal to the better feelings of the general body of the Native soldiery. So the Chief Commissioner determined to hold a grand Durbar. 1857.
April—May.

Lawrence was, at this time, resident in the Muriaon Cantonment. The Durbar was to be held in front of his house. At sunset, on the 12th of May, the Chief Commissioner, attended by all his principal military and civil officers, and by some of the chief people of the city, met the officers of the Native Army* in his garden grounds, and, addressing them in Hindostanee, appealed to all their best feelings as soldiers and as comrades. It was an imposing scene. The lawn was carpeted. The seats ranged for the visitors formed three sides of a square. Behind them stood groups of Sepoys eagerly watching the proceedings and listening to the words which fell from the venerable chief. And visible to all were the dresses of honour and the trays of presents that were to be given to the faithful soldiers, who had earned these rewards by their loyalty and devotion. May 12.
The Durbar
in Canton-
ments.

" I explained to them," wrote Sir Henry Lawrence, a few days afterwards, " our policy of non-interference with their religious prejudices, and appealed to the history of the last hundred years. I pointed out to

* About fifty privates from each regiment were also present.

them our strength at home, and the utter madness of their expecting to subvert our power. I showed what we had done, late in the day at Sebastopol, and how that it is equally possible to bring five thousand or thirty thousand Europeans to bear on India. . . . I said that I had come to Oude not for my own profit, but to help them and the country, and that by God's blessing we should get over our present difficulties." All this and much more, he said to them—especially reminding them of the fidelity of generation after generation of Sepoys, who had eaten the Company's salt, and had shared, in mutual confidence and comradeship with their British officers, the dangers and the privations of war. It was the plain, forcible eloquence of genuine sincerity. No words could have been better chosen. They were listened to with rapt attention, and they seemed to make a deep impression on the minds of the hearers. When he ceased, the dresses of honour and the purses of money were distributed, and the Durbar broke up. The English and Native officers conversed with each other; and the latter were voluble in their professions of devotion to the British Government. Perhaps they were sincere at the time.* But the question was, how long would the impression last? Sir Henry Lawrence said that the next fortnight would be one of great anxiety; but he little knew what it would produce.

At this time news was travelling through the country, which, when received from Agra on the 13th, was scarcely credited, in all its length and breadth,

---

* Mr. Gubbins says : " A number of Sepoys were standing round the space appropriated to the Durbar. We subsequently learnt that the re- marks which they were overheard to make were of a different character, and that they attributed the whole proceeding to our fears."

by the Lucknow Commissioner.* At the first blush, Lawrence pronounced the account of the disastrous tidings from Meerut to be greatly exaggerated. But the next day brought still more painful and more alarming intelligence. Delhi was in the hands' of the mutineers, and the sovereignty of Behaudur Shah had been proclaimed. It has been already told how, on being thus terribly assured of the calamity that had fallen on our people, he had telegraphed to the Governor-General for plenary military power,† and how, in reply, Lord Canning had cheerfully given Lawrence his unstinting confidence, and had placed the chief military command in his hands, with the rank of Brigadier-General. He was one of those who, in all great conjunctures, was eager to take upon himself the largest possible amount of responsibility. He was a man of a sensitive nature, and any proof of confidence in his superiors braced him up to new endeavours to show that it was not misplaced. With this plenary authority in his hands, he now felt that, if, with God's blessing, human agency could save the province—save the lives of our people and

---

* "We had greatly exaggerated accounts of Meerut doings," he wrote to Lord Canning on the 14th (I quote from his autograph letter). From this I may infer that the Delhi news had not then reached Lucknow. It reached Agra on the 13th or 14th (*ante*, page 198). Sir George Couper, however, writes to me: "We got the telegram on the afternoon of the 13th, and it informed us not only that the insurgents had occupied Delhi, but that they were trying to establish some sort of Government." Lawrence sent for his Secretary (Couper), and asked him what he thought of the news. Couper said that he believed that all the regiments in the army would revolt. Lawrence, who indeed had predicted the rising, seemed to be of the same opinion.

† Vol. i. page 613. It is another curious illustration of the conflicts of authority by which the writer of history is often beset that I have before me, written with reference to a similar assertion in Mr. Gubbins's "Narrative," a note by the man of all others whose testimony, on such a point, I should be most disposed to respect, asserting that Sir Henry Lawrence never did ask for this plenary authority, as it came unsolicited from Lord Canning. The words of Lawrence's telegrams are given in my first volume.

the authority of our Government—he would accomplish this great end. He would strive for the best; but he would prepare himself for the worst. There was little hope now that this epidemic of mutiny could be arrested. Assuredly it was no longer to be talked down. It was too probable, indeed, that the issue was now to be determined by strength alone—strength to do and strength to endure. Still, Sir Henry Lawrence, whilst neglecting no precaution which could contribute to the success of this last appeal, did not wholly abandon the thought that something might be done by conciliatory measures.

Want of
European
troops.

As a mere conflict of strength, the odds were heavily against us. What was our scanty European force has been shown. The Native force consisted of all arms — Horse, Foot, and Artillery—about seven thousand men.* How to utilise to the utmost our little body of English fighting men had been Henry Lawrence's first care. As it had never been dreamt that the English at Lucknow could ever be put upon the defensive, the troops had been posted here and there with reference to any other considerations than those which now presented themselves to the Chief Commissioner. The military Cantonments lay at a distance of three miles from the city, on the other side of the river. There the Head-Quarters of the Regular Infantry Regiments were planted; and at some distance beyond them were the Lines of the Seventh Cavalry. The road from the city to the Cantonments ran across an iron bridge; there was also a bridge, of masonry, at no great distance from it, and lower down the stream was a bridge

---

* I take these figures from the report of Captain Hutchinson, Military Secretary. The exact statement, referring to April 30, is six thousand nine hundred Natives and seven hundred Europeans, each exclusive of Artillery. The Native force includes the Police Battalions.

of boats. The iron bridge spanned the river near the Residency;* near the stone bridge was a commanding structure known as the Mutchee-bhawun. The barracks of the European soldiery, the quarters and the mess-house of their officers, lay a little way below the city, within a bend of the river, which there takes a circuitous direction. The Head-Quarters of the European and of the Native Regular troops were, therefore, at the two extremities of our position, with the great city between them. And in the city itself were posted the greater part of the Oude Irregulars, whilst detachments of the Regular Native regiments were continually on duty there, at the various public buildings of Lucknow.

It was now obvious to Sir Henry Lawrence that such a disposition of the troops was ill calculated to keep the Native soldiery in check, and to overbear them in the event of a sudden rising. It was deter-

1857.
May.

Disposition
of the troops.

---

* In a previous chapter (*ante*, page 203), reference is made to the extraordinary energy of Colonel Hugh Fraser, who took so distinguished a part in the defence of Agra, and an anecdote connected with Lucknow was then promised. There can be no fitter place than this for its introduction. I give it in the words of a brother officer of Engineers: "In 1842–3 Colonel Fraser was Engineer officer to the King of Oude. A cast-iron bridge had been ordered from England for the river Goomtee, some twenty-five or thirty years before, and its parts had been landed at the mouth of the river, some damaged, some wrecked. No one had ever faced the trouble of putting up this bridge, but Colonel Fraser at once took it in hand. He recovered the wrecked parts, brought all to Lucknow, got made in Calcutta and elsewhere the missing and damaged parts, and, in a few months of intense hard work, the bridge was put up. It was generally supposed the arches would collapse when the centres were struck, and Colonel Fraser, though certain his work had been well done, was very nervous on the subject. However, as he before told me he would do, when the time came for lowering the centre by driving out the wedges, he deliberately placed himself below with the workmen, and himself struck the last blows, with the intention of being crushed with the workmen if his work was to prove a failure. It stood, however, and stands to this day; though, I believe, hardly another officer in India could have been found voluntarily to undertake the work. Certainly many had the opportunity, and some expended large sums in the vain attempt to begin, but nothing really was done, in a long course of years, until Colonel Fraser took it in hand."

2 F 2

mined, therefore, as a first precaution, to diminish
the number of detached posts, and so to mix up Europeans and Natives as to render the latter comparatively innocuous.   Under the old arrangements, the
lives of all the European officers in the Cantonments
were at the mercy of an insurgent soldiery; and a
sudden rising in the city might have placed in the
hands of rebels and rioters all the treasure and all
the stores of the English ; and the general spoliation
might have been followed by a general massacre of
our people.   It was, therefore, determined that the
Thirty-second should evacuate their barracks in the
suburbs, where they were almost useless for purposes
of defence ; that a large detachment of them should
be posted in the Muriaon Cantonments, and the remainder quartered in those parts of the city which
were selected as our chief points of defence.   One of
these was the British Residency, and the other the
Mutchee-bhawun, which lay upon the main road high
up the river, at a distance of about a mile from
the Residency.   The Treasury was within the Residency grounds, close to the Banqueting-hall.   In it
were thirty lakhs of rupees in coin, and a still larger
sum in Government securities.   The abandonment of
this to the forbearance of a Sepoy-guard seemed to
be an invitation to them not readily to be declined.
The substitution of an European guard was therefore
urged upon the Chief Commissioner by Mr. Gubbins
with his wonted energy.   In this he was supported
by Captain Fletcher Hayes, then Military Secretary ;
but there was something to be said on the other side,
and Sir Henry Lawrence said it.   It was not improbable that such a movement would precipitate the anticipated revolt.   But when the subject had been discussed with Brigadier Handscombe and Colonel Inglis,

and both officers concurred in the propriety of the
recommendation, the Chief Commissioner withdrew
his objections; and Mr. Gubbins, who had been commissioned to make the necessary preliminary arrangements, now set to work to complete them with the
utmost possible despatch.* The first thing to be
done was to make room for the new occupants. For
not only were these European troops to be provided
with accommodation in the Residency buildings, but
large numbers of English women and children were
to find shelter there. To suit the Residency to these
altered conditions it was necessary that new dispositions should be made of well-nigh all the contents of
the buildings. Great collections of furniture were
to be removed; and the Government records and
other materials of the office establishment of the
Chief Commissioner, which had been kept in the
Banqueting-hall, were to be conveyed to other re-
ceptacles. All this could not be done without much
outward display of activity, which must have convinced the Sepoys at the Treasury that we were con-
verting the Residency buildings into barracks for
European troops. So Gubbins despatched a mounted
messenger to the Cantonments with a letter to Lawrence, urging him at once to send a party of the
Thirty-second with guns to the Residency; and on
the evening of the 17th the desired reinforcements
marched in, escorting the women and the sick.

The Mutchee-bhawun was an extensive edifice, of The Mutchee-
commanding appearance, the upper story of which is bhawun.

* It was on the 15th of May that _may_ have hastened Lawrence's reso-
Gubbins first made this proposal to lution to apply for plenary authority
the Chief Commissioner, and on the in matters military as well as civil.
16th it was discussed with Brigadier These contentions, indeed, were
Handscombe, who was then the frequent, and sometimes of a pain-
chief military authority. It is pos- fully acrimonious character.
sible that this conflict of opinion

1857.
May.

described as "towering above the surrounding buildings." It had been a place of no little importance in the earlier history of Lucknow; but in later days it had been used as a storehouse for tents and other public property, and had been suffered to fall into decay. The dilapidated condition of the building rendered it necessary that our Engineers should put forth all their strength in restoring and fortifying it. But it was doubtful whether any human effort could so strengthen the place as to enable it, before its capabilities would be tested, successfully to resist a siege. This at first was better known to the Natives than to ourselves. It was said by them that if the fire of our own guns did not bring down the place about our ears, the fire of an enemy would soon convert it into ruins.* Ere long this became patent to our own people, and the probabilities of the abandonment of the position, at some future period, were contemplated by Sir Henry Lawrence and his colleagues. Meanwhile, this capacious edifice was to be converted into a great storehouse and arsenal. Provisions of all kinds were bought up and carefully stored in it. All our available ordnance and ammunition were gathered up and secured.† The superintendence of

---

* Take for example the following from a report made by Kulb Ali Khan, extra-Assistant of Seetapore (June 20th), 1827:

"The reason for all these preparations for the attack of Lucknow is, that it is believed to be so weak that if it do not fall from the fire of its own guns, it will easily do so under a fire from the outside."—*MS. Records.*

† Lawrence's efforts are thus epitomised by one of his oldest friends, in a letter to the author, quoted in a former work: "Look at Lucknow. It was Henry Lawrence's foresight, humanly speaking, that saved every one of the garrison. But for him, I do not believe that one would have escaped. Three weeks before any one thought of the possibility of our ever being besieged in Lucknow, he saw that it might be the case. He laid his plans accordingly; got in all the treasure from the city and stations; bought up and stored grain and supplies of every kind; bought up all the supplies of the European shopkeepers; got the mortars and guns to the Residency; got in the powder and small ammunition, all the shot and

this latter work was intrusted to Lieutenant Thomas of the Madras Artillery; whilst Lieutenant James, the Chief Commissariat officer at Lucknow, put forth all his energies, and developed those of his department, in the collection of supplies. In this work he was greatly aided by Mr. Simon Nicolson Martin—a name pregnant with memories of two good men, who, perhaps, did more in their time for the alleviation of human suffering than any who have ever laboured in the East.* Mr. Martin was Deputy-Commissioner of Lucknow, and was well acquainted with the localities and resources of the place. Nor in this work was Captain Carnegy, Chief of the Oude Police, less conspicuous for his activity in collecting the means of a protracted defence. But it was not sufficient at this time to resort only to measures of internal defence. It did not escape the sagacious observation of Henry Lawrence that it was equally necessary to diminish the offensive power of the enemy by destroying such of the surrounding buildings as might afford shelter to our assailants and enable them to fire into our defences. The safety of our garrison demanded this precaution. So its execution was enforced. But Lawrence was a man equally just and tolerant; he had large human sympathies which no amount of wrong-doing on the part of others could repress. The demolition of a citizen's house seemed a harsh measure—but at all events its money value might be reimbursed to the

1857.
May.

shell, and the heavy guns; had pits dug for the powder and grain; arranged for water supply; strengthened the Residency; had outworks formed; cleared away all obstructions close up to the Residency, and made every preparation for the worst; and when, after the fight at Chinhut, the mutineers closed in on the Residency, and the whole population of the city and the province rose against us, they found the little garrison amply supplied with provisions, ammunition, and resources of every kind."

* Mr Martin was the son of Sir Ranald Martin, and godson of Mr. Simon Nicolson, the famous Calcutta physician, whose benevolence was equal to his skill.

owner. So he caused all the buildings sentenced to destruction to be appraised, before the work commenced, and every man was fairly reimbursed. But it happened that some of the most commanding buildings, and those most dangerous to the people within our line of defences, were religious edifices—towering mosques—from which a fire might be poured upon us with destructive effect. The expediency of demolishing these buildings was urged upon Lawrence by more than one of his advisers; but his answer was, " Spare the holy places." And the holy places were spared, to bring on us sad requital for our forbearance.

Feverish
symptoms.

Meanwhile the Native regiments in Cantonments were in an uncertain state of semi-mutiny. Events had not sufficiently developed themselves elsewhere to encourage a general rising of the troops at Lucknow. There was disunion, therefore, in the Lines. Whilst some were prepared to strike at once, others were for further waiting and watching. Although there were daily reports of a premeditated outbreak, first on one day and then another, the anticipated hour of danger passed again and again, and still the troops were quiescent. Was it possible to keep them so?

Disarming
proposed.

No man understood the Sepoy better than Sir Henry Lawrence. But to understand the Sepoy was to have a prevailing sense of his inconsistencies; and those who knew him best were ever the most perplexed as to the mode of treatment best suited to his constitution, whilst the little knowledge of brave and clever men tended to hasty judgment and counselled prompt action of the most hazardous kind. News came of the disarming of the Native regiments at Meean-Meer; and it was considered whether what had been done by a single white regiment in the Punjab might not be done also in Oude.* Lawrence believed that the Thirty-second could overawe the Native troops 'at Lucknow, and compel them to lay down their arms. But he was not Chief Commissioner of Lucknow—but of Oude; and although he felt that this bold stroke might be successful at the capital, he knew that such a measure would cause a general rising throughout the provinces and endanger our posts on the other side of the Ganges. The suggestion was, therefore, rightly negatived. Another question arose. If we could not overawe the Sepoys, might we not mollify and conciliate them? They had grievances—or they believed that they had grievances. There were many things dear to the Sepoy; but the dearest of all was his *tullub*, or pay. It was considered, therefore, whether a promise to raise the pay of Sepoys—Regular and Irregular— might not bring them round to their old state of contentment. All the chief officers, Civil and Military, in the City and in Cantonments, were consulted. The unanimous opinion was that the pay of the Oude Irregular Army, who did the same duty as the Regulars, should be raised. But with equal unanimity it was resolved that there should be no interference with the pay of the Regular Army.† The

---

* It must never be forgotten that the Punjab was bristling with European troops, and that what could be done safely in that province would have been dangerous, if not impossible, elsewhere.

† Mr. Gubbins says: "The proposal to raise the pay of the Regulars found no seconder but in the Secretary, Mr. Couper. It was the general opinion that the offer to increase the fixed pay of the Native Army, which had been so long established, would be attributed to fear, and would fail of the object desired. Sir Henry Lawrence probably came to the same conclusion, for the idea was abandoned." But Sir George Couper assures me that Sir Henry Lawrence was always opposed to this project, and that he (Couper) was of the same opinion. The officers consulted were Mr. Ommaney, Mr. Gubbins, Brigadier Gray, Major

distinction was obvious. So orders went forth to raise the pay of the Irregulars to a level with that of the Line.

Again and again it was reported that the Native troops in Cantonments were on the eve of rising, but our people had become so familiar with these reports that little importance was attached to them. Days passed and everything was quiet. The Sepoys, watched by the Europeans, went about their accustomed duties. But on the last day of May but one the long-meditated revolt had ripened. There was still division in the Lines, but the leading mutineers thought that they were strong enough for a successful movement against the Feringhees, and the firing of the nine o'clock gun on that evening was to be the signal for rebellious action. Sir Henry Lawrence was dining with his Staff in the Cantonment Residency House, when a Sepoy rushed in and reported that the game had commenced.* Presently, the sound of firing was heard. Lawrence and his officers at once sent for their horses. As they stood on the steps at the principal entrance in the clear moonlight, the subaltern of the Sepoy-guard at the Residency brought up his thirty men, and asked the General if he should load. "Load! yes, certainly," said Lawrence, "and take care of my property." The order was given, and as the men brought up their muskets in the act of loading, they levelled straight at the little group of officers waiting for their horses on the

Banks, Major Anderson, and Captain Carnegy. Lawrence discussed the question very fully with his Secretary at night—as he often discussed other matters during intervals of sleeplessness—and both concurred in opinion regarding the inexpediency of the measure. See Appendix.

* The first intimation of the intended rising was given to Captain Wilson, Assistant Adjutant-General, by a man of his regiment (the Thirteenth). The informer was one of those whom Lawrence had rewarded for having assisted in the capture of a spy. Nothing more was heard of him after the 30th of May.

REVOLT IN CANTONMENTS. 443

steps. And, perhaps, there was not one of them, who did not experience a feeling of relief, when the men shouldered their arms and marched off to defend the gateway.*

1857.
May 30.

The horses were brought round. Lawrence and his Staff mounted and rode for the Lines. The most active firing seemed to proceed from the position of the Seventy-first. On the right of that position Lawrence found three hundred men of the Queen's Thirty-second, with four guns of Major Kaye's† battery and two of the Oude Irregular Artillery, ready for action, and so posted as to sweep the Lines of the Seventy-first. At a little distance ran the road from the Cantonment to the city. It was of the utmost importance to command the great thoroughfare, so Lawrence took a company of the Thirty-second, with two guns (afterwards reinforced), and took post on the high road, thus effectually cutting off the communication of the insurgents with Lucknow. Meanwhile, the Sepoys were diligently at work, eager for the destruction of life and property. The red light of burning bungalows soon told the story of their activity as incendiaries, but as murderers they were less successful than they had hoped to be. Knowing that it was the time of the evening meal of the Feringhees, the mutineers rushed to the regimental mess-houses, but the officers on the first sound of the firing had made for their parade-grounds, so the massacre at the dinner-tables was escaped. Some were turned back by the firing; some succeeded in reaching the Lines. It was then apparent that there

---

* MS. Notes by a Staff Officer.

† Major Kaye himself was absent on leave at the Hills. On the outbreak of the mutiny, he joined the troops proceeding to Delhi, and commanded the detachment which took down the first siege-train. (*Ante*, vol. ii. page 189.) The Lucknow battery was commanded by Lieutenant Alexander, son of Sir James Alexander, K.C.B.

was division in the regiments. Whilst many Sepoys were bent on plunder and incendiarism, others remained true to their allegiance, followed their officers, and allowed themselves to be drawn up quietly beside the European camp. Most conspicuous among the mutineers were the men of the Seventy-first, but some of them, leaving their comrades, took post "next to the Thirty-second Foot." Three hundred Sepoys of the Thirteenth, under Major Bruere, bringing their colours and their treasure-chest, also fell in beside the Europeans.* The Forty-eighth, less active in their rebellion and less demonstrative in their loyalty, remained on their parade-ground, sullen and obstinate, refusing to march against the mutineers, but not openly siding with them. Vainly did Colonel Palmer endeavour to persuade them to march to the camp of the Thirty-second. Then seeing that they were rapidly deserting, he proposed that they should follow him to the Residency in the city. This proposal met with a nominal consent, and the Colonel and the colours entered Lucknow. But with the head-quarters of the regiment there went but a scanty following. Less than a hundred men marched into the city.

It has been said that, intent as were the mutineers on the murder of their officers, no great success attended their efforts at wholesale massacre. But the night was not without its attendant horrors. On hearing the first sound of the firing, Brigadier Handscombe, with his Staff, had ridden down to the European camping-ground. He had scarcely reached the left flank of the Thirty-second, near which the

---

* "The treasure was very gallantly saved by Lieutenant Loughnan, assisted by the Sikhs of the regi- ment." — *Gubbins's* "*Mutinies in Oudh.*"

Seventy-first Sepoys were posted, when a stray shot from the musket of a mutineer took fatal effect, and he fell dead from his horse. Lieutenant Grant, of the Seventy-first, was commanding the main picket in the centre of Cantonments, with a party drawn from different Native regiments, which for a time stood fast. But when a crowd of mutineers swept down upon them, they broke and joined the insurgents, and then Grant was hunted to his death. Vainly did a Soubahdar of the guard, and a few men less cruel than the rest, endeavour to save the white man by concealing him beneath a bed. A Sepoy of the Seventy-first tracked him, with the savage instinct of the bloodhound, and disclosed the hiding-place to his comrades. Then they dragged him out exultingly, and with bullets and bayonets soon completed their work. Lieutenant Chambers, Adjutant of the Thirteenth, whilst endeavouring to save the regimental magazine, was severely wounded. Lying helpless on the ground, he was several times fired upon by his men, but almost miraculously he escaped death. Fortunately, the Cantonment had been well-nigh emptied of its English women and children. One English lady, however, the wife of the Commandant of the Thirteenth Sepoy Regiment, had returned in defiance of orders, and had a narrow escape from violent death. Some Sepoys of the regiment, when the house was assailed in front, made a hole by which she could escape in the rear. Letting herself down through this aperture with her children, she passed the night in a dry ditch, and survived to tell the story of her adventures.

The following day was Sunday—that Sunday, the 31st of May, which is thought by many to have been fixed upon for a general rising of the Sepoys during the hours of our church service. The Lucknow mutineers had in the course of the night made their way to the race-course, near the Lines of the Seventh Cavalry, and thither the Europeans, with the faithful remnants of the Native regiments, followed at break of day. On reaching the open plain it was seen that a body of mutineers, some twelve hundred strong, were drawn up on the race-course, so our guns opened upon them with round shot, and they were soon in precipitate flight. Then our people gave chase as best they could—Cavalry, and Artillery, and Volunteers—and captured many of the flying enemy. On this day—as, indeed, on the preceding evening—Lieutenant Hardinge, with a body of Irregular Cavalry, did brilliant service, the record of which should not be omitted. "Hardinge," wrote Sir Henry Lawrence to Lord Canning, "is a splendid soldier. He led a few Horse several times through the burning Cantonments and through a crowd of mutineers. One shot at him within a foot, and then bayoneted him through the flesh of the arm. Hardinge shot the fellow dead. Wounded as he was he could not have had an hour's sleep, and yet he was the hero of yesterday's (Sunday's) work; and had we had any good Cavalry he would have cut up all the mutineers."

As it was, too many escaped. The Artillery, after the first discharge, do not seem to have fired a shot at the fugitives, and the Infantry never got within reach of them. A party of the Seventh Cavalry, who had gone out with our force from Cantonments, when they saw their comrades in front of them, went over to the enemy. And the morning's work was rendered memorable in the annals of crime by the brutal murder of a little Cornet of seventeen, who

Cornet
Raleigh.

had been only a few weeks with the regiment. Altogether, there was but a poor exhibition of our military strength. One of the finest soldiers who turned out against the enemy on that Sunday morning was, as often happened, a Civilian. Martin Gubbins, the Financial Commissioner, had ridden out from the city to communicate with Sir Henry Lawrence; and when he found there was still some fighting to be done, he attached himself, unarmed as he was, to the Irregular Horse, and was foremost in the pursuit. "Martin Gubbins," wrote Sir Henry Lawrence, "was another hero. He, with three horsemen,* did the work of a regiment, headed the rascals, and brought in six prisoners, for which I have given the men six hundred rupees." But the sun rose; the weather was insufferably hot; the pursuit was ended; the troops were withdrawn; and I am informed that not a single man of the enemy was killed until the hangman took in hand the prisoners whom we had captured.

But the foremost hero of the day was Henry Lawrence himself—the grandest act one as yet unrecorded. Our troops had pursued the enemy up to a place known as the "Hubshee-talao," where was a thannah, or police-station. The men were by this time utterly exhausted by heat, hunger, and thirst, and the General, seeing their condition, ordered them back under command of Colonel Inglis. He then rode on, accompanied by George Couper, Secretary and Aide-de-camp, who ever sat beside him in council or rode beside him in war. Couper, never forgetting the inestimable value of his chief's life, represented

---

* The actual number was four, including Gubbins's own Orderly. Gubbins, during the pursuit, got possession of the sword of a trooper who had surrendered.

that the enemy might be making a stand at this very place; but Lawrence, taking no heed of the suggestion, rode on, fearless and silent, to the appointed place. He had a great purpose in view. He believed that the mutineers were making for Seetapore, and he wished to write a letter to Mr. Christian, the Commissioner there, to warn him of the coming danger. The Thannadar supplied him with writing materials. The letter was written by Lawrence with a reed pen on the rude paper of the country, copied by Couper, and despatched by a camel-sowar, with offer of a large reward if he should bring back an answer. The man returned next day with the letter itself. It was too late. The troops at Seetapore had already broken into revolt.[*]

Much had not, in truth, been gained by the incidents of these two days. But if our troops had done little, the enemy had done less. They had run away in fear and confusion, and we had got rid—for a time, at least—of all the dangerous members of the Sepoy force — fortunately or unfortunately, a very large proportion of the troops in Cantonments. Writing on the following day to the Governor-General, Sir Henry Lawrence said: "We are now positively better than we were. We now know our friends and enemies. The latter beggars have no stomach for a fight, though they are capital incendiaries." But there were those who thought that, in this conjuncture, our professing friends might be as dangerous as our open enemies; and Gubbins again lifted up his voice for the disarming of the Native troops.[†] By this time, however, serious doubts had

---

[*] The story of Seetapore and of the fate of Mr. Christian, will be found recorded in the next chapter.

[†] Mr. Gubbins calculated that out of the four regiments only four hundred and thirty-seven remained faithful on the night of the 30th. Of these two hundred are stated to

begun to be entertained as to whether we were strong enough in Europeans to accomplish such a measure successfully; and, moreover, the military authorities seeing clearly what was before them—feeling that the time was not far distant when the English would be shut up in Lucknow, with an insurgent population around them; for there was rebellion seething in the districts as well as in the capital—knew that they could not hold out with their little handful of Europeans alone. To secure the services of a body of Native troops to take part in the arduous duties of defence, was, therefore, a necessity not to be ignored. So the principal military officers concurred in opinion with Lawrence that it would not be advisable to disarm the Native troops. It was not denied that there were strong arguments in favour of the measure; but, on the whole, it seemed to be more expedient to abstain from adopting it.

have been men of the Thirteenth. The numbers are probably somewhat understated. The "Staff Officer," in a revised copy of his book, says that three hundred men of the Thirteenth were true to the State. As he was Assistant Adjutant-General, and an officer of the Thirteenth, his testimony is most reliable.

CHAPTER II.

June, 1857.
Revolt of the
districts.

IT was now apparent that the worst that had been apprehended, even by the least hopeful, was rapidly overtaking our people in Oude. They had not to contend with the mutiny of a few regiments at the capital, but with a general revolt across the whole length and breadth of the province. " Of what is a

Victor Hugo. revolt composed ?" asks a great living writer, and proceeds to answer the question. " Of nothing and " of everything—of an electricity suddenly disen- " gaged, of a flame which suddenly breaks out, of a " wandering strength and a passing breath. This " breath meets with heads that talk, brains that " dream, souls that suffer, passions that burn, and " miseries which yell, and carries them off with it. " Whither ? it is chance work ; through the State, " through the laws, through prosperity and the inso- " lence of others. Irritated convictions, embittered " enthusiasms, aroused indignations, martial instincts " suppressed, youthful courage, exalted and generous

" blindnesses; curiosity, a taste for change, thirst
" for something unexpected . . . vague hatreds,
" rancours, disappointments, every vanity which
" believes that destiny has been a bankrupt to
" it; straitened circumstances, empty dreams, am-
" bitions surrounded with escarpments, every man
" who hopes for an issue from an overthrow; and
" lastly, at the very bottom, the mob, that mud
" which takes fire—such are the elements of riot.
" The basest and the most infamous beings who
" prowl about beyond the pale of everything while
" awaiting an opportunity; gipsies, nameless men,
" highway vagabonds, the men who sleep o' nights
" in a desert of houses with no other roof but the
" cold clouds of heaven, those who daily ask their
" bread of chance and not of toil, the unknown men
" of wretchedness and nothingness, bare arms and
" bare feet, belong to the riot. Every man who has
" in his soul a secret revolt against any act of the
" State, of life, or of destiny, is on the border line of
" riot, and, so soon as it appears, he begins to quiver
" and to feel himself lifted by the whirlwind."

1857.
June.

And so it was in Oude. When it was known that
the soldiery had revolted at the capital, their brethren
at the out-stations rose at once; and all classes, with
any power of rising, rose with them. Day after day
the saddest tidings of mutiny and massacre — of
English officers murdered, of property pillaged and
destroyed, of law and authority extinguished, of
anarchy triumphant—came in from the outposts and
filled our people in Lucknow with dismay. The new
Government had toppled down, like a house built of
cards.* It had no more substance or stability. Law-

The outbreak
in the dis-
tricts.

---

* I have borrowed this figure from a source the expression is more sig-
Mr. Gubbins. Coming from such nificant.

rence thought that he could clearly see in the movement evidences of general design and consistency. "Everything," he wrote to Lord Canning, with immediate reference to affairs at Fyzabad, "had been conducted with the utmost regularity, the Native civil officers taking prominent places; and the King of Delhi had been proclaimed. In all quarters we hear of similar method and regularity. . . . This quiet method bespeaks some leading influence." And again : " All the outposts are gone, and the rebels and mutineers are said to be closing in on us, though as yet all is quiet at Lucknow. Elsewhere, throughout the province, all is anarchy—the Talookhdars re-occupying the villages of which the summary settlement dispossessed them, and all men asserting their own rights." In the first ten days of June this great anti-revolution had been fully accomplished. Oude, so lately annexed by the British, had now to be conquered by them.

Seetapore.

The first place given up to revolt was Seetapore, the head-quarters of the Khyrabad Division. The station was defended by Sepoys of the Forty-first Regiment of Native Infantry and the Ninth and Tenth Oude Irregulars. The chief civil officer was Mr. George Jackson Christian, Commissioner of the Division, whom Sir Henry Lawrence had known, in old times, at Lahore. He was full of cleverness and of courage; but these qualities sometimes manifested themselves in undue self-assertion and impatience of control. Lawrence said of him that, when he was Secretary to the Lahore Board, he "tried to be a member of it;" and the new Oude Government was barely three months old when he was in fierce contention with Mr. Gubbins. Men of this stamp are always good for fighting. " Christian is doing very well and pluckily," wrote Lawrence at Lucknow to Charles Raikes at Agra on the 30th of May. On the very same day Christian had written to Raikes,* saying : " All quiet here ; and throughout my division the people seem well disposed, and the regular regiment here, the Forty-first, is quiet ; and I have in position nine hundred and fifty men, so that if things go wrong elsewhere, and they are tempted to rise, we could crush them in an hour." He spoke of the Irregulars and the Military Police, on whose fidelity he relied. But he knew that there were sources of danger from which the flames of insurrection might at any time arise. " The village system," he wrote, " which makes all men equal in their poverty, is now fairly on its trial in the disturbed districts, and Government has hardly a single man of influence to look to in them. Their Army is the same, a dead level —no gentlemen, no difference save in military rank. I love neither system ; but I hope our eyes will now be opened to Robertson's prophecy on the inevitable tendency of *our* system."† And even as he wrote, events were in the womb of time and well-nigh on the point of development, which opened our eyes very sadly to the fact that we had made a gigantic mistake. The Sepoys, Regular and Irregular, were

---

* Christian had married a daughter of Charles Raikes.

† He spoke here of the repeated protests of the late Mr. Thomas Campbell Robertson, who had been Lieutenant-Governor of the North-Western Provinces, against the system, so favoured by men of another school, of rooting out the landed aristocracy of the country. I was in habits of the closest intimacy with this excellent man for more than a quarter of a century ; and I know well the consistent sagacity with which he dwelt upon the injustice of destroying the influential classes and the evil consequences of such injustice, which we should ourselves experience, if the day of trouble should ever come to us, as he believed that some day it would. And after the insurrections of 1857—58, he spoke, very sorrowfully, of the manner in which his predictions had been fulfilled. Compare Christian's remarks with what is written in book viii., chapter ii., concerning affairs in Rohilkund.

rising on all sides; but if the great landed proprietors had been with us in this conjuncture, we
might have held our own against our assailants
instead of being helpless as children.

At Seetapore, the Sepoys, both of the Regular and
of the Irregular Army, protested their loyalty and
fidelity, and appeared to be pained by any manifestation of mistrust. An old Native officer, with
tears in his eyes, implored his European commandant not to cast away the confidence and to
break the bonds of a life of cherished comradeship;
and it would have been strange if such appeals as
these had not touched the hearts of Sepoy officers,
who, in camp and cantonment, and on hard-fought
fields, had shared their dangers and privations, and
had never known them to murmur. It was natural
that, to some extent, this confidence should have
been shared by the civil officers. In any case, it was
wise to simulate it. There was one precaution, however, which Christian, whatever appearance of mistrust it might create, felt himself bound to take. "I
have placed," he wrote to Captain Hutchinson on the
1st of June, "all the ladies, women, and children,
except some four, who refuse to leave the Lines of
the Forty-first Native Infantry, in my house, and
made all secure." But even this might be regarded
as a defensive measure against, not the Seetapore
regiments, but the muntineers from Lucknow, whom
it was supposed, or at least feigned, that their own battalions were eager to attack   Indeed, Colonel Birch,
who commanded the Forty-first, had marched his
men along the road to the capital on the first rumour
that the Lucknow mutineers were advancing, and
they had kept up a show of fidelity by actually firing
on the advanced guard of the declared insurgents.

This had checked the mutineers from Lucknow; and the Forty-first had been marched back to their Lines covered with honour as loyal soldiers.

1857.
June.

Thus passed the two first days of June in alternating confidence and doubt. Four guns were posted at Seetapore, and these, flanked by the Irregulars, had been posted between Mr. Christian's house and the Lines of the Forty-first. The house lay in the bend of a deep nullah, so it was free from attack in the rear; but that which prevented the enemy from attacking it, prevented our own people from escaping, and, therefore, it was unwisely chosen as a place of refuge. There had been signs of insubordination on those first two days of the month; on the third they were more unmistakable. On the morning of that day, Mr. Christian was informed by Major Apthorp that the Forty-first were seething into mutiny; but Colonel Birch still believed that the disaffection was only partial. The guns were, however, loaded, and the Irregulars warned; Christian still had confidence in the Oude levies and the Police, and he did not doubt the issue of the conflict.

June 3.
Mutiny of the troops.

The mutiny commenced in the wonted manner. A company was told off to seize the treasure. The Treasury lay at a distance of a mile from the Sepoy Lines, and whilst the plunderers were marching towards the spoil, the other companies assumed a menacing attitude and advanced in the direction of the guns. Colonel Birch, accompanied by Lieutenant Graves, rode off towards the Treasury, still hoping to arrest the mutinous madness of his men.*

* I have followed in these statements Captain Hutchinson's "Narrative of the Mutinies in Oude." The story is differently told by Mr. Gubbins, who says: "On the morn- ing of the 3rd of June, a cry was raised in the Lines of the Forty-first Regiment that the Tenth Irregulars were plundering the Treasury, and as the men were in a state of ex-

1857.
June.

The Colonel was shot dead; the Lieutenant, though wounded, was able to ride back to the Lines and to warn the other English residents in the station that the storm had burst, and that there was nothing for them but to escape with their lives. There was then a scene of terror and confusion, such as even the survivors of that fatal day find it difficult accurately to describe. The Regulars, the Irregulars, and the Mounted Police all fraternised. There were two feelings paramount among them—greed for the spoil, hatred to the Christians. The very name of the Commissioner and his family is said to have been so hateful to them, that the mutineers singled them out for swift destruction. When nothing more could be done by him for the preservation of life and property, Mr. Christian, with his wife and an infant in her arms, walked from his house to the nullah, or river, in its rear, and made for one of its fordable points. He had either crossed, or was preparing to cross the stream, when he fell dead, with his face on the ground, riddled with musket-balls. The poor wife then sat down beside the lifeless body of her husband, still holding her babe in her arms, and in a very little time, mother and child had been killed by the insurgents. Another child, gallantly rescued by Sergeant-Major Morton, was carried safely across the stream, and preserved for awhile, to die afterwards, a little captive in the Kaiser-baugh of Lucknow.*

Death of Mr. Christian.

citement, the Commander, Colonel Birch, who reposed the most entire confidence in his men, called out the two most suspected companies, the Light and Rifle, and led them to the Treasury. All there was found to be quiet, and the Colonel was about to return, when a Sepoy of the guard stepped out of the ranks and shot him in the back."

* Sir Henry Lawrence had pointed out in April the advantage of removing the Forty-first from Seetapore, as well as the Forty-eighth from Lucknow : " I told the Brigadier (Handscombe) that my remedy would be to send the regiment out of Oude. I shall be glad if your Lordship will permit the measure. Brigadier Gray, a Sepoy officer of

Meanwhile, other Christian residents had been effecting their escape or succumbing to the murderous fire of the enemy. Mr. and Mrs. Thornhill were killed. Lieutenant Graves, who had escaped with his life from the first discharge of musketry, was now slain, with his wife and child; Lieutenant Snell, with his wife and child; Lieutenants Dorin, Small, Greene, Dr. Marcus Hill, and others, shared the same fate. Sir Mountstuart Jackson and his two sisters, Mr. and Miss Birch (children of the Colonel of the Forty-first), and Mrs. Dorin, were among those who escaped from Seetapore.* They left behind them one of those scenes of terrible anarchy and outrage, which were even then becoming of such frequent recurrence, that the narrator is compelled to repeat the same story in well-nigh the same words. The houses of the English were gutted. All that was valuable and removable was carried off by the despoilers. The rest was broken or burnt; the buildings were fired, amidst shoutings and yellings, and all utterances of fiendish revelry; and not a Christian man, woman, or child was left alive in the place.

There were two smaller British stations in the Khyrabad Division—Mullaon and Mohumdee. In

---

forty years' standing, told me this morning that he had suggested the same step to Brigadier Handscombe. Indeed, he went further, and said he should like to see the Forty-first out of Seetapore. So should I; as we have two Oude corps there, and the less the Regulars and Oude Irregulars are together the better, inasmuch as their pay is different, whilst they are mostly men of the same caste and same part of the country. . . . Perhaps the Forty-first might march *via* Furruckabad

to Meerut, and the Forty-eighth to Cawnpore, either to remain there under its old Colonel (Sir Hugh Wheeler), while one of the corps there is pushed on, or it might move on to Agra or elsewhere." The result of this reference with respect to the Forty-eighth has been already shown (vol. i., pp. 586–7). The same consideration actuated the Chief Commissioner in regard to the Forty-first.

* What befel some of these fugitives will be told in a subsequent part of this narrative,

the former, Mr. Capper, of the Civil Service, was Deputy-Commissioner. Detachments of the Forty-first and of the Fourth Oude Irregulars were stationed there. In May, the Deputy-Commissioner had seen reason to doubt their fidelity, and had perceived also ugly symptoms of general fermentation throughout the district. "I wish," he wrote to Mr. Gubbins on the 29th, "that we could hear of the fall of Delhi, for deserters are coming in fast and spreading wonderful reports of the utter cowardice and alarm of the *sahibs* in the North-West. There appear, too, to be a good many corpses of Europeans lying on the Trunk Road; and it is time that they were buried. Their presence seems to cause alarm to all passengers, even more than the Dacoits. Every man who comes here has been thoroughly cleaned out by the Goojurs." Nothing could more strikingly illustrate the progress which the revolt had made, even at that early period, than these simple sentences, written at the end of May by the Deputy-Commissioner at Mullaon. A very few weeks before, a single white corpse lying by the road-side would have created the greatest excitement from one end of the district to the other, and would have been a subject of horrified comment in every English journal in the country. Now these unburied white corpses were spoken of with an indefinite plurality, all the more terrible for the coolness and quietude with which the report was made. Little more than a fortnight of this rough work had so habituated our officers to tales of blood, that the sensation once produced by the murder of one white man was greater than that which now followed the massacre of numbers. The Goojurs, too, the born depredators of the land, had found that their time had come; and with the

wonted impartiality of their race were plundering
alike friends and foes. It was plain that there was
small chance of the British officer holding his own
much longer in that isolated station. Still, reluctant
to fly, he held to his post for some days after the
evacuation of Seetapore; and then, seeing that the
troops were on the brink of open mutiny, mounted
his horse and rode unharmed to Lucknow.

Meanwhile, at Mohumdee, there was the germ of a
terrible tragedy. There Mr. J. G. Thomason, who
represented the third generation of a family distinguished in our Indian annals for good service, was
Deputy-Commissioner. His assistant was Captain
Patrick Orr, who had commanded, in the King's
time, one of the Oude Regiments. On the 1st of
June, the refugees from Shahjehanpore came into Mohumdee;* and thus the European party was largely
and dangerously increased. During the two next
days there were threatenings of a storm. On the 4th
the soldiery rose, sacked the Treasury, and released
the prisoners. It was time now for the Europeans to
seek safety in flight. The Sepoys were more of the
Oude Irregular Force. Captain Orr knew them well,
and he obtained from them the most solemn assurances that they would spare the lives of our
people. So, that evening, they went forth unharmed,
setting their faces towards Aurungabad. The women
and children were placed, some in a buggy and the
rest on baggage carts; and there seemed good hope
of deliverance. But on the following morning it was
plain that they had been betrayed. A party of the
Oude Irregulars was on their track. About a mile
from Aurungabad they declared themselves. Then
the carnage began. Resistance was impossible; escape

* The story of Shahjehanpore is told in book viii., chapter ii.

almost impossible. One man, however, escaped to tell the tale of the butchery. This was Captain Orr himself. "We all collected under a tree," he says, "and took the ladies down from the buggy. Shots were firing from all directions amidst the most fearful yells. The poor ladies all joined in prayer, coolly and undauntedly awaiting their fate. I stopped for about three minutes among them, but thinking of my poor wife and child here, I endeavoured to save my life for their sakes. I rushed out towards the insurgents, and one of their men, Goordhun, of the Sixth Company, called out to me to throw down my pistol and he would save me. I did so, when he put himself between me and the men, and several others followed his example. In about ten minutes more they completed their hellish work. Poor Lysaght was kneeling out in the open ground, with his hands folded across his chest, and though not using his firearms, the cowardly rascals would not go up to the spot until they shot him; and then rushing up they killed the wounded and children, butchering them in a most cruel way. With the exception of the drummer-boy, every one (of the Shahjehanpore party*) was killed, and besides poor good Thomason and one or two clerks. They denuded the bodies of their clothes for the sake of plunder."

Fyzabad.

At Fyzabad, Colonel Philip Goldney, of the Bengal Army, was Commissioner. I have spoken of him

---

* Captain Orr's list shows that there were eleven commissioned officers from Shahjehanpore, a quartermaster-sergeant, a band-master, and a drummer. There were eight women and four children of the party. Besides these, there were Mr. Jenkins, of the Civil Service, and Lieutenant Sheils, of the Veteran Establishment, who was shot, whilst riding Captain Orr's horse, before the general massacre commenced,

before, with the reverence of an old friendship, as a man of equal courage and capacity.* He had removed himself from Sultanpore, where his headquarters had been fixed, to Fyzabad, as the "more important position and exposed to the greatest danger." At the latter place were posted the Twenty-second‧Regiment of Native Infantry, commanded by Colonel Lennox; a light field-battery, under Major Mill, manned by Native gunners; the Sixth Oude Infantry Regiment; and a squadron of the Fifteenth Irregular Horse. After the wonted fashion, these troops, one and all, protested their fidelity. But Goldney, who knew the temper of the Sepoy Army, felt that a crisis could not be far distant, and, in view of the coming danger, tried to rally round him the "friendly Zemindars," and, by the help of a hastily fortified walled enclosure, sufficiently provisioned, to hold out till relief should come to save the lives of the people under his charge. There was talk, too, of sending the women and children to Lucknow. But both projects were abandoned under pressure of stern necessity. The "friendly Zemindars" were not disposed to fight against disciplined troops, and the road to the capital was too dangerous for the contemplated exodus of the helpless ones to be attempted.†

1857.

June.

---

* Vol. i. p. 280, foot-note. Mr. (Sir Charles) Wingfield was at Fyzabad, presiding over an examination committee, when news of the seizure of Delhi and massacre of the English arrived. That evening he dined with Colonel Goldney at the mess of the Twenty-second Regiment, N.I. Almost all the military officers at the station were present. There was no gloom or sadness over the party. They played whist and billiards after dinner according to their wont. But Goldney remarked to Wingfield on this gaiety at such a juncture and in view of the dangers that threatened them, adding, "How many of us will be alive a fortnight hence?" Within three weeks four-fifths of the light-hearted company had perished miserably.

† The state of feeling at Fyzabad in the third week of May is well represented in the following extract of a letter written by the medical officer of the Sixth Oude Infantry:

1857.
June.

The Oude
Talookhdars.

Our system, as Mr. Christian had said, was on its trial. If the great landholders—the Barons of Oude —had been with us at this time, our position would have been one of comparative strength. But our Revenue measures had hopelessly alienated their affections. The new rule of the English had prostrated them ; and though they might conceal their resentments for a time, it was well-nigh certain that the moment would come when they would throw off their disguise, and stand forth as the most bitter and unrelenting of our enemies. Foremost among these great Talookhdars was Maun Singh,* of Shah-gunj.

"Fyzabad, 19th May, 1857.—Here we are, in a jolly state of excitement, as we don't know but that Fyzabad may kick up a row and the Sepoys join in it any hour they like. We have no telegraph to Lucknow, and are dependent upon a foot-postman for news once a day. I need hardly say how we gallop from one bungalow to another when the post arrives, to see who has the latest news. We were certainly surprised at first to hear of the outbreak at Meerut, and then the troops joining the insurgents at Delhi ; but there had been signs of discontent for some time past in the Native army. . . . . . The thermometer is eighty-two degrees all night, and in the day (in the shade of course) a hundred degrees, and often more, and this, added to our excitement, keeps us nearly at fever heat. . . . . News just arrived here that we must prepare to make a stand if the worst comes; this is pleasant! and we, that is, all the Europeans, are to be lodged in one large house down by the river—what a spree! Post just in; all the Europeans at Delhi reported to have been murdered in the most horrible manner. People in Lucknow in great agitation." This is characteristic of the high animal spirits of our younger officers, and their confidence in the face of appalling difficulties. Even at a later

period, when the danger had thickened around them, the same spirit of confidence was manifested in all their letters.

* Maun Singh was the nephew and adopted heir of the well-known Bukhtawur Singh, often referred to by Colonel Sleeman. " Bukhtawur Singh," wrote the Resident in his journal, under date December 20, 1849, " has always been considered the head of the family, to whom Shah-gunj belongs; but he has always remained at Court, and left the local management of the estate and the government of the districts, placed under their charge in contracts or in trust, to his brothers and nephews. Bukhtawur Singh has no child of his own, but he has adopted Maun Singh, the youngest son of his brother, Dursun Singh, and he leaves all local duties and responsibilities to him. He is a small, slight man, but shrewd, active, and energetic, and as unscrupulous as a man can be. Old Bukhtawur Singh himself is the only member of the family that was ever troubled with scruples of any kind. . . . All his brothers and nephews are thorough-bred ruffians." This, however, must be taken with some limitations. Sleeman's picture of the Oude Talookhdars is much too highly coloured.

1857.
June.

The new Revenue system of the English had fallen crushingly upon him, burying him beneath the ruins of an once magnificent estate. The summary settlement had transferred to his tenants a large portion of the broad lands, which he had once owned, and he was declared a defaulter for the non-payment of Government dues which he believed to be illegally demanded from him. Our officers would have arrested him, but he was not to be found. Wronged and humiliated by the arbitrary proceedings of the English, he had gone to the vice-regal capital in search of redress—perhaps of retribution. Avowedly he went to Calcutta to take legal advice as to the possibility of obtaining a reversal of the harsh decrees of the British Government. It is more than probable that he took bitter counsel with Ali Nuckee Khan as to the great question of "what was to be done." What passed at the capital, and whom he saw on his homeward journey, we shall probably never know. He returned to Oude before the outbreaks at Meerut and Delhi, and was soon afterwards arrested and placed in honourable duress by orders from Lucknow.* The outbreak at Fyzabad found

* There seems to be some doubt as to the actual cause of Maun Singh's detention. Mr. Gubbins, Financial Commissioner, says : "At the beginning of the month, Rajah Maun Singh, Talookhdar of Shahgunj, was in confinement there. He had been arrested by order of the Chief Commissioner, in consequence of information telegraphed from Calcutta, which accorded with what had reached us at Lucknow." Captain Reid, Deputy-Commissioner of Fyzabad, says: "He was in close, but honourable confinement, having been placed under arrest by the Commissioner in obedience to orders from Lucknow. I was much opposed to this step; as, whatever may have been Maun Singh's conduct since, I had every reason to believe that he was then well affected to our Government." Captain Hutchinson ("Narrative of the Mutinies in Oude") writes, that "Maun Singh was in confinement on a *revenue question*, when Captain Alexander Orr, the Assistant-Commissioner, who had known him for several years, begged his release." One thing, however, is certain, namely, that at the end of May, and at the beginning of June, Maun Singh was under surveillance in Oude, and could not, therefore, have been intriguing at Calcutta. (See *ante*, book vii. page 36.) But he told Sir Charles Wingfield that he had

him under surveillance in that city. With Captain Alexander Orr, the Assistant-Commissioner, he had long been in habits of intimacy, and he now offered, if released from confinement, to shelter and protect Orr and his family in the Fort of Shah-gunj, which lay some twelve miles distant from the British station. Orr hesitated to accept an offer of this exclusive character, and urged that it should be extended to all who would accept it. Colonel Goldney consented to this; and then Captain Reid, the Deputy-Commissioner, accompanied by Orr, proceeded to Maun Singh's house in the city to discuss the whole question with him. Willing as the Rajah professed himself to be to shelter the whole of our women and children, he doubted his ability to do so, and he proposed, therefore, to limit his protection to the families of the civil officers. To this Reid demurred. He could not honourably accept such terms. So at last Maun Singh consented to receive all the families of our officers, on condition that their removal from the station to the Fort should be accomplished with the utmost possible secrecy. But when this decision was communicated to the military officers, they declined to accept the offer. They had more faith in the soldiery than in Maun Singh. They would not trust the one or show mistrust of the other. One only consented to send his wife and children to Shah-gunj, with the families of the civil officers.*

On the night of the 7th of June the exode of the women was safely accomplished. On the evening of the 8th the troops rose. Their first movement was to

---

visited Calcutta earlier in the year, for the purpose of taking legal advice as to whether any remedy were open to him against the injurious measures of the revenue officers of the British Government.

* The family of Captain Dawson, Executive Engineer, who went with his wife and four children to Maun Singh's Fort. The wives and children of the European Staff-sergeants were also sent to Shah-gunj.

seize the guns. The battery was drawn up ready for action, loaded with grape, a company of the Twenty-second on each flank, when the alarm was sounded from the Lines of the Oude Irregulars. The Golundauze lighted their port-fires, but before they could use them, the Infantry rushed in among them and pointed their loaded muskets at the heads of the gunners. Neither the commands nor entreaties of their officers could move them. The main body of the Twenty-second was now moving down, with the usual ominous shouts. It was clear that the game was lost. The Sepoys told the English officers that the guns were theirs, and that they were strong enough to turn us out of the country. They then escorted the officers to the Quarter-guard of the regiment.

Though the lead had been thus taken by the Infantry, the Cavalry were as ever the most vehement in speech and the most murderous in their desires. A Ressaldar of the Fifteenth Irregular Horse appeared to be the chief leader of the revolt. He was clamorous for the blood of the English officers, and the troopers generally accepted the invitation to murder. But the Artillery and Infantry resolutely refused to injure our people. Their forbearance went further than this. They assisted the Europeans to escape. They procured boats for them, and gave them money. All night long the English prisoners remained at the Quarter-guard; and in the morning they were escorted down to the river under an escort of the Twenty-second. The boats were there, but there were no boatmen; so the fugitives took the oars into their hands and left Fyzabad in safety.

But the danger was not yet passed. There are some things in this, as in almost every other narrative of regimental revolt, so inconsistent, as to be almost inscrutable. That the mutineers on that morning should have seized the public treasure, and laid their despoiling hands upon the private property of the English, was only in accordance with established rules. The work of plunder went on bravely as a matter of course. But it is not so easy to reconcile with these established rules the Sepoys' treatment of the persons of our officers. They not only permitted Colonel Goldney and his companions to depart unmolested, but aided their departure, as though desirous of securing their safety. Our people were at the mercy of the mutineers. Resistance was wholly impossible. They might have been slaughtered at any moment like a little flock of sheep. Not one could have escaped. But it is stated that scarcely had the English left Fyzabad, when the Twenty-second despatched a messenger charged with instructions to the Seventeenth, who were then on the banks of the Gogra, to intercept the boats, and to slay all the white people in them.* Certain it is that the Christian people were floating down to destruction. For they had scarcely gone thirty miles down the stream, when the inmates of the leading boats perceived that the right bank of the river was lined with Sepoys—Horse and Foot—whose intentions were too apparent. The narrowness of the stream at that point seemed to render escape impossible. The Azimgurh mutineers† opened fire upon them, with

---

* This is stated very emphatically by Mr. Gubbins: "Begumgunj, where the Seventeenth lay, is on the banks of the Gogra, and the current of the river sweeps underneath it. A messenger had been despatched by the Twenty-second Regiment to the Seventeenth to destroy them. Fearfully was the invitation responded to."

† These were men of the Seventeenth Regiment of Native Infantry, of whose revolt an account is given in vol. ii., 213—216, closing with the statement that, "flushed with success, they marched off to Fyzabad in military array, with all the pomp and panoply of war."

murderous effect, and there was nothing left for them
but to endeavour to escape on the opposite shore.
But the enemy crossed the river in boats; and it
only remained for our people to fly with their lives.
So Goldney addressed his companions, exhorting Death of
Colonel
Goldney.
them to save their lives by the only means still open
to the fugitives. "I am too old myself to run," he
said, "but you should do your best to escape." So
they sped across the country whilst the Commissioner prepared himself to die. And death soon
overtook him. It is said that, having been carried
before the Native officers of the Seventeenth, he
asked them if they meant to disgrace themselves by
the murder of an old man.* He was shot dead upon
the spot. Others from the two leading boats perished
in the attempt to escape. Lieutenant Currie, of the
Artillery, and Lieutenant Parsons, of the Oude Irregulars, were drowned. It is supposed that Major
Mill also was drowned. Adjutant Bright, of the
Twenty-second, shared the fate of Colonel Goldney.
The rest seem to have escaped to Amorah, where
they were joined by the fugitives from the fourth
boat. The party then consisted of eight. On the
morning of the 10th of June they had reached
Captan-gunj in safety. Thence they pursued their
hazardous journey, with good hope of ultimate deliverance. For the chief people of the villages,
through which they passed, had shown a friendly
disposition, and some had aided their escape by

---

* According to our English esti-
mates of old age, Colonel Goldney
was scarcely an old man when he
was killed. He entered the service
in the year 1820—probably at the
age of seventeen; and must have
been about fifty-four years old at the
time of his death. Mr. Gubbins
says: "It would be unjust to the
memory of this deserving soldier not
to mention that, from every account
that has reached me, he maintained
a most manly and gallant bearing
during these trying scenes at Fyzabad. He believed that he should
not survive them. But with a noble,
chivalrous feeling he resolved to remain at his post to the last."

2 н 2

1857.
June.

giving them money and mounting them on ponies. But these hopes were delusive; for as they sped onwards to the village of Mahwah-dabur,* the people rushed out, armed with swords and matchlocks, and fell mercilessly upon the fugitives. One only escaped to tell the story of this miserable flight. Sergeant-Major Busher outran all his companions, and by sheer bodily activity and power of endurance saved his life. The narrative he has written, which has every appearance of absolute fidelity, is the groundwork of all history relating to this particular episode of our troubles in Oude.†

Escape of
Colonel
O'Brien.

Thus has a mournful account been rendered of those who embarked in three of the four boats which started from Fyzabad on the morning of the 8th of June. There was yet another party of fugitives occupying the boat described in contemporary narratives as Boat No. 3, of whom no mention has yet been made. This boat was occupied by Colonel O'Brien, of the Oude Irregular Infantry, and by four other commissioned officers. By one of those happy thoughts, which come upon us in critical emergencies almost as divine inspirations, the whole party was saved. Not far below Fyzabad lies Adjoodhea, the ancient capital of Oude. The two leading boats dropped past this place. The third put in to shore, and secured a larger boat and a boat's crew. This enabled our officers to lie down, screened from observation, under the sides of the vessel. The enemy

---

* This was a Mahomedan village, held by a family that had discharged the office of Kagee. Our unfortunate officers, I am informed, were inveigled into it by two Mahomedan Government Chuprassies. One had preceded the party, declaredly to provide refreshments for them, but in reality to arouse the fanaticism of the people, and to plan the attack on the Christian fugitives.

† This narrative has been published in different shapes. It will be found in Captain Hutchinson's book. The account of the Sergeant-Major's subsequent adventures is extremely interesting and suggestive.

on the river-bank, who had fired on the two leading boats, did not know that the third had any white men in it.   So Colonel O'Brien and his companions made good their voyage to Dinapore.

The whole story of the retreat from Fyzabad is not yet told.   When the four boats, on the morning of the 9th of June, dropped down the river, Colonel Lennox, Commandant of the Twenty-second, remained with his wife and daughter during the early part of the day, and embarked with them in the afternoon.   It appears that Mrs. Mill was to have accompanied the Lennox family, but when the time for embarkation arrived, either purposely or accidentally, she lost the opportunity, and was left behind with her children.*   The Lennox family had not gone far down the river, when they were compelled to abandon their boat and to commence a foot journey to Goruckpore.   On their way they were made prisoners, and were about to be delivered over to the mutineers, when they were rescued by the followers of Mahmud Hoossein Khan,† who for more than a week sheltered and provided for them, until Mr. Paterson, the Magistrate of Goruckpore, sent an escort to convey them to that place.

In command of the station at Sultanpore was Colonel Fisher—familiarly known in India as " Sam

---

* Mr. Gubbins says : " Unwilling to expose her children to the sun, she had lost the opportunity of leaving the station with Colonel Lennox, and found herself left alone. She succeeded, however, in making her way alone through the country, and at length reached a British station. She had walked the whole way, wandering from village to village. The women in the villages were kind to her, but she lost one of her children from illness and exposure on the way."   Some interesting particulars of Mrs. Mill's escape will be found in the Appendix.

† This man afterwards (September, 1857), invaded Goruckpore when that district was abandoned by the Goorkah troops, and established his Government there. He subsequently surrendered himself to the British Government, and in consideration of his having succoured the family of Colonel Lennox, was allowed to go free,

Fisher." He was a member of a family which had furnished two generations of good and faithful ministers to the Anglo-Indian Church. His personal qualifications were of a kind to insure for him the highest measure of popularity. He had a splendid seat in the saddle; he was ardent and successful in all the sports of the field; he was a man of kindly and genial temperament, which endeared him alike to his own Christian comrades and to the Native soldiery. An officer of the Queen's Army, he was, I believe, the first man of that service ever appointed to the command of an Irregular regiment under the Company—the Fifteenth Irregular Horse. His second in command was Captain Gibbings. His Adjutant was Lieutenant Charlton Tucker, the youngest member of that family of Indian public servants whose name is synonymous with good work ever bravely done. The Eighth Regiment of Oude Irregular Infantry and a corps of Military Police were also in occupation of Sultanpore. On the 7th, anticipating the coming storm, Fisher despatched all the ladies in the station towards Allahabad, under charge of two officers. On the morning of the 9th, the troops rose. Fisher had gone down to the Lines, and had addressed the men, urging them affectionately to return to their duty, when one of the Nujeebs shot him in the back with a musket, and the fine old soldier, so much honoured, so much beloved, fell mortally wounded before the eyes of his own troopers, not one of whom would go to his aid; Captain Gibbings was also slain beside the dhooly in which Adjutant Tucker had placed the dying body of his Commandant. The death-agony was soon over; and then Tucker, being exhorted to fly for his life, mounted his horse and rode towards the

Goomtee, where he found hospitable refuge in the house of a Talookhdar of ancient family, who had been unjustly treated in the Settlement, and who, for the evil we had done him, returned to us only good.* Far different was the treatment to which our civil officers were subjected. Mr. Block, of the Covenanted, and Mr. Stroyan, of the Uncovenanted Service, flung themselves on the hospitality of a landholder named Yazeen Khan, of Sultanpore. This man professed friendship and received them into his house. But either with preconcerted treachery, or in an hour of fanatical repentance, he drove them from the shelter that he had offered to them, and caused them both to be shot to death.†

Thus all European authority was swept out of Sultanpore. And the usual festival was held. The houses of the English were sacked; all the portable property carried off; and then for a time the bonfires afforded plentiful amusement to the "babalogue." This done, the three regiments marched off to Nawab-Gunj, which was fast becoming the rendezvous of all the rebellious troops in the province—with what result will presently be told.

There was one other station in the Fyzabad Division. At Salone was posted the main body of the First Regiment of Oude Infantry. Captain R. L. Thompson commanded it. The chief civil officer was Captain Lousada Barrow, an officer of the

1857.
June.

Salone.

---

* His name was Roostum Sah. Mr. Gubbins says of him, that he deserved all the more credit, " as he had suffered unduly at the Settlement, and had lost many villages, which he should have been permitted to retain." Captain Bunbury of the Police Corps, with Captain Smith, Lieutenant Jenkins, and Dr. O'Donel of the Infantry Regiment, afterwards found shelter under the same roof. The whole were brought safely into Benares by Henry Tucker, the Commissioner of that place.

† Mr. Gubbins says: "This is the only instance of like treachery on the part of a petty Zemindar in Oudh which came to our notice."

Madras Cavalry, whose signal administrative capacity afterwards raised him to the Chief Commissionership of the province. All through the month of May and the first week of June the conduct of the troops was orderly, and their temper seemed to be good. In the districts, too, appearances were favourable. The landholders were paying up their Government dues as in the most tranquil times, and there was nothing to bespeak a coming convulsion. But when news came that the troops at Fyzabad and Sultanpore had risen, it was plain that the continued fidelity of the men of the First Irregulars was not to be expected. On the 9th of June there were signs of feverish excitement, and on the 10th the regiment rose—but with none of those worst signs of brutal violence that had distinguished so many similar risings in all parts of the country. The soldiery declared themselves to be masters of the situation, and proceeded to release the prisoners in the Gaol. But they respected the lives of their officers, and escorted them from the station—beyond which they were met by an influential landowner, named Humwunt Singh, who sheltered them for some days, and afterwards, with the aid of some other local gentry, enabled them to reach Allahabad.

Bareitch
Division.

The Bareitch Division comprised the districts of Bareitch and Gonda, situated upon the left bank of the Gogra, and of Mullapore, on the right bank of the river. Mr. Charles Wingfield* was the Commissioner of the division. A man of generous sym-

* Afterwards Chief Commissioner   Gravesend   in   the   House   of
of Oude, and now (1873) Sir Charles   Commons.
Wingfield, K.C.S.I., representing

pathies, not at all of the Thomasonian school, he had
seen with regret the operation of the new settlement
which had struck down the territorial aristocracy of
the province; and he had dealt with them more
leniently than had others. But when occasion required there had been no want of vigour in his administration. On one memorable occasion, in the
preceding year, he had greatly distinguished himself
by the pursuit and capture of a recusant Rajah, who
had defied the new authority of the British. His
ordinary place of residence had been at Bareitch—
the chief civil station; but he had removed himself,
in the preceding April, to Seerora, an old-established
military station in the time of the Native rulers,
where were posted in May, 1857, a regiment of
Cavalry, a regiment of Infantry,* and a horse battery
of the Oude Irregular Force. The troops were commanded by Captain G. W. Boileau.

When news of the disturbances at Meerut and
Delhi first arrived, there were the usual appearances,
and, indeed, the usual expressions of loyalty; and
for some weeks the troops performed their appointed
duties with their wonted observance of discipline. It
was necessary, however, to watch them closely, and
to be prepared for any emergency that might arise;
so frequent consultations were held between the chief
civil and military functionaries, who freely conversed
with the Native officers, and endeavoured to elicit
their opinions. But as news came in from station
after station, ever with fresh tidings of mutiny and
massacre, there seemed to be little hope that the
Bareitch Division would be exempt from the great
plague of insurrection which was afflicting the whole

* He was driven to change his his house at Bareitch was falling
residence by the circumstance that down.

province. So Wingfield, as a first measure of precaution, provided for the safety of our women, by
sending them under a guard of Cavalry, principally
Sikhs, to Lucknow; and then he concerted measures
for the retirement, in the event of a crisis, of our
Christian people to the strongholds of certain friendly
chiefs situated on the borders of Nepaul.

A false alarm, which may have been accidental, or
may have been designed, precipitated the rising of
the troops. News was brought in the night, that the
Infantry were arming. Since the departure of the
women, the officers had slept at the Commissioner's
· house, and when this message was brought they went
forth into the darkness to the Artillery quarters and
turned the guns upon the Infantry Lines. The
Golundauze obeyed orders, and seemed to be faithful
to their Government; but their was no need to try
the strength of their loyalty to the utmost, for the
Infantry made no demonstration, and the officers
went home to their beds—some declaring it to have
been a false alarm, others protesting that a seditious
design had been defeated by the attitude we had so
promptly assumed.

But a different story gained credence in the Infantry Lines. The Sepoys accused us of a design to
massacre them as they slept; and from that time the
nameless fear was upon them, that had so often been
the precursor of revolt. Then all branches of the
Force made common cause. And Boileau soon found
that he had ceased to command the troops at Secrora.
There was now nothing more to be done for the
maintenance of British authority. Sir Henry Lawrence had written to the chief civil and military
officers, saying: "Should a mutiny break out or
appear to be inevitable, you are at liberty to consult

your own safety." So Wingfield mounted his horse, and on pretence of going for his wonted evening ride, galloped with all speed to Gonda, where he found that the regiment posted there had not yet revolted.

Everything, indeed, had gone on in the old groove all through the month of May. Our civil courts had seen the wonted number of suitors, and discipline had been maintained in the Lines of the Sepoys But in the first week of June there was a perceptible change. It was plain that all classes were in a state of feverish excitement, girding themselves up for the coming struggle. The old belief in the indomitable power of the English was fast passing away.* Still there was no outward change. The Sepoys protested that they would remain true to their salt; and the majority of their officers believed them. But when the Commissioner brought in the discouraging news that the troops at Fyzabad and Secrora had revolted, it became evident that the troops, though they still protested their fidelity, would form a junction with their comrades on the first appearance of a mutinous body from either place. As all other roads were now closed, it was proposed that the regiment should be marched to Bulrampore†—some thirty miles distant —with the treasure. To this the men apparently at first consented; but the Sepoys said that they would fight the mutineers, when they might come,

---

* Mr. Wingfield says: "It was manifest that confidence in our power was fast departing; and Zemindars who had recovered their villages from Talookhdars at Settlement were writing to propitiate the latter or making preparations for flight. The Tuhseeldars had reported that the Sepoys had been overheard to express their determination not to allow the treasure to be removed," &c. &c.

† Mr. Wingfield had from the first the fullest confidence in the fidelity of the Maharajah of Bulrampore, which was amply justified by after events. He was made a Knight-Commander of the Star of India and a member of the legislative council of the Governor-General.

which really meant that they would fraternise with their comrades. So Wingfield with the civil officers rode on to Bulrampore. Captain Miles and his Adjutant, bent on making a last despairing effort to save their men from rebellion, still remained in the Cantonment. But, on the following day, they found that all their efforts were useless; so they also set their faces towards Bulrampore, together with some of the officers from Secrora.

One officer, however, still remained at the latter place, when all the rest had abandoned the Cantonment. This was Lieutenant Bonham of the Artillery, who commanded a battery of the Oude Irregular Force. He was a young soldier of great promise, and, for his years, of commanding influence. He kept his company together after the other branches of the service had revolted. But, although his courage commanded the respect and admiration of his men, it could not secure their fidelity. The Commissioner had gone. All the Infantry officers had gone. Everything portended that British authority was utterly extinguished. For a little while, however, the Infantry, without their own officers,* and subdued by the quiet gallantry of the young artilleryman, asked him to take command of them. They "made the most solemn promises never to leave him, and swore to protect him with their lives." Upon this Bonham consented to take command, and at once made his arrangements to march the Infantry and the guns into Lucknow. But these professions of loyalty were but short-lived. The Infantry soon

---

* I am informed that, on the preceding evening, the Infantry officers had been arrested by their men, and confined together in a house, with a guard over them. In the morning the guard was not relieved, so the men went off to their Lines, and the officers, very wisely, mounted their horses and escaped to Bulrampore.

became insolent in their demeanour, and there was
a marked change in the bearing of the gunners. Still
Bonham clung to his guns ; and, when the Infantry
advanced upon them, ordered his men to fire. The
order was not obeyed, and when Bonham himself
went to the battery to do the work, his men pointed
their carbines at him. There were some, however,
among them who were eager to serve him, and who
implored him to leave the place with the European
non-commissioned officers. They brought him horses,
and they brought him money, and urged him to fly
for his life. So at last, with a heavy heart, he turned
his back on his cherished guns and started for Lucknow, there to become, as will presently be told, one
of the most conspicuous heroes of the memorable
defence of that great city.*

Bonham had been cautioned to avoid the principal Bareitch.
ferry across the river, known as the Byram Ghaut,
which lay very near to Secrora, for there the main
body of the mutineers had taken up their position.
Not so our unfortunate people at the Bareitch station,
who took flight in that direction. Two companies of
the Gonda regiment were posted at the civil station,
under Lieutenant Longueville Clarke, a gallant young
officer who had shortly before distinguished himself
by the capture of a notorious freebooter named Fuzl
Ali. Mr. Cunliffe was the Deputy-Commissioner,
and with him was Mr. Jordan, an uncovenanted assistant. When they found that the head-quarters of
the regiment had revolted, there was no further hope
of the fidelity of the detachment ; so the Englishmen
mounted their horses and rode for Naupara, where

---

* He was accompanied by Farrier-
Sergeant James Bewsey, Assistant-
Farrier James Millar, and the Sergeant-Major of the Second Oude
Irregular Infantry, of whom Bonham
said that they all "behaved remarkably well throughout."

they had promise of friendly assistance. Disappointed in this, they turned back and rode for the Gogra, with the intention of making for Lucknow. They had disguised themselves in the costume of the country, and though the approaches to the Byram Ghaut were bristling with mutineers, they managed to escape detection and to gain the river. There they obtained a boat—it was said to be the common ferry-boat—and embarked with their horses. But a cry arose that some Europeans were escaping, and then there was a rush to the river-bank, and the Sepoys fired upon them. On this the Native boatmen took to the water; the Englishmen hid themselves, as best they could, under shelter of the sides of the boat; but powerless in this position to guide the vessel, they made no progress, perhaps they even drifted back, and Cunliffe and Clarke were shot to death. Jordan was dragged out of the boat, and suffered to linger for a few days, at the end of which he shared the fate of his comrades.*

Mullapore.

At Mullapore were no Sepoys; so there was no immediate fear of danger. But, after a little while,

---

* This story depends entirely upon Native evidence. Mr. Gubbins and Sir Charles Wingfield made every exertion to ascertain the truth; but their accounts differ in some respects, though in no material instance. Mr. Gubbins ("Mutinies in Oudh") says: "One of the young officers was engaged to a young lady at Lucknow, and the marriage was to have been shortly celebrated. The betrothed girl would not credit the story, and clung through the weary days of the siege to the hope that her lover would yet be found alive." The history of the great Indian rebellion is too sadly full of such romances. I cannot pass on without narrating a characteristic incident connected with this tragedy. Cunliffe and his companions were accompanied by the Native Deputy-Collector, a man of good parts, whom Mr. Wingfield had taken to Oude. He was a Pathan of an ancient family resident in Rohilkund. It was believed that he had cast in his lot with the European officers. When they turned back from Naupara he was captured with them at Byram Ghaut. His life was spared because he was a Native. He returned to Rohilkund, where family and national influences were too strong for him. He went into rebellion. His defection was proved by his own correspondence; so he was convicted and executed.

the wonted disorganisation of the Civil Government 1857.
manifested itself in the most unmistakable manner, June.
and our officers, powerless for good, prepared themselves to leave the station. They had been joined
by fugitives from Seetapore and other places; and
having obtained boats, were bent on making their
way—a long river journey—to Calcutta. This
hazardous experiment was arrested by information
that all the ghauts were closely watched by the
mutineers. So they quitted the boats, retraced their
steps by land, and made their way to the fortified
residence of the young Rajah of Dhowrerah at
Mutteeara, where they resided in safety for the space
of nearly two months. What were their subsequent
adventures will presently be told.*

One more story remains to be told, and it is the Durriabad.
more incumbent on me to tell it, as the record is
honourable to a brave and good soldier, who did his
duty nobly, and rendered good service to the State.
Durriabad was a district in the Lucknow Division.
The Fifth Regiment of Oude Infantry was stationed
there under the command of Captain W. H. Hawes.
He was much loved by his men, and he hoped that
they would remain staunch. But it was obvious,
before the end of May, that there was a growing
restlessness among them which might soon be developed into mutinous activity. Some three lakhs of
treasure were in Durriabad—an untoward circumstance, which greatly increased the difficulties of the
position. Hawes was eager to convey the coin to
Lucknow; but he felt that there was danger to

---

* The party—eleven in number— Mrs. Green, and Miss Jackson, from
consisted of Mr. Gonne, Deputy- Seetapore; with Sergeant-Major
Commissioner of Mullapore; Cap- and Mrs. Rogers, and the stepson
tain Hastings, from the same place; of the former; and a clerk in the
Messrs. Brand and Carew, from Mullapore office.
Shahjehanpore; Captain Hearsey,

others in his leaving the Cantonment.* This was approved by the Chief Commissioner. So Hawes stood fast, and on the 27th he wrote to Lawrence: "I feel my hands getting daily strengthened. . . . . I am steadily recovering the former strong hold I had in military discipline and proper subordination." Both the treasure and the prisoners had been brought into Cantonments, and Hawes believed that in a little while he could so restore loyalty to the regiment as to enable him to convey the money to the capital. But these hopes, like many others of the same kind, were delusive. The most favourable symptoms too often presaged a crisis. On the 9th of June he thought that the attempt might be made with safety. The carts were loaded with the treasure. The men marched out of Cantonments with a ringing cheer. But there was division among the Sepoys; and the treasure-escort had not gone more than half a mile towards Lucknow when mutiny broke out in their ranks. There were still some loyal men among them, but they could not resist the stern demands of their comrades, who fired upon them. So the coveted coin was carried back to Durriabad, and there was nothing left for the English but to betake themselves to flight.

They all escaped with their lives. Lieutenants Grant and Fullarton, with their wives and children, went off in an ecka, or Native covered carriage, and,

---

* "I have every hope," he wrote to Sir Henry Lawrence on the 25th of May, "of being able to hold my own and keep the treasure secure, so long as I can keep everything under my own eye and united; but as any harsh measure would very probably bring on an open revolt, I am desirous, for the sake of the European officers' families, not to show any apparent mistrust, or to bring on the crisis until obliged, or until I have felt my way a little more clearly. I could have taken on the treasure last night, but it would have been at the risk of leaving behind many mutinous spirits."—*MS. Correspondence.*

after some adventures by the way, being sometimes in great peril, they reached Lucknow in safety. Mr. Benson, of the Civil Service, also made good his way to the capital, riding the greater part of the way. The escape of Captain Hawes was a marvel. The Sepoys of his regiment, whom he had so much trusted and so kindly treated, fired upon him from all directions, sometimes by volleys, sometimes by the deliberate aim of single marksmen. But he rode on unharmed, and reached Lucknow without a wound. The English were cleared out of Durriabad. The mutineers remained there for some days, and then set their faces towards the great rebel rallying-ground at Newab-gunj; and the authority of the deposed King of Oude was proclaimed throughout the district.

1857.
June—July

Such were the principal incidents of mutiny and rebellion at the out-stations of Oude—incidents in their results most disastrous to the lives and property of the English, and most damaging to the fair fame of our nation. Everywhere our authority had collapsed. Everywhere our people, if not feeding the jackals and the vultures, were flying for their lives and imploring the mercy of those whom a little while before they had overawed and commanded. It was plain that we had but few friends in the province. Even those fugitives to whom shelter was given met with but scant courtesy and hospitality. Some, after much toil and travail, made their way to Lucknow; some escaped into Goruckpore, or were fortunate enough to reach Allahabad in safety; others perished by the way. Long time would it take to narrate all the incidents of these adventurous escapes, or the

General results.

1857.
June—July.

An episode of
captivity.

sufferings, often ending in death, endured by our people. One story, however, of captivity in Oude may be briefly told in this place—one episode in the great history of martyrdom.

Among those who escaped from the great massacre at Seetapore were Sir Mountstuart Jackson, a young covenanted civilian, and his two sisters—Georgiana and Madeline Jackson.* The personal attractions and engaging manners of these young people had won all hearts; and there were none whose fates, in this dreadful crisis in Oude, were invested with a wider and deeper interest from one end of the province to the other. In the confusion of the flight, the sisters were separated, and Madeline Jackson alone went with her brother. They were joined by Lieutenant Burnes of the Artillery—a young officer of great gallantry†—and by Sergeant-Major Morton, who had saved little Sophie Christian. These made their way towards Mythowlee, the estate of a " friendly Rajah," to which Captain Philip Orr had already sent his wife and child. On the morning of the 1st of June Mrs. Orr had arrived at Mythowlee, but was presently conveyed to the Fort of Kutchianee, one of those old strongholds defended by belts of jungle, in which the Oude Talookhdars had been wont to resist the authority of the King's officers. It was described as "a most dreary, desolate-looking building, devoid of the most common articles of furniture, and presenting a picture of the utmost discomfiture." In this wretched place Mrs. Orr was joined by her husband, who came in on the 5th of June—worn and weary, his clothes tattered and travel-stained, and with the blood of his

* Children of Sir Keith Jackson, and nephew and nieces of Mr. Colverley Jackson, who had been the first Chief Commissioner of Oude.

† He was son of Dr. Burnes, one of our earliest Scinde diplomatists —and nephew of Sir Alexander Burnes.

murdered comrades still upon them.* Their sojourn
in this inhospitable abode was but brief. They were
soon sent forth into the more inhospitable jungle.
Mountstuart Jackson and his party had arrived, and
their custodian alleged that, as the mutineers were
approaching, he could not conceal so large a party
of Europeans. So the Orrs went forth into the
howling wilderness. There they had scanty food
and little or no shelter; for if they had sought the
shades of the forest the tigers would have been upon
them; and at night they were compelled to burn fires
in an open space to keep the beasts of prey at a distance from them.

Meanwhile, the other party of Seetapore fugitives
were received into the Kutchianee Fort. They had
gone first to Mythowlee to claim the hospitality of
Loonee Singh, but had been refused admittance.
Burnes, however, would not be denied, and ere the
gate was closed, pushed through, weak and weary as
he was, and gained an entrance, to plead the cause of
his fellow fugitives. A blow on the head from one
of the Rajah's people covered him with blood; and
in this plight Loonee Singh took compassion on him,
and ordered him and his companions to be received
into the Fort. But the hospitality afforded to them
was of the most grudging kind. Sorely distressed as
they were—wanting everything and altogether in
evil plight—they were sent to herd in a wretched
cowshed,† and next day were despatched to the
gloomy fortress of Kutchianee.

* See the very interesting account   † Mr. Wylie's Narrative says :
of the "English Captives in Oude,"   "Their condition was sad, indeed,
compiled from the best sources of   completely worn out, as they were,
information by Captain Patrick Orr's by fatigue, their clothes in tatters,
brother. But Captain P. Orr says   without any shoes, and their feet
that the mutineers "let him have a   lacerated by the thorns of the jungle
horse and a few clothes" to help him through which they had passed."
on to Mythowlee.

There, after awhile, the bands of mutineers, who had been hovering about the neighbourhood, having dispersed themselves, the Orrs were again recalled to the Fort. There for some time the whole party dwelt together, hearing from all quarters evil tidings of the success of mutiny and rebellion, and of the sufferings of their fellow-countrymen. One only gleam of sunshine broke through the darkness. News came that Georgiana Jackson, whom her brother and sister had mourned as dead, was alive, but in captivity. And thus miserably passed the time from week to week and from month to month, till all spirit and all hope died within them, and they looked despairingly into one another's faces and said little, for there was no comfort to be interchanged. And thus June passed away and July passed away, and still there was no sign of deliverance. For a little while there was some reasonable expectation that a friend might be found for them in the depths of their sorrow; for the Wakeel of Loonee Singh of Mythowlee owed everything to Patrick Orr, who had raised this man—Zuhoor-ool-Hussun by name—from poverty to wealth by his good offices, and he had hoped that the kindness he had shown him might be returned. But the Wakeel never raised a hand or spoke a word to alleviate the sufferings of his patron, or of those who suffered with him ; and after a little while it appeared that the passive friend had become the active enemy of the English captives.

August came, and again there was a rumour of the coming of some detachments of rebel troops, and again the English captives were sent out into the jungle under a lying pretence that they would be safer there than in the Fort. But scarcely had they been driven out into the wilderness, when the Rajah sent a messenger to our enemies to tell them where

our people were to be found. It was plainly the
design to betray them; but the insurgents never entered the jungle. The cause of their forbearance is not easily explained.* But the result was that the fugitives were left unmolested. Perhaps it was thought that exposure to the sun, the rain, and the wild beasts of the jungle would soon do its work on the white people, and that death would come slowly and painfully, but not less surely, upon them. But death did not come upon them in the jungle, though all that makes life, as health and hope, was crushed out of them. They saw each other drooping day by day, or, as time went on, prostrated by jungle-fever, that left them weaker than before, and returned again and again to rack them. From the 6th of August to the 25th of October, they endured these torments; and then they were ordered to prepare for their departure, none knew whither, under a guard of the people of the Rajah of Mythowlee. Their preparations were very slender—for, in truth, they had nothing to take with them. They had no covering for their heads; no covering for their feet; scarcely any covering for their bodies, except some miserable rags. And when they tried to take with them an old sheet or some scraps of cloth, much prized in their pitiable state, the boon was brutally refused with blows.†

* The Orr Narrative, already quoted, says: "Will it be believed that two hundred and fifty men were actually afraid to accomplish the mission on which they were sent. They were actually afraid to encounter our small party, expecting a desperate resistance. Such was the report of the Passee—a report subsequently verified by the result, for the troops returned empty-handed to Lucknow, not having dared to penetrate the dreaded jungle, notwithstanding all the remonstrances of the Rajah." I can-

not say, however, that I am quite prepared to accept this view of the case.

† "Sergeant-Major Morton begged permission to take with him a piece of cloth which had served as a carpet, but was refused. Mrs. Orr had also wished to carry away a sheet with which to cover her head, as well as that of her daughter, but one of the cowardly ruffians accompanied the refusal with a blow, which felled her to the ground."—*The Orr Narrative. Edited by Macleod Wylie.*

Weak and fever-stricken, they were dragged out of the jungle, and on the roadside two of the common carts of the country were waiting for them. On these they were huddled together, and then they set forth on their nameless journey.

But the measure of their humiliation was not yet full. In a village through which they passed, preparations had been made by Zuhoor-ool-Hussun, who had now himself appeared upon the scene, to send the male prisoners forward in chains. . Perhaps it was in bitter remembrance of what had been done by us at Meerut that this last indignity was put upon our people. But whatever the secret cause in the eyes of our persecutors, it was a terrible success. It well-nigh killed one of the captives, and it crazed the brain of another.* It is significantly stated that the ingenious malice of Zuhoor-ool-Hussun reserved the heaviest pair of fetters for his patron; and, although Mrs. Orr went down on her knees to him, she was answered only by a brutal outburst of laughter.

The captives carried to Lucknow. It was soon apparent that their destination was Lucknow. On they went, a hundred and fifty men and a gun in front of them—a hundred and fifty men and a gun in rear of them. In the villages through which they passed they were made a show to be gazed at and to be mocked by the people. Their food, scanty and nauseous, was thrown to them, as if they had been dogs. Water was given to them grudgingly, or not at all. Nothing was omitted

---

* "At this gross indignity the mind of poor Burnes received a shock from which it never recovered. Sergeant-Major Morton, at the sight of the fetters, fell into a frightful convulsive fit, from which with difficulty he recovered under the attentions that could be paid to him by his fellow-captives. Death at one time seemed ready to terminate his sufferings."—*The Orr Narrative, ut supra.*

that could enhance their agonies both of body and of
mind. And ever as they went on their dreary six days' journey, there was a vague terror upon the captives of what lay before them at Lucknow. As they neared the capital, which was still in possession of the insurgents, a swarm of troops, both Horse and Foot, came out to meet them. The order was that the captives should be taken to the Kaiser-bagh, one of the old palaces of the kings, in which the enemy had a strong position. At a little distance from this place they were made to leave the clumsy vehicles on which they had sat, and to walk, or rather to stagger, through the streets, gazed at by an insolent crowd, which pressed upon them, rejoicing in their humiliation. It was, indeed, a ghastly procession. Orr carried his little daughter in his arms; Burnes carried Sophie Christian; Mountstuart Jackson was so reduced by fever and ague, that he could scarcely crawl to his new prison-house, and he had no sooner entered it than he fell down in a swoon. How the two poor English gentlewomen bore up against such trials it is hard to conceive. It is related that in the agonies of their thirst they shrieked for water, and that when at last their prayer was granted, it was brought to them "in such a vile vessel, that the ladies refused to pollute their lips by touching it."

Here, then, in a small apartment of the Kaiser- In the Kaiser-bagh. bagh the prisoners lay for some weeks. Literally, it may be said that they died daily—for they felt that each hour might be their last. The miserable plight in which they had left the jungle was now greatly aggravated. The men were emaciated and enfeebled both in body and in mind; the women, whose patient courage proved them to be true Christian heroines, tried to bear up bravely, for the

sake of those they loved ; but well-nigh everything
most revolting to an English gentlewoman was present to distress them. Their clothes were in rags.
They had no appliances of personal cleanliness. That
which has been said to be the glory of a woman had
now become her shame.* The only comfort that
came to them in their tribulation came from the
Word of God. They had not a Bible among them ;
but one day, whilst in the Kaiser-bagh, Mrs. Orr
sent for some Native medicines, and they were
brought to her wrapped up in a piece of printed
paper, which proved to be part of a leaf of the Book
of Isaiah. And the message, which came to them
through Mahomedan hands, was this :

" *They shall obtain gladness and joy; and sorrow
and mourning shall flee away. I, even I, am he that
comforteth you; who art thou that thou shouldst be
afraid of a man that shall die, and of the son of man
that shall be made as grass ; and forgettest the Lord thy
Maker, that hath stretched forth the heavens and laid the
foundations of the earth; and hast feared continually
every day because of the fury of the oppressor, as if he
were ready to destroy? and where is the fury of the
oppressor ? The captive exile hasteneth that he may be
loosed, and that he should not die in the pit, nor
that . . . ."†*

And the words of love, thus strangely and myste-
riously sent to them, comforted and strengthened
them in the midst of their sorrow. It seemed like a

---

* " Their clothes even in the
jungles had already been in tatters ;
they were now completely in rags ;
their hair was completely matted,
deprived as they had long had been
of combs and brushes."—*Orr Narrative.*

† Isaiah, chap. li., verses 11—14.
The paper was torn off before the
completion of the last verse. The
words are, " nor that his bread
should fail,"

promise of deliverance; and it was so—but only in part.

For, not long afterwards, the malice of the enemy discharged itself upon our persecuted people in a manner which it is terrible to contemplate. On the morning of the 16th November a party. of the Seventy-first Sepoy Regiment, fully armed and equipped, entered the dwelling-place of the captives, and said that they were bidden to take the gentlemen away. With difficulty, in their debilitated state, Jackson and Orr rose from their recumbent position, took a sad and solemn farewell of those who were so near and dear to them, and then with their comrades Burnes and Moreton, calmly suffered themselves to be bound. A rattle of musketry was presently heard; and although the gaolers assured our affrighted gentlewomen that it portended only the execution of some Native prisoners, the terrible truth soon became apparent to them. Our women and children had lost their protectors. Husband, brother, and guardians had been ruthlessly murdered, and the last state of desolation had come upon these poor helpless ones. A few days after this butchery another of the captives was delivered by death. Little Sophie Christian, who had for some time been reduced to an extremity of weakness by the ravages of disease, faded away so gently that those about her scarcely knew the time of her deliverance.* The prisoners in the Kaiser-bagh were now reduced to two

1857.
November.

Murder of
Jackson, Orr,
Burnes, and
Moreton.

---

* "Death passed his hand gently over her; her beautiful blue eyes closed as if in gentle repose, and before her companions were aware of the change her infant spirit had fled for ever from the scenes of danger and misery. Through the kindness of a man of the guard, himself the father of a large family, Mrs. Orr and Miss Jackson had the melancholy satisfaction of knowing that during the dark hours of the ensuing night the remains of the poor little orphan were carefully confided to the earth."—*Macleod Wylie—The Orr Narrative.*

women and one child; and such was the insignificance of the party in the estimation of the enemy, that this wretched remnant of the captive band had well-nigh perished from neglect. But time went on, drearily and sadly, until the year wore to a close, and still they lived and prayed and suffered; and great events occurred around them, of which they heard the fearful sounds in the almost incessant roar of the guns, and sometimes the crashing noise which told that the destructive missiles were falling closely around them. Of what all this portended they had but a dim notion, for the information which reached them was either wholly false, or distorted and exaggerated to our disadvantage; but so far as these poor women could understand their miserable environments, it appeared to them that whether the British or the Oude Government should be eventually triumphant, there was equally little prospect of their escape.

Then, whilst they ceased to hope for their own safety, and resigned themselves with Christian patience to whatsoever might be the will of God, their tender hearts were torn by the thought of what might be the fate of the little child who shared their captivity. So they resolved that they would endeavour to effect its deliverance, and cast about in their minds how this might best be accomplished. Among those who guarded them, or had influence over the guardians, were one or two less stern and cruel than the rest. One, indeed, had been their friend from the first of their captivity in the Kaiser-bagh. His name was Wajid Ali, and he was a Darogah of the Native Government. Counsel was now taken with him as to the best means of saving the child. The sympathies of a Native woman—a resident of Lucknow—were enlisted in favour of the child and her mother; and one day, after some earlier schemes had failed, the deliverance was accomplished. They stained the hands and the feet of the little girl so as to resemble those of a Native child, and the woman who was acting this good part wrapped her in a sheet, and with well-simulated weepings and lamentations carried out the precious burden as though she were taking the body of her own little one to burial, and thus eluded the vigilance of the guards. The little captive was taken to the house of Maun Singh, and after some days was conveyed in safety to the British camp in the Alum-bagh.

Then, after this, to the two who were left there was a season of weary suspense. Although British arms had been triumphant on every great occasion of conflict, the enemy still held positions in parts of the city and the suburbs, and might any day sweep in upon them with murderous intent. But Wajid Ali was still true to them, and when it was seen that the Kaiser-bagh was no longer safe, under the vigorous bombardment to which it was now subjected, he placed them in a palanquin, and, not without difficulty, conveyed them to another abode. But this was not beyond the reach of danger, so a second departure became necessary, and now they were housed beneath the same roof as Wajid Ali's wife and children, safe from the fire of our guns, but not secure against the assaults of the enemy. It was feared that the malice of the Moulavee would bring destruction upon them. Renewed exertions were, therefore, to be made to open communications with our people, so Mrs. Orr wrote a letter, to be delivered to the first British officer that could be found, and it was intrusted to the care of the brother-in-law of

Wajid Ali.   Providence favoured the effort.   For he had scarcely started when he came upon a detachment of the Goorkah force, accompanied by two English officers.   These were Captain M'Neill and Lieutenant Bogle, of the Artillery.   To read the letter was to grasp the suggestion of immediate action.   They hastened to the house where the captives dwelt, seized a palanquin, placed the Englishwomen in it, improvised a set of bearers from the ever-ready Goorkahs, and under charge of Captain M'Neill were carried through the narrow, tortuous streets, till the welcome sight of General Macgregor's camp at last assured them that they were safe, and soon in a tent pitched for them by the General, where all they needed was supplied to them.   They thanked God for their merciful deliverance.   Next day they were passed on to the camp of Sir James Outram.

CHAPTER III.

LUCKNOW IN JUNE—SIR HENRY LAWRENCE—HIS FAILING HEALTH—
MARTIN GUBBINS—NOMINATION OF A SUCCESSOR—PREPARATIONS AGAINST
A SIEGE—THE DISASTERS OF CHINHUT—DESTRUCTION OF THE MUTCHEE-
BHAUN—COMMENCEMENT OF THE SIEGE—DEATH OF HENRY LAWRENCE.

ALL these terrible disasters lacerated the heart of Henry Lawrence. He bore up as bravely as he could. But from the very commencement of his employment in Oude he had been in an infirm state of health. He had, indeed, as I have already shown,* intended to visit England in the early part of the year. The summons to Lucknow acted as a stimulant upon him; but stimulants are short-lived in their effects. As the month of June wore on everything around him had a depressing influence upon his exhausted frame and his sensitive mind. It was the worst season of the year. The removal from the Cantonment to the city made the June heats more oppressive to him. He was one who would never willingly spare himself, so long as he had any power of muscular exertion, or any capacity of clear thought. He went about from post to post at all hours, seeing everything with his own eyes, inquiring, examining, directing. His seat had

1857.
June.

* Vol. i. page 450.

been on the saddle; it was now on the cushions of his carriage. But the directing power was still the same. Outward action is good for the suppression of inward thought; and perhaps it sustained Lawrence for a time. And there was something that sustained him more—sustained him throughout all his trials—an abounding faith in the goodness of God and the efficacy of prayer. Often was he found upon his knees, by those who entered his room to convey information or to solicit instruction. Thus strengthened, he felt that the great deliverance would come, though he might not live to see it.

Martin Gubbins.

But it was obvious to those around him that he was growing feebler and feebler in body every day, and there was one man in the garrison, who believed, or pretended to believe, that he was growing feebler in mind. This was Mr. Martin Gubbins, the Financial Commissioner.* He was endowed with a high order of genius, nearly allied to madness. It was impossible not to recognise his great intellectual† qualities, as well as his consummate personal bravery; but his intellect was of an impulsive, an erratic character, such as to worry a chief, with all the responsibilities of the situation cast upon him. A man who, being second, thinks that he ought to be first, is a thorn in the flesh of him who has the supreme command. Martin Gubbins was such a

---

* See the following extract of a letter to Lord Canning: "You sent us a noble-hearted soldier as chief. And with him all promised well until it pleased God to send us this dire calamity. But Sir Henry Lawrence came to us attenuated and weak; and the severe mental anxiety which he has undergone has prostrated him greatly. Sir Henry Lawrence is no longer, I think, firm, nor his mental vision clear. How long, with little sleep, much anxiety, and overwork, any of us will retain clearness of judgment, who can tell?" —*Mr. Martin Gubbins to Lord Canning, June* 2, 1857. *MS. Correspondence.*

† I may say here that he visited me often (I think in 1858), and that I was greatly impressed by his intellectual attainments.

man. He was never quiet. He was never happy
unless he was in opposition. It might have been
said of him, in imitation of what was said of John
Lilburne, that, if he had been the only man left in
Lucknow, Martin would have quarrelled with Gubbins,
and Gubbins would have quarrelled with Martin.
He saw Lawrence fading away, and he hungered for
the empty chair. The Chief Commissioner knew it,
but he knew also that there was no man in the garrison more unfit to have supreme control. So he
telegraphed on the 4th of June to the Governor-
General, saying: " If anything happens to me during
" present disturbances, I earnestly recommend that
" Major Banks succeed me as Chief Commissioner, and
" Colonel Inglis in command of the troops, until better
" times arrive. This is no time for punctilio as regards
" seniority. They are the right men—in fact, the only
" men for the places. My Secretary entirely concurs
" with me on the above points."* He had at an earlier
hour of the same day drawn up a memorandum† in
other words, and more limited in its significance.
" If anything happens to me during present dis-
" turbances, I recommend that Colonel Inglis succeed
" me in command, and that Major Banks be appointed
" to the command of one of the posts. There should
" be *No Surrender*. I commend my children and the
" Lawrence Asylum to Government." It is obvious
that he had not then fully resolved to recommend
Banks as his successor in the Chief Commissionership.
It seems to have been an after-thought, or perhaps

1857.
June.

Major Banks.

* This is copied from a draft in
the handwriting of Sir George
Couper, and signed by Sir Henry
Lawrence.
† I take this from a copy in the
handwriting of Mr. A. Lawrence.

It does not seem to have been intended for a telegram, but as a
memorandum, in the event of his
death, to be read by his Staff and
communicated to Government.

1857.
June.

it was the result of a conference with his sagacious Secretary.

But from whatsoever source the recommendation proceeded, it was a wise and politic one. Major Banks was the Commissioner of the Lucknow Division. A little time before he had been one of Lord Dalhousie's most trusted officers. He was Military Secretary to that great statesman, then heavy with thought of the coming annexation of Oude. In the summer of 1856, the Governor-General was on a visit to the Neilgherry Hills. Thence in the month of June he despatched to the Home Government his exhaustive minute on the vast and still-increasing evils of Native misrule in Oude, and the duty of British interference. Nothing could be done until the decision of the Court of Directors should be communicated to him, but in the meanwhile it was expedient to make secret preparations for the deposition of the reigning prince and the extinction of the existing Government. To this end it was necessary, in the first instance, that a confidential officer should be despatched to Oude, to communicate with General Outram, our Resident at Lucknow, firstly, with regard to "the military preparations that might be necessary ; and, secondly, to the civil arrangements which might be subsequently required." For this important duty Major Banks was selected. He received his instructions on the 19th of July, and started on the following day for Calcutta, there to communicate with the President in Council, and afterwards to join Outram in Lucknow. He was a discreet and sagacious man ; but still it was Lord Dalhousie's duty to enjoin absolute secrecy.* Banks

* "And as it will be obvious to   Honourable Court shall have been
you that until the order of the   received, entire secrecy should be

did his work well to the absolute satisfaction of the
Governor - General, whose former high opinion,
evinced by the trust reposed in him, was greatly increased by the manner of its discharge. And not only
did the Governor-General entertain respect for his
Secretary; he felt a tender affection for him as a man.
All the softness of Dalhousie's nature was expressed
when he wrote to Banks and his wife. When, therefore, the great project for the extinction of the Native
dynasty in Oude had received the assent of the
Home Government, and the scheme of British administration had been prepared, it was certain that the
man who had been second only to Outram as a
pioneer of the great change, should have awarded to
him a place in the Government of the newly-acquired
province. He was appointed Commissioner of the
most important division into which the province was
partitioned—the Division of Lucknow—and being
therefore at the Head-Quarters of the Government in
constant communication with the Chief Commissioner, he soon won the good opinion of his chief,
who recognised in him a great combination of pru-
dence, sagacity, firmness, and courage. So Banks.
obtained, to his exceeding honour, the reversion of
the Chief-Commissionership of Oude.

This done, Lawrence felt great mental relief; but The Provi-
the physical weakness was increasing upon him, and sional Council.
he was at last persuaded by Dr. Fayrer—one of the

observed in the preparation of measures which the Government may
not, after all, be authorised to execute, you are requested to observe
absolute silence as to the duty on
which you are employed. Here and
at Calcutta, it will be a sufficient
answer to all curious inquirers, that
you are employed by the Governor-
General on public business, as to
which nobody has any business to
ask questions. Your departure from
Calcutta may be managed without
any one being aware of it. Surmises and suspicions of course cannot be prevented; but no communication for the purpose of your journey need be made except to those
already mentioned in this memorandum."—*MS. Document.*

brightest ornaments of the Indian medical service —
to take a few days of rest. He very reluctantly consented to make over the command, and appointed
a Provisional Council, consisting of Mr. Gubbins,
Mr. Ommaney, Colonel Inglis, Major Banks, and
Major Anderson. But only for two or three days
could Lawrence be induced to rest.* The strong
spirit asserted itself again; and a certificate was
wrung from Fayrer permitting him to return to his
work, on condition that he would spare himself as
much as was possible. But it was not possible for
him to spare himself. The eagerness of his nature
forebade him to cease from labour; his deep love for
his fellow-men would not suffer him to rest, so long
as he thought that he could do anything for them.

The brief interregnum had not been an uneventful
one. Gubbins had attempted a "coup" and failed.
He had tried, whilst at the head of the Provisional
Council, to eliminate the Poorbeah element wholly
from the garrison of Lucknow. He had recommended, from the first, the disarming of the Sepoy
regiments—but Lawrence had consistently opposed
the measure. As chief of the Provisional Council,
he now thought that he might carry out this che-

---

* " It was on the 9th of June that Lawrence appointed this Council. The order ran thus: 'As Dr. Fayrer states that it is imperatively necessary for my health that I should remain perfectly quiet for the next twenty-four hours, I appoint Mr. Gubbins, Mr. Ommaney, Lieutenant-Colonel Inglis, Major Anderson, and Major Banks to be a council to conduct the affairs of the province until I feel myself sufficiently convalescent to resume the Government.— H. M. LAWRENCE, June 9, 1857.' The Council sat on the 10th and 11th. On the morning of the 12th, Law- rence, eager to return to his work, obtained from Dr. Fayrer a certificate, somewhat reluctantly given, to the effect that, although he was capable of resuming his duties, he should be spared as much mental and bodily fatigue as possible. Upon this Mr. Gubbins recommended that the powers of the Council should be continued, but that all important questions should be referred to the General. Against this the other four members voted, and the powers of the Council ceased."—*Lives of Indian Officers.*

rished stratagem. So he obtained the consent of commanding officers to disarm the faithful remnants of their regiments and to send them on leave to their homes. But when Lawrence, to whom everything was promptly reported, was informed of this movement, he resolved at once, as far as was possible, to counteract it. He believed in the fidelity of the Sepoys, who had clung to us through good report and evil report, and he knew that he wanted them to aid in the defence of Lucknow. So it was partly from sentiment, partly from policy, that when he rose from his sick couch and resumed the command, he sent messengers after these home-going Sepoys, and brought numbers of them, with smiling faces, back to their posts.*

The sudden collapse of the Provisional Council of which Mr. Gubbins was the head, exceedingly disconcerted the energetic financial minister. He expected a longer reign, and he found that he had been "hoist by his own petard." Thus disappointed, he tried to persuade his comrades that Lawrence's policy was feeble, that it would be wise to adopt more vigorous measures, and to strike little blows in every possible direction. Referring to this on the day after his resumption of command, Lawrence wrote to Mr. Colvin at Agra: "Mr. Gubbins is perfectly insane on what he considers energetic manly measures. His language has been so extravagant, that were he not

Opposition of Mr. Gubbins.

---

* In a highly interesting memoir, written by Colonel Wilson (the "Staff Officer," to whom also I am much indebted), and quoted by Mr. Herman Merivale in the second volume of the "Life of Sir Henry Lawrence," it is stated that they "returned with tokens of delight, the honesty of which was verified by their loyalty during the siege." Mr. Merivale, however, quotes another manuscript document, written by Captain Edgell, also a staff-officer, in which it is stated that Lawrence approved of the disarming. That Captain Edgell himself approved of the disarming is certain, for Gubbins writes he was the only officer who supported him. I find that more than two years ago I had written the version of the affair given in the text, after conversing with Colonel Wilson and Sir George Couper.

2 K 2

really useful, I should be obliged to take severe measures against him. He is the one malcontent in the
garrison. All others, I believe, are satisfied that as
much energy has been evinced as circumstances
would permit." This has never been questioned by
any other than the man against whose counsel this
protest was delivered. The true policy at this time
was to defend Lucknow, which, it was certain, would
be ere long in a state of siege. Concentration, not
dispersion, was the great object to be attained. So
all the goings-out here and there that Gubbins recommended were for a time totally ignored.

There was one of these recommendations, however,
that we are bound to respect—Gubbins thought that
assistance might be sent to Cawnpore. How, in the
midst of all the tribulation at his own door, Henry
Lawrence could still find time to consider, and sympathy to deplore, the dangers and distresses of his
brethren at a distance, his correspondence in this
month of June largely testifies. It well-nigh broke
his heart to think that he could do nothing for
Wheeler and the Cawnpore garrison, whatever their
straits might be. What these straits were he hardly
knew—so difficult was it to obtain correct information from the other side of the Ganges. "We cannot," he wrote, on the 13th, "get certain tidings
from Cawnpore, although we have sent many messengers; but we have no reason to doubt that General Wheeler still holds his ground. The mutineers
hold the river bank for many miles below and above
Cawnpore, and search all passers. They at once
seized all the boats and drew them to their own bank.
Would that we could help the besieged—but our
numbers, and the distance, and the river forbid the
thought." Three days afterwards a letter was received

from Sir Hugh Wheeler, with an imploring cry for help ; and great as was his own need Lawrence would have sent it, if he had believed that the succours could ever cross the river in safety. "Wheeler asks for two hundred Europeans," he wrote on the 16th. "I would risk the absence of so large a portion of our small force, could I see the smallest prospect of its being able to succour him. But no individual here cognisant of facts, except Mr. Gubbins, thinks we could carry a single man across the river, as the enemy holds all the boats and completely commands the river. May God Almighty defend Cawnpore, for no help can we afford!"* Those were days when all men were scrambling for the few Europeans scattered about the country—when many thought of themselves, regardless of the fate of others, and clamoured for help which could be given only by inflicting heavy cost, perhaps ruin on the helpers. It would have been a question, even if it had been possible to cross the river, whether Lawrence would have been justified in sending so large a part of his little force to Cawnpore; but with the impediment, of which he spoke, looming so largely before him, it is simply a certainty that he would have been lamentably wrong; for he would have sent all these men to destruction.

But before the month of June was at an end, an event had occurred which changed the whole com- Advance of the enemy.

---

* He repeated this in almost similar words, at a later period, saying: "There was a report that the Nana had offered to escort the Cawnpore garrison to Allahabad, and that an armistice of two days had taken place in consequence. I sincerely trust that no such proposition will be attended to, as it would result in nothing but treachery and disgrace."

plexion of affairs at Lucknow. Having received intelligence on the 29th of the month, which left no doubt that the enemy were mustering in great force, about ten or twelve miles from the capital, with intent of marching forward to attack it, Lawrence determined on the following morning to go out in strength to make a reconnoissance, and, at all events, to demonstrate that the English were still capable of action. It was not without much thought and some reluctance, that he resolved to issue orders for a movement, which his ignorance of the actual strength of the enemy seemed to render at least hazardous. The scouts had reported the strength of the insurgent force at nine regiments of Infantry, one regiment of Cavalry, and twelve guns. Mr. Gubbins laughed the estimate to scorn, and wrote "What stuff!" upon the circular which communicated the intelligence to the chief officers of the garrison. That the irrepressible ardour of the Finance Commissioner prevailed over the military circumspection of the Brigadier-General is not to be doubted.* For, weeks past, Martin Gubbins had been urging upon the military authorities the expediency of a forward movement, and had in his letters to the Governor-General and others protested against the prevailing policy of inaction. To these counsels Lawrence yielded at last; and on the morning of the 30th of June, the flower of his force went forth along the road to Chinhut, but rather as a grand military promenade than with any definite thought of meeting the enemy. It was Lawrence's intention, indeed, only to proceed, along the great high road, as far as the Kokaralee Bridge, and

---

* See a note on this subject in the Appendix. If any further evidence be required, the reader need look back to Mr. Gubbins's letter to Lord Canning previously quoted in this book.

there, if no enemy were seen, to halt the force and to return to Lucknow.

The force that assembled under arms on the last morning of June consisted of three hundred men of the Queen's Thirty-second, under Colonel Case; about two hundred Infantry Sepoys, believed to be faithful to their employers; a hundred and twenty troopers of the Oude Irregular Horse, said to have been principally Sikhs; and a noble little band of Volunteer Cavalry, with the good blood of English gentlemen in their veins. Four guns of a light field battery (Europeans), and six guns of the Oude Native Artillery, with an eight-inch howitzer drawn by an elephant, were equipped to accompany the Force—in all about seven hundred men, one-half of whom were Natives. Sir Henry Lawrence took command of the whole.*

The morning was intensely hot; and the march was towards the rising sun. As often happens, some of the Europeans were in that unhinged, shaky condition with which the morning revenges itself on the constitution for the excesses of the preceding night, and nearly all were exhausted with much watching and work.† There are only two things in such a case that can restore the balance of outraged nature—time and

---

* See Brigadier Inglis's report, from which I have taken the details in the text; but the Staff Officer, a most reliable authority, speaks only of "a hundred and fifty of the Thirty-second from the Mutchee-Bahwun." I conclude that this is merely an accidental omission of those from the cantonment. The Staff Officer says that the howitzer was drawn by "*two* elephants;" Sir George Couper and Dr. Fayrer say by *one*. The point is of little importance except as illustrative of the difficulty of ascertaining the exact truth in respect of military details.

† An eye-witness writes to me: "They were worn out with the excessive labour which had been imposed on them in being under arms all day and all night for some weeks. I remarked to Lawrence as they stood on the Iron Bridge, just as the sun was rising and the word to move on was given, that they looked more like men who had just come off a hard day's work than just starting on one. It is certain they got nothing before starting."

further potations. But the stimulant of the morning dram was not served out to the men, and they marched out of Lucknow, for the most part, languid and dispirited, and with little heart for the work before them. Some dropped by the way. Others drooped, but toiled on. It was no thought of the enemy that caused them to flag. For there was a general feeling in the Force that, few as they were in numbers, they were more than a match for any multitude of the enemy that could be brought against them.

Thus the Force marched on to the Kokaralee Bridge, at which point the efforts of the skilled road-makers had ceased, and the onward route was loose and uneven, and muddy with much rain. Here the British Force was halted. No sign of an enemy had been seen ; and it was thought that the order would be given for the countermarch to Lucknow. Weary and thirsty, the men looked around for something to refresh them ; but there was nothing more supporting for the Europeans than the water in the leather-bags of the bheestees. They were in no mood to go further, on that hot June morning, and joyfully they stood with their faces towards Lucknow. But suddenly the order was issued for an advance to Chinhut.* So the regiments were again countermarched. Lawrence had placed himself at the head of the Force, and was bent on a further reconnoissance. So they struggled along the rugged causeway, and, about nine o'clock, they were approaching the village of Ishmael-gunj. Then it became clear that they were at no great distance from the main body of the insurgent army. Their round-shot were pouring

The battle of Chinhut.

* Captain Wilson, Assistant-Adjutant-General, was sent with this order to Colonel Inglis.

into our columns. So Lawrence drew up his troops. The Thirty-second lay in a hollow to the left of the road; in the centre, under charge of Bonham of the Bengal Artillery, the great howitzer was posted; to the right, a little in advance of the heavy ordnance, were the light European guns—and still further to the right the Irregular Cavalry and the Volunteers. For a little while there was a dubious conflict of artillery. The shells from the howitzer were sent bursting into the enemy's camp; and a continual stream of round-shot was poured in from our light batteries, but at too great a range to do much mischief in the ranks of the mutineers. To the fire of the British guns the enemy responded with "beautiful precision." But the battle was not to be fought in this way. After a brief lull, which made our people think that the mutineers were retiring, they were seen to extend themselves out, in both directions, Cavalry, Infantry, and Artillery, as though to outflank us both on the right and on the left. Then, for the first time, the British leaders knew with what they had to contend. The plain between Ishmaelgunj and Chinhut was one "moving mass of men." Steadily and compactly, as though on a field-day under a general of division, the Sepoy regiments, flaunting their standards, advanced to the attack.* Our field-pieces opened on their columns, but with little effect, and soon the battle became a rout.

It was, indeed, impossible to resist the rush of the

1857.
June 30.

---

* The following is from the very graphic account of an eye-witness, Mr. Lawrence, of the Civil Service, who was serving with the Volunteer Horse: "Regiment after regiment of the insurgents poured steadily towards us, the flanks covered with a foam of skirmishers, the light puffs of smoke from their muskets floating from every ravine and bunch of grass in our front. As to the mass of troops, they came on in quarter-distance columns, the standards waving in their places, and everything performed as steadily as possible. A field-day on parade could not have been better."—*Rees's Siege of Lucknow.*

swarming enemy. Miserably over-matched as we were, the main hope of our little party of British troops had been in their guns. But, unhappily, the greater number of our field-pieces were manned by Native artillerymen; and their treachery broke out in the hour of our sorest need. Some of the black gunners cut their traces and went off with the horses, over-turning the guns upon the field;* whilst the Native Cavalry turned and fled with all speed along the Lucknow Road. We had now only the companies of the Thirty-second, a few English gunners, and the Volunteer Cavalry, upon whom the General could rely to stem the onslaught of the insurgent multitude. The enemy had gained possession of the village of Ishmael-gunj, and were pouring a deadly fire of grape and musketry into our distressed people. Then came the time to storm the village. But it was a forlorn hope. The Colonel was shot down, and two of his officers fell mortally wounded beneath the dreadful fire of the enemy. Seeing this, the men of the Thirty-second, weary, dispirited, and weak for want of sustenance, who had been lying down in a hollow, rose up and fell back.† And the Native Infantry detachments, faithful among the faithless, posted on the right of the British Force, gave back a brisk shower of musket-balls in answer to the musketry of their countrymen.

But it was useless to maintain the unequal conflict. The enemy, having outflanked us, were endeavouring

---

* The current statement that all the Oude guns were so served, must be accepted with some limitation. I believe that only a part of the battery was served in this manner. One unpublished statement says that only two of the six guns were over-turned. Sir George Couper saw Captain Wilson (the "Staff Officer") spike two of them—the carriages of which were not overturned. Wilson did the work with the end of a bayonet.

† One highly credible informant assures me that they did not fire a shot.

to surround our little Force; and had they hemmed
us in on all sides, it would have been a merciful—a
miraculous deliverance, if a single man had escaped.
So Lawrence gave the orders for a retreat. It was a
disastrous, but not wholly an inglorious one. To
save the guns and the wounded was not possible in
the face of such overwhelming numbers. Three field-
pieces of the Oude Battery and the heavy howitzer,
in spite of all Bonham's heroic efforts, were left in the
hands of the enemy.* And many wounded men were
left helpless on the field to die where they had fallen,
or to be cut to pieces.

Among these was Colonel Case, who lay, with open
eyes, grasping his faithful sword in the agony of
death. Captain Bassano, who had sought for his
fallen leader among the dead and the dying, had endeavoured to remove him, and had proposed to bring
some of the men of his regiment to his aid. But the
wounded soldier had rejected all offers of assistance,
and when pressed further by his friend, had reminded
him, with a chivalry worthy of the dying Sydney,

Death of
Colonel Case.

---

* The conspicuous gallantry of
Lieutenant Bonham on this occasion
deserves more than this passing
notice. I cannot better repair the
omission in the text than by giving
the following details from Mr. Gubbins's "Mutinies in Oudh:" "The
European artillery limbered up and
went to the rear; and Sir Henry
Lawrence ordered Lieutenant Bonham to retire with the 8-inch
howitzer. Unfortunately, the elephant which was attached to the
limber had got frightened when the
firing began, and had run off with
it. Spare bullocks had been brought
out to meet such an accident, but
the frightened drivers had let them
loose. Lieutenant Bonham seized
the limber of a waggon, and mounting on the leading horse brought it
up to the howitzer. Dismounting,
however, to attach the limber to the
gun, the native riders galloped off
with it. At this time Captain Hardinge brought up the proper limber
with the elephant; but the animal
was so restless under fire that the
utmost exertions of the untrained
gunners failed to attach the trail of
the howitzer to the limber. The
enemy was pressing on, taking advantage of every break in the ground
and of every cover to pour in a
murderous fire of musketry. A
bullet struck Lieutenant Bonham,
who was carried off and put upon a
limber, and the howitzer was abandoned. At this time many of the
artillery-drivers detached their horses
from the guns and ammunition-
waggons and took to flight."

1857.
June 30.

that he was still commanding officer, and had gasped out his last orders by telling Bassano to rejoin his corps. A loving, tender-hearted woman was waiting for his return to the Residency, but the soldier was stronger than the husband in that awful crisis, and he would not take a man from his duty. He was a true-hearted, fine-tempered, English gentleman, of a genial nature, beloved by all who knew him; and there were few better soldiers in our camp.

Sir Henry Lawrence had been forward in the fight. He had moved from point to point unharmed amidst the thick fire of the enemy, and by his side his Secretary, George Couper, sinking the scribe in the soldier, had ridden on the battle-field as the aide-de-camp of his chief. In the crisis of the action, when the Thirty-second were falling fast and the activity of the enemy was at its height, Lawrence brought up a nine-pounder, and, though well knowing that there was not a shot in the tumbril, ordered the artillery-men to serve the gun and to light port-fire. By this timely display of fictitious strength he held the insurgents in check, until the Thirty-second had retired. The excitement of the action over, his physical weakness asserted itself, but the strong will sustained him nobly.* He had ordered out his carriage to meet him, intending, after the reconnoissance, to return in it to Lucknow; but the horses were needed for the guns: so he kept his saddle to the last, and rode on towards Lucknow.† He had been in the

* I am assured that the statement, so often repeated, that Sir Henry Lawrence, at the Kokralee Bridge, exclaimed, in great anguish of mind : "My God! my God! and I brought them to this!" is a pure invention.

† A different statement to this has been erroneously made, and, I am sorry to say, that in a former work I helped to give it currency. It was said that, after the battle of Chinhut, Lawrence was brought home on a gun-carriage. But Sir George Couper, an undeniable authority, assures me that the General

rear, endeavouring to animate the Thirty-second,   1857.
until he reached a narrow lane leading straight to   June 30.
the Iron Bridge. He then asked Inglis if he thought
he might make a short cut to the Residency without
detriment to his reputation as a soldier, to prepare the
people there for what was coming and make the necessary arrangements. Inglis answered that in his opinion
no possible blame could fall upon the General; so
Lawrence left him in command, and accompanied by
Wilson and George Couper galloped into the Residency—but they did not anticipate the head of the
retreating column by more than a quarter of an
hour.

At the Kokaralee Bridge, the scene of the morn- The retreat.
ing's halt, a large party of the enemy's Horse, having
doubled round our rear, had taken post with the object of cutting off our retreat. At first they were
taken for our own Cavalry, and all offensive movements against them were stayed. But when the
truth was apparent, Radcliffe's little body of Mounted
Volunteers went at them with triumphant audacity
and swept away the obstruction. Never was a nobler
charge of British horsemen against more tremendous
odds. Some thirty-five or forty sabres flashed in the
morning sun, as Radcliffe's loud, clear voice gave out
the stirring order, followed by that trumpet-note
which is dearest to the heroic heart. The enemy did

"rode on horseback every yard of the
way" to Lucknow. This is another
curious instance of the manner in
which error is circulated, and may
be perpetuated. In Captain Hutchinson's "Narrative of Events in Oude,"
which may be regarded as an official
document, an account of the Chinhut affair is given, as an extract
from the report of Brigadier Inglis.
In this it is stated that "Sir Henry

himself returned on a gun-carriage."
But on consulting the work again,
and comparing the passage with au-
thenticated versions of Inglis's report, I find that only a portion of
Hutchinson's narrative is derived
from that source—the latter part of
the extract being derived from some
private statement, though printed as
part of the official document.

not stand to bear the shock, but fled with their five hundred troopers and two field-guns to cover them.* Nor did the services of the Volunteers on that June morning end with that glorious exploit. It was theirs all along the road to cover the retreat of our Infantry as they fell back upon Lucknow. The heat was excessive; and our men, exhausted and parched with thirst, could scarcely drag their weary limbs along the road. Some jostled for seats on the limbers of the guns and waggons which had been saved; others sought a little help by holding on to the stirrup-leathers of the Volunteers. The water-carriers had deserted, and all sustenance was far from them. Indeed, they were in piteous plight. The insurgent Cavalry were following them—nay, sometimes getting a-head of them, and our wretched people had to fight their way against dreadful odds to the capital. Everything was against them. Even the muskets of the Thirty-second were so foul, that cap after cap exploded to no purpose upon the hammer, and men at last gave up discharging their pieces in despair.†

Weak as we were in European troops, this was a tremendous disaster. A hundred and nineteen of our little body of English soldiers had been struck down by the fire of the enemy or the fierce heat of the morning sun. All further possibility of offensive movements was now gone; and even bare defence was difficult against such odds. The insurgents

* See Mr. Lawrence's "Narrative," quoted by Mr. Rees.

† This is stated by Gubbins (page 212), but another informant assures me that: "They never tried. At least I never saw them, although I heard their officers imploring them to stand and return the enemy's fire." Gubbins refers to the retreat—not to the action at Chinhut—but the pieces must have been foul, when the regiment started, if at all.

came streaming on to the banks of the Goomtee, and as our people entered the Residency, fast and fierce came the round shot from the rebel guns. To those who had remained in Lucknow, whilst this unhappy expedition was in progress, and especially to the Englishwomen in the Residency, who watched the return of our beaten troops from its windows,* the moment was one of intense anxiety. The vast assemblage of the enemy could be clearly seen on the opposite bank of the river. In a little while they might swarm into the city. The Iron Bridge was commanded by the guns of the Redan Battery and the Stone Bridge by the fire from the Mutchee Bhawun.† But there were other means of crossing the river, and it was soon seen that whilst some were planting their batteries on the opposite bank, others were collecting boats lower down for the passage of the Goomtee. Before noon they had invested our positions. The streets were deserted by the people. Contemporary writers describe the aspect of Lucknow as that of a great " city of the silent"—the silence broken only by the boom of the cannon and the rattle of the musketry. The hum of voices and the clatter of wheeled vehicles were gone—and in their place was the roar of the battle. The audacity of the enemy was superb. The passage of the river accomplished, the mutineers speedily occupied the houses, in the most command-

1857.
June 30.

---

* Take as an illustration the following from Lady Inglis's journal. It should be premised that the writer was at the time suffering under the infliction of small-pox. "You may imagine our feelings of anxiety and consternation. I posted myself and watched the poor men coming in; a melancholy spectacle, indeed—no order, one after the other; some riding; some wounded, supported by their comrades; some on guns; some fell down and died from exhaustion not half a mile from our position. The enemy followed them to the bridge close to the Residency, which was defended by a company of the Thirty-second under Mr. Edmonstone, a gallant young officer. I could see the smoke of the musketry and plainly discerned the enemy on the opposite bank of the river."

† Gubbins, p. 215.

ing positions, near the Residency and the Mutchee-
Bhawun, and loopholing them in the most effective
manner, poured in upon us a tremendous shower of
musketry that never slackened, day or night.[*]

In this conjuncture it was one of Sir Henry Law-
rence's first thoughts to send off an express to Mr.
Tucker at Benares, inclosing a note to Brigadier
Havelock, acquainting him with the situation at
Lucknow, and urging him to press on to its relief.
" This morning," he wrote, " we went out eight miles
to meet the enemy, and we were defeated and lost
five guns, through the misconduct chiefly of our
Native artillerymen, many of whom have deserted.
The enemy have followed us up, and we have now
been besieged for four hours, and shall probably to-
night be surrounded. The enemy are very bold, and
our Europeans are very low. I look upon our position as ten times as bad as it was yesterday. Indeed,
it is now critical. We shall be obliged to concentrate,
if we are able. We shall have to abandon much
supplies, and to blow up much powder. Unless we
are relieved quickly, say in fifteen or twenty days,
we shall hardly be able to maintain our position."[†]
Thus were epitomised the day's disaster and its probable results. Lawrence's anticipations were abundantly fulfilled. Before the new month had commenced the enemy were raging against us on every
side; and it had become a matter of necessity to
abandon the Mutchee-Bhawun and to concentrate
all our force within the walls of the Residency.

Abandonment of the Mutchee-Bhawun.

But how was this concentration to be effected?
The ground between the Residency and the Mutchee-

[*] " The majority of the rebel force crossed at sunset, and it was a beautiful sight the way their Horse Artillery dashed across the bridge." —*MS. Memorandum.*

[†] MS. Correspondence.

June 30.

Bhawun was commanded by the enemy. To have
sent a messenger with a letter would probably have
been to have revealed, and, therefore, to have frustrated, our designs. Fortunately we were not without an alternative. The foresight of Lawrence's
engineers had caused the rude machinery of a telegraph to be erected on the roof of the Residency,
and the nature of the signals had been agreed upon
and was well understood between the inmates of the
two buildings.* But it was a service of difficulty and
danger so to work this improvised semaphore, as to
convey to the garrison of the Mutchee-Bhawun instructions to blow up the building and to withdraw
the garrison under cover of the night; for the insurgents, seeing our people actively employed on the
roof of the Residency, though probably not understanding the meaning of the movement, poured in
such a deadly shower of rifle-balls from a commanding position on the top of the Gaol, that it was not
until three hours had been spent, " under a broiling
sun and a heavy fire," that, mainly by the personal exertions of Captain Fulton and Mr. George Lawrence,
orders were conveyed to the Mutchee-Bhawun. Then
there was an interval of intense suspense at the Residency. The movement, upon which so much depended, was to be made at midnight. It was possible
that it might be suspected, or if not suspected, it
might be discovered by the enemy's sentries or scouts,
and our retreat thus intercepted. To avert such a
calamity, orders were issued by Lawrence to open, a
little before midnight, a distracting fire from all the
guns and mortars in our batteries, and thus to cover

---

* "It simply consisted of one black stuffed bags, each having its
post with a bar at the top, from own pulley to work it."—*Journal of
which were suspended in one row a *Staff-Officer.*

the retirement of the garrison. This was completely successful. By God's providence the hazardous movement was effected without the loss of a man. At the appointed time they marched into the Residency, bringing with them their treasure and their guns.* Had the enemy compassed our designs, it is probable that but few of our party would have escaped with their lives, and it is certain that the guns and the treasure would have fallen into the enemy's hands.

But it was necessary that our people on retiring from the Mutchee-Bhawun should leave much that was dear to us behind them. The building had been appropriated to the uses of a great storehouse and magazine. It was rich with commissariat stores; with powder and with small-arm ammunition. These could not be taken away by the retiring garrison; so arrangements were made to destroy them. The Mutchee-Bhawun and all its contents were to be rendered, so far as a great explosion could render them, unserviceable to the enemy. This work was intrusted to Lieutenant Thomas, of the Madras Artillery, who laid the train—and soon after Colonel Palmer and his men had secured themselves within the Residency-walls, a pillar of fire was seen to rise from the Mutchee-Bhawun. The welcome sight was followed by the sound of a loud explosion; and then presently was seen a great cloud of smoke which hung for some time in mid-air over the shattered building and proclaimed its evacuation. Two hun-

---

* The enterprise, however, nearly miscarried, owing to a misunderstanding. The story is thus told by the Staff-Officer. "A very serious accident had nearly happened. The leading men, finding the gates closed, shouted out, 'Open the gates,' and the artillerymen at the guns above, which, loaded with grape, covered the entrance, mistook the works for 'Open with grape,' and were already at the guns, when an officer put them right. The whole force came in without a shot being fired."

dred and fifty barrels of gunpowder, with large
quantities of small-arm ammunition, had been blown
up; and much good food for our people was sacrificed at the same time. But the junction of the garrisons was too great a gain for there to be much disposition to count the cost. The cheers which greeted
the arrival of Palmer and his followers showed how
intense was the satisfaction in the Residency. Every
man felt that a great danger had been escaped—that
a great deliverance had come; and thanked God for
the providential dispensation.

But a terrible revenge awaited us. On the morrow,
nay, on the same morning (for the Mutchee-Bhawun
was exploded after midnight), a great calamity overtook not only the Lucknow garrison, but the whole
British nation. At dawn of day, Sir Henry Lawrence had risen, and, with his wonted activity, had
superintended the new arrangements that had become
necessary, owing to the welcome accession of force
which the dark hours had brought him. He had
seen new detachments posted and new guns planted;
and when the morning sun had become oppressive,
he had returned to the Residency, and had laid himself down to rest on a couch in his sitting-room—or,
more correctly it should be said, to transact business
in a recumbent position, for it was only rest of body
that was allowed to him. His nephew, George Lawrence, was lying on another couch in the same room.
By the General's side stood Captain Wilson, Assistant
Adjutant-General, with one knee on the couch, reading an official memorandum, and waiting the orders
of his chief. There was also a Native servant in the
room. Whilst Wilson was still reading, a crashing
noise was heard; then the room was filled with
smoke and dust, through which nothing could be

1857.
July 1—2.

July 2.
Death of Sir
Henry
Lawrence.

2 L 2

seen. The Staff-Officer was thrown to the ground, but, on recovering himself, he cried out, "Sir Henry, are you hurt?" At first there was no answer ; but, after a little while, the feeble voice of the Chief Commissioner was heard to say, " I am killed !" And when the smoke cleared away, it was seen that the bed on which Lawrence lay was crimson with his blood. A shell from the howitzer, which Bonham had fought so gallantly at Chinhut, had exploded in the General's room, and a fragment of it had wounded him fearfully on the upper part of the left thigh.*

Dr. Fayrer was at once summoned to the General's assistance by Mr. George Lawrence, the only one in the room who had escaped unhurt. He found that Sir Henry had been removed to a small apartment, not so much exposed, adjoining the drawing-room, and there he lay on a couch near the window, surrounded by his friends. Though he seemed to be under the impression that even then he was in the agonies of death, he was talking quite calmly to the people about him. When Fayrer had examined the wound, Lawrence asked how long he had to live, and when the surgeon replied that his patient might survive for about two days, the sufferer expressed surprise and doubt, for he thought that his end was nearer at hand.† The most that human skill could do for him was to mitigate the pain of his dying hours. The amputation of the mutilated limb would have been fruitless—a doubtful operation on a

---

* It is a striking instance of the manner in which what is called "the doctrine of chances" may be falsified by actual events, that a shell had burst, on the preceding day, in the same room, between Lawrence and Couper, leaving both unhurt. When the former was exhorted to shift his quarters he answered that it was not likely that another shell would burst in the same room.

† Some accounts say *three*—but Dr. Fayrer assures me that he said " Forty-eight hours."

younger and stronger man, a cruel experiment on one so feeble and worn as the good General. The little life that was left in him might still be serviceable to his countrymen, and it was right to protract it to the utmost. He had work still to do, and he did it with all the firmness and collectedness of health. Death did not steal upon him like a thief in the night. He had already bethought himself of what was to be done in the event of the mortal blow descending upon him, and there was, therefore, no hurry or confusion at the last. He had obtained the sanction of Government to the appointment of Major Banks as his successor in the office of Chief Commissioner; and he now formally made over the charge to him. On Colonel Inglis he conferred the chief military command, associating with him Major Anderson in a kind of council. This done, he prepared himself to give his last instructions to his successors. But the position of the house in which he lay was so exposed to the fire of the enemy, that it was thought best to remove him to another; so he was carried, with all tenderness and care, to Dr. Fayrer's residence, which was less within the reach of the rebel guns, though open to their musketry. There his last hours were passed. There he prepared himself for the great change that was coming upon him.

And in those last hours, all that was admirable in the soldier, the statesman, and the Christian gentleman, was evinced with a grandeur and beauty of utterance that impressed the understandings and touched the hearts of all who were admitted to his presence, and made even those who had sometimes differed from him in life feel that a great and good man was passing away from the scene. The old watchword of Derry rung in his dying ears; and his last counsel was, "No surrender!" "Let every man," he said, "die at his post; but never make terms. God help the poor women and children!" The various detailed orders which he issued, some of a public, some of a personal character, were taken down by Major Banks. They showed alike the sagacity and the tenderness of the dying man. He thought much of those about him, now beleaguered in the Lucknow Residency—much also of those at a distance, his children, his kindred, his friends, and those "little ones," for whom he had done so much —the boys and girls of the Lawrence Asylum. When all his dying wishes had been noted down, he bade farewell to his comrades, asking forgiveness if he had offended any one by asperity of speech, and dwelling on the vanity of human greatness and the all-sufficingness of the Saviour's love. There was no one in that garrison so stern or cold as not to be melted to tears in his presence.

Except when, on one or two occasions, chloroform was administered to deaden the sense of pain, he remained in full possession of his faculties nearly to the last. He expressed great interest in the progress of the siege, and earnestly inquired, from time to time, into the events which were passing around him. Neither the booming of the guns, nor the rattle of musketry, seemed greatly to disturb him. The outer sense was deadened by the stronger inward sentiments of love of God and love of Man—strongest of all in his last hours. The sting of death was not in any thought of himself. He believed that he had done his duty; he knew that he had tried to do it. And he desired that on his tomb should be engraven the words, "Here lies Henry Lawrence, who tried to do his

duty." He added that he wished to be buried privately, "without any fuss." And so when, on the
morning of the 4th of July, after bidding farewell to
his comrades, he passed away to his rest, they covered
up the body until the shades of night had fallen
upon the scene; and then some European soldiers
were sent to remove the remains of their late chief to
a grave which had been prepared for him in a trench
within the Residency grounds. They lifted up the
coverlet and kissed him reverentially on the forehead; and then he was laid in the same grave with
some men of his old regiment, who had been killed
in the course of the day.

The character of Sir Henry Lawrence has been
imperfectly sketched at the very commencement of
this History. I do not think that I could write anything that can add to a reputation, than which there
is none purer or brighter in all the annals of our
great Indian Empire. Men of all classes and all characters mourned his death as a personal affliction.
And this sympathy, so strong, so general, was but
the echo or response to the catholic utterances of his
own sympathising nature. All men loved him because
he loved all men. It was this sympathy that so
especially suited him for the work of Indian Government. Without sympathy we may rule with power;
but we cannot govern with wisdom. It has been
observed elsewhere that he was wont to say and to
write that "it is the due admixture of Romance and
Reality that best carries a man through life;" and
that what he said and wrote he did—or rather he
was. It was the Romance of his nature that placed
him in the front rank of our Indian heroes, and to
some extent, indeed, has given him a place to himself in the great story of our national heroism. For

it is a special circumstance of Sir Henry Lawrence's career, that, though it has produced this great impression on the minds of men, it was not wholly a successful one. It was overclouded by failures and embittered by disappointments. And it was not, on the other hand, marked by any salient achievements of peculiar lustre. It had no Trafalgar, no Waterloo; no great peaceful triumph wrought out to the happy end. The student, of a future generation, when asked what Sir Henry Lawrence did, may not always be ready with an answer; but all will tell promptly what he was. And many, perhaps, will say that they do not quite know why of all men, of whom they had ever read in Indian history, he seemed to be the flower; but that they cannot help feeling it. It is a sentiment rather than a conviction, and no one cares to analyse or to explain it.

But that the Romantic did not overlay the Real, in the character of Sir Henry Lawrence, is shown by the estimation in which he was held for good practical work by the Governments under which he served. "We have suffered a sad loss," wrote Lord Canning to the President of the Board of Control. "Poor Henry Lawrence died on the 4th, of a wound received on the 2nd, and I do not know the person who can fill his place. Of all men in India, he is the one whose loss is least reparable at this moment. He would have been invaluable in the pacification of the troubled districts hereafter, both as a soldier and a civilian." And the Home Government paid to him, as a living statesman, the highest tribute that could be paid to one of their Indian servants. On the 22nd of July, a Court of Directors of the East India Company, not then knowing the calamity which had overtaken the nation, passed a Resolution appointing Sir Henry Lawrence to be Provisional Governor-

General "on the death, resignation, or coming away of Viscount Canning." I never saw so great unanimity in that assembly. No one then present doubted for a moment that Henry Lawrence was the man, pre-eminently qualified above all others, to succeed the ruler who was then bearing up so bravely against the manifold trials by which he was surrounded. And all sorrowed bitterly when they learnt that the commission which had been sent to him, under the most willing sanction of the Crown, had been addressed to one who, ere the letter reached Lucknow, had been many weeks lying in the grave. The sadness was shared by the whole nation. But though the great reward never reached him, not on that account is the example one less to be cherished. It is not less sweetly encouraging, because it "blossomed in the dust."

Days passed, and the fury of the siege continued. At every possible point on which guns could be posted, so as to bear upon our position, batteries were erected, and an incessant shower of shot and shell was poured. upon the British Residency and its outworks; whilst on all elevated places, as on the summits of mosques and mansions, skilled marksmen were planted, sharp-eyed and steady-handed, watching for the appearance of a white face beyond the cover of our defences.* Those defences had been

* "Our heaviest losses have been caused by the fire from the enemy's sharpshooters stationed in the adjoining mosques and houses of the Native nobility, the necessity of destroying which had been repeatedly drawn to the attention of Sir Henry Lawrence by the Staff of Engineers. But his invariable reply was, 'Spare the holy places and private property too as much as possible;' and we have consequently suffered severely from our very tenderness to the religious prejudices and respect to the rights of our rebellious citizens and soldiery." — *Report of Brigadier Inglis.*

greatly strengthened after the rough and ready fashion to which hard necessity had driven us.. There was nothing, of whatsoever value, so long as substance and solidity and power of resistance were in it, that was not turned to account by our people for purposes of temporary fortification. Tables and sideboards, wardrobes and chiffonieres, were gathered together and piled up as barricades. And some, when they brought forth the treasures of poor Fletcher Hayes's library,* to receive the assaults of the adversary's ammunition, must have thought, with some bitter-sweet reminiscences of their reading of the "Scotch novels" at home, of the defence of Colonel Mannering's house with the Dominie's cherished folios. Even the records of the Government were dragged from their hiding-places to afford shelter to our garrison, and many ponderous volumes, perhaps of no other value, were put to unexpected uses as muniments of war, making for the besieged paper-walls of serviceable thickness and strength.

Into the work of defence our people—officers and men alike—flung themselves with an amount of vigorous self-devotion seldom paralleled in the military history of the world. There was no duty to which officers, of whatever rank, did not apply themselves

---

* Captain Fletcher Hayes, of whom mention has been made in earlier parts of this history, had a passion for perilous enterprises. He was always eager to volunteer for some detached service. It has been seen that he was at Cawnpore up to the 26th of May (vol. ii., p. 296). He went thence intending to render assistance to Colonel Smith at Futtehgurh—but was dissuaded from fulfilling this purpose. He went to Mynpooree to take counsel with Mr. Power, whose position at that time (May 30) has been already described —leaving his men (Irregular Cavalry) at Bhowgaon under the command of Lieutenant Barbor. At Mynpooree he learnt that his men were disaffected—but he did not take much heed of the report, and waited till the morning of the 31st to join his troopers at Bhowgaon, accompanied by Captain Carey of the Seventeenth. On the way the troopers fell upon them. Hayes was cut down and massacred. Carey escaped to tell the tale.

with cheerful alacrity; there was no labour, however arduous or revolting, from which they shrunk in the hour of need; there was no danger from without or within to which they were not exposed. Day and night they toiled incessantly, seeing sorrowfully their little garrison diminishing, losing well-nigh every day one or more of their best men, but never faltering, never desponding. The fury of the enemy was but one of the many evils which they had to face. Cholera, Fever, Diarrhœa, Small-pox, the plague of boils and flies, the putrid stench from the rotting carcasses of horses and bullocks, the perpetual heat and the remorseless rain, affected our people more grievously than the fire of the insurgents. All men were soldiers at that time. The civil officers took post and sometimes command in our batteries, and the whole-hearted resolution and unfailing fertility of resource which they displayed placed them in the front rank of the warriors of the crisis. Mr. Ommaney, the Judicial Commissioner, whilst visiting the Redan battery, was killed by a round-shot glancing from a tree, which fractured his skull, at the very commencement of the siege. This was a heavy loss, but a still heavier one was in store for the garrison. Little more than two weeks after he had taken into his hands the chief conduct of affairs, Major Banks went out to visit Gubbins's battery. He had ever been active among the active—fearless among the fearless — visiting first one post and then another, in continual personal communication with his chief officers, seeing into all the details of the defence and encouraging the defenders. Thus he had proved himself worthy of the trust reposed in him by his sainted predecessor. But it happened disastrously that, on the 21st of July, he visited Gubbins's battery, where the lion-hearted civilian was working with his wonted energy. It was a great day with the enemy. They .were furiously attacking our principal posts, and calling forth all our activities of defence. .The works which the Chief Commissioner now visited were greatly exposed. The parapet was only breast-high, and it was necessary, for life's sake, to stoop when the enemy were firing into our battery. Banks had been often cautioned—but he was regardless of all warnings, and on this luckless day he seems to have been more than commonly mindless of his safety. He was a man of no great stature, but walking erect he was a fair mark to the enemy, and ere he had exchanged a word with Gubbins a bullet entered his brain. He fell heavily to the ground and never stirred again. When they tried to move him they found that he was stone-dead. The body was buried that night, sewn up in a white sheet. Death was too busy in the garrison to allow any more coffin-making.*

Others of these soldier-civilians, or civilian-soldiers, though ever under fire, escaped with their lives from the furious raging of the enemy. Mr. Martin Gubbins, the Financial Commissioner, more fortunate than his compeers, lived and served to make for himself a great reputation as a brave soldier and an able leader. The natural pugnacity of his character had now legitimate scope for exercise; and men who had resented his litigiousness on paper could not but respect his audacity under arms. Thornhill and Capper, of the same service, were wounded at their work; and George Couper, the

* We may fairly surmise that the shots which carried off the three chief people of the garrison in a space of less than three weeks were not purely accidental. The enemy, doubtless, had some active spies and tracked the movements of the British leaders.

Secretary, who had begun life as a soldier, was ready for any military duty that might be intrusted to him. And when no inspiriting soldierly work was required from him, he was content to perform the nauseous duties of the scavenger. It was no small thing—no small service to the garrison to look well to its sanitary condition. Many evil influences were against us. It was the hottest season of the year. Death came among our cattle—horses and bullocks—and their rotting carcasses were to be quickly buried. On one occasion, a stack of "bhoosa" had fallen and killed several bullocks, who lay beside it. The disaster of the loss of meat was overborne by the fear of the evil effects of the putrid carrion. So Couper went forth, with one or two staunch comrades, to dig graves and bury the dead. It was the hardest and foulest work that they ever had to do; and as they had neglected to take out with them either the stimulants which are so necessary to insure resistance to poisonous effluvia, or the milder drinks which repair the waste of exhaustion, they suffered fearfully from the unsavoury labour. These were days when men were ready for any kind of work, regardless of self, so that they could help the garrison. And so they toiled on side by side, those robust members of the two great Services; whilst others, whose names were not borne on the rolls of the Company, strove and suffered no less bravely than their enrolled countrymen, and many, who had come to Lucknow only to trade, died with arms in their hands.

But not to the masculine defenders of Lucknow was the heroism of the garrison confined. Numbers of English gentlewomen had followed the fortunes of their husbands to the Oude capital. The Residency

1857.
July.

The gentlewomen of Garrison.

was full of women and children. There was scarcely any kind of suffering—scarcely any kind of privation which they did not uncomplainingly endure. They saw the dead or wounded bodies of their nearest and dearest brought in from the outworks; they felt their children die in their arms. There was no place in which they were secure against the unrelenting fire of the enemy. Disease in its worst forms came upon them, and they bore up bravely against what, in the happiest homes, and with the most bountiful appliances, would have been anguish and bitterness, trying to the utmost the frailty of the flesh. Large numbers of their domestic servants had deserted at the commencement of the siege, and many, accustomed to all the delicacies and luxuries of a life in which every want was supplied, every wish anticipated, had now to perform for themselves menial offices, from which they would before have shrunk with dismay. But week after week, as the siege went on, these English gentlewomen suffered without a murmur. In their patience they were strong. But more than this, they were active in their ministrations. How they comforted and consoled one another — how they tended the sick and wounded—how they soothed the last hours of the dying, and carried help to those who needed it, though needing it themselves, has been gratefully recorded by men who survived the fiery trials of the siege to carry with them to their graves the memory of these gentle ministerings.

To one who thinks of the miserable straits to which the Cawnpore garrison were reduced by the total failure of their supplies, of the carrion on which they feasted, of the scanty water, to procure a cup of which might be death, a truthful record of the privations endured by our people at Lucknow must, in com-

parison, appear faint and feeble. But to Englishmen
and Englishwomen accustomed to live delicately and to fare sumptuously every day, the scarcity of wonted food, suited to the condition of those so reared, so spoilt by favouring circumstances, was distressing in the extreme. It was not that hunger gnawed them.* They were not starving. Strong appetites were not to be expected at such a time. But much of the food served out to them was coarse and unwholesome. There was a great want of good bread, for early in the siege the bakers had deserted in a body, and now indigestible chupatties took the place of the accustomed loaf. The gun bullocks for some time supplied meat to the garrison. Indeed, they were often shot by the enemy faster than the garrison could eat them, and it was sore tribulation to our people to dispose of the rotting carcasses. In some houses were good private stores of wine and beer and dainties, such as hermetically-sealed salmon and other European provisions; but, let the generosity of the owner be what it might, what were these among so many? Tea and sugar, of all things most prized by our women, soon became scarce; and ere long there was a failure of rum and tobacco, very distressing to the European fighting man. The loss of the ordinary "smoke" was severely felt. The habit was so strong that rather than smoke nothing many of our soldiers sucked pieces of ignited cane or wood, as schoolboys do, and found some solace in the tasteless substitute. Ever and anon, when some well-

---

* This refers to the earlier days of the siege. Speaking of a later period, one of my most trustworthy informants says: "They were next door to it (hunger). *There never was any bread.* And there were no servants to make chupatties of the coarse *bhoosa* (bran), which had therefore to be eaten almost uncooked. It was nearly as indigestible as the grass of the field, although undoubtedly there was enough of it."

furnished officer was struck down, there was a sale of his possessions by public auction, and a sharp competition for every article of food and clothing, at prices well described as "fabulous." At first, comparatively little anxiety on the score of provisions vexed the minds of the besieged; for it was believed that Havelock and Neill would soon bring the looked-for relief. But, as weeks passed, and no succours came, the thoughts of the garrison turned gloomily to a future, in which the supplies would be doled out in smaller and smaller portions, until starvation should stare them in the face.

But amidst these frequent disappointments there was no abatement of heart and hope. The men worked on and the women bore on, sustained by the certainty of a coming deliverance. This certainty seemed to sharpen the imaginations of the garrison, for many thought that they heard firing in the distance, and reported that the succours were coming when they were far-off. How it happened that the relieving force never came no one knew. A letter had been received from Colonel Tytler saying that they might be expected about the 8th of August; but days passed and weeks passed, and still the enemy taunted our people with their helplessness, declaring that they had driven back the relieving force, and would soon expel the garrison from their coverts. Many letters had been sent from Lucknow to which no reply had been received. But there was one man named "Ungud"—a noted scout—who succeeded where others failed. On the 15th of August he brought in a letter dated on the 4th, and partly written in Greek characters, saying: "We march to-morrow morning for Lucknow, having been reinforced. We hope to reach you in four days at furthest. You must aid us in every way, even to cutting your way out, if we can't force our way in. We are but a small force."* But with this letter the scout brought oral information to the effect that the whole of General Havelock's force had fallen back upon Cawnpore. There was great discouragement in this; and the recommendation that the garrison should cut their way out sounded then something like a mockery. The letter was addressed to Martin Gubbins, who took counsel with Colonel Inglis, and the result was that a letter was sent back in reply, stating that, hampered as they were with sick and wounded, with women and children, it was impossible that they should leave their defences. So still they waited and waited, doing their best to bear up against the disappointment, and, duly regarding the uncertainties of the future, husbanding their resources more and more every week. Half rations had become a fact—quarter rations were a prospective certainty, the advent of which could not be very remote.

All through the month of July, the fury of the enemy continued to increase. It was plain to those within our lines of defence that our assailants were not merely the men of the mutinous Sepoy regiments. The great Talookhdars had sent in their contingents, who were aiding the regular soldiery in their unremitting assaults. Now and again new batteries were planted in commanding positions, and our crumbling walls and battered roofs bore terrible witness to the destroying effects of their fire. This added grievously to the sufferings of the weaker portion of our people; for many of the upper rooms were

---

* As with many of the letters of that period it was written on very thin paper, in minute characters, and rolled up in a quill.

1857.
July.

rendered uninhabitable, and the women and children were forced to crowd together in the lower ones in a manner distressing especially to those whom sickness had rendered helpless and incapable. To the booming of the guns, and the crash of the fallen masonry, they had, by this time, become habituated, and even to the danger, to which they were exposed by the constant intrusions of shot and shell, they were becoming more and more insensible every day.* It is related, indeed, that many of the ladies of the garrison began to take quite a scientific interest in the artillery practice of the enemy, and came to be better judges of the weight of the projectiles which entered our buildings than the officers of the garrison themselves. But brave as they were in the face of all such perils, and patient under pressing privations, it was hard to keep a cheerful countenance under the domestic afflictions with which it pleased God to visit them. As July and August advanced, the children died off rapidly.† Others were born into the garrison—and not the least of the trials of our poor countrywomen were those which came upon them when the inevitable pangs of maternal labour were aggravated by exposure to the dire assaults of a relentless enemy.‡

But soon a greater danger than any that had gone

* "Balls fall at our feet, and we continue the conversation without a remark ; bullets graze our very hair and we never speak of them. Narrow escapes are so very common that even women and children cease to notice them."—*Rees's Personal Narrative.*

† *Aug.* 9. "The heat excessive; and children sank rapidly under the effects of want of good air, food, and exercise. Several deaths oc-

curred among them both yesterday and to-day."—*Diary of a Staff-Officer.—Aug.* 14. "Many cases of fever and several deaths among the children."—*Ibid.*

‡ *Aug.* 10. "Mrs. Ouseley had a little boy this morning, and Mrs. Barwell yesterday."—*Mrs. Case's Journal* ("Day by Day at Lucknow.") Mrs. Dorin was killed by the fire of the enemy.

before threatened the Lucknow garrison. On the 20th of July, a mine had been sprung by the enemy, near the Redan Battery; but it had done us no injury, and had perhaps been chiefly intended to create confusion and assist the enemy's advance.* Now, it was plain that the insurgents were strenuously endeavouring to undermine our chief positions, in the hope of terminating the siege by some grand explosions. If anything could have stimulated our Engineer officers to increased efforts for the general good, the effect would have been wrought by this stirring intelligence. But in truth no men could have toiled more zealously and assiduously than these had done from the first. Major Anderson was our Chief Engineer. A good officer, highly respected by the garrison, he had recently succumbed to the pressure of sickness, and those who watched him narrowly saw little hope that he would outlive the siege.† Happily, the officer who stood next to him was one of equal energy and capacity. Among the many brave men, whose wisely-directed labours tended so greatly to the security of our position and the salvation of our people, there was not one whose good deeds were more gratefully acknowledged by the garrison than those of Captain Fulton of the Engineers. He had been, from the first, indefatigable in

* It was intended to destroy the Redan, but failed. The musketry fire was kept up so thickly and persistently that the carrion-birds, attracted by the carcasses of horses and bullocks, fell dead from the surrounding trees.—*Statement of an Eye-Witness (MS.)*. The Redan Battery was commanded by Captain Lawrence of the Thirty-second Foot, commonly styled in the garrison "Sam Lawrence." Of this hero George Couper writes, " Strange to say, 'Sam,' although commanding one of the most dangerous posts, a volunteer, too, on every sortie, and one of the biggest men in the garrison, escaped throughout without a scratch."—*Notes to Mecham's Sketches.*

† He died on the afternoon of the 11th of August.

his endeavours to repair our damaged works, and otherwise to strengthen our defences; and now he had to give his first thoughts to the all-important work of counteracting the designs of the enemy to blow the English into the air. As quietly and guardedly as possible he had set about the preparation of his countermines; but the enemy knew well what he was doing, and did all that lay in their power to obstruct the efforts of our workmen.*

On the 10th of August the enemy sprung a second and a third mine. They made a prodigious noise and alarmed many of the women; but did very little harm so far as human life was affected by the explosion.† Two soldiers were blown into the road beyond our defences, but neither of them was injured. Subsequent experience, indeed, proved that it was a small matter to be blown into the air. But the first explosion did great damage to our masonry and timbers in the part of our defences opposite to Johannes's house.‡ When the smoke cleared away, the enemy pushed forward and occupied the buildings round the Cawnpore Battery; but so warm was the reception they received from our people that they

---

* *Aug.* 13. "Our mine near Sago's house was pushed on all night with the greatest possible speed. Every possible means was adopted by the enemy to prevent our miners working, and as only a wall and a few feet of ground divided the two parties, they resorted to squibs, rockets, brickbats, and lights at the end of bamboos to annoy our workmen."—*Diary of a Staff-Officer.*

† "About twelve o'clock, as I was sitting at the table writing, Carry washing our things and Mrs. Inglis working, we were suddenly alarmed by what appeared to us a great shaking of the earth, followed by a dreadful noise, such as I never wish to hear again. It was indescribable, and sounded as if the whole earth was coming against us; it was a mine exploding without doing harm."—*Mrs. Case's Journal.*

‡ "It blew in a great part of the house occupied by Mr. Schilling and the Martinière boys, and entirely destroyed our palisades and defences for the space of sixty feet. One of the heaviest timbers was pitched right on the top of the Brigade mess-house, among the officers and men of the Thirty-second, who occupied the post."—*Diary of a Staff-Officer.*

were unable to pass the line of our defences, and after a time fell back in despair. Nor were they more successful at the other point of attack near " Sago's House," where they were driven back with heavy loss and compelled to fire from discreet distances. All day long our garrison were under arms, suffering cruelly from the effects of the exhausting heat, but compelled to be ever on the alert, for the fury of the enemy never ceased even when night fell upon the scene. At nine o'clock, the insurgents, bracing themselves up for a crowning effort, attacked us at several points—at Innes's house, Anderson's and Gubbins's post—and so assured were they of the success of their assaults, that they brought up scaling-ladders with them ; but they were compelled to beat a retreat, leaving some of their ladders behind them. In the course of the day's operations, the howitzer, which Bonham had worked so well at Chinhut, and which was supposed to have slain Henry Lawrence, was brought to bear upon our positions, especially upon Innes's outpost. But the result of the day's fighting was that we lost three Europeans and two Sepoys killed, and five or six men wounded. The loss of the enemy must have been considerable, for a heavy fire of shot and shell supplemented the practice of our Infantry and carried slaughter into the Sepoy ranks. That they were greatly disheartened by the failure was believed. On our garrison, on the other hand, the issue had an invigorating effect. It taught them to despise the enemy even more than they had done before ; and it renewed their hopes of a successful resistance until the looked-for succours should arrive.

It was soon apparent, however, that the insurgents were resuming their mining operations in the neigh-

1857.
August.

Counterminu-
ing.

bourhood of Sago's house, so Fulton pushed forward a countermine with the utmost possible despatch, and on the 13th it was reported to be ready. The explosion was successful. The masonry building from which the enemy had started their mine was speedily a heap of ruins, and the groans of those who were buried beneath it declared the work it had done. Foiled at this point, the enemy commenced operations against another—and this time they were more successful. In the early morning of the 18th, they sprung a mine which shattered the outer defences of one of the squares in which the Sikh detachments were posted. A building in one corner of the square, on which we had a look-out post, was blown into the air;[*] and when the smoke cleared away, it was seen that a breach some ten or twelve yards long had been made in our defences. It was a moment of painful suspense and anxiety. A rebel leader mounted the breach, brandished his sword aloft, and called upon the crowd of insurgents to follow him into the works of the Feringhee. A bullet from the rifle of one of our officers on the roof of the Brigade Mess, where some of our best marksmen were posted, sent this man to his doom. Another rose to take his place, when instantly the same fate overtook him, and he fell beside his countryman in the breach. Then a great panic took possession of those behind their fallen champions, and not another man would advance.

---

[*] "By the explosion Lieutenant Mecham and Captain Adolphe Orr and one drummer were thrown into the air, but descended inside the square amidst the *débris* of the building, and escaped with little injury. The fourth, Band-Sergeant Curtain, of the Forty-first Native Infantry, was unhappily thrown outside the works, upon the road, where he was destroyed by the enemy."—*Gubbins*. Eight Christian drummers and a Sepoy were buried under the ruins, and one hurled outside and decapitated by the enemy.—*Couper's Notes*. An account written on the subsequent day and quoted in Wilson's Journal, says "six Christian drummers and a Sepoy.

There was no service, throughout these weary days of the siege, which called more nobly into action all the best qualities of our people, soldiers and civilians, or knit them more closely in the bonds of comradeship, than this work of counteracting the efforts of the enemy to destroy us by their mining operations. It is not easy to convey to the unprofessional reader a right conception of the toil and trouble of these subterraneous workings and explorations. Those who took part in these mole-like burrowings acquired wonderful powers of auscultation. They were continually on the alert to hear the clicking of the enemy's pick-axes, and would sometimes, in the midst of a conversation, suddenly throw themselves down, with one ear on the earth, to catch the suggestive sounds. Then there was the ingress into the shaft of the countermine, sometimes accomplished on all-fours like a beast, and sometimes horizontally on one's stomach, like a reptile; both at great expense of skin and flesh, by unavoidable excoriations. Men, after a time, became accustomed to the trials of the countermine, but a neophyte was sorely perplexed. It must have been a grand sight, if sight were possible, to see the officer in command of the burrowing party, or other "solitary sentinel," sitting, revolver in hand, at the end of the countermine, listening "to the enemy's miner coming closer and closer until his pick-axe actually pierced the gallery and exposed the disconcerted workman to the view." Then there was a crack of the pistol and an end to that man's work.*

As the month wore on, the labours of the garrison became heavier and heavier. Their numbers had

---

* See Sir George Couper's admirable descriptive letter-press to Captain Mecham's "Illustrations of the Defence of Lucknow," from which this is mainly taken.

greatly diminished, and their work had increased, for the heavy cannonading of the enemy kept up a continual process of destruction, and the necessary business of repairs, both to our residential buildings and our outworks, became more onerous every day. And ever as the toil increased, the strength of the toilers diminished. For the daywork and the night-work, the want of food and the want of rest, had well-nigh exhausted their powers. Many, indeed, be-coming wholly incapable of sustaining this continual pressure upon their bodily and mental energies,* had been compelled to take refuge in the Hospital. A new enemy about this time assailed them. Scurvy, induced by the absence of wholesome food, by hard work and continued exposure, struck heavily our people. Some were invalided; some, who tried to bear up, found their sufferings sadly aggravated, and soon succumbed to death. So great was the debility which accompanied the ravages of this dis-order, that it rarely happened that an amputation performed on a scurvy-stricken patient had any other than a fatal termination.

State of the
Hospital.
And it was a grievous aggravation of the suffer-ings of the sick and wounded that the Hospital was in a most exposed position. It lay between the Residency and the Baillie Guard, and shot and shell came crashing in at all times, and often with deadly messages to our poor people who lay helpless on

---

* "We had work nightly for at least three hundred men; as we had the defences to repair daily, supplies to remove from godowns which were fallen in from the effects of the enemy's shot, mines to counter-mine, guns to remove, barricades to erect, corpses to bury, and rations to serve out; but with our weak, harassed, and daily dimi-nishing garrison, we could seldom produce as working parties more than three fatigue parties of eight or ten men each relief; and the Euro-peans were capable of little exer-tion, as from want of sleep, hard work night and day, and constant exposure, their bodily strength was greatly diminished."—*Narrative of an Eye-Witness.*

their beds.* The upper story of the building had been rendered untenable at an early period of the siege. Hence the necessity of crowding and cramming in the basement, which whilst it increased the misery of the inmates, added but little to their security. But they were very patient under all these severe trials. "It was an affecting scene," wrote one who was familiar with every phase of daring and suffering during those "brave days," "to walk through the Hospital. The poor soldiers, and other wounded combatants, destitute as they were of everything that renders pain and disease endurable, were so patient and cheerful under their agony and afflictions, which the pitying beholder could only sympathise with without the power to alleviate. No murmurs, no grumblings were ever heard. If there was any complaint, it was that the sufferers had been incapacitated from taking further part in the desperate and holy struggle. If there was any expression of regret, it was that his fall had entailed additional duty on his dying comrades."†

The mining operations made new demands upon the few sound men with which it was difficult to comply; and the increasing activity of the enemy, whose numbers enabled them to employ a succession of fresh men on every kind of work, kept our people always on the alert. And so, as days passed, and still no tidings of the approach of Havelock's force came to them, they asked each other how long this strain on the resources of the enfeebled garrison could endure—how long thus reduced in number, thus exhausted by work and weakened by privation

---

* "The sufferers were constantly shot on their beds. In fact there was no spot, either in the sanctuary or throughout the entire defences, where a dying soldier or an ailing woman or child, could feel an instant's security."—*Couper's Notes.*

† Sir George Couper.

—they could hold out against an enemy that seemed only to become every day more numerous, more active, and more skilful, whilst not only our physical force, but the genius also which directed it, was rapidly fading away.

For ever as week followed week there was the same grievous catalogue of death and disaster in high places. The casualties in our upper ranks were of many kinds, but always with the same monotonous succession of nocturnal burials. Now, one of our best officers was shot by the enemy—now, by our own people in the confusion of the fight—now, by his own hand in a temporary paroxysm of insanity brought on by long-continued suffering. Thus Bruére of the Thirteenth fell with a rifle-ball through his chest, in the act of picking out a noted marksman of the enemy; thus Birch of the Fifty-ninth, "attached to the Engineer Department," received his death-wound whilst reconnoitring in the darkness, from one of our own European sentries; thus Graham of the Fourth Cavalry blew out his brains with a re-volver, not knowing what he did. Others, bearing up bravely as long as Nature could sustain them, sunk at last beneath their wounds or exhausting disease. Among these was Captain Simonds of the Artillery, who, though badly wounded, worked his guns as long as he could, and then laid himself down to die. It is recorded that, during a space of nearly three months, there was only one day in which a funeral party, rudely improvised, did not lay the body of one or more members of our garrison in the grave under cover of the darkness of the night.

Bonham of the Artillery. Conspicuous among the heroes of the defence was Lieutenant Bonham of the Bengal Artillery. He had been posted with his battery of Oude Irregular

Artillery at Secrora, in the Bareitch Division, when
the troops there broke into mutiny, and he had been
the last man to leave the station. It was only when
he had done all in his power to bring the Native
soldiery back to their allegiance, and had been assured by a faithful Soubahdar that not a man would
act against his comrades, that Bonham consented to
mount a horse that had been brought to him, and
accompanied by three European sergeants, to ride
for Lucknow. His arrival there was a very serviceable accession of strength, for Artillery officers were
much wanted, and Bonham's energies were of the
best kind. How he worked the great howitzer at
Chinhut has already been told. He was wounded
in that action, but wounds did not seem greatly to
disturb the robust artilleryman. He was soon at his
work again, one of the main pillars of the defence.
Fertile of resource, ever active, and regardless of
danger, he won the admiring approbation of the
whole British garrison. The extraordinary accuracy
with which he laid his mortars was a source of continual applause. There was a total absence of
howitzers, which was severely felt; but Bonham's
ingenuity enabled him to make one, by a clever
process of conversion, out of a mortar, and to work
it with admirable effect. Reckless of exposure, so
long as he could do any good work, he was wounded
a second time in the earlier part of the siege; and
again a third time, on the 30th of August, when he
was struck by a musket-ball, and so severely injured
that for awhile his services were lost to the garrison.

Bonham lived—to be neglected. But less or more
fortunate, another Addiscombe hero, another member
of those great Indian scientific corps, whose doings
in peace and in war have shed such lustre upon our

1857.
August.

Death of Ful-
ton.

reputation in India, men who have led great armies to victory and have constructed vast material works which have given plenty and prosperity to countries often before abandoned to famine and desolation. Fulton died at his work, with the harness on his back. He was the Chief Engineer of the garrison after the death of Anderson, and how, regardless of self, he toiled day and night, has already been told. He was generally to be found working in the mines, often coming into subterranean collision with the enemy, and by well-directed blows from his own hand diminishing the number of the miners; but this did not prevent him from visiting other points of our defences, and bringing his directing mind to bear wheresoever it was wanted. As brave as he was skilful, he was a tower of strength to the garrison; but men asked one another how long this could last in the face of such audacity of exposure. On the 6th of September he had escaped from an explosion,

with nothing worse than a contusion; but little more than a week afterwards, whilst reconnoitring in Gubbins's battery (for his presence was ubiquitous), the last deadly message came to him. A round shot struck him on the head.* And, perhaps, there was not a man in the garrison whose loss could have been more severely felt or more deeply deplored.

But relief—if not deliverance—was now closely at hand. Havelock's force, having overcome the prodigious difficulties in its way, was now rapidly

---

* The Staff-Officer, in his Diary, says: "He was a highly-gifted, cool, brave, and chivalrous officer, fertile in resources, and a favourite with both officers and men. His loss was acutely felt." The writer adds, in one of many manuscript notes written for me, which have greatly increased the value of the printed book, "No one did more towards our success. He was as brave as he was indefatigable in his endeavours to foil the enemy. He had many personal encounters with our foes underground."

advancing. Outram had joined the Army, whose
ranks were swollen by reinforcements from below—
and the long looked-for advent was now emerging
from the obscure distance. On the 22nd of September, Ungud, the noted scout, brought a letter
conveying the glad tidings that the relieving force
had crossed the Ganges. The news was at once communicated to the garrison, whose hearts were lightened by the cheering intelligence and who rejoiced
outwardly with a great rejoicing. Ungud was the
hero of the hour. He was greatly excited by his
success; for he had been fired upon as he entered
our works and narrowly escaped destruction. He
thought, however, that he had had enough of this
dangerous service; and he said to Brigadier Inglis,
" Now I have got back three times, I will go no more
—but live or die with you."*

And in truth the exigencies of the situation demanded that the help in trouble should be speedily
present. The rain was falling heavily and rendered
more untenable the buildings, already shaken and
shattered, to which we looked for some semblance of
shelter. Provisions and necessities of all kinds were
becoming wofully scarce. Our European soldiery
were reduced to a dram a day. At an auction, held
at the Residency, of the property of deceased officers, a bottle of brandy was sold for twenty rupees,
and a flannel shirt for forty. A few more weeks
would have brought us to the direst extremity. The
enemy, who seemed to have received intelligence of
the advance of our reinforcements, did not slacken
in their hostile activity. On the 25th, a sad calamity
occurred in our garrison. One of the very best of
our officers—one who had been ever foremost in

* MS. Note by the "Staff-Officer."

1857.
September.

Arrival of
Havelock's
Force.

attack and defence, whose cheerfulness, under all depressing circumstances, had set a gallant example—
Captain Radcliffe of the Seventh Cavalry—was mortally wounded, whilst in command of the Cawnpore
Battery. Thus another of the younger heroes of
Lucknow was swept away from the muster-roll of her
defenders.

The anxiety of the garrison now became intense.
There were many manifest signs, beyond the lines of
our defences, that our reinforcements were approaching. There was great commotion among the townspeople. They were seen, huddling about, with bundles in their hands, as if making themselves ready
for flight. Our own people, regardless of exposure,
flocked to all the best commands of observation,
using their glasses or straining their eyes to see all
that could be seen in the distance. The enemy, believing that we should make a sortie to meet Havelock's advancing force, kept up an incessant fire upon
all our points of egress. It was seen, too—most welcome of signs—that they were firing in a different
direction. Soon the glorious sight of our own people,
fighting their way through the streets of Lucknow,
sent such a thrill of joy through the garrison, as
perhaps never had been felt before. " Once fairly
seen," wrote one who was present and who still lives
to remember it,* " all our doubts and fears regarding
them were ended; and then the garrison's long pent-
up feelings of anxiety and suspense burst forth in a
succession of deafening cheers; from every pit,
trench, and battery—from behind the sand-bags
piled on shattered houses—from every post still held
by a few gallant spirits, rose cheer upon cheer—even
from the hospital many of the wounded crawled

* The " Staff-Officer"—now Brigadier-General Wilson.

forth to join in that glad shout of welcome to those who had so bravely come to our assistance. It was a moment never to be forgotten." And then in they came, those glorious Highlanders and Fusiliers— those gallant " blue-caps," alas! without their leader; and then there were all the greetings and hand- grippings of measureless welcome and delight. The women crept forth from their holes and hiding-places and rushed wildly about, grasping and sometimes kissing the hands of the sturdy warriors who had come to their relief, and praying God to bless their deliverers. There were eager inquiries made of what had happened elsewhere, during those long newless eighty-seven days within the defences of Lucknow when all the rest of the world was a sealed book to the garrison; and the first joy of the happy union was marred by the sad tidings brought to them from without. There were some who wished that they had never lived to see the day.*

Such was the first relief of Lucknow. How Have- lock's force fought its way from Cawnpore to Luck- now, achieving many victories, but encountering numerous impediments and obstructions which for- bade his turning them to account; how Outram with characteristic chivalry and generosity waived his right of command in favour of the General, who had for so long borne the burden and the heat of the day; how the glorious Neill was struck down on entering Lucknow, at the head of his men, by almost the last unerring shot fired by the enemy from their

1857.
September.

Sept. 25.

---

* " Wives, who had long mourned their husbands as dead were now restored to them; others fondly looking forward to glad meetings with those near and dear to them, now for the first time learnt that they were alone. On all sides eager inquiries for relations and friends were made. Alas! in two many in- stances the answer was a painful one."—*Journal of a Staff Officer.*

walled cover—must be told in another Book of this History. I have now to write of a great event, beside which even this first Relief of Lucknow sinks into comparative insignificance. A few days before Lucknow was relieved by Havelock, Wilson had captured Delhi.

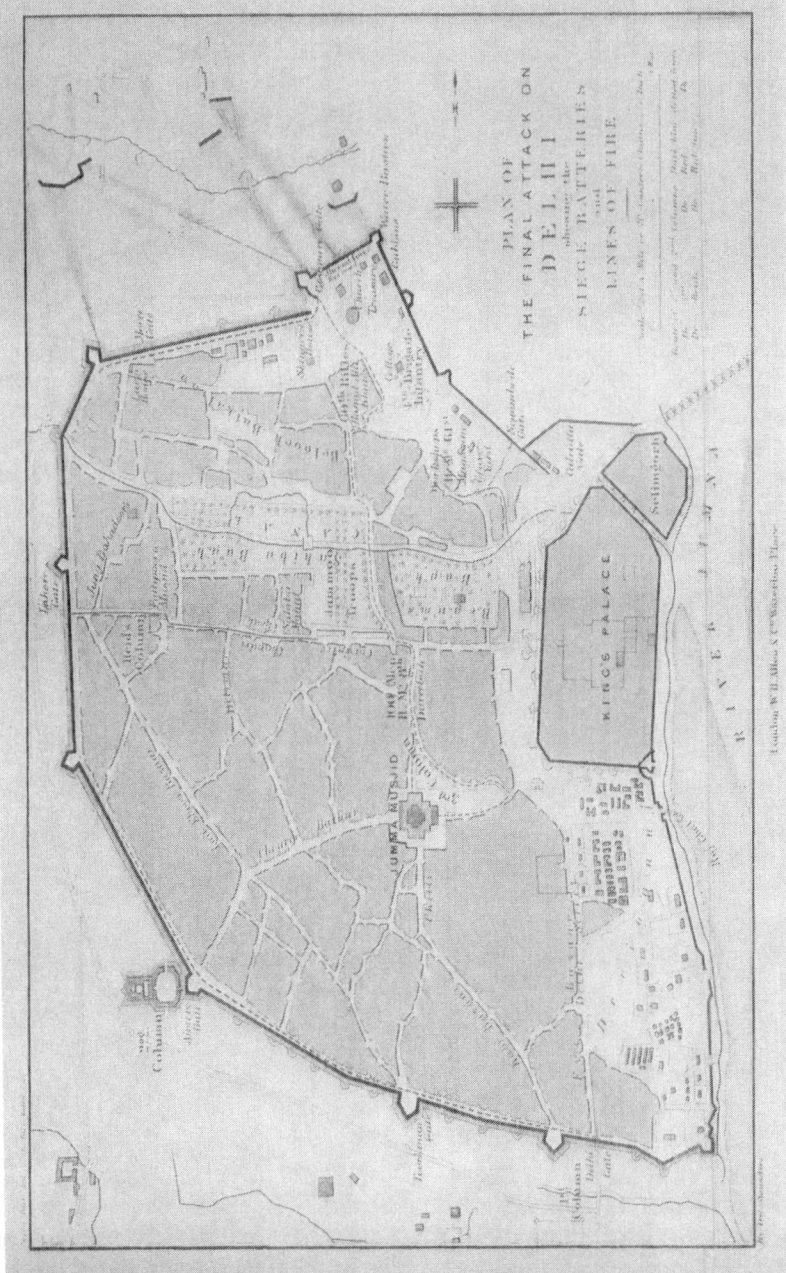

PLAN OF
THE FINAL ATTACK ON
DELHI
showing the
SIEGE BATTERIES
and
LINES OF FIRE

KING'S PALACE

JUMMA MUSJID

RIVER JUMNA

London W.H. Allen & Co. Waterloo Place

CHAPTER IV.

THE DAWN OF SEPTEMBER—ANXIETY FOR THE ASSAULT—WILSON'S CHIEF
ASSISTANTS—ARRIVAL OF THE LAST REINFORCEMENTS FROM THE NORTH
—THE QUESTION OF ASSAULT DEBATED—WILSON AND BAIRD SMITH—
THE FINAL ORDER GIVEN—ERECTION OF THE BREACHING BATTERIES
—EFFORTS OF THE ARTILLERY AND ENGINEERS—ALEXANDER TAYLOR.

THE time for resolute action had now come. In
the last volume of this History, I brought down
the narrative of the so-called " Siege of Delhi" to
the end of the month of August. But, up to that
time, we had been the Besieged and not the Besiegers. Of the wonderful heroism and the consummate patience—of the gallant actions then performed,
of the grievous sufferings then bravely endured, no
words can speak in language of sufficient admiration.
It was, indeed, this waiting game that tried the metal
of our people, all those long months, not of inaction, but of profitless activity—under burning suns,
under heavy rains, under constant exposure; wasting
human life, only to prove that we had lost nothing
of our old vitality. But all this was changed in
September. The dawn of that month saw our preparations nearly complete for the delivery of the
final assault. John Lawrence had despatched from
the Punjab the last of his succours, and, in the estimation of the general camp, the City of the Mogul

1857.
Septembe

1857.
September.
was doomed—and all who held high carnival in it,
in proud defiance of the English.

Neville
Chamberlain.
There were then, under the Chief Commander of
the Delhi Field Force, three men in the very prime
of life, who, holding high position in the Army, were
working strenuously to accomplish, with the least
possible delay, the great final consummation of the
assault on the doomed city. There was Neville
Chamberlain, who had been severely wounded, but
who had lost none of his pristine energy. As chief
of the Army Staff, he had been ever ready with sustaining and invigorating counsel; but his vigour was
tempered by a clear, sound judgment, and a just
appreciation of surrounding circumstances. If, looking from a distance at the work which lay before
Anson and Barnard, he took up the Punjabee war-
cry, and was disposed to censure what seemed to be
the weakness and reluctance of our leaders, a nearer
view of the actual difficulties of the position convinced him that he had greatly underrated them.
Eager as he had been for the assault, he had not
been long on Barnard's Staff before he confessed that,
with the scanty means then at our disposal, it was a
desperate enterprise. He was the man who first
described it, in language often afterwards quoted,
as the "gambler's throw." But nothing could have
moved him an inch from the ground which we had
taken up. The idea of a retrograde movement was
an abomination in his eyes. He knew that we needed
only a few more companies and a few more guns to
make Delhi our own; and he never ceased to do his
best, even when least capable of exertion, to persist in
this course of action. It was a fortunate circum-

stance, too, that at this time, when Chamberlain's _{*placeholder*} 1857.
wound necessarily kept him much in his tent, he had September.
the assistance of a young officer of the highest promise, whose great gifts were fast winning the confidence of his elders. In Captain Norman, of the
Adjutant-General's Department, there was a rare
combination of those qualities which make a wise
counsellor and a man of strenuous action. He had
all the enthusiasm and the enterprise of lusty youth,
and all the staid intelligence of mature manhood;
and there was scarcely a man in Camp who did not
recognise in him one of its leading spirits.

Then there was Baird Smith, Chief of the En- Baird Smith.
gineer Department, who was also enfeebled by much
sickness, and the distresses of a painful wound. He
had been struck by the fragment of a shell, when
superintending his work in the batteries, and he had
been lamed by the blow; but, when he ought to
have been on the sick-list, he was in the full swing
of active employment; when he ought to have been
in his tent, he was busy in the works. Worn to a
skeleton by the most weakening of all ailments, he
went about, when it was possible for him to go about
at all, saturated with opium and brandy, dragging his
maimed limb after him, with painful efforts; but
never losing his high courage, or the habitual cheerfulness of his demeanour.* Like Chamberlain, he

---

* See the following, from a private
letter written by Baird Smith after
the capture of Delhi: "An attack of
camp scurvy had filled my mouth
with sores, shaken every joint in my
body, and covered me all over with
livid spots, so that I was marvellously unlovely to look upon. A
smart knock on the ankle, from the
splinter of a shell which burst in my
face—in itself, however, a mere ba-
gatelle of a wound—had been of necessity neglected, under the pressing
and incessant calls upon me, and had
grown worse and worse, till the whole
foot below the ankle became a black
mass, and seemed to threaten mortification. I insisted, however, on being
allowed to use it until the place was
taken, mortification or not; and
though the pain was sometimes horrible, I carried my point, and kept up

1857.
September.

Alexander
Taylor.

John Nichol-
son.

had an assistant, who was one of the younger heroes of the Camp. In Alexander Taylor, his second in command, he found a man capable of any amount of work, and ready for any heroic enterprise. His energies were unbounded, his spirit unfailing; and it was truly a fortunate circumstance, that when the frailty of the flesh restricted Baird Smith's personal activities, Taylor was ever ready and eager to pass from point to point, and to display his bodily presence, which was always inspiriting and encouraging. There was little or no sympathy between Wilson and Baird Smith. They were men altogether cast in different moulds. But the General fully recognised the great attainments of the Chief Engineer; and though rarely outwardly courteous or orally compliant, practically yielded to his opinions.

And now united with these Two, and in daily counsel with them, was John Nicholson, a born soldier, who seemed to have come down to Delhi with a special mission to take it. He had chafed under the long delay, which had left the vast and guilty city so long in the hands of the mutineers. Patience was not one of his virtues. With great ardour commonly some impetuosity is combined. John Nicholson had not the cool temper and calm judgment of Neville Chamberlain. He overlooked all difficulties and ignored all responsibilities; and, perhaps, he did not always make allowance for those who clearly saw the one and were compelled to accept the other. He could not stand still. Active among the active, he was eager to execute any kind of work that might be entrusted to him,

to the last . . . . and to crown the pleasant catalogue, I was worn to a shadow by a constant diarrhœa, and consumed as much opium, with as little effect, as would have done credit to my father-in-law (De Quincey)."—*MS. Correspondence.*

until the day of final retribution should arrive, when he coveted, and believed that he would obtain, the post of honour at the head of the storming party. No man doubted his power, and no man envied his reputation. All felt that a great soldier had come among them, full-brained and lion-hearted; and they looked to him to lead them to victory.

In the early morning of the 4th of September the siege guns, drawn by elephants, appeared upon the l:idge, with an immense assemblage of carts laden with ammunition—sufficient, it was said, "to grind Delhi to powder." On the 6th, the residuary Rifles from Meerut marched into Camp, strong, healthy, and jubilant, welcomed by the inspiring notes of the band of the Fifty-second and the cheers of their old comrades. On the morning of the 8th, the Jummoo Contingent, promised by Gholab Singh and sent down by his son, made their appearance, with Richard Lawrence at their head, and were greeted by the General and the Commissioner. Then the spirits of all men rose, for they saw the beginning of the end. The days of waiting and watching were spent. Every man, every gun, every shot, every shell that could be sent down for the final assault had now reached its destination. There was no pretext for further delay. The waste of a single hour would have been a crime, for our troops were dying fast, and the enemy were escaping. The "real siege of Delhi" was now to commence.

There are men now living, as I write, who will never forget that crisis; there are others, gone to their rest, who were stirred to the very depths of their natures by a grand enthusiasm, which made

1857.
September.

Sept. 4–6–8.
Arrival of the last reinforcements.

Question of assault.

them cast aside every consideration of military discipline and decorum, and gird their loins up for that
which would have been to them either total ruin or
a grand reputation. They thought that the General
was wavering ; that even then he hesitated to issue
the orders for the final assault ; and had denial come
they were prepared to appeal to the Army, to have
put the Commander under arrest, and to have delivered the assault either under the direction of the
Chief Engineer, or of a Commander selected by
themselves. Eager among the eager was John
Nicholson, whose strong impulses were not to be
curbed, and who never scrupled to say what others
ventured only to think. "The game is completely
in our hands," he wrote to John Lawrence on the
11th of September ; " we only want the player to
move the pieces. Fortunately, after making all
kinds of objections and obstructions, and even
threatening more than once to withdraw the guns
and abandon the attempt, Wilson has made everything over to the Engineers, and they and they alone
will deserve the credit of taking Delhi. Had Wilson
carried out his threat of withdrawing the guns, I was
quite prepared to appeal to the Army to set him
aside and elect a successor. The purport of his
last Memorandum, in reply to the Engineers, ran
thus : 'I disagree with the Engineers entirely. I
foresee great, if not insuperable difficulties in the
plan they propose; but as I have no other plan
myself I yield to the remonstrances of the Chief.
Engineer.' The above are almost the very words used
by him." And, in truth, they were but little wrong.

But it is just that I should pause here for a little
space to make clear and intelligible, by reference
to documents before me, the facts out of which arose

this pregnant talk of the Camp. On the 20th of
August, Wilson, then in doubt with respect to the
sufficiency of his force for the capture and occupation
of Delhi, had written to Baird Smith saying:

GENERAL ARCHDALE WILSON TO COLONEL BAIRD SMITH.

" MY DEAR SMITH,—A letter has been received from the
Governor-General urging our immediately taking Delhi, and
he seems angry that it has not been done long ago. I wish
to explain to him the true state of affairs: that Delhi is
seven miles in circumference, filled with an immense fanatical
Mussulman population, garrisoned by full 40,000 soldiers
armed and disciplined by ourselves, with 114 heavy pieces of
artillery mounted on the walls, with the largest magazine of
shot, shell, and ammunition in the Upper Provinces at their
disposal, besides some 60 pieces of field artillery, all of our
own manufacture, and manned by artillerymen drilled and
taught by ourselves ; that the Fort itself has been made so
strong by perfect flanking defences erected by our own engineers, and a glacis which prevents our guns breaking the
walls lower than eight feet from the top, without the labour
of a regular siege and sap—for which the force and artillery
sent against it has been quite inadequate; that an attempt
to blow in the gates and escalade the walls was twice contemplated, but that it was considered, from the state of preparation against such an attack on the part of the rebels, such
an attempt would inevitably have failed, and have caused the
most irreparable disaster to our cause ; and that, even if we
had succeeded in forcing our way into the place, the small
force disposable for the attack would have been most certainly
lost in the numerous streets of so large a city, and have been
cut to pieces. It was, therefore, considered advisable to con-
fine our efforts to holding the position we now occupy, which
is naturally strong, and has been daily rendered more so by
our engineers, until the force coming up from below could
join to co-operate in the attack. That since the command of
the force has devolved on me, I have considered it imperatively necessary to adopt the same plan as the only chance of
safety to the Empire, and that I strongly urge upon his

1857.
August 20.
Lordship the necessity of his ordering General Havelock's or some other force marching upon Delhi as soon as possible. The force under 'my command is, and has been since the day we took up our position, actually besieged by the mutineers, who, from the immense extent of suburbs, and gardens extending nearly to the walls of the town, have such cover for their attacks, that it has been very difficult to repel them, and at the same time to inflict such a loss as would deter a repetition of them. They have frequently been driven back with loss, but they immediately take refuge under the grape fire of their heavy guns on the city walls, and, on our retirement, reoccupied their former positions ; every such attack upon them has entailed a heavy loss upon our troops, which we can ill spare, and has done us little good. I shall be reinforced by a siege train from Ferozepore by the end of this or beginning of next month, when I intend to commence more offensive operations against the city ; but I cannot hold out any hope of being able to take the place until supported by the force from below. As an Artillery officer, I have no hesitation in giving my opinion that the attack on Delhi, garrisoned and armed as it now is, is as arduous an undertaking as was the attack on Bhurtpore in 1825-26, for which 25,000 troops and 100 pieces of artillery were not considered too large a force. I enclose a return of the original force which was sent down to capture this strong place, and also a return of the present effective force, including sick and wounded, from which his Lordship will see how desperate would have been any attempt to take the city by assault, more especially as the mutineers keep a large portion of their force encamped outside the city walls, who, on our assaulting the city, could easily attack and capture our camp, with all our hospitals, stores, and ammunition, unless a strong provision was made against it. Something of this sort I intend forwarding to the Governor-General, and shall be glad if you will return this with such remarks and emendations as your experience as Chief Engineer suggests.

"Yours sincerely,

" A. WILSON.

"August 20, 1857."

After the perusal of this letter, Baird Smith drew up a Memorandum stating his reasons most emphatically in favour of immediate action. He contended that although there was always hazard in an assault, the evils of inaction at such a time, were so great, and the chances in our favour were so many, that it would be better to risk the enterprise than to shrink from it. He demonstrated, on scientific grounds, that, although the material resources of the enemy were far greater than our own, the superior forethought and skill, and the perfect union and combination, absent from the designs and operations of the enemy, would give us an immense advantage over them. He represented most urgently to the General that the breaches should be established and the assault should be delivered, with the utmost possible despatch, as the enemy once cognisant of our designs would strengthen their defences without and within the city and render its occupation impossible. To these arguments Wilson reluctantly yielded. The whole responsibility was thrown upon the Chief Engineer. The "ipsissima verba" used by the General were these: "It is evident to me that the results of the proposed operations will be thrown on the hazard of a die; but under the circumstances in which I am placed, I am willing to try this hazard—the more so as I cannot suggest any other plan to meet our difficulties. I cannot, however, help being of opinion that the chances of success, under such a heavy fire as the working parties will be exposed to, are anything but favourable. I yield, however, to the judgment of the Chief Engineer.—A. W." Baird Smith, transcribing the above, observed: "This, I think, every one would allow, places on my shoulders the undivided responsibility for the results of the siege. It would, doubtless, have lightened that burden greatly had I felt assured of the hearty support and concurrence of the General in command; but the withholding of these was no sufficient cause for hesitation, and I was too glad of even a qualified consent to immediate action to be careful as to the terms in which it was given."*

Baird Smith was not a man to shrink from the responsibility thrown upon him. To say that he cheerfully accepted it would be a faint recital of the fact; he eagerly grasped it. And there was not an officer under him, whose heart did not bound with joyous exultation when he knew that the work was to be begun. But Wilson was not wrong when he said that to attempt to erect our batteries so near the city walls, in the face of the enemy's fire from their inexhaustible artillery, was a hazardous undertaking. The eager gallantry of the Engineers believed all things to be possible. And it is by this noble self-reliance that great victories are achieved. But the Engineers, as will presently be shown, had set themselves a task which they could not accomplish. In the midst of that awful but glorious crisis, men saw through a glass darkly. But time has brought them face to face with the Truth. Some of the bravest and best of Wilson's officers, who, heated by the excitements and animosities of the Camp, had condemned this apparent reluctance to order the assault, looking back upon those troublous days, and calmly estimating the difficulties to be encountered and the

---

* Wilson's remarks are written in pencil on the copy of the "Memorandum by the Chief Engineer," which Baird Smith submitted to the General. It is now before me with Wilson's marginal notes.

responsibilities to be sustained, have since acknowledged that less than justice was done at that time to
the Commandant of the Delhi Force. All the principles of warfare were upon his side.   But these
principles have not been much regarded in India.
Everything has been gained by hard blows promptly
delivered in defiance of all principles of war.

Having once resolved to stand the " hazard of the
die," Wilson issued an Address to the Army, manly
and spirit-stirring, and wise in the cautions it conveyed.*   It spoke of the hardships and privations
undergone by the Army, and of the gallantry which
they had on all occasions displayed. It expressed
a cheerful hope that their great trials were now
wearing to a close, and that the grand reward was
close at their feet. It called upon the troops of all
arms to assist the Engineers in the arduous work
that lay before them—in the digging of trenches and
the erection of batteries. It appealed to the Artillery, who, it was said, would have "still harder work
than they had yet had, and which had been so well
and cheerfully performed." Then it spoke wisely and
sagaciously of the precautions to be observed after
the assault should have been delivered. It warned
the soldiers against straggling—it warned them
against indiscriminate plundering—it stimulated the
worst passions of the soldiery by reminding them
(or, as it is customary to say, "I need not remind
them") of the atrocious murders and cruelties committed by the enemy, and told them to spare the
women and the children, but to give no quarter to
the men. And it concluded with the words, " The
Major-General calls upon the Officers of the Force to

1857.
September.
Wilson's
address to
the Army.

---

* It is said to have been written by Baird Smith.

lend their zealous aid and efficient co-operation in the erection of the works of the siege now about to be commenced. He looks especially to the regimental officers of all grades to impress upon their men that the work in the trenches during a siege is as necessary and as honourable as to fight in the ranks during a battle. He will hold all officers responsible for their utmost being done to carry out the directions of the Engineers ; and he confidently trusts that all will exhibit a healthy and hearty spirit of emulation and zeal, from which he has no doubt that the happiest results will follow in the brilliant termination of all their labours."

And then began a work almost unparalleled in the history of modern warfare. That science, which has taught us how to make the siege of fortified places almost a certainty in the success of its results, was now of no service to us. The approach by parallels, so beautiful upon paper, and so effective in practice, was to us as if War and Science had been wholly divorced. The ring of fire closing in slowly, but surely, upon a doomed fortress, shutting up the garrison within its walls and reducing them to the necessity of surrender, was now to our English officers only a memory of the stirring pages of Napier and Jones. What they saw was an attacking force, scarcely one-third of the numerical strength of the enemy, who had still possession also of some important suburbs, without cover of any well-constructed trenches, bringing their guns within fire of the walls of Delhi, and pouring forth day and night an incessant shower of shot and shell, resolute to atone for the failure of science by gigantic physical efforts and an unexampled display of British pluck.

The plan of attack was that which Baird Smith had projected before he left Roorkhee, and of the efficacy of which his convictions had never been shaken. It was the plan which had commended itself to all our Engineer officers from the first establishment of our Army on the Ridge. Investment with our limited means being impossible, it was necessary to select a front of attack on which all our available breaching power could be brought to bear. The front to be assailed contained the Moree, the Cashmere, and the Water Bastions, with their connecting curtains. These works had, not many years before, been greatly strengthened and improved by our own Engineer officers, so that we well knew the force to be applied to their demolition. There were very important reasons for this selection—Firstly, because our left flank would be protected by the river, thus leaving us only the right flank to guard ; secondly, because the flanking fire from the city would thus be comparatively harmless, as only the Moree Bastion commanded the ground in front of it ; thirdly, because there was excellent cover to within a short distance of the walls.* The insurgents might have done more to increase both their offensive and their defensive powers, but they had failed to do so ; and it was permitted to us, therefore, to take advantage of their neglect.† Some thought, however, that when the enemy should see that we were preparing our batteries in earnest so as to bring a crushing fire from a short distance upon their walls, they would raise cover for a larger number of guns wherewith to

1857.
Sept. 7—13.
The plan of attack.

* MS. Memorandum by an Engineer Officer.   † Medley, page 73.

silence our batteries. It was manifest, therefore, that every hour was of the utmost importance to us; and so all our people went to work as if they had never had a day's fighting—never known a day's fatigue.

Construction of the batteries.

Then, night and day, worked the Artillery and the Engineers, as those services, with the lustre of long years of past activities upon them, had never, perhaps, worked before. The first thing was to construct the batteries behind which our guns were to work; the next was to get our heavy guns into position. Brownlow had charge of the Engineer's Park—Hogge of the Park of Artillery. Ever since his first appearance in Camp, Baird Smith had been collecting the materials of the batteries which were to cover the captors of Delhi. Immense supplies of gabions, and fascines, and sand-bags had been prepared, with scaling ladders and all else required for the later operations of the attack. The first heavy battery was traced out on the evening of the 7th,* and all through the night the work was being pressed forward as silently as circumstances would permit; but silence was, indeed, impossible. The large number of camels that were bringing down the *matériel* of the batteries, and the bullocks which were dragging the carts laden with ordnance stores, followed by the heavy guns, each with a team of forty floundering beasts, made such confusion, and the drivers, who are nothing if not clamorous, made such a noise, that it is marvellous that the enemy did not discover our designs and pour an unceasing fire

* There had been a light battery previously (evening of the 6th) erected upon the plateau of the Ridge to the left hand of the Sammy House. The object of this was to keep the ground clear and to protect the operations going on below. This battery contained eight light pieces —six 9-pounders and two 24-pound howitzers—under the command of Captain Remmington.

upon our toiling people. For a time all was secure; and things looked hopeful in the battery, when a heavy shower of grape came in from the Moree, and after a short interval another, too well-directed and too fatally destructive. Then the Engineers must have been much troubled in their minds, what would be the state of the working parties in the morning, if the insurgents should continue thus to molest us all through the night. It was, indeed, a terrible question. But the painful expectation of the renewal of the fire from the bastion soon died away, for there was not another flash, another sound; and the work went on without any further interruption. The carriage, and the cattle, and the drivers, and the camp-followers were cleared away before the morning sun shone upon the scene. The ammunition was stored. The guns were ready for work. But all the exertions of the Engineers, under the vigorous direction of the inexhaustible Alec Taylor, had not sufficed to fix the platforms on which they were to be mounted. No men could have done more; but they had set themselves a task which could not be accomplished in a single night, and so far the doubts of the General were confirmed. He had rightly forecast the difficulty; and when it was reported to him that it had arisen, he was disposed to withdraw the guns. But the man in command was not one to go a step backwards. Let the Moree batteries roar as they might, he would not give the order for the withdrawal of the British Artillery. So they gallantly faced the fire and went on with their work.

The battery—known as Battery No. 1—was at a distance of seven hundred yards from the enemy's works. It was divided into two parts connected by a trench. The right portion was constructed to cover five heavy guns and a howitzer, the special function of which was to demolish the Moree Bastion —our most obtrusive assailant all through the siege. The left contained four guns, intended to keep down the fire of the Cashmere Bastion. This battery was under the command of Major James Brind, who had virtually, indeed, commanded the heavy Artillery throughout the greater portion of the operations before Delhi,* who had always been foremost where work was to be done, and who, whilst careful in the extreme of his men, had exposed himself in a manner which had called forth the remonstrances of his friends. If there was any fault to be found with him, it was the glorious fault of doing too much. His restless bravery never halted. He did not know what it was to "stand at ease."† But this very activity, though sometimes wasted, suggested, when there was real work to be done, that Brind was the man to do it. He had now the honour, coveted by every artilleryman in the field, of commencing the

---

* I have before said (vol. ii. pp. 594, 595) that the services of the Foot Artillery, during the period which preceded the actual siege, have been insufficiently recorded. It seems that there were some official misunderstandings as to the authority, whose duty it was to report them, which caused them not to be reported at all.

† It was said of Major Brind that he "never slept"—and the statement was no great exaggeration. I am told that he more than once addressed his men, saying, as he shouldered a musket, "Now, you lie down and rest. Your Commandant will defend the battery." The same informant, himself an officer of the highest gallantry, often mentioned in preceding pages of this narrative,

said to me, "We talk about Victoria Crosses — Brind is a man who should be covered with them from head to foot." See also the letters of Major Reid, now (1875) Sir Charles Reid, one of the foremost of the Delhi heroes: "Battery No. 1 was commanded by my dear old friend, Major Brind, who had been constantly on duty with me on the Ridge, and who had given me most able assistance on the night of the Eed attack. Indeed, on all occasions the exertions of this noble officer were indefatigable. He was always to be found where his presence was most required; and the example he set to his officers and men was beyond all praise. A finer soldier I never met."

attack upon those works which had so long defied us. But on that morning, in that unfinished battery, it was a service of extreme danger. The morning light had fully revealed our designs to the insurgents, and laid bare our position. So they poured down from the Moree a pitiless shower of shot and shell, and sent out light guns with riflemen, to endeavour to take the battery in flank, whilst Brind's gunners, animated by his noble example, were working, unshaken and undismayed, to get their pieces into position. Only one gun was mounted when the fire commenced. Then "Brind dragged a howitzer well to the rear and fired over the parapet."* It was but a feeble response that he could return to the bellowing enemy; but he was resolute to give them something, and he knew that he would soon give them something more. Thus, ever as the sun rose higher and higher, the enemy fired and our people fell. But as gun after gun was mounted on its platform, the inequality of the conflict ceased; and then began that of which the insurgents behind their walls had had no former experience—perhaps, indeed, no conception. They had laughed at our long shots. But the close quarters to which we now brought our heavy guns, and the admirable manner in which they were served, gave altogether a new aspect to the operations before Delhi. The insurgents stood manfully to their guns. But the masonry of the Moree soon began to crumble; and ere the heat of the day had passed, the fire of the enemy had slackened, and before sunset it had feebly dwindled away into total quietude. But they had fired to some purpose. Our men were scarce, though our material was abundant, and the result of that first day's work was that

1857.
Sept. 7—13.

* Medley.

there were some seventy casualties in our trenches.*
Nor was it the fire from the Moree alone that distressed our people in the battery.   They were, also,
much molested by some light field-pieces and skirmishers of the enemy posted on our right.   These
enfiladed the battery and sometimes even took it in
reverse.   To meet these attacks and to protect our
position Brind brought down two field guns from
the rear.   Moreover, the mutineers, inspired probably by our Sappers, who to the number of eight
hundred had joined the insurgent force, ran a trench
along the plain in front of both sections of the battery, about midway between the city walls and our
position, from which they kept up a constant fire
and did some damage to us, as the battery had been
hastily erected without mantlets and with over-large
embrasures.†

Whilst the eighteen-pounders were thus blazing
away at the Moree, the twenty-four pounders in
the left section of the battery were directing their
fire on the Cashmere Bastion.   This section of the
battery was placed under the command of Major
Frank Turner, one of the best Horse Artillery
officers in the service.   But previous exposure
to the sun had broken him down; and an utter
failure of his powers of endurance compelled him
reluctantly to withdraw from the command.   He
was succeeded by Major Edward Kaye, who had
taken an active part from the beginning in all the

---

* "No. 1 Battery was unquestionably the key of the attack, and
on its success depended the opening
of Delhi to our assaulting columns.
The progress of the other batteries
depended essentially on its efficiency; and but for your moral
courage, clear perception, and un-
wavering resolution in arming and
working it, in spite of all obstacles,
consequences would have followed
causing the greatest embarrassment."—*Colonel Baird Smith to
Major Brind.—MS. Correspondence.*
† MS. Memoranda by Engineer
and Artillery Officers.

operations on the Ridge. Scarcely had the completion of the parapet enabled him to get his guns
in position, when a round shot from the Moree
shattered the skull of one of his subalterns—Lieutenant Hildebrand—and Riding-master Budd, of the
Horse Artillery, was soon afterwards disabled by the
fire of the enemy. But soon our guns were fairly
in position, and right good service they did, not
only by keeping down the fire of the Cashmere
Bastion, but by deluding the enemy into the belief
that our assault was to be delivered entirely from
the right. During the greater part of three days
this left section kept up a continued fire on the
enemy's works; but towards noon of the 10th its
operations were brought to a close by the internal
ignition of the battery. Hastily constructed of
fascines, made of very dry brushwood, it caught fire
from the blazing of our own guns. Every effort was
made to suppress the flames; but the efforts were
vain, for water was scarce and had to be brought
from a distance; and the water-carriers being much
exposed, going and coming, suffered severely from
the fire of the enemy. The Infantry on duty in the
battery (some details of the Kumaon Battalion) were
most zealous in their efforts, and suffered severely
from the musketry-fire of the enemy. Several, including Lieutenant Lockhart, who commanded the
party, were severely wounded. But, all to no purpose. The fire could not be mastered. So the guns
were withdrawn—and made ready for their removal
at night to No. 2 Battery. And thus the left section
of No. 1 became a thing of the past. It was not, however, a disaster of any moment. For that part of
the battery had done its work; and both the guns

2 o 2

and the gunners were wanted for service nearer to the real point of attack.

For by this time Battery No. 2 had been constructed — the left section immediately in front of Ludlow Castle and the right about eighty yards to the right front of the former. How it happened that the enemy had allowed us to take up such a position, within six hundred yards of the city, no one could explain, except upon the supposition that the insurgents, though never wanting in courage, were greatly wanting in wit. It was expected that we should have a hard fight for the ground, but our occupation of it was never contested. And yet this battery was intended to have, and in effect did have, a most potential effect upon the issue of the war. It was designed to crush the Cashmere Bastion and the adjacent works, and so to breach the walls as to open an entrance for our assaulting columns. It was to comprise, in the right section, cover for seven heavy howitzers and two eighteen-pounders; and in the left for nine twenty-four-pounders. The experiences of the first night had proved the impossibility of completing the battery and getting the guns into position before daybreak on the 9th; so the Engineers went more quietly to work, and there was not, during the darkness, much of a mischievous character from the enemy's guns to impede the operations of our working parties. On the second night the battery was completed and the guns brought into position. The right was to be commanded by Major Kaye; the left by Major J. H. Campbell.

When this Battery No. 2 had been completed,* it

---

* It was completed on the night of the 10th—11th, and the heavy guns from the left section of No. 1, then joined; others were brought down from the Park.

was not thought advisable immediately to unmask it. It was better to finish the other offensive works for the left attack, so that a simultaneous fire might be opened from both batteries. "The reason," said Baird Smith, "for delaying the opening of this battery until No. 3 has been armed, is that at present the siege works on the left are being carried on with very few casualties in consequence of the apparent ignorance of the enemy that any attack on that side is meditated."* So the works of No. 3 went on apace with little interruption. This battery was erected behind one of the buildings of the Custom House, at a distance of not more than a hundred and eighty yards from the Water Bastion, upon which our guns were to play. It was to cover six eighteen-pounders, under the command of Major Scott, who had commanded No. 14 Light Field Battery throughout the siege. If the building did not much protect our working parties, it greatly obscured the nature of the work on which they were engaged. The enemy never clearly knew what we were doing, but they felt that something was going on that portended mischief, and they poured in such an incessant shower of musketry, with occasional discharges from their mortars, that it was difficult and dangerous to work even under the cover of the night, and impossible after the dawn of day. The workmen were principally Natives and non-combatants, but they faced death as bravely for their Christian employers as if they had been English

1857.
Sept. 7---13
No. 3 Battery.

---

* Baird Smith had recommended that No. 3 Battery should be commenced before No. 2. (*Memorandum by Chief Engineer*), but General Wilson had objected to this, saying, "The commencement of No. 3 Battery before No. 2 is, I think, objectionable, and will cause a fearful loss of life from the untouched batteries in the Cashmere Bations. It would be much safer to silence the guns on the left bastion before erecting No. 3." (*MS. Notes*). Wilson was right. I am told, however, that in point of fact, No. 2 Battery did open fire before No. 3—indeed, before it was completely constructed.

soldiers.* There is nothing more true than that the calm courage of our Native adherents enabled us to recover India from their own countrymen.

Of a different character was the courage displayed by our allies from beyond the border. Our working parties were composed of men of all races—of all sorts and descriptions of people—whom we could press into our service ; for the labour was great and incessant, the heat was intense, and exhaustion soon came upon those who had to lift heavy weights. On the night of the 10th, no Sappers or Pioneers being available, Taylor had been compelled to employ the services of men drawn from two of our European regiments in the heavy howitzer battery. They worked heartily and effectively ; but soon after midnight they were failing from sheer exhaustion, and then the Directing Engineer bethought himself of our newly-arrived Jummoo Contingent, and sent a hundred and twenty men down to the battery. Elated with the thought of some fighting, to be followed probably by plunder, they streamed down, armed to the teeth. But when the true nature of the service required from them was explained, they looked askance at the shovels, and the sand, and the sand-bags, and murmured among themselves. So Medley, the Engineer, who had charge of the work, with those immediately under him, began cheerily and lustily to fill the sand-bags, and to do other coolies' work. Then the Commanding Officer of the Jummoo Detachment, feeling some compunctions of shame, followed the lead of the European officers, and presently all his men piled their

---

* "They were merely unarmed Native Pioneers, and not meant to be fighting men. With the passive courage so common to Natives, as man after man was knocked over, they would stop a moment, weep a little over their fallen friend, pop his body in a row along with the rest, and then work on as before,"— *Medley*, pp. 82, 83.

arms and laboured with the heartiest goodwill. All,
for some time, was quiet, as they worked under the
darkness of the night; but in the hour before the
dawn, there came from the enemy's position in front
a sharp shower of musketry, which so excited our
Dogra friends, that they seized their matchlocks and
discharged them with such impetuosity in the direction of their assailants, that they well-nigh shot down
all our people who were before them in the battery.
It was a mercy and a miracle that a bullet did not go
through Medley's head. The danger was too serious
to be repeated; so our impulsive allies were told
that if they wished to fight they were to go out into
the open, but that they had been brought into the
battery to work.

Whilst cover was being provided for our heavy
guns and howitzers, a powerful mortar battery was
in course of construction at the Koodsea Bagh. It
was one of the pleasantest places in the neighbourhood, shaded by orange and lemon trees, and odorous
with the perfume of the fruit. Sheltered on three
sides by a high wall, the position we had taken up,
though but two hundred and fifty yards from the
city, was but little exposed to the musketry fire of
the insurgents. There was some hard work for our
people in cutting away the trees; but the axe and
the bill-hook were plied with hearty goodwill, and
the ground was soon sufficiently cleared for the
erection of the battery and the planting of the
mortars. They were under the command of Major
Tombs, and he was not one to lose a minute in
doing good execution with his shells. Before the
batteries were completed for the left attack, he was
ready to open upon the lines between the Cashmere
and the Water Bastions. But his orders were not

1857.
Sept. 11.
to commence firing until the morning of the 11th, when it was expected that all the heavy guns and howitzers on the left would be fairly in position. Brind's battery all the time continued to pour in a destructive fire on the right, which so crippled the enemy, that the Moree Bastion and all belonging to it had become little more than a name.

There was great joy throughout the Camp, when it was known that the batteries for the left attack were so far completed that the work of breaching could be commenced. The circumstances of our position were such as to engender impatience. Those who did not know the difficulties with which the Engineers were contending, were disappointed that the breaching operations along the whole line of the enemy's works had not sooner commenced. Doubtless, the first forecast had been somewhat erroneous. Men, who are eager for the realisation of certain results, are wont to be over-sanguine in their calculation of the facilities of accomplishing them. But none could have worked with heartier zeal or more unflagging perseverance than the Artillery and Engineers engaged on that great work.

Scott's Battery.
On the 11th of September, Scott's heavy guns* had been dragged into position, under such a fire of musketry as might have deterred men of fainter hearts; and then, although the battery, from causes

* Norman says: "The establishment of Major Scott's battery within one hundred and eighty yards of the walls, to arm which heavy guns had to be dragged from the rear under a constant fire of musketry, was an operation that could rarely have been equalled in war." Under instructions received from the Chief Engineer, Scott had brought down his guns on the night of the 10th, but on reaching the site of the intended battery, after a difficult march, he found the works incomplete, or rather scarcely commenced. The ground had been cleared, but there were no signs of a battery. To have left the guns within such an easy distance from the enemy would have insured their destruction, so he was compelled to withdraw them before daylight.

to be presently displayed, could not be unmasked, 1857.
there was no longer any reason why the final attack Sept. 11—12.
should be longer deferred. And well was it for us
that there was no more delay. Mercifully the intel-
lects of the besieged had been dulled for a time. But
before our works were finished, they had woken up
to a sense of the expediency of mounting heavy guns
along the curtain between the Cashmere and the
Water Bastions, from which such a fire could have
been poured into our works on the left as to render
them wholly untenable.* But God's providence
arrested this calamity; the light had broken upon
the enemy too late.

At eight o'clock, the fire from our twenty-four-
pounders commenced. They were in the left section
of No. 2 Battery, under the command of Major
Campbell; and all the nine opened at the same
moment with terrific effect upon the Cashmere
Bastion. When the roar of this great first salvo had
ceased, up went three ringing cheers of triumphant
delight from the Artillery in the battery. We were
now breaching in earnest. When the smoke cleared
away, it was seen that the first discharge of our heavy
guns had brought down vast masses of masonry, and
that a few more such well-aimed blows would reduce
their boasted defences to crumbling ruins. The guns
on the Cashmere Bastion replied; and the enemy
at least had some revenge, for they severely wounded
the Commandant of the heavy guns, and sent him
crippled from the battery. But a little more of our
practice from both sections of the breaching battery,
aided by Tombs's mortars on the Koodsea Bagh,

* "So nearly were they being have assaulted at all, but must have
ready, that had the subsequent as- been driven from our batteries, or
sault been delayed for forty-eight had our men knocked to pieces
hours, I believe that we could not there.—*Medley.*

soon reduced them to silence. Then it was a grand sight to see the walls of Delhi falling to pieces, as shot and shell rained heavily upon them; the breach widening and widening as the eight-inch shells bursting on its crest, brought down whole yards of parapet, the cruel signs of a future desolation becoming more apparent every hour. It was something which all can understand, apart from circumstances of time and space. But only those who had waited for the great opportunity—who, for months, had been insulted by an enemy behind the walls, who had seen their comrades falling around them, who had toiled day and night under burning suns and drenching rains, and had seemingly made no progress towards the reduction of the great Imperial City, can thoroughly appreciate the glorious excitement of seeing, opening out before them, day after day, the road that was to lead them to the re-occupation of Delhi. It was a turning point in the life of our Anglo-Indian Empire such as not even those who had seen the great crisis at Caubul had ever witnessed before.

But there was heavier retribution yet to overtake the insurgents. An hour before noon, on the 12th of September, the advanced battery on the left (No. 3) was unmasked. It had been originally designed that it should open fire simultaneously with No. 2 on the preceding day; but it was found that this was impossible. The battery was constructed of sand-bags placed against the masonry of a part of the old Custom House. The walls had been so broken down as to admit of embrasures being made, through which it was intended that our guns should be pointed at the Water Bastion, only a hundred and sixty yards distant. These embrasures had been temporarily filled up with sand-bags, as a blind to the enemy, but, unfortunately, when our people began to remove them, it was found by the morning light that the embrasures, made under cover of the darkness, were so contrived as not to suffer our guns to be brought to bear upon the point intended. To Scott and Taylor this discovery was a bitter disappointment. It was necessary to reconstruct the cheeks of the embrasures, and thus to delay the opening of our guns upon the doomed city. Nothing could be more vexatious and embarrassing. Scott was eager to be first to open fire so as to dismount the enemy's guns at the very outset; but it was only too probable that if the battery were unmasked at mid-day, the insurgents would direct their heavy guns upon it before we could send in a shot. He was recommended to blow the sand-bags out of the embrasures, but this he refused to do, "being satisfied," as he said, " that the *débris* of the sand-bags would fall inwards, and seriously interfere with the accuracy of our fire." Whilst the question of the best mode of procedure was under discussion, a Sikh sapper, with calm courage, quietly proceeded to throw outwards the sand-bags before his own gun. The example was caught up by the gunners behind the other embrasures, and so rapidly was the work of clearance effected, that our guns opened upon the enemy before they had discovered our designs. Then went forth such a stream of heavy shot from our eighteen-pounders, as within that easy range, even if less skilfully directed, must have soon smashed the enemy's guns and pounded the Water Bastion into ruins. The effect was almost instantaneous. The once symmetrical bastion became a shapeless mass of earth and masonry. Then, for the first time, the enemy learnt what was the cannonade we could keep up, now that all our guns were in position, and the most sanguine must have despaired. All through the 12th and 13th the batteries on the left continued their breaching operations, under the direction of Kaye, Johnson,[*] Scott, and Tombs. The roar of fifty heavy pieces of ordnance was to be heard day and night without intermission. Never had our Siege Artillery a greater work before it. Never were guns more nobly served. Our trained gunners were few; but there was not a soldier in the camp who was not eager to handle a sponge-staff, or a portfire, or to bring up the shot and shell to the cannon's mouth. Among these volunteers none were more active than the Lancers. They soon became serviceable gunners, and every officer in charge of a battery was right glad to have their help. It was a service of no little danger, especially in the advanced battery, which was exposed to the incessant musketry fire of the enemy. We could silence their batteries, but we could not stop this skirmishing, and our people were all day long dropping beneath the assaults of the hidden marksmen. The utmost care had been taken to protect the inmates of the battery. Scott had mantlets on all the guns, and he strictly enjoined officers and men to keep themselves well behind them. Thus many lives were saved; but notwithstanding these wise precautions one lamentable casualty in the battery caused a great spasm of grief throughout the whole camp. Whilst working one of the guns, Captain Fagan, of the Artillery, an officer of the highest promise, and, for his years, of great performance, was shot through the head. He had mounted

---

[*] Captain (now Sir Edwin) Johnson, Assistant-Adjutant-General of Artillery, had taken the place of Major Campbell, disabled in the left section of No. 2 Battery.

a gun-carriage and was looking over the mantlet, 1857.
when Scott went up to remonstrate with him. It Sept. 7—13.
was said in camp, and Fagan himself thought, that
he " bore a charmed life." But scarcely had the Death of
words of caution been spoken, when a musket-ball Fagan.
entered his temple, and he fell death-stricken at the
feet of his commandant.*

It has been seen how, all this time, our Engineer Alec Taylor.
officers worked, with unflagging perseverance, in the
batteries. Alec Taylor was the heart and soul of
every movement — always cheery, always active,
never sparing himself—inspiring, aiding, animating
all by his noble example. It was impossible not to
admire—not to endeavour to imitate him. He never
complained ; he never faltered ; almost, it may be
said that he never rested. He had the sole executive direction of all the Engineering department of
the Siege Batteries, which opened the way to the
interior of Delhi. The younger officers of the Engineers swore by him, and in truth there was something almost divine in his wonderful fertility of resource and the self-sacrifice which he continually
displayed. He had studied the ground well, and he
had seized, with quick soldierly eye, upon the exact
points at which it would be desirable to erect our batteries. It was a happy stroke of genius to surprise and
divert the enemy by running up a battery (No. 1) in

* "When the enemy discovered the from front, flanks, and curtain proved
position and object of No. 3 Battery, the importance attached to it by
they at once placed heavy guns in them, and it was a matter of asto-
position on the opposite side of the nishment to all present that, thanks
river to take No. 3 in flank and suc- to the discipline and untiring devo-
ceeded in dismounting one of the tion of officers and men, the battery
18-pounders. Traverses were im- was able to open the required breach
mediately constructed which saved so rapidly (less than thirty-six hours),
the remainder, but the continuous so effectively, and at so small a sacri-
stream of shot, shell, and bullets, fice of life."—*MS. Memorandum by*
directed on this battery by the enemy *an Engineer Officer.*

a single night to play upon the Moree 'Bastion. It was Taylor's unaided idea—as was also the location of No. 3 Battery, the idea of which came suddenly upon him as an inspiration, and was worked out with wonderful promptitude and effect.

Baird Smith
and Taylor.
Among the many controversies which have grown out of this story of the Sepoy War, there is not one which it is more difficult to write of than the question as to whether the chief merit of the operations which resulted in the capture of Delhi is due to Colonel Baird Smith or to Captain Alexander Taylor. Such controversies are always painful ; for it is not easy to extol the merits of one without seeming to detract from the claims of the other. I believe the real historic truth to be this. Neither could have taken Delhi without the help of the other. Alec Taylor was the necessary supplement of Baird Smith. The large-brained chief of the Engineer Staff required just such a second-in-command to carry his plans into execution as he found in the noble-spirited Field-Engineer. The condition of Baird Smith's health was, as I have already said, such as would have sent most men to their beds. Lame from the effects of a painful and neglected wound on the ankle—suffering acutely from one of the cruel scourges of the country, which compelled him to drench himself with opium and brandy, he could not move about from place to place, so as to become a bodily presence, familiar to the eyes of men of all branches and all ranks of the army.* It has, therefore, sometimes been said : "We

---

* Baird Smith says that brandy was his daily sustenance, and that it had no other effect upon him than that of increasing his capacity for work. His brain was never clearer or more active. It carried him through the siege—but afterwards, rest and purer air enabled him to lay aside such dangerous diet.

never saw Baird Smith." Taylor, on the other hand,
though sometimes suffering from fever, was to be seen
everywhere. He had great physical activity and
powers of endurance to give practical expression to
the zeal and courage which animated him. But the
general directions for the conduct of our engineering
operations, often even in minute details, emanated
from Baird Smith. His thoughtfulness in respect of
everything that could in any way contribute to our
success is patent in the masses of manuscripts which
lie before me. In his own handwriting may be read
all his original conceptions and his amended designs;
but these last were rare, for it was but seldom, except
under pressure of altered circumstances, that he saw
any good reason for modifying his first projects. But
all these projects might have failed if there had been
a less able, a less active, and a less courageous officer
than Alec Taylor at the head of the executive
officers of the Engineer Brigade. He was one who
thought nothing impossible, and all men worked
under him with the heartiest goodwill, for he inspired and animated all who came in contact with
him in battery or in trench. Those who were above
him were equally impressed by his noble exertions.
"If I, survive to-morrow," said John Nicholson, on
the eve of the assault, "I will let all the world know
that Alec Taylor took Delhi." This was characteristic of the brave impulsive man, who never lived
to tell the story of the siege. But he erred, as he
did on a previous occasion of which I have spoken,
in not recognising the difference between a responsible and an irresponsible officer, whether at the head
of a regiment or the head of an Army.

No one acknowledged Taylor's services more un-
grudgingly than Baird Smith himself; but he could

not consent that History should accept the statement that the Chief Engineer had been in the background, doing nothing, whilst his first-assistant had gone to the front and done everything for the direction of the operations of the siege. "I think," he wrote to his wife some time afterwards, "that you may dismiss from your mind all sense of trouble about the injustice done to my work at Delhi. It is just as certain as that I am alive to say so, that from the day I joined, to the day I left, not a single vital act was done but under my orders and on my sole responsibility. And I know well that, but for my resolute determination, humanly speaking, there would have been no siege of Delhi at all ; and even that assault which gave value by its success to all the exertions that were made would have ended in deplorable disaster, had I not withstood with effect the desire of General Wilson to withdraw the troops from the city on the failure of Brigadier Campbell's column. Nobody does heartier justice to Taylor's devotion, capacity, and zeal than I do. No personal consideration would, for one moment, induce me to detract, even in the faintest degree, from them. But he was, throughout, my most able and most trusted subordinate, working wholly at my risk and on my responsibility in the one department intrusted to him —namely, the executive duties." And in another letter to a friend in the Royal Artillery he said: "I would not willingly do the very faintest injustice either to Captain Taylor or to any of the other junior officers of the brigade, to whose noble co-operation, given always without reserve and in the most cordial spirit, I was so deeply indebted, and for which I have done my best upon all occasions to express my gratitude. These feelings are especially strong in reference to Taylor, whom I found to be ever, not only the most energetic and competent of seconds, but in all relations a true and right-hearted gentleman. I should be ashamed of myself if I permitted any petty feelings to influence me in estimating his worth; and I feel assured that no credit which may be due to me will ever be really diminished by my doing the amplest and heartiest justice to every man who worked under my orders. But it was with myself alone that the entire responsibility for the conception, progress, and issue of the engineering operations in every essential point rested; and had we failed in our attack, this fact would have been recorded so often and so emphatically, that I should have had none to share the fatal consequences with me."* It is better that, in such a case, Baird Smith should be left to speak for himself. On the subject of responsibility there could be no doubt; and whatsoever question might arise as to the design and execution of the detailed operations of the siege, Alec Taylor was not a man to deny, that as the risk of failure was his chief's, so also should be the credit of success.

1857.
September.
Alec Taylor.

But the chapter, which I have just completed, is devoted mainly to the exploits of the Artillery. I have written in vain, if I have not shown what tremendous work lay before our gunners throughout that critical week; with what consummate courage they faced the unexampled dangers before them, and with what wondrous patience and calm skill they overcame all obstacles and opened the way for the entrance of the British forces into Delhi. I doubt

Services of the Artillery.

* MS. Correspondence.

whether there is any incident of History surpassing
in the boldness alike of its conception and of its execution this bombardment of the Imperial City of the
Moguls. But this was only the crowning work—
the grand culmination of weeks and months of toil
upon the Ridge, vexatious, harassing toil, rather demonstrative than effective, little tending to produce
any immediate results upon the enemy, to attract the
special attention of commanders, or to excite the admiration of comrades. In a little time the heavy-
battery service came to be regarded as part of the
routine work of the Camp. Its importance in keeping down the fire of the enemy and in arresting their
frequent sallies upon our outposts by showing ourselves continually on the alert, could not be over-
valued. To have slackened fire would have been to
encourage and embolden the insurgents; by leaving
them to believe either that our material resources
were on the ebb, or that our personal strength was so
reduced by death and disease that we were unable to
man our batteries. Few but those with scant knowledge of the position talked of this untiring energy as
" wasting our ordnance stores." Had our Rear been
closed, it would have been wholly different; but as
it was, we were never in any real want of ammunition, and we could afford to expend some powder and
shot without every discharge from our batteries palpably producing any great material results.

It is among the accidents of the Service, which all
good soldiers will cheerfully accept, that whilst one
by the very nature of his employment has opportunities of distinguishing himself and finding a niche
in some historical episode, by which his name,
perhaps, may be remembered in later days, another
is condemned to toil on, unnoticed, doing equally

good service to the State, but not of a nature to attract the regards of the Official Reporter or of the
Military Annalist. So it was, emphatically, with the
Bengal Artillery during the long so-called siege of
Delhi. The Horse Artillery and the Light Field
Batteries had opportunities of distinguishing themselves in dashing charges against the assailants of our
outposts ; but the Heavy Artillery on the Ridge had
no occasion of displaying their high qualities save
by their indomitable perseverance and endurance,
until the longed-for summons came to go down below
and to knock the main defences of the city to pieces.
How they did that work, when the time came, I have
endeavoured to show. That General Wilson, an old
and good Artillery officer, did not appreciate—
at least did not acknowledge—the magnificent services
of his own branch, as might have been anticipated,
alike from his sympathies and his experiences, was
generally felt by the regiment. His honesty, if not
his discernment, was conspicuous in this. But the
omissions apparent in the General's despatches caused
much bad feeling in the corps and led to some
painful controversy. Brind, with his wonted earnestness and directness of purpose, pleaded the cause of
his comrades in language which men in authority
were not accustomed to and did not approve. Some
wrongs were righted, but others remained unre-
dressed. It is enough to state that the Major Scott
of these pages, who fought his Light Battery so
nobly, before the day of assault, and then went down
to the post of danger, to command the most exposed
of the Breaching Batteries, still remains undeco-
rated.

CHAPTER V.

THE OCCUPATION OF DELHI—DIFFICULTIES OF THE ENTERPRISE—PLAN
OF ASSAULT DEVELOPED—THE STORMING COLUMNS TOLD OFF—DELI-
VERY OF THE ASSAULT—RESULTS—FIGHTING IN THE CITY—OCCUPATION
OF THE PALACE—DELHI TAKEN—ARREST OF THE KING—SLAUGHTER OF
THE PRINCES—DEATH OF NICHOLSON.

1857.
Sept. 13.
Preparations
for the as-
sault.

In the meanwhile, in Head-Quarters' Camp, upon
the Ridge, Wilson and Baird Smith were taking
counsel together as to the organisation of the assaulting columns, which were to move into the city, when
the breaches should be pronounced practicable.
Chamberlain was still confined to his tent, but he
went out sometimes in a dhooly, and was ever ready
to put forth sound opinions on all military questions,
both of principle and detail. One thing was certain
—that the universal voice of the Camp had proclaimed John Nicholson as the man of men to lead the
storming columns and to beckon them on to victory.
He had come down to Delhi surcharged with the
idea that he was ordained to plant the British standard
on the proud Palace of the Moguls or to die the
soldier's death at the head of his men. The decease
of Sir Henry Lawrence had given an increased so-
briety—indeed, solemnity—to his demeanour. If,
before this, he had been possessed by any vain ambi-

tions; if he had thought of the plaudits of his countrymen and the records of history, all this had passed away. He now thought only of the last words of his dying master—of the words which Lawrence wished to be engraved upon his tomb—and he also "tried to do his duty." He wrote that he wished to "get alongside" of Herbert Edwardes, that he might become more steadfast in his faith and tread more surely in the footsteps of his great exemplar who had died at Lucknow.

On the 13th, Taylor announced that the breaches were practicable. All was then ready for the delivery of the assault on the following day. The composition of the several columns had been minutely arranged. Their leaders were nominated. The precise direction which each column was to take, was laid down, and Baird Smith had mapped out on oil-paper for each commander a plan of the operations entrusted to him, and to the other leaders, to be taken with him for his guidance. A meeting of the principal officers was then summoned. All were present at the meeting, except Nicholson, who purposely or accidentally was down in the heavy batteries watching the effect of Scott's guns and Tombs' mortars.* He felt that his position was secured; and knowing that he was too prone to be

---

* A few days before he had written to the Punjab: "The Engineers have consulted me about the plan of attack though Wilson has not. They tell me they proposed to him that I should be consulted, and that he maintained a chilling silence. I imagine it is as I supposed, that he is afraid of being thought to be influenced by me. I care little, however, whether he receives my suggestions direct or through the Engineers. Like Barnard, he talks about the 'gambler's throw.' I think, however, we have a right to hope for success, and I trust that ere another week passes, our flag will be flying over the Palace minars. Wilson has told me that he intends to nominate me Military Governor, for which I am much obliged, though I would rather he had told me that he intended to give me command of the column of pursuit."—*MS. Correspondence.*

intemperate in speech, he might have thought it better not to be present at a discussion, in the course of which he might express some divergencies of opinion without becoming moderation. Whatsoever the cause, the meeting was held without his animating presence. Wilson unfolded his plans. Nothing could exceed the clearness of the whole design or the minuteness, which left nothing to be guessed at or puzzled over by commanding officers. Baird Smith's charts, some of which are now before me, were guideposts which no one could misunderstand. But there were some inquiries to make surety doubly sure— and some minute explanations in reply. Though satisfactory to the inquirers the answers added little to the original information. And the officers upon whom their several responsibilities had been thrown, quitted Wilson's tent eager for the coming struggle, and full of grand expectations of triumphant success.

The force was divided into four columns and a column of Reserve. The First Column commanded by Brigadier General Nicholson, was to consist of—

Her Majesty's 75th Regiment . . . 300 strong.
1st Bengal Fusiliers . . . . . . 250 ,,
2nd Punjab Infantry . . . . . . 450 ,,

Engineer officers attached, Lieutenants Medley, Lang, and Bingham *

This force was to storm the breach near the Cashmere Bastion and escalade the face of the bastion.

The Second Column was to be commanded by Brigadier Jones, C.B. It consisted of—

---

* Lieut.-Colonel Herbert com-   Jacob the Fusiliers, and Captain
manded the Seventy-fifth, Major   Green the Punjabees.

Her Majesty's 8th Regiment . . . 250 strong.
        „   2nd Fusiliers . . . 250 „
4th Sikh Infantry . . . . 350 „
Engineer officers attached, Lieutenants Greathed, Hovenden,
and Pemberton.*

1857.
Sept. 13.

This column was to storm the breach in the Water
Bastion.

The Third Column was placed under Colonel Campbell, of the Fifty-second. It was to assault by the
Cashmere Gate after its explosion by the Engineers
should have taken effect; and was thus constituted :

Her Majesty's 52nd Regiment . . . 200 strong.
Kumaon Battalion . . . . . . 250 „
1st Punjab Infantry . . . . . . 500 „
Engineer officers attached, Lieutenants Home, Salkeld, and
Tandy.†

The command of the Fourth Column was assigned
to Major Charles Reid of the Sirmoor Battalion, who
had held so long and so gallantly the post at Hindoo
Rao's house. It was to attack and to clear the suburbs of Paharunpore and Kishengunje and to enter
the city by the Lahore Gate. Its components were :

Detachments of European and
    Native Regiments.
Sirmoor Battalion.
Guides Infantry.
Detachment of Dograhs.

860 men, not in-
cluding Jummoo
troops.

Engineer officers attached, Lieutenants Maunsell and
Tennant.

---

* Lieut.-Colonel Greathed commanded the Eighth. The Fusiliers
were under Captain Boyd, and Captain Rothney led the Sikhs.

† The Fifty-Second were under
Major Vigors, the Kumaon Batta-
lion under Captain Ramsay. Charles
Nicholson commanded the Sikhs.

The Fifth or Reserve Column was commanded by Brigadier Longfield, and was thus composed :

Her Majesty's 61st, 250 men (Lieutenant-Colonel Deacon) ; 4th Punjab Infantry, 450 men (Captain Wilde) ; Wing Belooch Battalion, 300 men (Lieutenant-Colonel Farquhar) ; Jheend Auxiliaries, 300 men (Lieutenant-Colonel Dunsford) —Total, 1300 ; besides 200 of 60th Rifles, under Lieutenant-Colonel Jones, after they had covered the advance of the stormers.

But there was one thing more to be done before the assaulting columns could be let loose. Captain Taylor had reported that the breaches were practicable. But it was expedient that they should be examined by some picked Engineer officers. It was a service of some danger ; but there was not an officer in the brigade who would not have eagerly undertaken the duty. Lieutenants Medley and Lang were to explore the Cashmere breach and Greathed and Home were to examine the breach by the Water Bastion. It was a moonless night, but clear under the broad starlight. And as the gallant subalterns went forth to their appointed work, taking with them a few picked riflemen of the Sixtieth, the guns and mortars from the breaching batteries were still playing upon the enemy's defences, making night hideous with their roar, and well-nigh bringing the services of our exploring parties to a disastrous close. But at ten o'clock there was a lull and the perils of the Engineers were then limited to the assaults of the enemy. "The enemy's skirmishers were firing away on our right," wrote one of the exploring party (Medley), "some thirty yards from us, and the flashes of their muskets lit up the air as if they had been fire-flies. The shells and rockets of the enemy at one moment illumined the space around, as they darted over our heads and then left us in total darkness." But the work was done; the desired information was gained and the results of the explorations were duly reported to the Chief Engineer. The breaches would have been better for a little more cannonading; but Baird Smith determined that this would not countervail the evils of further delay; so he despatched a note to Wilson urging immediate action. The General wisely endorsed the recommendation, and the order went forth for the delivery of the assault on the morrow's dawn.

Before daybreak the whole assaulting force had assembled near Ludlow Castle, with the exception of Reid's column, which was to advance from the post at Hindoo Rao's and to clear the suburbs of Kishengunje and Paharunpore. Not a man was absent from his post; and few were present who were not eager for the coming affray. After the muster and the dram, they would have rushed at the breaches, with a cheery English hurrah! But, as almost ever happens, there were unexpected causes of delay, and when all were ready for the advance, the signal was not given. No soldiers, seeing their work clearly before them, can bear to wait. Nothing is more depressing than that hour of the "shuddering dawn"—a time when the vital power is ever at its weakest—when men wonder over unexplained delays, and curse their commanders for keeping them waiting. This period of expectancy, as night kindles into day, takes the eagerness for fighting out of them grievously, unless it be sustained by stimulants; and the effect of these, if not renewed, is transient and dangerous.* The reaction may be worse than the first craving. The cause of delay

* A double dram was served out to them.

was this. What Baird Smith had anticipated was now coming to pass. The insurgents having discovered our intentions had during the night, when our batteries were quiescent, filled up the main breach by which our columns were to enter Delhi. Skilled engineers were among them, who well knew the use of sand-bags, and moreover could improvise *chevaux-de-frise*. This had been done in the night; so orders went down, in hot haste, to the breaching batteries, to open fire again. This was done promptly and effectually; and soon the ramparts were cleared and our columns awaiting the appointed signal to advance.

Difficulties of
the position. Never, in the history of modern warfare, has an officer found himself in a position so environed and embarrassed with difficulties as that which General Wilson was now called upon to confront. The very thought of the responsibility before him had killed one general. A few weeks on the Ridge had sent another to his grave, and despatched a third for very life's sake to Simlah. But not one of them had attempted an assault. The two last had stood on the defensive; and even that was too much for frail humanity to bear up against. But Wilson, who had brought with him to Delhi all the enervating wear-and-tear of the first outbreak at Meerut, following closely upon a critical attack of small-pox, had toiled for months upon the Ridge, during the most trying season of the year, with all responsibilities upon him. His health, as time advanced, had failed him more and more; like Barnard, he was unable to obtain sleep, and some men, in like circumstances, would have followed Reid's example, and betaken himself to the nearest sanitarium.

But Wilson, though feeling painfully, and bitterly
deploring, his growing infirmities, determined not to
abandon his post. With a candour most honourable
to him, he confessed his physical prostration, and
the mental disturbances which accompanied it. He
was a man always of quick temper; but now, his
irritability had become chronic, and he had none of
that unfailing urbanity, that unceasing tenderness
for others, which had glorified the last days of Sir
Harry Barnard.* He was not, therefore, popular
with the Army—not even with his own branch of it—
and he was often thwarted by men in high places,
who knowing his difficulties and responsibilities
ought to have condoned his infirmities and supported
him. The situation was cast upon him; he did not
seek it. And with his high sense of duty and love
of country, he would have given over the command
to another, with all its high promise of honours and
rewards and historical renown, if he had known one
of sufficiently high rank equal to the work before
him.

And now the critical moment had come when a
great deed was to be accomplished or a desolating
failure was to stain the annals of our country. The
strongest brain might have been disturbed—the
strongest nerves might have been shaken by the
prospect which lay before Wilson on that September
morning. With the Heavy Artillery at our disposal it
had been no impossible work to breach the defences of
the city. With the indomitable pluck of the British
soldier it might be no difficult work to carry the
breaches thus opened. The difficulty was to commence
after the carriage of the defences of the city had been
accomplished. It was said that Baird Smith knew

* Vol. ii., pp. 541, 542.

Delhi well.   And in truth he did.   He knew
the state of the defences thoroughly; but it was
doubted whether he knew as much of the interior
of the city—the great imperial capital of India, with
all its vast piles of buildings, its numerous covered
places, its streets, its lanes, and its bazaars.   This,
however, was a mistake.   He knew Delhi well, inside
and out.*   But had he known the city as it was before the siege, how could he, even with the help of
spies, know what changes had been wrought since in
May we were expelled from Delhi? Of all our officers
the man who knew most was Sir John Metcalfe,† our
City Magistrate, ere the storm burst upon us and
swept all authority away.   His information was ever
most reliable, and it was freely given.   But even he
could not say what might have been done, during
those four months of Native occupation; what open
streets might have been turned into blind alleys—
what houses might have been raised for better command of observation and of fire—what spaces might
have been cleared, what batteries erected, in prospect of the inevitable day of assault.   We knew only
that the enemy relied not on their moral, but on
their material resources—not on the number and

* Hear Baird Smith himself on the subject: "I mentioned to you in a former letter that I had been person- ally familiar with the localities about Delhi for fully sixteen years. Two of the canals under my charge ter- minate there, on flowing through the heart of the city and throwing out branches in different directions through Delhi. In connexion with this work different plans of improve- ment or extension had been sub- mitted to me and I made it part of my duty to examine the localities carefully. It was only in the month of September preceding the mutiny that I spent ten days at Delhi, and almost every day was occupied in examining parts of the city. My camp was pitched upon the ground we carried our operations over, and on the whole I had, before I joined the force at all, a tolerably minute knowledge of the important features of the ground both inside and out- side the place."—*Letter to General Lefroy, MS.*

† Generally known and described as Sir Theophilus. Theophilus was a family name borne also by Sir Charles and Sir Thomas.

strength of their men, but on the number and
strength of their houses. Wilson saw that the
crowning victory was to be gained only by overcom-
ing these material resources. His columns had to
fight their way to the Palace, to plant the British
Standard on its walls, and to secure the person of the
King. He knew that our troops had no appetite for
street fighting, and he had a causeless lack of confidence in the officers and men of his Force. What
wonder then that broken in body and in spirit, by
the toil and exposure of months and the ever-
present, wearing sense of the responsiblility that
lay upon him, he should have shuddered, as he looked
down, through the grey dawn of that September
morning, on the great city which lay before him;
and that thinking of the paucity of troops told off
for the assault and the scarcity of available fighting
men left for the protection of his Camp on the Ridge,
he should have painfully doubted the success of the
enterprise on which he was launched.*

. 1857.
Sept. 14.

The general design of the attack was this: the
Infantry, divided into four columns and a column of
Reserve, each guided by Engineer officers,† were to
cross the ditch at different points by the aid of
scaling ladders, to clear the outer defences of the
city, taking possession of all bastions, guns, and
gateways, and establishing defensible posts. This
having been accomplished, it was to be left to the

General de-
sign of the
assault.

---

* I find in the Laureate's last
work, "Queen Mary," the following
words, much to my purpose:

"Stupid soldiers oft are bold.
Poor lads, they see not what the ge-
neral sees,
A risk of utter ruin."

† Nicholson had recommended
that two or three Artillery officers,
with some gunners, should accompany each of the leading columns to
work the captured guns (*MS. Mem.*).
The suggestion appears to have been
a good one, and it was turned to
account.

discretion of commanding officers, under the general
direction of Nicholson, to determine whether, " dependent upon the circumstances of the moment, and
the resistance of force," it would be advisable to direct
the columns to clear the streets of the city in their
front and vicinity, or to wait for the arrival of Artillery to aid them. The roads to the Palace and Selim-
Ghur having been rendered practicable, a vigorous
bombardment of those places was to be undertaken
with the least possible delay, every available mortar
being conveyed into the city and placed in the Magazine or other suitable positions.* It was impossible to
calculate the amount of resistance except upon the
spot, so no one could say how much time it would
occupy to clear the inner defences of the city,
the streets and squares, and covered buildings, and
to bombard the Palace of the Moguls. But it was
the general conception that all this might be accomplished, and the person of the King secured, within
three or four days from the time of our first delivery
of the assault. It was thought, however, that much
might be done on the first day; as the enemy, panic-
struck and confused, dreading the terrible retribution
which would descend upon them, might betake themselves to sudden flight, and clear the way for the
advance of the English. Baird Smith's maps had indicated the points within the city at which the several
columns, after clearing the outer defences, were to
take post; and the Delhi Gate, beyond the Palace,
was assigned to the First Column. It will appear,
as the narrative advances, how erroneous was this
forecast.

The assault commenced.   It was a fine still morning. As day broke and the
columns took up their positions, awaiting the ap-

* MS. Memorandum in handwriting of General Wilson.

pointed signal, the heavy guns were still thundering at the defences, keeping down the enemy's fire, and enlarging the breaches for our entrance. Nicholson's column was on the left of the Koodsea Bagh. Jones, with the Second Column, was a little space to Nicholson's left. These two formed the Left Attack. Some way to the right on the road leading towards the Cashmere Gate was Campbell with the Third Column; and the Reserve were somewhat behind them. Eager was every man for the signal—the sight of the Sixtieth Rifles rushing to the front, and the sound of their bugle-call. For fast poured the shot from the ramparts of the enemy, and our people of the leading columns were ordered to lie down on the ground and wait. When the time had come for the advance, Nicholson, who directed the general attack, went over to Jones, and, placing his arm on the Brigadier's shoulder in token of comradeship, asked him if he was ready to move. Having received a prompt answer in the affirmative, he rejoined his own column. Then the order was given, and the voice of our heavy guns, which had been roaring at their loudest, suddenly dropped into silence; the Rifles sounded the advance; the regiments started up, and with a cry of exultation surged onward, and, in the teeth of a heavy fire from the enemy's works, steadily went up the slope of the glacis.

Whilst the First Column were thus establishing themselves, the Second under Brigadier Jones of the Queen's Sixty-first were doing their work gallantly and well. The fire of the enemy fell heavily upon them as they ascended the glacis, and the slaughter was terrible among the brave fellows of the ladder party, guided by the Engineers Greathed and Hovenden, who were the first to fall, wounded but not

The Second
Column.

mortally, beneath the pitiless storm of the insurgents.* The column was divided into three sections.
Colonel Greathed, of the Eighth Foot, commanded
the first section, of which his splendid regiment
formed the principal part. Captain Boyd was at the
head of the second; and Brigadier Jones brought
up the Reserve. The stormers carrying the ladders
were led by Captain George Baynes and Lieutenant
Metje of the Eighth. When the signal was given
for the advance they rushed forward from a covert
of rose-bushes, behind which they had been partially
hidden from the sight of the insurgents, who had
gathered more thickly on the walls and were ready to
sweep us down as we advanced. And awfully they
did their work. The Grenadiers of the Eighth
went forward manfully with the ladders on their
shoulders, but so encumbered could not fire a shot;
and they had no covering party.† Thus exposed
naked to the fierce fire of the enemy, they fell fast
upon the slope of the glacis or the edge of the ditch.
One volley brought down five of our ladder-men.
When Metje and some of his followers picked up the
ladders and went forward they also were struck down
and disabled. So fearful, indeed, was the carnage
that when Baynes found himself opposite the Water
Bastion, the seventy-five men who had started with

---

* Welby Greathed, when wounded, hid himself among the rose-bushes that his brother might not see him.

† There was a sad mistake about this. One of the leading officers of the column thus explains it. "The supporting party of the Second Bengal Fusiliers instead of following the leading stormers to the left towards the Water Bastion, had gone straight over the breach in the Curtain. This was the result of the divided command in the storming arising from a mixture of regiments. Thus the storming party was left without any support, and their situation would have been very critical, if the company of the Fifty-second Light Infantry, which was sent by Colonel George Campbell to clear his left flank, after he had got into the town, had not cleared the bastion of its defenders, and allowed the remnant of the Eighth stormers to make their way in."—*MS. Memorandum.*

him on their perilous mission were reduced to only
twenty-five. For two days these twenty-five men,
without a commissioned officer—for Metje had been
carried wounded to the rear and Baynes had been
disabled by sharp sickness—held their position in
the Water Bastion under Sergeant Walker, and did
excellent service.

Then came the difficulties of the escalade. On
the crest of the glacis our men were falling fast. So
furious was the fire of the enemy, and so heavy the
shower of stones and bricks from the crumbling
walls, which the maddened insurgents poured upon
us, that it was difficult, for a little time, to plant the
ladders in the ditch so as to ascend the scarp on the
other side. Medley of the Engineers, who led the
ladder party of the First Column, received a ball in
the fleshy part of the arm. Fortunately the bone
escaped; and his brave heart would not suffer him
to halt in his work for mere bodily pain, however
acute. He went on with the storming party. Two
or three ladders, after this brief check, were thrown
down into the ditch, and presently the wall beneath
the breach was gallantly escaladed. The column was
divided into two sections. One composed mainly of
the Bengal Fusiliers under Jacob, was personally
commanded by Nicholson himself. The other, of
which the Seventy-fifth Queen's were the chief components, was led by Colonel Herbert of that regiment.
Determined that his leadership should be not a
name, but a fact, Nicholson went on in advance of
his men, followed by Jacob and Greville of the
Fusiliers, and was the first to mount the wall. The
other section of the column pushed on with like
eagerness. Lieutenant Fitzgerald, of the Seventy-
fifth, was the first to ascend, but he was shot

down, in the moment of victory, and died the hero's death at the head of his men. Others not less gallant and, often, not more fortunate, took his place ; and soon both sections of the First Column had gained the ramparts, carried the breach near the Cashmere Bastion, and taken up their position at the Main Guard.

Advance of the Second Column.

The main body of the Second Column went steadily on, and having made good its entrance by the breach in the Cashmere Curtain, went forward, at the double, across the open space, inside the Cashmere Bastion, where they inclined to their Right. Then seeing some men rushing into the city on his Left, Jones cried out to them to "bear away to the right along the ramparts." They were at that time running at the topmost of their speed, the men with Jones being partly of Nicholson's column and partly of his own. As they were proceeding along the road leading to the Caubul Gate, the Brigadier's bugler cried out that the enemy were firing down the streets. This fire was speedily answered, and the insurgents left remaining on the ramparts ran like hares before us and so escaped the fire of our eager soldiery. In the Moree Bastion the gunners made bold resistance ; standing to their guns with a gallantry worthy of the great school in which they had been taught. But our English Infantry went in amongst them, bayoneted them as they stood, and cast them dead or dying from the ramparts into the ditch below. Then our people leapt up exultingly on the parapet of the Moree Bastion—that grand defence of the enemy, from which for months an unceasing shower of shot had been poured in upon the besiegers ; and waved their caps rejoicingly to their comrades on the Ridge.

Thence they had a prevision of what was going on elsewhere. They saw the Sepoys in their white dresses, huddling on confusedly from Kishengunje, and they saw the Cavalry and Horse Artillery forming up, under Hope Grant, and sustaining a heavy fire from the insurgents in the suburbs. The column then advanced to the Caubul Gate, where Jones having ascended to the summit of it, ordered a party of his men to fire down the streets on each side of the Canal. The order was promptly obeyed, and one of the enemy's deserted guns was turned on the Lahore Gate, from which the enemy had been keeping up a galling fire, whilst the houses adjacent to the Caubul Gate and along both sides of the Canal, were occupied by our own people. The Caubul Gate was now secure, and it remained for us only to plant the British flag on the summit of it. This was done under Jones's orders, by a private of the Sixty-first, whom he rewarded in the presence of his comrades.* The regimental bugle-calls were then sounded; the different corps were gathered together; and men shook hands with and congratulated each other and somewhat marvelled that any were alive.

1857.
Sept. 14.

* Unpublished letter from Major-General Jones to Sir Archdale Wilson, March, 1864. This was written, at the suggestion of Colonel (now Sir Edward) Greathed, in consequence of an error in Wilson's Delhi despatch, in which he says: "The firm establishment of the Reserve rendering the assaulting columns free to act in advance, Brigadier-General Nicholson, supported by Brigadier Jones, swept the ramparts of the place from the Cashmere to the Caubul Gates, occupying the bastions and defences, capturing the guns and driving the enemy before him." Wilson sent the letter to me (for which purpose, indeed, it was written) and confirmed the truth of it. Greathed, who commanded the Eighth under Jones, wrote to the latter: "As I was close to you from the time we got up to the top of the breach together, until you had finally caused the troops to re-form and rest at the Caubul Gate, I am perfectly aware that the clearing of the walls, ramparts, and bastions was performed solely under your orders, and that Nicholson did not join us until some time after at the Caubul Gate, when the work had been accomplished."

The light of these first congratulations was soon darkened by the gloomy thought of their diminished ranks. They had done their work nobly and well; but how many brave men and good soldiers had been left, dead or dying behind them; how many friends and comrades had been lost to them since the dram had been served out in the early morning. The enemy fought well to the last, and the bloody instructions which we had taught, were returning to plague the inventors. Alas! for our shattered columns.

It was not until after the flag had been planted on the Caubul Gate that Nicholson joined the Second Column. He had diverged from the intended line of advance to suppress a brisk fire of musketry, from some houses on his left flank, between the Cashmere and the Moree Bastions, which was severely harassing his people. Having turned aside for the reason stated, as men must at times under heavy pressure of circumstances, and entered the town, he did not meet Jones at the Caubul Gate until more than an hour after the Second Column had reached it. The enemy then observing our inactivity, regained somewhat of their courage and began to pour in a sharp fire of musketry and cannon-shot.* The men of the Second Column were then resting from their work. Misunderstanding the quietude of their demeanour, the young Brigadier-General exclaimed, "The men are not in hand." Upon this Greathed fired up and

---

* "The Lahore Bastion kept up a steady fire on us from a twelve-pounder, which we could not silence, and a couple of guns were brought to bear on us from a side street; but fourteen men of the Seventy-fifth ran down and took one of them; the other was taken away, and we received no further molestation from that quarter. A gun was also brought to bear upon us from the end of the long straight street which led down directly to our position at the Caubul Gate; and this pelted us throughout the day with round shot and grape. In short our position was a ticklish one."—*MS. Memorandum by an Officer of the Eighth Foot.*

said, "What do you want done? Tell me and I'll soon show you that they are in hand." Nicholson then, whose words had conveyed a meaning beyond what he had probably intended, made some wise suggestions as to the positions of the enemy and the disposition of our troops and then went back to join the First Column. Jones had received orders to remain at the Caubul Gate until he might hear tidings of the fall of the Jumma Musjid; so he got his men well lodged in houses commanding the approaches and waited for the signal to advance.

Meanwhile, a sad misadventure was befalling us in the First Column. Still annoyed by the fire from the Lahore Gate, Nicholson determined to take it, and got together a number of men of different regiments to follow him on this enterprise. It has been said that there were officers without their men and men without their officers, so that they were a "mere rabble." It was a hazardous duty that loomed before them; for the way from the Caubul to the Lahore Gate lay through a narrow lane swept by artillery and commanded by houses occupied by the enemy. If there is one thing to dishearten the British soldier more than all else it is the thought of street-fighting. He can receive a charge of Cavalry with a loud hurrah. He can march steadily on the enemy's blazing batteries and scale their ramparts, or enter the breaches in their walls, as though it were mere play-work. But he is not used to street-fighting. He does not know what barricades may have been suddenly thrown up; he does not know what masked batteries may be erected: and he fancies that every house is full of a hostile soldiery, and that every window is an embrasure, at which a skilled marksman may be placed, and with aim steadied by the sense of his own security.

And so it was now. Nicholson's column having entered the outskirts of the city, found itself in a long narrow lane lined with marksmen on both sides, and commanded by some more distant positions of the enemy. It was soon obvious that some of the enemy's guns had been brought forward to scatter confusion in our ranks, and, in our helplessness, to send back the advanced columns to the Ridge. The men were falling fast. Major George Jacob of the First Fusiliers, an officer of distinguished gallantry, received his death-wound; but refused to be carried to the rear.* Captain Greville and Lieutenant Speke, doing duty with the Fusiliers, were struck down,† and other officers fell disabled and helpless under the enemy's fire. Then there was something of a waver —a pause. The British soldier found himself in the position which he most hated. It was not fair fighting. He was in a trap. Nicholson saw it all— saw what was depressing the hearts and checking the onward movement of our fighting men. So he drew himself up to his full height, and with his sword raised high above his head, called upon his men to follow him. To some at least of the defenders of Delhi, that face and figure must have been familiar. Others saw a man of commanding presence, whose position at the head of the column, and whose gestures of command, indicated that he was a great

---

* See a very interesting letter from an officer of the regiment, quoted in Hodson's "Twelve Years of a Soldier's Life": "Again the word was forward, and leading on the men, my glorious friend George Jacob was mortally wounded; he, poor fellow, was shot in the thigh, and died that night. As he lay writhing in agony on the ground, unable to stand, two or three men went to take him to the rear, but a sense of duty was superior to bodily pain, and he refused their aid, desiring them to go and take the guns."

† The writer above quoted says of Speke that he was "gentle everywhere but in the field." Speke never recovered from his wounds. Greville happily was spared.

chief. His lofty stature rendered him so conspicuous, that if he had been a private soldier, some rifleman at a window or on a housetop would have taken deadly aim at him, and he would have sent one more hated Feringhee to his account. But it was not a single life that he took ; it was the life of a whole army.

Nicholson was shot through the body. He knew at once that he had received his death-wound ; but he begged that he might not be carried back to Camp until the capture of Delhi were secure. This, however, was impossible, and he was gently removed to the Hospital on the Ridge. The surgeons who attended him were doubtful of the final issue, for the ball had not touched the lungs. But he had got the death-chill upon him—the worst sign of all; and there was really no hope for him. He could not help chafing, too, under the miserable infliction which had taken him away in the very hour of the grand fulfilment of his hopes, and rendered him helpless as a child. It was a sad addition to his own sufferings to know that his brother, Charles Nicholson, who had commanded the Punjabees, in the First Column, had been brought into Camp with a shattered arm, and that nothing but amputation could save him. He was a fine gallant soldier of high promise, but his lofty stature had made him a sure mark for the enemy, and the promise could never be fulfilled.*

1857. Sept. 14.

It was the apportioned duty of the Third Column to enter the city through the Cashmere Gate; and

The explosion of the Cashmere Gate.

---

* Charles Nicholson survived the operation, but he never altogether recovered from the effects of his wounds, and soon passed away. Sir Hope Grant speaks of him as one of three young officers worthy of especial mention—Probyn, Watson, and Nicholson.

to this end a party of Engineers was told off to blow in the gate with powder-bags. The officers appointed for the performance of this hazardous duty were Lieutenants Home and Salkeld. The non-commissioned officers were Sergeants Carmichael, Burgess, and Smith. With them went a party of Native Sappers. It was broad daylight when they started. Leaving Ludlow Castle at the double, headed by a party of the Sixtieth Rifles, they reached the road leading to the Customs House, where they opened out: the Sappers under Lieutenant Home, and the carrying party with the powder-bags under Lieutenant Salkeld — Sergeant Smith bringing up the rear. Forward they went, at first unseen by the enemy, straight upon the Cashmere Gate, followed by the Sixtieth Rifles and the other components of the column under Colonel Campbell, awaiting the explosion and prepared for the deadly work before them. Home, with his bugler, was first down into the ditch. The danger of the enterprise was then upon them. The designs of the exploding party had been perceived by the enemy; and as they crossed over the broken drawbridge leading from the outer to the inner gate a brisk shower of musketry was poured upon them. But they made good their hazardous march to the point at which the explosion was to be effected. Many were the brilliant episodes of adventure which illustrated the siege of Delhi; but not one more heroic than this. Home had planted his bag, but on Carmichael advancing with his powder on his shoulder, he was shot down by a death-dealing musket-ball. Smith then went forward and placed his dying comrade's bag in position, having also placed his own, and prepared the fuzes for igni-

tion. Salkeld stood ready with a slow match* in his
hand, but as he was lighting it, he was struck down;
a bullet in his arm and another in his leg had sent
their death-messages to him. In falling, he held out
the match and called on Smith to take it. Burgess,
who stood nearest to Salkeld, took the match but
could not ignite the charge. Smith then was in the
act of giving him a box of lucifer-matches, when
Burgess was shot down by a bullet through the body.
Smith was now alone, or thought he was alone, for
he had lost sight of Home for some time. The
moment was a critical one; but he had succeeded in
striking a light and was applying it, when a portfire,
which it was thought had been extinguished, went
off in his face. There was a confusing fog of smoke
and dust as he scrambled down into the ditch, and
presently a roar and a crash, significant of a deed
accomplished. The gate had been shattered by the
explosion, but not with the destructive effect that
had been anticipated by the assailants or by those
from whom the design had emanated. It was enough,
however, for the Third Column, which awaited this
signal to advance, and the stirring sounds of the bugle
sent them forward to do their work, the Rifles leading the way.†

Sliding down into the ditch, his back to the wall,
and groping his way amidst the obscuring dust and

1857.
Sept. 14.

* Most accounts state that it was
a portfire. It was really a slow-
match as stated in the text.

† Lieutenant Medley writes:—
"The bugle sounded the advance,
and then with a loud cheer the Fifty-
second charged through the broken
gateway." I wish I could accept
this statement unreservedly. But I
am bound to add that Sergeant
Smith, in an unpublished memorandum given in the Appendix, says:
"They did not go fast. Their bugler
had sounded fifty times at least, and
some ten minutes elapsed before any
one came." It was not only known
at Head-Quarters, but throughout
the army, that there had been some
backwardness.

the masses of falling masonry, Smith placed his hand on some one whom he could not discern and cried out, asking " Who are you?" He was answered by Lieutenant Home, who said he was unhurt. When the dust had somewhat cleared away they went together to minister to Salkeld; but as there was a fire of musketry then bearing upon them, the gallant sergeant told his lieutenant not to expose himself, as he would remain behind to tend the wounded. Having full confidence in Smith and being all eagerness to go forward, Home, after giving some brandy from his flask to Salkeld and Burgess, joined the column and went ahead. Salkeld at first refused to be moved; so Smith and the bugler, who had remained with him, placed the dying officer's head upon a powder-bag and bound up his wounds, as best they could, with improvised bandages torn from a puggery. Smith then went to the rear to obtain some stretchers, and not without threats and the display of a drawn sword succeeded in obtaining the use of two, a third having been taken from him by an officer of the Rifles. Upon one of these Salkeld, now too feeble to resist, was placed, and sent to Camp under charge of the bugler, with strict injunctions not to leave him until he should have seen the wounded man in the hands of a surgeon. But human skill could do nothing for him, and after lingering for a few days the fine young soldier was laid in the grave. Burgess was placed upon the other stretcher and sent under care of a Naick to the hospital, but they had not proceeded far before he died. For these achievements Home, Salkeld, Smith, and the Bugler Hawthorne were promptly rewarded by General Wilson with the Victoria Cross. Neither of the two gallant subalterns lived long to enjoy their honours. Salkeld had passed away from the scene of mortal strife, before Home, on the 1st of October, was killed by the premature springing of a mine, after the capture of the fort of Malagurh. And the explosion well-nigh cost us, in the sequel, another life, which would have been greatly mourned. George Chesney, who was Brigade-Major of Engineers, and one of the most promising of the younger officers of that noble Engineer Corps,* went, after the explosion, with a party of Sappers to restore the broken bridge, of which mention has before been made. Whilst making for the gate, a heavy shell from one of the enemy's batteries at Kishengunje burst in the air, some twenty yards off, severely wounding Chesney, who received a shrapnel bullet through his right side and in his arm.† Renny of the Artillery, whose Native troop had withstood all trials and temptations and shone forth with conspicuous loyalty from first to last,‡ met the Engineer as he was returning. Then he and Fulton of the Artillery finding that the wounded man with some assistance could walk, helped him on to Ludlow Castle, whence he was conveyed to Camp, and by the skill and care of the surgeons saved to do good service to the State.

1857.
Sept. 14.

Having carried the Cashmere Gate, Campbell's

The Third Column.

---

* Now Lieutenant-Colonel Chesney, President of the Engineering College at Cooper's Hill.

† It is stated in MS. accounts that some men of the party were killed. I believe that this was a mistake. Chesney was in advance of his party when the shell burst.

‡ In pursuance of the principle and practice of the time, the guns were taken away from Renny's troop and restored after the fall of Delhi. The gunners were all Hindostanees, but they were as ready to fight against the Poorbeah rebels as if the enemy had been of a different colour and a different race. It is a remarkable illustration of the scant justice done to the Artillery, that no mention was made of Renny's troop in any of the despatches.

column, followed by the Reserve, streamed onward towards the city. It was a grand sight to see their compact masses, moving forward, like hounds in the hunting-field, and carrying everything before them.* The point to be gained was the Jumma Musjid, which Campbell had been commissioned to take. The capture of this place was to have been the signal for the further advance of the First and Second Columns. But it was a duty of far more difficult accomplishment than it had been thought to be. Campbell, a right-good soldier, intrepid and well-skilled, had the inestimable advantage of the personal guidance of Sir John Metcalfe, who knew neither fear nor pity and was ever eager to push forward in the great work of retribution. He had the plan of the city with all its turns and windings at his fingers' ends; and now he knew well how to lead the column, by a devious way, so as to encounter little opposition on the road. It passed on unharmed until the great street of the Chandna Chouk was reached and the Kotwallee seized by our people. Then fast fell the fire of the insurgents upon them, and it was found impossible to take the Jumma Musjid without such heavy loss as we could ill endure; so the column fell back to the vicinity of the Church and joined the Reserve, which had followed it through the Cashmere Gate and was pressing forward into the heart of the city.

The Fourth Column.

Up to this time, if the success of our operations had not been complete, there had been no disastrous

* An officer of the Second Column, who saw the advance says: "The sight at this moment was beautiful. We could see the two columns on our right up the breach and the Cashmere Bastion; like a swarm of bees, or rather like the horses of the Sun all abreast—then like hounds topping the fence into a gorse cover they disappeared into the town."—*MS. Journal.*

failure. But the fortune of war was now turning against us on the Right, in a manner little expected. The Fourth Column, commanded by Major Charles Reid, whose gallant and most serviceable exploits in command of the important position at Hindoo Rao's house have been already narrated in this work, was struggling with unforeseen difficulties. It was to have cleared the suburb of Kishengunje and entered the city by the Lahore Gate.* It was an enterprise of no little difficulty and danger. But he had a detachment of the Sixtieth Rifles; a detachment also of the Sixty First and of the Bengal Fusiliers. He had some of Daly's Guides, and he had great reliance on his little Goorkahs. Their indomitable spirit was something beautiful to behold. They had expended themselves so freely, during months of fearless fighting, at the post which they never quitted, that there were but few efficient men, at Hindoo Rao's, on the eve of the assault. The improvised hospital in the back rooms of the building was full of sick and wounded, and all who could move were eager to take part in the coming assault. When Reid went in amongst them, lying, as they were, on the floor, for there were no cots for them, and told them what was to be done on the morrow, sorrowfully adding that he could muster scarcely a hundred of his Goorkahs for service, all sprung up as if the word of command had been given to them and volunteered to

---

* In a letter to the Reverend Mr. Rotton, Chaplain and Historian, Reid says that he was to have entered the city by the *Caubul* Gate. But Norman, who was Deputy-Adjutant-General, has recorded that the Fourth Column was to enter by the Lahore Gate (*ut supra*, 583). The two statements are not irreconcilable. The fact appears to be that the enemy held the Lahore Gate in force and were not disposed to evacuate it. It would have been a dangerous experiment for Reid, weakened by much fighting in the suburbs, to attempt to carry it.

follow him into the field. Some were wholly unfit for such rough work; but of the hundred and fifty men, who had been reported ineffective, ninety-five mustered for active service on the morning of the assault. So Reid's heart was gladdened by the thought that he was taking with him two hundred of the sturdy little Goorkahs who had clung to him so nobly from the first.

The Jummoo troops.

At five o'clock the column was mustered and moved forwards in high spirits. Unfortunately, however, it was overweighted with Jummoo troops. John Lawrence had said that they might be trusted, and in ordinary circumstances they might have been. But their ways were not as our ways; and the great principle of cohesiveness was unknown to them. The original conception of the General had been that this Contingent might act independently, as a substantive force, carrying the Eed Gate and suburb of Paharunpore and spiking the enemy's guns in position there, whilst Reid with his picket was to support this attack, after leaving a sufficient number of men for the defence of Hindoo Rao's house. But Baird Smith saw at once the error of this and asked, "Is the Jummoo Contingent to make this attack as a Principal and not as an Auxiliary Force? It consists of untried troops with no interest in our cause. It is not a Native fashion to take guns, and I greatly fear the results. If Major Reid leads and the Jummoo troops support the attack, I should expect it to be quite successful."* The good sense of the General yielded to this suggestion and the original programme was reversed. But even in this secondary position our allies soon demonstrated their deficiency in those

* Autograph notes by General Wilson and Colonel Baird Smith.

very qualities which we most needed in such a conjuncture. There was a hitch. Reid had been promised three guns, but when the time came there were
only gunners enough to man one of them. He was
not now going in defiance of the principles of warfare
to take a single gun into action, so he ordered the
Artillery officer to make inquiries and to endeavour
to obtain more gunners. Whilst he was awaiting the
result he heard musketry fire to the right, and learnt
that the Jummoo troops, on their way down from
Camp, had become engaged with the enemy. Any
further delay then would have been hazardous in the
extreme. So Reid determined to advance without
the promised artillery.

The enemy had prepared themselves for his reception. When within a short distance from the canal
bridge, Reid discovered that the insurgents had erected
a breastwork across the road and another running
parallel to it. Trained in our English schools of discipline, they knew well the advantage of reserving their
fire ; so they did not open upon us until our people
we rewithin fifty yards of their cover, when they poured
in a heavy well-directed volley of musketry from the
foremost breastwork. Thus assailed, Reid at once
sent forward the British Riflemen and the Sepoys of
the Sirmoor Battalion, who headed his column, and
dislodged the mutineers from the breastwork and
drove them into the road. For some time the enemy
stood irresolute, uncertain of the next movement,
seemingly hesitating as to whether they should fall
back on the further breastwork or should attack our
Jummoo allies on the right. Then was seen the result of the miserable accident or mismanagement
that had caused the column to go forward without
guns. If Reid had been able to open upon the

1857.
Sept. 14.

Confusion of
Fourth Co-
lumn.

enemy with grape from the Horse Artillery pieces, he could have cleared the road at once and would have hurled back the reinforcements which were pressing onwards to the aid of their comrades. As it was, he presently found himself opposed to some fifteen thousand men, of all kinds, surging on to overwhelm him. In the crisis, which then threatened the gallant leader of the Fourth Column, Reid was making his dispositions, firstly for a false attack upon the enemy, in the front of the Kishengunje batteries, and secondly, for a real one, in front, flank, and rear, when he was smitten down by a bullet, which struck him on his head, and incapacitated him from further command. The officer next in rank was Major Lawrence, who had brought down the Jummoo troops, ten days before, to Delhi. As Reid was being carried to the rear, he met the Punjabee officer, made over the command to him, and explained his plan of attack. "Up to this time," he wrote afterwards, "all was going on admirably; the troops were steady and well in hand, and I made sure of success. I was not a little surprised to hear, about an hour afterwards, that the columns had retreated—that the Jummoo troops had lost their guns and were flying back to Camp."*

---

* Norman says that "the Cashmere Contingent (Jummoo troops) were so sharply attacked by the insurgents, who were in great force, that, after losing a great number of men, and four guns, they were completely defeated and fell back to Camp. Major Reid's column met with the most strenuous opposition, greatly increased, doubtless, by the failure of the Cashmere Contingent, and the enemy were so numerous and so strongly posted, that after the loss of many men and officers, the Commander, Major Reid, having been carried away severely wounded, Captain Muter, Sixtieth Rifles, the next senior officer, judiciously withdrew the troops to their former post at Hindoo Rao's and the Subzemundee." The variance between these two statements is obvious. It may, perhaps, in some measure, be explained by the fact that Major Lawrence came to Delhi, not in a military but in a political capacity. I find no mention of this affair in Mrs. Muter's interesting volumes.

But although this was a disastrous failure, it was not an ignominious one.   There was no better soldier —no braver gentleman, in all the Camp than Charles Reid. Nothing could have been more skilfully devised than his plan of attack, which was unhappily only half developed. Circumstances were against him. He had failed to obtain the light field-pieces, which would have so greatly promoted his success; he had been grievously thwarted by the eccentricities of his Cashmere Allies; and the enemy were not only mighty in numbers but were posted so strongly and so judiciously as to have all the advantages of ground on their side.   But our own troops —European and Native—the European detachments, the Goorkahs, and the Guides fought splendidly; and there was more than one of those acts of heroic personal enterprise, which are seldom wanting in such episodes as this, to lighten up the surrounding darkness. One of these incidents, a mournful one, may be narrated here.   A party of the enemy sheltered by a breastwork were firing heavily upon our people, when some officers with a handful of men made a rush upon the work to take it. Foremost of these was young Murray of the Guides,* who had been wounded in June and July, who had gone to the Hills to recruit and had returned to Delhi a few days before the assault. Speeding onward with impulsive bravery, the grim message of death met him, in the pride of his youth and the flush of his daring. He was shot through the chest and fell dead upon the field. Almost at the same moment, Captain M'Barnett, attached to the Fusiliers, a good officer,

* The Commandant of this distinguished corps, Major Henry Daly, was then at Hindoo Rao's recovering from his wounds. He was able to take charge of the Picket for a time, though, as he said, able neither to ride nor to run.

ever eager for work, was shot down never to rise[*]
again on this side of the grave—Altogether the loss
on our side was heavy. Europeans, Guides, and
Goorkahs all suffered severely. The sturdy little
fellows of the Sirmoor Battalion left forty of their
comrades behind them.

Gallantry of the enemy.
The enemy fought well—never better than on this
occasion. They were in truth no contemptible opponents. Our finest soldiers are ever the most prompt
to acknowledge the merits of their adversaries. On
that morning of the 14th of September two of
our greatest warriors, crippled in previous fights, and
all-eager for the battle, were condemned to be on-
lookers only in this momentous crisis. Neville Chamberlain and Henry Daly were at Hindoo Rao's house.
Both had carried their wounds thither, thinking that
they might be of more service to the State than they
could possibly be in Camp. Day had not broken,
when Chamberlain went down to the famous Picket
to see Reid's column started and to be a present help,
if any time of trouble should come. When the
operations against the enemy in the suburbs were
fairly commenced it was broad daylight. Chamberlain, Daly, and Khan Singh, Rhosa,[†] went to the top of
Hindoo Rao's house and watched the progress of the
conflict. From this elevated position a stirring scene
was visible below in the early daylight; and Chamberlain, whose quick soldierly eye took in all the details of the struggle below, could not but admire the
dashing manner in which the Native officers rode in
among the ranks of the mutineers, urging them and
leading them on to the battle against the British and

* Captain M'Barnett was an officer of the Fifty-fifth Native Infantry.
† This man was a Sikh chief, who
had fought against us at Chillian-
wallah. He offered his services to us,
when the mutiny broke out, and went
to Delhi with Daly and the Guides.

the Jummoo troops. Nor was his admiration, in this conjuncture, without some feeling of anxiety. For it seemed at one time that the enemy might break through our Subzee-mundee defences, carry the undefended battery below Hindoo Rao's house, and take possession of the post itself, with its Hospital and its Magazine. So critical, indeed, was the aspect of affairs that Chamberlain summoned the Native guard to the roof of the house, that it might better defend the entrance to the Magazine. And the three wounded officers prepared to take post with muskets in their hands. Happily Reid's people held on, when they reached the Subzee-mundee line of defences and the present danger was averted ; so Chamberlain and Daly descended from their plateau and strenuously exerted themselves to keep order among the excited assembly of mixed races below.* It is not questioned that about this time, our position on the Right was in great danger. Reinforcements of any sufficient strength could not be sent from the Camp,† and the Picket at Hindoo Rao's was itself called upon to afford assistance to others in this emergency. It was plain that we had received a severe check, which might have been turned to terrible account against us, and would have been, but for an incident which must now be narrated in detail.

1857.
Sept. 14
Chamberlain
and Daly.

* Among the troops at Hindoo Rao's house were a part of the Kumaon Battalion. They were in a somewhat disorderly state, when Chamberlain, reproving them for their noise and confusion, addressed them as a *Pultun* (regiment) and called forth an indignant, half-insolent rejoinder : " We are not a regiment, but a battalion." Chamberlain's answer was prompt and to the point : " Then show yourselves worthy of the distinction." Order was at once restored.

† I believe that the Belochee regiment were first to arrive. They were steadfast in their loyalty and fought well. Captain Bannerman was killed.

2 R 2

1857.
Sept. 14.
The Cavalry
Brigade.

The siege of a fortified city rarely affords much opportunity for a display of the great qualities of the Cavalry branch of an army. It is mainly the work of Engineers, Artillery, and Infantry. But when a city cannot be invested, and therefore the enemy are not shut up within the walls—when, as in this case, they can come out at one end of the place to fight, and go out at the other to escape, the mounted branch may do excellent service.* Seeing clearly the need of our troopers, especially for the protection and support of Reid's column, Wilson had called upon Hope Grant; and Grant, than whom there was no better soldier in Camp, eagerly donned his sabre and his spurs and prepared himself for the battle. The Brigadier took with him two hundred men of the Ninth Lancers, and four hundred Sikh horsemen, and awaited orders from the General. The orders soon came, and Grant marched his men down to a position under the walls of the city, covering the whole of our batteries, which before had been unprotected. At this time the enemy at Kishengunje had just defeated Reid's column, and elated with success were raging furiously against us. Availing themselves of the cover afforded by numerous houses and gardens in the vicinity, they poured

---

* There was a skirmish on the 11th, in which the Punjab Horse greatly distinguished themselves. The enemy's Cavalry in the Kishengunje suburbs had suddenly attacked one of our pickets; seeing this, Watson, the heroic commander of the First Punjab Cavalry, turned out at once, with his troopers and a few of the Second, and went at the insurgents at "tip-top speed." It was a wild helter-skelter affair; but the enemy could not stand the rush of our horsemen. Some forty of them were left dead on the field. Our own loss was slight, but Watson himself encountering one of the enemy's most intrepid swordsmen in hand-to-hand fight, received a swashing sabre-cut on the head, which glanced off his helmet, and clove his left cheek and upper lip. He was also slightly cut on the shoulder. But he was not a man to take heed of anything much less than a death-wound; so he had his face sewn up, and went about his work as before. The scar will go with him to the grave.

in a brisk shower of musketry upon our line of Cavalry and strove mightily to dislodge us. So Tombs's troop of Horse Artillery was ordered up, to open fire on these mischievous insurgents. This was done, promptly and well, at a range of two hundred yards, and the occupants of the sheltering houses were compelled to fall back. But there was a still more dangerous enemy. The Lahore Gate, which had been a source of such grievous trouble to our Infantry, was still untaken. So the enemy, at a distance of some five hundred yards, turned a twenty-four-pound gun, charged with grape, upon our horse-men, and soon had cause to exult in their success.[*]

It must have been a grand sight then to have seen these troopers and their officers, drawn up in battle array, stern and immovable, to face the deadly fire of the enemy. There they sate, firm in their saddles, "ghastly motionless as if they slept," whilst the unerring grape-shot streamed upon them and made dreadful openings in their ranks. There was scarcely a man, who had not caught the noble spirit of their commanders, Hope Grant, Drysdale of the Lancers,[†] Tombs of the Artillery, Watson and Probyn of the Punjab Horse. The courage of the Ninth Lancers was never surpassed. Not only were they under the immediate command of an intrepid soldier, but their own Colonel commanded the brigade. When Grant commended their sturdy gallantry under fire,

---

[*] It was at this time that Sir Hope Grant says that he saw Nicholson on the ramparts and exchanged greetings with him. "He called out to me that fighting was going on well for us in the town, and that he was on his way to attack the Lahore Gate." I am informed, however, that it was not Nicholson, but Colonel Greathed, who spoke to Hope Grant from the ramparts. Both, however, may have spoken to him.

[†] Captain Drysdale commanded the detachment of Lancers. Hope Grant says of him that he was "a gallant officer and a thorough Scotch-man."

they replied that they were ready to take as much more of it as he liked. Forty-two men and six officers were struck down. Rosser of the Carabineers, who had been so eager to carry to Delhi the first tidings of the revolt at Meerut, and who now was acting as Hope Grant's aide-de-camp, fell with a bullet in his forehead, which all regarded as his death-wound. Others were slightly wounded. Eleven officers of the Lancers had their horses killed under them. Nor were the Artillery under Tombs less exposed or less steadfast under their exposure. Animated by the noble example of their commander they were equal to any daring and ready to face any danger. The Punjabees, to whom the situation was new, for they were not familiar with grape-shot, lacked nothing of the steadfastness of their white comrades, and never flinched from the merciless fire. Watson's Cavalry lost few men, for they were clothed in slate-coloured uniform, and the neutral tint was of good service to them, placed as they were between the white jackets of the Lancers and the scarlet uniform of Probyn's Horse. For two long hours the brigade stood firm as a rock, and as one after another fell riddled with grape or canister there was no wavering in the ranks. Every man pressed his knees more tightly on his saddle and took a firmer grip of his reins. There was nothing else in their demeanour to distinguish this grand scene of defiance and endurance from an ordinary Cavalry parade. I may be wrong, but I think that this Heroism of Patience is grander far than the active gallantry displayed in a perilous charge. It is far easier to rush at an enemy in the fine enthusiasm of battle, than to stand steadfast on a given spot, for an ungiven period, waiting for the order or the opportunity to move, whilst swept by the fire of a hidden enemy. It is the waiting that tries the man. And never were men more tried, or more patient under trial, than the troopers of Hope Grant's Brigade.

After a while the enemy's fire began to slacken. Those within the works were, perhaps, diverted by other emergencies, and those in the open were kept back by the guns of Tombs and Campbell, afterwards reinforced by Bourchier. The Brigadier had made a requisition for some infantry to aid him; but only from the Picket at Hindoo Rao's house could any footmen be obtained. A party of two hundred and eighty of the Guides and Goorkahs—staunch as Europeans—were then placed at his disposal, and his nephew, Frank Grant, brought them down to the points where they were most needed.* But there was not much for them to do. The enemy were ceasing to prevail against us, and the General gave orders conditionally to the Cavalry Brigadier to withdraw to the neighbourhood of Ludlow Castle. Grant had done a good morning's work. The presence of the Cavalry Brigade alone prevented the enemy, who had driven back the Fourth Column, from advancing along the open ground between the Ridge and the City, and taking the whole of our Left Attack in flank.

Little more could be done by Infantry or Cavalry against the enemy on that day. Our assaulting columns, though not wholly successful, had done some good work. They were much exhausted by fatigue,

---

* Sir Hope Grant (" Incidents in the Sepoy War") writes: " Though the officer in command of that post, Chamberlain, who had partially reco- vered from his wounds, was himself short of men, he placed at my disposal two hundred and eighty men of his little force."

and much depressed by the mortality that surrounded them. They saw the dead gathered up and the dying carried off in long strings of doolies to the hospitals in the Camp. Never were our medical officers more saddened by the sights brought before them ; never have they shone more brightly in all the best manifestations of professional skill and manly devotion ; never have they striven more mightily in the God-like work of alleviating human suffering. The result of that morning's fighting was that sixty European officers and nearly eleven hundred men were either laid in the grave, where burial was possible, or carried disabled to the hospitals.* But among those who remained after that day's carnage, although the desire to avenge their slaughtered comrades was strong, nothing could be done, for exhaustion had disabled them ; and they were not fit to undertake the perilous work of penetrating deeper into the city. It would not have been wise to attempt any further offensive operations at such a time; but on the morrow, refreshed and recruited, they might force themselves into the heart of Delhi and plant the British standard on the proud Palace of the Moguls. The Artillery, however, to whom the morning had been comparatively one of inactivity, were eager to lay their mark upon the city itself, as they had before done upon its defences. And Brind, Salt, Renny, Hamilton, and others, under the direction of Wilson, who had fixed his head-quarters in Skinner's house,† turned all

* It would be a very close approximation to the truth to say that the casualty list on the 14th was this : *Europeans*, eight officers killed, fifty-two wounded. Rank and file : one hundred and sixty-two killed and five hundred and ten wounded. *Natives* : killed, one hundred and three ; wounded, three hundred and ten.

† A life-like picture of Wilson and his Staff, at this time, is given in the following extract from the Journal of an Artillery Officer : "Towards evening, Frith" (of the Artillery—Wilson's brother-in-law)

their available means to account, in shelling or battering the buildings which it was most important to
take or destroy, or in endeavouring to disperse such
of the enemy as were still eager to act on the offensive.

To a General, strong-bodied and strong-minded in
such a juncture, there would have been in the aspect
of affairs which presented itself to his eyes and to his
understanding, after the assaults of that memorable
morning, much to cause the most profound anxiety.
To Wilson, feeble as he was at that time, from circumstances already narrated, the half-success of the
enterprise was disheartening in the extreme. When
he rode down, with his Staff, to the city and, map in
hand, learned distinctly all that had happened, his
first thought was that the only hope of preserving
his army from utter destruction, was to withdraw his
columns to their old position on the Ridge. Baird
Smith had also gone down to the city. He was at Wilson's elbow, near Skinner's house, when the General
put the critical question as to what was then to be done
—asking whether he thought we could hold what we

came to me and said, ' The General
wishes you to fire some shells just
over the top of Skinner's house (in
which the General and Staff were),
as the enemy had just got into the
houses there close by.' I pointed
out that I had no regular scales and
weights and that it was a ticklish
operation, because I knew not what
posts were held by us beyond, in the
direction of the Moree Bastion. I,
therefore, went with him to Skinner's house, and in a large hall I
found Johnson, Norman, Anson, and
the rest of the Staff and told them
I wished to speak about the order I
had got. They told me that in that
case I had better speak to the General myself, for they had rather not

go near him, and pointed to him at
the other end of the hall, where he
sat balancing himself in a chair, with
his face to the wall, on which his feet
rested. I told him my errand and
he said ' Come, and I will show you
what I want, and I followed him to
the flat roof of the house, where,
creeping to the edge, we looked
down on the houses beyond, where
we could see the enemy firing at our
field guns and a strong picket in the
street at the gate, who even came
and fired upon us. After looking at
the state of affairs and hearing what
I had to say, he told me I had better
leave it alone; and going back to
the hall resumed his old contem-
plative position."—*MS. Records.*

had taken. The answer of the Chief Engineer was prompt and decisive, "We *must* do so."* The General, who had before bowed to the decision of a man whose genius he could but recognise, although personally he disliked his "obstinacy," did not now oppose the suggestion. The Chief Engineer had taken, so far as he could take it, the responsibility on himself, and if the aspect of affairs had been still worse, he would not have shrunk from upholding the counsel, which he had tendered when he was more hopeful of immediate success. It is possible that other officers, at a later period, may have urged similar opinions upon the General. Neville Chamberlain from Hindoo Rao's house, sent down a strong appeal in favour of continued action. But it was to Baird Smith's opinion that Wilson deferred, and the merit of the "holding on" is due to the brave pertinacity of the Chief Engineer.†

The morrow was a miserable blank. Delhi was full of spoil—of gold and silver and precious stones and all the rich fabrics of the looms of the East. All these things had been promised to the

---

* I have the clearest possible proof of this in a memorandum, written for me by a Field Officer, who heard the conversation: "I got some men together," he writes, "and cleared the way for the guns to enter. General Wilson and his Staff passed through the gate soon after this. I joined them, and accompanied them to the vicinity of Skinner's house. Whilst standing there reports were brought to the General that some of the attacking columns had been checked in their advance. . . . Wilson appealed to Colonel Baird Smith, asking him if he thought we could hold what we had taken. The reply was clear and decisive that we *must* do so."

† See *ante*, page 575, for Baird Smith's own statement. I have read in print, some fabulous accounts, with fancy pictures, of the General, propped up by Chamberlain and Seaton, in the city, and forced by them to do what was right. Chamberlain was at Hindoo Rao's house, and Seaton, whose irrepressible desire to see what was going on, took him down to the scene of our operations, was soon sent back to Camp, by the infirmity of the flesh, "so sick and faint that he was more than two hours returning, and when he got to his tent he felt as if he should never rise again from his bed."

army as " Prize." Upon the action of the first two days depended, in no small measure, the value of the booty to be divided; for the people were huddling out of the city with all the property they could carry off and burying the rest, with a distant hope that some day they might recover it. But there was one kind of property which all were fain to leave behind and to which our soldiery after that long waiting on the Ridge and the excitement of that fierce assault upon the defences of Delhi was more alluring than all. A black or a green bottle filled with beer or wine or brandy was more precious than a tiara of diamonds. The enemy knew this too well; and with the subtlety of their race had purposely left the immense supplies of intoxicating liquors, stored in the city, open to the hand of the spoiler. The result was more terrible than strange. The Europeans fell upon the liquid treasure with an avidity which they could not restrain. And if the insurgents had then seized the opportunity as cunningly as they had made it, it is hard to say what calamity might have befallen us. But the good Providence, which had so often confounded their wisdom, frustrated their plans, and turned their victories into defeats, now again strangled this pet project in the womb. With the great suburb of Kishengunje still in their hands; with the Lahore Bastion and numerous strongholds within the city still held in force by them, whilst our Camp on the Ridge was occupied by a scanty body of troops, many of them invalids or convalescents, a stroke of generalship on the part of the enemy far below genius point, might, at that time, have caught our whole army in the toils, and left the Mogul triumphant. On that miserable Fifteenth of September, a great cloud hung over us. It was the hour of our sorest peril and our extremest need. For the first and last time during this great struggle the destinies of the English in India trembled in the balance ; and no human wisdom could foretell the issue.

It was not strange, therefore, that. Wilson, who had doubted, from the first, the expediency of the assault without further reinforcements, and who, on the preceding day, after the failure of the Third Column and the Reserve to penetrate the city, followed by the repulse of Reid's troops, had thought of withdrawing his forces to their old position, should now have felt burdened with a weight of anxiety enough to crush him to the ground. He could scarcely have gone more nearly to the act of withdrawal without positively accomplishing it ; for he had made arrangements to cover the retreat of the assaulting columns. But having once recognised the wisdom of the adverse councils tendered to him, he flung away all thought of receding, even if greater disasters should overtake him. It seems to have been little more than a petulant utterance ; a hasty inception ; the growth of an irritable and nervous temperament wrought upon by hostile circumstances. A little mature thought convinced him of the disgrace and humiliation of going back to be again besieged. What Clive had said a hundred years before, of our position in India, was in this crisis eminently true, "To stand still is danger ; to recede is ruin." There was nothing for us, in such a conjuncture, but to go on.

But there could be no going on with any good hope of victory, whilst so many of our fighting men were wallowing like swine in the filth that had been set before them. No sustained efforts could be made for the reduction of the city, until they had been

delivered wholly from the temptation of the intoxicating liquor. In a similar emergency Havelock, at
Cawnpore, had made over all such stores to the Commissariat. But Wilson could not follow this example.
It was necessary to act promptly, and the Commissariat had other duties to perform. It must have
been sorely against the grain that the General issued
an order for the destruction of the liquid fire, which,
if often a baneful enemy, is not seldom a most serviceable friend. But there was clearly no alternative.
So the streets ran with spirits, and wine, and beer; the
dust licked up the stimulants so much needed for our
hospitals,* and a large amount of valuable Prize was
sacrificed to the necessities of the hour.

The great object was gained. The troops shook
themselves free from the humiliating debauch, which,
prolonged for another day, might have sent many to
the grave and many to the hospital. But there was
still the omnipresent thought that, at almost every
turning, new stores might be found, as we advanced
further into the city; and the fear of such a result
sat heavily upon the mind of the General. But
on the 16th, though he was obviously suffering
under much depression of spirit, he recognised some
hopeful appearances in the general aspect of affairs.
During the preceding night the enemy had evacuated
Kishengunje, and now the great Magazine was falling
into our hands. Wilson personally superintended
the operations. His experience as an Artillery officer
must have been very serviceable at a time, when the
chief work was to be done by the scientific branches

* " It was deplorable to see hundreds of bottles of wine and brandy,
which were sadly needed for our
sick, shivered, and their contents
sinking into the ground. Wine
which had fallen to threepence the
bottle soon rose again to six shil-
lings."—*History of the Siege of
Delhi by One who was There.*

of the Army.   And it must have gladdened his heart to see the immense supplies of Ordnance stores which now came into his possession.   The grand exploit of the Artilleryman Willoughby* was none the less grand, because the material wealth of the Delhi Arsenal had been but little diminished.   It was chiefly the small-arm magazine that had suffered by the explosion in May.   It was thought in the British Camp that the insurgents must have been sorely put to it for copper-caps; but large quantities were still in store when the English entered the city.   It was no profitless morning's work that placed all these guns and mortars and ammunition again at our disposal; but it did not seem to rouse Wilson, who wrote still in great despondency:

"16th September, 2 p.m.

" We took possession of the Magazine this morning, with the loss of only three men wounded.   This advances us a little, but it is dreadfully slow work.   Our Force is too weak for this street fighting, when we have to gain our way inch by inch, and of the Force we have, unfortunately there is a large portion besides the Jummoo troops in whom I can place no confidence. . . . . What gives me, however, most trouble, even more than the enemy, is the immense quantity of wines, spirits, and beer which is discovered, and which our fellows, European and Native, get hold of before we can destroy it and make beasts of themselves and incapable of doing their duty.   I find myself getting weaker and weaker every day, mind and body quite worn out.   The least exertion knocks me down.   I walk with difficulty and fully expect in a day or two to be laid altogether on my bed.   This is very sad and frets and worries me. . . . The rebels who so long attacked Reid's Picket from Paharunpore, evacuated the place last night, leaving their heavy guns behind.   How I wish Reid could have driven them out on the 14th and joined in the attack on the city. . . . . We have a long and

* See vol. ii., pp. 90, 91.

hard struggle still before us. I hope I may be able to see it out."

It was in the very nature of things that it should be a long and a hard struggle. Nothing else could be reasonably expected. To think of the great city itself, with all its impediments—of the teeming population, of the military and religious elements, of the still pervading sentiment of loyalty to the House of Delhi even in its decline, was to be convinced of the difficulty of the enterprise. It is a sentiment as old as heroism itself, that the difficulty of an enterprise makes its pleasurable excitement in the hour of action, its glory in the hour of accomplishment. And few men would have felt this more than Wilson, if it had not been for that great failure of the body, to which the mind of every man, great or small, is compelled to succumb. Still, little by little, though his dejection was great at the outset, he began to look more hopefully upon the aspect of affairs. Time was his best ally. There was no sign of any offensive action on the part of the enemy to cause serious inquietude. On the other hand, it was plain that they whose evacuation of the city had been arrested by our inactivity after the assault, had begun to discern the wisdom of flight. A few desperate men, not madmen or "fanatics," but brave soldiers and loyal subjects of the Throne of Delhi, might hold out for a time and die at their posts : but large bodies of soldiers and citizens were flocking out of the city, some with much property and others with only their lives in their hands; whilst our Artillery and Engineers were putting forth their strength, in strenuous endeavours to bombard all the great buildings of Delhi, and to occupy the houses which afforded cover to the enemy and impeded our progress into the city. But what seemed the easiest operation of all was in reality a most difficult one—the bombardment of the chief buildings of Delhi. Mortars, and shells, and fuzes were abundant; and there was no lack of experienced gunners; but it perplexed our best artillerymen to determine the elevations, as they could only vaguely surmise the distances, and there was some fear of dropping a loaded shell in the midst of an assembly of our own people, or sending it clean over the building on which it was intended to lodge.*

The Engineer Brigade. Ever to the front, ever active, ever fertile in re-sources, the Engineer Brigade had much work to do, and did it well in this conjuncture. It had been terribly shattered during the assault. One after another the subalterns attached to the different columns had fallen beneath the fire of the enemy. Few had escaped the perils to which they had been exposed.† But happily Alexander Taylor was alive, though not unhurt, for a bullet had struck him painfully on the chest on the morning of the assault.‡ And there was work for his active brain in devising the best means of securing what we had gained and in superintending their execution. All the professional resources

* *Ante*, page 617, *note*.

† " I found our Doctor at the General Hospital," writes Medley, " and then heard, as he exclaimed on seeing my bandaged arms, ' What, another of you!' that I was the eighth Engineer officer that had already claimed his good offices to-day." Salkeld and Tandy were killed—the former, as already related; the latter on the withdrawal of the Third Column and Reserve from the attempt on the Jumma Musjid.

‡ As Field-Engineer he had accompanied the Brigadier - General and the First Column of Attack, and when Nicholson, as above related, visited the Second Column, he left the troops immediately under him and all operations that might be necessary to the charge of Captain Taylor, in case the signal were given, during the absence of his chief, for an advance—a contingency which actually occurred. The assault on the breach was delivered under the direction of the Field Engineer.

of " those who were left," were brought into play, to 1857.
intrench the different commanding positions, as they Sept. 16.
fell from time to time into our hands. The outer
openings, as in the College premises, were closed with
sandbags, leaving loopholes for our fire. Barricades
were thrown up across the roads, leading to posts
likely to be attacked. Houses were garrisoned and
loopholed. Implements and stores of all kinds, necessary for immediate use or of probable requirement
were furnished, and nothing was left undone that the
sagacity of science could suggest, for the retention
of the posts which we had captured, but which might
be wrested from us.[*]

On the evening of the 17th, the general state Sept. 17.
of affairs was this. Our troops had endeavoured State of affairs
to advance up the streets towards the Palace— in the city.
the grand object of all our movements—but in
almost every instance they had been repulsed. There
was still some heart left in the insurgents. Many
had evacuated the city by the gates of egress, either
in search of the personal safety of the moment, or
with some ulterior designs of mischief in other parts ;
but enough were still left in the city to render the
advance of our weak force a work of difficulty. The
Magazine and the Bank had been captured and occupied. But the Lahore Bastion[†] was still in the
enemy's hands. No advance had been made in that
direction since Nicholson had fallen. It was evident

---

[*] This refers to what was done on the day of the assault. After the assault, as already shown, Baird Smith removed his Head-Quarters to the City. He found that his Lieutenant had anticipated all that he desired to be done. Taylor, then worn out with exhaustion from the preceding eight days' hard work in the Batteries, and suffering much from his wound, was compelled to betake himself to his bed until the latter part of the 17th, when he re-turned to fling himself into his work with all his old energy unabated.

[†] This is called by some writers the Burn Bastion. It led to the Lahore Gate. I have adhered to uniformity by calling it the Lahore Gate throughout the narrative.

that the appetite of our troops for this kind of fighting had not improved, and that our attempts to gain
our ends by open force must be superseded by some
more insidious system of attack. The exposure of
our few fighting men was by all means to be avoided.
They had seen enough of it already. They courted
no more; and if they consented, it was with manifest
reluctance.

Taylor's ope-
rations.
So Taylor, who had returned to the city after his
two days' rest in Camp, suggested at Head-Quarters
that each brigade should be ordered to work, under
the guidance of the Engineer officers attached to it,
not along the open streets, but through the sheltered houses, during the advance; using them as
means of communication; fortifying all commanding
buildings as soon as they could be secured; and
placing garrisons in them. The project met with
willing concurrence and consent; and Taylor and
his subalterns went about their work with the
thoughful activity that had characterised all their
proceedings. But the progress was not rapid. On
Sept. 18. the evening of the 18th they were little further advanced than on the morning. The cause was not
very remote; nor was it very unintelligible. The
veterans of the different brigades did not fall in very
readily with the views of the young Engineers or
cheerfully recognise their temporary supremacy.
So situated, Taylor, with the concurrence of the Chief
Engineer, went to the General and drew from him
an order to the Brigadier commanding at the Caubul
Gate to place at the disposal of the Field Engineer a force of some five hundred men, European and Native, to carry out the above-mentioned design; and early on the 19th the advance
began in earnest. This was not one of the least of

the great services of Alec Taylor. Some thirty
houses, important both by their size and their position, fell into his hands, and were duly barricaded
and garrisoned. Nothing could have been more satisfactory than the result, especially as it was attended
with but trifling loss on the part of the assailants.
The houses thus taken were principally detached
houses with surrounding premises, very favourable
to our operations, for the occupants were exposed to
a flanking and cross fire from the troops occupying
the houses which we had already taken in the rear.
Working onwards in this insidious but most effective
way, our people towards nightfall found themselves
in possession of a building, behind the gorge of the
Lahore Bastion, which so entirely commanded it
that the enemy, seeing their danger, were fain, after
firing a few shots, to escape under cover of the night;
and so the Bastion became our own. But so great
was the terror, which the very name of this formidable work had inspired in the hearts of our men, that
although the bastion had fallen thus easily into their
hands, and there was no opposition, there was a
manifest reluctance on the part of our soldiery to
hold what we had taken. It was hard to restrain
them from leaving the Bastion.

In the meanwhile an attempt had been made to
carry the Lahore Gate by assault. Edward Greathed,
of the Eighth, who had worked cordially with the
Engineers in their house-to-house visitations, was
eager to carry the Lahore Gate, which had so long
defied us. It appeared that this might be done,
without encountering the dreaded opposition of the
Lahore Bastion, by a route of a less hazardous nature.
Greathed was appointed by Brigadier Jones to command the attack, and Colonel Pelham Burn, who had

Attempt on
the Lahore
Gate.

2 s 2

been selected to be Military Governor of Delhi after its occupation by the English, was requested to accompany the detachment.* Greathed took with him a party consisting of some details of the Eighth and Seventy-fifth Queen's and of the Bengal Fusilier Regiments, accompanied by a couple of guns. It was arranged that, on the sound of firing being heard, supports should be sent on from the Caubul Bastion by a narrow lane under the ramparts. The force made good its way without difficulty to the narrow street leading into the Chandna Chouk, but the enemy were posted in force behind a gate at the end of it, which was unexpectedly flung open, for we thought that our movements were unknown, and a six-pounder gun was brought to bear upon our advancing detachments.† On this Greathed ordered up a gun under Lieutenant Harington and directed the men of the Seventy-fifth to charge under cover of the smoke, when the gun should be fired. But the Seventy-fifth did not charge. The Eighth were then ordered to the front, but they also refused to charge ; and the Artillery were left to be fired at by the insurgents, who exhibited more gallantry than our own people. The noble example of our officers could not induce their men to display that fine onward feeling—that regulated impetuosity—which alone can command success under such trials as this. They hated the kind of work which they were called

---

* Burn, who had distinguished himself in Afghanistan, and who had afterwards approved himself as an excellent administrator in one of the great Public Departments at the Presidency. He was a general favourite with the Bengal Army. At Delhi he appeared only as a volunteer ; and having no fixed position could not avail himself of his rank, But he was very useful as a field officer, and General Wilson spoke of him as one of his best officers. He accompanied Nicholson's column on the morning of the assault.

† In this attack Lieutenant Bristowe of the Seventy-fifth was killed.

upon to spring at, and they shrunk back when they ought to have flung themselves upon it. Greathed saw at once the temper of his followers—if followers they could be called who would not follow: he saw the Artillery suffering from the musketry of the enemy ; he knew the value of life at such a time too well to needlessly expend it, and wisely, though most reluctantly, he determined to withdraw his men from the unequal encounter before they. had sustained any heavy loss. But a new difficulty confronted him, for the men seemed equally unwilling to advance or retire. To give assurance to the rest by covering their advance, Burn had taken the detachment of the First Fusiliers to occupy the houses in the narrow street. So with this aid Greathed was able to withdraw his men in an orderly and creditable manner. It was another illustration of the national character in its soldierly aspects. They did not know what they were fighting against, and the unseen danger assumed, in their imaginations, proportions, the reality of which would have been contemptible in the open field.*

There was nothing to exhilarate or to encourage the General in all this. Indeed the crowning misery of all was the thought of the backwardness of the troops under his command. He need not have thought much about numbers, if the hearts of the few were in the right place. Had Wilson been assured of the temper of his men, he might have taken a more cheerful view of the prospect before him. But how this last failure saddened him his letters clearly evince :

---

* In a letter before me this is described as the " sagacious instinct of the British soldier, which teaches him what can be and what cannot be done." But the *Audace, audace—toujours audace!* is better than this.

"Delhi, September 18th, 1857.

" We are still in the same position in which we were yester-day. An attempt was made this morning to take the Lahore Gate, but failed from the refusal of the European soldiers to follow their officers. One rush and it would have been done easily, but they refused to make it. The fact is our men have a great dislike to street fighting; they do not see their enemy, and find their comrades falling from shots of the enemy who are on the tops of houses and behind cover, and get a panic and will not advance. This is very sad and to me disheartening. We can, I think hold our present position, but I cannot see my way out at all. I have now only 3100 men (Infantry) in the city—with no chance or possibility of any reinforcement. If I were to attempt to push on into the city they would be lost in such innumerable streets and masses of houses, and would be annihilated or driven back. It is true that a great number of the enemy have bolted, but they have still a large camp out between the Delhi and Ajmere Gate, and those who have bolted may possibly return when they find we cannot make any progress. Again in our favour we have possession of nearly all their guns, shot and shell, except those they have in the bastions still in their pos-session, and we are bombarding from an easy distance, Selim-gurh and the Palace. . . . It has been a hard task imposed upon me, almost too hard; both mind and body are giving way. Since the night of the 13th I have certainly not had five hours' sound sleep, and nature cannot stand it. I trust, however, and think, I have done my duty. May Almighty God still support me in doing so . . . This is a very doleful letter, but the state of my mind and body perhaps make me more depressed than I should be. . . . ."

" Camp before Delhi, 19th September.

" . . . . I came up to Camp last night in hopes of getting a good night's sleep—I was not, however, very successful. Brain, nerves, and body have been too much strained to quiet down so quickly. I am going back to the city immediately, but shall try to get back here to-night to sleep. . . . We are progressing more satisfactorily—bombarding the city and gradually seizing strong posts in advance of our present position. The King evacuated the Palace yesterday afternoon with most of his followers, finding it too hot to hold him; report says very few are left in it. He is gone to a place near the *Poorana Killah* (Old Fort), outside the city. We have met with a very heavy loss in taking what we have done. I have not yet seen the returns, but hear the total loss in killed and wounded is full 1150 men, including 46 officers. The killed are only about 250. Brigadier-General Nicholson is a very great loss to me—I have no one who can supply his place. I am very much afraid we shall lose him. He was not going on at all favourably yesterday. . . . ."

But when Wilson returned to his Head-Quarters in the city, glad tidings awaited him. Taylor reported the success of his operations, in working from house to house and making grand progress with little loss. The occupation of the Lahore Bastion was an important step in advance; and the General, determined not to lose what we had gained, sent some officers of his Staff to spend the night in the Bastion, or to remain there as long as might be necessary to secure its continued occupation. But there was no attempt on the part of the enemy to recover it. The night passed peaceably away. When day dawned on the 20th, arrangements were made to resume the tactical operations, which had so far been crowned with such complete success. But those who were on the look-out were struck by the deserted aspect of the streets. Some adventurous explorers then went out to ascertain more certainly the position of affairs in the city, and they found that the place was well-nigh abandoned.

The Lahore Bastion being secured, the fall of the Lahore Gate speedily followed. A body of the Sixtieth Rifles rushed at it; and its defenders, finding that "the game was up" with them, from one end of the city to the other, evacuated the work which had so long defied and frustrated the best efforts of our troops. The story of the Lahore Gate is a curious one. It is the story of a lost opportunity. After the first onslaught of the Second Column, the Brigadier, scarcely knowing the importance of the position, found himself on the Lahore Bastion. A bold front, in the confusion and half-panic which had then set in among the defenders, might have carried everything before it and saved all after-trouble and disaster. But Jones had received his orders. He had gone beyond the point at which he had been directed to await tidings of the fall of the Jumma Musjid; so in obedience to orders he fell back and lost the golden opportunity. Emboldened by our inaction at such a time the enemy clung to the work with desperate pertinacity, and for six days held it to the infinite discomfiture of the besiegers. Nicholson had been the only leader of a column, who had, previous to the assault, personally gone down to the breaching batteries, studied the effect of their operations and taken a comprehensive ocular survey of the breaches through which we were to push our way on to victory. But, it may be doubted whether even that "born General" knew much of the position or the designs of the enemy within the ramparts, which Brind, Scott, and others with their heavy guns were battering with such wonderful effect. There were few to whom the advance into the city had not appeared to be a much easier operation than after-events proved that we were justified in anticipating. In affairs of war, it is hard to say what great issues may depend upon some accident of the moment. Had this cruel Bastion and the Lahore Gate, with or without orders,

fallen to our arms on the 14th of September, when 1857.
the Second Column first advanced on these works, Sept. 20.
Delhi would have fallen sooner; and Nicholson might
have survived the siege.

But, whatsoever the misadventure may have been Occupation of the Palace.
at the outset, the capture of the defensive works
of Delhi was now complete. There was an almost
general rush inwards. The cry was "To the Palace! to the Palace!" The occupation by British
troops of the great home of the Moguls was the only
genuine proclamation of victory. Our scouts had
brought us intelligence that the Royal Family had for-
saken their old asylum, and had become fugitives
and outcasts huddling together in the suburbs, not
knowing what to do. The Reality of Indian warfare was now at an end in Delhi; we were about
to see the Romance. Hope Grant sent Hodson to the
General to convey to him the glad tidings that the
city was evacuated.[*] Wilson sent at once a party
under Jones of the Sixtieth Rifles to blow in the
gates of the Palace and of the Selim-gurh. The
powder-bags aided by our guns, did the work with
but little difficulty. A few desperate men remained, moved either by religious enthusiasm or
by military devotion, to die at their posts in the Palace of the Moguls. It is related that a sentry was
found at each gate, with his musket on his shoulder,
grim and immovable, prepared for his doom.[†] No one
found in the imperial premises was left alive. The
British standard was hoisted. And the Englishman

[*] Whether this was the first intimation that reached Head-Quarters
I do not know. I follow here only
the statement of the Cavalry Brigadier. Sir Thomas Seaton also says
that he reported it himself at Head-
Quarters. Many others, doubtless,
did the same.

[†] Aitkin of the Artillery shot one
of them. See in Appendix, an interesting account of the capture of
the Palace and Selim-gurh.

celebrated his victory by ordering dinner to be laid in the Elysium of the Dewan-Khas, with its lustrous marble walls and lovely arabesques, triumphs of that barbaric art, beside which the best effort of the nineteenth century Englishman is but as a Caliban to an Ariel. I know not whether any harmonious spirit, "tired of war's alarms," celebrated and enlivened the occasion by a burst of song, with the well-known adaptation of the words, which our people now saw around the cornices of the Dewan-Khas, but they knew that the famous "Elysium on Earth" was their resting-place and the enemy who had mocked us was no more.*

To the weary warriors of Delhi the best Elysium at that time must have been Rest. There was little or nothing in the material environments of the place strongly to impress the captors with a sense of its splendour or its beauty. We saw it at the worst in the hour of its decadence and humiliation, with the well-remembered pollution of half a century upon it. But since the early days of May, the Mogul, before a puppet, had become a potentiality; and Delhi, one of our greatest civil and military stations, where the old imbecile King and his multitudinous family had so long lain prostrate at our feet, for four long months, had snorted defiance at us, garrisoned by our own army. But now Delhi again was occupied by our British troops. The usual accompaniments of retribution and spoliation could not be wholly absent from such a siege as this. But if there had been no failures,

---

* Moore's poetry is better than his authorities. Quoting Franklin, he informs his readers that around the exterior of the Dewan-Khas in the cornice are the following words in letters of gold on a ground of white marble: " If there be a Paradise on earth, it is this, it is this." The inscription is in letters of *black* marble *inside* the hall; and I can find no other account of its having been otherwise.

no checks; if our legions had entered the imperial
city, which had so long defied us, with a grand rush,
sweeping everything before it, the results would have
been terrible. Hatred of the inhabitants and greed
for the spoil would have borne their accustomed
fruits. But the delays to which we had been compelled to submit gave altogether another character to
the first partial and then complete occupation of the
city. When on the 20th of September Delhi fell
into our hands it was little more than a vast solitude.
The cry of *Væ Victis!* therefore, was never raised. It
was the desertion of the enemy that made us victors
at all. There could, happily, therefore, be no wholesale retribution. But during that week of incerti-
tude, when our half-successes were almost counter-
balanced by whole failures, and no man knew what
might be the issue of these vicissitudes, opportunities arose for the assertion of our retributive strength;
and the temptations, if not irresistible, were most difficult to resist.

Seldom, if ever, since War began, had there been so
much to exacerbate and infuriate an army, as then
inflamed the brains and fevered the blood of the men,
who found themselves in the blood-stained city. No
reader of this narrative needs to be told what were
these exciting influences. But when we come to
weigh the heavy burden of unutterable guilt, of
which our women and children were the victims,
against the cruelty and inhumanity of the aveng-
ing power, we see how light were our reprisals. Still
it must always happen, both in the West and the
East, that the miserable consideration still remains
that the innocent must suffer for the guilty. Many

1857.
Sept. 20.

Treatment of
the con-
quered.

who had never struck a blow against us—who had tried to follow their peaceful pursuits—and who had been plundered and buffeted by their own armed countrymen, were pierced by our bayonets, or cloven by our sabres, or brained by our muskets or rifles. In this instance, I have said, there were aggravations, which have not stirred the hearts of our western warriors. From western warfare there has been absent that which in the East has been most perilous of all, the difference of colour. The very sight of a dark man stimulated our national enthusiasm almost to the point of frenzy. We tolerated those who wore our uniforms and bore our arms, but all else were, in our eyes, the enemies and persecutors of our race. So it sometimes happened that during the first days of our occupation of Delhi, many innocent men were shot down or otherwise massacred. Some of the best and bravest of our officers sanctioned, if they did not take part in these outrages; and it is doubtful whether they could have controlled the excesses of their fighting-men, especially when they were maddened by much drink.

I know only one instance of slaughter on a large scale, which was made the talk of the Camp. Major James Brind, Brind of the Batteries, was sent into the city on the most ungrateful duty of burying the rotting carcases which were polluting the atmosphere of certain parts of Delhi. He took with him a detachment consisting of Artillery and Infantry, mainly, if not wholly, Natives of the country. Among them were forty Sikh artillerymen. The duty thus fixed upon him was of a sanitary, not a retributive character. But it happened that, as he was proceeding to his unsavoury work, news was brought to him of " a brutal attack " which had been made upon a party

of Muzbee Sikhs, in one of the lanes between the 1857.
Delhi and Ajmere Gates. At this time he fell in Sept. 14—20.
with Brigadier Jones, who had commanded the 'Second Column of Attack, and he asked to be reinforced,
if needed, by some European Infantry, that he might
dispose of the men who had committed these outrages and others which Jones reported. The Brigadier
promised to aid Brind, and approved of retributive
action. A wounded Sapper was with difficulty persuaded to lead the way to the spot where these
" murderers " were located. When Brind got among
them he made short work of the chastisement to be
inflicted upon them. Among the traitors were
" Syuds and various classes of debauchees." Many
of the enemy were slain on the spot, and others,
" against whom blood-proofs, as also relics of our
murdered countrywomen, children, and other Christian residents" were to be found on their persons or
in their houses, were reserved for more humiliating
punishments. Following the example set by Neill at
Cawnpore, he kept these men " to labour in cleansing
our polluted lines before their final punishment."
The number slain by Brind's detachment ranged
from a hundred and fifty to two hundred men. As
a pleasant set-off to this, Brind had the satisfaction
of reporting that he had " sent out of the city many
hundreds of women, children, and helpless male
inhabitants—blind and decrepit."* It is not clear
whether the men thus " slain " were our revolted
Sepoys or civil inhabitants of Delhi. It does not
appear to me, however, that the fact of their having
certain articles in their possession was any proof of
their having murdered the English people, to whom

* Major James Brind to Colonel Gaitskill, commanding Artillery.—
MS. Correspondence.

they had belonged. The goods might have been purchased at a prize-auction, or might have come into their possession by some very innocent accident. It was not the first or the last time, when mere possession has been treated as a proof of forcible spoliation attendant on "treacherous murder."* There was not a kinder-hearted, as there was not a braver man in the Delhi army than James Brind; but he was a man of an excitable temperament, and he had been working day and night in the batteries, under a fierce sun, seldom or never sleeping all the time. And he had ever before him the memory of the fact that his brother had been killed at Sealkote by the treacherous connivance of his own servants.†

There is other testimony, which, though not so officially authentic as this, is very strong and reliable, to the effect that many innocent men were destroyed, after the occupation of Delhi, by our infuriated troops. An officer, who served throughout the siege, and who has given us the best account of its chief incidents now before the public, says, " Our men treated these (the women and children) with kindness and sympathy, but many of the citizens were shot, clasping their hands for mercy. It was known, too, that a large proportion of them had all along wished us well."‡ And Colonel Bour-

---

* There has been a story, long time current, to the effect that a number of wretched villagers were hung up, because they had some new *pice* in their possession (a neighbouring treasury having been looted); but it appeared afterwards that the copper coins had been paid to them, for milk, vegetables, grain, &c., by a detachment of our own people. I have no authentic evidence of the truth of this story—so I merely relate it as something very like truth. In the language of the day every Native of the country was a traitor—if he turned against us. The Sepoys, who had received our pay, and had been drilled and disciplined by us, were, in some sense, rebels and traitors—but all the other inhabitants of Delhi who did *not* strive mightily against us were, assuredly, rebels and traitors. All their loyalty was due to the Mogul.

† *Ante*, vol. ii. p. 629—631.

‡ "History of the Siege of Delhi

chief of the Artillery, in his published narrative says: "Some men were caught going out of the Cashmere Gate disguised as women and were hung; whilst several bheesties, or water-carriers, detected in bringing in drugged liquor for the troops, were likewise disposed of."* The enormity of endeavouring to escape the fury of the assailants by huddling out in petticoats is not very clear. The device was one not altogether unknown, or unpractised, in like emergencies, by our own officers. It might have been better to have given these epicene creatures the benefit of the doubt. It is a pleasure to the Historian to be able to add that from the mass of manuscript documents before him he can clearly derive the one gratifying fact, that the women and children were almost uniformly respected. A stray shot might, now and then, inadvertently have carried death with it; but no intentional outrages were committed. A distinguished officer of the Eighth, which formed part of the Second Column, writes: "The Eighth took possession of a large house, the basement and court of which was filled with women and children, evidently of a respectable rank of life, who were naturally much frightened.† But they had no reason to be so, for our good fellows treated them as if they had been their sisters and passed them out carefully and kindly on their way to the Cashmere Gate, which was all, indeed, we could do for them." I

by an Officer who served there."— This very able writer observes: "Helplessness ought to be respected in either sex, especially in those who have never done us wrong. It is as unmanly for an officer to drive his sword through a trembling old man or a soldier to blow out the brains of a wounded boy, as to strike a woman."

* "Eight Months' Campaign in India against the Bengal Sepoy Army, by Lieutenant-Colonel Bourchier, C.B."—afterwards Sir George Bourchier, K.C.B.

† This was Jung Behaudur's house. The Eighth had afterwards to evacuate it, as the building was required for other purposes.

could add many other proofs of the forbearance of our soldiery ; but this may be taken as a sample of the whole.

Plundering the city.
The reign of unlicensed plundering had begun at an early period. The Sikhs, among whose traditional day-dreams the sack of Delhi had ever been prominent, now found themselves within reach of the realisation of their fondest wishes. No scruples restrained them. They had no conception of a Prize Agency beyond the grand cardinal principle that it was the duty of every man to gather up what spoil he could get and to keep it as long as he could. Their natural astuteness, aided perhaps by some experiences elsewhere, had taught them how to discern the lurking-places of concealed treasure. It might be buried beneath the floors of their houses or bricked up in their walls. In the former case it might be ascertained by pouring water through the crevices, for if the space below were excavated it would soon filter down ; if not it would return to the level of the floor. In the latter, the wall might be sounded, as a physician sounds the chest of a patient; and the results of this process of auscultation were very convincing to our Sikh comrades. To what extent their surmises were justified can only be conjectured. But nothing was more patent than the energy of their endeavours, for almost everywhere battered walls and wrenched up floors told plainly what they had done. It was clearly ascertained, too, that large quantities of plunder were handed over the walls to their brethren below, and that afterwards numbers of laden carts passed out at the opposite gates of the city. It has been stated, indeed, that their countrymen would not believe in the fall of Delhi until they had ocular demonstra-

tion of the " loot." But it is not to be thought that 1857. the Sikhs were the only recipients of unauthorised Sept. 14—20. Prize. Sepoys of other nationalities and camp followers of all, went in remorselessly for what they could clutch. And our own European soldiery in a lesser degree took part in the unlicensed spoliation. But they had not the same discriminating eye for booty as their Sikh comrades, and they were seldom richer in the end ·for their contempt of the Prize Agents and their evasions of the Provost-Marshal.

The Head-Quarters' Staff, Military and Civil, were Death of Hervey Greathed. now fixed in the Palace. But there was one absent from the party, whose work at that time had developed into peculiar interest and importance. It was truly a sad thing that just at this point, when all things were working on, surely if not rapidly, to the complete occupation of Delhi, the subversion of the Mogul, and the proclamation of the Queen's authority, the man who, from the very beginning, had superintended all the political and civil transactions connected with our position at Delhi was suddenly stricken by cholera. The Pestilence that walketh in the darkness had laid the cold hand of death upon Hervey Greathed. He was a man in the prime of his life, with the flush of health on his cheek; with strength and activity in every movement. The published extracts from his family correspondence show how cheerful he was throughout the long months of the siege, how friendly and sociable he was with his comrades, especially his old friends from Meerut, and how lovingly he dwelt with his brothers. It was a luxury during that long dreary period of waiting to have an old friend or relative of any

1857.
Sept. 19.

degree with whom to converse and to exchange sympathies. But the Greatheds had no such scanty consolation ; for the three brothers, Edward, Hervey, and Welby were all in Wilson's camp, performing different duties, but seldom, for a day, apart.* Nothing could be more cheery than the manner in which the civilian wrote of this pleasant family intercourse. And as it did much to sustain the spirits of the Triumviri, so also it must have sustained their health. But the brightest and the lustiest are often those to succumb first to the approaches of cholera ; and on the 19th of September, whilst full of hope, eager for the crowning action, and never doubting the final issue of the great contest, all that was mortal of Hervey Greathed lay in the pale stillness of death. He was buried in the graveyard near Ludlow Castle —the first to find a resting-place there.

Capture of the Royal Family.

The English had now captured the Palace ; but where was the King? If any man in our Army could track him down, that man was Hodson of Hodson's Horse—the famous partisan leader, who had the fierce courage of the tiger unsubdued by any feelings of human compassion—who might have grown

---

* Much mention is made of Welby Greathed, the Engineer, and of his bold projects for a coup-de-main, in Barnard's time, will be found in the second volume of this History. He was severely wounded in the assault (ante page 592). Edward Greathed was Lieutenant-Colonel of the Eighth Foot. Wilson, at no time very prodigal of praise, spoke of him as one of his best officers of his force. His subsequent career in India will be detailed in the last volume of this history. He was created a Knight-Commander of the Bath in 1865. Hervey Greathed himself was a man of high promise. He had passed out from Haileybury first of his term, and was held in great estimation by all under whom he served, especially by Mr. Colvin, who was in confidential communication with him almost to the day of the Lieutenant-Governor's death. He was at Meerut, when the mutiny broke out, and went to Delhi with Wilson's force. See vol. ii., pages 68 and 183.

into something good and great, had years, which bring the philosophic mind, taught him the might of mildness and the glory of forbearance. As it is, viewed by such light as is cast by his antecedents on his character and conduct at this time, he appears as a man labouring under a strong sense of intolerable wrong, excited and exasperated by what had befallen him, feeling that he was under a cloud, but firmly resolved to blaze through it, with the light of some heroic enterprise that would cause the past to be forgotten. He had nothing but his character as a fighting man left to him; but this was of the finest temper. He had been dismissed from political employment in the Punjab for truculent injustice to a Native chief and had been pronounced wholly unfit ever to exercise any civil power.* Another grave charge had been brought against him, which I am not competent to discuss. But there was not a stain upon the brightness of his sabre. In critical conjunctures such men are of eminent service to the State. They will do deeds which some would shrink from in fear and others would abstain from on principle. Wilson was not unwilling to give him *carte blanche* to deal with the Royal Family as he might think fit—with the single reservation that the life of the old King was to be spared.

Hodson, who had been appointed executive Chief of the Intelligence Department, had done his work right well with the aid of some notable Native spies, the chief of whom was Rujjub Ali, who rendered excellent service to the English by the intelligence and sagacity with which he obtained and communicated information regarding the movements of the

---

* See *ante*, vol. ii. p. 182.

1857.
Sept. 18.

enemy throughout the siege. But we owed much also to a traitorous, or as it was the fashion to say a "loyal" member of the House of Delhi, the Meerza Elahee Buksh, who was the father-in-law of the late heir-apparent. This man, who was said to be more "respectable" than the majority of his kinsmen, was also more sagacious. He had no dream of the restoration of the lost honours of the House of Delhi. Believing that the English would triumph in the end, he saw clearly that his own interests would be best served by covertly aiding the Infidels, whilst assuming the part of a friendly adviser of the Mogul. The game which he played was distinguished by no little Oriental astuteness. The leaders of the Army were eager to carry off the King with them. They pleaded that although want of provisions compelled them to leave the city, outside the walls, they could, if it were necessary, ravage the country, supply themselves, and make a great war against the English. And they had well-nigh succeeded, when the wily Meerza, who had persuaded the poor old man to accompany him to his house, where

Sept. 18—19. they spent the night, had not used all his efforts to keep the King from joining the Insurgents. He was satisfied that "a real fidelity required him not to let the King go with the Army." So with "great effort" and "extreme endeavour," when Bukht Khan and other chiefs of the Imperial Army met Behaudur Shah and the Princes at Hoomayoon's Tomb, the Meerza "made so many good arrangements that neither the King nor his sons did ever listen to them, and none of them have ever gone with the officers of the ungrateful regiments."* All this and much more was

* These are a translation of Elahee Buksh's own words as given in a manuscript statement before me.

communicated to Hodson principally through the
Moonshee Rujjub Ali. It was plain that the wily
Meerza had got the whole Royal Family in his toils,
and that it needed now only that the bold heart
and the strong hand should be brought in aid of
this crouching treachery. By specious representations Elahee Buksh held them in gentle bondage at
the Tomb of the Emperor Hoomayoon with its surrounding structures, a suburb in itself, beyond the
modern city. It was the way out of Delhi, and
large numbers of the Insurgents were still flocking
there for safe egress, carrying off what property
they could, but glad to escape even with their
lives. It was thought that amidst this crowd of
people, the King and his family, swayed by later
counsels, might escape. So Hodson galloped down
to Head-Quarters and obtained reluctant permission
from the General to take a party of his own men to
Hoomayoon's Tomb and bring in, without injury or
insult, the last of the Mogul Emperors. Taking
fifty of his troopers he rode off, elated with the success of his mission, and passing the ruins of the ancient city of Delhi, made his way to the asylum of the
prostrate monarch. There was then little risk either of
escape or resistance; for the King, under guidance of
Zeenut-Mehal, was already treating for his surrender.
Still it was hard to say what terrible crisis might not
be evolved at such a time, out of the desperation of
those about him. It was necessary to move cau-
tiously; so Hodson concealed himself and his men
in some ruined buildings near the gateway of the
Tomb; whilst he sent his emissaries on to convey his
instructions to the royal fugitives. Two weary hours
dragged away—hours of painful suspense—before
they brought back an answer. The King consented

to give himself up to Captain Hodson, on assurance received from that officer's own lips that his life would be spared.

So Hodson went forth from his resting-place and stood out before all, in the open space near the beautiful gateway of the Tomb, a solitary white man, among so many, awaiting the surrender of a King and the total extinction of a dynasty, the most magnificent that the world had ever seen. It was then but a title, a tradition; but still the monarchy of the Moguls was a living influence in the hearts of the Mahomedans of India. And, truly, a grander historical picture was rarely seen than that of the single British subaltern receiving the sword of the last of the Mogul Emperors in the midst of a multitude of followers and retainers grieving for the downfall of the House of Tamerlane and the ruin of their own fortunes. Grand as was the central incident in itself, it was rendered still grander and more impressive by its gorgeous historical background—"the magnificent gateway with the milk-white domes of the Tomb towering up from within"*—the gateway through which, preceded by the Queen and her son, for whom the wretched old man had endured so much and was now perishing, passed the palanquin containing the last poor remnant of royalty on its way to a living tomb. Hodson pricked on with drawn sword, to meet it and called upon the King to give up his arms. The old man asked if he was "Hodson Behaudur," and asked for a renewal from the Englishman's own lips of the promises made by his herald. This was done; and

---

* See a letter addressed to Hodson's brother in "Twelve Years of a Soldier's Life." The writer is probably Captain M'Dowall, of the Bengal Fusiliers, and second-in-command of Hodson's Horse, who could use his pen as well as his sword.

Hodson formally guaranteed the personal safety of 1857.
His Majesty and of the son of Zeenut-Mehal. The Sept. 21.
Imperial arms were then surrendered to the Englishman, who made them over to his orderly, observing
that if any attempt were made to rescue his prisoner
the King would be shot down like a dog. Then the
procession to the city commenced. It was a slow
and dismal march along five miles of road; and it
might have been a critical one, for a vast crowd
followed the palanquins and their escorts during the
greater part of the journey. They seemed hushed
and overawed—rather wondering than excited—and
gradually slunk away as they neared the Lahore
Gate. Hodson and his captives then passed up the
great street of the Chandna Chouk to the city.
Meeting Saunders, the principal civil officer left to
us at Delhi, Hodson made over the prisoners to him
and went to report himself to the General. Wilson
received him in his usual way, with a sort of bluff
heartiness, which few in Camp understood, for there
was more kindness in his heart than appeared upon
the gritty surface; and said, " Well, I am glad you
have got him, but I never expected to see him or
you again!" But when the royal arms were given
up to him Wilson told his subaltern to select any
that he wished to possess as memorials of the adventure. One of the swords which he took had adorned
the side of Nadir Shah, the other had been worn by
the Emperor Jehanguire.

I wish that the record of Hodson's exploits had Slaughter of
ended with this narrative of the capture of the King. the Princes.
It would have gladdened the heart of the daring
subaltern to have been ordered or permitted to shoot
Behaudur Shah like a dog or to strike him down like
an ox in the shambles. But this congenial occupa-

tion was not conceded to him. His captive was a miserable, infirm old man, much wrought upon by evil advisers; the slave rather than the master of circumstances, the shadow of a name turned to evil purposes.* To have used brutal violence towards such a poor feeble creature would have been little more manly than the slaughter of a woman. But the game of royalty-hunting had not yet been played out. Some of the King's sons, or near relatives, who were believed to have taken an active part in the insurrection and in the massacre of our people, were still to be tracked down. They were in the prime of life—if life, spent in that great reeking stye of the Delhi Palace could ever be said to have a prime—and no pledges or promises had been made to them. They were lawful game and Hodson knew where to find them. So he got Wilson's permission to hunt down the Shahzadahs and sent to his Second-in-Command, M'Dowall, to bring up a hundred troopers. He promptly obeyed the summons, and Hodson mounted, eager for the affray. The Princes were at Hoomayoon's Tomb where the King had been captured on the preceding day. With them were some thousands of followers, including a number of Mussulman fanatics, who called upon them in the name of the Prophet to resist the infidel intruders; but they thought it better to sue for terms—hoping at least that their lives would be spared. Hodson would grant them no terms—would make no promises of any kind. He commissioned his emissaries† to say that "he had

---

* Hodson himself spoke of the Behaudur Shah as a mere puppet, a "ruse." "He is old and well-nigh impotent, and is only used as an authority for all the acts of rebellion and barbarity committed by his sons." Yet he admits that he would rather have brought in the king dead than alive.

† These delegates were the notorious Moonshee Rujjub Ali, who was the very life of Hodson's Intelli-

come to seize the Shahzadahs, and intended to do so, dead or alive." After two hours spent in useless negotiation—mere idle talk leading to nothing—the delegates of the British Government as it was then represented by Hodson, reported that the Princes were coming out in covered bullock-carts. Soon the wretched captives appeared, made one last despairing appeal for their lives, and were sent on towards Delhi guarded by our troopers on both sides of the way.*

Having seen his prisoners fairly started, Hodson, with his remaining Sowars, passed the precincts of the Tomb, and in a loud voice, called upon the people assembled there to surrender their arms. It is true that the multitude were but the "scum of the Palace," weak, nerveless, heartbroken people, who had seen their King carried off from the midst of them, and yet in their pitiful prostration had not courage to strike a blow in his defence. Still there were at least six thousand of these miserable creatures within the precincts of Hoomayoon's Tomb, and a rush of the surging multitude might have overwhelmed the little body of Hodson's Horse. But the commanding attitude and authoritative utterance of their intrepid leader overawed the congregated numbers; a great fear fell upon them; they felt that it was hopeless to endeavour to resist the power of the White Man, now that he had shattered their defences, dispersed their fighting men, and established

gence Department, and the "loyal" member of the Delhi Family, willing to betray his kinsmen for his own ends.

* Meerza Elahee Buksh had a principal hand in this. "At night," he says, "when I went to Hodson Sahib, he told me to bring to him the Meerza Khazar Sooltan, Meerza Mogul, and Meerza Aboo-Bakr. I answered that I had already made arrangements for that. He might find them any time he liked. . . . Then (22nd September) according to the order of Hodson Sahib, I brought those three above-mentioned from the sepulchre to him. Having taken them with the King's property with him, he returned, and was very pleased with me."—*MS. Records.*

himself in the Palace of the Moguls. So they sub-mitted almost without a murmur; and in less time than Hodson had dared to anticipate, they were quietly collecting their arms, their horses and carriages, and under the supervision of the troopers gathering them together in the centre of the square.

Up to this time all that had been done by Hodson was worthy of a Christian Warrior. He had captured the Princes; he had disarmed their followers; and in doing so he had confronted great dangers, from the thought of which most men would have shrunk appalled. But, whether he had gone out with any foregone intentions to kill his captives, or whether any sudden emergency arose, which rendered it necessary for the public safety that they should be forthwith executed without the formality of a trial, Hodson resolved that he would shoot them down like dogs. When he left Hoomayoon's Tomb, fearing that some misadventure might have befallen the escort on the road to Delhi, he galloped forward to overtake them. As he neared them a little way outside the city he saw that a crowd was pressing on the guard and he thought that a rescue would be attempted.* Upon this Hodson rode in amongst them, and addressed his troopers, so as to be heard by the multitude, saying that the prisoners were the butchers who had murdered our women and children, and that an outraged Government had now ordained their punishment. So he ordered the Shahzadahs to quit the cart in which they had been placed and strip themselves to their under-vestments. They tremblingly obeyed and were ordered back to the cart. Then either thinking that his Sowars might not obey him,

---

* It is not stated whether these, or any of these, were armed men.

or rejoicing in the work of carnage, he took a car- 1857.
bine from one of his troopers, and deliberately, with Sept. 22.
his own hand, shot to death his unarmed and
unresisting captives. This done, he rode with his
prey into the city, and ordered the corpses of the
Princes to be flung out and exposed to public view
in front of the Kotwallic. And there they remained
till the bodies rotted and stank, and it was necessary,
for health's sake, to bury them.

I have told this story, briefly and plainly, as it is Estimate of
narrated by the only two European witnesses, who Hodson's con-
were present at this terrible execution—Hodson him- duct.
self and his Second-in-Command, M'Dowall. I cannot,
for a moment, question the truth of their evidence.
But after a full consideration of the incident, as thus
recorded and accepted, I cannot resist the conviction
that Hodson, in thus stripping and shooting the
Princes, committed an act which no good man can,
at this distance of time, approve. That the men so
suddenly sent to their account were members of the
House of Delhi, was shown upon the testimony
of that loyal kinsman of the King, who had been
bought over, and who had accompanied Hodson for
the purpose of identifying his prisoners. But that
these identical men were promoters or prime agents
of the massacre of our women and children, Hodson
seems to have had no satisfactory proof, to justify his
summary execution of the suspects. Their trial,
probably, would have educed some pregnant truths
illustrative of their conduct and of the conduct of
other members of the Imperial House—facts now,
perhaps, lost to us for ever. It was no uncommon
thing in those days to execute the wrong man. I
have heard terrible stories of these "mistakes"—
stories not to be told unless supported by over-

whelming evidence. Hodson was the last man in
the Camp to trouble himself much about evidence.
He believed that it was his mission to take an active
personal part in the infliction of dire retribution
upon the House of Delhi. On the last day of
August he wrote: " If I get into the Palace, the
House of Timour will not be worth five minutes'
purchase, I ween; but what my share in this work
will be no one can say"—and on the 23rd of September he wrote again with exultation, saying, " In
twenty-four hours I disposed of the principal members of the House of Timour the Tartar. I am not
cruel, but I confess that I did rejoice in the opportunity of ridding the earth of these ruffians." He
said that he would sooner have brought in the old
King dead than alive. He would fain, indeed, have
ridden into Delhi with the head of Behaudur Shah
at his saddle-bow.

It is not to be questioned, therefore, that Hodson,
as portrayed by himself, was a man of a truculent
and sanguinary disposition, delighting in such deeds
as this. He was gratified by the execution and proud
in the remembrance of such exploits. There is no
sign of his having been pained by the thought of
them. He scarcely supposed that they required any
justification. But as they were altogether of an
abnormal character, he felt that the propriety of
such an act as the massacre of the Princes might be
questioned by men in authority more scrupulous
than himself. He set forth therefore, firstly, that the
General had told him that he did not wish to be
troubled with the prisoners; and, secondly, that if
he had not killed them, their adherents would have
killed him. But it is not fairly to be assumed that
Wilson hinted at the summary execution of the pri-

soners. He probably meant only that they should be made over at once to the civil authorities. The other plea has certainly much weight, if the emergency was as great as is stated. But at that time the people were so prostrate, and the Princes themselves so powerless for evil or for good, that it is little likely that any serious effort at rescue, resistance, or retaliation would have emanated from such a body, in the presence of Hodson and his well-mounted, well-armed troopers. They had not heart for such an encounter. The fact that so large a body of men had succumbed to Hodson and readily surrendered their arms at Hoomayoon's Tomb, shows the hopeless imbecility to which the adherents of the Imperial House had been reduced. And if Hodson thought that with his heroic band of horsemen he could not have guarded his prisoners and dispersed the mob, with a great slaughter, he must have thought more meanly of his own prowess and of his splended regiment than did any other man in Camp.

But what was thought of this achievement by his comrades? "I cannot help being pleased," wrote Hodson, on the 25th of September, "with the warm congratulations I receive on all sides for my success in destroying the enemies of our race. The whole nation will rejoice." But in the February following he wrote in a different strain. "I made up my mind at the time to be abused. I was convinced I was right, and when I prepared to run the great physical risk of the attempt I was equally game for the moral risk of praise or blame." The truth is that, at the time of the capture of Delhi, when men's blood was fevered with anger and hatred, and their faces flushed with shame and indignation at the thought of the measureless cruelty of our enemies, some of the best and wisest of our countrymen in India looked with excited approval upon what they came afterwards to regard with calm regret. And although Hodson at one time believed that the "whole nation" would rejoice, I may aver without hesitation, that the general feeling in England was one of profound grief, not unmingled with detestation. I never heard the act approved ; I never heard it even defended.

All danger was now at an end. All doubt was now at an end. The King was a captive. The city was a wreck. It had been a week of ceaseless anxiety— of tremendous care. Whatever might have been said or thought at the time, Wilson did not exaggerate the difficulties of the situation. I repeat here at the end, what I said at the beginning, of this narrative of the Siege*—for Justice may reiterate itself without offence—that after the excitements and impetuosities of the hour had passed away, after the eager irresponsible audacities of the younger heroes of the siege had been calmed down by the subduing influence of Time, and that great crisis in our national history had become a tradition, many of the best soldiers of the Delhi Army frankly declared that, the longer they lived, the more convinced they were, that justice had not been done to the General, who had commanded them. Men, whose blood was at fever-heat, looking only from certain fixed stand-points at details within their circumscribed view, and not seeing even the whole significance of those details, were not in a position, neither were they in a temper, at the time, to take a calm and comprehensive view of the great expanse before the General. I have ob-

* *Ante*, pp. 554—555.

served during a period of many years the progress of this reaction. Sooner or later Time will ever bring in its revenges. 1857. Sept. 22.

⌐ But the fact that he had taken Delhi did not seem much to rouse him from his depression. He was profoundly thankful to the Almighty for the great deliverance ; but he scarcely seemed to rejoice in his victory. There can be no stronger proof of the heavy clouds of gloom which enfolded him, that no thought of honours or rewards—of the realisation of fame or fortune—as the captor of Delhi, seems to have possessed him at this time. He was too much broken down to long for anything but perfect repose. In his private letters he said little of himself. Not a particle of ambition or greed entered into them. Seldom has a man in such a position been so little egotistical :—

"The Palace, Delhi, 22nd September, 2 P.M.

"The plot thickens. Yesterday evening the King and his favourite Begum, Zenut-Mehal, gave themselves up and are now my prisoners. I have not allowed them to return to the Palace, but they are in honourable confinement in Zenut-Mehal's house. To-day Hodson and his Horse surrounded Hoomayoon's Tomb, in which some of the Princes had taken refuge with nearly all the women of the Palace. Three of the Princes, Mirza Moghul, Mirza Abboo Bakr, and Mirza Rezi Sultan, were taken and shot. The two former have been the most virulent against us. Hodson as a partisan officer has not his equal. To-morrow morning a movable column of about 2800 men move in the direction of Muttra, under Colonel Greathed, in pursuit of the flying rebels. If Havelock could only relieve Lucknow and move up this way, the whole rebellion would be put down I believe at once. I have sent a party of Irregular Cavalry in the direction of Meerut to my old battle-ground on the Hindun River to reconnoitre in that direction. I have not a single moment that I can call my own and cannot write you a long letter. . . . . Hodson has presented me with the King's sword, dagger, and matchlock . . . . I have just heard the party I ordered to the Hindun (the Mooltanee Horse) have refused to march. You see what materials I have to work with!

> "23rd September, Palace, Delhi.
>
> " . . . . . We are, I hope, going on smoothly. Order is getting gradually restored, though the discipline of the troops has, I am sorry to say, got sadly disorganised. Such a heterogeneous force as I command was certainly never before collected together — Beloochees, Afghans, Sikhs, Pathans, Dograhs—all of whom have been bred and taught to consider plunder of an enemy legitimate, and will not be restrained. The Europeans are so badly commanded from the loss of most of their old officers, as to be quite as bad, if not worse. I hope, however, it will soon quiet down. Burn is Military Governor of the city and is exerting himself well . . . . I am completely done and can't carry on much longer. I have written to J. Lawrence to tell him I am quite unequal to the task now before me and that I wish some younger and more competent man may be sent to relieve me. . . . . That fine fellow Nicholson died to-day at one o'clock; if he had been spared what an assistance he would have been to me."

Death of John Nicholson. During nine days John Nicholson lay dying in the Camp upon the Ridge. He had been removed to a bungalow for greater comfort and quiet. Now and then, it was said, upon medical authority, that he was a little better. But he chafed under the great misfortune that had fallen upon him. He could not rest for thinking of the doubtful issue of the final struggle. He was continually inquiring how the attack was going on—and was very readily excited by the news that was brought to him. On one occasion the vehement impetuosity of his passionate nature broke through all restraints. When told that there had been some talk of retiring, the dying hero exclaimed, "Thank God, I have still strength enough to shoot that man."

If he had lived, calmly to review all the events of this momentous siege, with its chances, its perils, its responsibilities, he would never, to himself or to others, have justified such words. And if he had ever got beside Herbert Edwardes, both men would most earnestly have condemned them. But the passionate vehemence of the natural man overbore all restraints, and there may have been something of the delirium of fever which rendered him scarcely responsible for his words. There were few of the more earnest spirits in Camp who were not moved by like seething indignation, at the thought of withdrawal from Delhi; but they did not express their anger and shame in the same truculent language.

These outbursts greatly enhanced his fever and increased his pain, and it was found necessary to give him large doses of morphia to secure him temporary rest. When not under the influence of the drug, he continued to inquire after the progress of our offensive operations, tidings of which Chamberlain, who had gone into the city with Wilson, frequently sent to his dying friend, through the "good Surgeon Mackinnon." And whenever he could leave the city he was beside his friend, gentle as a woman in his ministrations, and ever speaking words of hope and encouragement, to cheer him on his dying bed. Once or twice, as time wore on, warmed, perhaps, by the cheering intelligence which he received from the city, he rallied a little; and again his friends entertained some faint hopes of his recovery. But there was really no hope. He was wearing away to his rest.

And so days passed, and the complete occupation

of the great imperial city was every day approaching the final issue. The tidings brought to Nicholson's bedside were, every day, more and more assuring. He lived to hear that the Palace of the Moguls was occupied by British troops. He lived to hear that Behaudur Shah was a prisoner in our hands. He lived to hear that Hodson had, with his own hands, shot down the Princes like dogs. He lived to hear that Edward Greathed had been ordered to command the column of pursuit—a command which he himself had coveted. But he felt now that the world was passing away from him, and he thought much of those whom he was leaving behind; especially of his aged mother at Lisburne, and of Herbert Edwardes and his wife. "Tell my mother," he said, "that I do not think we shall be unhappy in the next world. God has visited her with a great affliction, but tell her she must not give way to grief." And of Edwardes he spoke, "Say that if at this moment a good fairy were to give me a wish, my wish would be to have him here, next to my mother." This was on the evening of the 22nd of September. On the morrow morning he rendered back his soul to his Maker.

Thus died John Nicholson, in the prime of his life, amidst a great wail of the universal Camp. He was a man *sui generis*. There were features of resemblance in his character to some characteristics of other heroes of the time. He had much of the high sense of duty—the stern conscientiousness of Henry Lawrence, with something more of the impetuosity of temper which that great man so often deplored. There was much also of the fearlessness of responsibility and the contempt of authority that sometimes made Neill a thorn in the flesh of those above him.

But the whole massive manhood of Nicholson had no perfect resemblance, in Camp or in Council, present or past. And the reason was this; his character was not yet fully developed. He was growing into something other than he was when he fell—something more perfect, more complete, more harmonious in its consistency. Some qualities might have been toned down and others might have ripened—each and all for the better. But before the fruit was ripe it fell to the ground. It is not difficult, however, to perceive what would have been the ripening effect of time. The very desire to get nearer to Herbert Edwardes and to think more of Henry Lawrence reveals clearly to us what would have been the growth of the future—what India lost in that final encounter. He had been so much associated with the affairs of Afghanistan and the Punjab, that his comrades and others in Lower India knew but little about his worth. They had a general idea that in the Punjab there was a man of great promise named Nicholson. It has been said that the Queen's officers were jealous of his high reputation. But there were brilliant exceptions to this. Hope Grant said; of him as Nicholson lay dying that he was "like a noble oak. riven asunder by a thunderbolt.* It must have been painful to the senior officers of the Force to be superseded by so young a man; but there were no complaints, for all admitted the grandeur of his character and his fitness for the work on which he was employed. But it is true that the Punjab was the home of his renown. The Natives of the district which he had governed, regarded him almost as the embodiment of an Avatar—as something little

* " Incidents in the Sepoy War," by General Sir Hope Grant.

2 U 2

short of Godhead itself—as a hero-saint to be adored and worshipped. When he chastised his followers, they regarded it as an honour—for he could do nothing wrong in their eyes. It has been said that such is the prodigal growth of English manhood of the noblest type, in Camp and in Council, that when one great man passes away from the scene, his place is soon filled by one of equal worth. I do not think that it is so. As I write, eighteen years have passed away since Henry Lawrence, Neill, and Nicholson fell beneath the fire of the enemy; but I do not know the men who have replaced them. Nurtured by the grand old East India Company— knowing nothing of purchases and exchanges and Civil Service Commissioners, they went to the front by the unaided force of their own personal heroism. They flung aside, as if it had been a feather, the dead-weight of the seniority system. They knew little, if anything, of the art of war. But they knew how to do the right thing at the right time, and gained victories, when, according to all scientific principles, they ought to have been ignominiously and disastrously beaten.

Then from city to city, from cantonment to cantonment went the chequered tidings; Delhi had fallen, the King was a captive—but John Nicholson was dead.

₊ Much that I wished to say in this chapter has unavoidably been left unsaid. But it is proposed to return to Delhi in the first chapter of the next volume. It is but an episode in this story: but it is a very important episode; and demands more than common consideration.

APPENDIX.

NOTES AND ILLUSTRATIONS.

[Vol. iii. p. 9.]

ACT No. XIV. of 1857.

PASSED BY THE LEGISLATIVE COUNCIL OF INDIA.

(*Received the assent of the Governor-General on the 6th June, 1857.*)

AN ACT *to make further provision for the trial and punishment of certain offences relating to the Army, and of offences against the State.*

WHEREAS it is necessary to make further provision for the trial and punishment of persons who endeavour to excite mutiny and sedition among the Forces of the East India Company, and also for the trial of offences against the State : It is enacted as follows :

I. Whoever intentionally seduces or endeavours to seduce any Officer or Soldier in the service or pay of the East India Company from his allegiance to the British Government or his duty to the East India Company, or intentionally excites or stirs up, or endeavours to excite or stir up, any such Officer or Soldier, or any Officer or Soldier serving in any part of the British Territories in India in aid of the Troops of the British Government, to commit any act of mutiny or sedition ; and whoever intentionally causes, or endeavours to cause, any other person to commit any such offence—shall be liable upon conviction to the punishment of death, or to the punishment of transportation for life, or of imprisonment with hard labour for any term not exceeding fourteen years ; and shall forfeit all his property and effects of every description.

II. Whoever shall knowingly harbour or conceal any person who shall have been guilty of any offence mentioned in the preceding section, shall be liable to imprisonment, with or without hard labour, for any term not exceeding seven years, and shall also be liable to fine.

III. It shall be lawful for the Governor-General of India in Council, from time to time, by Order in Council, to empower every General or other Officer having the command of Troops in the Service of Her Majesty or of the East India Company, or any of such General or other Officers, to appoint General Courts-Martial for the trial of any person or persons charged with having committed an offence punishable by this Act or by Section I. or Section II. of Act XI. of 1857, and also to confirm and carry into effect any sentence of such Court-Martial.

IV. Any General Court-Martial, which may be appointed under the authority of this Act, shall be appointed by the Senior Officer on the spot, and shall consist of not less than five Commissioned Officers, the number to be fixed by the General or other Officer appointing the Court-Martial. The Order in Council may direct that a General Court-Martial to be appointed under the provisions of this Act shall consist wholly of European Commissioned Officers or wholly of Native Commissioned Officers, or partly of European Commissioned Officers, and partly of Native Commissioned Officers; and in [such case the Officer appointing the Court-Martial shall determine whether the same shall consist wholly of European Officers or wholly of Native Officers, or partly of European Officers and partly of Native Officers.

V. Sentence of death or other punishment to which the offender is liable by law, may be given by such Court-Martial, if a majority of the members present concur in the sentence ; and any such sentence may be confirmed by, and carried into effect immediately or otherwise by order of, the Officer by whom the Court-Martial shall have been appointed, or, in case of his absence, by the Senior Officer on the spot.

VI. It shall be lawful for the Governor-General in Council to countermand or alter any Order in Council which may be issued under the authority of this Act.

VII. It shall be lawful for the Governor-General in Council, or for the Executive Government of any Presidency or place, or for any person or persons whom the Governor-General in Council may authorise so to do, from time to time to issue a Commission for the trial of all or any persons or person charged with having committed within any district described in the Commission, whether such district shall or shall not have been proclaimed to be in a state of rebellion, any offence punishable by Sections I. and II. of Act XI. of 1857, or by this Act, or any other crime against the State, or murder, arson, robbery, or other heinous crime against person or property.

VIII. The Commissioner or Commissioners authorised by any such Commission, may hold a Court in any part of the district mentioned in the Commission, and may there try any person for any of the said crimes committed within any part thereof, it being the intention of this Act that the district mentioned in the Commission shall, for the purpose of trial and punishment of any of the said offences, be deemed one district.

IX. Any Court held under the Commission shall have power, without the attendance or futwa of a Law Officer, or the assistance of Assessors, to pass upon every person convicted before the Court of any of the aforesaid crimes any sentence warranted by law for such crime; and the judgment of such Court shall be final and conclusive; and the said Court shall not be subordinate to the Sudder or other Court.

X. If a Commission be issued under the authority of this Act, any Magistrate or other Officer having power to commit for trial within the district described in the Commission may commit persons charged with any of the aforesaid crimes within such district for trial before a Court to be held under this Act.

XI. Nothing in this Act shall extend to the trial or punishment of any of Her Majesty's natural born subjects born in Europe, or of the children of such subjects.

XII. This Act shall not extend to the trial or punishment of any person for any offence for which he is liable to be tried by the Articles of War.

XIII. The word " Soldier." shall include every person subject to any Articles of War.

XIV. This Act shall continue in force for one year.

SIR THOMAS MUNRO ON THE INDIAN PRESS.—Page 14.

" Owing to the unnatural state in which India will be placed under the foreign Government, with a Free Press and a Native Army, the spirit of independence will spring up in this army long before it is even thought of among the people. The army will not wait for the slow operation of the instruction of the people, and the growth of liberty among them, but will hasten to execute their own measures for the overthrow of the Government and the recovery of their national independence, which they will soon learn from the press it is their duty to accomplish. The high opinion entertained of us by the Natives, and the deference and respect for authority which have hitherto prevailed among ourselves, have been the main causes of our success in this country, but when these principles shall be shaken or swept away by a Free Press, encouraged by our juries to become a licentious one, the change will soon reach and pervade the whole Native Army. The Native troops are the only body of Natives who are always mixed with Europeans, and they will, therefore, be the first to learn the doctrines circulated among them by the newspapers ; for, as those doctrines will become the frequent subject of discussion among the European officers, it will not be long before they are known to the officers and troops. Those men will probably not trouble themselves much about distinctions regarding the rights of the people and forms of government, but they will learn from what they hear to consider what immediately concerns themselves, and for which they require but little prompting. They will learn to compare their own low allowances and humble rank with those of their European officers, to examine the ground on which the wide difference rests, to estimate their own strength and resources, and to believe that it is their duty to shake off a foreign yoke, and to secure for themselves the honours and emoluments which their country yields. If the press be free they must inevitably learn all this and much more. Their assemblage in garrisons and cantonments will render it easy for them to consult together regarding their plans. They will have no difficulty in finding leaders qualified to direct them ; their patience, their habits of discipline, and their experience in war, will hold out the fairest prospects of success ; they will be stimulated by the love of power and independence, and by ambition and avarice, to carry their designs into execution. The attempts would no doubt be dangerous, but when the contest was for so rich a stake they would not be deterred by the danger.''

ESCAPE OF THE CONVICTED SEPOY FROM FORT WILLIAM.—
Page 36.

[This incident greatly distressed Lord Canning, who wrote to the President of the Board of Control, saying :]

" It is most deplorable that the man who tampered with the Sepoy, and who, after trial and conviction was placed under guard of the Fifty-third (Queen's), should have escaped. A court-martial is now trying the officer of the guard. But it is probable that he is not so much to blame as the officer who put the prisoner in irons which were too large for him that he slipped his hands and feet out, or as the sentry who failed to keep watch. It will of course be said that the prisoner was allowed to escape as soon as he had turned his evidence to account."

This does not seem to have induced greater caution, for I find Mr. Peacock, on the 17th, calling attention to the disgraceful manner in which things appeared to be managed in the Fort. " It came to my knowledge," he adds, " quite by accident, late last night, that on the previous evening a carriage had been stopped going into the Fort, and some men, who were in it, had been apprehended in endeavouring to carry papers to one of the State prisoners. I also learn that the papers were lying folded up in a piece of paper, not even tied, in the officer's room' at the main guard, so that any of them might easily be abstracted during the officer's absence. And this, too, after the escape of the prisoner on Sunday night."—*MS. Records.*

GENERAL LLOYD AT DINAPORE.—Page 110.

[An exculpatory letter from General Lloyd is referred to in a note to page 110, where it is stated that the vindication will be found complete in the Appendix. The extreme length of the communication has, however, suggested the expediency of giving only those passages in which the General explains his own act. The rest merely confirms the accuracy of the narrative given in the text :]

" On the 25th July, 1857, I was far from well, and on that day the crisis occurred here, and in consequence my manner may not have been as firm and decided as it used to be. But my acts will, I think, bear the strictest scrutiny; and although from my gouty feet I am physically unequal to active bodily exertion, I assert that in judgment and intellect I am fully equal, if not superior, to any of the younger commanders at Dinapore. The way I have been vilified and abused by the press forces me thus to assert my own qualifications in a style which might otherwise be thought unbecoming. However, the shortcomings of some of those who had previously talked much, but when the time came did little, have been visited very hardly on me; and the difficult nature of the country, and the peculiar one of the locality of the Dinapore Cantonment at this season, as well as the small available European force at Dinapore, have been quite lost sight of by those who have seen fit to publish their dogmatical opinions as to what should or should not have been done on the occasion of the late outbreak here."

"As I was quite aware of the likelihood of a mutiny of the Native troops here, and feeling sure that in such an event they would make off towards Arrah, I, in June last, issued written instructions relative to the course to be pursued by the European troops acting against them, and this was fully made known to Colonel Fenwick, the commanding officer of the Tenth, who was then the senior. Subsequently, Colonel Huyshe, of the Artillery (senior to Colonel Fenwick, though I was not aware of this till after the 25th July), and I took an early opportunity to inquire from him whether he had made himself acquainted with the orders given and arrangements for meeting an outbreak—whether Lieutenant Smithett had told him all these things—and I received a reply in the affirmative, and the Colonel said the bullocks could be harnessed in a moment, as they were close by, in the tanyard, or old magazine yard, and he would not be caught napping—an expression I particularly remarked."

"I had no horse in Cantonments. My stable was two miles distant, and being unable at the time to walk far or much, I thought I should be most useful on board the steamer with guns and riflemen, in which I proceeded along the rear of the Native lines, the river being only two hundred yards, or thereabouts, distant from the right of the advancing column of guns and Europeans, and expecting to get some shots at the Sepoys on shore, or escaping by the river. Considering that I had fully previously given instructions for the attack and pursuit of the Sepoys by the guns and Her Majesty's Tenth, under their respective commanding officers, I left it to them to follow up the mutineers by land. On embarking, I sent Captain Turner, D.A.A.G., to order the guns to advance, as I thought they were long in setting off, and I sent Lieutenant Nedham, D.A.Q.G., to order the commanding officer of the detachment of Her Majesty's Thirty-Seventh Foot to place himself under Colonel Fenwick's orders."

" The mutineers' position being on the road from Patna *viâ* Phoolwaree towards Arrah, with the road to Gya open in their rear, it was uncertain which road they would take, or they might have taken all three, and visited the three places. Two guns and a detachment were therefore sent off to protect Patna, leaving only five hundred men and four guns at Dinapore. The high road to Arrah was quite impassable for guns, and even the Infantry would have had a difficult and slow march along it to reach the Kholwur Ghaut on the Soane. It is perhaps to be regretted that some were not sent that night or next morning, but only a small party, in comparison to the strength of the mutineers, could have been detached ; no guns could have gone, and as the mutineers avoided the road, and kept to the fields, where they could scarcely have been effectively followed by a small party of Europeans, they would probably not have been of much use. However, as the readiest means of following them, to prevent their crossing the Soane, I, next day, the 26th, sent off some riflemen in a steamer up that river, expecting that at this season there would have been sufficient water ; but unfortunately the steamer could not get up high enough, and returned in the evening without having effected anything."

" Early next morning the commander of the steamer changed his mind, and said he could not tow two flats, consequently the party had to be reduced by a hundred men, and therefore Colonel Fenwick remained, and sent Captain Dunbar in command, an officer of whose unfitness for such a command I suspect Colonel Fenwick may have been aware ; at any rate he subsequently proved himself to be utterly so. He marched his men fasting (though he might have given them a meal, as he had taken three days' provisions with the detachment) towards Arrah, pushed on against advice and common sense in the dark, got his column into an ambuscade from which they were suddenly fired upon by the rebels, and were thrown into utter panic, broken, and scattered."

THE MUTINY AT FUTTEHGURH.

[The subjoined is the letter from Colonel Smith referred to at page 299 :]

"Fort Futtehgurh, July 1st.

" Au magistrat de Mynpoorie, ou à un officier European attaché à une armée de soldats Europeens. Nous avons été fortement assiegés dans le Fort de Futtehghur, par une force d'Insurgents, pendant la dernière semaine et nous avons peu d'espoir de continuer le siege si nous n'avons du secours de suite. Nous sommes en tout 100 personnes : 32 hommes, et 70 femmes et enfans. Nous vous supplions de venir de suite à notre secours, nous sommes en très grand danger. We are in great danger and plead for speedy help. We are more than one hundred—32 men, 70 women and children, against 1000 insurgents.

"G. A. SMITH,

"Colonel Commanding."

"R. Thornhill, July."

[This was addressed to "Any Officer commanding or attached to a European Force or to the Magistrate of Mynpoorie or Agra." It was on the receipt of this at Agra, I believe, that Major Weller made the offer mentioned in the text to lead a force to Futtehgurh.]

THE ADVANCE ON CHINHUT.—Page 502.

[In a brief Memoir of Sir Henry Lawrence, written by the author, a few years ago, the following note upon this subject is given, the correspondence being quoted from the originals in his possession :]

" Upon this subject, Mr. Gubbins has written in his book : ' Upon his death-bed Sir Henry referred to the disaster at Chinhut, and said that he had acted against his own judgment from the fear of man. I have often inquired, but I never learnt .the name of any one who had counselled the step which resulted in so severe a calamity.' This may be true; but it is not quite the whole truth. It is probable that no one especially recommended this individual movement ; but it is certain that Mr. Gubbins himself was continually urging Sir Henry Lawrence to send out a force to meet the enemy. But what he certainly did with respect to this particular affair was to ridicule the idea that the enemy were advancing in any formidable strength. When the news of the advance of the mutineers was first brought in, the circular that went round for the information of the chief officers of the garrison stated that the man who brought the information said he could not speak with certainty as to the numbers, but that he heard there were eight or nine regiments of infantry and one of cavalry, with twelve guns. Mr. Gubbins appended four notes of exclamation to the passage, and wrote beneath it, ' *What stuff!*—M. G. ;' and not satisfied with this, endorsed the paper with the same words. But we now learn from Mr. Gubbins himself ('Mutinies in Oudh,' pp. 189, 190) that the rebel force consisted of nine and a half regiments of Infantry, twelve guns, and seven or eight hundred Cavalry. It must be added, in the cause of historic truth, that after the death of Sir Henry Lawrence, Brigadier Inglis took some pains to elicit the facts, and that letters were addressed to several staff-officers on the subject. One answered : ' I could not positively state that Mr. Gubbins addressed a letter to the late Sir Henry Lawrence urging him to send troops to Seetapoor, or to Chinhut, or to Cawnpore, or anywhere else, but I have a decided though general impression that he did do so ; and, if I am not mistaken, Mahommedabad and Nawabgunje, on the Fyzabad road, might be included in the list of places to which Mr. Gubbins thought it would be beneficial to send troops. . . . . I have so often heard Sir Henry Lawrence talk on this subject, especially dwelling on the pertinacity with which Mr. Gubbins pressed him, that I could, without much difficulty, show, if necessary, the line of argument the Brigadier-General adopted.' Another wrote : ' Several times the Brigadier-General (Lawrence) asked me how I could equip detachments of Europeans which Mr. Gubbins proposed sending to Seetapore, Cawnpore,

Mulleabad, and Nawabgunje ; and if it were possible to transport them within certain fixed times on elephants. On these occasions I perfectly remember Sir Henry appeared irritated and annoyed, and always pronounced such expeditions most rash, unsafe, and utterly impracticable. The feasibility of the proposed enterprises was openly discussed by all the members of the Staff, both in Sir H. Lawrence's room, and often at his table, and I always heard that Mr. Gubbins had advocated the movements.' A third said, in reply : ' I have the honour to state, for the information of the Brigadier commanding at Lucknow (Inglis), that I perfectly remember that in the latter part of June last many letters were received by the late Sir H. M. Lawrence from Mr. Gubbins. Several of these letters were given me to read, but not all, as they did not belong to my department, but to that of the Military Secretary. I, however, generally heard the purport of them discussed, which was the advisability of sending an European force over to Cawnpore, at another time to Seetapore and Chinhut, and also the advantages to be gained by sending a force out to meet the rebel army at Nawabgunje. I always heard the late Brigadier-General express himself as strongly opposed to the above movements.' And again another officer, who had peculiar opportunities of observation, said : ' Sir Henry Lawrence did from time to time complain to me that the indomitable personal courage of Mr. Gubbins, his excessive zeal and ardent temperament, had caused him to be the over-earnest, importunate, and too public advocate of military movements which, according to Sir Henry's personal judgment, could only have ended disastrously. He more than once deplored to me, as a calamity which weighed down his spirits, that owing to the chivalric ardour and the eloquent fervour with which Mr. Gubbins urged his views, and the publicity which he gave to them, the Finance Commissioner had come to be regarded by some of the more spirited and less experienced officers of the force, as the real man for the crisis.' Nothing further need be said to explain the meaning of Lawrence's dying words."

CAPTAIN NORMAN AND COLONEL SEATON.

At page 547, mention is made of the high qualities and distinguished services of Captain (afterwards Sir) Henry Norman, Assistant-Adjutant-General of the Army. I gladly avail myself of the opportunity to rectify an error, in which I was led by a previous writer. It is stated at page 573, vol. ii., that Colonel (Sir Thomas) Seaton was, after Chamberlain was wounded, "appointed to officiate as Adjutant-General." No such appointment was ever made. Nor is there any statement to that effect in Colonel Seaton's memoir ("From Cadet to Colonel"). The duties of the Adjutant-General's office were carried on by Captain Norman, under the general direction of Colonel Neville Chamberlain, who, although physically incapacitated by his wound, was never unequal to the duty of giving sound advice and suggesting wise instructions.

HINDOO RAO'S HOUSE.

[The following is portion of a letter from Sir Charles Reid to the author, relating to the famous Picket at Hindoo Rao's house, of which frequent mention has been made in these pages :]

"The true key of our position in front of Delhi, and upon the holding of which the success or failure of the siege depended, was *not* the Subzee-mundee, as stated p. 518, vol. ii., but Hindoo Rao's house. The latter post (which by the way be it said was *not* on the extreme right of my position, there being one battery and two pickets beyond it) commanded the Subzee-mundee by about 150 feet, as well as the Grand Trunk Road. Had the rebels once taken Hindoo Rao's house, a glance at the map will show that our camp lay open to the enemy's guns, and our position would have become an untenable one, and we must have retreated in disgrace. That this was evident to the rebels appears from the extraordinary efforts made by them to obtain possession of the

Ridge, especially the highest point, viz., Hindoo Rao's house, and as Baird Smith remarks, it was 'the one great feature of their operations from which they never departed.' Not less than twenty-six separate attacks were made on the right of the Ridge by the enemy in order to obtain possession of the house—one of which lasted one whole night and a day. I allude to the grand Eed attack on the 1st and 2nd of August, and another from the 6th to the 13th of August, *vide* General Wilson's despatch of the latter date : ' A constant worrying attack night and day by both Infantry and Artillery.' Neither of these you make mention of, which I think must have been an omission. The Eed attack, in my opinion, was the crisis and turning point of the whole siege, and for the sake of the gallant officers and men who served under me I would fain hope it is not too late to mention it, as the history does not go further than the operations in August, in which month it occurred."

"There were several gallant deeds on the part of officers and men who served under me on the Ridge which I made mention of in my letters and notes, and which I cannot but think you would wish to bring forward in your admirable work—viz., Minto Elliot's gallant conduct with a sergeant and a gunner on the 23rd of June, recommended for Victoria Cross."

[No one can regret more than the author of this work, the material exigencies which have compelled him to leave so many brave deeds unrecorded. I have already said that I could not have yielded to my inclinations without extending this work to a length which would scarcely have been acceptable to the reader. It should be remembered that I have not attempted to write a History of the Siege of Delhi, but of the Sepoy War in all parts of the country.]

THE EXPLOSION OF THE CASHMERE GATE.—Page 601.
" Sept. 14, 1857.
" THE party for blowing in the gate, the Sixtieth Rifles leading, went off at a double from the Ludlow Castle, until

VOL. III. 2 x

they arrived at the cross road leading to the Customs, and the men, when they opened out right and left, the Sappers going to the gate led by Lieutenant Home and one bugler, Lieutenant Salkeld, with the party carrying the powder a few paces behind, the three European non-commissioned officers, and nine Natives with twelve bags of 25 lb. each. My duty was to bring up the rear, and see that none of them remained behind. Lieutenant Salkeld had passed through the temporary Burn Gate with Sergeants Carmichael and Burgess, but four of the Natives had stopped behind the above gate and refused to go on. I had put down my bag and taken my gun, and threatened to shoot them, when Lieutenant Salkeld came running back and said, ' Why the d—l don't you come on ?' I told him there were four men behind the gate, and that I was going to shoot them. He said, ' *Shoot* them—d—n their eyes, *shoot* them !' I said, ' You hear the orders, and I will shoot you,' raising the gun slowly to ' present,' to give fair time, when two men went on. Lieutenant Salkeld said, ' Do not shoot ; with your own bag it will be enough.' I went on, and only Lieutenant Salkeld and Sergeant Burgess were there; Lieutenant Home and the bugler had jumped into the ditch, and Sergeant Carmichael was killed as he went up with his powder on his shoulder, evidently having been shot from the wicket while crossing the broken part of the bridge along one of the beams. I placed my bag, and then at great risk reached Carmichael's bag from in front of the wicket, placed it, arranged the fusee for the explosion, and reported all ready to Lieutenant Salkeld, who held the slow match (*not a port-fire*, as I have seen stated). In stooping down to light the quick match, he put out his foot and was shot through the thigh from the wicket, and in falling had the presence of mind to hold out the slow, and told me to fire the charge. Burgess was next him, and took it. I told him to fire the charge, and keep cool. He turned round and said, ' *It won't go off, sir ; it has gone out, sir*' (not knowing that one officer had fallen into the ditch). I gave him a box of lucifers, and, as he took them, he let them fall into my hand, he being shot through the body from *the wicket also*, and fell over after Lieutenant Salkeld. I was then left alone, and keeping close to the charge, seeing from where the others were shot, I struck a light, when the port-fire in the fuse went off in my face, the light not having gone out as we thought. I took up my gun and jumped into the ditch, but before I had reached the ground the charge went off, and filled the ditch with smoke, so that I saw no one. I turned while in the act of jumping, so that my back would come to the wall to save me from falling. I stuck close to the wall, and by that I escaped being smashed to pieces, only getting a severe bruise on the leg, the leather helmet saving my head.

" I put my hands along the wall and touched some one, and asked who it was; 'Lieutenant Home,' was the answer. I said, ' Has God spared you? Are you hurt?" he said, ' No,' and asked the same from me. As soon as the dust cleared a little we saw Lieutenant Salkeld and Burgess covered with dust ; their lying in the middle of the ditch had saved them from being smashed to pieces and covered by the *débris* from the top of the walls, the shock only toppling the stones over, which fell between where we stood and where they lay. I went to Lieutenant Salkeld and called the bugler to help me to remove him under the bridge as the fire had covered upon us, and Lieutenant Salkeld's arms were broken. Lieutenant Home came to assist, but I begged him to keep out of the fire, and that we would do all that could be done. Lieutenant Salkeld would not let us remove him, so I put a bag of powder under his head for a pillow, and with the bugler's puggery bound up his arms and thigh, and I left the bugler to look to him and went to Burgess, took off his sword, which I put on, and done what I could for him. I got some brandy from Lieutenant Home and gave to both, also to a Havildar (Pelluck Singh), who had his thigh shot through, and was under the bridge by a ladder that had been put into the ditch by mistake by the Rifles. Lieutenant Home got out of the ditch, leaving me in charge of the wounded, and went to the front after the Rifles had gone in, and the Fifty-second followed them : THEY DID NOT GO FAST ; their bugler *had sounded fifty times at least, and some ten minutes had elapsed before any one came, and the Rifles returned and went in first.* I then went to the rear for three stretchers and brought them, one of which was taken from me for an officer of the Rifles. I had to draw my sword and threaten to run any one through who took the other two. I put them into the ditch, and with the bugler's assistance got Lieutenant Salkeld into one and sent him with him, charging him strictly not to leave him until he had placed him in the hands of a surgeon, and with the assistance of a haick who had come to the Havildar, got Burgess into one and sent the haick with him, I being scarcely able to walk, and in a few minutes he returned to say he was dead, and ask for further orders. I told him to take him to the hospital. After assisting to clear away the gate and make the roadway again, I went on to the front to see what was going on. It will be seen that Carmichael did not live to get up to the gate, and that Sergeant Smith did not run up as he was there and placed the bags and arranged the fuse for the charge, and was there when all were gone or shot down. The bugler took charge of Lieutenant Salkeld at my request, and came to our tents when recommended for the (Victoria) Cross, to thank me in the presence of my comrades for being the means of him getting it.

"JOHN SMITH."

CAPTURE OF THE PALACE AND SELIM-GURH OF DELHI.—
Page 633.

Extract from the Journal of an Artillery Officer.

" Near the Calcutta Gate I met Captain Aitkin with a small party of Wild's Punjabees, who told me he was going on as far as he could, and I returned to the Magazine where we saw Aitkin and his party advance, first to the bridge leading to Selim-gurh, and then right on along the road winding round it, and shortly after we saw them appear in the corner tower whence the last heavy gun had been fired ; and I reported the matter at once. In the mean time Colonel Longfield of the Eighth, a fine old soldier with whom I had marched from Jullundur, came to the Magazine and told me a column was forming to blow in and assault the Palace Gate, and soon after it was blown in and the place captured. But before that Aitkin and his party had got into Selim-gurh, and had spiked the guns there and obtained possession of the gate leading into the Palace, having shot the sentry at the gate on his post. For this act Aitkin has never got the credit he deserved. He afterwards, however, got the V.C. in the more fortunate region of Oude. I sent Lieutenant Evans in after the storming party to report the state of affairs, and then went myself to the Palace Gate, where I found Major R. Ramsay commanding the Kumaon Battalion. While talking to him, word was brought that the enemy were attacking the other, or Duriao-gunge Gate of the Palace, so Ramsay fell in a party of his battalion and we doubled off to the gate, which we found closed, while a large party of the Sixtieth Rifles and Kumaon men formed a semicircle some way off in the yard in front of the gate at which they were firing, while shots were being returned from a small opening between the two leaves of the great iron-covered gate, which did not close completely for the lower four or five feet. We found two of the Sixtieth and three Kumaonees all shot through the legs by this fire, so, getting alongside the wall I ran into the gateway, knowing the gates were musket-proof, and putting the muzzle of my revolver just over the muzzle of a musket that appeared in the chink, I pulled the trigger and the owner of the musket went down with a grunt. Presently after there was a rush and scuffle outside with shouts that we were not to fire, and I found a party of Punjabees had got possession of the gate outside. On opening the gate, we admitted Captain Stewart, whom I did not know, but addressed as Hodson, whom he greatly resembled. And so ended the siege of Delhi, and I flattered myself the troop had done its duty. Afterwards I went to the Jumma Musjid and found Major Brind in possession, having, with characteristic energy, organised and headed the party that pushed on and seized that post.

[The following was published in the last edition of the Second Volume of " The History of the Sepoy War."]

ADDENDA TO VOL. II.

THE CARABINEERS ON THE TENTH OF MAY.

IT was stated in the first edition of the second volume that the turning out of the Carabineers at Meerut on the 10th of May, 1857, was delayed by the slow process of a regimental roll-call. This Colonel Custance denied, and supported his denial with an overwhelming amount of documentary evidence. I therefore wrote him the subjoined letter, with permission to publish it :

"Penge, Surrey, Dec. 20, 1870.

" Sir,—I am perfectly convinced, by the documentary evidence which you have afforded me (I should have been satisfied, indeed, with your own denial), that the statement at page 65 of the second volume of my 'History of the Sepoy War,' to the effect that on the 10th of May, at Meerut, there was a roll-call of the Carabineers (then under your command) before they moved out against the Sepoy mutineers, was based upon erroneous information. As the passage was written some years ago, I cannot, without a laborious search, which I have not yet had time to make, ascertain the authority or authorities on which the statement was made ; but whatever the authority may have been, I regret that I should have been, however unintentionally, the means of giving publicity to a statement at variance with the fact. I need not add, that I wish to do all that lies in my power to correct the error in future issues of my History ; and all the more willingly, as I have reason to believe that the story which I have published was commonly accepted as a fact before the appearance of my book. I may add to this that from a careful perusal and collation of the several documents which you have sent me, containing the evidence of officers and non-commissioned officers of your regiment, it appears that the Carabineers, when proceeding towards the lines of the Native battalions, were countermarched, by order conveyed to you by a staff-officer, and marched towards the gaol, which lies, at a considerable distance, in a different direction. It seems that on reaching the gaol, it was found that the prisoners had already escaped, so the Carabineers were marched back again towards the Native Lines. On their return, darkness having set in, they lost their way, although under the guidance of the staff-officer who had directed you to the gaol. That this was the real cause of the tardiness with which you reported your arrival on the general parade to the Brigadier is sufficiently plain from the evidence which you have afforded me. I have much pleasure in informing you that I am perfectly satisfied of the truth of these statements.

"You may make any use of this letter that you may wish.

"I am yours faithfully,

"J. W. KAYE.

"Major-General Custance, C.B."

[After this had been published, I received another letter on the subject, which I also feel bound to publish ; and I am the more willing to give it publicity, because the record is highly honourable to the splendid regiment (though in May, 1857, owing to accidental circumstances, it was not in the height of its splendour) which Colonel Custancé then commanded. I thought when I last saw it, on the occasion of Lord Mayo's funeral, that such a regiment might have demolished at least half of the Native Cavalry of Bengal :]

"Junior U.S. Club, Pall Mall, London, Feb. 27, 1871.

"DEAR SIR,—On return home I have looked over my memoranda of Meerut and Delhi in 1357, and have carefully read the passage in your History to which Colonel Custance, of the Carabineers, takes objection. As I can personally vouch for certain points, I here state them.

"The Carabineers turned out with extreme rapidity. I ought to know, for it was I who ordered a sergeant of the regiment from the bridge close to the parade of the mutineers to run to Colonel Custance himself, and I sent a rifleman also to the Brigade Office. This was the first intimation given, as the firing, in which Colonel Finnis and others were killed, was then proceeding. This sergeant afterwards told me that Colonel Custance had 'instantly ordered out his regiment,' and, on reaching his house myself a few minutes later, I saw the regiment on its parade rapidly getting ready, *and I heard the roll called in the troop nearest me,* an important duty which no good sergeant will omit on any occasion, as he cannot report his men present if he has not ascertained it.

"Colonel Custance and his regiment had to await 'orders,' and if any delay took place it was, I imagine, owing to the very late arrival on the scene of General Hewitt from his house, distant a long way off, and from whence, half dressed,

and upset mentally and physically, he had been brought by
Lieutenant Warde, Eleventh Regiment, N.I.   He was very
old and feeble.   The Carabineers were in broad daylight
ordered not to the mutineers' parade-ground close by, but to
the prison some miles off, and the services of Colonel
Custance and of his fine regiment, both of them able and
ready to obey any order long before it was issued, were lost
pro tem.   I myself saw the regiment drawn up and ready for
orders, and I do not believe the slightest delay occurred when
those orders were received by Colonel Custance.

" After the Carabineers had left their parade, I rode across
both the parade-grounds of the two mutineer regiments to
try to reach the house of Mrs. Chambers.   Lieutenant Shelley
and another officer wished to accompany me, and the former
lent me his Arab.   As I crossed, the Sepoys were then
plundering my regimental magazine; some on their knees,
and all crying, ' Quick, brother, quick ! Delhi, Delhi !' and
I saw a stream of Sepoys and troopers going off towards the
Delhi road.

" The Sepoys took little notice, but I saw several officers
lying dead, and one dying raised himself as I passed.   I had
almost reached the house of Mrs. Chambers, then in her
verandah, and looking at me, when five or six Native troopers
spread out to cut me off, and forced me back.   Even then but
few shots were fired at me.   I returned to Colonel Custance's
house, and then went to the Artillery Lines, and earnestly and
repeatedly begged General Hewitt to let me ride to Delhi
and give warning.   Colonel Smyth and Major Harriott were
by, and the latter urged the General to send me, but he
refused ' unless I obtained Colonel Wilson's permission.'
That officer was actively engaged in the station, a very large
one, and I, owing to being misdirected, could not find him ;
and I corroborate his statement in your History that he did
not know that evening for certain ' where the enemy had
gone.'   You retain General Hewitt's, Colonel Smyth's, and
Major Harriott's letters stating that I offered to ride through
the mutineers to Delhi ; and General Hewitt states I did so
at 7.30 P.M., 10th May, 1857, but this was my third and last
offer to him, after an hour and a half had been lost by him
in sending me again and again to Colonel Wilson for permission !

" The above proves the correctness of your narrative both as to the fact of the ' roll-call,' and that the enemy could have been attacked in broad daylight on their own parades, and followed up to Delhi. That they were in a state of ' scare,' I could myself testify.

" Both Colonel Custance and his fine regiment were in ample time to have attacked the mutineers, and were quite ready for action ; and it was, I submit, no fault of either that the regiment was ordered off elsewhere, and our kith and kin left to perish.

" I saw Captain Rosser, Carabineers, late the same evening, and on my stating that I had nearly reached Mrs. Chambers, he said ' I will follow them now with a troop,' and, for aught I know, made the offer, but the enemy had then about four hours' start.

" As I was the only officer who offered to ride through the mutineers to Delhi alone, and who traversed the city early next morning from end to end (alone also), to secure the prisoner alluded to in your History, I naturally felt deeply hurt at my reception by General Hewitt, who insisted I was romancing (until the prisoner corroborated my assertion), and that the city was full of armed men. It is of course possible that there were many armed men, but I did not see them, and they were quiet enough, though a rabble at once surrounded me.

. . . . .

" If you think of referring to Colonel Custance in an introductory chapter to your next volume, or elsewhere, this note —fully corroborating the accuracy of your History—is at your service. If the evidence of an officer in my humble position can be of any avail, you can make what use you please of this letter now or at any time. Thanking you for your personal courtesy to myself, and with best wishes for the success of your important work,

" I remain, yours faithfully,
" H. Le Champion,
" Captain 101st Foot,
" Late Le Champion Möller,
" 11th Regiment, N.I."

[I have submitted this letter to General Custance, who writes that the roll-call which Captain Möller heard must have been that of the unmounted men of the regiment. Here I must leave the question for the judgment of the public.]

[As regards Captain Rosser's offer to take a detachment of Cavalry and some Horse Artillery guns to Delhi, on the night of the 10th of May, I should state that I have received a letter from Mrs. Rosser, enclosing one from her husband, written shortly after the outbreak, most distinctly asserting that he made the offer, which has been denied by the authorities ; and I must admit that all I have heard, since the first edition of this work was published, strengthens the conviction that the offer was made, though not, perhaps, in accordance with those strict military rules, which though recognised in quiet times, must be departed from in a great crisis.]

THE METCALFE HOUSES.

"6, St. James's-terrace, Harrow-road.
"March 1, 1871.

" DEAR SIR,—There appears to me to be a slight confusion in a matter of detail at p. 543 of the second volume of your Sepoy War, which possibly may be worth mentioning to you in case you wish to inquire further into it. There are *two* Metcalfe houses—one outside the Cashmere Gate, the other at the Kootub, which, you know, is eleven miles from Delhi.

" The former (with which alone you are concerned here) was not, *as far as I know*, an adaptation of, or built on the site of, or in any way connected with a Native building. Lord Lawrence could doubtless tell you all about it. I have only known it since the rebellion ; but there is enough of it left to show that it is a thoroughly English building, and I have always understood that Metcalfe built it from top to bottom for himself. I do not think there are even any remains of Native buildings in " Metcalfe's Compound," and the remains in the Koadsiah-bagh somewhat nearer to the Cashmere Gate are, I believe, considerably more recent than the time of Akbar. The rooms in *this* Metcalfe House have never been let at so much a day. One wing of it has been repaired, and is let by the month as an ordinary dwelling-house.

"The Metcalfe House *at the Kootub* is a fine Native tomb adapted to the requirements of a European residence. I cannot find it in our friend Syūd Ahmud's Asaroossunnadeed, but in a small English guide-book I see it is said to have been the tomb of Mohammed Koolee Khan, one of Akbar's foster-fathers. *This* Metcalfe's House is (or *was* a couple of years ago when I was at Delhi) used as a dâk bungalow, some small charge a day being made for the rooms. If I am right in the above, the question as to the removal of the tomb-stone becomes of no importance ; but I may mention that though the stone must have been removed from this tomb (for it is not in the centre hall where it ought to be), the passage from Sleeman in your note may refer, and I *suspect* does refer to another tomb close by.

" That other tomb is the burial place of Adum Khan, a man who made a great figure in the reign of Akbar. It would be termed " magnificent," with much more propriety than Metcalfe's tomb. The stone in it has been removed from the centre and placed in the verandah outside, and I have a dim recollection of hearing that it had been removed by one of the Delhi officials many years before, and that the feelings of the people were hurt by the thing. Adum Khan was not the foster-brother of Akbar ; but, as you probably are aware, he slew one of Akbar's *foster-fathers*, and was executed in consequence. The story is a long one, and Sleeman may have fallen into some confusion about it. Lord Lawrence, I dare say, could tell you which tomb Blake had done up for himself. Or, if you wish, I could get certain information for you from Delhi or from Syūd Ahmed.

" Assuming that my conjecture is wrong, and that a portion of the Delhi house was a converted tomb with the slab removed, as at the Kootub, I should consider your remarks most just. With the exception of a few celebrated shrines, which are the fashion, and the burial-places of their own families, the Mahomedans are, for the most part, indifferent about the desecration of tombs. The Zemindars often use them as dwelling-houses or as cattle stalls. The fine tomb of Toog-luck Shah was occupied in this way until a few years ago, when we swept all the abomination out of it. But though they will stand desecration by others, they are up in arms at once if a European official attempts it, and they are probably right in making the distinction.

" As I am writing to you I may take the opportunity of mentioning, with reference to the words ' baba' and ' beebee' (page 354), that the latter word is universally used by Natives who live in contact with Europeans for our word ' baby,' of which it is no doubt a corruption, while the word ' baba' is used for older children, or for children young and old indifferently. ' Beebee' is used also in its proper sense of a lady or wife, but not *commonly.* A Native would generally speak of a lady as a ' mem sahib.' I speak with reference to the country from Delhi up. It may be otherwise lower down. I do not know whether it is worth while troubling you with this letter; but you seem so anxious to insure accuracy down to the most trifling detail, that even a hint of so slight an inaccuracy may be acceptable.

" Yours truly,
" D. Fitzpatrick,
"Late Officiating Deputy-Commissioner of Delhi.

" J. W. Kaye, Esq.

" P.S.—You do not appear to have seen the papers of the trial of Hajee, the man referred to in your note at page 79. Sir J. Metcalfe almost severed his head from his body at Arah Seran some time after the capture, and left him for dead.* He, however, survived by something scarcely short of a miracle ; but the mark, a fearful chasm in his neck—a curiosity from a surgical point of view—enabled us to trace him. I had the satisfaction of committing him for trial just before I left, and he was executed shortly after. I have always understood that he struck the first blow. I think Bucktawur said so on the trial."

* The less said about this affair the better.

END OF VOL. III.